Levant

Levant

Splendour and Catastrophe on the Mediterranean

PHILIP MANSEL

Yale

UNIVERSITY PRESS

New Haven & London

First published in the United States in 2011 by Yale University Press.
First published in Great Britain in 2010 by John Murray (Publishers),
an Hachette UK Company.

Copyright © 2010 by Philip Mansel

Yale University Press books may be purchased in quantity
for educational, business, or promotional use. For information, please e-mail
sales.press@yale.edu (U.S. office) or sales@yaleup.co.uk (U.K. office).

Typeset in Bembo by Hewer Text UK Ltd, Edinburgh

Printed in the United States of America

Library of Congress Control Number: 2011920105
ISBN 978-0-300-17264-5 (hardcover : alk. paper)

A catalogue record for this book is available from the British Library.

This paper meets the requirements of ANSI/NISO Z39.48-1992 (Permanence of Paper).

10 9 8 7 6 5 4 3 2 1

Contents

There are few greater pleasures than to extricate oneself from the caulked circumference of a ship and step forth upon the quay of a Levantine city.

Eyre Evans Crowe, *The Greek and the Turk; or,*
Power and Prospects in the Levant, 1853

THE LEV.

Constanti

Salonica

Gallipoli

GREECE

Aegean Sea

Piraeus

Athens

Sr

Chios

CRETE

Mediter

N

W E

S

0   100   200   300
Miles

El Alam

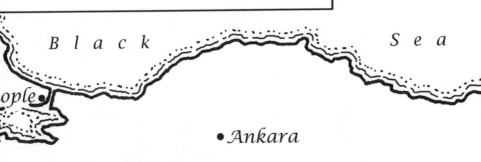

ANT, C.1930

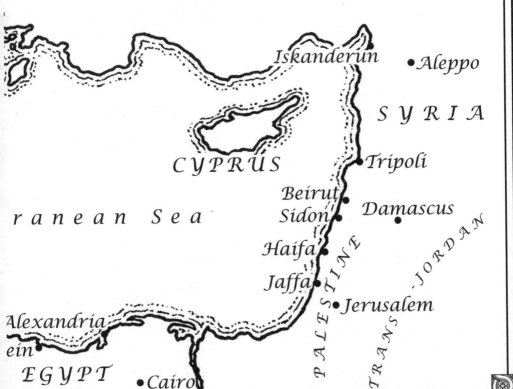

Black *Sea*

nople•

•*Ankara*

A N A T O L I A

yrna
•*Aydin*

T U R K E Y

•*Iskanderun*   •*Aleppo*

S Y R I A

CYPRUS

Tripoli

ranean Sea

Beirut
Sidon   *Damascus*

Haifa

Jaffa

PALESTINE

TRANS-JORDAN

Alexandria
ein

•*Jerusalem*

EGYPT   •*Cairo*

Introduction

THE LEVANT IS an area, a dialogue and a quest. Just as the word 'Orient' derives from the Latin *oriens* meaning 'rising', so Levant comes from the French word for rising – *levant*. For western Europeans, *le Levant*, the Levant, *il Levante* became a synonym for the lands where the sun is rising – hence the lands on the shores of the eastern Mediterranean: what are now the modern states of Greece, Turkey, Syria, Lebanon, Israel and Egypt, which from the sixteenth century to the twentieth were part of the Ottoman Empire.

A Western name for an Eastern area, the Levant was also, by implication, a dialogue between East and West: therefore – after the Muslim conquests of much of the eastern Mediterranean in the seventh century – between Islam and Christianity. Gibbon called the eastern Mediterranean 'the coast which had so long resounded with the world's debate'[1] – the debate between Christianity and Islam, which now resounds louder than ever.

In this book the Levant is described through the history of its three key ports: Smyrna, Alexandria and Beirut. They were, by the nineteenth century, the largest, richest and most international in the area, with the exception of the imperial capital, Constantinople. They were also the most revealing. By their location on the coast of the Mediterranean, in what are now Turkey, Egypt and Lebanon, they were on the front line between the Ottoman Empire and Europe, between East and West. They challenge stereotypes about cosmopolitanism and nationalism, and give a new view of the region's history. They were simultaneously windows on the West, generators of revolt against it, and targets for its battleships. Rather than being incompatible antitheses, in the cities of the Levant cosmopolitanism and nationalism could flourish at the same time, in people as well as in cities.

Smyrna, Alexandria and Beirut were at the heart of the Levantine dialogue. At once Mediterranean and Middle Eastern, Ottoman and European, nationalist and international, they were mixed cities, where mosques, churches and synagogues were built side by side. Often they had no clear Muslim or Christian majority. Their history explains why France and Britain were present in the region for so long. In a divided society, where the government could not provide essential services and protection, cities and individuals turned – in some cases still turn – to foreign 'saviours'. Foreign consuls in these cities often had as much power as local governors – as the latter often complained, while also using consuls' services, or taking refuge in a foreign consulate, when it suited them.

The cities' names also reflected the Levantine dialogue. Smyrna and Alexandria derived their names from their Greek past. The first is believed to have been founded by Greek colonists in 688 BC; the latter was founded by Alexander the Great in 331 BC. Beirut's name comes from an ancient Phoenician word for a spring. In contrast, the names of the great inland cities Aleppo, Damascus, Baghdad and Cairo are Arabic in origin. Except for Aleppo, these cities have an aura of sanctity; Damascus was compared to paradise by the Prophet himself. Baghdad and Cairo were planned imperial capitals, founded by Muslim caliphs, in AD 762 and 969 respectively.[2] They were government, mainly Muslim, cities – as different from the ports of the Levant as Washington is from New York.

Far from, and often flouting the orders of, the imperial capital, Constantinople, frequently administered in separate units removed from the jurisdiction of the provincial capital, dynamic and different, the cities of the Levant were protagonists in the dialogues between cities and states, ports and hinterlands, as well as between East and West. Cities are a third way between states and individuals, laboratories of new worlds, economic, cultural and political. The 'soft power' of cities can influence their inhabitants more than the 'hard power' of states. A square or a quay can be a political document as well as a geographical location. Europe without Paris, or the Levant without Smyrna, Alexandria and Beirut, would have had totally different histories. Galvanizing the entire region, the Young Turk revolution of 1908 cannot be understood without its incubator, Salonica, another Levantine port which will be described in these chapters.

Diversity and flexibility were the essence of Levantine cities. They could be escapes from the prisons of nationality and religion. In these cities between worlds, people switched identities as easily as they switched languages. Examples include Muhammad Ali Pasha, who in the early nineteenth century turned Alexandria from a wasteland into a cosmopolis, and whose grandson Khedive

Ismail declared that Egypt was part of Europe; the Baltazzi family of Smyrna, which was at once Greek, Ottoman and European; the great poet Constantine Cavafy in Alexandria, who, like many other inhabitants of these cities, selected what he wanted from different identities and languages; the trilingual writers of Beirut, who use Arabic, French and English. Some of the cities' schools and universities were by intention international, helping to make Smyrna, Alexandria and Beirut cultural beacons in the Levant. By reaction, they also produced some of the great nationalists of the period. The 'first shot' in the Turkish war of liberation in 1919 was fired in Smyrna; the Egyptian national hero Gamal Abdul Nasser was born in Alexandria.

The Levant was also a mentality. It put deals before ideals. For the Middle East, Levant and Levantinism were the equivalent of what Patrick Leigh Fermor sees as the role of Romiosyne – the Byzantine world and attitudes which survived under the Ottoman Empire – for Greece: standing for a world of 'shifts and compromises', 'a preference for private ambition over wider aspiration', for empiricism over dogma. Some considered Levantines 'synonymous with duplicity'.[3] Others admired Levantines precisely for their lack of ideals. Thackeray liked Smyrna, which he visited in 1839, because 'there is no fatigue of sublimity about it'.[4]

Smyrna, Alexandria and Beirut conformed to Cicero's description of port cities. He wrote in *The Republic*, praising Rome for not being one of them, that port cities share 'a certain corruption and degeneration of morals ... a mixture of strange languages and customs ... the lust for trafficking and sailing seas ... The delightfulness of such a site brings in its train many an allurement to pleasure through either extravagance or indolence'.[5] In the end, however, in all three cities, the zeal of nationalism has triumphed over the 'lust for trafficking' and 'allurement to pleasure'.

Levant is not only a history of three key cities, and the ways in which they reflected dialogues between East and West, cities and states. It is also a quest: to find out whether, as many inhabitants claimed, these cities were truly cosmopolitan, possessing that elixir of coexistence between Muslims, Christians and Jews for which the world yearns. Were they global cities before globalization, early examples of the mixed cities now emerging from Los Angeles to London? Or, below the glittering surface, were they volcanoes waiting to erupt – as, in the twentieth century, catastrophe in Smyrna and civil war in Beirut suggest.

Beirut is today the last Levantine city, the last city where neither Christianity nor Islam dominates. 'Parity' rules. However, the increasing religious polarization of different districts, the assassinations of politicians and writers since the murder of the former prime minister and international businessman Rafic Hariri in February 2005, and the rise of the Shia 'Party of God', Hezbollah, in the city's southern suburbs suggest that Beirut may become as homogenized as the others.

I

The Vineyards of Pera

May the said Frenchman travel freely in the lands and seas here
designated, dependent on our glorious empire ... may he as he
wishes enter, leave or reside here in conformity with our sovereign
orders and may he everywhere be accorded help and protection.
Firman of February 1788, issued in 'Constantinople
the well protected' to Charles-Sigisbert Sonnini

THE MODERN LEVANT was born from one of the most successful alliances in history: between France and the Ottoman Empire. From the
sixteenth century to the early twentieth, the history of the region and its
cities would be dominated by the changing balances of influence – political, cultural and economic – between Constantinople and Paris.

At first an alliance between France and the Ottoman Empire appeared
impossible. Jihad had been one of the foundations of the Ottoman
Empire and a reason for its rise from Anatolian principality to world
power, stretching from Hungary to Yemen, Algeria to Azerbaijan. The
Empire included not only the ports of the Levant, but also north Africa,
the Balkans and most of the Middle East. It was proud to include many
races and religions, both in its capital, Constantinople, and in its army.[1]
However, the Ottoman sultans also called themselves *gazis* or holy warriors, and their wars – like the Arab conquest of the Levant in the seventh
century – appealed to Muslims bent on following 'the path of God' and
winning plunder or martyrdom. After the Ottoman acquisition of Syria,
Egypt, Mecca and Medina in 1517, the sultans were in addition 'servant of
the Two Holy Places' and caliph of the Muslims. An inscription over the
door of the Suleymaniye, the mosque that Suleyman the Magnificent built
dominating the Constantinople skyline, called him 'the caliph resplendent with divine glory who performs the commands of the hidden book'.
The power of the Ottoman Empire, many of its Muslim subjects believed,
showed that God wanted it to be the last empire, as Muhammad was the

last Prophet.[2] Islam was one of the foundations of the Empire, in which Muslims occupied the highest positions.

If the Ottoman Empire had a tradition of jihad, no country had a stronger crusading tradition than France. The king of France was 'the Most Christian King', the 'eldest son of the Church.' The model king, St Louis, had led one crusade against Muslims, to Egypt in 1249, and died on a second, in Tunis in 1270. King Charles VIII had entered Naples in 1494 determined to conquer the Ottoman Empire and proclaim himself Roman Emperor. As part of an unsuccessful effort to relieve the Ottoman siege of Rhodes, a French force had attacked Beirut in 1520.[3]

In both France and the Ottoman Empire, however, realism outweighed religious zeal. Strategy was the reason. Formed by a line of military sultans out of conquered kingdoms and sultanates, the Ottoman Empire could seem both illegitimate and fragile. However triumphant it appeared, it had not destroyed the identities of the conquered nations, nor their memories of a glorious, pre-Ottoman past. European maps continued to show, within the frontiers of the Ottoman Empire, places called Greece, Bulgaria, Armenia, Syria and Egypt. A Venetian diplomat reckoned that the Empire was composed of forty conquered kingdoms.[4] Its greatest enemy, by the sixteenth century, was Emperor Charles V, head of the House of Austria, Holy Roman Emperor, king of Castile, Aragon, Naples and Sicily, and master of the Low Countries and parts of the New World. He had ambitions to conquer North Africa, and more. One of his many titles was King of Jerusalem, and he was assured – as many later Christian rulers would be – that Christians in the Ottoman Empire were eagerly awaiting his armies' arrival.[5]

Charles V also threatened France. His dominions surrounded it, and he and King François I were rivals for control of Italy. When François I was captured by the forces of Charles V at the Battle of Pavia on the Lombard plain on 24 February 1525, he turned for help to the 'asylum of the universe', the Ottoman sultan Suleyman the Magnificent.[6]

Alliances with Christian powers had always distinguished the Ottoman Empire since its forces first crossed into Europe in the 1350s as allies of Genoa. Jihad meant not only war on behalf of Islam, but also any meritorious effort – above all, the inner struggle to control 'the lower self' and follow the precepts of Islam. In his wars to establish a Muslim state, the Prophet had made truces; so could his successors.[7] Against Charles V, the Caliph of the Muslims and the Most Christian King were natural allies. The letters between the two were carried by secret agents, such as the Croatian noble Niccolo Frankopan, often (when crossing Habsburg or neutral territory) travelling under disguise, with letters hidden in the soles of their boots. Antonio Rincon, a former rebel against Charles V in Spain, was murdered by Habsburg agents near Pavia on 3 July 1541, as he was travelling back to Constantinople with a project for a Franco-Ottoman alliance.[8]

In his letters to François I, Suleyman urged his 'brother', 'king of the country of France', to take heart: 'It is not surprising that emperors are defeated and taken prisoner ... Take courage and do not be cast down. Our glorious ancestors and our illustrious forebears, may God illuminate their tombs, have never ceased from making war to repulse their enemies and conquer countries ... Day and night our horse is saddled and our sword is girded.' In 1526, partly in response to a plea from François I's mother, Suleyman attacked Charles V's brother-in-law King Louis of Hungary, defeating and killing him at the Battle of Mohacs. The end of Hungarian independence for the next 400 years was an early consequence of the Franco-Ottoman alliance.[9]

The first of the many tough and brilliant French ambassadors to be 'sent to the Levant to reside as our ambassador at the gate of the Grand Seigneur' was Jean de La Forest, a Knight of St John, who had learned Greek in Italy from the Byzantine exile Theodore Lascaris. He arrived in Constantinople in 1535. Despite frequent disputes, and the disapproval of religious zealots in both countries, for 250 years the French alliance remained one of the few fixed points in European diplomacy. The king of France, it was said, had only two friends in Europe – the Ottoman sultan and the Swiss. Thanks to the alliance, the Ottoman Empire – and therefore Mecca and Medina – had become part of the diplomatic system of Europe. For their part, ambassadors, consuls and dragomans (or interpreters) became part of the Ottoman government system: they received a living allowance, and the right to use guards from the Ottoman elite force the janissaries and government messengers.[10]

Suleyman wanted a formal written alliance, but, mindful of some Catholics' view of their relationship as 'an infamy',[11] François I, and his successors, eluded the request. Nevertheless, what a later French ambassador in Constantinople called 'the union of the lily and the crescent' was repeatedly called an alliance, by both sides.[12] In 1672 the French ambasssador the Marquis de Nointel boasted that France was 'the most powerful, the oldest and the most faithful friend of the Porte [the Ottoman government]', and referred to 'the French alliance which has lasted for one hundred and thirty-seven years' – since 1535.[13]

The Franco-Ottoman alliance helped provide the Levant with a framework. The grant by the sultan to the king of France of concessions or capitulations (so called because they were written in chapters, or *capitulae*) was to be the legal basis of Europeans' presence in the Levant, and of the growth of its international trade. The Ottoman versions – headed by the sultan's gold *tughra* or monogram, with his name and the epithet 'always victorious' – were known as *ahdnames* or pacts, guaranteed by the sultan's oath. If grand strategy was the original reason for the French alliance, commerce was the reason for the French capitulations – and soon became one of the driving forces of the alliance. French merchants were Christian foreigners who needed a legal framework in which to operate in the Ottoman Empire, outside sharia law. Foreigners' legal status in Middle Eastern countries is still an issue today, especially in Iraq and in Iran; in the latter, the legal extraterritoriality that Americans were granted by the Shah helped turn Iranians against him. The Ottoman system was based on Islamic and Byzantine tradition. Already since 1454 the Venetians living in the Empire had been placed under the authority of an official known (as he had been under the Byzantine Empire) as the bailo. He was at once their protector with the Ottoman government and their administrator, police chief and judge. He was also the resident Venetian ambassador and spymaster, and appointed Venetian consuls throughout the Empire.[14]

Capitulations established freedom of commerce between the two states; extraterritoriality for French subjects – who, for all crimes except murder, could be judged by their own laws in their consuls' courts, rather than in Ottoman courts – freedom of dress and worship; and freedom from forced labour, from Ottoman taxation, from collective reponsibility for individual nationals' crimes, and to reclaim prisoners held on Ottoman ships. All officers of the sultan throughout the Empire were ordered to observe the capitulations. Discussed in 1535–6, they were finally issued in 1569.[15]

In theory, as Islamic tradition required, capitulations were concessions granted, on request, by an individual sultan to an individual monarch and his subjects. They could be temporarily withdrawn. They were not binding on a sultan's successors,[16] and had to be renewed in each reign, as French capitulations were in 1581, 1597, 1604, 1673 and 1740. In practice, however, capitulations continued to be observed even if there was no renewal. They were bargains between states, the result of French diplomacy and threats to withdraw from trade and negotiations in the Levant, as well as of Ottoman power. The first French capitulations, in 1569, had eighteen articles; the last, in 1740, when France had just helped the Ottoman Empire recover territory in the Balkans, had eighty-five, including clauses extending French religious protection over Catholics (which France interpreted to include local Catholics) and Christian holy places in the Levant.[17] The capitulations enabled the cities of the Levant to become, by the nineteenth century, experiments in coexistence between different races and religions – cities which, as contemporaries remarked, had few parallels anywhere else in the world.

After 1536 the French ambassador established his embassy near that of the Venetian bailo in what were called 'les vignes de Péra' – the vineyards outside the walls of the predominantly Christian district of Galata in Constantinople. (They are now submerged by the shops and apartment blocks of Beyoglu, although vines still grow in some courtyards.) Pera became a diplomatic centre for Europe and a model for the cities of the Levant. Poland was another Ottoman ally, and with Polish support – since both Poland and England were anti-Habsburg – an English embassy was established in Pera after 1576, on the initiative of some English merchants.[18] Both countries were united by fear of the increase in Spanish power after Philip II inherited Portugal in 1580. Moreover, English tin and lead helped the Ottomans in making munitions. Blending trade and strategy, the Levant Company paid ambassadors, while the Crown controlled them. Despite French and Venetian hostility, capitulations were granted to England, on the French model, in 1582.[19] United against the Habsburg monarchies, England and the Empire became so close that in 1596 the English ambassador Edward Barton and a large suite accompanied the Grand Vizier, the Sultan's deputy, on campaign against Habsburg forces in Hungary.[20]

Against the opposition of its commercial rivals Venice, France and England, the Netherlands was the next foreign power to establish itself in the Levant: the Ottoman Empire, aware of their commercial and strategic uses against Spain, was an active agent in the process, even sending envoys to the Netherlands. The first Dutch ambassador, Cornelis Haga, arrived in 1612, and capitulations were granted that year. The first Dutch embassy was near the site of the present Dutch consulate, among 'les vignes de Péra', on what was then known as Strada Maestra and is now one of the city's principal shopping streets, meeting places and fashion parades, Istiklal Caddesi. Far from being treated as necessary evils, foreign embassies were welcomed to Pera. The mufti of Istanbul, the senior Muslim scholar in the Empire, was often visited by foreign ambassadors.[21]

In other cities – ninth-century Baghdad or twentieth-century Belfast – ethnic and religious segregation was or is normal. A modern social scientist has written that groups prefer to live as a majority in their own street or district. 'People like to live with others who belong to the same culture, share values, ideals and norms, respond to the same symbols and agree about child rearing ... and life style.' With their desire to protect women from prying eyes, traditional Muslims were, and are, especially keen on segregation.[22] Christian Europe could be even more rigorous. To 'protect' Venetians from Jews, and Jews from Venetians, from 1516 to 1797 all Jews in Venice had to live in a ghetto (a word of Venetian origin) like a small separate city. By law, they were locked inside it every night from 6 p.m. until dawn, and were forced to pay Christians to guard it.[23]

By its diplomatic relations with Christian powers, however, the Ottoman Empire created a Levantine interzone, first in Pera, then, as they grew in importance, in the ports of the Levant. There were many obstacles. Catholics and Orthodox, Muslims and Christians, were often hostile to each other. What have been called 'the small insults of daily life' were frequent. Boundaries between races and religions were clearly marked – by dress as well as by laws and customs: the tight multicoloured clothes and changing fashions of the European contrasted with the unchanging monochrome flowing robes of the Ottomans. The former wore hats (and later wigs); Muslims turbans; Christian subjects of the Ottoman Empire black wool caps or kalpaks.

Christians and Jews were forbidden to ride horses. Despite the prestige attached to the post of ambassador in Constantinople, it was considered, one Venetian ambassador wrote with feeling, as 'above all others full of inextricable difficulties'. Muslims called the ambassadors' janissary guards 'swine-herds'.[24] In 1614 Cornelis Haga complained, 'If I were to tell about the injury and the unpleasantness that the French, the English and the Venetian who have after all been known here through so many years are every day exposed to, even in Constantinople, instead of a letter I would have to write a bulky book.'[25]

By 1650 Galata's Muslim minority may have become a majority. Churches were sometimes converted into mosques. In 1600 there were twelve Catholic churches in Galata; by 1700 only six.[26] Although many churches have been built subsequently, today only the Dominican church of St Peter and St Paul, a few yards down from the Galata Tower, predates the Ottoman conquest in 1453, although it has been moved and reconstructed as a result of fires on five occasions. Like other Istanbul churches, San Piyer Kilesi, as it is now known, is still surrounded by high walls for protection.

However, first in Pera, later in the other great Levantine cities of Smyrna, Alexandria and Beirut, there was more interaction between worlds, however pragmatic and superficial, than anywhere else. In Morocco and Iran, the rare foreign embassies were isolated in diplomatic ghettos, in cities far from the capital, such as Essaouira or Tabriz. In nowhere but the cities of the Levant did large numbers of Muslims, Christians, and Jews live together over many centuries.

Indeed, life in Pera provided compensations as well as insults. 'Les vignes de Péra' – facing Topkapi Palace across the Golden Horn – had no rivals, in Europe or Asia, as a centre of diplomacy, information-gathering and inter-action between the Muslim, Catholic and Orthodox worlds. Pera drago-mans, for example, established standards of translation for the hitherto unknown language of Turkish.[27] Pera was an also an experimental labora-tory for religious and racial coexistence. There were no ghettos. Despite his complaints, Cornelis Haga remained in Constantinople until 1639. He bought and 'adorned' a house, married a Dutchwoman, and became so 'corrupted by their [Perotes'] manners', in the opinion of the English ambassador Sir Thomas Roe, that he became the 'shame of ambassadors'.[28] Evidently, despite the 'injury and unpleasantness', he had learned to enjoy himself in Constantinople. In 1609 the great English traveller George Sandys found western Europeans living in the city 'freely and plentifully'.

As well as money and power, sexual freedom was another attraction of the Levant. One Venetian bailo wrote, 'The liberty of Turkish living, the lasciviousness of the Turkish women and the corrupt customs of the renegades would have the power to make a saint a devil.'[29] Wives rarely accompanied husbands to the Levant; Frenchwomen were forbidden to do so by the French government. However, foreigners did not have to 'lie alone'. In a form of temporary marriage, like the *urfi* marriage becom-ing popular in Egypt, Lebanon and Iran today, it was possible to purchase 'the beautiful daughters of the Grecians' from their parents as temporary partners: the transaction known as *kabin*, later by derivation 'mariage à la cabine', was legalized by the Ottoman judge or kadi in his registers. The Greek girls were 'exceedingly obsequious' to their lovers, since if returned to their parents they would be regarded 'as a worn garment'.[30]

This was one of many examples, throughout the Levant until the nine-teenth century, of Christians and Jews using Muslim courts. They also did so in inheritance cases, since daughters could inherit more easily under sharia law than under European laws. Some even became Muslims to facilitate a marriage or a divorce.[31] Conversely, local Christian and Jewish courts showed the influence of sharia law and Ottoman custom. Without Ottoman authorities complaining, Muslims often used foreign consuls' courts, since they were cheaper than Ottoman ones.[32]

In the Levant, Ottomans and foreigners were also connected by trade. Venetian merchants sold textiles (often to the palace), glass, paper (until the nineteenth century most paper used in the Levant came from Italy), cheese and – a particular necessity – clocks and watches. Constantinople exported textiles, smoked fish, dyes and grain.[33] People of different religions and nationalities not only walked and shopped on the same streets, but also drank with each other in Pera's shops and taverns. Italian families of Galata like the Testa and Fornetti provided dynasties of dragomans for Western embassies: the Salvagos served Venice (the bailo of Venice lived in a house belonging to them), the Fornettis France, while the Testa family, with exceptional dexterity, served, sometimes simultaneously, Venice, the Netherlands, Austria, Prussia and Sweden.[34]

As in other capitals, hospitality was a political instrument. Ottomans frequently visited ambassadors and attended embassy banquets, just as, partly for the sake of the music, they also attended church services. (At Christmas, some brought flowers as presents for the Christians.)[35] European diplomats and merchants were invited to the houses of the grand vizier, the mufti and other officials, where they might discuss the political and religious issues of the day. Sometimes they went hunting together. One bailo kept what he called 'a continual tavern in my house and I very often needed to set three or four tables a day'.[36]

In time Pera became a new Andalusia – that lost world of cultural and religious *convivencia* in southern Spain, before the narrowing of minds in the fourteenth century. Since Pera was a diplomatic centre, its culture was less intellectual and more political than that of Andalusia. The French embassy in particular helped ensure that, in France between 1480 and 1630, four times as many new books were published on the Ottoman Empire and its system of government as on the New World.[37] In 1548–50 one ambassador, Gabriel d'Aramon, welcomed five writers to his embassy: Pierre Gilles, André Thévet, Guillaume Postel, Nicolas de Nicolay[38] and Pierre Belon, the father of French zoology.[39]

With its need for foreign embassies, and officially recognized non-Muslim minorities, the Ottoman Empire provided a more stable framework for interaction than the emirates of southern Spain. There were no special days reserved for Christians and Jews in the baths of Constantinople, as there had been in Andalusia (although there were efforts to ensure they did not use the same towels and razors as Muslims). Residential apartheid was less strict.[40] Even in 'tolerant' multi-faith Andalusia there had been religious massacres. In western Europe, massacres and executions on account of religion were frequent – in London in the 1550s under Bloody Mary; in Paris during the massacre of St Bartholomew's Eve in 1572; in Spain at the ceremonial auto-da-fé held in the seventeenth century in the main square of Madrid before the king and queen.

In 1526, after the fall of Granada in 1492, Muslims in Spain were, contrary to treaties, obliged to convert to Christianity. In 1609–14, in a frenzy of 'religious cleansing', the descendants of these Muslim converts, to the number of about 80,000, were expelled en masse; most ended up in the ports of North Africa, where they established distinct Andalusian communities.[41] In Russia, which had begun to conquer Muslim territories in the 1550s under Ivan the Terrible, the 'Agency of Convert Affairs' on the Volga used massacres, forced baptisms and the destruction of mosques to convert Muslims.[42] From the Ottoman conquest until 1770 there were no massacres of Christians or Jews in the cities of the Levant. Indeed, the proportion of Christians in the population rose from 6 per cent in the sixteenth century to 20 per cent in the early twentieth. Another reason for the demographic change was Muslims' use of abortion and disdain for precautions against plague.[43]

After the elimination of religious minorities, religious uniformity continued to be enforced in most European countries with hysterical severity. In Spain, no Jewish worship was allowed between 1492 and 1967. In London, Catholics had to worship in the chapels of foreign ambassadors from 1559 until the construction of the first Catholic churches in the 1840s. In Paris, Protestant worship was forbidden from 1685 until 1788. In theory, after 1569 France gave Ottomans of all religions reciprocal privileges of trade and residence; however, Muslims had to wait until the nineteenth century to live and worship in Paris or Marseille as freely as the French could in the Levant. The first mosque in Paris was inaugurated in 1926 – for patriotic reasons: to honour the Muslims who had died for France in the First World War. Even in Amsterdam, the freest city of the seventeenth century, although synagogues were built after 1639, Catholics had to worship in 'secret churches' hidden from the street. Only the cities of the Levant contained mosques, churches and synagogues side by side.

Partly because of European intolerance, few Ottoman Muslims travelled to western Europe: the two great attractions of holy places and classical antiquities did not exist for them in Christian Europe as they did for Europeans in the Ottoman Empire. Moreover, they found Christian Europe frightening. There was no Levant for Muslims in Europe: no system of protecting embassies, capitulations or janissaries, and no places of worship for them. Muslims were insulted, spied on, assaulted, or worse.[44] Only in Venice could Muslims live and trade in peace, as is shown by the allocation to them in 1618, as their residence, market and warehouse, of the palace later called the Fondaco dei Turchi, on the Grand Canal.[45] Even in Venice, however, although there was a prayer hall in the Fondaco, there is no mosque, and never has been.

The Levant was defined not only by geography, diplomacy and the capitulations, but also by language: first by lingua franca – *lisan al-franji* in Arabic – after 1850 by French. Lingua franca was a neutral language born of the need to communicate when neither European states nor the Ottoman Empire possessed many speakers fluent in the other's languages. Proof of the networks of trade and diplomacy linking the European and Muslim shores of the Mediterranean, and of Muslims' desire to communicate with Europeans, it was essentially simple Italian, without tenses or syntax, or distinction between masculine and feminine. It included, depending on location, French, Provençal, Castilian, Turkish and Arabic words. Its origin may have been the necessity to communicate in ships and households full of sailors or slaves speaking different languages.[46]

Lingua franca was a spoken, not a written, language – of direct daily contact, not of literature or holy books. Its omnipresence in the Levant had been ignored or minimized by scholars and writers until the recent pioneering book of Jocelyne Dakhlia. Moreover, its widespread use from the Middle Ages to the nineteenth century disproves the notion of two hostile worlds, or that Islam had become a closed world.[47]

Travellers, with their direct experiences of ports and cities, however, were more realistic. They wrote of lingua franca as the language 'which is in use throughout the Levant' (du Chastelet des Bois, 1665); 'generally understood on all the shores of the Levant' (La Guilletière, 1675); 'in use among seamen in the Mediterranean and merchants who go to trade in the Levant and which is understood by people of all nations' (Abbé Prevost, 1755). A character in *Don Quixote* – Cervantes knew lingua franca from his years as a slave in Algiers – calls it 'a mixture of all languages which we use so that we all understand each other'.[48]

Here are a few examples. 'Ti voler per questo?' meant 'Do you want to buy this?' 'Ti star consul o non star?' – 'Are you consul or not?' 'Christiani star furbi' – 'Christians are cunning.' 'Ven acqui' – 'Come here.'[49]

Lingua franca was spoken by admirals and ambassadors in Constantinople; by the merchants of Smyrna and the sailors of Alexandria; by the rulers of Tunis and Algiers; by slaves and their owners. Janissaries were said to 'commonly understand what is called Lingua franca'. Molière used it in *Le Bourgeois Gentilhomme* in 1669. Rousseau knew some words of it – he had relations who were watchmakers in Pera. Byron learned what he called 'Levant Italian', as well as Italian itself, when he spent the winter in Athens in 1809–10.[50]

Through trade and diplomacy the Ottoman Empire was embedded in the diplomatic system of Europe. More than other Muslim empires, the Ottoman Empire also facilitated travel, making the Levant more accessible than many Christian states. Like the capitulations, travel in the Levant depended on embassies. If an embassy purchased for a traveller a travel pass generally known as a *yol emri*, or an imperial firman, headed by the *tughra* of the reigning sultan, the traveller could travel round the Empire, and enter mosques, with ease. When an official was shown the document, he touched the *tughra* to his lips and forehead in token of loyalty.

The message of these travel documents changed little over the centuries. One issued in 1631 stated that 'our sovereign wish is that you receive [these travellers] with respect and a good welcome'.[51] A firman obtained in 1800 by a British consul required officials to allow two British officers 'to be conveyed in a hospitable manner with a courier for known purposes and to be provided on their journey with necessaries for travelling and the customs of hospitality to be observed towards them'.[52]

Provided the traveller's manners were good, his presents acceptable, and no war was raging, Ottoman officials in the Levant were generally polite and hospitable. In Beirut in the early nineteenth century William Turner found 'the Aga was very civil and begged that if I had need of anything here which he could do for me I would not fail to apply to him.'[53] In 1812 Byron (an admirer of Islam, who wrote more poems on Turkish than Greek subjects) wrote to his friend William Bankes, who was setting off on his travels, these words of advice: 'Be particular about firmans – never allow yourself to be bullied – for you are better protected in Turkey than any where – trust not the Greeks and take some knick-nackeries for presents – watches, pistols etc etc to the Beys and pashas ... You will find swarms of English now in the Levant.'[54]

The Levant was both accessible and alluring – hence the number of travellers' accounts quoted in this book. It became better known to Europeans than many closer destinations. In London and Paris, prints of the temples at Baalbek, a few days' travel from Beirut, were published earlier than images of the ruins of Diocletian's palace at Split on the Dalmatian coast. Even Palmyra, in the middle of the Syrian desert, was rediscovered (in 1691, by an English merchant of Aleppo called William Halifax), and recorded in paintings, earlier than Paestum, south of Naples.[55] A favourite destination for travellers, well positioned for visiting the ruins of Ephesus, was the city of Smyrna, known as 'the pearl of the Levant'.

2

Smyrna: The Eye of Asia

The ports of the Levant, you know that they are what is richest and most populous! Smyrna, what wealth!

Tsar Alexander I to General Comte de Caulaincourt, ambassador of Napoleon I, 12 March 1808

ASIA AND EUROPE meet in Izmir. It lies at the end of a long gulf on the west coast of Anatolia, where the Mediterranean projects furthest into the western tip of Asia. In addition to location, Izmir has the advantage of anchorage. Watered by six rivers, the Gulf of Izmir is so wide and deep that the largest ships could, and still do, sail in close to the shore.[1] If Constantinople seemed destined by nature to be the capital of a great empire,[2] Smyrna, as Izmir was widely known until 1922, seemed equally destined to be a great port.

Smyrna had been one of the most brilliant Greek cities in Anatolia, a nursery of mathematics, and reputedly the birthplace of Homer. The largest and most Romanized of the cities of Asia Minor, under the Roman Empire it was called 'the joy of Asia and the ornament of the Empire'.[3] It was also seat of one of the earliest churches, founded by St Paul himself on his visit in 53–6. Pillage and decay had been its subsequent fate. Successively attacked by Seljuk Turks (1082), Genoese (1261), the Knights of Saint John (1344), Timur (1402) and Venice (1472), since 1425 Smyrna (the Turkish name Izmir is derived from the Greek for *eis teen Smyrna* – 'into Smyrna', as Istanbul is derived from *eis teen polis* – 'into the city') had been part of the Ottoman Empire. It was then no more than a small market town, serving the surrounding region. In 1580 it had around 2,000 inhabitants. The main buildings were grouped among classical ruins, below the massive hilltop fort known as Kadefekale, or Velvet Castle, founded in the Hellenistic age and rebuilt by Byzantines, Genoese and Venetians, and around a lesser fort by the sea, built by Mehmed II, the conqueror of Constantinople.

The principal port of the region was on the island of Chios, six miles off the Anatolian coast.[4]

After 1600, however, Smyrna enjoyed a second golden age. Other ports were helped by their governments. The grand dukes of Tuscany, for example, proclaimed Livorno a free port, open to Jews and Muslims, in 1591. The French government fostered Marseille, giving it the monopoly on French Levant trade in 1661.[5] Smyrna, however, was made by merchants. From 1600 it was freer and more cosmopolitan than its hinterland, capable of defying the sultan's commands and the economic and religious restrictions of the Empire.[6]

Its rebirth was due to merchants' desire to evade the Ottoman government's controlled economy, customs dues and price restrictions. As early as 1574 Constantinople was suffering shortages because Ottoman ships, sailing from Egypt with provisions for the capital, unloaded at Smyrna – where they could get better prices than the imperial government's artificially depressed prices, imposed throughout the Empire at official weighing stations.[7]

By the end of the sixteenth century, the Ottoman navy, neglected by the Empire's prolonged and simultaneous land wars against the Habsburg monarchy and Persia, was on the defensive. It was said that God had given the land to Muslims, the sea to the infidels.[8] Some feared that 'before very long' Europeans would use their control of the high seas to 'rule the lands of Islam'.[9] The Aegean was infested with English, Maltese, Barbary and Dalmatian pirates, who from bases on the islands of Paros or Delos hunted ships and people – often with support from local Christians. An English ambassador boasted that English ships could 'harry the commerce on the coasts and islands of Turkey and . . . seize the shipping of Syria and Alexandria at will.' No one was safe.[10]

Foreign and Ottoman ships took advantage of the chaos to land surreptitiously near Smyrna to buy local products such as grain, raisins and figs. The imperial government in theory prohibited the export of grain, in order to provide its subjects with cheap food, but the demands of the market in Europe, especially in famine years, outweighed the decrees of the Sublime Porte.[11] The market – and the spread of brigandage in Anatolia – helped the city loosen government control. In 1593 the Porte complained that the black grapes of Izmir were not available 'immediately' for the palace; they were being picked by locals – including Muslims – and made into wine for their own consumption.[12]

Chios, hitherto the main port of the region, lay at the junction of shipping routes between Constantinople, Alexandria and the western Mediterranean, and was the residence of Venetian, French and English consuls. It was the most international of the Aegean islands. Three and a half centuries of Genoese rule after 1204 had given it networks of contacts in the Mediterranean, and independence of spirit. Already paying tribute to the Ottoman Empire since 1528, in 1566 it had passed under direct Ottoman rule, on the grounds that some Chiots had helped the Knights of Malta during the Ottoman siege of that island.[13] However, Chiots continued to dress and live 'in the manner of the Genoese', and enjoyed so much freedom that their island hardly seemed part of the Empire.[14]

In 1610 George Sandys found the inhabitants 'in a manner releast of their thraldome, in that unsensible of it ... Never Sunday or Holy-day passes without some public meeting or other where intermixed with Women they dance out the day and with full crowned cups lengthen their jollity ... the streets do almost all night long partake of their Musick.'[15] Other travellers praised the beauty, licence and cleanliness of the women (the women of Lesbos, however, were described as 'the ugliest sluts that ever I saw saving the Armenian trulls of Constantinople').[16] The stone houses were the most elegant in the Levant. The port had a fine stone esplanade where foreign ships moored.[17] 'The climate of Scio is delightful and the air more salubrious than that of any other islands in the Levant,' wrote the English traveller Thomas MacGill.[18]

Chios silk was sold throughout the Levant; the wine ('agréable et stomacal') was excellent; the island's lemons were the finest in the Levant; but its most prized speciality was, and still is, mastic or chewing gum, formed from the resin of the small green bushes which grow on the island's southern hills. The bushes then belonged to the sultan and produced four different kinds of gum, the best of which was reserved for the ladies of the harem.[19] The island's communities lived well together. Many of the 10,000 Muslims spoke Greek. Some of the 100,000 Greeks wore turbans; as on other Aegean islands, they had the right to ring the bells of their churches. The island also contained 3,000 Catholics. However, it was exposed to attack: in 1599 the Grand Duke of Tuscany had tried to seize it. Trade moved to Smyrna.[20]

In 1592–8 the first substantial building of modern Smyrna, the Hisar Cami or Castle Mosque (now embedded in the bazaar), was built by the sea. The year when Smyrna replaced Chios as the principal port of the region can be dated thanks to the Ottoman customs registers read by Daniel Goffman. In 1604/5 customs revenue from Chios surpassed that from Smyrna by 1,064,025 akces to 981,854; in 1606/7 Smyrna's customs revenue surpassed that of Chios by 1,332,733 akces to 600,192.[21] In 1610 George Sandys wrote, with typical prejudice, that Smyrna's 'beauty is turned to deformity, her knowledge into barbarism, her religion into impiety'. Nevertheless, he found that the city was frequented by foreign and local merchants. Locals settled there partly to flee the great Anatolian rebellions of the early seventeenth century, led by brigands and peasants (possibly with Shia sympathies), which, at times, threatened Constantinople itself.

Smyrna too had been attacked by rebels, but was defended by 'certain English ships that lay in the road': by 1595, within thirteen years of the establishment of diplomatic relations with the Ottoman Empire, English ships were entrenched in the carrying trade in the Levant. 'The principal commodity of Smyrna is Cotton-wool which there groweth in great quantity.' (Izmir is still surrounded by cotton fields today, though foreign competition – and the cost of Turkish labour – make them increasingly unprofitable.)[22]

Abundant and succulent figs were another product. Ripened in the sun-drenched valleys of Anatolia, they were, and still are, dried, packed and exported to Constantinople and Europe. A later traveller would find that 'the misfortune of the society of the merchants of Smyrna' was that they talked of nothing but figs.[23] In August and September the loudest sound in the city would be the 'terrific hammering' of men making barrels for transporting dried figs. Other cities were built on cloth, or silk; Smyrna was built on figs.[24]

European diplomacy, as well as market forces, helped the rise of Smyrna. In 1610 the imperial government ordered the city's market inspector to search the holds of French ships for contraband goods such as beeswax and muskets. The French reacted by producing certificates counterfeited or purchased in Constantinople. Ottoman authorities had to be circumspect in their inspections, thanks to orders not to 'injure, seize and threaten' the French. French capitulations had been renewed and extended in 1604, and the Ottoman Empire still needed France as an ally against the King of Spain and the Holy Roman Emperor.[25]

The arrival of consuls confirmed Smyrna's tightening links with Europe. By 1612 a Venetian consul and a Dutch vice-consul had arrived, and in 1619 the French consul in Chios was transferred to Smyrna.[26] The most important French consul in the Empire, his jurisdiction extended over Anatolia and many Aegean islands, where he appointed vice-consuls.[27] The Venetian consul helped Franciscan monks rent and restore a Greek church in 1597. At the height of the Counter-Reformation, the Catholic Church was determined to reconquer other Christians. Louis XIII, the king of France, Venice's rival as protector of Catholics in the Ottoman

Empire, helped Jesuits and Capuchins move to the Levant. A Jesuit church was built in 1623; Capuchin monks made a chapel for the French consul in 1628. Both orders at the same time began to teach and to proselytize elsewhere in the Levant, especially in Beirut and the semi-autonomous Christian area to the east, called Mount Lebanon.[28]

The leaders in Smyrna's international commerce, from the beginning, were French, Dutch and English merchants. Partly because it was difficult for them to trade in European ports, Muslims were excluded. On his way to Jerusalem in 1621, Louis Deshayes de Courmenin noted that, while Turks, Greeks and Jews lived inland, foreign merchants' residences lined the seafront and their owners 'live in great freedom'.[29]

Antiquities as well as commerce linked Smyrna to Europe. In the Ottoman Empire, Muslims' view of history was dominated by the Koran, by the figures of the Prophet Muhammad and his companions and successors, and by pride in the Ottoman dynasty. Christians, however, had two pasts. They were inspired not only by the teachings of Jesus Christ and the Apostles, and the prophets of the Old Testament, but also by pagan Greeks and Latins: Homer, Aristotle, Tacitus and others. Maps show the extent to which Europeans lived in the classical past: some marked cities' ancient Greek or Latin names more clearly than their modern ones.[30] Escorted by janissaries lent by their consul, it was easy for Europeans from Smyrna to visit the ruins of Ephesus, or to buy Greek and Roman coins and medals, and engraved gems, in the bazaar.[31]

In 1625, by leave of the Ottoman authorities, the English ambassador in Constantinople, Sir Thomas Roe, organized expeditions to Smyrna, Ephesus and the surrounding cities and islands to look for 'marbles hidden in the ground' for the Duke of Buckingham and the Earl of Arundel – the first major collections of classical antiquities in the British Isles were formed in the Ottoman Empire. In 1628, as he was leaving the Ottoman Empire, Roe went to Smyrna in person, to supervise 'collecting and lading' the marbles on to ships bound for England.[32]

In other cities like Constantinople and Aleppo, in order to assert Muslim and Ottoman supremacy, Ottoman authorities built mosques with distinctive Ottoman domes and minarets, to dominate the skyline. Smyrna's appearance was more commercial than religious. The spacious sweep of the bay, surrounded by wooded mountains, was filled with white-sailed ships, taller than the tallest buildings, and hundreds of 'little trafficking barks'. Surrounded by orange, lemon and mulberry groves, vegetable gardens and vineyards, the city was built on land so low and flat that it seemed to rise straight from the sea.[33] Within the city walls, houses made of wood, wattle and unbaked brick climbed from the shore up the slope of the hill to the massive castle on the crest, past dark-green patches where cypresses marked the presence of a Muslim graveyard. The houses were so similar that from the castle the city seemed to be a single red-brown roof.[34]

A new fort confirmed Smyrna's growing prosperity, and the Ottoman government's growing interest in it. On 28 September 1644, Maltese galleys had seized an Ottoman fleet on its way from Constantinople to Egypt, murdered the Sultan's trusted chief black eunuch on board, enslaved pilgrims, then sailed to Crete and sold the proceeds. Thereby they triggered a war for Crete between Venice and the Ottoman Empire. In the 1650s the Venetian navy took Lemnos and Samothrace and threatened Constantinople itself. Therefore in 1656–7 a fort, guarded by a cannon big enough to contain an entire man, was built at the entrance to the Gulf of Smyrna by Grand Vizier Mehmed Köprülü, to stop Venetian ships attacking and merchants cheating Ottoman customs by taking on loads there. It had a garrison of 200 men paid from the Smyrna customs revenue. Departing ships had to stop to present a certificate proving that they had paid taxes and received customs clearance.[35]

One of the greatest of Ottoman writers, and the only one to devote himself to travel, was Evliya Çelebi. His travel book is a fundamental source for the Ottoman Empire. Born in Constantinople in 1610, he had been told in a dream to travel. Capable of reciting the Koran in eight hours (though, like most Ottoman Koran reciters, he did not know the Arabic in which it is written), he was son of the Sultan's chief jeweller and a boon companion of Murad IV. He despised 'tricky Franks [Western Europeans]', 'treacherous' Jews and Armenians, and hoped God would perpetuate the Ottoman Empire until the end of time. Nevertheless, he also criticized Ottomans' use of torture and the Sultan's Stalin-like insistence, during rebellions, on quotas of heads from provincial governors. Moreover, he had an enquiring mind and tried to check some of his data.[36] He was aware of Smyrna's non-Muslim past: he believed that Alexander the Great had founded the city, and knew that Franks dug for buried treasure there. He commented, about one castle, 'It does not remain from the unbelievers' – as if much else did.

In 1671, at the age of sixty, he visited Smyrna. In the *Seyahatname*, which he composed for his patron Melek Ahmed Pasha, he wrote that the city supported a tax farm of 200,000 gold coins. Order was maintained by detachments of the Sultan's elite forces of janissaries and *bostancis*, and by local cavalry under the captains commanding the two fortresses. The city's chief officials were a kadi, to administer Muslim religious law, the *gümrük emini* in charge of customs, and for civilian affairs a *mutesellim*, based in Manisa, 100 miles to the north-east. It was not the capital of a province.[37]

Evliya praised Smyrna as the most celebrated port in the Empire, because of the number of ships loading and unloading there – although he did not like the noise made by the firing of a cannon each time a vessel arrived. When foreign fleets sailed in from Marseille, Amsterdam or London, thousands of small boats rushed out, eager to cut out the middleman and exchange local silk and camel hair, or fresh grapes and peaches, for cloth, tin and household goods such as mirrors, plates, needles and knives.[38] Red was the most popular colour: one boat from Marseille contained 22,000 red cloth caps.[39] Evliya counted 82 *hans* or inns 'like castles', and admired the wealth of the city merchants, both Muslim and non-Muslim. Three thousand six hundred shops paid taxes once a week to the market inspector, and to the janissary police known as 'the six sticks'. In addition there were 40 coffee houses, 70 soap factories, 200 taverns and 20 *bozahanes* selling a fermented alcoholic drink made of wheat – the interdiction against drinking alcohol was, for many Muslims in the Levant, a fiction.[40]

Evliya complained that Smyrna resembled an ocean of people. The streets were so crowded that people rubbed shoulders and it was impossible to walk comfortably. Alexander Drummond, who visited the city a hundred years later, agreed. Smyrna was 'not at all handsome; for the streets are so narrow they scarce deserve the appellation of lanes, as dirty at all times as kennels, and so crowded where the business of the Franks is carried on, that one cannot pass without great difficulty'. Streets changed direction from house to house; in the market they were lined by wooden stalls with owners yelling the prices of cabbages or melons. Camels and mules were the main means of transport. People had to stand aside in the lanes, to allow them to pass or to kneel down to be unloaded.[41] Even the main thoroughfare of the Frank district, called Frank Street, parallel to the coast, was 'dirty, ill-paved and narrow', with a gutter running down the middle.[42] One of the characteristics of houses throughout the Ottoman Empire, from Damascus to Sarajevo, was the *cumba* or projecting window – built out of love of light, and of watching street-life.[43] In Smyrna some *cumbas* protruded so far that they almost touched each other across the street, and stopped light from reaching below.[44] There were no large streets or squares.

Further confirmation of Smyrna's international importance came during the vizierate of Fazil Ahmed Köprülü. He may have been shocked by the difficulty of using Smyrna as an Ottoman base during the war to conquer Crete from Venice. The Empire built back. In 1676 he built the Vizier Han near the sea – partly from remains of the Greek theatre in the upper city. A massive walled rectangle with two storeys of bedrooms for travelling merchants, above arcaded courtyards full of shops, it is still an impressive building.[45] He also built a double aqueduct and fountains to ensure the city's water supply. Until the end of the Empire his *waqf*, or charitable trust, including markets, warehouse and shops, was one of the main employers in the city. In 1675 a wooden customs house, where merchants were henceforth obliged to have their goods examined by Ottoman customs officials and pay their dues, was built on pylons out in the sea, with stairs so that goods could be unloaded directly from a boat – thus the Ottoman authorities hoped to check fraud. Further signs of increased imperial control were the transfer of Smyrna from the authority of the Kaptan Pasha, or head of the Ottoman navy, to the province of Aydin, a Muslim city one hundred miles inland, and the reallocation of its tax revenue to the Sultan's mother.[46]

If foreigners dominated Smyrna's trade with Europe and with distant Ottoman ports such as Alexandria and Sidon (half the French ships arriving in Smyrna had set out from other Ottoman ports), Ottomans controlled trade with smaller ports of the Empire and with the interior. Principal hub of a vast network of inland trade routes, Smyrna's rise was helped by European merchants' certainty that their products would find buyers there. Smyrna was, as contemporaries wrote, where Asia came shopping for Europe.[47]

The inland trade routes were used by caravans of camels – since the Ottoman conquest of Syria and Egypt in 1517, camels had spread to Anatolia.[48] From Persia, via Aleppo, on journeys that took up to seven months, caravans of 1,500 camels and horses at a time brought opium, silk and Indian textiles – as well as Armenian immigrants working in the associated trades. They returned with spices and European goods like scissors, mirrors and watches. The area around Ankara supplied mohair (goat or camel hair); Smyrna and the surrounding region provided carpets, rhubarb and mastic from Chios, as well as figs, raisins, wine and cotton.[49] Again international politics favoured Smyrna: from the 1620s these caravans began to avoid the great inland trading city of Aleppo because of a return of Iranian–Ottoman wars, the difficulty of evading customs dues, and the horror of its port city Iskanderun, described as 'the cemetery of the Franks'. Surrounded by marshes, its air was vile and the people 'worse than Devils'.[50]

Smyrna soon developed different districts for Greeks, Jews and Armenians as well as Turks and Franks. Like Pera, from the beginning it was a city of churches and synagogues, as well as mosques. There was what seemed to astonished Europeans 'an entire freedom of religion'.[51] In accordance with sharia law, churches could be built or rebuilt provided that the Ottoman authorities were satisfied there had originally been a church on the same site: given the number of ruined Byzantine churches in the city, modern churches could obtain permission with little difficulty. Government architects issued permits specifying how and in what dimensions they were to be built.[52]

Smyrna even acquired its own Christian shrine. By 1654, perhaps as a result of an anti-dervish movement by the Ottoman authorities, a dervish shrine had been occupied by Christian monks. Religious tradition being 'as easily manufactured as perpetuated', it re-emerged as the burial place, shrine and church of St John Polycarp – the fourth bishop of Smyrna, who had been burnt alive by Roman authorities in AD 167. Hidden behind walls and usually inaccessible, the church, now seat of the Roman Catholic archbishop and called Aziz Polikarp Kilesi, still holds services today, although the congregation rarely numbers more than ten. It contains a revered black Madonna encased in silver, and its floor is laid with the elegant inscribed tombstones of the Catholic merchants of the city, rescued from an abandoned cemetery.[53] In Smyrna as in Pera, Muslims entered churches – even lighting candles – to hear the music or to gain divine protection in addition to that implored for in mosques.[54]

Smyrna was both Ottoman and European. By 1700 it had three Catholic, two Greek and two Armenian churches, and eight synagogues.[55] In some streets you could hear the sound of the organ playing in Catholic churches.[56] In Frank Street you might be in a Christian country. You could hear Dutch, English, Italian, French and particularly Provençal being spoken, and see Jesuit and Capuchin monks in their distinctive robes. Whereas Ottomans always wore turbans or, in the case of Christians or Jews, caps, in the Frank district men wore hats.[57]

As early as 1610 the Porte was complaining that Jews were moving to Smyrna from Salonica and Manisa and should be sent back 'immediately'. They were prominent in tax farms (many sources of government revenue were farmed out to the highest bidder, to speed collection) and in customs.[58] The first printing press in Smyrna was a Jewish one, using the Hebrew alphabet, which started working there in 1649.[59] A Jewish printer from Smyrna, who had been printing in Spanish (the daily language of Ottoman Jews, most of whom descended from Jews expelled from Spain in 1492), later printed the first English book in the Ottoman Empire: the copy made by Paul Rycaut (English consul in Smyrna from 1667 to 1678) of the capitulations renewed in 1662 between Charles II and Mehmed IV.[60]

Smyrna even produced its own Levantine Messiah. Sabbatai Sevi was born in Smyrna in 1626, the son of a Jewish broker working for English merchants who had come from Greece around 1614. A manic-depressive visionary, in 1648 he proclaimed himself the Messiah and – having failed to consummate two marriages to humans – married himself to the Torah during a banquet. Driven from his native city by outraged rabbis, he then wandered round the Mediterranean. On his return to Smyrna in 1665, he declared himself King of Israel, the Sultan Sabbatai Sevi, who will 'take the kingship from the ruler of Turkey'.[61] This assertion of power and royalty – as local Jews were feeling economically vulnerable as Christians became more numerous and prosperous – made him popular. He walked through the streets of the city surrounded by a bodyguard of 'the frenzied rabble', who listened to him as if he was the voice of God.[62]

Hysterical scenes of mass public penance, in expectation of the impending end of the world, spread from Smyrna to Jewish communities as far away as Poland. Even rabbis believed the Sultan would abdicate in Sabbatai's favour. Master of the Jewish community of Smyrna, he abolished fasts and declared his two brothers kings of Judah and Israel and emperors of Rome and Turkey respectively. Synagogues began to pray not for the Sultan but for 'the King of Kings, the Sultan Sabbatai Sevi'. He was sexually as well as politically liberating. He commanded his followers to send him their virgin daughters, whom he returned a few days later, swearing he had not touched them.[63] Accusations – not entirely unfounded – that his followers practised free love, or ritual wife-swapping, continued down to the twentieth century.

The Ottoman government soon reacted. Brought before the Sultan in Edirne in September 1666, Sabbatai renounced his royal pretensions. Finally, given the choice of conversion or impalement, he tore off his Jewish cap and adopted the Muslim turban. Known as Aziz Mehmed Efendi, he died in exile in what is now Montenegro in 1676. Back in Smyrna, many of his followers remained in 'dejection of the spirit' and returned to orthodox Judaism. Others continued to believe in Sabbatai Sevi even though he no longer believed in himself. They thought only his shadow on earth had become Muslim: his body and soul had been taken to heaven. Some of them, as Sabbatai had advised, converted to Islam, assumed Muslim names and outward practices, but remained secret believers in Judaism or in Sabbatai: they retained Jewish dietary rules and a tendency to marry in their own community and to use Ladino and Hebrew prayers in secret.[64] Known as *dönme* or 'turned',[65] they remained numerous and powerful in Smyrna and Salonica, and were to exercise considerable influence on the Young Turk revolution and the Turkish Republic.

Despite the vitality of its Christian and Jewish communities, Smyrna was a predominantly Muslim city – its prosperity encouraged Muslim immigrants from the countryside, for whom mosques had to be constructed. Evliya Çelebi's account of the city is dominated by triumphant Muslim statistics. He counted 310 mihrabs or prayer niches in the city, 77 masjids (prayer halls), 40 madrasas and, by the sea, a large open-air prayer space capable of holding 100,000 men. Unlike churches and synagogues, mosques were used day and night. The 'Bearded Mosque', built over the shops of the perfumers, was never free of congregations. Its beauty resembled that of a white pearl. The Ahmed Aga Mosque, built in 1668, by the port at the beginning of the new bazaar, had coloured glass from Constantinople 'worthy of King Suleiman': when the sun shone it was like an emerald. 'Its splendour illuminates the city of Izmir.' Mosques were built by el-Hajj Yussuf, Sheikh Mustafa Faik Pasha, Ahmed Agha's mother and many others. Evliya records as something unusual a mosque not containing a prayer area on the side reserved for women.[66]

Other prosperous Muslim merchants mentioned by Evliya were Mahmud Efendi, Hasan Aga, Kucuk Huseyin Aga and Ahmed Aga. The tomb of Marcus Fabius served as a fountain in the hospitable garden of Ahmed Aga.[67] Ahmed shared a taste for classical antiquities with one of the richest merchants of the city, called Imamoglu, who arrived from Ankara in the mid seventeenth century with a few bales of goat hair. By the end of his life he owned flocks of sheep and goats, more slaves and houses than he could count, and many of the vegetable gardens outside the city. However much he was offered, Imamoglu would not sell the marble statues he discovered under his properties.[68]

Smyrna showed that, even at the height of its power, the Ottoman Empire could rule with a light touch. In the 1670s the Empire had just taken Crete from Venice, and Podolia from Poland; it was preparing to attack Vienna itself. Yet in Smyrna Evliya was awed by the wealth and power of the Franks and their consuls: 'The ships of the Franks come so often that half of the city of Izmir is like Frengistan [Europe]. If someone hits a *gavur* [a Turkish word for non-Muslim], everyone immediately surrounds him and takes him and brings him to the consular judge or the *keffires* [unbelievers] execute him. And at that time the Muslim people become invisible, so that at this time it seems a dark Frank place like Malta.'[69] Malta – home of the Knights of St John, whose duty and trade was to raid Muslim (and sometimes Christian) shipping throughout the Levant – was a synonym of horror for Muslims, owing to the thousands of Muslim slaves it contained. It was easy for the Knights to discover who were Muslims on board a captured ship and take them as slaves 'as they are circumcised', wrote Richard Pococke, who witnessed such an event in 1739.[70]

Consuls were the key power-brokers in the Levant. In Smyrna, as in Pera, to enhance their status as well as to protect their persons, they were escorted by janissaries holding six-foot-long ivory-knobbed staves with which they beat the ground, as well as by their own liveried footmen. Consuls were expected to keep open house for travellers and merchants – which cost little, since food and wine could be had 'almost for nothing'. Living in what seemed like 'a small palace', the French consul served French, Spanish and Italian as well as local wines, and received guests 'to the sound of bottles and flagons'. He also possessed a library with the latest gazettes.[71]

Paul Rycaut demonstrates consuls' importance as cultural transmitters, like ambassadors in Pera. Born in London in 1629 of Dutch origins, he came to Constantinople in 1661 as secretary to the English ambassador Lord Winchilsea. In 1667 he made his entry as English consul into Smyrna escorted by a hundred merchants and six trumpeters: in the Levant, as in Europe, music was a sign of power. He occupied himself with commerce, antiquities, and negotiating anti-piracy treaties with the rulers of Algiers, Tunis and Tripoli. He also began to write his pioneering books on the Ottoman Empire: *The Present State of the Ottoman Empire* (1667), *The Present State of the Greek and Armenian Churches* (1679), *The History of the Turkish Empire* (1680) and *The History of the Turks* (1700). Rycaut spoke Turkish, ancient and modern Greek, Latin, French and English. His books were based on Ottoman registers and on such Levantine informants as a palace employee originally called Albert Bobowski, the imperial dragoman Mamucha della Torre, the Sultan's doctor Dr Marcellini, and a Smyrna friend called Sheytan Ibrahim, who had been governor of Egypt and was later commander-in-chief of Ottoman forces in Hungary. Despite errors, *The Present State of the Ottoman Empire* was translated into French, Italian, Dutch, German, Polish and Russian. Thus Smyrna was not only 'the eye of Asia', but also one of Europe's eyes on Asia.[72]

Rycaut devoted his career to the Ottoman Empire; he admired the grand vizier Fazil Ahmed Köprülü, and praised Ottoman discipline and charity. In 1675, after the renewal of the English capitulations – which remained in force until 1923 – he wrote, 'The honour and privilege which Our Nation enjoyeth here and security of our persons and Estates under the Turkes ... is beyond the example of former times.' However, he was as prejudiced against Ottomans as he was against other foreigners. He felt that the Ottoman Empire would 'never be nourished by softness and the arts and blandishments of Peace', wrote that a Turk 'is not capable of real friendship towards a Christian', and considered that one reason for the banning of books printed by or for Muslims in the Ottoman Empire (Jews and Christians could and did print books) was its government's fear of 'that subtlety of Learning which is inconsistent with as well as dangerous to the grossness of their Government'.[73]

In reality there were other reasons for the interdiction: the difficulty of printing Arabic script; fear of scribal unemployment; love of calligraphy. The French scholar Antoine Galland said that, when a book by the Arab scientist Ibn Sina was available in a cheaper printed edition, buyers still preferred manuscript versions. Perhaps the main reason was the conviction that the Koran is the literal word of God, and calligraphy the supreme art. To own a beautifully written manuscript of the Koran was meritorious. When printing by Muslims was allowed, in 1727, it was on condition that no religious work was printed.[74] For the same reasons there was no printing in the Persian and Mogul empires.

Thus, until the spread of printing and accurate French maps (such as the superb collection of plans of the ports of the Mediterranean by Joseph Roux, printed in Marseille in 1764, and dedicated to the French foreign minister the Duc de Choiseul) in the late eighteenth century, the Ottoman Empire had no easy access to reliable maps. The absence of printed books also limited education. Literacy in the Empire is thought to have been around 1 per cent before 1800, rising to perhaps 15 per cent by 1914.[75] Most people in the Ottoman Empire were cut off from contemporary information revolutions.

Rycaut noted too that in Smyrna 'the Greeks have also an inclination to the Moscovite beyond any other Christian prince, as being of their Rites and Religion, terming him their Emperor and Protector, from whom according to ancient Prophesies and modern Predictons they expect delivery and freedom to their Church.'[76] Indeed, confirming the fragility – and, for some, the illegitimacy – of the Ottoman Empire, in the seventeenth century Ecumenical Patriarchs, no doubt reflecting the desires of their flock, repeatedly sent secret messages from Constantinople to the Tsar in Moscow, at risk of their lives, asking him to invade and liberate the

Orthodox, suggesting appropriate moments and routes. (The messages, in Greek, are still in the national archives in Moscow.) Greek dreams of liberation by Russia increased the built-in combustibility of the Levant.[77]

If consuls lived like princes, Western merchants – in all there were perhaps five or six hundred French, English, Dutch and Venetians in Smyrna in 1678 – lived like lords.[78] In theory, foreigners were forbidden to own property in the Ottoman Empire. However, Smyrna was a law unto itself. By the mid seventeenth century foreigners had country houses in the nearby Greek villages of Buca and Bornova, and entertained themselves by hunting and shooting – boar, bears, ibex, duck.[79] The English merchants were the richest; they imported their own hounds to hunt hares, and were said to drink as much wine as all the other foreigners together.[80]

In the seventeenth century Smyrna's international trade was dominated by the Dutch and the English. The Dutch displayed in the Levant the same energy which had led them to establish trading posts, from Nagasaki to New Amsterdam, as New York was called when it was founded in 1626, at roughly the same time that Smyrna became a great port. Dutch merchants became famous for disputes with their consul, liaisons with local women, and banquets.[81]

The most prominent Dutch family of Smyrna, the de Hochepieds, served as consuls in Smyrna and ambassadors in Constantinople. Daniel Jean de Hochepied, 'gentle, civil and insinuating', the Dutch consul from 1688 to 1723, was so respected that he was called 'Monsieur le Consul', as if he were the only one. When he died, thousands of Muslims, Greeks and Armenians as well as Franks attended his funeral. His wife, Clara Catherine, had been brought up in Constantinople, where her father, Justinus Colyer, Dutch ambassador from 1668 to 1682, had in 1680 secured the renewal of the Dutch capitulations, at vast expense. Madame de Hochepied's connections with the Sultan's mother were so good that in 1710 she helped obtain a firman authorizing the construction of a new church for the Franciscans of Smyrna. Although themselves Calvinists, the Hochepieds became the church's official protectors, thereby raising their prestige in the city and the Dutch community.[82]

Sons inherited parents' networks. The Hochepieds' son Daniel Alexander, born in Smyrna in 1689, succeeded his father as Dutch consul in 1723, and assembled a fine collection of medals and antiquities. His brother Elbert de Hochepied was Dutch ambassador in Constantinople in 1747–63.[83] A later de Hochepied was Dutch consul and Austrian vice-consul in Smyrna in 1796–1810 and 1814–24.[84] The family did not leave Smyrna until after the 1922 catastrophe.

English merchants bought Ottoman silk and sold English cloth. Generally youngest sons of gentry families, with shares in ships called *Smyrna Factor* or *Levant Merchant*, they dominated the Levant Company in London. On retirement to England, they had often made enough money to purchase a country estate or marry a daughter into the peerage.[85] They had been sufficiently confident, by 1646, for disputes between parliamentarians and royalists in Smyrna to put 'the whole town ... in an uprore'. The Porte had been powerless to stop them.[86]

Whereas foreign merchants in Aleppo lived shut up in their own *hans* at night, like undergraduates in Oxford colleges,[87] in Smyrna they lived in houses of their own. Often made of stone, these looked 'tolerably handsome' compared to the 'inelegant, inconvenient' houses of the locals. They generally had one front on Frank Street; behind were warehouses, terraces and, sticking out into the sea, wooden galleries and lavatories.[88] Europe was more of a reality in Smyrna than in most European cities: in Smyrna, Europeans were said to live in 'a most particular union undisturbed by any difference of Religion or nation or any party feeling, even in wartime'. Almost all kept open house.[89] Either to avoid insults, or to counter the effects of the heat, most wore Turkish dress, with a hat to show they were Christians. As in Constantinople and other Levantine ports, the principal common languages, until the 1830s, were Italian and lingua franca.[90]

When Galland reproached some French merchants with not learning Turkish, they replied that they had so little contact with Turks that they did not need to. Also, in Smyrna merchants used Jews, many of whom spoke Turkish (Sabbatai Sevi's father, for example), as middlemen in trade. 'All trade is conducted through Jews,' wrote the French botanist Pitton de Tournefort in 1702. In all, in addition to lingua franca, twelve languages could be heard in the streets of Smyrna: Turkish, Arabic, Persian, Armenian, Greek, Russian (spoken by slaves), Hebrew, Italian, Portuguese, French, English and Dutch.[91]

In Smyrna the working day was broken for Muslims by the five ritual prayers; for Franks by breakfast at eight, dinner at one, and a siesta. Supper at eight was followed by visits to each other's houses. As in Pera, networks of visits linked consuls, foreign merchants and prominent Turks. When the Kaptan Pasha visited Smyrna with his fleet of galleys, during his annual inspection of the Aegean islands, of which he was governor, he expected to receive visits and presents of telescopes or brocade from local merchants.[92] However, visits rarely stretched into meals. Turks sat on cushions rather than chairs, and ate with their hands rather than knives and forks. It was easier for non-Turks to smoke pipes or drink coffee than to dine with them.[93] In November 1670 the Rev. John Covel noted a dinner with a rich Turk, 'a very courteous man and friendly to all our Nation', as an exceptional event. Covel sat down 'Taylor like, crosse-leg'd' on a carpet, enjoyed the 'good, plain, wholesome food', and later wrote, 'All things being so quite different from our own way of living did very much surprise me with wonder and delight.'[94]

Although heads of guilds in Smyrna were generally Muslim, Christians and Muslims worked together in, for example, the dyers' or carpenters' guilds. The relative silence of the central archives suggests an absence of conflict in the workplace: when it occurred, it usually opposed Smyrna craftsmen – Muslim, Christian and Jewish – against those of foreign origin or working for foreigners. In 1685 the Dutch consul obtained an order from the Porte to stop a Smyrna tailor from harassing the Dutch tailor who was making clothes for the Dutch. In 1817 Smyrna carpenters complained about attempts to stop them from working in the Frank quarter.[95]

The Muslim women of Smyrna remained in a world of their own. Covered from head to toe in white veils, with a black cloth masking the face, except for small holes for the eyes, they were dominated by family and piety. They were free to make expeditions to the bazaars for shopping, or to graveyards to pray at their relations' tombs and drink coffee. Behind their veils, they appeared 'inelegantly protuberant to the English eye'.[96]

The Christian women of Smyrna, however, according to one visitor, provided 'the most admirable collection of charming feminine faces I have ever seen'.[97] Evliya Çelebi wrote of the *gavur* 'beloveds' (*dilbers*) that 'when young Muslim men see their sweet-smelling and dishevelled locks their minds become ruined and confused.' Later visitors were equally enthusiastic: 'The Smyrniote ladies thus blending oriental and Frank manners and customs are considered extremely attractive.'[98] Combining the grace of Italians, the vivacity of Greeks, and the 'stately tournure' of Ottomans, they possessed 'almost irresistible fascination'.[99] Sitting out in the evening in the Rue des Roses, they were admired, for having lips like coral, eyes like fire and 'looks which pierce your brain'. Until the switch to European fashions in the 1840s, they wore jewels and gold coins in their headdress so 'the suitor can reckon as well as admire the object of his affection'.[100] Moreover, they were 'particularly attentive to strangers'. Smyrna was said to be the paradise of sailors.[101]

Like Pera, Smyrna acquired a reputation, still extant today, for sexual freedom. Until the middle of the twentieth century, women of the Greek mainland were suspicious of Smyrna women for being too clean (*pastrika*) – almost whores.[102] The city's reputation inspired one of the most famous playwrights of the eighteenth century. Carlo Goldoni's *L'impresario di Smirna* (1759) is a comic play about the desire of a rich Turkish merchant of the city to form a company to mount an opera there – driven by desire for the singers' bodies rather than their music. The play is a warning against ruinous passions.[103]

The wine in Smyrna was as good as the women. The French and the English inhabitants were generally in good humour, considered the French traveller Monsieur Poullet in 1668, because 'the wine there is so exquisite that unless you are naturally doltish, you have to lose there all the malignity of melancholy.'[104] The English would oblige guests to drink when they did not want to, attacked the French consulate shouting 'French dogs' and further insults, or set fire to Frenchmen's clothes. Some even proclaimed themselves Muslim.[105] On the quays, taverns were open all night: people danced 'à la française', 'à la grecque' or 'à la turque'. By the 1660s the season of revelry before the four-week fasting season of Lent, known throughout Catholic Europe as carnival, was celebrated at Smyrna, as in Pera, with such frenzies of drinking and dancing that Turks thought the revellers mad. (Probably carnival came to Smyrna from Catholic Europe rather than, as on the Greek islands, being a relic of the pagan past.)[106] In the eighteenth century European consuls tried to stop Turks frequenting the taverns of the Frank quarter, where they could enjoy 'the most absolute freedom ... to commit every kind of outrage'.[107] Even for the Ottoman government, Smyrna and wine were synonymous. If, on occasion, the grand vizier tried to ban the sale of wine in Constantinople, he issued orders that customs officials were not to interfere in any way with foreigners' wine in Smyrna.[108]

From 5,000 in 1600, the population had risen to 30,000–40,000 in 1650 and to around 100,000 in 1700, perhaps distributed in a ratio of seven Turks to two Greeks, one Armenian and one Jew.[109] Despite its narrow lanes and stinking alleys, most travellers liked Smyrna. Evliya praised it for the sweetness of the air and water, the wealth and hospitality of its merchants, and the quality of the soap and the honey.[110] The French traveller and jeweller Jean-Baptiste Tavernier wrote in 1634, 'Smyrna is today for trade by both sea and land the most famous city of all the Levant and the most famous market for every merchandise going from Europe to Asia and from Asia to Europe.' Pitton de Tournefort, who visited it in 1702, sent by the French government to investigate the plants of Anatolia, called it 'one of the richest store-houses in the world'.[111]

Smyrna was so rich that it could affect international politics. The English attack in peacetime on the Dutch 'Smyrna fleet' in 1664 was a signal for war to break out between the two countries. The French destruction of the Anglo-Dutch 'Smyrna fleet' off Gibraltar in June 1693, when over 100 ships were captured or sunk, was a catastrophe that brought down the responsible Secretary of State, the Tory Earl of Nottingham, and helped lead to the creation of the Bank of England in order to finance a new fleet. Louis XIV had been so eager for news of the action that he asked for his door to be broken down when it arrived.[112]

Travellers called Smyrna 'the pearl of the Levant'. In reality it was also a city of earthquakes, plagues, fires and massacres – so frequent that only its inhabitants' resilience, and the unsuitability of rival ports, can explain its continued prosperity. Most years in the eighteenth century saw outbreaks of plague. The plague of 1739–42, for example, claimed 20 per cent of the population, that of 1759–65 about 50,000 lives (half the city), that of 1784 thousands more, that of 1812–15 some 45,000.[113] There was little knowledge of hygiene. Greek priests were allowed to sell on the clothes of dead plague victims, thereby spreading the infection.[114] As in Constantinople, in times of plague most Turks remained in the city, trusting in God, despite the groans from the dying in the street. If they could, Franks and local Christians withdrew to the country, or shut themselves in their houses for periods of months at a time known as 'the closure'. They obtained provisions by letting down baskets on string, or from foreign ships through the galleries at the back of their houses, without anyone touching land. Letters were fumigated with nitre and brimstone.[115] A relic of these plague months are the massive walls, designed to keep out infection, still surrounding the gardens of Bornova.

Earthquakes shook the city in 1688 and 1788; the second may have claimed 15,000 lives. The kadi was suspected of involvement in a fire which destroyed two-thirds of the city in 1742. There were further fires in 1752 and 1763. In 1787, worried by the imminence of another Russian–Turkish war, the Franks set up their own police force to put out fires in their quarter.[116]

Other disasters were man-made. Below Smyrna's smiling surface was a volcano waiting to erupt. In 1678 Galland attributed the relative peace in which the different communities lived among each other to the 'rigour' of Ottoman laws: in their hearts even Christians of different sects, as well as Muslims and Jews, hated each other 'mortally' – all the more fiercely for being obliged to pretend not to.[117] Any sign of Christian pride could arouse Muslim anger. In 1636, for example, when an English ship arrived in the port flying a flag with the red cross of St George, people raged 'that the *gavurs* should not dare wear their cross aloft in the port of the Grand Seigneur'. After three or four days' rioting, the foreign consuls went in a body to the kadi and said that, if it did not stop, they would leave. The kadi then 'appeased the fury of the people', by means unspecified. The presence in the harbour of sailors from North Africa, or the Kaptan Pasha and his fleet, often triggered riots. Drunken sailors would attack Franks or their churches on Frank Street.[118]

During the War of the Holy League, opposing the Holy Roman Empire, Poland and Venice against the Ottoman Empire in 1683–99, as Austrian and Polish armies plunged into Ottoman territory in the Balkans, and even Louis XIV sent agents to decide which Ottoman cities would be easiest to seize, Venice – by no means a spent force – conquered much of Greece. On 28 April 1694, 14,000 Venetian soldiers seized Chios, expelling its Muslim population and threatening Smyrna itself. Smyrna's defences, Galland had noticed in 1678, were as weak as those of most Ottoman cities. If Venice were to attack the city, there were fears of a retaliatory massacre of Christians – and the plundering of warehouses – by Muslims. The Levantine system swung into action. Presumably with the knowledge of the Ottoman authorities, certainly with the approval of his English and Dutch colleagues, the French consul persuaded the Venetian admiral to withdraw his fleet.[119] The war in Europe opposing France and England and the Netherlands was overlooked. On this occasion the possibility of Muslim attacks on Smyrna Christians had acted as a deterrent against attack by a foreign power – in effect as insurance for the entire city. Fear of massacre prevented invasion.[120]

The only result was that on Chios, abandoned by Venice on the arrival of an Ottoman fleet in February 1695, conditions for Catholics deteriorated. A few were hanged. Catholic churches were destroyed or converted into mosques or Orthodox churches. The Ottoman authorities forbade Catholics from wearing hats or Genoese dress, and obliged them to salute the humblest Muslim.[121]

In the eighteenth century France dominated the foreign trade, as it did the foreign relations, of the Ottoman Empire. Although the Levant trade had declined in relative terms compared to world trade, Smyrna had become the largest and wealthiest port of the Empire, surpassing Constantinople itself. In the period 1748–89 one in four ships leaving Marseille went to Smyrna – the biggest of all foreign ports for French international trade. Smyrna's trade linked it more closely to Europe than to the Empire itself. With France Smyrna's trade was valued at 20 million livres; with Constantinople at 7 million. By 1740 there was a a quay along the sea, to which 'the small boats come up and load at their doors'.[122]

Some merchants who arrived in Smyrna from France and the Netherlands in the eighteenth century still have descendants trading there today, such as the Guys, Pagy, Giraud and Keun families. The many branches of the Giraud family descend from Jean-Baptiste Giraud. He arrived from Antibes in 1780, married Hélène, daughter of the last Venetian consul, Luigi Cortazzi, in 1787,[123] and himself − by inheritance from his father-in-law, since Austria had annexed Venice − became Austrian consul. Thus the French-speaking 'second Levant' of the nineteenth century was connected by marriage to the Italian-speaking 'first Levant' of the previous centuries.[124] The Catholic Aliotti, d'Andria and Marcopoli families were of Venetian or Genoese origin. They came from Chios to Smyrna in the late eighteenth or early nineteenth century, working as consuls and merchants, often at the same time.

Though Smyrna prospered, after 1750 the Ottoman Empire appeared close to disintegration. It had begun its long retreat in the Balkans. Conversions to Islam, still frequent in the seventeenth century, collapsed thereafter. After the renewal of France's capitulations in 1740, France had greater privileges − and rewards to offer its clients − than before. The Empire knew it was weakening. Ottoman officials themselves began to employ French, rather than Ottoman, ships for transport, and used French consuls and ambassadors as intermediaries with their own government.[125]

Amiral de Bauffremont, later 'vice-amiral ès mers du Levant', toured the Levant with the French fleet in 1766. A magnificent picture, now in the Musée de la Marine in Paris, commemorates his procession through Smyrna to visit the *mutesellim* or governor, along Frank Street, on 28 September 1766, escorted by janissaries, naval officers, dragomans and French merchants, and watched by 'Madame la Consulesse de France avec les dames de la Nation' and 'all Smyrna'. The procession frequently came to a halt to enable Turkish servants to sprinkle the Admiral with perfume and orange-flower water. The picture is a glorification of the Ottoman−French alliance. Bauffremont had just been received by the Kaptan Pasha on board his flagship, with coffee, sorbet and jam and offers of service 'for me personally as well as for the King's vessels … The Grand Seigneur could not do too much for the Emperor of France his friend.'

Yet Bauffremont no longer trusted in the Empire's future. In his 'journal de campagne', while praising Smyrna for its pleasures and 'douceur des mœurs', he wrote, 'On all sides one sees revolts … everything announces its decadence and the end perhaps nearer than we think ... The Grand Seigneur is extremely hated by his subjects.'[126] It is not foreign intervention in the Ottoman Empire which is surprising, but that more of it did not take place sooner.

In 1768, outraged by Russian interference in Poland, and encouraged by the French government and its own public, the Ottoman Empire declared war on Russia, for the third time since 1700. In 1769, in one of the most remarkable naval feats of the century, a Russian fleet had sailed from St Petersburg round Europe, through the Strait of Gibraltar, into the eastern Mediterranean; the island of Paros in the Aegean became its base. It was the beginning of the end of the Ottoman Empire. Ottoman forces no longer showed the skill and valour which had helped them to defeat Russia in 1711, Venice in 1715 and the Habsburg monarchy in 1739.

With Russian help, a rising in the Peloponnese occurred during which cruelties were perpetrated on both sides. Both Muslims and Greeks fled to the safety of Anatolia.[127] Russia controlled the eastern Mediteranean. Twenty-four Russian ships burnt the Ottoman fleet at Çeşme, fifty miles from Smyrna, on 7 July 1770. Defeat in the Aegean meant blood on the streets of Smyrna, for Greeks' 'fanaticism' for Catherine II was well known.[128] They believed ancient prophecies that they would be liberated by a fair-haired race from the North, that the Marble Emperor who slept below the Golden Gate of Constantinople would rise and restore the Byzantine Empire.[129] In Smyrna on 8 July, spurred by a fanatical customs official called Ibrahim Aga, Muslims killed thousands of Greeks and the Dutch dragoman. Many Christians took refuge on foreign ships moored in the harbour.[130] Like the Venetians in 1694, however, and for the same reason, the Russian fleet in 1770 abstained from attacking Smyrna, to save Christian lives. In this Asian city, Europe could be a political reality. On 2 August, according to a Russian officer, 'a small vessel came under the admiral's stern, filled with English, French and Italian merchants who came express from the several consuls at Smyrna to intreat Count Orloff [the Russian commander] not to come with his fleet before the city as they greatly feared that the consequences would be a general massacre of all the Christians.'[131] Nevertheless, the possibility of what the consuls, in a joint letter to their ambassadors in the capital, called 'absolute chaos' and further massacres by 'the city's mob' persisted.[132] From being a haven of commerce, Smyrna had become a powder keg.

In June 1772 and again for five months from October 1773 to February 1774 Russian ships seized Beirut – the first mainland Levantine port to be occupied by a foreign power since the crusades. It was then a city of about

5,000 whose main fort was a former crusader castle, itself built with stones from Roman temples. The city was sacked; its inhabitants were forced to bow to a portrait of Catherine II erected above the main gate of the city walls.[133]

Russian ships threatened Constantinople itself. The forts of the Bosphorus and the Dardanelles were repaired with the help of French engineers, supplied by the French ambassador, the Comte de Saint-Priest; the French consul in Smyrna helped organize the restoration of the forts guarding the city. The capital's food supply also depended on the French ambassador, who organized the transport of wheat from Salonica on French ships: Ottoman ships would have been seized by the Russian fleet.[134]

By the Treaty of Kuchuk Kainardji of 21 July 1774, Russia was allowed to establish consulates throughout the Ottoman Empire and began to claim, on the basis of a misinterpretation of one clause of the treaty, the right to protect its Orthodox Christians: in reality the Russian government had merely been granted the right to build a Russian Orthodox church in Beyoglu or Pera.[135] Ottoman defeats in the war of 1768–74 made plain the weakness of the Ottoman Empire which travellers and diplomats had long been proclaiming. The Ottoman government, fearful and ill-informed, retreated into passivity. The Sultan referred decisions to the religious authorities. The Grand Vizier and different consultative councils also feared to take decisions, and relied on advice from the French ambassador.[136]

In 1776 the mission of the Baron de Tott, a French officer who had helped refortify the Bosphorus forts in 1772, now sent 'to inspect the ports of the Levant', hid a secret pupose, based on oral instructions from Louis XVI and the Minister of Marine – possibly unknown to the rest of the French government. Tott was told to find ways to conquer Egypt and Beirut – the latter's strategic importance had been revealed in the recent war. Tott's report reflected his own and his master's desires more than strategic reality.

Alexandria, the key to Egypt, was protected only by 'a fortress with towers of a very bad construction, which the presence of one of the King's ships would compel to surrender immediately'.[137] A prosperous international port until the sixteenth century, the city now had a population of only about 15,000, although many ships still called at the harbour, often carrying pilgrims on their way from North Africa to Mecca. Since it was a port exposed to attack by Europeans, living there could be seen as a form of jihad, making the city more attractive to pious Muslims. Mosques were built around the tombs of Muslim holy men who had died in Alexandria, such as Abu al-Abbas al-Mursi (from Murcia), Sidi Bishr and Sidi Gabr.[138] Most people lived on a narrow promontory outside the old city walls. The modern port was surrounded by a waste of broken columns and buried cisterns – relics of the centuries when Alexandria, with its lighthouse, library and museum, had been the first cosmopolis, the centre of the trade and learning of the classical world.

Egypt itself had been misgoverned for centuries, under Ottoman suzerainty, by the Mamelukes, a military elite recruited from Caucasian slaves. According to Tott, it would be 'very easy to conquer', and could be controlled by 15,000 French troops. Tott returned to France with detailed maps of cities and forts, and operational plans – which, having survived the Revolution, would be taken out of ministry files in 1798 to be used on Bonaparte's Egyptian expedition. He later published memoirs in which he described the Turks as barbarian fools whose empire was on the edge of extinction. French plans were common knowledge. When the French consulate moved from Cairo to Alexandria in 1777, many in Egypt were convinced it was a sign of an imminent French invasion.[139]

From Smyrna, however, the Empire's future looked different. The French consul-general in Smyrna, Charles-Claude de Peyssonnel, came from a family of dragomans and consuls from Marseille. His father had been consul in Smyrna in 1747–55; he himself served there in 1766–78.

In his writings, Peyssonnel goes beyond clichés about Ottoman barbarism and Western superiority. He stresses the Ottoman government's eagerness for the French alliance and French technicians, and Turks' desire for contact with Westerners, shown by their attendance at embassy receptions and their adoption of foreign drinking and eating habits. Above all he claims that, far from being barbarians, 'there is perhaps no government in the world more human than the Turks', which represses the populations less, which demands fewer taxes, which imposes more moderate levies on commerce.' He carefully explains why, at certain times, interpreters had been killed.[140] He compared the Empire to 'an infinitely robust tree which could dry up under the care of a negligent and inexpert gardener but which under an attentive and clever cultivator can in a short period recover all its sap, its youth, its freshness and raise its proud head above all those which surround it'.[141]

3

Smyrna: Massacres and Merriment

I never saw such unrestrained laughter and merriment combined
with so much natural grace.

Pauline Countess Nostitz, 1835

IN 1782 RUSSIA and Austria had begun to plan to divide the Ottoman
Empire; Catherine II hoped that her grandson Constantine would
become emperor in Constantinople. Smyrna survived unscathed the
Ottoman war against them in 1787–92. The Ottoman alliance with
Sweden prevented a Russian fleet entering the Mediterranean as in 1769.
The Ottoman Empire proved its resilience, as many of the landmarks of
Europe were swept away. Poland was divided between Russia, Austria
and Prussia. The French monarchy, whose servants like Bauffremont and
Tott had so often prophesied the demise of the Ottoman Empire, was
itself overthrown in 1792. Paris suffered a reign of terror.

In 1797 Smyrna endured its own reign of terror — a second warning,
after the massacre in 1770, of the fragility of the Levant. A murder which
might have been of little consequence elsewhere led to an explosion in
Smyrna. In the Levant, intercommunal tensions could be so bitter that
they weakened the authorities' desire to stop killing and looting. The
outbreak also reveals the extent of local resentment at the way capitulations — the foundation stone of the Levant — were being abused to protect
criminals. By the end of the eighteenth century foreign embassies and
consulates were selling certificates of diplomatic protection, or *berats* —
which included freedom from Ottoman taxes — originally meant for their
employees, to hundreds of local Christians and Jews — sometimes Muslims
too — in search of security and protection: further proof of an erosion in
confidence in the Ottoman Empire. For example, the Canetti family —
Jews living in Edirne, ancestors of the writer Elias Canetti — purchased
protection from the Dutch embassy. The British ambasssador Sir Robert
Liston was said to earn £3,000 or £4,000 a year this way.[1]

In 1796 'vagabond Sclavonians' (mainly Dalmatian subjects of Venice) had begun to 'infest' Smyrna, leading to an increase in the number of taverns and 'aqua vita shops' – 'nurseries for thieves'.² Throughout the Empire the janissaries stationed to keep law and order in its principal cities had become fomentors of disorder and extortion. The combination of the two sources of disorder was fatal.

On 12 January 1797, during an exhibition in a local theatre by Italian acrobats travelling under the protection of the imperial (Austrian) consul, a janissary guard was murdered by two Greeks from the island of Cephalonia (and therefore Venetian subjects), who had wanted to watch without paying. The murder went unpunished, despite the authorities' demands. The Venetian and Russian consuls (the latter under suspicion as so many Greeks claimed Russian protection) and their dragomans denied all knowledge of the murderers' whereabouts; the culprits, Mathieu and Antoine Pana, had fled by boat. Long festering with resentment at Venetians' lawlessness, the city was now in a state of 'fermentation'. The kadi told the dragomans that, unless the murderer was delivered, he could not be responsible for the consequences.

On 15 January janissaries paraded their murdered comrade's blood-stained shirt through the streets, 'menacing they would have the blood of the xians' according to the British consul Francis Werry. Six hundred janissaries entered Frank Street with 'bundles of wood', set fire to a Christian *han* at one end, began killing anyone they met, and drove away fire guards and fire engines (including one belonging to the French consulate) coming to extinguish the fire. A southerly wind helped the fire spread in the Frank, Greek and Armenian quarters. In the words of the imperial consul-general Baron de Kraemer, who had urged his colleagues to hand over the murderer, 'All you heard on all sides were the sounds of gunfire, accompanied by terrible shouts which with the awful cries of the dying and wounded formed an atrocious scene.' Only four European houses, and two British warehouses, escaped, thanks to faithful janissaries; all Frank Street, many churches and nine consulates were destroyed. Up to 1,500 Christians – mainly Greeks – lost their lives, including an entire school burnt with sixty pupils inside. Christian children were sold as slaves. All Franks and many others took refuge on foreign boats anchored in the bay. By the evening, with no one left to massacre, the janissaries withdrew to the customs house, to contemplate the progress of the fire they had started.

The crews of the Venetian and some of the Russian ships in the harbour – more Dalmatians – landed in the city to join in the pillage and murder, breaking open the remaining warehouses in search of loot. Werry wrote, 'In the midst of peace and living under the protection of Capitulations we have been treated as savages only could treat enemies in the most furious rage of War. The savage behaviour of the Natives has been nearly equalled by the atrocious behaviour of the crews of the shipping there in the Bay.' The authorities were powerless, cowardly or malevolent. 'Contrary to all former practice neither Mullah, Musellim nor any Turk official was present' to help fire extinguishers or protect Christians. 'Our personal safety on that unfortunate day was the effect of mere chance.'[3] The next day, in a characteristic move to fix the historical record, the local authorities forced local inhabitants to sign a petition to the central government stating that the events were an accident of little importance.[4]

Help finally came from one of those families of notables, and tax farmers, with some of the attributes of hereditary nobility, who were beginning to modernize some Ottoman provinces. They were called Karaosmanoglu. Thanks to their administration in the province of Aydin since the late seventeenth century, inhabitants there were said to 'look better and indeed are better than any others in the country'.[5] Among the richest individuals in the empire, with control of much of south-west Anatolia and its caravan trade, in charge of tax collecting for the central government, *mutesellims* of Manisa for much of the eighteenth century until 1816, the Karaosmanoglus had invited thousands of Greeks from the islands and the Peloponnese to work on their lands, and even built churches for them. In Smyrna they constructed two *hans*. The French consul Peyssonnel would invite them to balls and plays, and would send them his doctor when necessary. For his part Karaosmanzade Hajj Mustfa Aga invited Peyssonnel to tilting parties. He would end letters to his 'très illustre et très sage et très digne et très sincère et très véritable amy et très renommé consul de France à Smyrne' with 'may the Lord grant you precious gifts and long life', and greetings to the consul's wife, daughter and sons.[6] The Karaosmanoglus had already helped to protect Smyrna against brigands in 1739 and to restore order in 1770, and were supporters of the reforming sultan Selim III. In 1792 a Karaosmanoglu had been appointed *kapici bashi* or chief chamberlain. They could supply the central government with 2,500 troops. Urged to intervene now by a letter from the consuls, they restored order, punished offenders, and instituted a new form of government for the town.[7]

'It is all over with Smyrna ... Smyrna is lost for ever,' wrote the Venetian dragoman Joseph Franceschi, beggging in tears to be relieved of his job. He blamed above all 'les esclavons' and the Venetians for 'since a long time' provoking the Turks – a judgement with which Russian ships' captains agreed.[8] By order of the Sublime Porte on 15 May, all unmarried Venetian subjects from the Ionian isles and Dalmatia – described as 'people of a savage rebellious description habitually addicted to heinous practices' – were expelled from Smyrna and other seaports. On 19 May eighteen Turks and three Venetians were executed. Turks were forbidden to bear arms.[9] The extinction in the same year of the Venetian Republic by General Bonaparte, and its annexation by the Habsburg monarchy, ended centuries of Venetian presence in the Levant. As Austrian subjects, Venetians and Dalmatians were henceforth under stricter control: in the nineteenth century they would be replaced, as principal troublemakers in the ports of the Levant, by Maltese.

Protected by its location, and its trade, Smyrna soon recovered its prosperity and insouciance. By one estimate, in 1813 the population had reached around 130,000: 70,000 Turks, 30,000 Greeks, 15,000 Armenians, 10,000 Jews, and perhaps 5,000 Franks.[10]

That year an English banker called J. O. Hanson, who had not experienced the horrors of 1797, found that 'the police of Smyrna is good and the city generally tranquil. Murders are seldom heard of ... For months together the sky is cloudless.'[11] In this period, from Sarajevo to Damascus, merchants had views of Constantinople painted on the walls of their stately stone or wooden mansions: it was the centre of their world. The remarkable uniformity of style throughout different regions of the vast empire is probably explained by the fact that the murals were painted by teams of itinerant craftsmen from the mountains of Macedonia, moving from patron to patron. In Smyrna, however, in a new pulpit for Hisar Cami and in the water fountains of two new *hans*, the Donertaş (1805) and the Cakaloglu (1813–14), views of Smyrna itself were painted.[12]

Passing through on a pilgrimage to Jerusalem in 1806, Chateaubriand compared Smyrna to 'another Paris', 'an oasis of civilization, a Palmyra in the middle of the deserts of barbarism'. He admired the merchants' wives for wearing the latest fashions from the Rue du Faubourg Saint-Honoré.[13] Others praised the food: 'I have seen nowhere in the Levant tables served with more choice and even profusion than at Smyrna,' wrote J. M. Tancoigne.[14] Like other visitors, he found that by 1800, if not earlier, Franks were as much at home in Smyrna as in Marseille. With the confidence of wealth, they felt the city belonged to them, as well as – or, since they contributed so much to its prosperity, more than – to its Turks, Greeks, Armenians and Jews.[15] In this sense – in making different races and religions feel it was their city – Smyrna was indeed cosmopolitan.

Hanson wrote:

> From a long residence many of the Merchants have become as it were naturalised in the place. Many of them speak Turkish [an improvement on the past] and all of them Greek, French and Italian. Most of them are married to women of the country and display much elegance and hospitality in the arrangement of their houses and their reception of travellers. During my stay at Smyrna it was customary in two families resident there to give Public evenings once a week ... These parties I found particularly agreeable ... We met early without ceremony or form and passed the evening in music round games or cards ... An introduction to one family infallibly leads to the acquaintance of the whole society.

On first arrival you were immediately given coffee and sweetmeats, as in a Greek or Turkish home; houses were heated by Turkish charcoal-burners.[16]

After a low period in the early nineteenth century, British merchants' fortunes were recovering. Charlton Whittall, founder of a famous English dynasty which stayed in Smyrna and Constantinople until the 1980s, arrived from Liverpool in 1809. He soon acquired a fortune and a wife, Madeleine Giraud, daughter of the Austrian consul. Thanks to the Whittalls' and other foreign merchants' country houses, with well-kept gardens and 'masses of beds of flowers', Bornova and Buca were beginning to look like English rather than Greek villages – though with Turkish guards to keep out brigands. In the summer, when Smyrniots moved there to avoid the heat and plagues of the city, there were parties every night: not one family would stay at home.[17] A French visitor, Maxime du Camp, complained, 'It is sad to run away from them [the English] everywhere, only to find them unexpectedly under the Asian sun.'[18] As well as making fortunes, Whittalls made discoveries, of ancient coins, new species of animals, or flowers, such as *Fritillaria whittallii*. In 1906 five Whittalls would be part of the Turkish team at the Olympic Games in Athens.

After the events of 1797, the Franks established an instititution of their own, called the club or Casino, by the sea next to the British consulate. Open every evening from eight, it was described by Thomas MacGill in 1808 as 'one of the best regulated places I ever knew', with a reading room, French papers, a billiard room, card tables 'and several small rooms for private conversation.'[19] Five guineas a year was the subscription; travellers paid nothing unless they asked for 'wine, liquors or supper'. Lord

Byron himself visited it with his friend John Cam Hobhouse, during their grand tour round the Ottoman Empire, on 8 March 1810.[20]

During carnival season, balls were held there twice a week, with up to 300 people, 'consular and naval uniforms of every country', and 'bewitching ladies' in Greek dress: after dancing, their postures could be 'positively indecent'. These balls were more enjoyable than their equivalent in Constantinople, which were marred by 'jealousy, stiff court etiquette and a foolish idea of superiority', particularly if ambassadors or, worse, ambassadresses came with their miniature courts.[21]

Even this institution dedicated to pleasure, however, reflected national tensions. Prominent Turks were admitted to the Casino. The governor attended the balls – choosing to drink rum and brandy, on the grounds that they were not, like wine, specifically forbidden by the Prophet.[22] At one ball given by the British consul the Turkish governor drank to the prosperity of Smyrna – and to Franks' share in it.[23] But, however rich they were, despite years of petitions, Greeks, Armenians and Jews were excluded from the Casino – as were ships' captains of all nationalities.[24] Social prejudices were as violent as racial ones. In 1819 Greeks established their own casino or Greek club (with gambling for higher stakes) opposite a Greek church on Frank Street.[25]

At the same time as it assumed the role of 'Paris of the Levant', Smyrna was becoming a great Greek city again. There was no continuity between the new Greek city and its classical or Byzantine past: commerce in the Ottoman Empire was its basis. Greek merchants of Smyrna had become rich enough to found modern Greek schools there (partly to defend Greeks against Catholic proselytism) in 1733 and 1808.[26]

Particularly after the end of the Russo-Ottoman war of 1768–74, increasing numbers of Greeks came from the Aegean islands to work in Smyrna: they could be recognized by 'the insolence of their gait and their noisy gaiety'.[27] The Greek spoken there resembled that of the islands more than that of Anatolia. Greeks' growing importance was signalled by the construction – theoretically illegal under sharia law – of new (rather than rebuilt) churches in 1772, 1778, 1799, 1801 and 1804.[28] The Greek language, and Greek wives and servants, became so common that Smyrna's English families began to speak English with a sing-song Greek inflexion – and to scatter their conversation with Greek as well as French words.[29]

The leading figure in the Greek Enlightenment – the first to teach a sense of modern nationalism to his fellow Greeks – was Adamantios Korais. Born in Smyrna in 1748, and educated with the help of the Dutch chaplain Bernhard Keun, he left to set up business in Amsterdam in 1772, and lived in Paris from 1788 until his death in 1833 – a living link between Smyrna, the European Enlightenment and Greek independence.[30]

Greeks were acquiring capital as well as education. Leading Greek merchants of the city included members of the Ralli, Baltazzi and Argenti families. They profited from the fact that western Europe was finally beginning to open its ports to Ottoman merchants. By 1782, at the latest, they had offices in Marseille and Trieste. The British government finally allowed what were called 'Ottoman bottoms' (i.e. ships) to reach London in 1797, despite the opposition of the Levant Company. The rise of the Greeks was helped by the collapse of French trade as a result of the wars of the French Revolution and Napoleon's continental blockade, and by their neutral status, as Ottoman subjects, during those wars.[31]

By 1803 Korais believed that French, the language of educated Europe, was as commonly spoken by Greeks as Italian. More modern Greek schools were being founded, and foreign books translated and printed. Some Greek areas of the Ottoman Empire, such as the Peloponnese, Hydra, Chios and Ayvalik, further up the Aegean coast from Smyrna, enjoyed considerable autonomy.[32]

By 1813 there were over 600 ships owned by Greeks from the Ottoman Empire. Greek sailors filled the lower ranks of the Ottoman fleet. Greek ships sailed even to Montevideo, making huge profits on cargoes of wine and hides.[33] Defying Ottoman regulations, even when Greek regions, or Constantinople itself, were threatened with famine, Greek merchants 'without mercy', in search of large profits, exported wheat on fast light ships to France or the Duke of Wellington's army in Spain: 'The poor's blood they sucked like wild beasts … Both Greeks and Turks Allah beseeched' according to a poem by a Greek priest. The Greeks of Smyrna had their own flag: five alternating stripes of blue and white. The Muslims' flag was red, green, red; other Greeks had red, blue, red.[34] The Greeks of Smyrna also had their own 'Senate' of twelve notables who met in a church to regulate the payment of taxes to the Ottoman government and such matters as starting a bank or importing a fire engine.[35]

In 1818 – at a time when the Greek Phanariot aristocracy was at the height of its power and confidence in Constantinople, helping to run Ottoman diplomacy and the principalities of Wallachia and Moldavia in what is now Romania – the Chiot merchants of Smyrna showed a similar spirit. They organised the city's textile trade to their advantage, at the expense of Europeans.[36] A book published in Vienna in 1817 by a Smyrniote Greek teacher called Constantinos Oiconomos boasts of the 'glory' of Smyrna and Hellenism. The birthplace of Homer, formerly the first and most beautiful city of Asia, he wrote, had become the seat of excellent Greek schools and new churches, a source of prosperity and enlightenment for the Greek nation. His own school, however, was closed in 1819, owing to the hostility of the Ecumenical Patriarch and a Greek mob to 'modern philosophy'.[37]

The Armenians of Smyrna were also growing in numbers and confidence. An Armenian printing press was established in 1758, a modern school in 1799, a hospital in 1801.[38] A wealthy Smyrna Armenian family called Tatikian ran a lithographic press which published prints representing the city's different nationalities and professions.[39]

After 1800, independent states had begun to appear in different corners of the Empire. In 1803–5 Wahhabis – enemies of all Muslims but themselves – had sacked the Shia shrines in Najaf and Karbala and even Mecca and Medina. For four years the holy cities were closed to pilgrims.[40] In 1804 a revolt in Serbia, at first against janissary oppression rather than Ottoman sovereignty, started that nation on its long road to statehood: under Ottoman rule, it had never lost its sense of identity. In Constantinople rebellious janissaries, jealous of his New Order army, deposed the reforming sultan Selim III in 1807. In 1808 Napoleon I and Alexander I planned to divide the Ottoman Empire. Salonica would go to Austria; the East Balkans and Constantinople to Russia; the ports of the Levant to France.[41] In 1809 a Greek text proclaimed, 'The Ottoman state finds itself today in its death throes and can be compared to a human body gripped by apoplexy.'[42]

On his travels in the Ottoman Empire with Lord Byron, John Cam Hobhouse noted in his diary on 9 December 1809, 'We have observed the professed hatred of their masters to be universal among the Greeks.' Byron dreamt that Greece might still be free, and translated the sanguinary poem of the nationalist martyr Rigas, often sung by Greeks in front of uncomprehending Turks:

> Sons of the Greeks, arise!
>
> .   .   .   .   .
>
> Sons of Greeks! let us go
> In arms against the foe,
> Till their hated blood shall flow
> In a river past our feet.[43]

The drop in profits, after the end of the continental blockade and of their neutral status during the Napoleonic wars, sharpened Greeks' appetite for independence: over half the members of the nationalist Friendly Society founded in Odessa in 1814 were minor merchants.[44] On 25 March 1821 the Archbishop of Patras launched a revolt, long anticipated by foreign travellers and consuls, which took the Ottoman authorities by surprise.[45] Probably by premeditated design, the entire population of around 20,000 Muslims and Jews in the Peloponnese was then killed – perhaps in order to make it impossible subsequently to make peace with the Ottoman government.[46] The news aroused fury in the Empire.

Shocked by betrayal by a race they had trusted, Sultan Mahmud II and some of his officials reverted to the language of jihad. They felt more insecure than they appeared. The Levantine synthesis broke down, and Muslims were encouraged to take arms. Greeks were killed in the streets of Constantinople simply for being Greek. The Sultan selected the names of wealthy Greeks (especially those to whom he owed money) from a list which he had obliged his chief dragoman, Prince Moroussi, to compile. He then had them executed one by one, including Moroussi himself; the Ecumenical Patriach was hanged from the gate of the Patriarchate courtyard.[47] Slaves were sold in the markets, and heads piled at the gate of Topkapi Palace, 'in quantities never seen and heard of before', boasted the Sultan. 'I am very pleased. May god almighty always grant victories to the Muslims everywhere. Amen.' Greek officials and sailors were dismissed or hanged, and replaced by Muslims. The Sultan wrote, 'Under the present circumstances there can be no trust in the Greek *millet* [community] and especially in the *reaya* [subjects] of the islands ... After this conspiracy of the Greeks it is not permissible to employ them in the Imperial Navy. It is most necessary to recruit Muslim sailors. Find and fetch them right now.'[48]

In mercantile Smyrna there was no revolt. Nevertheless, the dispatches of Francis Werry reveal the city's vulnerability, and the speed with which, as in 1770 and 1797, race and religious hate could flare up – and die down again. On 8 April 1821, drunken janissaries began to threaten Christians, openly attacking the Spanish consul. On 11 April armed Muslims, many from Crete (where Muslim converts from Christianity were keen to attack Christians), appeared in the streets. The consuls, the kadi and the governor's council met 'in the greatest harmony', and in 'full costume' – often in the Casino – 'to insure the tranquillity and safety of the city'. The British consul was part of the Ottoman as well as the British government machine. He encouraged the authorities to be 'on the best of terms with the Franks particularly so with us' by communicating to them 'every information that I receive'. Greeks fled towards the sea looking for boats.

Some jumped into the water to save themselves from Turks. Such was their economic dominance that 'trade of course has become entirely paralysed.' Much of the town seemed 'entirely abandoned'.[49] The Russian consul wrote that no one paid anyone and it was hard to find bread, especially for the poor. He blamed foreign ships for spreading news of Greek atrocities.[50]

Greek ships were not only attacking Turkish ships in the Aegean – in 1821 they killed the Imam of Mecca and his wives on one of them – but were also removing Turks from British and Maltese ships to kill them. Werry feared that Greeks would attack Smyrna itself.[51] In an attempt to prevent further violence, he tried to stop news of massacres, by Turks or Greeks, from spreading in Smyrna. On 17 May two British ships of war arrived; but, the consul reported, 'killing has been the order of the day and night too.' Volunteers from inland Anatolia, on their way to suppress the rising in the Peloponnese, as well as Muslims from Crete, ferocious and hungry for spoils, were often 'the chief instigators', rather than Smyrna Muslims.

On the feast day of St Constantine, founder of Constantinople, sixteen Greeks were shot dead in the bazaar. 'So very very deluded are these fanatic people', wrote Werry, 'they yesterday openly congratulated each other (the lower orders) on the approach of the morrow as the day appointed by heaven to liberate them from the Ottoman yoke and restore their Race of Princes to the throne and possession of Constantinople. The Turks who entered on their fast of Ramazan yesterday heard this and began their fast in the evening with human sacrifices and I fear much this will be followed up.' To preserve order the Porte agreed to the consuls' request, made through their ambassadors, to keep the moderate and pliable Hussein Pasha as governor. More Greeks shut and sealed their shops and fled to the safety of foreign ships in the harbour.

When news arrived that Greeks had taken an Ottoman ship, Turks started firing on Greeks on the marina or shoreline – hunters pursuing humans 'as their prey', in the words of the Russian consul: perhaps 160 were killed. As the city slipped out of control, Muslims also turned on their own authorities. The governor barricaded himself in his house in despair. The kadi was murdered. Ten or fifteen a day were being killed. The words 'horror' and 'panic' reappear regularly in the dispatches of the British consul. On the morning of 18 June the British and French consuls embarked their nationals on board ships in the harbour.

There were now two separate Smyrnas: land Smyrna, in chaos; sea Smyrna, on ships in the harbour. Land Smyrna had guns; sea Smyrna money. Land Smyrna could not function economically unless the floating refugees returned. Sea Smyrna had nowhere to go. Finally a deputation from the city asked the refugees to return and open their shops. Thus in 1821, out of necessity, the Levantine synthesis survived.

On 2 August Werry reported with relief, 'The governor pasha has adopted measures to punish the Turks. No murder of the Greeks has been known some days past. The shops are all open and the Greeks as gay as ever. They are an extraordinary set of people.' The alternation of massacre and merriment was a characteristic of Smyrna, later the subject of a song by a Greek from a Smyrna family, Mikis Theodorakis. On 17 September, 'The continuation of quiet and tranquillity daily inspires confidence in the Christian inhabitants, trade revives, commensurate as disorder ceases.'[52] An added guarantee was that Dutch, English, French and Austrian ships, with large guns, were anchored in the bay. There were more killings in November, on news of further massacres in Greece, but the violence began to die down. Race tensions nevertheless remained so high that, Werry wrote, 'such is the temper of the mass of Turks it would excite a general insurrection if a Mussulman was put to death for killing a Greek giaour [unbeliever].'[53]

In Smyrna the Levantine synthesis survived; in Chios it drowned in blood. The story could serve as a parable of the lethal consequences of nationalism. Content with their commercial Levantine life, most Chiots did not want Greek independence, let alone to fight for it. They had wider horizons. On 25 March 1822 a fleet from the rival island of Samos with 1,500 soldiers landed on Chios and began to kill Turks. The Greek massacre was answered, on the orders of Mahmud II,[54] by a massive counter-massacre. On 11 April Turkish troops, some in a state of near-mutiny, landed and massacred or burnt alive as many as 25,000 Chiots, including hospital inmates, and enslaved 50,000 others, mainly women and children (including a future grand vizier, Ibrahim Edhem) – causing a fall in price due to a glut of slaves on the market: Werry reported that Smyrna was full of them. The population of Chios sank from 120,000 to around 25,000. The Rev. Robert Walsh, chaplain of the British ambassador Lord Strangford, found the city stinking of death, human and animal. There was no one in the streets. The elegant stone villas had been pillaged. 'Among the rubbish lay skulls, arms and half consumed bodies amid paper, books and broken furniture.' 'Weltering' bodies resembled 'heaps of rags'.[55] Glass cases in monastery antechambers on Chios still display victims' skulls and bones to the curious visitor.

Chios was the first Levantine paradise to be destroyed. The Greek island which least wanted independence suffered most because of it. A pattern had been established, which would be repeated in Smyrna in 1922: initial Greek attack; Turkish hyper-retaliation, to the detriment of long-term Turkish interests. Soon after the massacre the British government began to treat Greeks as belligerents; Delacroix's picture and Victor Hugo's poems inspired by the massacre of Chios expressed French revulsion.[56]

Chios was the first example of a phenomenon which would transform the Levant in the twentieth century: the 'unmixing of peoples'; flight to the West; subsequent submerging of identities in the host country. Many Chiots – such as the Ralli, Calvocoressi and Skilizzi families – fled to London, where, until the mid twentieth century, they formed a separate community with its own businesses and traditions, such as marrying Greeks and living in Bayswater.[57] Others chose Smyrna, Odessa or the small Catholic island of Syros in the Cyclades, one of the Ottoman Empire's many autonomous enclaves, on which two monasteries benefited from French protection. On Syros, Orthodox immigrants from Chios built a new city which they called Hermoupolis, after Hermes, god of commerce. For the next fifty years, replacing Chios, Syros would become a Levantine Hong Kong, with the largest port, most imposing mansions, and best schools and theatre in Greece.[58]

Greek pirates in the Aegean continued to take Ottoman ships. In June 1822 they burnt the Ottoman flagship off Chios, killing the Kaptan Pasha and many sailors.[59] Candarli, north of Smyrna, was taken in 1823, Beirut was attacked in 1826, Iskanderun was sacked in 1827, the same year that Alexandria itself was threatened.[60] When the French ambassador Comte Guilleminot came to Foca near Smyrna to persuade the Kaptan Pasha to ensure the safety of the Franks of Smyrna he had to travel by land: Greek pirates controlled the seas.[61]

Finally, pushed by public opinion horrified by the massacres of Chios, further brutalities in the Peloponnese, and the festooning of Constantinople buildings with Greek body parts,[62] France, Britain and Russia took action in favour of Greek independence. (In contrast, fearful of Russian expansion, Austria remained pro-Ottoman – Trieste merchants profited from the Greek War of Independence to increase their share of commerce with Smyrna.) On 9 September 1827, Admirals de Rigny and Codrington, in command of the French and British fleets in the eastern Mediterranean, while paying courtesy visits to the Ottoman authorities in Smyrna, planned a joint attack on the Ottoman fleet. On 20 October 1827 at Navarino, on the west coast of the Peloponnese, British, French and

Russian ships, without a declaration of war, destroyed seventy ships of the Ottoman fleet. It was a disaster worse than Çeşme in 1770.[63]

Shocked by the infidels' treachery, in 1828 the Sultan declared jihad. Infidels and Muslims were natural enemies. Representing the wishes of 'the entirety of the Muslim nation', 'the Sublime State of Muhammad', as he called the Ottoman Empire, would not tolerate the 'unspeakable nonsense' of a Greek government: 'perhaps they will turn our mosques into churches tolling their bells.' He claimed that infidels planned to eradicate Muslims from the surface of the earth.[64]

Frightened for their lives – de Klezl, the senior Austrian dragoman, was beaten to death – the French, British and Russian ambassadors and their staffs, for the first time in the history of the Empire, left Constantinople: the affairs of their countries were looked after by the Dutch embassy, whose chargé d'affaires was the old Levantine interpreter (who knew every language but Dutch) Gaspard de Testa.[65] Jihad led to further Ottoman defeats. Finally, in 1829, as Russian armies neared Constantinople, the Ottoman Empire signed a peace treaty. It recognized the newly independent kingdom of Greece, a small state limited to the islands of the Cyclades, the Peloponnese and southern Thessaly. Most Greeks remained subjects of the Ottoman Empire. The ambassadors returned.

After the massacres, Smyrna had resumed its cosmopolition appearance and its habits of merriment, which some inhabitants – who had attended the Casino throughout – had never dropped.[66] Already, in 1818, the city's first Catholic archbishop had arrived. In 1824 the first newspaper in the Ottoman empire, *Le Smyrnéen*, later renamed *Le Courrier de Smyrne*, was founded by a young French merchant called Alexandre Blacque, who used it to attack Greek independence. Like an earlier Smyrna Frenchman, Charles de Peyssonnel, he defended the Ottoman Empire and called for European tolerance towards Islam. Blacque's career shows how closely Franks could interact with Ottoman society. In 1831 he was summoned by the Sultan to Constantinople, where he would found the first regular newspaper in the city, in both French and Turkish, called *Le Moniteur ottoman*.[67] In 1833 Smyrna was linked for the first time by a regular steamer service, first to Trieste, then to Marseille. Only two years later did a steamer (called *Levant*) begin to make regular journeys between Smyrna and Constantinople. Services to London began in 1840, to Alexandria in 1844.[68]

At the same time the British chaplain Francis Arundell, author of *Discoveries in Asia Minor*, noticed that wooden houses were giving way to 'palaces of stone erecting in all directions'. The bazaar could now supply

'most of the comforts and luxuries ... from London and Paris'.[69] New
schools for boys and – for the first time – girls, opened by American
missionaries after 1830, 'threw the whole Smyrniot population into
amazement' – though at this stage they were attended only by Christians.
The missionaries felt 'Smyrna is comparatively a free city' and brought a
printing press.[70] One, however, feared the city for having 'a moral atmosphere wholly corrupt'.[71]

Travellers from homogeneous nation states like France and England
were attracted to Smyrna's variety of 'national character, language,
costume and complexion', which they believed to be greater than in any
other city on earth[72] – a claim Constantinople and Vienna would have
disputed. The marina, dominated by consulates flying the flags of their
respective nations, was praised for displaying 'the distinctive features of
almost every Nation of the East, and the whole wider range of human
passions, modified by as wide a range of accidents'.[73]

Sometimes there were 200 merchant ships and 1,500 camels in the
city at the same time. Usually at least one British man-of-war from the
Mediterranean fleet was anchored in 'the roads' among the merchant
ships, for the British consul – characteristically – felt that only a British
ship of the line 'being permanently stationed in this Bay' could guarantee
law and order.[74] Since a treaty against France in 1799, Britain was a formal
Ottoman ally; therefore the Ottoman government instructed local authorities to supply the British fleet at current prices.[75] Sometimes officers gave
a 'naval ball' on two boats lashed together.[76] At other times blue-jacketed
sailors, known as 'tars', came on shore, where, in the words of one of
them called George Hawthorn, in the space of two days by 'purchasing
pipes, purses, tack, otto [attar] of roses, Greek caps, mouth pieces, bowls of
tobacco and silk fishing lines and what with cheating Jews and Greeks (the
latter being worse than the former), taking the Turkish baths, smoking,
coffee-drinking etc etc we successfully got rid of all significant money.'[77]

In his great Levantine novel *Anastasus* (1819), based on his travels round
the Ottoman Empire in 1796–8, Thomas Hope described bare-chested
Turks on the quays in Smyrna wearing 'costly elegant clothes', scarlet dye
on their lips and shadow round their eyes. They had 'a confident look, an
insolent and sneering tone, and an insolent yet swaggering gait'. Modest
women avoided them, and respectable men always gave way.[78] To James
Emerson, another traveller, Turks appeared to be 'the finest looking
race of men in the world', with their brightly coloured traditional dress,
turban, and sword- and pistol-stuffed sashes; in comparison, Europeans
in coats and pantaloons cut 'a miserable figure'.[79] Referring to Turkish

SMYRNA: MASSACRES AND MERRIMENT

porters, who used a quilted cloth pad to ease the pressure of the loads they
carried through the streets on their backs, a later traveller called Francis
Hervé wrote, 'I never saw such immense chests and shoulders as these
men have; in fact their arms and legs are in the same proportion. They
often appeared to me like colossal satyrs. Their shirts are always open at
the chest, displaying a mass of hair almost like the fur of some animal.'
Despite or because of their strength, they were 'a remarkably quiet, civil,
inoffensive people'.[80]

The variety of hats and caps in Smyrna amazed one visitor:

The swelling kalpack of the pondering Armenian, the pointed black
sheepskin cap of the pale faced Persian, the rich turban of the old
Osmanly, the fez worn by the unwilling follower of the modern
Mussulman fashions, the sugarloaf [turban] of the dervish and no less
lofty one of the zeibec [armed Anatolian mountain-dweller], the low
brimless cap of the Greek papas, the broad-brimmed straw of the Yankee
skipper, the smaller and more rakish one of the British tar, the cocked
hat of the naval officer, monks with shaven crowns, Jews with kerchief
bound brows, and Greek and Italians in every variety of head dress ...
The very bustle alone may keep the spectator in good humour.[81]

Smyrna offered a variety of sounds as well as costumes: jackals howling in
the hills, barking dogs, and in some seasons croaking frogs.[82] Visitors were
advised that, if surrounded by dogs baring their teeth, the best course to
adopt was to go to a baker's shop and buy them bread.[83] Inside the walls
of Smyrna, the cries of sherbet and fruit sellers mixed with British sailors'
songs, Greeks singing ballads or 'chattering and screaming over a pack of
cards' in a café, and the muezzin's call to prayer.[84]

The cosmopolitanism of the city was helped by the late-flowering tolerance of Mahmud II. As the Greek War of Independence came to an end,
he had adopted a new identity, and a modern, semi-Western dark-blue
military uniform. Instead of the traditional turban, he wore a crimson
wool cap or fez – already much used by sailors in the Mediterranean.
The Ottoman Empire experienced a dress revolution. On 28 June 1829 a
British diplomat, R. C. Mellish, reported from Constantinople:

What engrosses everybody here is the extraordinary change which is
daily taking place in the manners of this people ... Very few years
more, and not a turban will exist. Grand Vezir, Reis Efendi [official
dealing with foreign affairs], Ulema [religious authorities], employees of

every description, now wear the red cap, cossack trowsers, black boots and a plain red or blue cloak buttoned under the chin. No gold embroidery, no jewels, no pelisses. The Sultan wears a blue jacket, cossack trowsers, black boots and the red cap like the others.[85]

The Sultan started to lift restrictions on Christians and Jews, and to proclaim equality before the law. In a firman of July 1829 he stated, 'There will in the future be no distinctions made between Muslim and *reaya* and everybody will be assured the inviolability of his property, life and honour by a sacred law and my sublime patronage.' Such sentiments were frequently repeated. Some of his subjects began to call him the '*gavur* sultan'.[86]

His son Abdulmecid, who succeeded him in 1839, was a gentle sybarite, who accelerated the modernization of the Empire. On 2 June 1842 Catholics in Smyrna were allowed, for the first time since the Ottoman conquest, to celebrate the great Catholic festival honouring the Holy Sacrament, known as the Fête Dieu, in what would henceforth be an annual procession through streets decorated with orange blossoms and tapestries. It was led by the consuls' and governor's bodyguards, or kavasses, in full dress. Then came schoolchildren, representatives of Catholic confraternities and consuls' dragomans, followed by the Archbishop under a dais, a statue of the Virgin Mary, escorted by 300 schoolgirls, the Catholic clergy and notables, and the consul-general of France and the commander of the French ship in the harbour, representing what Ottoman officials now acknowledged to be the official protecting power of the Catholics of the Empire. Each time the procession paused in front of an altar erected in the street, French and Austrian ships in the port fired a cannon in salute. The procession was watched by amazed crowds and escorted by Turkish soldiers. The governor himself was in the streets to assure order.[87]

Smyrna – like Paris, St Petersburg and Odessa – was proof of the strange resilience of cosmopolitan cities during the rise of nationalism in the nineteenth century. Louis Fauvel, the former French consul in Athens, who had helped 'collectors' like Lord Elgin remove antiquities, did not believe that modern Greeks deserved to be emancipated. In 1828 he left for Smyrna, where he spent his last years living on a meagre government pension, cursing modern Greek nationalism, surrounded by models of ancient Athens.[88]

Indeed, the independence of Greece led to an emigration of Greeks to Smyrna. Brigandage flourished in independent Greece more than in the Ottoman Empire. Thousands of Greeks decided that they preferred 'groaning under the Turkish yoke' and prosperity to independence and poverty. As Alexander Kinglake wrote in *Eothen* in 1834, 'There is a greater field for commercial enterprise, and even for Greek ambition, under the Ottoman sceptre than is to be found in the dominions of Otho [the first king of Greece].'[89] Smyrna had many times the population of Athens. By 1840 (or by some counts 1870), for the first time since the fourteenth century the number of Greeks in the city surpassed the number of Turks. In a population of about 130,000 there were approximately 55,000 Greeks, 45,000 Turks, 13,000 Jews, 12,000 Franks and 5,000 Armenians.[90] It was indeed, as Turks called it, *gavur* Smyrna – infidel Smyrna. A minority had become a majority. Smyrna's true rival was not Athens, the impoverished Greek capital, but another Levantine port: Alexandria.

4

Alexandria: The Key to Egypt

The life of the dynasty is the life of its city.

Ibn Khaldun, *c.*1380

MODERN SMYRNA HAD been made by merchants. Modern Alexandria was the creation of one man: Muhammad Ali, pasha of Egypt from 1805 to 1849.

When Muhammad Ali came to power in 1805, Alexandria had sunk below even its late-eighteenth-century level. The population was about 6,000. Passing through on his way back from Jerusalem in 1806, Chateaubriand found it, in contrast to Smyrna, 'the saddest and most deserted place in the world'.[1]

'Alexandria has the fewest attractions for a traveller who wishes to indulge more senses than his curiosity than any place I have ever yet beheld ... The country has no appearance of culture; everything seems sunk in apathy,' wrote another traveller, William Birch, in 1810. Surrounded by the remains of its classical glory, the city presented 'a sense of wretchedness unequalled even in this land of desolation' according to Thomas Jolliffe in 1817. There was only one inn.[2] When Muhammad Ali died, in 1849, Alexandria was a city of over 100,000: at once a port, a cosmopolis, and the key to the future of Egypt.

Like Alexander the Great, Muhammad Ali came to Egypt from the other side of the Mediterranean. He was born in 1770, in the port of Kavalla on the main road from Constantinople to Salonica, in what is now north-eastern Greece, where the family's large Ottoman house can still be admired today. His father was a Turkish merchant selling local tobacco to Egypt.[3] Muhammad Ali first saw Egypt in 1801, as a volunteer officer in an Albanian regiment sent to fight the French invaders.

Three years of French occupation since the invasion in 1798 had achieved little in Egypt except to alienate the Egyptians. Muhammad Ali's rise to power has better cause to be considered 'the beginning of the modern Middle East' than the arrival of the French: he inherited neither men nor ideas nor institutions from Bonaparte. French forces left Egypt in 1801 after their defeat by a British–Ottoman army outside Alexandria (the first land battle won by a British army against a French revolutionary army). A sign of Britain's emergence as a world power, and readiness to intervene in the Levant, was its use in this campaign of Malta as its Mediterranean base, and of British-officered regiments from the Cape of Good Hope and India.[4]

After 1801, the Albanian regiments in Egypt – around 5,000 men – became one of Muhammad Ali's power bases in the struggle between Ottoman authorities, Mameluke soldiers, local factions and foreign powers which was reducing Egypt to ruin: Albanians' obedience to Ottoman authorities had been diminished by lack of pay.[5]

Cairo was another power base. Longing for an end to chaos was as great as in France in 1799, when, on his return from Egypt, Bonaparte had seized power in the *coup d'état* of Brumaire. The great historian Abdul Rahman al-Jabarti was a scientist and religious expert, from a family of Azhar sheikhs, who recorded events in his classic work *Wondrous Men and their Deeds*. Although he wrote that the French were wicked unbelievers, he admitted that within a few years of their departure people were so angry with Egypt's misgovernment that 'all' longed for the country to be occupied by any European government, whatever its nationality.[6]

Finally Muhammad Ali – 'the Albanians' chief', as the French consul called him – was proclaimed pasha of Egypt by the *ulema* of Cairo on 12 May 1805 without a shot being fired. He was a skilled manipulator. He promised the senior Ottoman official in Egypt, the Kaptan Pasha, that he would pay a higher tribute, always obey the Sultan, and protect the poor. He also produced signed (but some signatures were falsified) declarations from notables begging the Sultan to keep him in power.[7] In return for official recognition, the Porte demanded that he suppress the Wahhabi revolt in Arabia.[8] The great Egyptian power vacuum had been filled. In the next forty years Muhammad Ali was able to do in Egypt what other local rulers elsewhere in the Ottoman Empire hoped to do: to establish a dynasty on a stable territorial base.

More than any contemporary Ottoman governor, Muhammad Ali soon made himself absolute master of his province. By September 1807 his forces had defeated and expelled a British army of 8,000 which had occupied Alexandria that March – persuaded by an over-excited British consul, Mr Missett, that another French invasion was imminent.[9] In the eyes of the Egyptian people and the Ottoman government, the British defeat made Muhammad Ali a hero. Alexandria, previously under a separate governor, was formally placed under his authority. A sign of Muhammad Ali's foresight was that he returned British prisoners of war instead of, in accordance with Ottoman practice, executing or enslaving them: he knew British goodwill would be useful in the future. By another stroke of luck, the pro-British Mameluke chief el-Elfi died the same year. Only then, Muhammad Ali said, did he feel that he had conquered Egypt. In 1809 he felt sufficiently secure to bring over his wife and children from Kavalla. The dynasty was beginning.[10]

Success followed success. On 1 March 1811 he entertained Mameluke officers to a festival in the citadel of Cairo, to celebrate the appointment of his son Tusun to command the army leaving to fight the Wahhabis in Arabia. As they were walking up a narrow passage, 450 Mamelukes were gunned down by his Albanians; 1,000 more were killed in Cairo.[11] By 1815 Muhammad Ali had established a semi-independent government in Egypt, with his own chief eunuch, pipe-bearer, grand master of ceremonies, and keeper of the seal. There were six departments – of foreign, military, naval, financial, commercial and educational affairs – and a consultative council. Since the departments consisted of a few officials with chairs or cushions, and files, they could and did follow the ruler wherever he went.[12] Muhammad Ali's rise in power was matched by a rise in status. By 1819 or earlier, he was called, by foreign consuls and visitors as well as his own officials, not vali or governor of Egypt, but His Highness the Viceroy.[13]

Lack of prejudice distinguished Muhammad Ali from other Ottoman governors. His early illiteracy – he taught himself to read in 1815 at the age of forty-five[14] – may have liberated him from some of the mental constraints shackling some literate Ottomans. As early as 1812, when Muhammad Ali was introducing quarantine measures, the French consul remarked that he 'eagerly seizes every opportunity to shake the yoke of prejudices'.[15] His remark in 1825, when permitting Christians to ring church bells in Egypt – that, among so many religions, it would be a great misfortune if one was not the right one – suggests a certain scepticism.[16]

The official in charge of foreign affairs – and customs revenues – and the Pasha's chief interpreter was an Armenian from Smyrna called Boghos Yussuf Bey, the first of many Armenians to run Egypt's foreign affairs, who had begun as dragoman of the British consul in Smyrna. In 1810, like many other ambitious young men in the Ottoman Empire, drawn to the rising sun, he had moved to Egypt. His gentle manners and excellent French won universal praise.[17] The French consul called him 'an all-powerful man whom the consuls should conciliate more than the pasha himself if they do not want to be exposed to all sorts of unpleasantness'.[18]

The French consul, a Piedmontese with the manners and appearance of a courtier, called Bernardino Drovetti, was another Christian with influence on Muhammad Ali. Drovetti, the jealous British consul noted, 'goes wherever Mehemet Ali goes'. As early as 1806 Drovetti had written to the French Foreign Minister, Talleyrand, 'This man has gigantic ideas.'[19] After 1809, Muhammad Ali was the first non-Christian ruler to send batches of young men to be educated in Europe: first to Italy; after 1826 to Paris. An Egyptian college was established there on the advice of Drovetti, since he believed the schools were better and Paris was the great theatre to observe men. For Muhammad Ali, as for most contemporaries, France was more attractive as a source of culture than a conquering empire. By 1848 over 300 Egyptians, including the Pasha's sons Halim and Hassan and his grandson Ismail, had been educated in Paris, London or Vienna.[20]

Muhammad Ali was also in advance of other provincial governors in his interest in new ways of making money. He became a merchant as well as a governor. He soon ended the Ottoman system of tax farms, establishing a land registry and a government monopoly on the sale of wheat. Peasants had to sell their crops at fixed prices to government agents. He first began to visit Alexandria frequently in order to sell directly to foreign merchants the wheat, rice and other vegetables which he had requisitioned from Egyptians, in exchange for gold, tin, iron, textiles and other European goods. He then sold on the European goods to Egyptian merchants at prices fixed by himself.[21] By 1810, despite decrees prohibiting the export of wheat from the Ottoman Empire, wheat from Egypt, via Alexandria and Malta, was supplying Wellington's army fighting French forces in Spain. Napoleon's consuls were horrified.[22]

Muhammad Ali soon had his own commercial agents in Venice, Malta, Smyrna and Bombay, and had established cotton and silk factories in Egypt. Cannon, gun and bullet factories were also set up. By 1811 he was believed to be the richest pasha in the Empire. He refused to obey orders from the Porte which went against his own private interests.[23]

In contrast to its former apathy, by 1817 the port of Alexandria presented 'an active scene of ships building, vessels loading and taking in their cargoes, with heaps of grain and bales of goods piled up along the shore. But the European stranger is particularly struck with the crowds of naked porters that ply their busy task and the swarms of horrid beggars that constantly importune and harrow up the feelings of his heart.'[24] In 1820 a traveller arriving by sea saw a forest of masts in the port, flying the flags of the different trading nations, and on the right, among a few scattered palm trees, up to 200 white windmills.[25] As Alexandria rose, Egypt's other ports – Damietta and Rosetta – fell, losing population as well as trade.[26]

After wheat and cotton, another bulk export from the port of Alexandria, for the next hundred years, was antiquities. Muhammad Ali was proud of having established what the British consul Henry Salt called 'extraordinary tranquillity and security of person ... throughout Egypt', and willingly gave Europeans permission to excavate and export 'colossal heads', sarcophaguses, obelisks, even sections of temples. Consuls devoted considerable time to collecting antiquities; the British and the French, in particular, were eager to outdo each other. On one occasion, when Muhammad Ali hesitated to grant the required firman, Salt threatened him with a suspension of 'all friendly communications between us'. Most Egyptian antiquities now adorning the British Museum and the Louvre, and the obelisks given by Muhammad Ali and his successors to the cities of London, Paris and New York, were loaded in Alexandria.[27]

In order to hasten modernization, Muhammad Ali believed in employing Frenchmen in Egypt, as well as in educating Egyptians in France. On the initiative of Boghos and Drovetti, a system of quarantine to prevent the spread of plague was introduced in Alexandria in 1817 – twenty years before the rest of the Ottoman Empire.[28] In 1818, with the help of the French engineer and architect Pascal Coste, a forty-six-mile-long canal was begun to connect Alexandria to the western branch of the Nile. Workers were paid well, so they flocked in large numbers – perhaps 100,000 at any time – although casualties were appalling. The canal was inaugurated in February 1821 and named Mahmudiye, in honour of Muhammad Ali's increasingly resentful suzerain Sultan Mahmud II. Still in use today, it improved Alexandria's access to its hinterland and its drinking water, and enabled cultivation to spread in the surrounding countryside: Alexandria was freed from the constraints hindering its growth for the previous 200 years.[29]

More confident of his control of Cairo, and desiring to trade in person with foreign merchants, Muhammad Ali began to spend more time in Alexandria after the extermination of the Mamelukes: in 1811 six weeks, in 1812 two months, in 1818 four months. From 1812 he had it fortified, although Henry Salt called the fortifications 'too weak and far too extensive to be of any use in case of a siege'. By 1822 he was said to be spending all the time there: that year the consuls-general moved their offices from Cairo to Alexandria.[30]

In 1830 the Russian consul reported that Muhammad Ali and his eldest son, Ibrahim Pasha, a brilliant general twenty years younger than his father, were alternating between Cairo and Alexandria.[31] In the eighteenth century a place of exile from Cairo, under Muhammad Ali Alexandria became Egypt's unofficial capital, a synonym for its government as 'London' and 'Paris' were for the British and French goverments. Under his descendants it remained Egypt's summer capital, where the government and the embassies moved every June to escape the heat of Cairo, until the final departure of Muhammad Ali's great-great-grandson King Farouk from Alexandria in July 1952.[32]

Muhammad Ali chose to build his palace on the western edge of a promontory protruding out of the peninsula on which Alexandria was built. It is called Ras el-Tin (the Cape of Figs). If Alexandria is in, but not of, Egypt, Ras el-Tin is in, but not of, Alexandria. Almost entirely surrounded by sea, it is in another world: a suitable choice for a man with colossal ambitions, and Mediterranean roots.

In 1811–17 the palace was built in what was called 'Rumi style', in wood and plaster, with wide, projecting eaves, and protruding rectangular windows, probably by traditional craftsmen architects from the mountains of Macedonia. There were two sections: a harem, like a walled convent, and a divan or office and reception building. Soon, however, reflecting changes in the Pasha's habits, and the influence of an architect from · Livorno called Pietro Avoscani, the palace exterior and interior began to look more European. Gas lighting was supplied by Thomas Galloway, representative of a firm established locally. The arrival of a billiard table in 1827 astonished Alexandria. Royal portraits, a mosaic table and chandeliers next appeared: presents from King Louis-Philippe of the French, the Pope, and the East India Company. In another break with tradition, portraits of Muhammad Ali's own family were also hung on the walls. A marble bathroom and staircase were installed. By the end of his life, although he slept on a mattress on the floor, the furnishings of the Pasha's bedroom were entirely European.[33]

Outside the palace were a semaphore which took his orders to Cairo in forty-five minutes,[34] sentries, palm and banana groves, ministers' houses, guards' barracks, and a long avenue of acacias leading to Alexandria.[35] An English tutor of one of Muhammad Ali's descendants loved Ras el-Tin for its 'beautiful gardens shaded by palm and acacia glowing with flowers of rare scent and splendour, freshened with cool streams and fountains', the sound of waves from the harbour, and the 'ever changing picture as the great ships come and go or tiny Arab boats scud across its glimmering surface. Altogether a more charming situation cannot be imagined; and the charm once felt can never be forgotten.'[36]

Under Muhammad Ali, Ras el-Tin was the centre of Alexandria. It was an architectural and human epitome of the Levant, like Frank Street in Smyrna or the Grand' Rue in Pera. The Pasha kept open house. He liked visitors who brought him news from Europe or Alexandria: an English naval officer found that he was 'fond of gossiping and said to be informed of everything that is either said or done in Alexandria. He has many friends among the Franks.'[37] No warning was needed before going to the palace.[38]

Particularly in 1821–9, when its War of Independence made Greece an unappealing destination, a stream of foreign travellers and writers came to Egypt, fascinated by Muhammad Ali and his reforms as well as by its antiquities. It was said of John Barker, a Smyrna merchant's son who became British consul-general in Alexandria in 1827–30, and a confidant of Muhammad Ali and Ibrahim, that, because of the number of British travellers in Egypt, 'like Lucullus's Mr Barker's table was always laid and dinner ready at any hour.' His motto was 'a watch, spying glass or pair of pistols properly administered removed every species of ill will.'[39]

Perhaps no country has inspired a greater number of travel books, in a shorter period of time, than Egypt under Muhammad Ali.[40] The Pasha for his part tried to use foreign visitors – who included figures as various as Disraeli, Marshal Marmont and Horace Vernet (his companion Monsieur Goupil-Fesquet took the first daguerrotype in Egypt, at Ras el-Tin on 7 November 1839, eleven months after the discovery had been first demonstrated in Paris) – to convey a favourable image in Europe, in order to further his ambitions.[41]

It was normal for a traveller to be presented to the Pasha immediately on arrival in Alexandria. James St John wrote in 1834, 'Any person who has leisure and knows no better mode of employing it, may go every evening to the palace, whether he have business there or not; and if he does not choose to force himself upon the pasha he can enter into any of the other magnificent apartments which are lighted up as well as the audience chamber and converse if he please with some of the numerous company there assembled.' Boghos Yussuf Bey's nephew Nubar, later three times prime minister of Egypt, compared the palace of Ras el-Tin to a public café, where people went if they had nothing else to do. It was frequently described by travellers.[42]

Francis Schroeder told how he and his friends ascended

a handsome wide stairway of marble, crossed several huge halls and corridors and at length found ourselves in a large oval-shaped saloon decorated, carved, painted and emblazoned; set round with rich satin ottomans ... plentiful Arabic inscriptions [from the Koran] and arabesque adornments ... and here we were in the presence of the hero of the East ... His face is regular and handsome, showing none of the effects of years; his lip firm; head erect and well set; complexion hale and hearty, and the eye ... yet undimmed.

The Pasha looked ten years younger than his age and was slightly under average height. His manners aroused admiration, in an age which considered them as important as dress. They were 'quick and lively; he laughs often and heartily and is quite free from that solemn dullness so characteristic of the Turks.'[43]

The fullest description comes in the memoir of Charles Murray, who served as British consul-general in Egypt from 1846 to 1853. He admired Muhammad Ali's 'high breeding and winning manners' and the 'strange wild fire' in his bright grey eyes; the Pasha had 'a straight nose with rather wide nostrils; his mouth was broad but well shaped; beneath it a massive chin covered with a grizzly beard completed a countenance on which the character of a firm but determined will was indelibly stamped.' His hands were small and delicate. He generally wore yellow slippers, loose blue clothes, a cashmere sash, and a white turban; no jewels, not even an earring. After 1838, he replaced his turban with a modern fez, and after a visit to Constantinople in 1846 he adopted the semi-Western costume introduced there twenty years earlier by Mahmud II.[44]

Generally he sat in a corner of his reception room overlooking the port, on the right end of a large divan or *sedir* lining the room. He passed the time watching the port through his telescope, talking, drinking coffee and smoking. His pipe – the most luxurious item in his palace – was seven and a half feet long, with a diamond-encrusted stem, silver tassels, and a gilt bowl resting on a silver saucer.[45]

With consuls, he was 'especially civil and fond of having them about him' – most of the day, every day. Sometimes they were invited to dinner.[46] When he wished, wrote Henry Salt, 'his manner has a charm that it is difficult to conceive without witnessing', flashing his eyes and flattering his interlocutor that they were talking together as friends.[47] He talked of everything – the number of people massacred by Egyptian forces in Greece compared to British forces in India, or the custom of kissing the Pope's toe: 'And so people kiss his toe? How extraordinary to

LEVANT

kiss a mufti's toe. If I went to Rome, would they compel me to kiss his toe?'[48] Occasionally he discussed methods of government: 'You must be aware of how many opposing interests I have to consult, how many prejudices to surmount, how delicate is the affair! If the matter comes to the attention of the Porte I would give it a blanket denial ... I can find very few to understand me and do my bidding. I am often deceived and I know that I am deceived. I have been almost alone for the greater part of my life.'[49] He might also talk of his ambitions: 'If your Government supports me – as I hope – if it will acknowledge me when occasion comes as an independent prince, I shall be satisfied. You will some day – not far remote I trust – reside here in another capacity than that of Consul' – in other words as ambassador from one sovereign to another.[50]

Years later Vincent Benedetti, who had started his career in French diplomacy in Alexandria, also recalled the 'singular charm of this court at once rustic and familiar'.[51] Money formed part of the charm. One reason for Muhammad Ali's move to Alexandria had been his desire to buy and sell. Al-Jabarti claimed that he thought only of money and taking other men's profits.[52] James St John found that 'every look, word or smile of the pasha is subjected to an arithmetical calculation to ascertain its value in piastres.' Some foreign merchants, imitating the Ottoman *temena*, kissed the fringe of the Pasha's divan and pretended to gather up the dust from his feet to their forehead. 'Here therefore', St John added, 'the monarchical principle may be contemplated in all its naked beauty divested of the manifold disguises cast over it in Europe by the history of courtly manners.'[53]

Foreigners were more likely to be present at the palace than devout Muslims. One popular Alexandria preacher, of Algerian origin, Sheikh Ibrahim, had built a mosque in the city in 1824 and ran the leading Koranic school there. In his sermons he denounced innovations; when he claimed that meat butchered by Christians and Jews could not be halal, he was temporarily exiled.[54] A rebellion by a sheikh who called himself the Mahdi, and Muhammad Ali an infidel, was crushed.[55] No Islamist opposition was allowed. Alexandria lost that truculent autonomy for which it had been known in the eighteenth century. A French consul wrote that Muhammad Ali had bought most of the *ulema*; those opposed to his projects were exiled.[56] Once one of the most fanatical provinces of the Ottoman Empire, where travellers had felt 'surrounded by hostilities',[57] under Muhammad Ali Egypt became one of its most tolerant.

Inside themselves, however, many Muslims resented Muhammad Ali's fondness for foreigners. Al-Jabarti complained that Christians, 'the enemies of our religion', had become 'the companions and intimate friends of His Highness'. Christians, in al-Jabarti's opinion, suggested new taxes, helped the Pasha's commercial enterprises, obtained the best jobs and houses, and even employed Muslims as servants.[58]

Foreigners were especially influential in the army and the navy. In 1819 a bankrupt former colonel in Napoleon's army called Joseph Sève, presented to Muhammad Ali by Pascal Coste, began to help train the Pasha's army; in order to increase his authority over his soldiers, he converted to Islam and became known as Soliman Pasha. The New Order army of Selim III was one influence on Muhammad Ali's army; a French military mission of fourteen sent in 1824 under General Boyer, who had served in Egypt in 1798–1801, was another. Boyer saw the Pasha daily, but also had a secret mission from the French Prime Minister Jean-Baptiste de Villèle 'to prepare the events which ought one day to put us in possession of this country'.[59] In order to impress French public opinion, Charles X hoped to emulate Bonaparte's conquest of Egypt. Soon the army, about 100,000 strong, appeared at reviews to be a well-disciplined force, Drovetti complacently reported, 'entirely on the French model'.[60]

This 'astonishing' new conscript army, as Henry Salt called it,[61] was raised at a cost rarely mentioned by the consuls and merchants of Alexandria. Charming to Europeans in his palace, Muhammad Ali could be cruel, even by the standards of his age, outside it. On his expedition to Arabia in 1811–13, when Mecca and Medina were recovered for the Sultan, he out-slaughtered the Wahhabis themselves.[62] When an officer resigned in protest at the number of rebels killed in Crete, the Pasha confessed 'as for the number of executions, it is my fault, it is my sin.'[63]

Muhammad Ali was as much an imperialist as any European ruler. At first he had recruited soldiers in Syria and the Balkans.[64] In 1820–22 he conquered the Sudan, and he might have contemplated taking Ethiopia too if Henry Salt had not warned him that the conquest of such an ancient Christian kingdom 'would probably involve him with the English government'.[65] Although the conquest of the Sudan extended his rule almost to the sources of the Nile, it was essentially a slave raid, designed to seize Africans for his army – or, as he wrote, 'to fetch us blacks to use in the affairs of the Hejaz and other similar services'. He considered them more valuable than jewels. Most died on the horrific land journey up into Egypt, as most of those on 'the Atlantic passage' from Africa to America also died. The revenue of the Sudan, however, continued to be paid to Muhammad Ali in slaves until his next visit, in 1838.[66]

After 1822 Muhammad Ali turned to the peasants of Egypt. His officers led raiding parties on villages. Peasants were taken from their homes, with ropes round their neck, listed, conscripted into the army, and disciplined. So intense was peasants' love of their homes and families that the valley of the Nile was compared by a visiting French officer to a vale of tears.[67] Another deplored 'the most cruel oppression and exactions that people ever submitted to'. Villagers showed their loathing of conscription by flight, rebellion or self-mutilation (cutting off a toe or finger, or blinding themselves with rat poison). Some refused to marry, so as not to have children who would be subject to such torture.[68] The Pasha commented that men who put rat poison in their eyes were beasts in human form who should be sent to forced labour for life; as further punishment, another member of their family should be conscripted to replace them. Women who helped them should be drowned or executed.[69]

The navy also used conscripts. More than any other city of the Levant except Constantinople itself, Alexandria became a naval base, as it still is. Muhammad Ali's fascination with the navy, as well as with making money, had been another reason for his move to Alexandria and construction of the palace at Ras el-Tin. Many officers in the navy were Europeans, and wore European tunics with a Muslim turban. From 1822 the chief trainer of the navy was a Dalmatian formerly in French service called Villenich; the head of the navy, Osman Bey, also knew French. A naval school was established by Ras el-Tin in 1826. Its 1,200 pupils would include Muhammad Ali's own son Said, who would later become a 'man mountain' deformed by fat: his father's instructions to him to lose 'a corpulence hateful to all eyes' had no effect. The director of the port of Alexandria was Besson Bey, also formerly in the French navy. Besson, with another French officer called Koenig, was in charge of Said's education and ensured that he spoke good French.[70]

In 1829, with the agreement of the French government, Louis Charles Lefèbvre de Cérisy left France for Egypt and, as director-general of naval constructions, began to supervise the construction of a new arsenal, between Ras el-Tin and the city. Employing as many as 5,000, including workers from the French naval base at Toulon, the arsenal was another Levantine Tower of Babel: 'French, English, Italians, Maltese, Arabs, Turks, Armenians, Copts, Arabs of the desert all work together and understand each other as best they can.' The workforce also included women, conscripts and prisoners. On occasion they were subjected to medical experiments. To this day, in Egyptian Arabic, the Turkish word for harbour, *liman*, by which the Alexandria arsenal was called, is a synonym for prison.[71] When an English resident of Alexandria saw peasants being led through the streets, 'chained neck and neck with hands in two holes of wood' because they had fled their villages, they may have been on the way to the *liman*.[72]

To outsiders, the long range of stone buildings, where masts, rope and uniforms were made and stored, looked 'like an overgrown English manu-factory'. Stones from the classical ruins, and Muslim cemeteries, outside the town were used to construct the arsenal, the docks and four stone slipways for building ships. The arsenal's nearest rival was its equivalent in Constantinople.[73]

In the summer Muhammad Ali spent much of the day inspecting the arsenal. When he was not there in person, he was often watching it through a telescope from a special wooden bathhouse built for him jutting into the sea from the garden of Ras el-Tin. He appreciated the sea breeze and being able to talk in his bathhouse without being overheard.[74] In fact Muhammad Ali's move to Alexandria had medical as well as political and commercial motives. One reason, according to the French consul in 1811, had been his doctors' desire for him to take sea baths – the fashionable cure being prescribed, at the same time, for George III at Weymouth and for the future George IV at Brighton.[75]

The navy became an obsession. When the German traveller Prince Pückler-Muskau visited Alexandria during a Muslim festival and heard the deafening thunder of ships' cannon firing in celebration, 'as if Alexandria were a volcano emitting its fire on every side', he wrote that 'the genius of the man who holds sway here seemed to dwell upon the waters.'[76]

The palace, the army and the navy were not the only modernizing forces in Alexandria. The city itself, as Muhammad Ali intended, created its own dynamic. Outside the palace and the arsenal was a boom town, like two other 'windows on the West' with vast hinterlands, to which Alexandria was sometimes compared: St Petersburg and Odessa.

In 1820 it had been much as Chateaubriand had found it in 1806. The streets were dirty, irregular and unpaved. The houses had a 'dull insipid appearance', with flat roofs. The Turks and Egyptians did not mix with the few hundred foreigners living in what was called, as in Smyrna, 'the Frank quarter'. A lantern and stick at night were necessary 'as a protection against insult'. The local women were covered in black or blue cloaks. Only the nose and eyes were visible:'even the points of their fingers could not be seen'.[77]

After 1825, however, wrote the Russian consul, every day 'we see some fresh innovation in the European style destined for the improvement of the city or for public utility.' In 1829 government administrations were ordered to keep accounts in European numerals. A tribunal of commerce was established in 1826, with four Muslim, two Catholic, one Greek, one French and one Jewish member.[78] In 1831 a public-health office was founded in a room in the French consulate.[79]

Consuls' access to information and technology enabled them to perform a double function. They could both interfere in Ottoman provinces on behalf of their own governments and be used by the Ottoman government itself as substitute executives, to bypass inefficient or disobedient officials: another example of flexibility of nationality in the Levant. With the rise of the number of their nationals living in Egypt, moreover, each consul began to consider himself, as Henry Salt wrote, 'a sort of king. Every Consulate here is a little Government and all those residing in the country are considered to be under its exclusive Protection.'[80] Soon it was said that consuls in the Ottoman Empire were more important than ambassadors in Europe.[81]

Consuls could change the course of history. In Algiers on 29 April 1827, during a quarrel about money owed to the dey of Algiers by the French government, the French consul, Pierre Deval (born in Pera in 1758, of a family of dragomans),[82] was beaten by Hussein Pasha, dey of Algiers, with three blows from the handle of his fly-whisk – 'violent blows' acording to the consul, 'light blows' according to the Pasha, who also claimed the consul had insulted Islam and the Sultan. Three years later, using this humiliation as a pretext (though in reality, to try to increase his government's popularity, having previously considered invading Egypt for the same purpose), Charles X sent French troops into Algeria: they did not leave until 1962. Charles X used Napoleon's plans of Algiers, as Bonaparte had used Louis XVI's plans of Egypt, for his conquest. French regimes changed; French desire for expansion in the Mediterranean did not.[83]

An outward sign of the power of the consuls and the modernization of Alexandria was the creation of 'the only cleanly and airy' square in the city, the first modern square in the Middle East. It was parallel to the eastern harbour, between the Ottoman city on the peninsula and the remains of the classical city inland. More spontaneous than planned, by 1813 it was described as a 'large square near the sea ... improved and covered by the Europeans who come here to breathe the sea breezes'. It was soon known as the Place d'Armes, as troops drilled there. By 1828, when some consuls came to live there, it was called the Place des Consuls, or Grand' Place.[84]

In the early 1830s it was redesigned as a formal rectangle by a political exile from the Papal States called Francesco Mancini. He also laid out a surrounding area of straight, wide streets – in defiance, as Mohammed Awad has written, of the crooked streets of the adjoining Ottoman city.[85] Large stone complexes known as *okallas* (later versions of which still line it), containing courtyards, shops, apartments and, on the upper floors, some-times as many as 600 inhabitants – in effect, nineteenth-century shopping malls – were constructed round the square, often on Muhammad Ali's orders. Shops had 'all the productions of Europe'.[86]

Soon the square contained the French, American, Swedish and Greek consulates; two comfortable hotels, the Hôtel d'Europe (where the Prince of Wales would stay in 1868) and the Hôtel d'Orient; and houses with French windows and *portes cochères*. The streets of the old town were full of camels. Round the Place des Consuls, according to English visitors in 1843, 'Carriages of every description filled with smartly dressed ladies are to be seen driving about at all hours.' By then a straight street three miles long, the Rue de la Porte de Rosette (now Freedom Street), traversed the entire city, along the old Ptolemaic road from the Gate of the Sun to the Gate of the Moon.[87]

Ceremonial confirmed consuls' rise in status and the city's interna-tionalization. In 1803 consuls' houses in Alexandria had been attacked by local soldiers for daring to fly their country's flag, as consuls did elsewhere in the Levant. The consuls had fled to the safety of Ottoman ships in the harbour, until the soldiers were punished.[88] Under Muhammad Ali consuls flew ostentatiously large flags from their roofs.[89]

From 1811 new consuls-general began to make a state entry into the city, riding a horse sent from the Pasha's stables. In 1833 the new British consul-general, Colonel Patrick Campbell, entered Alexandria with an Arab guard of honour, dragomans and 'a number of naval officers with the whole body of British residents', saluted by cannon from the ships in the harbour and Qaitbey Fort guarding the harbour entrance, and by ships' bands playing French and Arab music; he then made a speech in praise of 'the friendship and good understanding which now so happily prevails between the two countries', as if Egypt were independent.[90]

The first Greek consul-general after independence was one of the driv-ing forces behind the revival of the city. He was a friend of Muhammad Ali called Michel Tossizza. He first became head of the Alexandria Greek community, and later built a porticoed classical house at the head of the Place des Consuls, designed by the court architect, another Italian radi-cal living in Egypt, Pietro Avoscani. Tossizza and the Pasha had been friends since Kavalla, where the Tossizza family is said to have advanced the young Muhammad Ali a loan at a crucial moment. Michel and his brother Theodore also helped in the construction of the first Greek school and hospital in the city, ancestors of institutions which still exist today.[91]

The Swedish consul-general was another Greek friend of Muhammad Ali, called Yanni Anastasi. He too lived on the Place des Consuls. He had arrived in Alexandria from Lemnos in 1809, and helped Henry Salt collect Egyptian antiquities. He became the richest and most respected merchant in Egypt: in 1847, for example, he purchased the entire gum crop of Sennar in the Sudan from Muhammad Ali for £80,000. As he went up in the world, Yanni Anastasi became Giovanni Anastasi, finally the Chevalier Jean d'Anastasy.[92] Both d'Anastasy and Tossizza were cosmopolitan merchants with agents in other Mediterranean ports such as Marseille and Livorno.[93]

Like Smyrna, Alexandria was becoming Greek again – more Greek than at any time since it had surrendered to an Arab army in 642. The Greeks first arrived in large numbers in Alexandria as slaves, after the massacre of Chios in 1822, and Ibrahim Pasha's campaign in the Peloponnese in 1826. Michel Zizinia, for example, founder of the Zizinia district, had been a slave from Chios called Tsisinia. Greeks also came voluntarily to Alexandria as to Smyrna, in order to make their fortunes. Greeks' success was partly due to language. Muhammad Ali never learned Arabic: until the 1860s Turkish, not Arabic, was the first language of the dynasty, court and government in Egypt. Since Greek immigrants (and Boghos Yussuf Bey, the foreign minister) came from areas of the Ottoman Empire with large Turkish populations, they probably knew Turkish. Since Syrians and Egyptians came from Arabic-speaking areas, without large Turkish populations, they were unlikely to know it.[94] Greeks also worked, in large numbers, as gardeners and builders in Alexandria.[95]

An outbreak of cholera in 1834 confirmed the consuls' power. They had already helped establish and enforce permanent quarantine controls in 1828. In 1834 Muhammad Ali asked the consuls to deal with the cholera and offered Colonel Campbell, the British consul-general, 20,000 soldiers to establish a cordon sanitaire. However, thinking all precautions useless, Egyptians hid the sick and the dead and the disease spread: 20,000 may have died. Writing that 'these ignorant people do not discriminate between good and evil and desire to spread disease in the great city of Alexandria', and alarmed by the death of a woman in his harem, Muhammad Ali fled to the safety of a ship, his son Ibrahim Pasha to upper Egypt. The consuls, however, had streets widened and slums demolished.[96]

Alexandria was a court city as well as a naval and commercial port, and Muhammad Ali ran it though one of his sons-in-law, another immigrant from Kavalla, called Moharrem Bey. From 1828 Moharrem Bey was governor of the city, an admiral in the fleet and *kapici bashi* or grand chamberlain of the Pasha; by the time he died, in 1847, he owned large estates outside Alexandria.[97] In 1834 Muhammad Ali set up the Commissione di Ornato or Board of Works to supervise the construction of roads and buildings, and, as the city expanded, to allot land to those he favoured. Like the arsenal, and the commercial tribunal, the Ornato institutionalized Alexandria's cosmopolitanism. Its first president was the Greek consul Michel Tossizza. The other consuls, leading merchants and an Egyptian sheikh were the other members.

Muhammad Ali looked after the spiritual as well as the material welfare of Alexandria Europeans. Behind one side of the Place des Consuls the Catholic church of St Catherine, built in 1634, was given more land and rebuilt in 1834.[98] The only religious building on the square itself was the English church dedicated to the apostle of Egypt, St Mark. Its foundation stone was laid by the British consul-general Colonel Campbell on 16 January 1840 'in an area conceded by the munificence of the Viceroy Muhammad Ali', as a Latin inscription proclaims above the entrance. Designed in Anglican Arabesque style by James Wild, it was finished by 1854. With many memorial tablets to long-dead commandants of the Alexandria City Police, it is a museum of British Alexandria, though services are now in Arabic and Dinka as well as English.

Alexandria was becoming part of the world economy. The harbour usually contained at least 200 ships. The 'merchant vessels and ships of war with outspread sails and colours flying, entering or leaving the port', were surrounded, as in the port of Smyrna, by numerous smaller 'jerms, feluccas and pilot boats scudding with large white sails along the shore'. 'Filled with Arabs, Turks and dirty Italians', these would approach the larger boats 'chattering bargaining, wrangling'.[99] In 1835 the construction of a new quay along the main western harbour facilitated the expansion of commerce. By 1839, at £2,825,880 p.a., the value of trade going through Alexandria alone was equivalent to the value of all trade going through the whole of Egypt ten years earlier.[100] The number of European firms established in Alexandria rose from 23 in 1822 to 69 in 1837.[101]

Europeans in Alexandria came from many backgrounds. They included Italian political exiles; followers of the radical economic doctrines of Henri de Saint-Simon, known as Saint-Simonians; and, after the failure of the Warsaw rising of 1831, Polish officers of fortune. British merchant families, such as the Barkers, Peels and Carvers, continued to run businesses in Alexandria until their expulsion and expropriation after the

British–French–Israeli attack on Egypt in 1956. A member of a famous Marseille shipping family, Jean-Baptiste Pastré worked in Alexandria from 1825 to 1835; after his return to Marseille 'he came to dominate the trade between the Nile and the Rhône to the point where it was almost his private domain.'[102]

After Constantinople and Smyrna, Alexandria had become the third Levantine cosmopolis. Like them, it was an accumulation of contrasts. The Muslim Egyptian population was growing as a result of the jobs available, and the flight of peasants from the countryside, to escape conscription and marauding Bedouin. In the old Ottoman city on the promontory, 'a promiscuous crowd of men of all colours and costumes – gorgeous, fantastic, wretched, many of them nearly naked – with their loud confused din of outcries and vociferations, form a scene that is quite unbelievable. One's head soon grows dizzy with the strange sights and strange sounds.' As well as camels, jugglers, women in large blue mantles, with white veils over their faces, waddling 'like walking woolsacks', and troops of dogs – 'lean, wolfish and prick-eared' – Alexandria also contained soldiers, officers in brilliant uniforms, and running footmen. The population in 1834 was around 36,000, excluding the garrison of over 5,000 men.[103] In the old city the year was, and still is, marked by religious festivals – Ramadan, the Prophet's birthday and the two Eids – and by local Muslim saints' days with shows and games. Its long association with Islam may explain why, despite Muhammad Ali's tyranny, Alexandria was never regarded by Egyptians as an alien intrusion in their country, as St Petersburg was by some Russians.[104]

In the new city there were 4,886 Europeans and they were increasingly visible.[105] As early as 1834, Cérisy declared, 'Everyone has building mania and we already have several houses which would be magnificent even in Paris.'[106] Ali Mubarak, a native-born Egyptian who would serve as minister of education in 1868, admired foreigners' houses, which were the 'model of architectural magnificence', and noted that Alexandrians began to abandon their former way of life. He attributed the revival of Alexandria to the generosity of the dynasty.[107] However, wealthy Alexandrians were not yet willing to obey Muhammad Ali and send their sons to be educated in Paris, preferring to send porters' sons instead; the Pasha punished the parents by making them help remove the mounds of rubbish surrounding the city.[108] Foreign travellers arriving from Cairo or anywhere else in the Levant, seeing in the 'broad airy streets' of the modern part of Alexandria people wearing European clothes and speaking

European languages, felt, as they would for the next hundred years, that they were in Europe.[109]

Alexandria was beginning to revive as a centre of learning. The first printing press in Egypt, after those brought and removed by the French occupiers, and Muhammad Ali's government press established in Bulaq near Cairo in 1820, was the European press owned by Signor Draghi in Alexandria. In 1824 it published the first English book in Egypt, *Egypt: A Descriptive Poem*, by Henry Salt. Alexandria also had a book club and library, founded in 1827 on the Place des Consuls;[110] a government newspaper printed in French and Arabic; and a postal service, established in 1820 by Signori Merati and Chini. The first stamps in Egypt had inscriptions in Italian.[111]

By 1840, according to Clot Bey, a doctor who in 1825 had moved to Alexandria from France and become Muhammad Ali's chief medical officer, there was a European hospital (founded in 1817 on Drovetti's initiative), one French and one Italian theatre, and eight or ten European restaurants; ice for the restaurants of Alexandria came from the mountains of southern Turkey. In 1820 Baroness von Minutoli, wife of a Prussian envoy, had complained, 'Society at Alexandria offers but very few resources ... all the gossiping of a little country town.' Twenty years later, however, Clot's account reads like a foretaste of Lawrence Durrell's *Alexandria Quartet*. Perhaps he was trying to attract visitors from Europe: 'It [Alexandria society] likes pleasure and parties, and often meets at brilliant soirées and balls ... morals are fairly relaxed in Frank society; love affairs there are not rare.'[112]

Carnival came, from Smyrna or Italy, to Alexandria under Muhammad Ali. During the carnival season, many private and public balls were given, often by consuls, who considered them an obligation; invitations were easy to obtain. As in Smyrna, there were also parties at a European 'Casino'. At some balls, wrote a traveller called C. Rochfort Scott, after watching Muslims waltzing with consuls' daughters, 'such was the variety of character and costume that it was with difficulty I could persuade myself I was not at a real fancy dress ball.'[113] The theatres were small and not good. One performance of Bellini's *Norma* compelled the French journalist Jules Coignet to leave after forty minutes.[114]

Alexandria was acquiring a reputation for luxury and sensuality which would last until the 1960s.[115] Marshal Auguste Marmont, who in 1834 had returned as Muhammad Ali's guest to visit the city which he had governed for the French Republic from November 1798 to August 1799, noted in the streets a large number of 'filles publiques', whom he assumed to be for

Egyptian workers; 'Their faculties are said to be prodigious despite their extreme poverty and their astonishing sobriety.' He also enjoyed the parties in the grandiose Italianate mansion of Jean d'Anastasy.[116] While other guests admired the collection of antiquities, Vincent Benedetti admired a beautiful Greek slave, a survivor from the massacres on Chios who had been sold to d'Anastasy. In Alexandria most wealthy foreigners, as well as Egyptians, owned slaves, except the English and 'the more respectable among the French'.[117] Benedetti married her. In 1864 Comtesse Benedetti, one of the most beautiful women of the Second Empire, accompanied her husband to Berlin, where he was appointed French ambassador – an embassy that lasted until the Franco-Prussian war. Thanks to Alexandria, a slave from Chios could become an ambassadress in Berlin.[118]

As the city expanded and modernized, it began to be surrounded by another city, of mud huts among the classical ruins. Since travellers were interested in the ruins, they saw for themselves, at close quarters, the plight of the poor. The huts – single rooms six feet high, covered in white plaster – reminded Florence Nightingale of an army of white ants.[119] To an American called David Millard their 'most filthy and squalid appearance' presented a picture of 'extreme wretchedness'.[120] James St John called them 'inferior in comfort and appearance to dog kennels or pig sties', even to 'the cabins of the Irish'.[121] Their inhabitants lived among animals – cows, goats and 'dogs that rush out at strangers as if driven by hunger to search for prey' – and their poverty seemed to have gone 'beyond the limits of the possible'. The men were only just covered by rags; their half-naked children were thin and diseased, with swollen stomachs. There was little vegetation, just 'one melancholy interminable waste of sand', broken by the occasional palm tree.[122]

Extreme poverty explains why travellers complained of 'the rapacity of the boatmen who like all other classes at Alexandria are never satisfied'; 'the importunate extortion of the donkey boys and beggars of Alexandria'; or that 'the word baksheesh [tip] accompanied by a significant gesture was so often and emphatically repeated ... that we at once concluded it to be the corner stone of the language.'[123]

5

Alexandria: Bid for Empire

Egypt is our possession and its inhabitants are but our slaves.
Ibrahim Pasha to Muhammad Ali, 5 September 1832

ALEXANDRIA WAS NOT only capital of Egypt. It was also seat of a
bid for empire. As Alexandria under Cleopatra challenged Rome, so
Alexandria under Muhammad Ali challenged Constantinople, for the empire
of the East. Muhammad Ali was inspired by the decay of the Ottoman
Empire. He saw an opportunity to use one province of the Empire to
conquer the rest.

Muhammad Ali was an exception in his time and culture. The Porte
itself had paid tribute to his success and efficiency in Egypt. After he had
suppressed the Wahhabi revolt in Arabia, it turned to him to suppress rebellion in Greece. On 10 July 1824 Ibrahim Pasha had set sail from Alexandria
with a fleet of 163 ships (many built for his father in Marseille or Livorno)
and an army of 16,000 to subdue the Peloponnese. At first he had enjoyed
considerable success. Egyptian ships came and went continually between
his army and Alexandria.[1] The city was on the front line. Twice, in 1825
and 1827, Greek ships attacked Egyptian ships in Alexandria's harbour.
On the first occasion Muhammad Ali was so enraged that he rushed down
to the harbour, commandeered a vessel, and for a week searched in vain
for the attackers.

Despite the racial and religious war in Greece, and the destruction of
the Egyptian fleet at Navarino, special patrols in Alexandria protected
Franks and Greeks from attacks by Muslims bent on revenge. Muhammad
Ali's authority and his personal guarantee ensured that, unlike Smyrna in
1770 and 1821, Alexandria remained in 'the most perfect tranquillity'.[2]
Under government protection cosmopolitanism survived.

In 1830 Muhammad Ali subdued another rebellion for the Porte, in
Crete. Then he turned to Syria. Like Egypt in 1805, it was a province
ready for plucking. As early as 1812 he had included Syria in what the

British consul already called his 'ideas of conquest and independence'. In 1825 he was planning to seize Damascus, Yemen and the Arabian Gulf.[3] Attack was the best means of defence. Both in 1807 and 1820 the Porte, alarmed by Muhammad Ali's ambition, had tried to remove from his authority Alexandria and the Nile ports: they had previously formed a separate province, and officials like the kadi and the port captain had been appointed directly from Constantinople, rather than from Cairo.[4] The Porte also tried and failed to dismiss him from the governorship of Egypt itself: first in 1806, then in 1822.[5]

The fate of another independent Albanian governor, Byron's admirer Ali Pasha of Janina, was a grim warning. Like Muhammad Ali, he too, as the Ottoman Empire weakened, had created a large army, become an international merchant exporting wheat, and established close relations with foreign consuls and Greeks, and he may have aimed to establish his own monarchy. Yet he and his sons were killed on the Sultan's orders in 1822.[6]

Differing world outlooks were another source of conflict between the Porte and the Pasha. Like a later pasha from the Balkans, the founder of the Turkish Republic Mustafa Kemal himself (born in Salonica in 1888), Muhammad Ali had a modernizing mentality. He shared some of the attitudes, towards the Ottoman Empire, of European travellers and diplomats now regarded as condescending racists. In 1822, in a letter to his nephew Ahmed Pasha Yeghen, Muhammad Ali denounced the Ottoman state as 'feeble and rampant with problems because of its viziers' obsession with ceremonies and tradition'. The Sultan, he wrote, was a bigot in the hands of the *ulema*, too bigoted to employ Franks in positions of authority, rather than merely as technical advisers.[7]

During the war against the Greeks, Ibrahim Pasha saw the Ottoman army and navy at first hand. 'They are so helpless and inefficient they cannot even fix the masts of their frigates,' he wrote to his father in 1825: Greek sailors who had previously manned the Ottoman navy had deserted to fight for independence, so Turkish sailors were inexperienced.

Ottomans and Muhammad Ali lived in different worlds. Just before the combined Ottoman–Egyptian fleet was blown sky high at Navarino in 1827, the Grand Vizier wrote to Ibrahim Pasha, 'Victory does not depend on the number of ships but on the strength of men's hearts.' Muhammad Ali in contrast believed that 'Wars are won not only by depending on God and trusting in Him but also by putting all possible human effort into it ... God has ordered us in His Book not only to stand up to the enemy but also to spare no effort in confronting him.' He believed that in the art of war 'the Europeans are way ahead of us.'[8]

Muhammad Ali was the first agricultural reformer in the Middle East. He changed the landscape of Egypt, introducing pineapples, bananas, mangoes, figs, vines and orange groves. He took a personal interest in cotton, sending soldiers into the plantations to help with the harvests.[9] In the four years after his introduction in 1820 of long-crop Jumel cotton, annual cotton production rose from 944 to 228,078 hundredweight. More than any other commodity, cotton would be the basis of Alexandria's economic future.[10]

New plants and crops were planted in and around Alexandria, particularly around the palaces built for the Pasha's sons and grandsons and the villas of the rich. The palace of Moharrem Bey was surrounded by palm and orange groves, figs and pomegranates. Boghos Yussuf Bey learned to create new types of orange tree.[11] The Sultan, on the other hand, had the richest country in the world and, in Muhammad Ali's opinion, did nothing with it.[12] Muhammad Ali and his son were like a team of modern managers taking over an antiquated subsidiary company, appalled at their predecessors' mismanagement, eager to import the latest foreign techniques and to make a bid for independence from head office – or take it over.

Finally, on 4 November 1831, after factories in Egypt had been working overtime for months, the attack on Syria began. Ibrahim sailed from Alexandria to Jaffa with a fleet of thirty ships, some of them built in the Alexandria arsenal, bearing his staff, cannon and supplies. The army advanced overland. The coast ports, including Jaffa and Sidon, surrendered that month. After a seven-month siege, on 27 May 1832 the great fortress city of Acre, which had withstood Bonaparte's army in 1799, was stormed by troops led by Ibrahim Pasha in person; Damascus fell a month later. Ibrahim continued his advance north, taking Adana on 31 July.[13] At the Battle of Konya on 21 December 1832, 15,000 Egyptians defeated an Ottoman army of 50,000. The Grand Vizier himself was taken prisoner. On 1 February the Egyptian army reached Kutahya, en route for the Bosphorus.[14] Ibrahim Pasha's victories were due to his own leadership, his excellent second-in-command Suleyman Pasha, the devotion he inspired among his officers – who were better paid than in the Ottoman army – and his well disciplined modern army. Rivalries in the Ottoman high command, and its fatal habit of following the advice of religious leaders, also helped.[15]

From all corners of the Empire, people turned to the victors. Anatolia was more sympathetic to Muhammad Ali than Syria, which some diplomats attributed to its ingrained tolerance. In Anatolia, Turks, Greeks and

Armenians (whom Turks then called 'a people of camels', since they were docile and hard-working) lived easily together, compared to the fanatacism of Syria. The Karaosmanoglu dynasty and Smyrna itself briefly paid homage to Ibrahim Pasha, until the foreign consuls – still the key power-brokers – persuaded the city to revert to its imperial allegiance; the consuls acted for the Ottoman Empire, following their governments' orders, although they believed it was about to disintegrate.[16] The Sultan suspended Muhammad Ali from his governorships; the Sherif of Mecca, head of the Hashemite dynasty, which considered itself the oldest in the world, declared the Sultan the enemy of Islam.[17]

Even the Ottoman Empire in Europe, Muhammad Ali boasted, was waiting for him, and he had many supporters in Constantinople itself. He halted his son's advance only to spare bloodshed and consult the powers of Europe. The arrival of Russian troops on the Bosphorus, to protect the tottering Sultan, was a more compelling reason to hesitate.[18] The Levant was again 'the world's debate' – not between Christians and Muslims, but between rival Muslim dynasties, and the rival European powers support-ing them.

In May 1833 a truce signed at Kutahya, brokered by French and Russian diplomats, restored Muhammad Ali to the governorships of Egypt, Crete and the Hejaz and appointed Ibrahim governor of Damascus, Aleppo, Tripoli and Acre and to a financial post in Adana – to enable the Egyptian navy to use wood from the Cilician mountains.[19] Never before had one family controlled so much of the Ottoman Empire.

Ibrahim Pasha introduced the first orderly government Syria had enjoyed since the eighteenth century. He had more incentive than pashas whose terms of office had been limited to a few years. In accordance with his father's policy, he built barracks and hospitals, raised the status of Christians and Jews, and let them serve with Muslims on consultative councils.[20]

His chief local ally was the emir Bashir II Shihab, ruler of the area east of the ports of Beirut and Tripoli, known as Mount Lebanon. His dynasty had been in power since 1697, in the double capacity of Ottoman tax collectors and leaders of the Druze (a heretical sect, following a secret version of Islam, which had lived in Mount Lebanon since the eleventh century), and is still active in Lebanese politics today. In the second half of the eighteenth century, perhaps under the influence of a Christian doctor, his branch had converted to Christianity, although he continued to profess Islam in public, to please his Ottoman suzerain. Emir Bashir, whose manners and bearing impressed vistors even more than Muhammad Ali's, from 1804 to 1840 ran a mini-state with a population of 213,000, where he may have hoped, like Muhammad Ali and Ali Pasha, to establish his dynasty on a firm territorial base: 130,000 were Maronite (practising a local form of Christianity which had acknowledged the authority of the Pope since the crusades), 65,000 Druze, and a few Muslims.[21]

The conflict between Muhammad Ali and the Sublime Porte operated on three levels. The crux was the Pasha's desire to start a dynasty – his dynastic ambition would be one of the foundations of Egypt's independence. Sometimes he liked to present himself as the Empire's best servant. In February 1832 he declared of the Sultan, 'I have nothing against his dynasty which is the only legitimate one ... I do not desire the Sultan's throne,' though he claimed all were calling for him. However, in August 1832, elated by victory, and referring to his seizure of power in 1805, he declared, 'I conquered Egypt by the sword and it is the sword which will take it from me. The Arabs are all for me and they are worth more than the Turks. I am waiting for anything, I am ready for anything.'[22] At times he urged a fatwa to depose the Sultan, who would be replaced by his son Abdulmecid.[23] He even considered making a 'religious *coup d'état*', bringing the Sherif of Mecca to Cairo, proclaiming him caliph, and kissing the hem of his robe. He said Arabs needed a religious revolution to regenerate them.[24]

Some historians have claimed that independence was merely a manoeuvre to increase his bargaining power with the Sublime Porte. However, from his correspondence with Ibrahim preserved in the Egyptian National Archives in the Cairo citadel and published by Khaled Fahmy, as well as from innumerable conversations reported by foreign consuls, Muhammad Ali and Ibrahim clearly often considered independence. In 1832 Ibrahim urged his father to mint his own coins, have the Friday sermon read in his name in mosques, and declare 'Egypt's independence' – as one ruler of Egypt, Ali Bey, had done in 1772.[25] In 1833 Ibrahim called independence 'a vital question which takes precedence of all the others'. Without it 'all our efforts would be vain and we would remain under the yoke of this perfidious power which does not stop oppressing us with its ridiculous demands and its requests for money.'[26] To his soldiers he once declared, 'What have I or any of you benefited by the Sultan? ... Have we not all eaten of the bread of Mohammed Ali ... Egypt is his and he won it by the sword; we know no sovereign but Mohammed Ali.'[27]

The clash also reflected a struggle of personalities within the Ottoman governing class, between Muhammad Ali Pasha and his personal enemy Husrev Pasha. Both had competed to be governor of Egypt in 1801–5.

On 20 August 1825, when Husrev, as Kaptan Pasha, visited Muhammad Ali at Ras el-Tin while the Ottoman fleet was refitting in the port of Alexandria, Henry Salt saw them competing 'with gentle violence' to make the other take the best seat, to be first to blow flies from the other's face with their fly-whisk. He was not deceived. He commented that their rivalry 'has contributed materially and must contribute to its [the Empire's] ruin.' During the Greek War of Independence, Husrev Pasha was said by Muhammad Ali himself, in letters to the Porte, to have sabotaged Ibrahim's victories by 'neglect and inaction'. Muhammad Ali called Husrev, in a circular to other pashas, 'the sole author of all the woes which have successively befallen the Empire, a person swollen with venom'.[28]

Race tensions, the hidden wiring of Ottoman history, also contributed to their rivalry. Husrev was an Abkhazian from the Caucasus, said to loathe Albanians like Muhammad Ali.[29] Yet race might also keep Muhammad Ali loyal to the Ottoman Empire. Muhammad Ali considered himself a Turk. The definition of a Turk was, then as now, political, cultural and religious as well as ethnic – it could include Circassians, Albanians, Bosnians or Kurds, if they thought of themselves as Turks, spoke Turkish, followed Islam, served the Ottoman Empire, and were not Arab.[30] As Khaled Fahmy has shown, a sense of racial superiority pervades Muhammad Ali's correspondence: 'The Turks are members of our race and ... must remain close to us all the time,' he wrote in 1822, when explaining why he could not use them as soldiers but had to conscript Egyptians. He compared Egyptians to 'wild beasts'.[31]

Turkish hatred for Arabs is ancient and enduring. The Ottomans had a proverb that they would forgo all the sweets of Damascus if they could avoid seeing the face of an Arab. Many converted Slavs, Greeks and Albanians became viziers and pashas. Almost no Arabs (unless they also had non-Arab blood) did.[32] In Egypt, 'the last Turk considers he has the right to dictate orders and knows how to make himself obeyed. There reigns a deep hatred and animosity between those two races,' wrote a Russian diplomat in 1837.[33] Egyptians in their turn disliked 'the Turks', whom al-Jabarti considered an alien group.[34]

Muhammad Ali's regime was based on race. His officers were Turks, as Turks were 'entitled to rule.' No Egyptian was allowed to rise above the rank of captain in the army or the navy. Again showing his imperialist sympathies, he compared Egyptians' role to that of Indian soldiers under British officers in India. Turkish prisoners of war were recruited as officers into Muhammad Ali's army in preference to Egyptians. He paid better than the Sultan. A colonel in the Ottoman army was paid sixty times more than a soldier; a colonel in the Egyptian army 500 times more.[35]

The army was called the Jihadiye army of Egypt – although its only 'jihad' was against Muslims. Muhammad Ali made no appeal to Egyptian nationalism. It did not yet exist – although it may have been festering in the army, where Egyptian soldiers were discriminated against and humiliated by Turkish-speaking officers.[36]

With his 'Turkish' power structure and mentality, regarding Constantinople as the centre of the world, Muhammad Ali may have considered his role as a servant of the Ottoman sultan – and access to recruitment in Ottoman lands and to Ottoman honours – more advantageous to his dynasty than independence. Despite his outbursts of contempt, he may also, as he frequently stated, have felt a degree of loyalty to the empire from which he came.

Moreover, as European empires advanced on Egypt, the Ottoman Empire offered a form of protection from their ambitions. Muhammad Ali was alarmed by what he called the 'misery' and 'decline' of Muslims.[37] The Bey of Tunis, he felt, had become 'the slave of France'.[38] Ibrahim too feared 'the ruin of our family' and 'the partition of Islamic lands'.[39] The fate of Algiers – once known as al-Mahroussa, 'The Fortunate', the stronghold of jihad – was a warning. Throughout the 1830s the French government was extending its control, settling European colonists on Muslims' land, destroying mosques and schools. A new European city, built on a grid plan, with a large open square on which French soldiers drilled, appeared beside the kasbah or old Arab city. Soon the church of Notre Dame d'Afrique dominated the skyline. Popular songs lamented:

> O tears for Algiers and its houses,
> The Christians inhabit them, their state has changed!
> They have degraded everything, spoiled all, the impure ones!
> Scattered the bones of our fathers, tied their horses in mosques.[40]

On the other side of Egypt, forestalling Muhammad Ali's ambitions in the area, British ships bombarded Aden in 1839 and seized it from the Sultan of Lahej. The first Arab possession of the British Empire, it was to remain one of the busiest ports on the Indian Ocean until the departure of British troops in 1967.

The struggle between the Pasha and the Porte was also an international struggle. Both sides asked for foreign help, and used foreign diplomats as messengers and negotiators. The period of foreign domination, from which the Middle East has not yet recovered, was caused not only by foreign empires' expansion, but also by rulers' repeated requests for foreign support, and notables' regular demands for foreign diplomatic protection.[41] Without it they felt they had little security of life and property, without foreign education little hope of meeting the challenges of their time.[42]

Dissatisfied with the growing power of Russia, Prussia and Austria in Europe, France supported Muhammad Ali, whom some Frenchmen regarded as the successor and avenger of Bonaparte. Moreover, France was beginning to trade more with Egypt than with the rest of the Ottoman Empire. A steamer service between Marseille and Alexandria began in 1835. In conversations with French diplomats, Muhammad Ali presented himself as a hero keen to secure his place in history, a new Bonaparte who would do what the French government decided. His pride in what he called his 'Muhammad Ali-ness' was shown by the fact that the only words embroidered on his troops' red flags were 'Muhammad Ali'.[43] As he had told Henry Salt, 'Mehemet Ali is no Pasha – has no title – is plain Mehemet Ali. I have never put any other inscription on my seal than – Mehemet Ali.'[44]

For Britain, Prussia, and Austria, however, the Ottoman Empire was indispensable for the system of Europe, preferable to the alternatives of chaos or partition. The European consuls in Alexandria, the European ambassadors in Constantinople, and the special envoys sent directly from London, Vienna and St Petersburg to Alexandria constantly supported Ottoman power.[45] In 1829, when Britain and France – not for the last time – were about to send fleets to protect Constantinople from an approaching Russian army, the Duke of Wellington stated, 'The Ottoman Empire exists not for the benefit of the Turks but for the benefit of Christian Europe.' The French foreign minister General Horace Sébastiani, a former ambassador in Constantinople, wrote in 1832 that the dissolution of the Empire would be dangerous for the peace of Europe.[46]

Britain in particular feared that the expansion of Muhammad Ali's power would drive the Ottoman Empire into alliance with Russia – as indeed happened in 1833: as a safeguard against Ibrahim Pasha's advance, 5,000 Russian troops camped at Buyukdere on the Bosphorus. The British Foreign Secretary, Lord Palmerston, wrote to Colonel Campbell in Alexandria of 'the importance which His Majesty's Government attaches to the maintenance of the integrity of the Turkish empire as an object of European interest'.[47] Moreover, the laissez-faire economic attitudes of the Ottoman Empire, enshrined in the Convention of Baltaliman of 1838, were considered more favourable to British trade than the interventionist policies of Muhammad Ali – although the British merchants of Alexandria constantly praised him to their government.[48]

Finally, on 25 May 1838, Muhammad Ali, complaining that he had been the most obedient vassal in history, told the French consul-general Monsieur Cochelet, and later the others, that he wanted independence: 'I am old, I want to be assured before I die of the future of my family. I want the power I have founded to pass into its hands.' He also mentioned the future of his factories, his schools and his fleet. He was prepared to pay £3 million to the Porte for independence.[49] To Michel Tossizza he said that he did not want 'to leave after his death to the discretion of the Sultan his great political and natural family which the Sultan would want to exterminate with him'.[50] He was proud of his reforms. But his priority was not Egypt, nor the Arabs, nor the Ottoman Empire, nor Islam, but what he and Ibrahim called 'our Sublime Family', 'my dynasty' – 'to carve a place for my family and my dynasty's families in history that will be remembered in four or five centuries' time'.[51]

Meanwhile, Ibrahim Pasha's introduction of conscription, on the Egyptian model, had led to revolts in Syria. Many Muslims detested him. He was less traditional in his habits than his father. He sat 'à la franque' on a chair, rather than 'à la turque' on a divan, ate with a spoon and fork, and drank large quantities of wine in public: his father drank only in the secrecy of the harem.[52] In Beirut, Sheikh Fadlullah denounced the introduction of quarantine as 'contrary to the teachings of Islam ... there is no power nor might except in God the exalted and Great.'[53]

War with the Sultan began again. On 24 June 1839 at Nezib, east of Aleppo, the Ottoman army engaged Ibrahim Pasha's forces. Nezib was a Levantine prequel to the Franco-Prussian war. Prussian officers, including Helmuth von Moltke, the architect of victory in 1870, tried to advise the Ottoman army, French officers the Egyptian. Fighting against the Sultan's orders and Moltke's advice, the Ottoman commander Hafiz Pasha was routed, losing his cannon and his baggage.[54]

The victory was followed by another Ottoman catastrophe. At the funeral of Mahmud II on 2 June 1839, Muhammad Ali's enemy Husrev Pasha had seized the grand vizier's seal of office. The Kaptan Pasha was another of Husrev's enemies.[55] He sailed with the Ottoman fleet from Constantinople and, instead of engaging the Egyptian fleet, proceeded to Alexandria. On 14 July 1839, saluted by many cannon, he landed, rode to Ras el-Tin on Muhammad Ali's horse between files of troops, and knelt to kiss the hem of the Pasha's robe. Muhammad Ali raised him, kissed him, and said, 'Welcome, my brother.' They then went arm in arm to drink coffee and smoke pipes, sitting on the divan in the reception room, from which they could see the combined Ottoman and Egyptian fleets, now under Muhammad Ali's orders, in Alexandria harbour.[56] Yet Muhammad Ali again shelved his plans for independence. On 16 July 1839 he made a speech before the officers of the two fleets, reaffirming his Ottoman loyalties: 'My children, we are all one and the same nation. From now on no one should say "I am Egyptian, I am from Constantinople"; we all have only one and the same faith and only one sovereign. We must show union to restore its force and grandeur to the empire. It is to this end that all our efforts should tend. Our Sultan is a beautiful unblemished diamond.'

The Ottoman officers then asked permission to wear Egyptian uniform. Muhammad Ali said they were free to do so, but not obliged to. He explained that, whereas in Constantinople people had adopted Frank dress but kept Turkish heads, he had kept Turkish dress but acted with a Frank head.[57] Clearly he was playing with his variety of identities and loyalties – imperial, religious and national – in a way characteristic of the Levant. While fighting the Sultan, he remained attached to the Ottoman Empire. For the next year and a half the politics of Europe centred on the Levant.

While Muhammad Ali hesitated, Britain, as the Pasha had foreseen as long ago as 1830, was the main impediment to his success: 'Wherever I turn she is there to baffle me.'[58] Palmerston and the British ambassador in Constantinople, Lord Ponsonby, had become the Pasha's personal enemies: they found his naval ambitions and his friendship with France intolerable. In 1840 revolts began to break out in Lebanon, encouraged by a British agent called Richard Wood, sent from Constantinople by Ponsonby. Alexandria was in the eye of the storm. Muhammad Ali began to fortify the city. A national guard was formed and began to drill on the Place des Consuls.

Muhammad Ali claimed he was fighting Lord Palmerston, not the British. He boasted to the truculent new British consul-general, Mr Hodges, who had replaced Campbell (considered too favourable to the Pasha), that he could make all Ottoman provinces revolt. Hodges replied that he would be pulverized. Rival French and British naval squadrons cruised among the islands of the Aegean.[59]

On 22 August 1840 the French consul announced publicly at Ras el-Tin that there would soon be war in Europe.[60] From Paris, Adolphe Thiers, the nationalist Président du Conseil, advised Muhammad Ali not to abandon Syria. He even wrote that 'the honour of France' depended on it. Normally lucid and moderate, like many leaders dealing with the

Middle East Thiers lost touch with reality. He advised Muhammad Ali to work day and night on fortifying Alexandria, and wait for spring. France would then have 600,000 men under arms.[61]

In August an Ottoman envoy called Rifaat Bey arrived in Alexandria by steamboat from Constantinople. Muhammad Ali refused to accept his terms to withdraw from Syria and return the Ottoman fleet. He was again dismissed as governor. On 23 September, to Muhammad Ali's fury, since he had refused to accept the Ottomans' improved offer of Egypt as a hereditary province, and southern Syria for life, all foreign consuls except the French left Alexandria. A British naval squadron, which had wintered near Smyrna, was stationed outside Alexandria, harassing arriving and departing ships. Muhammad Ali's fleet proved an expensive illusion. Cochelet advised against it sailing out of Alexandria harbour, fearing it would be destroyed by the British squadron. When Muhammad Ali asked for a French admiral to be sent to command it, and 8,000 soldiers and sailors, the French government refused.[62] The French government merely sent an engineer named Commandant Gallice (called Colonel, to please the Pasha), to direct the fortifications of Alexandria and all the military engineers of Egypt. Working at the same time for the Pasha and the French government, Gallice Bey was soon convinced that, with the 400 cannon in position on the existing forts, the city could be defended.[63] Thiers's special envoy Count Walewski, however, considered that Alexandria could not resist a British attack unless defended by 800 French artillerymen under a French general. They never came.[64]

In September 1840 Syria became the focus of a joint Ottoman–British–Austrian attack on Muhammad Ali's forces: a now forgotten conflict which at the time nearly became a world war. While Ottoman troops approached from the north, British and Austrian ships hovered off the shore. A proclamation by the British admiral Charles Napier was translated into Arabic by Richard Wood: 'Syrians! Great Britain, Austria, Russia and Prussia in conjunction with the Sultan have decided that the rule of Mehmet Ali shall cease in Syria. Charles Napier.' Soliman Pasha, the commander of the Egyptian troops (formerly Colonel Sève of the French army), replied, 'Beirut shall fall into your power only when reduced to cinders.'[65] Seeing which way the wind was blowing, Emir Bashir, ruler of Mount Lebanon, switched sides from Muhammad Ali back to the Ottomans, as readily as, a few years earlier, he had switched faiths, from Islam to Christianity.[66]

Meanwhile, war fever swept France and Germany. There was talk of a 'fatal divorce' between the two. Heine wrote that Thiers had awoken Germany from its lethargic sleep. From this crisis date the famous nationalist songs 'Die Wacht am Rhein' and 'Deutschland, Deutschland über alles'. Paris crowds cried, 'Guerre aux Anglais, ils ont pris notre Beyrout!' Newspapers called for war not only to support Muhammad Ali but also to reconquer the left bank of the Rhine, which France had lost after the fall of Napoleon in 1814.[67] However, in a sign that France would not fight, on 10 October the French fleet withdrew to the safety of French waters.[68] The Royal Navy was too strong. Moreover Louis-Philippe was too intelligent to link, as he said, the fate of France to the authority of the Pasha of Egypt.

In the Royal Navy's attack on the great fort of Acre on 3 November, technology triumphed over humanity. The cannon of the Royal Navy, 'vomiting forth huge volumes of flame', were so deadly that, Commodore Smith reported to Palmerston, 'every living creature within the area of 60,000 square yards ceased to exist.' When they hit an ammunition magazine, it erupted like Mount Vesuvius. On 5 November Acre surrendered.[69]

The peace of Europe depended on decisions taken in Alexandria. On 22 November 1840 Commodore Charles Napier moored his ship HMS *Powerful* in the harbour. On 26 November he had an audience with Muhammad Ali. When asked for his credentials, he replied that 'the double-shotted guns of the *Powerful*, with the squadron under his command to back him, his honour as an Englishman, and the knowledge he had of the desire of the four Great Powers for peace, were all the credentials he possessed.' He advised the Pasha to accept the terms offered by the Porte. If he did not give up Syria and the Ottoman fleet, he might lose everything: 'Egypt is not invulnerable; he may rely upon it, Alexandria itself may be made to share the fate of Acre and His Highness, who has now the opportunity of founding a dynasty, may sink into a simple Pasha.'[70]

Boghos Yussuf Bey meekly replied for his master that, although 'convinced that Syria in his hands might still furnish great resources for the Ottoman Empire', 'in no case has His Highness intended to place himself in opposition to the will of the great powers of Europe.' On 27 November a convention was concluded for the immediate evacuation of Egyptian troops from Syria. The Ottoman fleet would be returned when Muhammad Ali received a guarantee of dynastic heredity in Egypt. Ponsonby and his official superiors complained of Napier's independent actions, but in the end they backed him up. Once Ibrahim Pasha had been master of Syria. As he retreated back to Egypt, no one bothered to salute him.[71]

On 29 October Louis-Philippe had dismissed Thiers. In the Chamber of Deputies, the French poet and politician Lamartine called the French humiliation in the Levant 'the Waterloo of French diplomacy'. In one month, Louis-Philippe had lost his popularity and Muhammad Ali had lost Syria. Because of his pacific policy in 1840, until the revolution of 1848 (to which it contributed) Louis-Philippe no longer dared review the Paris National Guard, for fear of hostile demonstrations.[72]

During the ensuing negotiations the Ottoman and Egyptian governments, and the European powers, were in continuous consultation. All admired Muhammad Ali's dignity in adversity and lack of *amour propre*. Forgetting previous outbursts of fury, and oaths that he would 'never' leave Syria, he proclaimed that he was 'always disposed to sacrifice what I possess and even my life in order to conciliate the good graces of His Highness'.[73] In February 1841 the Ottoman navy returned to Constantinople, to the joy of its sailors – and of Alexandrians alienated by their lawless behaviour.[74]

Finally, after much renegotiation, a *Hatt i-sherif* or imperial proclamation dated 1 June 1841 arrived in Alexandria on a Russian boat from Constantinople. It stated that, in gratitude for 'the loyalty and servitude you have demonstrated to me and the interests of my empire', and 'the zeal and sagacity by which you are characterized as well as the knowledge and experience which you have acquired in the affairs of Egypt', the governorship of Egypt would be made hereditary. In accordance with the system prevailing since 1617 in the Ottoman dynasty, it would be inherited by the eldest male among Muhammad Ali's descendants – not by primogeniture. The governorship of the Sudan was not to be hereditary. Muhammad Ali's status and independence were reduced. The Ottoman Empire and Egypt would henceforth share the same flag, coinage and uniforms, and follow the same internal laws and international agreements. The Pasha of Egypt would enjoy no special titles or ceremonial status, and would appoint officers only to the rank of colonel. His army was to be limited to 18,000, and no ships of the line were to be built without Ottoman permission. In other words, he would no longer have the means to invade other Ottoman provinces. A quarter of gross government revenue was to be paid by the Pasha of Egypt to the Porte.[75]

On 7 June a 100-gun salute from the Pasha's cannon announced the ceremonial proclamation by the Pasha's secretary Ismail Bey of the new *Hatt i-sherif* in Ras el-Tin. Decorations were handed out. Muhammad Ali's son Said sailed for Constantinople with presents for the imperial family and the ministers of the Porte.[76]

Muhammad Ali's bid for Syria had failed – though he said it was the loss of Crete which he regretted most. Once his pride and joy, his navy was left to rot in Alexandria's harbour.[77] However, he had expanded the territory of Egypt to include the Sudan, and had established not only a new dynasty – one which would last longer on its throne than the other new nineteenth-century dynasty, the Bonapartes – but a new state.

In the last years of Muhammad Ali's life Alexandria continued to expand. An English journalist called Bayle St John, who arrived there in 1846, found 'a perfect rage for building in Alexandria'. Entire quarters had been added 'as if by magic ... Everywhere else almost the bricklayers and masons are at work.'[78] The population had risen from 60,000 in 1840 (of whom about 12,000 were soldiers and 8,000 sailors) to 104,189 in 1848, the first year that a proper census was conducted. Some 22.5 per cent were from Alexandria itself, the rest being Egyptians from Cairo and the Delta. Around 5 per cent were Europeans; the remaining 7 per cent came from other provinces of the Empire.[79] Alexandria had grown faster than any city in the Empire. In comparison the population of Alexandria's rivals was stagnant: Cairo had around 230,000 people, Damietta and Rosetta around 25,000 and 15,000 respectively.[80]

Like St Petersburg and Odessa, Alexandria attracted foreigners, fostered trade, and spread modernization and education. Muhammad Ali had made the city a machine for transforming Egypt. He compared it to Paris. It had become a city with a future.[81] Ali Mubarak hoped it would become the greatest commercial centre on earth. Who holds Alexandria, it was believed, holds Egypt.[82]

However, the key to Egypt might be its downfall. Success and accessibility can be as fatal to a city as decline. Thanks to the personal authority of Muhammad Ali, Alexandria had so far mixed races and religions with remarkable ease. But, just as Smyrna, by attracting massive Greek immigration, also imported Greek nationalism, so Alexandria, by encouraging European immigration, might attract foreign armies like those which had conquered Algiers and Aden. Both Smyrna and Alexandria were potential time bombs. Even in 1785, when foreigners in Alexandria were being harassed by Mamelukes, they had threatened the Ottoman government: if it did not resolve the situation, their own governments would do so. An Ottoman expedition arrived to restore order a year later.[83]

Alexandria was easy prey. France had seized it in 1798, Britain in 1807. Palmerston threatened Muhammad Ali with a bombardment or blockade of the city in 1833, 1838 and 1840.[84] During his visit in 1850, Flaubert wrote that he considered it impossible that, with British troops already in

Aden, Britain would not shortly become mistress of Egypt: 'Remember my prediction.'[85]

Muhammad Ali was popular with Europeans. All admired his ability to enforce law and order. Even in 1840, when the Royal Navy was threatening Alexandria, and bombarding Egyptian troops in Syria, the British overland mail service through Egypt to India continued uninterrupted. When the British consul-general fled to the safety of a gunboat, Muhammad Ali told the British residents he would be their consul and protector – and kept his word.[86] Nevertheless, and despite the small number of Europeans living in the city, European consuls began to challenge his authority.

The years 1800–1830 saw a hardening of British imperial attitudes in India, caused by growing wealth and power, and the rapid expansion of British territory. Relationships between British men and Indian women, once common, became unacceptable. It was the take-off moment for Britain's imperial century. A similar process began to take place a few years later in the Levant. In 1843 the consuls threatened that, if Muhammad Ali did not dig a Suez canal (already suggested during the French occupation in 1799), one might be dug without his consent.[87]

In January 1847, despite Muhammad Ali's protests, six drunken British sailors, wanted for murder by the Egyptian authorities, were removed from Alexandria on a British ship. Against the letter of the capitulations, on their own initiative rather than their governments', European consuls and residents were claiming total extraterritoriality, and freedom from the jurisdiction of local courts.[88] Travellers sometimes complained of European Alexandrians' 'love of ostentation' and 'presumptuous judgements', perhaps heightened by their pride in their city's past. This ostentation and presumption were also the basis of their politics.[89]

If Alexandria was an ambiguous legacy, both strengthening and threatening, Muhammad Ali was an ambiguous ruler. On the one hand were his achievements in dragging Egypt into the nineteenth century. He diminished fanaticism, encouraged education, transformed agriculture. On the other hand, he often oppressed Egyptians while favouring foreigners. His rush to industrialize, like his bid for empire, was often wasteful and counterproductive as well as inhuman. Taxes and prices rose precipitously. 'All classes of the inhabitants of Egypt', wrote the French consul, were reduced to 'extreme poverty', worse than any previously seen there.[90] Al-Jabarti wrote with distaste that 'the Pasha', as he called Muhammad Ali, had made himself 'absolute master of Egypt', and tried to raise money 'by all methods ... The Pasha does not like to be crossed on any matter.

He wants his slightest desires to be executed without any comment.'[91] Opposition to his orders was considered 'dangerous in the extreme'.[92]

While praising Muhammad Ali's energy in reconstructing, embellishing and fortifying Alexandria, the final judgement made by al-Jabarti was that 'if with the energy, generosity of character and qualities of direction and organization with which God had endowed him, he had possessed the sentiment of justice, this man would have been unique in his time and the wonder of his age.'[93] It is possible that al-Jabarti experienced Muhammad Ali's injustice for himself: by one account, after spending the evening with the Pasha, and annoying him by the freedom of his comments, the greatest modern Egyptian historian was strangled and his body tied to the feet of an ass.[94]

Nevertheless, when they heard the news of the Pasha's death in Alexandria on 2 August 1849, Egyptians' displays of grief surprised many observers. The British consul-general wrote, 'The attachment and the veneration of all classes in Egypt for the name of Mohammed Ali are prouder obsequies than any which it was in the power of his successor to confer.' He heard many say that 'if Allah would permit me, gladly would I give ten years of my life to add them to that of our old pasha.' 'The old inhabitants remember and talk of the chaos and anarchy from which he rescued this country; the younger compare his energetic rule with the capricious vacillating government of his successor; and all classes, whether Turks or Arabs, not only feel but hesitate not to say openly that the prosperity of Egypt has died with Mohammed Ali. In truth, my Lord, it cannot be denied that Mohammed Ali notwithstanding all his faults was a great man.'[95]

6

Beirut: The Republic of Merchants

Beyrouth is a Levantine *scala* [port], a bastard, a mongrel.

A. A. Paton, 24 February 1841

MUHAMMAD ALI WAS the founder of modern Beirut, as well as modern Alexandria. When Egyptian soldiers occupied it in 1831, it was a labyrinth of narrow streets, and overhanging mansions, with 'excessive filth prevailing', packed inside thick crusader walls.[1] When they left, nine years later, it was beginning to be a modern city.

Beirut was distinguished from neighbouring ports, not – like Smyrna – by the prominence of foreign merchants, nor – like Alexandria – by a modernizing pasha, but by the power and number of its Christians, and the proximity of Christian Mount Lebanon. Hence Flaubert's comment, when he arrived in 1850, 'There is something in the air which makes you at once think of the crusades.'[2]

Mainly Muslim in the sixteenth century, Beirut had thereafter become a mixed city.[3] Visiting it in 1660, the Chevalier d'Arvieux, a merchant in Smyrna who later became French consul in Aleppo, wrote, 'The city of Beirut is sombre, its streets are narrow and very dirty in winter. It is quite populous, the greater number of its inhabitants are Greek [Orthodox] Christians and the commerce of this city is very considerable.' In the evening, inhabitants would drink wine and sing in their gardens, and, except for the Jews, 'all the citizens of Beirut, whatever religion they are, live well together. They are polite, visit each other and arrange parties of pleasure. Even the people is not wicked [*méchant*] as in Sidon.'[4] In contrast to inland cities like Jerusalem and Damascus, there were no religiously zoned districts; mosques and churches were built side by side, the double-domed Orthodox church of St George next to the Omari Mosque (the former crusader church of St John) in 1767.[5]

In addition to Orthodox Christians, Beirut contained a small number of Maronites. They were a local Christian group who since the crusades (which they had supported) had acknowledged the supremacy of the Pope. They lived mainly in Mount Lebanon, which rises a few miles from the sea, visible from the Beirut corniche. To this day the remote wooded valleys, villages and monasteries of the mountain are a separate world from the cities of the coast. Maronites' sense of superiority to their neighbours was fostered by historians, most of them monks glorifying their Church.[6]

In addition to Maronites, the mountains of Lebanon contained Druze, Syriacs, Ismailis, Shia Muslims in the south (where roads are now lined with posters of imams and ayatollahs) and, up the coast to the north, Alawis or Nusayri, the community of the Assad dynasty ruling Syria today. To Ottomans the mountains were 'the refuge of villains'; to their inhabitants they were a refuge from Ottomans.[7] The Maronites in the mountains enjoyed greater security of life and property than the people of the plains, under direct Ottoman rule, whom Richard Wood, the British dragoman and later consul, called 'wretches in a state of starvation and nakedness'.[8]

The proximity of rival religions at a strategic crossroads inspired a mating game of seduction and exploitation still being played today. Using emotional language to mask self-interest, each religious group tried to seduce a foreign power; each foreign power searched for suitable local protégés. Outside interference was matched by inside desire for more of it.

In 1639 – at the height of the Counter-Reformation – the King of France, Louis XIII, had officially taken under his 'protection and special safeguard' the Maronite patriarch and 'all the Maronite Christians of the said Mount Lebanon', and offered to help them to come to Christian countries for study or 'other purposes'. He instructed French consuls and vice-consuls to protect them – an unprecedented intrusion in the internal affairs of an ally. For their part, many Maronites agreed with a later patriarch who wrote, imploringly, 'We have in the East no protection, refuge or safety outside the throne of France and its representatives in the Levant.' Already, like some Greeks in Smyrna, they hoped for foreign intervention to free them from Ottoman domination. Some suggested that, instead of wasting time and money on small territorial gains in Europe, the King of France should think of conquering Syria. Thus began France's connection with Lebanon which has lasted to this day. The Ottoman government was not informed.[9]

After 1799, foreign merchants trading with Syria moved from Sidon and Tripoli to Beirut, encouraged by the proximity of Emir Bashir II, whose authority started outside the city gates.[10] Beirut had the further advantages of a healthy climate and easy access to the mountains for those fleeing plague or Turks. By 1808, with a population of about 7,000, it had replaced Sidon as the main port for Damascus. In 1811 the French consul wrote, 'The commerce of this town is increasing daily.'[11]

Beirut maintained its traditions of autonomy and good Muslim–Christian relations – perhaps because numbers were evenly balanced. As a mixed port competing with a predominantly Muslim capital, Beirut was already in opposition to Damascus, as it still is today. The local mufti had more authority than officials sent from the capital. The French consul made a famous remark in 1827. He wrote that Beirut was 'a republic of merchants who have their [own] strength and their [own] laws'.[12]

These wealthy merchant dynasties, like the feudal dynasties of Khazens and Shihabs, helped shape modern Beirut. They included the Muslim Bayhum and Barbir families; the Orthodox Sursock, Bustros, Tueni and Trad; and the Greek Catholic Pharaon and Zananiri. The last two families had begun to move between Syria and Egypt in the eighteenth century. Many Beirut merchants used foreign consular protection to help them compete with foreign merchants – for example in the silk trade. Their foreign connections, language skills and geographical position between Europe and Asia helped give Beirut merchants their competitive edge. From the beginning, unlike in Smyrna and Alexandria, the big money in Beirut was local.[13]

The conquest of Syria by the forces of Muhammad Ali in 1831–2 installed a government favourable to merchants and modernization. Lamartine, who stayed in Beirut in 1832–3, found it a paradise, with its views of the mountain and the sea, and he enjoyed complete security of property and travel – although his daughter Julia died there of the plague.[14] The city was governed by Mahmud Nami Bey, an Egyptian officer of Circassian origin, who had studied in France, and by a newly appointed town council divided equally between Muslims and Christians. Some streets were cleaned and paved.[15]

Between 1830 and 1840 customs receipts quadrupled. In 1835, the year a jetty was built, 310 ships entered the port; in 1838 there were 680. The British consul found Beirut 'transformed from a third-rate Arab town into a flourishing commercial city – the residence of Europeans of various nations'. Sixty-nine firms were established there by 1839, half of them foreign. The new security of life and property, he wrote, encouraged 'native capitalists' 'to embark their fortunes in commercial speculations which formerly they did not venture to do'.[16]

The first members of the shipping and insurance firm of Heald arrived in 1837. They were dismayed by Beirutis' love of gambling and all-day picnics, but their descendants are still there today.[17] Merchants began to leave the cramped quadrilateral of the old city and build villas in the surrounding countryside.[18]

In 1836 an American and in 1839 a Russian consulate joined the French, British and Austrian consulates already established in the city. By their very presence, consuls increased inter-communal rivalries and external intrigues. The Russian consul was instructed to help Orthodox pilgrims and the Orthodox church.[19] The Jumblatt dynasty, wealthy from the silk trade, had for two centuries been Druze feudal lords in the mountains. In 1839 some members came to Beirut to ask British officials if they could be ruled by Great Britain – in order to achieve prosperity similar to India's. Druze desire for a British connection continued for many decades.[20]

For far longer Maronites had been playing a similar mating game with French consuls. Indeed, from 1655 to 1758 the Khazen dynasty of Maronite landowners, who had founded many monasteries and the first Maronite church in Beirut, had been French consuls in the city.[21] Another community was the Greek Catholics, Orthodox in ritual, but acknowledging the authority of the Pope. After 1841, formally recognized as a separate community, their numbers swollen by immigrants from Aleppo hostile to Greek domination of the Orthodox Church there, they were protected by Austria.[22]

Consuls in Beirut behaved as arrogantly as their colleagues in Alexandria. Huge flags flew from masts outside their residences. They had so many dragomans, scribes, guards, and Christian and Jewish protégés that Muhammad Ali complained that they removed 'half the city of Beyrouth from the authority of the local government'. To demonstrate that they were his equals in rank, they refused to remove their hats in Ibrahim Pasha's presence.[23]

Consuls also had their uses, however. From 1834 strict quarantine measures were introduced by a committee including the European consuls, the Egyptian commander Soliman Pasha, who, like Muhammad Ali, acted as a merchant as well as a governor, and his aide-de-camp the Comte d'Armagnac. Nevertheless, cholera continued to plague the city until after 1900.[24]

As in Egypt under Muhammad Ali, in the 1830s there was a green revolution. The beauty of the countryside around Beirut seduced foreign visitors. Some wanted never to leave. Flaubert's friend Maxime du Camp wrote in 1849, 'It seems to me that one can live here happy, just by looking at the mountains and the sea.'[25] Below snow-capped mountains with clusters of cedars lay 'a plain varied by small hills covered with cottages and enriched with olive, palm, orange, lemon and mulberry trees and vines'.[26]

Surrounded by gardens, and umbrella pines, the city seemed to 'spring from an ocean of verdure', and to be 'embedded in the greenest and coolest of bowers'. Inside the walls also was an 'extraordinary profusion' of trees and shrubs.[27] The British consul in Aleppo in the 1840s, John Barker, of the famous Levantine dynasty, helped introduce potatoes, tomatoes, greengages and plums to Syria, and improved the strains of mulberries and oranges.[28]

The administration of Muhammad Ali earned the admiration of foreigners and merchants, but the abhorrence of the people administered. In addition to greater efficiency and equity in taxation between Christians and Muslims, Egyptian rule brought forced labour, conscription, higher taxes, state monopolies, and the confiscation of wheat and silk crops.[29] There were repeated uprisings.

As elsewhere, a foreign occupation worsened relations between communities. In 1838–9 the Egyptian government used Maronites, for the first time, to fight a Druze rebellion. Previously checked by dynasticism or patriarchy, sectarianism was now emerging as the basis of the country's political order, as it still is today. The old Druze–Maronite entente began to break down, neighbours to be regarded as traitors. Modernization led to less, not more, toleration.[30] Representatives of what were called the 'nations' of Druzes, Christians and Shia wrote to the new young sultan, Abdulmecid, and to foreign ambassadors in Constantinople, asking for help against the tyranny of Muhammad Ali.[31]

In 1840, in an extreme example of consular interference in local politics, Richard Wood, who had studied Arabic in a Maronite monastery, organized the Lebanese revolt – in which the part he played was more vital than T. E. Lawrence's would be eighty years later in the Arab Revolt. An American missionary wrote of Wood, 'His word was law throughout the land.' Acting as a servant of the Ottoman and the British governments, he persuaded both Maronites and Druze to rise against the Egyptian occupiers.[32]

As part of their strategy to force Muhammad Ali to withdraw from Syria, in September 1840 nineteen British, seven Ottoman and four Austrian ships – the British now powered by steam – moored off Beirut, cutting Egyptians' communication with Alexandria. On 10 September on the 'smooth sandy beach' of St George's Bay, in scenes which anticipated the Lebanese civil war of 1975–90, within view of the snow-capped peaks of Mount Lebanon they landed troops, artillery and muskets for the Maronites.[33] Lieutenant-Colonel Edward Napier, an eyewitness, wrote:

Never was the confusion of Babel better exemplified than in the scene presented at that time by the Port of Beyrout – naval officers in cocked hats – English tars and Austrian marines – filthy Turkish soldiers with their slouching gait and the large and graceless fez drawn over their besotted and unmeaning countenances – Druses and Maronites with their rich and gaudy dresses – the large turban, flowing cloak and loose silken drawers – whilst the girdle contained a perfect armoury of weapons – all hurrying to and fro – strings of ungainly camels, some kneeling to their loads.[34]

Commodore Charles Napier, his brother, commanded 7,000 men from Mount Lebanon, helped by 1,500 British marines and sailors under Richard Wood and Captain Baldwin Wake Walker. Like many Levantine cities, Beirut's sole fortifications consisted of 'a wall with a few weak turrets mouldering to ruins and mounting very few guns', and two castles dating from the crusades, themselves partly built with columns from Roman ruins. Little had been built since.[35] After a brisk three-day shelling on 11–13 September by British and Austrian ships, destroying part of the crusader walls and castle, and killing many soldiers, 11,000 Ottoman troops landed on 19 September. Because Britain and Austria were allies of the Sultan, bombardment did not produce a massacre of local Christians by Muslims, or fear of massacre, as in Smyrna. On 9 October, after another bombardment which spared neither the hospital nor the French consulate, Soliman Pasha and 2,000 Egyptian and Albanian troops in Beirut surrendered to Emir Bashir, at the head of Ottoman soldiers and mountain Lebanese, 'universally tall, stalwart and well developed ... of bold expression of countenance, set off with an immense moustache'.[36] It was not only British and Austrian intervention, but also the unpopularity of Ibrahim Pasha's rule, and the contribution of Emir Bashir and his troops, which made Muhammad Ali lose Syria.

In his final report on this forgotten conflict, Commodore Charles Napier anticipated the creation of modern Lebanon by eighty years. He wrote to Palmerston that, if the region of Mount Lebanon was expanded to include the ports of Sidon, Beirut and Tripoli, it would be 'most advantageous to them and most beneficial to the interests of England'.[37]

After 1840, Beirut changed almost as rapidly as Alexandria. In 1842 it became the official seat of the vilayet of Sidon. The town council established by Ibrahim Pasha continued. In 1846, according to the French consul, there were 9,000 Christians, 9,000 Muslims, 850 Druze and 250

Jews.[38] In 1847 a Society of Arts and Sciences was established there. In 1851 a missionary called Charles van de Velde saw ships coming from Tyre and Sidon 'every day ... with building materials taken from the ruins'; Beirut's own ruins had been exhausted.[39] The Earl of Carlisle called it 'the only place I have yet seen in the Ottoman dominions which exhibits the genuine signs of positive progress'.[40]

On the Place des Canons, outside the city walls, European carriages began to appear. Education is a key to the rise of Beirut. Catholic orders such as the Franciscans, Capuchins, Lazarists, Jesuits and Frères des Ecoles Chrétiennes for men, and an avalanche of orders for women (Notre-Dame de Sion, Notre Dame de Nazareth, Sœurs de Besançon, Sœurs de Saint-Joseph, Filles de la Charité), established schools, conscious that the future belonged to whoever provided the best education. They taught in French. Whatever the French government's policy towards the Catholic Church at home, it always protected and subsidized the work of French Catholic orders overseas, as the most effective means of spreading French culture and prestige: anticlericalism was not for export.[41] In addition, Protestants established the American School for Girls and the British Syrian School for the Blind (the first in the Levant), the Orthodox the National College, and the Greek Catholics the Patriarchal College.[42]

F. A. Neale, who lived there from 1842 to 1850, was a thorough though hostile observer. Outside the crusader walls,

> stupendous new mansions, the property of opulent merchants, were daily being built, cafés, country villas and steam factories for silk. As the inhabitants grew more wealthy, greater attention began to be paid to dress and fashion ... There are few who cannot converse freely in Italian, the lingua franca of the East ... and some of the grandees occasionally give a ball with a sumptuous supper, to which all the elite of every religion and costume are invited. On these occasions the pasha's band generally attends and right well do they execute their duties.

Houses began to contain furniture and knives and forks. A theatre and newspapers were started.[43] When Muhammad Ali's son Said Pasha, ruler of Egypt, visited Beirut in 1859, he stayed in the princely mansion of the Bustros family, in preference to the Ottoman governor's residence.[44]

Beirutis enjoyed promenading in the evening on the road west going to Ras Beirut, the promontory where the American University now is. Boys swam in the sea. People smoked the nargile 'chatting away merrily' on chairs. Women squatted in groups on the ground and 'aspiring youths ... in the picturesque dress of their country' walked to and fro or practised riding on Arabian horses. At night the silence was broken by 'the yelp-ing and barking and growling and snapping' of dogs, the 'dismal howling of a troop of jackals' and the 'perpetual din' of military bands playing retreats and roll calls in the Ottoman barracks.[45] Making a comparison which would soon become familiar, Neale called the city 'a perfect Syrian Paris'.[46] Variety and flexibility were the essence of Beirut, as of Smyrna and Alexandria. Coming from further east, Beirut seemed like a European city; arriving from Europe, visitors felt they were in 'a new world'.[47]

The port too was becoming busier. Passengers were carried ashore by 'half-naked natives'. On shore 'a scene of hurry, scurry and bustle meets [the traveller] at every step – steamers arriving – steamers departing – merchants hurrying to save the mail – clerks running with bills of lading and bills of exchange – goods being landed and others being shipped, brokers bustling and a thousand other incidents connected with a commer-cial town – a European air of business runs throughout'. The shops were full of foreign goods. The difference between 1835 and 1855, wrote one traveller, was like that between night and day. Beirut had doubled in size and become a city. Merchants might lounge on the divan with coffee and nargile, but they had European books on their desks. Another reason for the rise of Beirut was that Christians trusted its mercantile board, with members 'of every nationality and creed', created to resolve disputes.[48] The value of imports and exports combined rose from 10 million francs in 1825 to 38 million in 1845, and 77.5 in 1862.[49]

However, economic growth was accompanied by, and helped to cause, massacres. As the power of the feudal dynasties weakened, the Maronite clergy were becoming more confident, more literate, and more pro-French. In 1841 Richard Wood wrote that the different sects were 'particularly remarkable for the great hatred they bear to each other'.[50] In 1842 the Ottoman government abolished the Shihab 'emirate' – the Shihabs being dismissed like servants – as it had long desired.[51]

In 1842–5 for the first time, partly on the advice of European govern-ments, administrative reforms introduced 'confessional representation as a constitutional principle into Lebanese public life', as it still is. The Mountain was placed under one Maronite and one Druze sub-governor, dependent on the Ottoman governor in Beirut.[52] A tradition of coexist-ence – of Muslims praying in churches and Christians invoking Allah and Muhammad – was beginning to break down. The arrival of Catholic and Protestant missionaries, as well as foreign consuls, also deepened the chasms between religions.[53]

In May 1860, at a time of economic protests by Maronite peasants against Druze landlords, Druze began to attack Maronites in the mountains, as they had in 1840. Another Levantine catastrophe was imminent. Random murders turned into massacres sparing neither age nor sex. The Druze made up in ferocity for what they lacked in numbers, cutting up Christians like firewood. Seventeen members of the Shihab dynasty alone were killed. Finally, one Druze chronicler wrote, 'They set fire to all the villages and farms in the district, and left them like smouldering lava whose ashes the wind carried into the air, and thus the vast district became desolate wasteland, where only the crows croak and the owls hoot.'[54] Around 15,000 died in Mount Lebanon. Two hundred villages were destroyed; there were 100,000 refugees. Many Christians fled to Alexandria, strengthening the Syrian community there.[55]

Events can be seen through the eyes of the wife of the Comte de Perthuis, a French businessman living in Beirut. She knew Beirut well, having visited it in 1853, and kept a diary. They lived in a half-Arab, half-European house on the old walls. On 29 May 1860 Druze and Maronites working on the road her husband was building to Damascus suddenly began to quarrel: there was a 'horrific noise of lamentations, cries of fear and shootings'. As they would in 1958 and 1975, Beirut streets emptied.

From her windows, with incomparable views of mountains and the sea, she could see Christian villages burning in the distance. Her servants were in agonies of fear for their families. 'All night you can hear the sound of firing in the distance.' Druze believed there was a Christian insurrection committee in Beirut, backed by the French consul. News arrived of Druze destroying Christian villages, going from house to house with torches. Christian refugees flooded into the city and camped in the foreign consulates. Druze women compensated for their inability to fight in person by encouraging, or shaming, the men into further atrocities.[56]

Beirut became a city of fear. On 25 June, Madame de Perthuis reported, 'Muslims of the city have been in great agitation since the morning and the Christians maddened with terror.' A Muslim had been found murdered. His father threatened the French consul with a knife. 'The exaltation of Muslim women is above all hideous.' Beirut Muslims declared they were ready to kill Christians. A leading Muslim merchant, Omar Bayhum, and other notables calmed the crowds, as did the arrival of Ottoman troops on a warship and the execution, with the approval of the European consuls, of the alleged Christian murderer. Beirut could not feed all the refugees, so food was distributed from consulates and monasteries. Like Smyrniots in their crises, many Beirutis took refuge on boats. The Comte de Perthuis ran a relief committee; his wife sewed clothes. She wrote, 'In the Saray [the governor's residence] they have lost their heads. A Municipality does not exist in Beirut. One is improvised in the form of a committee as head of which they appoint my son.'[57]

Bloodshed spread to Damascus. At the time of the Greek uprising in 1821, Damascus Muslims had protected local Christians from the Sultan's order to kill or 'humble' them. By July 1860 they resented Christians' growing prosperity, and use of foreign trade and consulates to promote it: Muslims in the provinces, unlike the Ottoman government in the capital, had few foreign friends. Christians were beginning to be regarded as traitors and a danger to the Empire. Even a Greek Catholic chronicler called Mikhail Mishaqa complained that 'ignorant', 'humble' Christians had begun to behave with 'insolence' as equals of 'exalted' Muslims. Muslims massacred local Christians and sacked their houses. The Christian quarter in Damascus became a corpse-strewn mass of rubble; around 5,000 died.[58]

On the arrival of refugees from Damascus in Beirut – sometimes 3,000 in one day – each community came forward to welcome those of its own persuasion.[59] Thanks to the refugees, Beirut henceforth until the 1920s had a clear Christian majority, between 58 and 66 per cent. While the Muslims were almost entirely Sunni, most of the Christians were Orthodox, with substantial Maronite and Greek Catholic minorities.[60]

Catastrophe led to European intervention. On 18 and 22 July, French and British warships arrived off Beirut. In agreement with other European powers, on 16 August 7,000 French troops under General d'Hautpoul, who had served under Ibrahim Pasha in 1840, arrived to protect the Christians. Lebanon was now militarily under European protection, as it had been politically since 1842. Beirut was divided. The Maronite Patriarch and Christians petitioned for French troops to stay; the Muslims of Beirut petitioned for them to leave at once.[61] A former grand vizier called Fouad Pasha arrived at the same time on a special mission from the Sultan and punished Druze and Muslim perpetrators of the massacres, including Ottoman officials and soldiers and Druze chiefs of the Jumblatt dynasty.[62]

Fouad Pasha was a skilful and conciliatory negotiator, more than a match for European commissioners and consuls. He stopped the French army marching on Damascus. It left in June 1861, jeered by Muslims but lamented by Maronites and the widows of the murdered Christians. On the surface Beirut resumed its role as an Ottoman city. Between 5 and 9 July 1861 on the Place des Canons thousands of Beirutis greeted the accession of the new sultan, Abdulaziz, with a series of festivals, fireworks and military reviews; each corporation in its costume danced in front of the consuls and Fouad Pasha. Shops were festooned with flowers and candles. Women sang from the rooftops.[63]

On 18 July 1861, however, a new internationally guaranteed regime in Mount Lebanon – in effect a state in embryo – was proclaimed by Fouad Pasha at a grand Ottoman ceremony in the pine forest outside Beirut. Henceforth the governor-general of Mount Lebanon had to be an Ottoman Christian from outside the region, chosen after consultation with the European powers by the Ottoman government. The independent gendarmerie established for Mount Lebanon, with French instructors, is the oldest armed force in Lebanon today.[64]

7

Alexandria: Khedives and Consuls

People speak every language there, you see every kind of costume
there, you see all the races of the East and the West, this variety, this mixture, this pell-mell itself forms the true character of
Alexandria.

Eugène Poitou, *Un hiver en Égypte*, 1860

O N 30 JANUARY 1863 an Egyptian soldier riding along the quay by the
port of Alexandria made his horse rear. It hit a passing Frenchman;
he fell to the ground. The Frenchman struck back at the Egyptian, and
was taken to the nearest police station by Egyptian soldiers. Recently
victorious in wars with Russia and Austria, France under Napoleon III
was at an apex of arrogance. The French consul-general, Monsieur de
Beauval, outraged that Egyptians had dared lay hands on a Frenchman,
threatened that, unless he obtained 'satisfaction', the French navy would
bombard Alexandria. Three days later, watched by officers and sailors of
the French navy 'en grande tenue', in front of the French consulate on
the Place des Consuls, the Egyptian soldiers involved were put in a public
pillory. Their weeping commanding officer was transported in chains to
twenty years' imprisonment. Confirming the message of Egyptian humiliation and French supremacy, an official Egyptian request for the consul's
transfer was refused.[1]

This confrontation, one of many between consuls and Egyptians, shows
that Alexandria, like Smyrna and Beirut, was on a fault line between
empires. Consuls in Alexandria, and other Levantine cities, behaved as
if they were the Emperor of Russia. They were 'above everything': their
watches, it was said, controlled the sun.[2]

Alexandria was becoming a diarchy where the Egyptian government
and the European consuls both exercised authority. If a European committed a crime, his consul arrived on the scene, with his own armed kavasses
(often Montenegrins or Albanians in national dress, appreciated for their

size and loyalty), and took the criminal and the investigating policemen to his consulate. There the consul conducted his own investigation and established his own version of events.[3]

In 1858 foreign consuls won an additional privilege: to keep ships known as *stationnaires* in Alexandria harbour (as European ambassadors did in the Bosphorus) in case of 'emergencies'.[4] Since the local post was not trusted, France, Italy, Austria, Russia and Greece also established their own post offices in Alexandria, as they did in Smyrna and Beirut; stamps bore the superscriptions 'Poste Française Levant' or 'Oesterreichische Post'.[5]

In a further European abuse of power in Egypt, Europeans – unlike Egyptians – carried guns and knives, sometimes issued by the consuls themselves, despite their frequent promises to implement the law against bearing firearms.[6] In 1871 a French consul's ordinance formally encouraging French nationals to resist Egyptian policemen by force shocked even his fellow-consuls.[7]

As well as running their own mini-states, European consuls also helped run Alexandria itself. As in the sixteenth century, Pera, Constantinople's predominantly Christian diplomatic and commercial district, remained a model for the cities of the Levant. After the victory of the Ottoman Empire, France, Britain and Piedmont over Russia in the Crimean War, it entered a second golden age. A reforming decree, extending one of 1839, promised Christians and Muslims equality before the law, in place of their separate legal systems; equal liability to military service and access to government positions; and freedom from confiscation. Mixed courts to judge cases involving both religions had come into existence in 1847. In 1867 a new law regulating property rights allowed foreigners, in theory as well as in practice, to own property in the Ottoman Empire. A hundred thousand Europeans moved to Pera in the years 1839–79; for a time the Ottoman capital had a Christian majority.

The European influx helped transform Pera into a modern city. In 1857 the sixth municipal district of Constantinople, with power to levy local taxes, was established in Pera by the Ottoman government. Records were kept in both French and Ottoman, but French was the language of deliberations. An early president of the municipality was Blacque Bey, son of Mahmud II's publicist from Smyrna. In the next five years Pera was, both metaphorically and literally, cleaned up. Shops and houses were pulled down, streets widened and paved, drains laid. In 1863–5 most of the old Genoese walls of Galata were demolished – although fragments can still be seen today from the Galata Tower, embedded in modern buildings.[8]

In June 1869 the Egyptian government proposed to establish in Alexandria a similar municipality to Pera's, with tax-raising powers and separate departments for police, health, roads and finance. By then, about a quarter of Alexandria's population came from Europe. Bowing to their wealth and power, eight of the thirteen members of the new municipal commission were to be non-Egyptians who had lived in Alexandria for over five years. Acknowledging the reality of diarchy, the proposal was sent for approval to the consuls (who included two Alexandrians, the Belgian consul Menandre de Zizinia, and the Portuguese consul Max de Zogheb). Despite the proposed European majority, on 22 July 1869 the consuls denounced what they called the plan's 'profound infractions of consular jurisdiction and existing usages'. In plain English, they did not want Europeans to pay an 8 per cent city tax, and they feared the power of the government-appointed president of the commission. They also claimed, without proof, that Muhammad Ali had given foreigners exemption from property taxes – exemptions said to cost the Egyptian government £500,000 a year.[9] The reform was killed.

Consuls did, however, accept reforms if they were proposed by Europeans. British merchants were dissatisfied by the state of the port of Alexandria. An 1864 petition to the British consul-general survives, complaining that 'both in the railways and custom house there is an utter absence of proper organization while a shameless corruption reigns everywhere,' leading to 'heavy loss and extreme annoyance'.[10] In 1869, the same year that consuls refused the municipal commission, they accepted Alexandria exporters' and importers' proposed 'mixed provisional municipal and commercial committee', set up with Egyptian government help, to repave roads round the port so that transports no longer stuck in the mud.[11]

The dynasty as well as the consuls supported the modernization of Alexandria. Europeans had been working in the palace, and princes receiving a partly European education, since the 1830s. When forced to choose during the British invasion of 1882, most of the dynasty would side with European powers against the Egyptian government and people.

Muhammad Ali, however, had been succeeded by the only Egyptian ruler, until Nasser in the 1950s, who stood up to European powers. As the eldest male in the dynasty, Abbas, grandson of Muhammad Ali, was appointed vali of Egypt on 12 November 1849 at the age of thirty-seven, at a ceremony held in Constantinople, where he had stopped on his way back from a pilgrimage to Mecca. Having held official positions in Cairo,

Lebanon and the Sudan during his grandfather's reign, he had considerable political experience. In his opinion Muhammad Ali's reforms had been too brutal, and too European. He dismissed many officials – even the chief medical official, Clot Bey – cut others' salaries, and closed government factories. 'Order and the strictest economy' reigned, wrote the Egyptian Armenian Nubar Pasha (a key witness of this period, three times prime minister, in 1878, 1884–5 and 1894–8) many years later in his memoirs. Neglecting Alexandria, because it contained too many foreigners – or because of a prophecy that he would die there – he built his own palace city of Abbasiya north-east of Cairo, and other palaces in the Egyptian countryside. He sometimes kept a consul waiting for days before granting him an audience. He said he preferred to be slave of the Sultan rather than the consuls.[12]

While strengthening his Ottoman connection, Abbas remained master of Egypt, keeping an army larger than that allowed by the *Hatt i-sherif* of 1841, and fostering an Egyptian identity among his officers and officials. The tax burden on the poor lessened; agriculture flourished.[13] The first railway line in the Middle East was begun by British engineers between Cairo and Alexandria in 1854. It opened on 1 January 1857 – in time to transport British troops going to suppress a nationalist rising in India. Proud of his dynasty's modernizing record, Abbas boasted that, if it ruled the valleys of the Euphrates and Tigris, they would be flourishing like the valley of the Nile – and generating higher revenue for the Porte.[14]

On 16 July 1854 Abbas was murdered by two of his Mamelukes at his isolated palace of Binha in the Nile delta. Either he was 'in the middle of his debauches' (no guards or servants were present) or the pages wanted revenge: Abbas had sent them from the palace to work in the stables, for having laughed at the chief eunuch. Some of his household hoped that, as Abbas had intended, he would be succeeded by his son Ilhami Pasha, rather than, in accordance with the *Hatt i-sherif*, by the eldest male of the dynasty, Abbas's uncle Said Pasha. They concealed Abbas's death and instructed the governor of Alexandria to recall Ilhami, who had just sailed for Europe. Instead, the governor informed Said, who was proclaimed vali of Egypt in Alexandria with the support of the consuls.[15]

Alexandria was transformed by Said's reign of nine years, from 1854 to 1863. Said had often visited Europe, where he had won a reputation for generosity and credulity. He spoke excellent French and English. The French consul wrote that 'from every corner of Europe, at the first news of the death of Abbas Pasha, people have come en masse to fasten on Egypt as if it is a new California ... His inquisitive mind is always ready to let itself be seduced by the grandiose phrases which are constantly repeated in his ear.' Soon 30,000 Europeans a year were said to be arriving.[16] Nubar Pasha had close ties with European immigrants, since he was at this time director of Egypt's state railways and himself a businessman. He called them 'active, intelligent and determined people who needed ingenuity to survive. Constantly searching for business deals, they naturally looked for them where they could be found, that is to say in the palace of the viceroy, the centre of preparation of all commercial transactions with the government.'[17]

Under Said the Egyptian government became, in Nubar's words, 'a regime of laissez-aller and complete lack of self respect'.[18] Said was the victim of his own character, as well as of Europeans' financial and technical skills. Since he invariably yielded to pressing demands, his reign saw government contracts produce 'incredible' profits, and Alexandria businessmen make equally incredible fortunes and lawsuits.[19] Consuls often supported their nationals' claims on the Egyptian government, and shared the profits. During an audience at Ras el-Tin, a consul-general shivered by an open window. Said Pasha said, 'Cover yourself, cover yourself; if you catch cold your government will ask me for an indemnity.' Henry Bulwer, British ambassador in Constantinople, called the aggressive attitude of the consuls the prime source of corruption in Egypt.[20]

Said's most important contract was for the creation of the Suez Canal. It was signed in Alexandria with his old friend Ferdinand de Lesseps. Lesseps came from a family with extensive Levantine connections: his father had been French consul in Alexandria; his brother Jules was Paris agent of the Bey of Tunis. Lesseps had first met Said in 1831 when serving as French vice-consul in Alexandria – where he had also found, in the consulate archives, plans for a Suez canal drawn up during the French occupation in 1798–9. The friendship had been reinforced by Lesseps's secret presents of food when Muhammad Ali was trying to force Said to lose weight.

On the day he returned to Alexandria, 7 November 1854, Lesseps was received by Said. On 30 November the convention was signed.[21] By the time the canal was opened, by Lesseps's cousin the Empress Eugénie in November 1869, the French-dominated Compagnie Universelle de Suez had charged so much money, and used so much forced Egyptian labour, that it had helped ruin the Egyptian treasury and many Egyptian lives (though fewer died than for the construction of the Mahmudiye canal or the Egyptian railways). The Suez canal rapidly became an international waterway even more vital than the Bosphorus and the Dardanelles. Most of the profits went to the canal company rather than the Egyptian government.[22] None of Said's predecessors as governor of Egypt, nor any Ottoman sultan, would have agreed to the construction of the canal. They knew that, once established as the main British route to India, it would be a further inducement for the British government to occupy Egypt.

In the nine years of Said's reign the number of Europeans in Alexandria quadrupled. By 1864 there were 50,000 to 60,000 – a quarter to a third of the population: 15,000 Greeks, 15,000 Italians, 10,000 French, the rest mainly Maltese and Syrians from the Ottoman Empire (who in Alexandria were beginning to be considered Europeans).[23] In 1865 two French visitors could write, 'The European colony is really mistress of Alexandria. All the nations of the globe have furnished their contingent to this bizarre reunion of colonists, differing in appearance and habits and without any other connection than an immense desire to enrich itself promptly and a profound disdain for the institutions of the country.'[24]

Confident in their power and wealth, the English had the reputation for despising everything unconnected to themselves and their race.[25] The inscription on the tomb of Sir Henry Edward Barker – grandson of John Barker, consul-general in the 1820s – who was born in Alexandria in 1872 and died there in 1942, is an epitome of condescension: 'Proud of his country and a staunch believer in her destiny of service to the world, he spared no effort to bring to Egypt and especially to his birthplace Alexandria some measure of the blessings Great Britain herself enjoyed.'[26]

Italians in Alessandria d'Egitto (as they called it, to distinguish it from Alessandria in Piedmont) tended to be emigrants from Sicily and the south – their economies had been disrupted by their conquest by Piedmont in 1860. Their strong wines, bare-legged women, and sharp knives – often used in murders – shocked Alexandrians, from the ruler down.[27] Stonemasons in Alexandria and Egypt often came from Bari or Barletta in Apulia. Traditional builders from the mountains of Albania and Macedonia were replaced by Italian architects, such as Pietro Avoscani, and Francesco Mancini; some of the city's grandest buildings look as if they could be in Genoa or Naples.[28]

The Greeks lived slightly apart from the others, with their own institutions and cafés, and a large white cathedral, built in 1848–56 (and recently restored by the Onassis foundation). At home in Alexandria – as one British vice-consul wrote, its very name gave them right of domicile – their first loyalties were, nearly always, to Greece.[29] After 1860 the Greek consul-general was automatically head of the community. They went to their own Greek schools, and at this stage rarely married non-Greeks, even if they were also Orthodox.

In addition Alexandria contained an important community of Syrians: by 1870 or earlier, through trade and property deals, the Sursocks, Debbanes, Zananiri and Zoghebs – all originally from Lebanon or Syria – had become some of the richest families in the city.[30] The fact that they spoke Arabic – and until the 1860s often wore Arab dress – did not stop them sharing Europeans' disdain for Egyptians. Indeed, some showed their desire to distance themselves from Arabs by adopting French as their principal language in public, while continuing to use Arabic at home. They rarely hid their wealth. Hence the following alleged exchanges between Alexandria Syrians. To the question

'Votre père, je crois, est mort centenaire?': 'Non, non, millionaire!' Or, to a question about a statue, 'C'est Andromaque?': 'Ma ché, en dromaque? C'est en marbre et elle m'a couté fort cher!'[31]

The Zoghebs became one of the most enduring and cosmopolitan of Alexandria's merchant families. Max Zogheb had arrived in Alexandria from Syria in the 1840s to sell pistachios. He wore Arab dress, and could at first speak only Arabic and a few words of lingua franca. In time he became the Portuguese consul, a millionaire and a papal count, with a magnificent house on the Rue Sherif Pasha (decorated with his new-won coronet) called the Palais Zogheb (now the Toksha school). His wife, Comtesse Catherine de Zogheb, who could barely write her own name, decided to change out of Arab into Frank dress only in 1876, for the wedding of her daughter Rosine. Some members of her family wondered why her children resembled the doorkeeper Hassan more than her husband. Another daughter, Isabelle, Madame Mihalla Pasha, became a lady-in-waiting to the wife of the Khedive – the Zoghebs had left their roots far behind.[32]

The total population of Alexandria rose from 181,000 in 1865 to 213,000 in 1872 and 232,000 in 1882, nearer in size to Cairo than at any time since 1400.[33] One reason for the dramatic rise was 'white gold' – cotton. As American cotton production dropped during the civil war of 1861–5, Egyptian cotton exports grew. In one year cotton doubled in price, and some merchants doubled or trebled their capital. On 30 June 1862 the *Times* correspondent wrote from Alexandria (where there had been a correspondent since 1849, earlier than in any other city outside Europe) that there was nothing to report but 'an appearance of prosperity, the reality of which it is difficult to see any reason to doubt'.[34] The cotton boom brought more ships to Alexandria: about 1,000 a year before 1850, 1,500 in 1855, 2,000 in 1860, 2,500 by 1865. The quays filled up with bales of cotton, sacks of grain, chests of tea, and bags of spices.[35] Between 1862 and 1872 the number of British ships visiting Alexandria doubled; their cargoes were worth more than twice the value of all Alexandria's other cargoes combined.[36]

Alexandria had become a world port; it was not yet an elegant city. London and Paris had recently installed sewerage systems and eliminated the possibility of another 'great stink', such as had infested London in 1858.[37] Alexandria, however, as travellers frequently complained, was one of the dirtiest cities in the world. Unpaved streets resembled rivers of mud, especially in winter. In Pera men and women wore galoshes to avoid getting their feet dirty. In Alexandria they had to hire donkeys: the donkey-drivers became one of the city's most important guilds. Over the city hung a permanent smell of garbage and excrement, 'tenacious as remorse', in the words of the Paris journalists Messieurs Sacré and Outrebon. The city's mortality rate was the highest in Egypt.[38]

Alexandria was in the middle of economic, demographic and cultural revolutions. It was surrounded by shanty towns of deracinated peasants. Beggars were common. Yet violence tended to be within or between immigrant groups – for example, Greeks versus Jews. Maltese had the reputation 'throughout the Levant' of being 'connected with all that is turbulent, fanatical, dishonest and immoral'.[39] They tended to fight Italians, rather than Egyptians, who were at this stage peaceful, or intimidated.[40] In 1857 the British consul complained of the powerlessness of the police: the city contained 'whole streets of the lowest possible kind of Wine Shops, Taverns and houses of ill fame kept by Maltese, Greeks, Italians and Frenchmen ... Daily ... corpses are found floating in the harbour for which no one can account and for whom no one cares.'[41] By 1868, however, there was a 'European commissioner' in each district 'to settle small claims', and Italians were being recruited into the Egyptian police, to help it deal with Europeans' crimes.[42]

There were fewer riots in Alexandria than in many other cities. In Europe, thousands died during the revolutions of 1848 in Paris, Vienna and Berlin, Milan, Venice and Rome. In 1857 Delhi rose against the British. In 1858, in the cosmopolitan Red Sea port of Jeddah, riots killed, among others, the British vice-consul and the French consul and his wife. Many thousands died, and many monuments were burnt, in Paris, 'the capital of civilization', during the final week of the Commune in May 1871. Fights in Marseille between French inhabitants and Italian immigrants took place almost every day; in 1881 they caused many Italians to return to their homeland.[43]

Shared prosperity, as well as the dynasty's cosmpolitan ethos, may have helped lessen Alexandria's tensions. As the French journalists Sacré and

Outrebon wrote in 1865, the different elements in the city were gradually becoming, if not a nation, at least a society, whose elements were slowly modifying each other. Moreover, unlike Smyrna or Algiers, Alexandria was not a segregated city. It contained mixed areas such as Dogana and Attarine, where poor Europeans and Egyptians lived side by side. Sometimes they did the same jobs. In 1872, of 641 fishermen registered in Alexandria, 40 were Maltese, 30 Greek, 250 Italian and 321 Egyptian.[44]

Said Pasha died in January 1863. He loved the city so much that he was buried beside his mother in the Nebi Danwil Mosque – the only ruler of the House of Muhammad Ali to be buried in Alexandria rather than Cairo. He was succeeded by his nephew Ismail.

Ismail Pasha had some of the 'peculiarly fascinating manner' and intelligence of his grandfather Muhammad Ali.[45] He came to the throne with ideas of retrenchment and modernization. But, even more than Said, he developed into an ambitious spendthrift, with a weakness for Europeans. He gave estates to consuls, even of lesser powers like Portugal and Sweden, and confiscated land from the family of Ibrahim al-Sheikh to present it to the Catholic church of St Catherine near the west side of the Place des Consuls.[46] As in the reign of Muhammad Ali, the antechambers at Ras el-Tin filled day and night with Europeans proposing expensive schemes; and Ismail lacked Muhammad Ali's sense of reality.[47]

In 1865 a collapse in cotton prices and an outbreak of cholera caused thousands of Alexandrians to panic. Ships could not unload their cargoes before they were boarded by people desperate to leave the city.[48] Ismail Pasha himself said to a crowd of anxious European businessmen gathered at Ras el-Tin, 'Bonsoir, messieurs!' before boarding his yacht for a prolonged holiday.[49]

By 1866 Egypt had recovered. In return for large payments in Constantinople, Ismail had secured the succession to the governorship of Egypt for his eldest son, Tewfik, rather than, as hitherto, for the oldest member of the dynasty. (A year later, also in return for large sums, he obtained the further distinction of the title Khedive or Master for himself and his successors.) He returned in triumph on board his latest extravagance, the yacht *Mahroussa* – the *Well-guarded*. Built in England in 1865, on the model of the royal yacht the *Victoria and Albert*, it is still moored in Alexandria harbour today: it played a crucial role in the coup of 1952, by removing King Farouk to Europe.

The following quotation, from a private letter written during Ismail's reign, expresses both consuls' power in Alexandria and Alexandria businessmen's exploitation of Egyptians. André Dervieu had arrived in Alexandria from Paris in 1860 and became a banker to Said and Ismail, whom he frequently saw in private: like many government officials and businessmen to this day, he spent hours on the train between Cairo, where he went to see government officials, and Alexandria, where he was a pillar of the French community and a member of the French consular court.[50] On 9 May 1866 he wrote to a colleague in Paris, 'We are all waiting with impatience for the return of the Viceroy. Our consuls are determined to push him to a settlement of his debts to the European merchants. It is no longer paper that he is going to have to give but money and he will be able to find it in the pockets of his fellah [peasants] who have been burying it away for so many years.'[51]

Dervieu later quarrelled with Ismail. Having made 5 million francs in Egypt, he built a lavish house near the Parc Monceau in Paris, where he died a papal count, thanks to his many benefactions to the Catholic Church.[52] Other immigrants, however, remained in Alexandria. They built villas in Ramleh (Arabic for The Sands) to the east of the city, and in the Rue Rosette, going south-east from the Place des Consuls, which are now among the architectural attractions of the city. Edwin de Leon, for many years US consul in Alexandria, called them villas of 'every possible variety of architectural caprice ... from Khedivial palaces built in utter scorn of all the orders of architecture to Swiss chalets, square boxes and houses of as confused plans as the dreams engendered by undigested suppers'.[53] From 1863 the 'Alexandria and Ramleh Railway Company Limited' began to build a tramline to connect Ramleh to the city centre. Tram stops' names usually commemorated the wealthy owners of nearby properties – Bulkeley, Mustafa Pasha, Bacos, Zizinia. In 1863 the Zizinia family built a church dedicated to St Stephen: it gave its name to the famous San Stefano hotel and casino which opened nearby in 1887. Consuls and ministers came from Cairo to spend the summer there, and, until construction of a special building called Wizara in the Rue d'Aboukir, the council of ministers used to meet there. In 1870 the Khedive Ismail also built a palace at Ramleh.[54]

Alexandria was being modernized. It was the first city in Egypt with street numbers. In 1866, ten years after Pera, gas lighting arrived, and in 1871 a cotton exchange, designed by Avoscani, was opened by the port. Called Minat al-Bassal or the Port of Onions, it was like a vast *han* with several courtyards: one, unnoticed by most Christian visitors, enclosed a small tomb to a Muslim sheikh, where Muslims still come to pray.[55] Until 1961, with the bourse on the Place Muhammad Ali, it was one of

Alexandria's two commercial hubs. It was there and in the surrounding warehouses that raw white cotton from the Delta and Upper Egypt was weighed, separated according to quality, pressed, and packed into bales by workers singing as they trod it down with their feet. Over a hundred years the routine changed little. One of the last surviving cotton brokers, John Nahman, remembers:

> The sacks were placed on a big trestle table, eight-sided. Men stood behind each sack of a particular grading (from 'extra good', through 'fully good plus', 'fully good minus', down to 'good to fully good minus'), tossing the cotton, to the rhythm of a tambourine, on to the centre table. There the cotton was mixed, according to length, colour, silkiness, number of knots, to match the foreign buyers' purchase orders. Some people could tell the difference down to the sixteenth of a grade merely by the appearance. The cotton on the trestle was then tossed into the air, mixed and watered. A master standing in the middle ordered which man should throw his bale's content on to the trestle at the exact minute in order to get the perfect mix according to the buyer's wishes in Manchester, Lille or Ghent. Once the mixture had been 'blended' to perfection, the trestle was emptied and the cotton was taken nearby to be moulded into compact bales ready for export.

Like all cities at that time, Alexandria treated workers as expendable. 'The mortality rate from the cotton particles in the air was very high.'[56]

Modernization continued. In 1871 new quays were begun; the bourse moved to the Palais Tossizza on the Place Muhammad Ali. The brokers, buying and selling cotton at one end and stocks and shares at the other, made so much noise screaming, shouting, waving, spitting and bidding, in French, that, from the street outside, they sounded like devils in agony.[57]

In 1873 a triumphant equestrian statue of a turbaned Muhammad Ali, made in France by the sculptor Henri Alfred Jacquemart, was unveiled in the middle of the Place des Consuls by the governor of Alexandria. It was the first statue erected in a public space in a Muslim country. The Khedive had to obtain a fatwa from the reforming theologian Muhammad Abduh to silence some Muslims' hostility.[58] The statue of Muhammad Ali was an equivalent, as a symbol of Alexandria's role as a window on the West, to the towering equestrian statue of Peter the Great erected ninety years earlier in St Petersburg.

The Place Muhammad Ali, as the Place des Consuls was renamed, became 'the rendez-vous of the entire city, the Boulevard des Italiens, the

Canebière, the goal of every business deal and every excursion'.[59] Every race and class – Greeks, Africans, Arabs and Europeans, rich and poor – passed through: 'They all growl, agitate and shout in a strange tumult of sounds and colours. One also learns to admire many varieties of rags,' wrote the Parisian journalist Gabriel Charmes in 1880.[60]

In 1876 a new legal system called the *tribunaux mixtes*, or mixed courts, set up at the instigation of Nubar Pasha, removed legal jurisdiction in cases involving foreigners and Egyptians from the consular courts, which had exercised it, under the capitulations, since the sixteenth century. The *tribunaux mixtes*, however, followed European, particularly French, law. In the appeal court there were seven foreign, and only four Egyptian, judges. Official languages were Arabic, French, English and Italian.[61] The *tribunaux mixtes*, 'more than any other agency', as the English anti-imperialist Wilfrid Scawen Blunt wrote, became hated for putting Egyptians in bondage to European or Levantine moneylenders.[62] A symbol of Alexandria's role as Europe's bridgehead – or Trojan horse – in Egypt, and of the Place Muhammad Ali as centre of Alexandria, the headquarters of the *tribunaux mixtes*, inaugurated in 1887, was a massive classical building, looking like a grimmer version of Buckingham Palace, erected on the Place Muhammad Ali in 1886–7.[63]

Within two years, the *tribunaux mixtes* were threatening the Khedive himself. Alexandrians were amazed to learn that some officials from the new courts, in search of payment, had tried to seize the furniture in the Khedive's palace at Ramleh.[64] Alexandria had gained a foreign legal system at the same time that it was losing some of its Muslim character. There were only 312 Koranic students in Alexandria in 1878, compared to 4,838 in the city of Tantah, in the Delta, and 7,695 in Cairo.[65] In addition to the *tribunaux mixtes*, Alexandria contained Egyptian sharia and government (*mahkamah*) courts; consular courts, for cases involving foreigners only; and Orthodox, Coptic, Armenian and Jewish courts, for cases involving members of those religions only.[66]

The diarchy between the Khedive and the consuls exploited the mass of Egyptians and paved the way for the British occupation. However, it also made Alexandria freer from government control than Cairo. It became a political and cultural laboratory, as well as an international port. Dervieu could publish pamphlets criticizing Khedive Ismail there. The most famous newspaper in the Arab world, still flourishing today, *Al-Ahram* (*The Pyramids*) was founded in Alexandria in August 1875 by two Maronites from a village near Beirut: Salim and Gabriel Takla. Seventeen other Arabic newspapers also started in Alexandria in 1873–82.[67]

The Belgian consul Comte Menandre de Zizinia built a palace for himself on the Place Muhammad Ali, and the elegant classical Zizinia Theatre, designed by Avoscani, on the Rue Rosette in 1862.[68] In 1876 the theatre put on one of the first Arabic-language plays performed in Egypt, a patriotic work to raise money for Egyptian troops wounded while fighting for the Ottoman Empire in the Russo-Ottoman war of 1876–8.[69]

By then, however, Egypt was threatened with foreign financial control, or invasion. Bankruptcy was one reason. Between 1863 and 1876 Egypt's foreign debt rose from £3 million to £91 million. It was to an international bankruptcy commission that on 23 August 1878 Khedive Ismail made his remark, so revealing of his dynasty's aspirations, 'Mon pays n'est plus en Afrique: nous faisons partie de l'Europe actuellement.'[70]

After the imposition of Franco-British financial control, and a ministry headed by Nubar Pasha in 1878, the situation deteriorated further. Khedive Ismail was caught between the Ottoman sultan, the French and British governments, his own extravagance and absolutism, and the Egyptian army – which, as in other countries without representative institutions, acted as an expression of popular feelings. Army discontent increased as European creditors of the Khedive were paid immediately and in full. Egyptian officials and soldiers were paid late, or, as part of the European-imposed economy drive, dismissed. On 18 February 1879 a military demonstration in Cairo encouraged Ismail to dismiss Nubar and the British and French representatives in the Egyptian government. In response, on 26 June 1879 a telegram from the Sublime Porte in Constantinople, drafted at the request of the French and British ambassadors, arrived in Cairo. It was adressed 'to the ex-Khedive Ismail of Egypt'. On the advice of the French and British consuls-general, Ismail abdicated that day.

Most European journalists in Egypt were, as so often, manipulated by government officials on the spot.[71] An exception was a radical Swiss journalist called John Ninet, who had helped manage Muhammad Ali's cotton plantations. He described the ex-Khedive's departure from Alexandria four days later with his harem, on the *Mahroussa*. Having lost control of the country to foreign financiers, Ismail was regarded as 'odious' by Egyptians – even prosperous merchants were heard to call him 'the dog'. Rather than crossing the city, he went straight from the railway station to the port. The people who came to bid him farewell had benefited from his rule – businessmen, judges and consuls. There were few Egyptians, outside the ranks of saluting soldiers. 'All' were said to be delighted by his fall. Many would have preferrred his successor to be, in accordance with tradition, the eldest of the dynasty – his great-uncle Halim, youngest son of Muhammad Ali. Before 1866 Halim had been heir to the throne and commander-in-chief of the army, but he had since moved to Constantinople. Instead, as he had planned, Ismail Pasha was succeeded by his eldest son, Tewfik. Married to his cousin Emina Ilhami, Tewfik was even more European in outlook than his father. He had no harem, employed an Italian private secretary called De Martino Bey, and had long enjoyed close relations with the French and British consuls.[72]

The position of ordinary Egyptians, improving under Abbas and Said, had become 'insupportable' as Ismail had raised taxes to try to pay his debts. Poor Egyptians were treated as beasts of burden, to be taxed at will. In 1849 Flaubert had already noted that, in Alexandria, anyone wearing a clean coat struck anyone wearing a dirty coat, or no coat at all.[73] Thirty years later, officers and officials were still striking Egyptians in the street with whips or canes if they were in the way – as Egyptian soldiers can be seen doing in newsreels of political demonstrations in the 1920s. An early Lebanese radical, Faris Chidyaq, in a satire published in 1855, wrote that Turks in Alexandria had decided in council that the most comfortable form of transport was an Arab's back.[74]

Egyptian nationalism had been strengthened by the government itself when it wanted more autonomy from the Ottoman Empire. In 1858 and 1869, official directives had encouraged the use of Arabic, rather than Turkish, as the government language. Said Pasha had begun to promote native-born officers. One of them, the future leader of the 1882 revolution, Ahmad Arabi, the son of a village sheikh, well-built with 'a fine presence', had accompanied him as adjutant on a pilgrimage to Mecca in 1861.[75]

Egyptian-born officers' resentment of Turkish-speaking senior officers was increased by their experience of those officers' incompetence during the Ethiopian war of 1875 (when Khedive Ismail had failed to establish an Egyptian empire in East Africa). Between Egyptians threatened by dismissal and the Khedives' favoured Turkish and Circassian officers loaded with presents 'sucked from the blood of the poor Egyptians and from the sweat of their brows', as Arabi later wrote, an abyss widened.[76]

Like Smyrna in 1821 and Beirut in 1860, Alexandria became a volcano ready to explode. In 1879 the departing British financial commissioner Sir Charles Rivers Wilson and his wife were threatened by an angry mob.[77] Soldiers demonstrated outside Ras el-Tin Palace against the privileges of their Circassian officers. When the batteries of the shore forts, recently strengthened by Khedive Ismail, saluted ships arriving in the harbour, foreign-born Alexandrians were seen to shudder with apprehension.[78]

The first riots in the 'normally so peaceful' city of Alexandria – where the garrison was, incredibly, only 800 – took place in 1881. Greek anti-Semitism was virulent in the Levant, especially at Easter – in 1847 an Athens crowd had sacked the house of a British citizen, Don Pacifico, partly because he was Jewish, leading to a blockade of the city by the Royal Navy.[79] In Alexandria on 23 March 1881, just before Easter, a Greek boy was found dead in the harbour. He had probably fallen in and drowned. Although no signs of violence were found on his corpse, the boy was hailed as a 'martyr'. Greek crowds surged through the streets and into houses, attacking and insulting Jews: they believed the ancient 'blood libel', that at Passover Jews killed Christian children in order to use their blood in cooking. The Ecumenical Patriarch himself wrote a letter from Constantinople to condemn Alexandrian Greeks' 'absence of all intellectual culture'. Fifteen hundred extra troops were sent from Cairo under the command of the Minister of War. Yet Greek newspapers of Alexandria continued to publish incendiary anti-Jewish articles. When a Greek agitator was arrested, traders surged out of the bourse on the Place Muhammad Ali to free him. Some Jews fled for safety to the French or British consulates. The city was put under a state of siege. Finally the agitation, so revealing of Greek aggression, died down.[80]

In addition to Greek nationalism, Egyptian nationalism grew in reaction to Europeans' tightening grip on Egypt. Alexandria was still a predominantly Muslim city, with, in 1872, 100 mosques and only 12 churches and 3 synagogues.[81] A famous Muslim speaker in Alexandria was called Abdullah Nedim. Born in Alexandria in 1843, founder of a Young Men's Patriotic Association in 1878, in 1881, encouraged by the freedom of the city, he began to publish in Alexandria pamphlets calling for Muslim renewal.[82] Another Muslim, Sheikh Hamza Fathallah, warned Egyptians of the fate of his own native city, Tunis. It had been occupied by French forces, and declared a French protectorate, in 1881. He also attacked Europe as a source of socialism and anarchism.[83] Public opinion turned to Arabi. Appointed minister of war thanks to army pressure on a reluctant Khedive in February 1882, he was hailed as 'al-Wahid', 'the Only One', the saviour of his country. The army began to dominate Egypt.[84]

Insulted and humiliated by his own soldiers, Khedive Tewfik turned for advice to the French and British consuls, with whom, behind his ministers' backs, he had long been in communication.[85] By March 1882 he was determined to move to Alexandria and there await release by France and Britain from what he called 'this nightmare'. To encourage foreign intervention, he told the consuls – incorrectly – that the Prime Minister had threatened a massacre of Europeans.[86]

The British government began to plan intervention. Far from being acquired 'in a fit of absence of mind', as some British politicians liked to boast, or in rivalry with other powers, Egypt was acquired by careful planning – with the encouragement of Europe. Military force was applied to defend economic interests and win votes. In 1879 the British government had considered occupying Egypt, but had been too busy fighting Zulus, at the other end of Africa, to do so. A Liberal government came to power in 1880. Sir Charles Dilke, the new Undersecretary of State at the Foreign Office – protesting his government's respect for 'the liberties of the Egyptian people' – was determined to show British voters that Liberals could be as imperialistic as Tories. Lord Hartington threatened to resign from the Cabinet if a 'forward' policy was not pursued.[87]

The Prime Minister, Gladstone, had a personal incentive for intervening, as he realized when adding up his fortune in December 1881. He had an exceptionally large holding in Egyptian government bonds: £40,567, or 37 per cent of his entire portfolio. Sixty-five other MPs also had investments in Egypt. Thanks in part to the British occupation of Egypt, these investments would prove more profitable than many British stocks.[88] The need to 'protect the Suez Canal' was another factor influencing British policy.[89] In degrees impossible to measure, strategy, 'the market' and vote-winning encouraged Britain to occupy Egypt. The fate of the Khedive and of the Europeans in Alexandria would be a pretext.

The events of 1882 read like the 'chronicle of an occupation foretold'. A British official in Cairo told London what it wanted to hear: 'There is a strong and growing feeling among both foreigners and many Natives that the best and indeed the only issue out of the difficulties with which Egypt is beset would be its occupation by England.' That winter Alexander Bruce Tulloch, from the recently formed Army Intelligence Department, visited Egypt to examine forts, barracks and possible landing places around Alexandria. If his memoirs are to be believed, Egyptians were aware of his intentions, and laughed when he told them that he had come on holiday, to shoot snipe.[90] Although both Muhammad Ali and Ismail had strengthened Alexandria's defences, these had been weakened by the city's expansion and the use of military land for commercial buildings.[91]

On 20 May 1882 British and French gunboats anchored off Alexandria, while a joint naval squadron moved to Crete. Their orders were to communicate with the consuls-general, support the Khedive, and land

a force if 'the safety of Europeans' required it.[92] The Khedive regarded
Europe as a friend; most Egyptians regarded it as an enemy. Arabi was
supported by most of the country, including *ulema*, young officials like
Saa'd Zaghloul, the future hero of the 1919 revolution, and even some
members of the Khedive's dynasty. Many wanted a written constitution
to replace khedivial absolutism.[93]

On 25 May the British and French consuls-general demanded a change
of ministry and Arabi's departure from the country.[94] Arabi resigned as
minister of war. On 27 May, following a meeting of nationalist officers
in Alexandria, General Toulba Pasha interrupted Tewfik and told him
the army recognized only the Porte and would not accept Arabi Pasha's
resignation.[95]

On 29 May, Tewfik told the British consul-general in Cairo, Edward
Malet, that he no longer felt safe there. For the sake of his family, Malet
reported, he would do nothing 'without consulting my French colleague
and me'.[96] On 3 June, however, he reappointed Arabi as minister of war
with almost dictatorial powers.

The mood in Alexandria frightened many Europeans. On 30 May the
British community requested the British government 'to provide efficient
means for the protection of their lives. Every day's delay increases the
dangerous temper of the soldiery and their growing defiance of discipline.' The British consul, Charles Cookson, discussed with other consuls
a plan of defence for the Place Muhammad Ali, prepared by British and
Greek naval officers.[97] Between 2 and 5 June six more French and British
warships arrived in Alexandria harbour.

Arabi, who received the Grand Cordon of the Ottoman order of
Mecidiye in June, was in correspondence with two of the Sultan's aides-
de-camp, who warned him above all to avoid Egypt falling into the hands
of foreigners.[98] On 8 June the Sultan's special envoy Dervish Pasha arrived,
to cries of 'God give victory to the Sultan!' Arabi considered the Khedive
an apostate from Islam, and hoped the Sultan would depose him. In the
end, however, putting monarchy before Islam, or preferring to be on
the winning side, the Sultan would side with the Khedive and denounce
Arabi as a rebel.[99]

Running west from the Place Muhammad Ali to the port, the Rue
des Sœurs began with a convent – hence its name – and finished with
what a British soldier would call 'infamous dens of vice and debauch-
ery'.[100] On 11 June outside the Café Crystal, at the port end of the street,
a Maltese man quarrelled with his Egyptian donkey-driver, to whom he
had refused to pay the fee requested. Each insulted the other's religion, as,

Ninet wrote, 'happens every day'. After the Maltese drew his knife (or, by one account, revolver) and killed the driver, there was an explosion.[101] An Egyptian crowd, including policemen and skilled artisans such as butchers, tailors, carpenters and sherbet sellers, began to attack Europeans, whom they identified by their hats and clothes. Hatred of rich foreigners was one of their driving forces. Among their cries were 'O God, succour the Lord of Islam and destroy the depraved unbelievers!' and 'Long live the Sultan!'[102] The same day, addressing a large meeting in the city, Abdullah Nedim declared the Khedive unfit to rule.[103] Alexandrian Greeks began arming themselves, using funds provided by a rich banker called Ambroise Sinadino.[104]

Some, however, including Arabi's admirer Wilfrid Scawen Blunt, believed the Khedive and the governor of Alexandria, Omar Lutfi, deliberately allowed the riots to escalate, in order to show that Arabi could not maintain order, and thus provide a pretext for Franco-British intervention.[105] In reality no conspiratorial explanation is necessary: the surprise is not that riots took place, but that, given the incendiary proximity of armed Europeans and simmering Egyptians, they had not occurred sooner.

Egyptians armed themselves with long wooden sticks called nabouts. Along Frank Street and Strada Nuova and the quays, they hit Europeans as hard as they could. Europeans fired on Egyptian soldiers and policemen, sometimes from windows. Looting broke out. By the afternoon the riots had reached the Place Muhammad Ali.[106] The British and Greek consulates handed out more weapons to their nationals. The Greek consul, Monsieur Rhangabe, whose red beard made him 'look like an Englishman', was hit. The British consul, Cookson, received head wounds, bruises and a broken finger. The British consulate was described as 'in a state of indescribable confusion, women and children crowded in everywhere, weeping and terrified'.

The British vice-consul, Henry Calvert, telegraphed that the police did not interfere to protect Europeans: 'Governor and consuls have been concerting measures.' The consuls asked Admiral Sir Beauchamp Seymour, commander of the Mediterranean Squadron, not to land sailors as they might provoke further violence – thus the foreign ships proved more of a provocation than a defence for Europeans in Alexandria. Replacing the police, Egyptian troops began to patrol the streets to restore order, and even helped Europeans to take refuge on ships in the harbour. Arabi did not want to give Britain a pretext to attack – and was too honourable, or weak, to force Europeans to stay in the city and act as a human shield against foreign fleets, as they had in Smyrna in 1695 and 1770.[107]

On 12 June rioting continued in the lower town. Cookson began to recover, as his injuries were 'not serious'. In all about 50 Europeans had been killed and perhaps 250 Egyptians – proof of Europeans' superior firepower: the massacre of Europeans was also a massacre of Egyptians. Egyptian deaths were easier to ignore by journalists, since, in accordance with Muslim tradition, Egyptians were buried at once, while Europeans were not. The European consuls asked remaining Europeans not to carry firearms – further proof, from their own representatives, of their aggressive behaviour.[108]

On 13 June, as was his habit, the Khedive arrived for the summer in Alexandria, accompanied by Dervish Pasha and the foreign consuls-general. By then the harbour was filling up with foreign boats and warships – Dutch, Austrian, American, Russian, Turkish and Greek, as well as French and British.[109] By 17 June, 20,000 Alexandrians had fled for safety to these ships, including Syrians like the Taklas, and Greeks such as the Benaki and Cavafy families. Egyptian notables also began to leave the country. In the general *sauve qui peut*, after 13 June Egyptian police and soldiers kept disorder to the minimum.[110]

On 20 June Arabi arrived in Alexandria to a hero's welcome. The next day he drove through the streets in the same carriage as the Khedive – although in Cairo he had made speeches denouncing the monarch and the dynasty.[111]

By 9 July all who wanted, including many refugees from Cairo, had 'gone afloat'. Banks and hotels throughout the city were padlocked. Only two or three shops were still open. The few remaining Europeans were officials, doctors and nurses.[112] Thus one condition for foreign occupation of a Levantine port – removal of local Christians to prevent their massacre – had been fulfilled. The British 'Channel Squadron' had moved to Malta and been placed under Seymour's orders; some of its ships proceeded to Alexandria.[113]

Having been sent to protect Alexandria, Admiral Seymour now claimed he needed protection from it. Personally infuriated by the death in the riot of his 'body-servant' Strackett,[114] he threatened to bombard the city unless its surrounding forts were dismantled and British forces were allowed to occupy them. The Egyptian cabinet, meeting with the Khedive and Dervish Pasha at Ras el-Tin, decided to resist. It was a national resistance, ordered by the legal government of the country.[115] Gladstone, so eloquent in his denunciations of 'the Bulgarian atrocities' committed by Turkish irregular troops in 1876, now authorized his own 'Egyptian atrocity' – which would result in greater loss of life.

On 10 July all remaining foreign ships left Alexandria harbour, 'foreseeing the bombardment and occupation of the city which the English will perform tomorrow', a young French sailor called Didier Girard wrote in his logbook. By a secret agreement with the British fleet – probably because the Chamber of Deputies had not voted the necessary credits for a French intervention, or because the French government and the Chamber were happy for Britain to bear the cost and responsibility of protecting European lives and financial interests in Egypt – the French fleet sailed away from Alexandria to Port Said, with the staff of the French consulate on board.[116]

At seven on the morning of 11 July Admiral Seymour sent a signal to the great ironclad battleship HMS *Alexandra*: 'Attack the enemy's batteries.'[117] One by one, every ship of the fifteen-ship force joined in the bombardment of Alexandria. Soon they were covered by a mass of white smoke. 'The spectacle was magnificent ... terrible and awe-inspiring and in spite of myself I trembled with excitement,' wrote de Kusel Bey, an Englishman working in the Egyptian customs. The deep booming of the British guns was answered by the rattle of Egyptian artillery, firing from the forts with what Tulloch called 'uncommonly good shooting'. British firing was indiscriminate but effective. Moreover, there were few Egyptian cannon and artillerymen, and by 11.30 these had been silenced. After the bombardment, all the bands on the foreign men-of-war in the distance, in an outburst of shared imperialism, played the British national anthem.[118]

The bombardment reduced to ruins the harem at Ras el-Tin, much of the surrounding district and of the Dogana and Attarine districts, the Place Muhammad Ali, and Rue Sherif Pasha. Soon the sky turned red from fires, some started by British shells, others by Egyptian looters. Columns of smoke rose above the city. Each time Egyptian soldiers tried to extinguish the fires, more bombs from 'the floating monsters' set them alight again, according to John Ninet, who was an eyewitness.[119] A change of wind helped spread the fires. Egyptian troops, and large numbers of Egyptian Alexandrians, began to leave the city in 'one vast stream of fugitives'. Europeans had left the city by boat; Egyptians fled by train, many riding on the roofs and buffers of the carriages.[120] In all about 60,000 Egyptians fled from Alexandria, mainly to Cairo, which was still ruled by the nationalist government.[121]

After the bombardment, there was a sinister three-day gap before the arrival of British forces, perhaps because so few were available. In it, Alexandrians enraged or emboldened by the bombardment, and Egyptian soldiers, continued looting and began killing. The consulates, the French and Austrian post offices, buildings belonging to the dynasty, the 24,000 square foot Sursock block, the houses of the Comte de Zogheb and Nubar Pasha and many Egyptian merchants' houses were burned and looted, as well as shops, schools and hospitals.[122]

On 11 and 12 July the main sounds in Alexandria were the crackle and roar of flames, the crash of falling buildings, and howling dogs. Arabi left on 11 July, the last Egyptian troops around 1 p.m. on 12 July.[123] Alexandria turned, in the words of an official in the British consulate, into 'a Dantesque Inferno, alight almost from end to end, the flames running riot from street to street without any attempt to check them being made, with wild figures here and there pillaging and looting and ghastly corpses swollen to gigantic proportions lying charred and naked in the road-ways.'[124] Another witness called it 'a pandemonium of hell and its devils ... I never saw anything so awful.'[125] Among the ruins were libraries of finely bound books, torn and trampled;[126] pyramids of rubbish, broken glass and furniture; and cats and dogs 'maddened by thirst and starva-tion'.[127] The only object untouched was the statue of Muhammad Ali on horseback, who seemed to survey the ruins around him with disgust.[128]

The photographs of an Italian Alexandrian, Luigi Fiorillo, sold in an album called *Souvenir d'Alexandrie ruines*, would make the staunchest im-perialist blush: gutted mosques, churches, schools and consulates (British guns destroyed both the British and the French consulate); dismantled forts; piles of rubble; empty streets with no sign of life, not even a stray dog, except for a token European posed to give scale.[129]

Finally, on 14 July, 400 British sailors and marines landed with a Gatling gun, and entered the city, under Commander Hammill of the *Monarch*. As more ships arrived, more sailors and marines landed, including Germans, Americans and Greeks, to guard their consulates and help the British. They were joined after 17 July by soldiers from the British garrison in Cyprus.[130]

By 20 July there were about 3,800 British soldiers, sailors and marines in the city.[131] Lord Charles Beresford, commander of the gunboat *Condor*, acted as provost marshal, with 'absolute power of life and death, or to flog or to blow down houses or to do anything I thought fit'. He used an Arabic-speaking British merchant of the city called F. C. Haselden as his interpreter, and soon established police posts throughout Alexandria.

The Place Muhammad Ali became a shooting range, with humans as targets. Outside the Palais Tossizza, Beresford dispensed 'summary justice'. Egyptians were condemned as plunderers, incendiarists and rebels. Some were tied to trees in the square, shot, and buried beneath them in mass graves.[132] Dead artillerymen were buried in more mass graves outside Ras el-Tin. The totals speak for themselves. Five British troops died; between 350 and 2,000 Egyptians – probably more. By 19 July Beresford claimed he had established 'perfect order'.[133] Protected by British guns, Europeans began to return to Alexandria.

Meanwhile Arabi had made the fatal error of returning to Cairo and not securing the king on the political chessboard, Khedive Tewfik. To avoid the British bombardment, and wait to join the winning side, on 11 July Tewfik had withdrawn from Ras el-Tin to the Mustafa Pasha Palace in Ramleh, which had once belonged to his radical uncle Mustafa Pasha Fazil.[134] An American general in the Egyptian Army, General Charles Stone, and his ministers were in attendance. The ladies of Tewfik's harem are said to have bribed Arabi's troops with their jewels to let him leave Ramleh. The Khedive and his ministers returned to British-occupied Alexandria on 13 July, escorted by cavalry. According to Ninet, he was received by defiant cries of 'Long live Arabi! Down with Tewfik!' On 16 July he finally dismissed Arabi as minister of war.[135]

British sailors and marines, as well as some of his own troops, guarded him at Ras el-Tin. On 20 July the commander of the Naval Brigade, an ambitious young naval captain called Jack Fisher (later First Sea Lord and inventor of the 'dreadnought'), wrote home, 'I have now command of the city and sea forts of Alexandria and I have also charge of the Khedive ["such a nice man, a perfect gentleman"] and am responsible for his safety; and that is why I am living at Ras el tine with my headquarters here.'[136] Another future war leader present was Lieutenant H. H. Kitchener, who had volunteered, while surveying Cyprus, to join the attack on Alexandria: his fluent Turkish and Arabic were useful in reconnaissance.

While Britain secured Alexandria, Cairo proclaimed jihad. Calling the Khedive a despicable traitor, and denouncing the British for plundering Egyptians' property and 'raping' their women, the Egyptian official gazette urged, 'Make haste, O people of Islamic ardour!' and quoted the Koran: 'Fight the unbelievers who are near to you and let them feel a rough temper in you and know that Allah is with those who show piety!' Egypt's problems, it declared, were caused by its rulers' lack of piety. On 29 July, Tewfik was deposed by a congress of notables, including sheikhs of the Muslim university al-Azhar in Cairo and the Coptic Patriarch. He was not replaced. The country functioned relatively well; the canal remained open to shipping, until attacked by British forces. Arabi's government was a national movement, supported by some members of the khedivial dynasty and the Turco-Circassian elite, as well as Egyptians. If British forces had withdrawn, a clandestine note reveals, the Khedive's own ministers would have joined Arabi. Under British command, Alexandria was prepared to resist Egyptian forces, which hovered outside the city.[137]

But God was on the side of the big battalions. By 1882 Britain was the supreme world power, under fewer restraints than the United States today. Having recently sacked both Delhi (1857) and Peking (1860), it would not withdraw from Alexandria as easily as it had in 1807. On 20 July the British cabinet, claiming that any occupation would be temporary, decided to send an army to Egypt to 'restore the khedive's authority'.[138] Gladstone called it 'a European duty': as his biographer Richard Shannon has written, 'Europe became a fig leaf to cover the nakedness of empire.'[139] The expeditionary force, under Sir Garnet Wolseley, proved better organized than the army sent thirty years earlier to the Crimea. On 12 August the Brigade of Guards, under Queen Victoria's favourite son, the Duke of Connaught, landed at Alexandria, marched through the city, and camped in Ramleh.[140] Arriving on a mediation mission from Cairo, when he saw the size of the British army in Alexandria, Ali Mubarak, 'the father of Egyptian education', joined the Khedive. In his account of 1882 he later blamed Arabi, not the British bombardment, for the burning of Alexandria and the flight and sufferings of its inhabitants.[141] On 12 September, at Tell el-Kabir between Cairo and the Suez Canal, the Egyptian army was defeated by British and Indian forces. There was less subsequent resistance than during the French occupation of 1798–1801 or during the French occupation of Tunisia in 1881. On 15 September 1882 Cairo fell.[142]

Alexandria's role as both summer capital and cosmopolitan port had been a determining factor. Bringing different communities into proximity, it helped provoke racial and religious explosions. Making the Khedive accessible to foreign navies, it facilitated intervention on his behalf. When news of Cairo's fall reached Alexandria, Europeans shouted 'Viva Inghilterra!' and embraced British soldiers 'frantically'. Bands played 'God Save the Queen' and the khedivial hymn in turn.[143] On 25 September, after the dramatic summer in Alexandria, Tewfik returned to Cairo, driving in an open carriage with the Duke of Connaught, Sir Garnet Wolseley, and Sir Edward Malet, through streets lined with British troops.[144] In a congratulatory letter to the Foreign Secretary, Lord Granville, Malet expressed the importance of electoral considerations in the invasion of Egypt: 'You have fought the battle of all Christendom and may I also venture to say that you have given the Liberal party a new lease of popularity and power.'

The Gladstone government had wiped away the shame of the retreat from Afghanistan in 1881.[145]

Meanwhile, so distrusted were Egyptians that Alexandria was guarded for a time by a force of 1,000 mercenary Swiss and Bosnians. For once a Levantine city had its own army; but Coles Pasha of the Egyptian police considered them 'a very scratch lot' and soon sent the Swiss back.[146] Conditions in the city were described by John Cavafy, one of the sons of the Greek cotton merchant Peter Cavafy, writing to his brother Constantine, the future poet, who had moved for safety with his mother to Constantinople. On 12 August John Cavafy wrote, 'Alexandria alas is much changed but the streets are becoming orderly and passable'. On 17 September, 'The stench of our streets, – I referred to some time ago – was produced by the opening and repairing of the sewers but all that is now over, and the authorities have succeeded so well in piling up the ruins and gathering all the stones and rubbish together, that positively the damage done appears much less now, than when I arrived.'[147]

As usual, the Place Muhammad Ali was a gauge of events in Alexandria. It was covered in wooden huts, serving as temporary shops. The Royal Oak bar had a female orchestra, members of whom, in the words of a British soldier, helped 'the gay soldier ... quaff the foaming ale'. Few Egyptians could be seen in this area, except those wearing European dress. Donkey-drivers, however, reappeared, crying, 'Me very good donkee, Johnny, take him.' When rebuilding started, male workers were joined by women who, 'in long blueish gowns', could be seen 'climbing up the ladders with their loads'.[148]

Below the cultivated surface, Alexandria could be a brutal city. Between comments on the Bible and the difficulty of obtaining literary magazines, John Cavafy wrote to Constantine that one detachment of marines had 'shot down every Arab as they went along'. Their business associate, Watson, eager to get back to his office, 'had a revolver and did something in that line of business too'.[149] *Le Phare d'Alexandrie* called Arabi 'a little Attila'; on 2 October 1882 John Cavafy expressed the hope that he would hang:

> For to see a man swing
> At the end of a string,
> With his neck in a noose, is a very rare thing.

(I quote from memory and am not sure about the last line). I read in the *Times*, the other day, that there is only one course of procedure with Araby left to England, i.e., to hang him. I hope they'll do it here. What a sell if they let him go Scot free! It is not at all unlikely. – The English are such fools sometimes![150]

To the fury of many Alexandrians, including the Khedive himself, Arabi was exiled to Ceylon, and was later allowed to return to Egypt to die in peace.

European Alexandria began to recover self-confidence. Greeks entertained their British 'saviours' to banquets and '*après-midis dansants*'. On 24 October a Greek millionaire from Chios called John Antoniadis, later knighted for his services to Britain, gave a banquet for Sir Garnet Wolseley. On 30 October John Cavafy wrote, 'Alexandria is becoming quite brisk again.'

There may be arguments in favour of the British Empire. The bombardment of Alexandria and occupation of Egypt are not among them. They show how often the British Empire, far from 'making the modern world', as Niall Fergusson has claimed in *Empire* (2003), thwarted it. Egypt's development was distorted by seventy years of British occupation.

This is not historian's hindsight: it was a view expressed at the time by many British officials. One radical, John Bright, resigned from the cabinet. Walter Miéville, later president of the Maritime and Quarantine Council in Alexandria, wrote that the 'financiers of Europe were the real instigators of the bombardment ... The fatal mistake of our government has been to bombard the forts before the landing force for the protection of the city had arrived'.[151] C. F Moberly Bell, an Englishman born in Alexandria in 1847, who had since become the *Times* correspondent there, wrote that the bombardment was 'an egregious blunder' which led to 'atrocities which rival those of the Commune'.[152] General Sir Garnet Wolseley himself, in a private letter to his wife on 10 September 1882, denounced 'that silly and criminal bombardment of Alexandria which Lord Northbrook [First Lord of the Admiralty] and the Admiralty concocted'.[153] 'Silly and criminal' is a phrase which could apply to many episodes in the British occupation of Egypt, up to the attack on the Suez Canal in 1956. Arabi's government in 1882 had been correct to call the bombardment 'inhuman and useless', as contrary to international law as the British occupation was contrary to national dignity.[154]

After the bombardment came the settling of accounts. Under the presidency of Yaqub Artin Pasha, a nephew of Nubar, the Indemnities Commission made 9,000 payments, mainly to Europeans and Levantines who had fled the city, including the Cavafy family. The Egyptian taxpayer paid. Coles Pasha admitted there were 'many frauds'. Some claims for lost belongings were so extreme that one commissioner protested, 'Did the ladies flee naked?'[155]

8

Alexandria: British Years

Egypt is now in that giant Anglo-Saxon grasp which no human
force, once it has seized a foreign land, whether it is a rock like
Gibraltar, a point of sand like Aden, an island like Malta or an
entire world like India, can ever again dislodge or remove.

Eça de Queiroz, 1883

AFTER 1882 THE power of the consuls in Egypt reached its apogee.
As was shown by the decision to spare Arabi Pasha's life, the real
ruler of Egypt was not Khedive Tewfik but the British consul-general
in Cairo, Evelyn Baring, later Lord Cromer. His authority was based on
the British army of occupation, about 5,000 strong, and the 400 or more
British officials who, behind a legitimizing screen of Egyptian ministers,
ran the country.

At first Baring had proposed an occupation for twelve months:
Gladstone promised evacuation five times in 1882–3. Appetite grew with
eating. The strategic value of Alexandria was one argument for keeping
Egypt. By 1887 Baring thought that Britain should leave Cairo in three
years and Alexandria in five. This constantly extending departure date
eventually changed into the assertion that Britain had no right to abandon
its 'duties' in Egypt: in plain English, it would stay as long as it wished.[1]

The great Portuguese novelist Eça de Queiroz – coming from one of
the oldest European empires – had few illusions about them. Having
admired Alexandria as 'the Levantine city par excellence', the queen of the
Levant, he considered that Gladstone had done it more damage than any
Roman emperor or Christian mob. 'The world is becoming Anglicized.
The English are everywhere, that is why they are detested, they never
integrate or de-Anglicize themselves.'[2] Indeed, complaints of English
insularity and disdain were as frequent in Egypt as in India or China. 'It is
because of their manners they are not liked,' said Prince Muhammad Ali,
younger son of Khedive Tewfik.[3]

Alexandria had entered its British period. Until 1947, British battleships were anchored in the harbour, British troops garrisoned in the city, living in barracks in the districts of Ras el-Tin, Mustafa Pasha, Moharrem Bey and Sidi Bishr. British officials held many key positions in the city. The director of the port was Sir George Morice Pasha, in office since 1879. In 1914, of 451 men in the Alexandria City Police, 108 were British.[4]

Nevertheless, Egypt had a sufficiently strong identity, and Britain a sufficiently light hand, to avoid either a protectorate or annexation. Ottoman suzerainty and the Khedive's pliability also helped. A separate Egyptian government and army continued to exist throughout the British occupation. Unlike the French in Algeria after 1830 or the Italians after 1911 in neighbouring Tripolitania, the British in Egypt were not colonists who settled in the country and expropriated its people. They were either capitalists come to run businesses or government servants. British officers and officials serving in the Egyptian administation or armed forces, including both Gordon and Kitchener 'of Khartoum', wore the Ottoman fez as a sign that they were – however contemptuously – servants of the Sultan and of his vassal the Khedive.

The Khedive and his court and ministers, with the consuls-general, continued to spend every summer in Alexandria: the former in and around Ras el-Tin, the ministers and consuls in the Hotel San Stefano. Like most rulers of his dynasty, Tewfik was 'very fond' of its second capital. Pointing with pride at the ships and houses and minarets reflected 'like a city in a dreamland' in the moonlit water outside the palace of Ras el-Tin, he said to his sons' tutor Alfred Butler, 'Where will you find anything like that in Cairo?' But 'all the pashas and people around him were fretting after Cairo'. So, like many other monarchs, every autumn he reluctantly returned to his capital.[5]

Tewfik's son Abbas Hilmi succeeded him in 1892 at the age of eighteen. Every June Abbas Hilmi would enter Alexandria in state, escorted by cavalry. His arrival would be celebrated by a ball in his honour given by the merchants of the city – the richer of whom then left to summer in Europe, away from the heat of Egypt. Their European travels are shown by the fact that their newspaper, *Le Phare d'Alexandrie*, was on sale all year in Vienna, Paris, Rome and Florence, and in the summer at Carlsbad, Marienbad, Vichy, Athens and Naples. For them, Khedive Ismail's boast about Egypt being part of Europe was true. Their Alexandria was part of Europe, which they knew far better than Egypt.[6]

The Khedive built himself yet another palace, called el-Montazah – 'The Pure' – on a pine-covered promontory to the east of the city. A monstrosity reminiscent of one of King Ludwig II's castles in Bavaria, the vast columned *haremlik* building (for women and children), extended in the 1920s, is surmounted by 'Florentine' campaniles with superb views of Alexandria. The surrounding park, now used by a hotel, was filled with kiosks, dovecotes, beehives, and mulberry and pine trees. Inside, the decoration and furniture is in the ultra-gilt 'Louis Farouk' style preferred by the Muhammad Ali dynasty.[7]

Even in his own palace, however, the young Khedive felt surrounded by British spies and agents: treason, he later wrote, poisoned the atmosphere.[8] The bourgeoisie was asleep, the press flaccid, the peasants occupied with their own troubles: he began to devote his energies to his private business empire. Reverting to his dynasty's Ottoman roots, he preferred to spend many summers in a palace on the Bosphorus, far from Alexandria and his nemesis Lord Cromer.[9]

After the bloodshed of 1882 Alexandria entered what has been celebrated as a golden age of cosmopolitanism. By examining certain institutions and individuals, it is hoped to find out whether Alexandria's cosmopolitanism was real or imaginary. Was Alexandria a city of conviviality, whose inhabitants crossed frontiers between races, religions and languages and, as E. Breccia, director of its Archaeological Museum, claimed, showed mutual respect in daily life and 'a touching solidarity' in misfortune? Or was it a segregated city, where, as Murray's *Handbook* stated, hostile or indifferent communities were connected only by money?[10]

The most visible cosmopolitan institution, which influenced many levels of Egyptian society, was the monarchy itself. Abbas Hilmi was a polyglot who, like some members of his family to this day, knew Turkish, Arabic, Persian, English and French. The Khedive's household included European, Arabic and Turkish offices, and an English secretariat. The head of his Arabic office, Ahmed Shawqi, was an adored national poet, whose lines were famous as soon as they were published.[11] On his first visit to the Alexandria municipality, then lodged in a school in the Rue Rosette, which had been a present to the Khedive Ismail from the foreign community of Alexandria, Abbas Hilmi expressed (probably in French) his belief in cosmopolitanism: 'In my good city of Alexandria I want there to be neither foreigners nor natives, but only Alexandrians, rivalling and emulating each other for the progress of their city.'[12]

The career of the Khedive's cousin Prince Omar Toussoun, a grandson of Said Pasha, shows that cosmopolitanism remained part of the dynasty's ethos. Known as the 'Prince of Alexandria', his principal residence was a palace by the Mahmudiye canal, now a school. The first president and for long only Muslim committee member of the Alexandria Sporting Club, from 1890 to his death in 1944 he bridged many worlds. A Muslim interested in non-Islamic history, a professional geographer and archaeologist, president of both the Alexandria and the Coptic archaeological societies, he wrote articles on the city's Graeco-Roman as well as its Muslim past. Always ready to attend prize-givings at the city's schools – Egyptian, Jewish or Christian – he was also head of over eighty charitable societies, including the Young Men's Muslim Association, the Nubian Salvation Society, and the Society for the Poor of Alexandria. From his many charities he was known as 'the father of the fellah'. His private band, wearing velvet uniforms as they went to play at an employee's wedding, was a familiar sight in the streets of Alexandria. He was an able administrator of his estates, and a good shot. A representative of the modernizing, charitable aspects of the Egyptian monarchy, overshadowed by King Farouk's unhappy end, Prince Omar Toussoun was both cosmopolitan and patriotic: he advocated wearing the fez as a symbol of national pride.[13] Coles Pasha considered that, if the Prince had been Khedive, 'there would never have been any Egyptian Question.'[14]

In addition to the dynasty's, other cosmopolitan households were common in Alexandria – and statistically important when domestic service was one of the largest employment categories. Rich merchants of Alexandria would frequently employ Greek or Italian maids (generally from the Greek islands or Istria), an Italian cook, a French or English governess, Egyptian gardeners and valets, and drivers and secretaries of any nationality.[15] Marriages between members of different races or religions were not common – perhaps at most 10 per cent of any community, at this stage, married 'out'.[16] When Gaston Zananiri's father, a Greek Catholic of Syrian origin, married Marie Ines Bauer, daughter of a Hungarian Jewish atheist and an Italian mother living in Alexandria, the quarrel with the rest of his family lasted thirty years.[17] However, another form of intimacy was common: living in the same household, following the same routine, eating the same food.

Lewis Henry Birch, for example, was an English merchant living in 'Bleak House' in Ramleh, built in 1884, with an office on Place Muhammad Ali. President of the Alexandria Sailing Club, chairman of the Anglo-Egyptian Investment Company, the Anglo-Egyptian Banking Company and the Alexandria Cotton Transport Company, and a member of the municipal council, he employed an Egyptian secretary and a European secretary and 'held the khedivial seal', probably to run the Khedive's private fortune.

His wife was English, his cook Indian, his valet Egyptian: his Sudanese servants wore white turbans, his Egyptian servants red tarbooshes.

His own headgear reveals the variety of lives he led. He possessed bowler hats, straw hats, felt hats, top hats; a grey top hat for the races; a small yamulke for courtesy visits to the rabbi (unthinkable in Europe); and a tarboosh for visits to the palace, meetings of the municipal council and the Council of Rural Affairs, and parties given by the governor of Alexandria. Thus, on official occasions, like Gordon and Kitchener, he paid deference to the all-important outward display of Egyptian identity.[18] In 1907 the Khedive gave him a state funeral in Alexandria.

The Alexandria municipality was another cosmopolitan institution. Aborted by the consuls in 1869, it was finally established in 1890 – when the British-backed administration, after eight years' occupation, felt strong enough to make foreigners pay taxes. It was another first for Alexandria – the first, and for long the only, autonomous municipality in Egypt. It had twenty-eight members: eight appointed by the Egyptian government, six elected by those paying the new municipal tax, three elected by exporters, three by importers, eight by property-owners. Of elected members, no more than three were allowed to be of the same nationality; appointed members were usually Egyptians.[19] Internal municipal documents were always in French, public ones in French and Arabic. From the start it was multinational. In 1892 a civil servant called Joseph Chakour, a Lebanese Maronite born in Alexandria, educated in France and married to a German, was the first director-general of the municipality. Nubar Pasha told him that his post made him less than an Undersecretary of State, but far superior to a prime minister. Members of the council included Sydney Carver, Sir John Antoniadis, Aristide Sinadino, Ambroise Ralli, Baron Jacques de Menasce, Muhammad Bey el-Adl, Ali Bey Hussein. Eight were Egyptians, six Greek, four English; from the start there were complaints that some members did not know Arabic.[20]

Foreigners shuddered at the idea of taxation. Backed by the French consul, the Jesuit college of Saint François Xavier refused to inform the municipality of the number of its pupils, let alone to pay taxes. For the municipality, Keller Pasha protested, 'The city is your fatherland. The prosperity of Alexandria is therefore your prosperity.'[21]

The municipality let non-Egyptians run the city. In 1912 there were protests that there were only 357 Egyptians among the 2,713 general voters. Nevertheless, cosmopolitanism brought efficiency as well as exploitation. Cairo began to demand its own municipality on the model of Alexandria – a privilege it did not obtain until 1949. Since Nasser's presidency, both cities have been run directly, without autonomous institutions, by the Egyptian government.[22]

Alexandria was also a city of cosmopolitan clubs: the president of the Cercle Khédivial, established on the Place Muhammad Ali in 1886, was Baron Jacques de Menasce; the president of the Cercle Muhammad Ali, on the Rue Sherif Pasha, was G. A. Benaki. Members enjoyed deep armchairs, billiards, gambling, and newspapers in every language of the city. The Cercle Khédivial admitted Egyptian princes, ministers, foreign diplomats and British (but not Egyptian) officers 'on permanent basis without ballot or entrance fee'.[23]

Both closed after 1961; but the Sporting Club remains an oasis of playing fields and tennis courts in Alexandria today. It was founded, in 1890, by Coles Pasha of the Alexandria City Police; in contrast to the Gezireh Sporting Club in Cairo, which excluded Egyptians until after 1918, it always had some Egyptian members.[24] Alexandria also had its own Archaeological Society, Desert Exploration Society and sailing, swimming and tennis clubs.

Most clubs were international. The Union Club was founded in 1904 on the initiative of Lord Cromer to provide British officers with an alternative to the Muhammad Ali and Khedivial clubs, where gambling had led to 'regrettable incidents'. Restricted to British nationals, with reciprocal arrangements with British clubs in London, Athens and Khartoum, it had 350 members and dining, billiard, reading and smoking rooms. Closed in 1956, it has been outlasted by the Greek and Syrian clubs, both of which are still among the city's leading meeting places, since both serve alcohol.[25]

There were also separate welfare organizations for every nationality living in the city (and for subdivisions such as Cretans and Cypriots), as well as the 'Victoria House and Nurses' Home established [in 1887] by the British community as a memorial of the jubilee of Her Most Gracious Majesty' – a neo-Tudor exception among the city's many neoclassical, neo-Venetian and neo-Mameluke buildings. It served as a home for the retired English and Scottish governesses of Alexandria, and a place where aspirant governesses could find employers.[26]

In addition to the monarchy, the municipality, clubs and households, business generated another form of cosmopolitanism. By 1900 Alexandria was the third port of the Mediterranean in volume of traffic, after Genoa and Marseille. It was not only the commercial capital of Egypt, but also contained the administrative headquarters of the Egyptian customs, posts, ports and quarantine system, as well as of the hated *tribunaux mixtes*.[27] Continuing its astonishing growth rate, the population rose from 232,636 in 1882 to 444,617 in 1917. Foreigners formed between 20 and 25 per cent of the population – and many Egyptians had foreign blood.[28]

A list of some of the famous individuals born in Alexandria suggests the variety of nationalities inhabiting it. They included the Italian Futurist poet Giuseppe Marinetti (1876), Rudolf Hess (1894), Jean Ross (1912 – a model for Christopher Isherwood's Sally Bowles), Eric Hobsbawm, (1917), Gamal Abdul Nasser (1918), Mohammed Fayed (1929), Omar Sharif (1932) and the singer Georges Moustaki (1934). Companies formed in this period included the Bank of Alexandria, the Alexandria General Produce Association and the Bank of Egypt. In 1905 the French visitor A. B. de Guerville wrote that 'Egypt has entered an era of incredible wealth; it is the golden age ... Alexandria has for brain a bank safe and for heart a wallet, both being stuffed with bank notes.' The 'palpitating heart' of the city was the bourse on the Place Muhammad Ali, with its stark bilingual inscription on the pediment, in French and Arabic: Bourse/Borsa.[29]

Money not only drew people to Alexandria, but ensured the city was swiftly rebuilt. The magnificent cross-shaped Passage Menasce was erected by the Italian architect Antonio Lasciac on the Place Muhammad Ali in 1883–7. The streets in the centre were widened, paved, and equipped with sewers and gutters.[30] In the east of the city the Nouzha Gardens were laid out, like a European municipal garden, in 1902–6.

A corniche began to be constructed in 1907. The tram system spread as outlying areas were laid out with villas, often on land expropriated from poor Egyptians by companies headed by prominent business dynasties such as those of the Bacos, Choremi and Salvago families. The buildings resemble elegant, white neoclassical ocean liners. The Sursock, Salvago and Tawil villas in the quartier grec are outstanding. The superb Villa Cordahi in Rushdi, east of Alexandria, built in 1907 by an Italian architect called Aldo Marelli, has a porch supported by caryatids, robed maidens like those of the Erechtheion in Athens; inside rooms open off a neoclassical atrium.[31]

The most compelling relics of Alexandria's cosmopolitan century, however, are the tombs of the notables in the Greek, Greek Catholic, Coptic, Latin and Jewish cemeteries, side by side in an immense rectangle in the district of Chatby. The mausoleums of the Sitivandi, Aghion, Zervudachi and Cordahi families are extravagant assertions of wealth and grief. Statues of angels and goddesses and busts of the deceased stand between obelisks, pyramids, classical columns or Mameluke domes.[32] Like similar cemeteries in Istanbul, they are challenges in stone to today's Muslim city, reminders that a large part of the city's population was once

Christian or Jewish. Inscriptions are in Latin, Italian, French or Hebrew, rarely Arabic.

The smartest street in Alexandria was Rue Sherif Pasha (now Salah Salem), which runs south-east from Place Muhammad Ali. Lined with palatial three- or four-storey Italianate buildings, it was often packed with carriages (and later with the most recent models of luxury cars). It acquired what Ronald Storrs called 'something of the brilliant narrowness of Bond Street'. Storrs was an English official in Egypt who considered himself 'a natural Levantine', and increased his salary by writing opera reviews for an Alexandrian newspaper.[33]

The raised terrace of the Cercle Muhammad Ali at one end, shielded from the street by a classical colonnade and balustrade, was a much-feared centre of gossip, known as 'the belvedere of snobbery'.[34] Rue Sherif Pasha also contained the palatial edifices of the Banca di Roma and the National Bank of Egypt, as well as La Maison Baudrot, a famous café opposite the Cercle Muhammad Ali. Calling itself 'the establishment of the elite', it had been started in 1884 by Giacomo Groppi, the man who introduced crème Chantilly to Egypt. He sold it in 1906 to a Frenchman called Auguste Baudrot, and moved to Cairo, where he established the legendary Café Groppi. Baudrot held concerts and had special rooms for bridge-players.[35] Next door was a bookshop called Cité du Livre, owned by a Greek Jew from Salonica, Nessim Moustaki, father of the singer Georges Moustaki. It was so packed with books, and signed photographs of famous writers, that it was difficult to move. In the basement was a small bedroom from which Moustaki sometimes emerged, shining-eyed, with a female customer.[36]

Further down Rue Sherif Pasha were the city's best jewellers, Horowitz, and most elegant shops: Old England; Maison Française; Hannaux, 'where one could find anything one's heart desired'; and Whitehead & Morris, the firm of stationers and printers which in 1922 would publish the first edition of E. M. Forster's *Alexandria: A History and a Guide*.[37]

Alexandria's wealth and cosmopolitan atmosphere encouraged innovation. It was not just a business city. Money was also invested in culture. The Baron de Menasce not only founded a synagogue, a Jewish school and the Khedivial club, but also gave a building to house the Alexandria municipal library.[38] In 1892 a museum was founded with the help of the Ralli and Menasce families; in accordance with Alexandria's self-image, its antiquities were Greco-Roman, rather than Islamic or pharaonic.[39] The same year Egypt's first feminist paper, *Al-Fatat*, started in Alexandria. In January 1897 the first cinema in Egypt was opened there by the Frères Lumière – the same year that Egypt's first brewery, the Crown, was established in Alexandria. The first film shot in Egypt was a short documentary called *Place des consuls à Alexandrie*.[40]

The excellence of its schools also distinguished Alexandria, as it did Smyrna and Beirut. In 1897, twenty-two years after establishing a university in Beirut, Jesuits founded a school in Alexandria. Although staffed by Catholics, it attracted Jews, Muslims and Orthodox pupils, including Zoghebs, Sursocks, Menasces and Rolos. Catholics contributed less than half the pupils. The tolerance of Alexandria is shown by the fact that Jesuits could not force non-Christian pupils there to attend church services, as they did elsewhere: 'Alexandria is not Beirut,' wrote one official.[41]

In 1901, with the help of the municipality, a Universita Populare di Alessandria was founded, at the same time as a new journal, *Le Lotus*. The initiative for the university came from Alexandra de Avierino, whose family ran Alex. G. Avierino Frères, Grands Magasins d'Habillement. She wanted 'to awaken Egyptians to the demands of modern times'. Courses were open to all, without distinction of sex, race or religion, and were in every language, including Arabic. There were evening lectures: for example, 'Etudes sur l'ancienne Alexandrie' by Alexandre Max de Zogheb, delivered there on 3 December 1902.[42] Other famous schools in Alexandria included Notre Dame de Sion, established by Catholic nuns in 1880. Alexandria also had schools run by, and for, Germans, Greeks, Italians, Jews, Scots and American Protestants. Their imposing buildings still form a ring of cultural power statements around the city.

The most famous school in Alexandria – the only British institution remembered there with affection – was Victoria College. The idea came from Sir Charles Cookson, the British consul-general wounded in 1882. In keeping with the city's commercial ethic, he made the school into a dividend-paying limited company, in order to attract financial backers. The foundation stone was laid by Lord Cromer himself on 24 May 1906, on a site in Siouf, an oasis east of Ramleh, surrounded by desert and palm trees, in the presence of the foreign consuls, 'members of the European and native communities', and Christian and Jewish – but not Muslim – dignitaries. The school was opened by the Duke of Connaught in 1909.[43]

Victoria College gave a conventional British education – classics, Shakespeare, games and speech days. Often called 'the Eton of the Middle East', it began to attract Egyptians, and non-Egyptian Arabs. Like many Alexandrian institutions, it was both communal and cosmopolitan. In this British school, French was widely used; the school motto came from an Alexandrian Latin poet called Claudian: 'Cuncti gens una sumus' – 'Joined

we are one people.' In 1930 its magazine proclaimed the school's cosmopolitan ethos: that, despite the variety of nationalities and religions among
its pupils, it contained 'no germs of national or religious animosity'.[44]

In theory it was a secular school. Religious instruction, in Islam,
Judaism or Christianity, was given only if parents requested it. Like other
Levantine schools, Victoria College was not simply a vehicle of cultural
imperialism: it was also a window on the outside world, which could
help individuals to open their minds, and find the means with which to
challenge imperialism. Early pupils included both supporters and opponents of the British presence in Egypt and the Middle East: Rallis, Rolos
and Barkers; but also the sons of Mahmoud Sami al-Barudi, prime minister of Arabi Pasha in 1882; George Antonius, Syrian author of *The Arab
Awakening* (1938), the first account in English of Arab nationalism from
an Arab point of view, and an eloquent defence of Palestinians' right
to their own country; Youssef Chahine, the famous director of, among
many other films, *Alexandria . . . Why?* (1978) and *Alexandria Again and
Again* (1989); and Mohammed Farghaly, from a great Alexandrian trading family.[45] Known as 'the cotton king', Farghaly would be the youngest
man and the first Egyptian to preside over the Cotton Exchange, and
a member of the municipal council. Famous for his Rolls-Royce and the
carnation he always wore in the buttonhole of his white suit, he would
live in the ultra-modern Villa Farghaly Pasha, where his cocktail parties
gathered 'all the official world, all of high finance and "le tout Alexandrie
mondain".[46]

Victoria College was for members of the elite who could afford it.
British officials had done nothing for Egyptian popular education:
Egyptian ministers were obstructed by the inspector of education, Mr
Dunlop, former headmaster of the Alexandrian Scottish school, a bully
accused of retarding Egyptian education for a generation.[47]

Despite its cosmopolitan institutions and habits, Alexandria also remained
community-centred. Different individuals and groups reflected these two
tendencies according to the combination, at any given time, of politics,
economics and personalities: any interaction was possible. Any general-
ization can be contradicted. There were different types of cosmopolitanism and nationalism – institutional, professional, or class-based – and they
changed from generation to generation and individual to individual.

Some rituals in Alexandria emphasized demarcations between communities. Every day, the muezzins' call to prayer replied to church bells'
summons to services. Every year before Passover the number of police on

duty in Jewish areas was doubled – to prevent anti-Jewish riots like those of 1881. Special covered carriages for women were added to trams during Muslim festivals.[48]

In the most cosmopolitan city of the age, Paris, foreign residents – for example, the parents of President Sarkozy or of former Prime Minister Balladur – became French after one or two generations. In Alexandria, however, in a crisis nationality could fall like a sword, dividing groups from each other as it had in 1882. The museum director E. Breccia claimed only that Alexandria could weaken chauvinism and religious fanaticism, not that it made them disappear.[49] In 1906, an English banker called Mr Rowlatt at once saw a dispute about the governor of the National Bank of Egypt in racial terms. In a private letter, he wrote, 'The Jews never really showed but probably behind his back were more violent than the Greeks … Both Jews and Greeks have been biding their opportunity to speak up.'[50]

The Greek community in particular reveals Alexandria's combinations of nationalism and cosmopolitanism. The defeat of Egyptian nationalism in 1882 led to an influx of Greeks. They were not colonialists, but they were imperialists through their links to the British Empire. Relatively small in numbers – at most 30,000 in a city over ten times that size – the Greeks considered themselves the richest and most successful community in the city, with nine primary and two secondary schools, two hospitals, two orphanages, a sports club, and after 1902 their own chamber of commerce. There were at least twenty-four different Greek organizations in Alexandria, such as the Corporation of Greek Grocers of Alexandria and its Suburbs, the Hellenic Nautical Circle and the Ptolemy Hellenic Scientific Syllogos.[51]

Greeks' houses in Alexandria were famous for silver, porcelain, Persian carpets, French pictures, and a 'flower-garden of lovely girls'. Sometimes a Greek house was so immaculate that a maddened husband would spill tomato sauce on the marble floor.[52] The Benakis were one of the richest Alexandria Greek families. Born on the island of Syros, from a family which had fled the massacre of Chios in 1822, Emmanuel Benaki had come to Alexandria in 1863 after several years working in Liverpool. Soon Choremis, Benakis & Company was the greatest cotton exporter in Egypt, with offices throughout the country and a head office in Alexandria, mainly staffed by Greeks.[53]

Emmanuel Benaki – 'the king of the bourse' – was also administrator-general of the Bank of Alexandria, founded with other Greeks (Choremis,

Salvagos and Zervudakis) in 1872.[54] In 1884 the Benaki family could afford to move out of a flat in the Rue Sherif Pasha to a luxurious villa on the Rue Rosette. Their wealth, in their opinion, enabled them to live like *grands seigneurs*, to be generous to Greek charities, to ensure that Greek schools and hospitals were the best in the city. They considered themselves an aristocracy.[55]

Indeed, families like the Zoghebs and Benakis – and the Muhammad Ali dynasty itself – show that wealth, privilege and ambition are enough to form an aristocracy. Antiquity is inessential. A rhyme in Alexandria went:

> Chio, famous for its raki,
> Is even more so for its great men.
> Who sent us Benaki?
> Chio famous for its raki.[56]

The Benakis gave *bals masqués*, commemorated in elaborate photograph albums. The house would be smothered in roses and jonquils; guests dressed as courtiers of Louis XIV. At one ball in 1886, where 'all the most select society of Alexandria' was present, Panteli Salvago left his diamond-studded black velvet hat under a bed, 'so great was Alexandria Greeks' indifference to their wealth and prodigality'. (His hostess sent it back the next day.)[57] During carnival, Alexandrians would pack balconies to throw flowers and confetti on to elaborate floats and orchestras processing in the annual 'corso' round the Place Muhammad Ali, down the Rue Sherif, Pasha, into the Rue Rosette.[58]

In the Benaki household, the servants were Greek, Egyptian or Italian. The governess and many household objects – furniture, silver, glass, linen, Pears' soap, needles – came from England. 'We grew up with respect for any English product,' remembered Emmanuel's daughter Penelope, born in 1874 – later, as Penelope Delta, a famous Greek children's writer. Out of office hours the men rode, shot and played polo; the women played cards and made and received visits – especially on Sunday – and did charity work. Living in Alexandria, they knew French and English at least as well as Greek, and considered themselves more modern than mainland Greeks.

During the Arabi revolution of 1882, however, the Benakis had taken refuge on a Greek boat and visited Greece. Penelope Delta remembered those days as the happiest of her life – perhaps for the freedom from family control, as well as the excitement of nationalism. Her family became Greek nationalists as well as cosmopolitan Alexandrians. In addition to their villa in Alexandria, they bought another outside Athens.[59]

From Madrid to Moscow, nationalism was becoming a religion, followed more fervently, in many cases, than Christianity or Islam. Reflecting the spirit of the age, and Hellenic traditions, Penelope Delta wrote that her family considered 'anything Greek holy and sacred ... The adjective Greek was for us something superior, extraordinary, luminous, adorable.' Their business she described, not in financial but in national terms, as 'the power and glory of Hellenism'.

Egypt was still in theory part of the Ottoman Empire; but Benaki sons volunteered to fight for Greece in the wars of 1897 and 1912 against the Empire (as did many other Alexandria Greeks – their names are inscribed on memorial tablets in the courtyard of the city's Orthodox patriarchate). The Benakis despised most other Alexandrians. Syrians were 'Levantines'. Jews, wrote Penelope Delta in her memoirs, were considered to have the Devil inside them. As for poor Egyptians – 'we had the greatest contempt for the fellahs and regarded them almost as cattle. Not only was it permitted to hit an Arab; it was almost required. I remember my father striking a gardener, Giouma, because he had been rude and after he had been hit he kissed my father's hand and jacket. They were animals.'

Everyone did it, including Egyptians. One of her cousins saw Hopkinson Pasha, the handsome and courteous commandant of the Alexandria City Police in 1902–17, director of the Alexandria municipality in 1917–23, hitting a fellah in the face with his horsewhip at a tram station: 'these kinds of scenes and others like them took place every day.'[60] Like the Greeks of Ptolemaic Alexandria, who, for the first hundred years, allowed only selected Egyptians entry into their city, the Benakis knew little of Egypt except how to exploit or – depending on the point of view – develop its economy. Emmanuel Benaki often toured villages in the Delta, inspecting the cotton crop.[61] Egyptians hardly appear in Penelope Delta's memoirs or novels, except as objects of pity or disdain.[62]

Chairman of the Cercle Muhammad Ali, head of the Greek community in 1901–11, Emmanuel Benaki nevertheless left his city in 1911. He became the Greek minister of finance, then mayor of Athens, where he built another lavish villa opposite the royal palace. Generous as well as patriotic, he helped finance, among many Greek institutions, an orphanage, a hospital and schools. He had been persuaded by his friend the charismatic Greek politician Emmanuel Venizelos to help make a dynamic, modern Greece.[63] Penelope Delta considered Alexandrians 'dolls', and came to dislike the city where her family had stopped her divorcing for fear of scandal. The man she loved – the Greek vice-consul Jon Dragoumis – also hated Alexandria: 'I have never suffered so much as here; Christ did not suffer more in Jerusalem,' he wrote. In Athens, where she moved in 1916, she found fame and independence as the first Greek children's writer. Her novels have titles like those of her near-contemporary G. A. Henty: *For the Fatherland* (1909), *In the Days of the Bulgar-Slayer* (1911).[64]

The magnificent collections of Iznik plates, Ottoman carpets and textiles, Coptic and Greek portraits, and works of art from the Ottoman Empire with which her brother Anthony Benaki decorated some of the rooms of his house on the Rue Rosette showed a taste for Islamic art unusual at the time, especially among Greeks brought up on tales of the massacre of Chios and the Greek War of Independence. However, the collection left Alexandria, with Anthony Benaki, in 1927. The museum which he founded in 1930 is not in Alexandria, where the fortune which paid for it was made, but in the Benaki mansion in Athens.[65]

The greatest poet of modern Alexandria, Constantine Cavafy, like his friends the Benakis, combined nationalism and cosmopolitanism. Constantine's half-Phanariot family came from Constantinople, where his great-grandfather had been a secretary to the patriarchate; the family name Kavafy, like many Greek and Arab family names, is of Turkish origin, from *ayakkabici*, the Turkish for shoe-seller. While they had relations in Vienna, Venice and Trieste, the Cavafys' wealth was based on Britain and cotton. Cavafy's father's company, P. I. Cavafy & Co., had offices in Alexandria, Constantinople, London and Liverpool. Constantine was born on 29 April 1863, in the family apartment in the Okelle Zizinia near Rue Sherif Pasha. The Cavafy family flourished financially and socially, but the death of Peter-John, the poet's father, in 1870 forced the surviving members of the family to move to England in 1872. In 1876, due to the incompetence of the poet's elder brothers, the family business was dissolved; in 1877 Madame Cavafy and her younger children returned to Alexandria. Nevertheless, English remained one of the family languages. They wrote letters to each other in English as well as Greek. Constantine is said to have spoken Greek with a slight English accent – though his brothers also complained of the 'most intense stupidity and ignorance' of some British in Egypt.[66]

After 1885 Constantine started to publish poems and articles in Greek, and in 1892 he was hired as a clerk in the Third Circle of Irrigation at the Ministry of Public Works of Egypt. He had failed to secure British naturalization, and his Greek citizenship excluded him from any permanent position. Cavafy managed to hold this temporary position (renewed annually) for thirty years. In addition he worked at the Alexandria bourses from 1894 to 1902. He also gambled. These sources of income, along with some shrewd investments, enabled him to live in comfort for the rest of his life.

Alexandria was Cavafy's home. After 1885 he travelled abroad only six times: once to Paris and London in 1897, five times to Athens. In 1908, after his mother's death and the departure of his brothers, he began to live alone in a flat in the Rue Lepsius, near the Rue Sherif Pasha, at the age of forty-five. Soon he limited his social life and devoted himself to poetry.

Cavafy remained in Alexandria even though he found it dull and backward. In a note dated 28 April 1907, he confessed, 'I am used to Alexandria now, and odds are I'd stay here even if I were rich ... (still I'm not absolutely certain I'd stay here) because it's like a homeland, it connects me to my life's memories. But oh! how a person like me, someone so different, needs a big city! London, for example ...'[67] Cavafy may have realized that in other cities his life might resemble his life in Alexandria. For him cities were made by individuals, as well as by economic, military and political forces. In 'The City' he wrote:

> You said: 'I'll go to another country, go to another shore,
> find another city better than this one.
> Whatever I try to do is fated to turn out wrong
> and my heart lies buried as though it were something dead.
> How long can I let my mind moulder in this place?
> Wherever I turn, wherever I happen to look,
> I see the black ruins of my life, here,
> where I've spent so many years, wasted them, destroyed them totally.'
>
> You won't find a new country, won't find another shore.
> This city will always pursue you. You will walk
> the same streets, grow old in the same neighborhoods,
> will turn gray in these same houses.
> You will always end up in this city. Don't hope for things elsewhere:
> there is no ship for you, there is no road.
> As you've wasted your life here, in this small corner,
> you've destroyed it everywhere else in the world.

Cavafy's poems are about Greek kings and heroes, Greek cities and ports, and what he called 'the splendour of our Byzantine heritage': Ulysses, the later Ptolemies, the Byzantine emperor Manuel Komnenos and others. Neither pharaohs nor Islam nor the Muhammad Ali dynasty interested him: of the first he said, 'I don't understand these big immobile things.'

Cavafy always wore the straw hat of the Greeks, not the tarboosh of the Egyptians.[68]

Yet Cavafy's poems are not exclusively Greek. His are cities on the edge of Asia or Africa. Their inhabitants are Greek in manners and language, but Egyptian or Asian at heart: Beirut, Smyrna, Antioch with its 'notorious life', Alexandria with its 'unsurpassable sensuality'.[69] About Greece itself – 'the tight-lipped little kingdom overseas' – according to his friend E. M. Forster, 'he could be very caustic.'[70] Unlike poets in Athens, in Alexandria he developed a Greek of his own, a mixture of demotic and puristic, with his own spelling and punctuation.[71] He is a Levantine. His poems are pervaded by a sense of vulnerability. Hostile armies are about to break through; Mark Antony ponders his defeat, before killing himself. The jewels in the Byzantine emperor's crown have been replaced by coloured glass. 'Can we really consider ourselves safe in Amisos?' he asks: 'The town isn't very well fortified, and the Romans are the most awful enemies.' His cities' brilliance is heightened by their proximity to peoples their inhabitants regarded as barbarians. In 'Waiting for the Barbarians' he writes:

> And now what will become of us without Barbarians?
> Those people were some sort of a solution.[72]

Cavafy wrote at the high noon of British power in Egypt, between the 1890s and 1920s. Yet Cavafy's cities were under threat. Riots took place between Greeks and Italians, and Greeks and Egyptians, in 1899 and 1904. Some streets, on certain occasions, resounded to cries of 'Death to Christians!' or 'Death to Jews!'[73] In 1907 a protégé of the Khedive and the Sultan, Mustafa Kamil Pasha, founded the Egyptian National Party in Alexandria; at mass meetings, he made speeches calling for the end of British occupation and 'Egypt for the Egyptians!'[74] In 1908 the Young Turk revolution galvanized Muslims throughout the Ottoman Empire.

Cavafy was conscious that, as he wrote in 'The God abandons Anthony', he might have to 'say farewell to her, the Alexandria that is leaving'. Indeed, like the Benaki collections, the Cavafy Archive – his manuscripts, papers and photographs – said 'farewell' to Alexandria after his death in 1933, when it was moved by his heirs to Athens.

Cavafy also wrote about another form of life on the edge. In another first for Alexandria, he was the most daring homosexual poet of the early twentieth century – the first to describe the furtiveness of homosexual life in those days. Here again, as in his concentration on Greek history and literature, he reflects the chasm between Europeans and Egyptians in

Alexandria. Homosexuality was not, then, regarded in the Levant with the outrage current in Europe. In 1806, reporting the pursuit into the French consulate of a young Frenchman by a Turkish admirer, the French consul in Smyrna complained of 'infamous turpitudes unfortunately so common among orientals'.[75] Charles Napier had witnessed 'the most open and shameless manner' in which Ibrahim Pasha 'followed his inclinations'.[76] When the Dutch consul Mr Ruyssenaers had complained to Said Pasha of the prevalence of homosexuality in Egypt, the Pasha is said to have replied that, before complaining, the consul should try it himself – in every position.[77] In the Ottoman Empire in general – in part because of the near-impossibility of love affairs with Muslim women – poets, including the Egyptian chronicler al-Jabarti, had celebrated the beauty of 'moon-faced' young men, with 'glances like daggers'.[78]

Cavafy, however, had little knowledge of Arabic or Turkish, and, as far as is known, kept his lovers, like his poems, European. He may have known little of relaxed Egyptian attitudes to what he calls, with affected reprobation, 'the most audacious erotic desires, the lascivious impulses of my blood', his 'stringently forbidden amorous inclination'.[79] He enjoyed no equivalent of the handsome ticket-collector Muhammad el-Adl, whom Cavafy's friend and admirer E. M. Forster – working in Alexandria for the Red Cross in 1916–20 – met on the tram to Ramleh. Muhammad helped inspire Forster to write *Alexandria: A History and a Guide* – although Forster too, like Cavafy, sometimes wrote that he was wearied 'beyond expression' by the city, 'so colourless and banal'. The foreigner crossed racial frontiers; the Alexandrian did not.[80]

Hired rooms, closed cabs and secret embraces in shops give bite to Cavafy's poems. His tone is haunting:

> The room was cheap and sordid,
> hidden above the suspect taverna.
>
> .   .   .   .
>
> ... From below
> came the voices of workmen
> playing cards ...
>
> And there on that common, humble bed
> I had love's body, had those intoxicating lips,
> red and sensual,
> red lips of such intoxication
> that now as I write, after so many years,
> in my lonely house, I'am drunk with passion again.[81]

143

Poems on 'The beauty of unnatural attractions' and 'cheap debauch-ery' were (after 1919, and particularly after the death of his last sur-viving brother in 1921) published in Alexandria, by a civil servant, in literary magazines like *Nea Zoe* or *Grammata*, or privately printed in separate sheets which he would then send to friends and critics. The first complete edition was published as a book in Alexandria in 1935, two years after the poet's death in the Greek hospital.[82]

Ruthless and materialistic in some ways, Alexandria could be tolerant and progressive in others. In all other cities except Paris, Cavafy's poems would have provoked horror or imprisonment. There was no English or German Cavafy. E. M. Forster stopped publishing novels as he felt unable in London, the largest city in the world – the city which Cavafy had dreamt of inhabiting – to write about homosexual love. Alexandria was not only a city of khedives and consuls. It was also a city ahead of its time.

Cavafy wrote about men. At the time, Alexandria was better known for women. For example, Coles Pasha, of the City Police, wrote in his memoirs that Alexandria contained 'some of the prettiest and best dressed women in the world ... A Greek woman in a costume straight from Paris is certainly very hard to beat as regards looks!'[83] Some were so beautiful that men would hire chairs outside churches in order to watch them leaving Sunday mass.[84] Looking at people was indeed, as Cavafy's poems confirm, one of Alexandrians' favourite occupations. An Australian soldier called Hector Dinning wrote that in Alexandria, without pyramids or caliphs' tombs, there was no distraction from 'the occupation of first importance, looking upon the living'.[85]

Alexandrian women had a reputation for being easy-going. For that reason some mainland Greeks hesitated to marry a Greek woman from Alexandria or Smyrna. Alfred Butler, the English tutor of the Khedive's sons, claimed that women 'have no reverence for tender years and even before little boys and girls they talk and joke about such things as no lady in England would even know'.[86]

Nevertheless, it was not easy to conduct love affairs with women. Some men turned to domestic staff or brothels. One lady made her maids sleep under her bed – considering it the only place safe from her predatory relations. Alexandria had its own 'bureau des filles publiques' which tried to limit the spread of sexual diseases. Egyptian women were more likely to be infected, as they started 'working' younger. European women, having already experi-enced 'all sorts of infections', according to the bureau, 'present a certain degree of resistance'.[87] Despite many government orders to suppress the slave trade since 1854, a few slave dealers also operated from private houses in Alexandria, keeping stocks of fifteen to twenty slaves at a time, some of whom were sold to brothels.[88] The Société Pour la Suppression de la Traite des Blanches, founded in Alexandria in 1905, tried to stop the trade in European women. It repatriated many, and saved 2,253 children from brothels.[89]

Off the Rue des Sœurs were winding side streets with hotels where rooms could be hired by the hour. 'Women of all ages waited for clients,' remembered Gaston Zananiri: 'in front of some of these rooms were men, young or old, sometimes handsome, often ugly, men, always men.' In nearby *cafés chantants*, taverns and gambling dens, as much as in the city's wealthy households, 'all races mingled'.[90]

Races could mingle because they had the first prerequisite for cosmopolitanism: a common language. Whatever their origins, most Alexandrians knew at least some words of Arabic. In addition, the city had an international language in which the different communities could speak to each other. Until the 1860s it was Italian or lingua franca. In the words of Murray's *Handbook*, 'Next to the local language Italian will be found most useful throughout the Levant.'[91] Until the mid twentieth century, Alexandrian Arabic contained many Italian words, such as *bosta* ('post'), *gambari* ('shrimps'), *torta* ('cakes'), *roba vecchia* ('old clothes'): local ears found Italian sound combinations more appealing than Greek or French ones.[92] Hence one Alexandria hostess's remark, offering a visiting English peer a piece of cake, 'Lordy! Lordy! Do have some torta!'

After the 1860s, however, French replaced Italian. From Mexico to Persia, it had the attraction of being the language not only of diplomacy, culture, science and modernity, but also of a great power. From the 1830s it had been one of the languages of the Ottoman Ministry of Foreign Affairs. French was spread throughout the Levant by French schools and priests, and by the lack of an alternative international language. The area experienced what one contemporary called 'galloping gallomania'.[93]

By 1912 the enormous total of 108,112 pupils were receiving an education in French establishments in the Ottoman Empire.[94] Of 28,000 children being educated in Alexandria, about 12,000 went to government schools, 9,000 to other foreign schools, and 7,000 to French-language schools; French was also taught in almost all government and foreign schools. All foreign schools also, by 1912, taught the dominant local language, Turkish, Armenian or Arabic.[95]

In Lebanon the French language became so common that some Lebanese spoke it better than Arabic. In 1907 the French consul-general in Beirut boasted that 'soon the conquest of Syria by our language will be accomplished and irrevocable.'[96] In Constantinople by 1913 French was described as 'universal'. 'It was all French! Everyone spoke French!' remembered one centenarian English inhabitant of the city at this time. French was so universal that the Turkish language, hitherto receptive to Arabic and Persian, was flooded with French words: *randevu* ('rendez-vous'), *kriz* ('crisis'), *metres* ('mistress') and many others. By 1970 a total of 5,600 French words had entered the Turkish language.[97] French became as characteristic of the Levant as foreign schools, or the sea.

Further linking Alexandria to the outside world, after 1860 French became the official language of communication for the city's different foreign communities, both between themselves and with the Egyptian government. Ismail Pasha wrote in French to his representative in Constantinople, an Armenian called Abraham. In conversation, in his 'curious slipshod French', every sentence ended 'comme ci, comme ça, etcetera'. For example, when a lady's breasts fell out of her corsage after a very low curtsy at a court ball, he said, 'Mais, madame, il ne faut pas perdre ces belles choses-là, comme ci, comme ça, etcetera.'[98] Street signs and official documents in Alexandria were in Arabic and French; shop signs were often in French alone. Most customers and shop assistants understood it.[99] Vendeuses in Orosdi Back, the chain of department stores established by Hungarian refugees after the failed Hungarian revolution of 1848–9, with branches in Alexandria, Beirut and Smyrna, often spoke Arabic, Italian, English or Greek, 'and always French'.[100]

Even more than in France itself, where the regime had many enemies, the Third Republic was revered in the Levant by progressive Greeks, Turks, Arabs and Jews alike. 'France the educator, civilized France, France the friend of the Orient, France which has broken the chains of slavery of all oppressed peoples' was regarded as a synonym for freedom and progress. The sufferings of Algeria and Tunisia under French colonial rule were ignored. A French education was considered a sign of modernity and, for some, a way of distancing themselves from Arabic and joining what they considered a superior culture.[101]

Paris became, after Constantinople, the second capital of the Levant, and the favourite residence for its political refugees. 'We loved Paris just as one is in love with a person, body and soul,' wrote the Turkish novelist Abdulhak Sinasi Hisar. Yahya Kemal, an influential Young Turk revolutionary who lived there in 1903–12, also remembered, 'In my dreams Paris especially shone like a star brighter than any dreams.' Some compared

Paris, enlightened and sublime, to Mecca itself.[102] Britain ruled the waves; France ruled hearts and minds.

French might be used, as their consuls often complained, by Greeks and Italians even when writing to their fellow nationals. In reaction the Dante Alighieri Society was founded in 1898 by the Italian government to 'Italianize our colonies bastardized by French feelings and the French language'. In the twentieth century many Egyptians and Lebanese would choose to write in French rather than, or as well as, in Arabic: Albert Cossery, Andrée Chedid, Amin Maalouf.[103]

In 1911 Lord Kitchener arrived by battleship in Alexandria, the city he had helped to occupy in 1882, to take up a new position as British consul-general in Egypt. An embodiment of the British Empire at its zenith, contrary to regulations he wore his red field marshal's uniform, rather than blue-and-gold diplomatic uniform. However, when presenting his credentials to Khedive Abbas Hilmi at Ras el-Tin, he spoke French.[104] If he had used English, he would not have been understood.

9

Beirut: The Jewel in the Crown of the Padishah

Arise O Arabs and awake! You are up to your knees in mud.
Ibrahim al-Yazjii, Beirut, 1878

IN ALEXANDRIA, BRITAIN was the occupying predator/saviour. In Beirut France hoped to assume that role, with the active encouragement of much of the Christian population. Both cities reflected the struggle between local powers and foreign empires for the future of the Levant.

In the last third of the nineteenth century French political and financial support for the Maronite 'nation' increased. While still owing allegiance to the Ottoman Empire, Lebanon had entered a French sphere of influence. An Ottoman governor called Hamdi Pasha wrote of French desire to acquire 'the whole of Syria as a cardinal principle of their policy in the region. The fulfillment of this objective depends upon the power and influence of the Maronite clergy, who nourish desires for independence and feel strongly attached to the French.' Soon Paris had prepared a plan of conquest for what a French consul called 'an essentially French country'. 'A little bloodshed and it is all over,' wrote another French official.[1]

By its magnetism, Beirut became the unofficial capital of the new mini-state of Mount Lebanon. Lebanese wintered in Beirut; Beirutis summered in the mountains. The capital of Mount Lebanon was moved from Beiteddine in the mountains to Baabda, six miles from Beirut, where the president of Lebanon now lives; the governor also built a residence in the city itself. Calling Beirut 'the key to Lebanon', he wanted to annex it to Mount Lebanon. Mount Lebanon began to acquire institutions such as the administrative council made up of four Maronites, three Druze, two Orthodox, one Greek Catholic, one Shia and one Sunni, as well as a system of elections still in use in Lebanon today: for example, voters still have to return to their village of origin.[2] Taxes were low; the Ottoman Empire, despite its deplorable finances, subsidized the mountain, rather than the other way round. Consuls continued to behave like potentates, with 'pretensions which the ambassadors in Constantinople never had'. Otherwise the situation remained relatively peaceful.[3]

Despite the years of peace, however, the 1860 massacres were not forgotten. They heightened Christians' fears throughout the Levant, and caused a mass migration of Syrian and Lebanese Christians to Egypt. When policemen tried to arrest a murderer in Pera, Christians convinced themselves a massacre had started and fled in panic. There were similar panics in Smyrna.[4]

After 1860, peace spurred economic and cultural development in Beirut. In 1863 a good road over the seventy miles between Beirut and Damascus was finished by the Comte de Perthuis's company. Soon there were daily stage coaches between the cities.

Beirut became a great publishing capital. The first press had been established in Beirut in 1751, by Orthodox priests.[5] In 1834 the second Arabic press in Beirut was brought by American missionaries from Malta – the same year in which they took Greek and Armenian presses from Malta to Smyrna. At first the press too printed mainly the Bible and Christian texts, but it was soon being used to publish material for government offices and local merchants.[6] In 1857 two Christian Beirutis established their own press, which also began to print the first non-offical Arab newspaper in Beirut, *Al-Haqiqa* or 'The Truth'. At this stage more newspapers and periodicals were published in Beirut than in any other Arab city.[7] The city was being launched on its career as the intellectual capital of the Arab world. By the end of the century, Lebanon had over twenty presses – three-quarters of them in Beirut – which had published several thousand books in Arabic.[8]

Beirut also became the educational as well as the printing capital of the Arab world. In 1823 the first American missionary school had opened: its main opponents were not Muslims but local Catholics.[9] In 1835 one of the first girls' schools in the Ottoman Empire was established by Americans in Beirut.[10] In 1866 the Syrian Protestant College was established by American missionaries led by the Rev. Daniel Bliss, in the terraced campus which is one of the last green oases in Beirut today. Like many schools founded in the region, it not only acted as a vehicle for a form of cultural imperialism – the curriculum was essentially American, and at first Muslim students were obliged to attend Christian prayers and eat non-halal food – but also provided students with the weapons with which to challenge that imperialism. It became a cradle of Syrian nationalism.[11] In 1882 students protested when a professor who had discussed Darwin's theory of the origin of species was dismissed.[12]

A new municipal council, based on the municipality set up in Pera in 1857, was established in 1868, with equal numbers of Muslim and Christian members – twenty-two years before Alexandria obtained its municipality. Its first head was Nami Bey, son of the officer who had governed the city for Ibrahim Pasha in the 1830s and had remained in Beirut.[13]

Beirut continued to attract more schools and colleges. In 1875, partly because of rivalry with the Protestant missionaries, Jesuits founded a school in Beirut, ancestor of the Université Saint-Joseph today. With medical and theological colleges, a printing press, a faculty of oriental studies, and a newspaper, it seemed 'perhaps the most lively and active place in the city' to the French writer Louis Bertrand. It published both French and Arabic books and the review *Al-Mashriq*.[14] Other foreign schools – for girls as well as boys – were started, such as the German School of Deaconesses (1862); the American School for Girls (1866); the Collège Notre Dame de Nazareth (1869); and an Orthodox school, financed by Russia. An Ottoman college patronized by Muslims from all corners of the Empire was founded in 1895, a French law college in 1913.[15] Thus Beirut's role as an arena of rivalry between religions worked to its advantage; it helped make Beirut the university city of the Levant and the centre of 'the Arab renaissance'.[16] Many Muslims attended Christian schools, since they were considered the best. Few Christians attended Muslim schools.

Between 1860 and 1890 – later than in Alexandria – rich Beirutis adopted the outward signs of a European way of life. The first European tailor opened a shop in 1878: tailcoats soon replaced kaftans.[17] Tables, chairs, mirrors, knives and forks, and European food and wine were advertised in local newspapers. Separate bedrooms and dining rooms were created, often opening off a large central hall. In contrast to traditional courtyard houses with plain outer walls, after 1840 Beirut houses, built by local craftsmen, were generally square. The main decorative feature was pointed triple arches in the centre of a wall, supported by narrow columns and enclosing ogival windows, often looking out to the sea. The rich could afford glass windows, marble floors and roofs of red tiles, first imported from Marseille, then made locally.[18]

Beirutis believed their city was destined for a great future. They were aware, as one newspaper article put it, of the 'honey in this bee hive'. They had been furious at its demotion in 1862 from acting capital of a province to subordination to Damascus. Rivalries between cities could be as influential as rivalries betwen states or religions. Then as now, the two cities had different interests. Damascus lived from agriculture and the pilgrimage to Mecca, Beirut from trade and education.[19]

In 1888, partly as a result of Beirutis' repeated protests and petitions, Beirut became capital of a province again, directly answerable to

The French consul, accompanied by merchants of his nation, is presenting the kadi (chief Muslim judge) of Smyrna with a copy of the capitulations, governing conditions of French nationals' residence in the Ottoman Empire, and regularly renewed at vast expense, c.1690. Until the 1920s, life in Levantine cities was marked by the capitulations and by frequent meetings between foreign consuls and local authorities.

The number of ships in the harbour at Smyrna, c.1880, is a sign of the trade boom in the city after the completion of the quay in 1876. In the foreground is the main Ottoman barracks. When it was demolished in 1960, rats infested the city for weeks.

The van Lennep family of Smyrna, *c*.1765. Far left, Justin Leidstar, father of Anna Maria van Lennep, sitting centre holding her latest child, next to her husband, David van Lennep, who after moving to Symrna in 1731 had become one of its richest shipowners. Some of the family wear Ottoman dress, others European. The van Lenneps remained merchants and consuls in Smyrna until their departure for the United States after the 1922 fire. Elizabeth Clara, standing on the right, later married an English Smyrna merchant, Isaac Morier, and was mother of James Morier, author of *The Adventures of Hajji Baba of Ispahan* (1824).

The quay at Smyrna, *c*.1910, at a time when it was regarded as the commercial capital of the Ottoman Empire. Camels remained a common mode of transport until the mid twentieth century.

Greek troops landing on the quay at Smyrna, 15 May 1919. On the left is an image of the national hero Eleftherios Venizelos. Three and a half years later, Greek troops abandoned Smyrna to its fate.

Entry of Turkish troops into Smyrna, 9 September 1922, passing the abandoned kit of the Greek army. For the next four days, until the outbreak of the fire, the city enjoyed a semblance of normality.

Fire rages in Smryna, 13–16 September. The quay or Cordon had been lined with cafés and hotels. The fire was used by the Turkish authorities to expel or kill the city's Greeks and Armenians, who were blamed for starting it.

Greek refugees leaving Smyrna, end September 1922. Many men between the ages of fifteen and forty-five were deported into the interior of Anatolia.

Most of the centre of Smyrna was burnt, except the Turkish and Jewish districts.
It was many decades until the last blackened ruins were removed.

Salonica after the fire of August 1917. It destroyed 10,000 houses – mainly in Jewish
and Muslim quarters – and 70,000 people were made homeless. Many Jews and
Muslims subsequently emigrated. The Greek Prime Minister, Venizelos, regarded the
fire as an opportunity to Hellenize the city.

Seated left to right: Muammar Uşakligil, one of the richest businessmen of Izmir, his daughter Latife and her husband, Mustafa Kemal, c.1924. Latife was eager to help Mustafa Kemal in his modernization programme, but they divorced after two years and her family moved to Istanbul.

Visit of Prime Minister Venizelos of Greece to President Mustafa Kemal Ataturk of Turkey, Ankara, October 1932. Both Venizelos and Kemal had contributed to the end of Smyrna. Subsequently they inaugurated an era of peace between their countries.

Pietro Canonica's equestrian statue of Mustafa Kemal, erected in 1931 on the ruins of Izmir, near the site of the Grand Hotel Kraemer Palace.

View of the Place des Consuls, Alexandria, *c.*1880. Laid out in the 1830s, it was the first modern square in the Middle East. The building at the end, originally residence of the Greek consul-general Michael Tossizza, became the bourse, the economic heart of the city. From its balcony on 26 July 1956 Nasser would announce to a delirious crowd the nationalization of the Suez Canal.

Statue of Muhammad Ali on the Place des Consuls (later Place Muhammad Ali), *c.*1880. Inaugurated on 16 August 1873, a tribute to Muhammad Ali's role in the revival of the city, it was the first statue erected in public in a Muslim country. On the right is St Mark's, the English church.

British marines in the ruins of Alexandria, 1882. After much of the city was destroyed by a British naval bombardment, British troops occupied Alexandria in July 1882, in order to 'restore the authority of the Khedive'. They did not leave Alexandria until 1947, Egypt until 1956.

Night raid on Alexandria, November 1941. During the Second World War, Alexandria was a vital war base for the Allies fighting in the desert and the Mediterranean. Unlike Cairo, which was treated as the capital of a neutral country, Alexandria was subject to frequent Axis air raids.

Constantinople. Acre, Nablus, Tripoli and Latakia were subordinated to Beirut. The population rose, mainly through immigration from the hinterland, from 46,000 in 1860 to 130,000 in 1914 – a rate of increase less startling than Alexandria's, but astronomical considering its 1800 base of 6,000.[20] As a result of its new status as a provincial capital, Beirut became, in the words of the future president Bsharra al-Khoury, 'an ocean of bureaucrats ... Office in those days was everything.'[21]

The Ottoman sultan Abdulhamid II, who reigned from 1876 to 1909, frequently used Islam as a political weapon. His palace city of Yildiz, on a hill above the Bosphorus, became a centre for Sufi Muslim orders and preachers, who were paid to preach devotion to the Ottoman sultanate throughout the Muslim world. However, he also favoured the mainly Christian city of Beirut. His motive was probably a desire to 'break and decrease' foreign influence in this Levantine port, home to French schools and companies, by re-Ottomanizing it – and also to keep Syrian patriotism split between Beirut and Damascus.[22] Moreover the Melhames, a Maronite family known to their many enemies as the 'mal famés', provided a living link between Beirut, their native city, and the Sultan's palace of Yildiz. They had houses in both cities, between which they regularly commuted. Salim Melhame was minister of forests and agriculture; Nejib of public works and commerce and also in charge of one of the Sultan's police forces; Philip was a senator; Habib a councillor of state.[23]

As it became more modern, Beirut was re-Ottomanized: the Empire built back. In 1851–6 a massive imperial barracks had been built on a hill above the city: it is now the Grand Saray, the president of Lebanon's official residence. In 1884 the main government building or Petit Saray, seat of the provincial government, was inaugurated on the west side of the main square, then called Place Hamidiye after the Sultan. The Hamidiye Public Garden in the middle of the square acquired kiosks and a military band.[24] A lighthouse was erected in 1889, one of the 150 'phares de l'empire ottoman' which stretched round the eastern Mediterranean. Abdulhamid also built in Beirut, as in other provincial capitals, hospitals, schools, a school of arts and crafts, drinking fountains, police stations, and an Ottoman post office, to compete with foreign ones. An ornate neo-Ottoman clock tower, on the hill by the barracks, was designed by the municipal engineer, Yussef Aftimos, a pupil of the Syrian Protestant College, who had worked in the USA.[25]

At the suggestion of the local governor, the clock tower had two faces with Arabic numerals and two with Latin numerals. For 'the Muslim population', the former showed 'Islamic times' – with each day beginning at sunset, from which hours are measured (the clock setting was changed once a week, to keep pace with the change in the time of sunset). The latter showed '*alafranga*' time, with the day beginning at midnight.[26] Thus two time systems, and attitudes to time management, existed side by side in the same city. Visible from afar, built of local stone and marble, the tower was inaugurated on 31 August 1899 at a grandiose ceremony with speeches in Turkish and Arabic in honour of the Sultan's 'resplendent and eternal nature'. It was erected not only to encourage punctuality in his subjects, but also to compete with the clock tower in the grounds of the Syrian Protestant College, which showed only European time. In Beirut, religion divided time, as so much else.[27]

In 1889–94, pushed by local merchants such as the Sursocks, a modern port, quay, jetty and breakwater with warehouses were built by the Compagnie Impériale Ottomane du Port, des Quais et des Entrepôts de Beyrouth, directed by the Comte de Perthuis and Salim Melhame. As in Smyrna and Salonica, ships could now berth directly by the quay. Most of the old crusader fort and the city walls were razed in the process. In 1889 gas lighting and in 1907 electric trams were introduced. In 1895 the city was connected by train to Damascus, and in 1903 a railway line directly on to the quays was opened. Trade boomed.[28]

One of Beirut's principal exports was people. Through the ports of Beirut and Tripoli streamed thousands of Lebanese and Syrians – perhaps 10,000 a year, or a total of 300,000 between 1880 and 1914 – who left in search of wealth and security abroad; among them, in 1902 on their way to Mexico, were the parents of Carlos Slim, now (2010) 'the richest man in the world'. Migration was organized by 'brokers' who travelled from village to village, with tales of fortunes to be made overseas. (Some organized journeys which, to clients' surprise, ended in Africa rather than America: the present speaker of the Lebanese parliament, Nabih Berri, was born in Sierra Leone.) Since 95 per cent of the emigrants were Christians – more likely than Muslims to have the education and contacts to facilitate success in other Christian lands – the proportion of Christians in the population began to diminish.[29]

The apogee of Hamidian Beirut was the visit in November 1898 of Kaiser Wilhelm II, accompanied by an enormous retinue. He was on his way from Constantinople to Damascus, where he made a speech proclaiming his friendship for the world's 300 million Muslims. The German alliance ultimately led to the fall of the Empire. At the time it seemed to protect it from European predators. To cheering crowds, the Kaiser and Kaiserin visited German schools and hospitals and the park outside the city and inspected troops. The Kaiser declared Beirut 'the jewel in the crown of the padishah [the Ottoman title for the Sultan]'.[30]

By 1907 the port of Beirut was on a level with Salonica, handling 11 per cent of the trade of the Empire. As in Salonica, there were strikes and labour unrest. The Sultan sometimes favoured the workers over the port company and the bosses. Workers would shout at their bosses, 'You are not in France here, you are in Turkey,' and sometimes won disputes. The British consul-general called them 'the scum of the Levant'.[31] Two new buildings by the port, opened in 1900 and 1906 respectively, demonstrated its growing links with Europe: the Orosdi Back department store and the new local branch of the Ottoman Bank. With mansard roofs and classical ornaments, they looked like buildings in France.[32]

At the same time as it emerged as a commercial and intellectual capital, Beirut was becoming, like Alexandria and Smyrna, famous for what one inhabitant called 'magic taverns, wine, perfumed beds'. Already in 1860 Madame de Perthuis had noticed that 'our soldiers introduce the unknown habit of cabarets.' Smart society – now so big that it could no longer all fit into Madame de Perthuis's salon at once – began to go to a theatre organized by French soldiers. In winter she dined out a lot and attended carnival balls: she noted that 'the Shihab family has long since lost its influence and its wealth.'[33] In their enormous mansions, the Sursock, Bustros and de Fraij families received visits and gave parties.[34]

In a forest on the edge of the city, Rustum Pasha, an Italian convert to Islam who was governor-general of Mount Lebanon from 1873 to 1883, had laid out an 'English garden'. A band played in the evening; the Pasha exchanged compliments with ladies in the kiosk; it became 'the meeting-place for the elegant of both sexes'.[35] In 1893 a racecourse was founded on the outskirts of the city.[36] By 1900 Beirut had eighteen hotels and forty brothels: inmates of the latter were, in theory, inspected three times a week.[37]

Beirut remained a mixed city, with Muslims, Christian and Druze intermingled in the same districts, although Muslims tended to live in the west, Christians in the east. For most of the time it appeared peaceful and increasingly prosperous. Below the surface however, like other Levantine ports, Beirut was a time bomb. Even under the strict rule of Abdulhamid, whose soldiers paraded through the city and whose spies were ubiquitous, tensions between Christians and Muslims led to riots and murders, sparked by games or quarrels, in 1872, 1881, 1888 and 1896. At times there were revenge murders by a Muslim or a Christian on alternate nights.[38] Each community, one Ottoman governor of Mount Lebanon complained, made it a point of honour to hide their criminals from the police, or send them to America. There was a 'ferment of religious discord'. In riots between Muslims and Orthodox in March and September 1903, seven Christians and fifteen Muslims died; 20,000 Christians temporarily fled to the safety of Mount Lebanon. The vali was suspected of involvement.[39] As in 1860, a bloodbath was averted by the mediation of the notables, and the arrival of two American warships, misinformed that the American vice-consul had been murdered.[40]

With the spread of modern schools, for the first time memoirs, novels and autobiographies open windows into hearts and minds hitherto masked by religious and social conformism. Edward Atiyah came from the cultivated Christian bourgeoisie: his father had converted to Protestantism to show his modernity, and to facilitate access to the best education in Beirut. He paints what may be an overdramatic picture of Beirut as a city of conflict. Even when there was 'neither fanaticism nor aversion there was always the tendency to regard yourself under a religious rather than a national denomination'. Out of fear of Muslims and admiration for Europeans' power and culture, 'everything European came to be regarded with almost religious veneration' – particularly after the Armenian massacres of 1895 and 1896 in Constantinople, provoked by Armenians' desire for more rights, or independence, had revealed how quickly the Ottoman government could switch from tolerance to ferocity. Beirut's population swelled with Armenian refugees.[41]

Brawls between Muslim and Christian gangs in the streets of Beirut produced 'a haunting sense of insecurity', heightened for some Christians by the presence in public of Muslim women shrouded in black. A Christian leader called Osta Bawli ('Mister Paul'), famous for his bodyguard of kaftan-wearing lieutenants with dagger-stuffed sashes, was murdered in 1896 while walking on the corniche with a friend. He received the equivalent of a state funeral in Beirut. Frenzied crowds sang anti-Muslim and anti-Ottoman songs, encouraged by the cries of women from balconies. Just before the body was lowered into the ground, a smartly dressed young man, with a rose in his buttonhole and a scented handkerchief in his pocket, 'walked up to the coffin, bent over the dead man's face and kissed it'. Two weeks later he entered a tobacco shop and shot three Muslims (presumably identifiable by their dress) – to revenge his beloved, not because they had committed the murder. He then vanished, probably abroad to escape a vendetta.[42]

Osta Bawli had been one of Beirut's *qabadays*, from a Turkish word meaning 'strongman'. They were key figures in the criminal underbelly of the city. They were at once gangsters involved in smuggling and gambling; informal leaders and arbitrators for their district or community; and bodyguards, often working for consuls or notables. They were famous for flamboyant dress, rampant moustaches, and violence. One *qabaday* killed three custom officials: 'bribery and intimidation, however, soon removed all danger of prosecution.'[43]

Atiyah preferred Alexandria to what he called the 'sordid human sore of Beirut', its dirty narrow streets and slimy gutters. For him Alexandria was the true meeting place of East and West, a modern Westernized city. While many Syrians already thought and spoke in French, as a Protestant he hoped that Syria 'would come under British rule' – until he worked in the Sudan and experienced for himself 'the arrogance of domination' of the British 'sons of god'.[44]

10

Smyrna: Greeks and Turks

> Western civilization is invading with giant steps all layers and all
> classes of society and so Smyrna illuminates like a beacon all the
> other provinces of the Ottoman Empire.
>
> Charles de Scherzer, *La Province de Smyrne considérée au point de
> vue économique, culturel et intellectuel* (Vienna, 1873)

IN ALEXANDRIA, BRITAIN was the predator/saviour. In Beirut, France
was preparing to assume that role. No foreign state, however, was
awaited with more longing, by more of the city's inhabitants, than Greece
was in Smyrna.

At first, however, Smyrna seemed destined to continue its cosmopolitan,
commercial destiny. One structure came to symbolize that role: the massive
stone quay called the Cordon. Its construction had been the greatest single
urban project in the history of the Ottoman Empire. The idea came from
the Société des Quais de Smyrne, formed by a group of Smyrna businessmen: Baron Alliotti, A. Spartali, Herr Kraemer and Monsieur Cousinery.
Replacing the old wooden quay and projecting jetties, the Cordon was built
fifty yards into the sea in 1867–76 by Dussaud Frères, a private company of
Marseille, which specialized in transforming Mediterranean ports: it also
built quays at Marseille, Toulon, Algiers, Trieste and Port Said.

Like the spread of the French language and schools, the Smyrna
Cordon was a sign of French predominance in the Levant. British oppos-
ition had been almost as strong as it had been to the Suez Canal; but in
Smyrna, as in Alexandria, French influence won, with backing from the
Ottoman government.[1] The main engineer of the Cordon was a Greek
called Polycarpos Vitalis, who also worked on the quay at Salonica.[2]
Despite British attempts at takeover, the quay and the port continued to
be French-run until 1934.

Using granite blocks shipped from Naples or the Anatolian interior,
demolishing the shore fort built four centuries earlier by Mehmed the

Conqueror, the company pushed back the sea from the old Frank houses on the marina, making a quay two miles long and thirty yards wide. A customs house and telegraph, passport and quarantine offices were built on a jetty protruding from the quay. Two harbours with protecting break-waters were built beside it. Dussaud Frères also paved the entire area and built a road parallel to the quay.[3] Soon what the Smyrna merchant Richard van Lennep called 'the most beautiful and palatial houses with façades of white marble', built three or four storeys high in an elegant neoclassical style, stretched from the konak, or governor's palace, to the promontory known as Alsancak or La Punta. A rare surviving example, built in 1875–90 for the Armenian Spartali family, is now the city's Ataturk Museum.[4]

The Cordon became the main 'sight' of Smyrna. Visitors were fasci-nated.[5] Under the titles 'Mouvement du port', 'Smyrne le port et les quais', 'Vue du Cordon', 'Types turques', postcards showed it lined with ships, their masts as tall as the neighbouring minarets and church towers, and covered with bales of cotton and crates of figs. In all the cards, men wearing Western hats far outnumber those in the Ottoman fez.[6]

Individuals' contrasting perceptions of a city, and Smyrna's blend of East and West, are reflected in some messages. On one view of the city, the sender writes, 'Smyrna is a charming city which we will leave with regret. There you are completely in the East.' On another, the writer asks, 'Would you not think yourself just as well in front of a view of a great European city?'[7]

Towards sunset, in the northern section known as Bella Vista, hundreds of strollers walked up and down, ladies displaying the latest Paris fash-ions, young men showing low shoes and 'coquettish silk socks'. It was even livelier than the Grande Rue de Péra.[8] Later in the evening, wrote a French consul, 'a compact crowd of every age and every nationality' walked up and down under the gas lights.[9] According to a guidebook of 1881, 'The quay ... is the favourite promenade in the evenings and up to a late hour at night. The numerous cafés along it are brilliantly lit up and form the rendezvous of motley costumed crowds while strains of oriental as well as European music are heard on all sides.'[10]

As Lisbon created fado, and New Orleans jazz, Smyrna, more than any other Levantine port, created its own sound: a blend of modern Greek and Turkish music called Smyrnaika or rebetiko. Each group living in the city left its mark on rebetiko: zeybeks, Greeks, Turks, Armenians, Jews, Italians, Andalusians, Bulgarians, churches, synagogues, dervish lodges and taverns.[11] It was the music of rebels, particularly appreciated by the *qabadays* or *dais* (Greek), the toughs who, as in Beirut, worked in the harbour and in the evening gambled and fought with each other.

At the end of the nineteenth century the city was swept by a frenzy for the mandolin, violin, guitar and zither. A French visitor wrote, 'Nowhere have I seen so many barrel organs'.[12] A Wallachian called Giovanakis was famous for his 'sweet violin'. A certain Papazoglu, a musician in one of the cafés on the Cordon, remembered, 'We had to know a song or two from each nationality to please the customers. We played Jewish and Armenian and Arab music. We were citizens of the world, you see.'[13]

Some cafés were called *amanedes*, as the singers, pausing during improvisation, shouted aman! aman! (Turkish for 'Help!' – to indicate that the singer could no longer bear the pain expressed in his song). Different both from the light Italian music of the theatres and salons and from traditional village music, rebetiko songs mixed Western polyphony and Eastern monophony. Rebellious in character, they described the sufferings of the poor and of prisoners, the torments of love, or the pleasures of hashish – for that reason an authoritarian Greek government would forbid them in 1936:[14]

> Won't you tell, won't you tell me
> Where hashish is sold?
> The dervishes sell it
> In the upper districts.[15]

In Smyrna songs, women were coquettes or tyrants:

> Your black eyes that gaze at me,
> My dear, lower them, because they are killing me.

Some songs hint at love across religious boundaries:

> I feel like changing my faith,
> So I can rush into the harem and grab you,
> Flirtatious little Turkish girl.

Often they lament the faithlessness of the beloved:

> Don't you swear, you liar, and do not go on crying.
> Oh, Oh, Oh!
> The same vows I heard you give to someone else the other day.
> And your own eyes that glance at me.
> Oh, Oh, Oh!
> I can tell from their colour they are untrue.
>
> You stay up all night at the *cafés chantants*, drinking beer, Oh!
> And the rest of us you are treating as green caviare.[16]

In all there were twenty-eight hotels, cafés and brasseries along the Smyrna Cordon. At first dismissed in Murray's *Handbook* as 'inferior and dirty ... not very suitable for English people',[17] they soon improved. One of the finest was the Sporting Club, built in 1894 by Polycarpos Vitalis. It had spacious rooms, its own garden and orchestra, and a famous terrace, from which members watched the sunset over glasses of raki.[18] Another was the Hôtel des Deux Auguste, later called the Grand Hotel Huck: in the winter season the Cercle Européen, as the old Casino was now known, held balls there. The Café de Paris was French, the Alhambra and the Poseidon were Greek, but drinking beer in the Café Hoffmann you might be in Vienna. Run by an Austrian from Trieste, the Grand Hotel Kraemer Palace ('Pilsener Bier. Jeder Abend Musik'), four storeys high and eleven windows wide, with an adjoining glass-covered café, was the largest.[19] Every man who could afford it went to the cafés: Greeks and Turks, locals and Europeans. If there were brawls, they usually involved outsiders – Turkish soldiers returning from service in Tripoli, British sailors drunk on leave.[20]

The writer Norman Douglas visited the city in 1895. He was seduced:

Smyrna – whatever it may now have become – seemed to be the most enjoyable place on earth. That fascinating bazaar, the variegated crowds about the harbour, eastern bustle and noise; or if you were in softer mood, there was the cemetery with its glorious cypresses, or the Greek quarter full of pretty girls, far prettier than those of Greece itself ... The fortnight in Smyrna ... proved to be one of the happiest of my life; I was in a state of beatitude and aware, not afterwards but at the very moment of the fact.

He particularly enjoyed one café near the Cordon, with a 'cheap but attractive' floor show, where you could 'pick up a girl or anything else you fancied'; a restaurant above, where you could take the object of your desire for dinner; and bedrooms on the upper floors, to which you could both retire for 'an hour's rest': 'you paid your money and you got your key. Why are such delectable places not commoner?'[21]

Smyrna, like Alexandria and Beirut, represented freedom from the nation state. For Dimitri Argyropoulo the Cordon was a sweeter, more indolent version of the Canebière, the main thoroughfare of Marseille. 'It is both the Europe of the Orient and the Orient of Europe.'[22] Turks were attracted to it as much as Greeks – perhaps even more, as, needing special passports from the Ottoman government to travel inside the Ottoman Empire, as well as abroad, they were less likely to know similar cities. In his memoirs the Turkish writer Naci Gundem wrote that it was the Cordon that made Smyrna Smyrna. From sunset until midnight it was like 'a fairy-tale country', with 'a magic atmosphere which made the most sombre and depressed souls end by laughing'.[23] 'If Smyrna is the eye of Asia,' it was said, 'the quay is the pupil of the eye.'[24]

By night the quay was devoted to pleasure, by day to trade. All day the Cordon was busy with ships unloading cargoes, and goods wagons or camels bringing figs and cotton from the interior directly on to the quay for loading. In a practice known as *disbarco*, however, many ships moored out at sea in order to save on port fees, and used local barges to land cargoes.[25] By one estimate the agricultural production of Anatolia quadrupled between 1845 and 1876; the percentage of Ottoman international trade passing through Smyrna rose from 7.5 per cent in 1850 to 30 per cent in 1873. By 1900, 55 per cent of all Ottoman exports went through Smyrna. Huge warehouses were built near the Cordon: the city was not only the eye of Asia, but its storehouse.[26]

The number of ships visiting the port rose from 1,295 in 1863 to 2,465 in 1900. Seventeen shipping lines called at Smyrna. Their names are typical of the period: the Hamidiye Line, Khedivial Mail, Deutsche Levante Linie, Messageries Maritimes, Austrian Lloyd, Peninsular & Orient.[27] As early as 1850 a French newspaper of Smyrna, *L'Impartial*, had lamented that, thanks to the frequency of steamboats, life had become 'a rush without end'.[28] Smyrna was on the tourist route. Messages on postcards sent from Smyrna might read, 'Leaving tomorrow for Rhodes and Aleppo, beautiful weather kind regards' or 'Just leaving Smyrna, sunshine and calm sea, very hard to buy much passing through quickly as we do, one ought to stay in the country some time to get things cheap.'[29] As in other Levantine cities, foreign powers opened their own post offices. The Austrian and the French handled most items.[30]

Smyrna's traditional commerce in figs, raisins and cotton was joined by opium. Consumption boomed after the Opium Wars (1839–42, 1856–60), started by Britain to force the government of China to let British merchants sell opium directly to the Chinese. Barker Brothers advertised themselves as 'Opium, fruits and general produce merchants Smyrna Turkey'. Dutch merchants of Smyrna, like the van Lenneps, exported opium directly to the Dutch colonies in Indonesia.[31] The city was swept by a fever of opium trading: 'not only in the offices and bazaars but on the streets, in the coffee-houses ... Even women and maid servants meddled with it,' reported one Dutch inhabitant.[32] As part of Europeanization, Smyrniots themselves, however, had begun to prefer wine to opium.[33]

Smyrna was not an island moored off the coast of Turkey. Economically, culturally and politically, its connections to the hinterland, as well as to the outside world, were increasing. The port was fed by the Smyrna–Aydin railway, the second line to be built in the Ottoman Empire, after that between Alexandria and Cairo. Four British businessmen had won the concession on 23 September 1856, in order to speed the delivery of the fruit of the valleys to the port.[34] On 30 October 1858, on his way back to retirement in England, the great ambassador Stratford Canning, recently created Lord Stratford de Redcliffe, laid the foundation stone of the Smyrna station. After the successful conclusion of the Crimean War (for the outbreak of which many considered him partly responsible), his speech revealed his world vision, and taste for self-congratulation.

The foundation stone, in his opinion, 'might be said to have inserted the keystone of the arch at which he had for so long laboured, for the consolidation of European interests with those of Turkey'. He foresaw a time when Calcutta might be joined to London by railway and 'the Ottoman as now the British dominions may be intersected throughout by a network of iron communication'. He hoped for 'a progressive diminution of abuses, prejudices and national animosities ... I need hardly tell you, gentlemen, that Europe has more than ever a deep stake in the regeneration of Turkey. Western civilization is knocking hard at the gates of the Levant.' He feared 'that fierce struggle of partition which our ablest statemen have long struggled to avert ... It cannot be denied that by reason of successive errors and calamities Turkey is feeble and embarrassed.' However, he concluded, 'Don't despair. Was Rome built in a day? ... Was British liberty the work of a single age? ... I cannot more appropriately conclude than by proposing a toast to which I have no doubt you will all most cordially respond – success with three times three and one cheer more to the Smyrna and Aidin Railway!'[35] Finished in 1866, the railway soon integrated the Meander valley into the booming Smyrna economy.

In addition to the port, the town itself was enjoying a boom. New districts with European houses were built in the north and east of the city.[36] Across the Gulf of Smyrna the smart new district of Cordelio or Karshiyaka, soon connected by ferry to the city centre, was particularly favoured by Turks. They included the wealthy Evliyazade family, two of whom served as mayors of Smyrna – Evliyazade Hajj Mehmed and 'Gavur' Refik, one of the founders of the Smyrna Jockey Club, mayor in 1913–18 – and another wealthy family long established in Smyrna, the

Katipzades, one of whom, Adnan Menderes, became prime minister of Turkey in 1950–60.[37]

Long before the reforms of Mustafa Kemal in 1923–38, Smyrna Turks were breaking with traditions. The manners and customs of the city were as effective in changing mentalities as government decrees. Whereas Greeks tended to build houses in 'Chios style', with a raised first floor, Turks built in Parisian style, with Western furniture and special rooms in the house – rather than separate *selamliks* in the garden – in which to receive guests. Tevfik Nevzat, an editor of *Hizmet*, visited cafés on the Cordon with his unveiled wife; as a political radical, he was later exiled to Adana by the Sultan, and executed.[38] Muslim women of Smyrna were famous for not following the Islamic dress code, which had been reinforced by Abdulhamid. Despite repeated injunctions to return to sharia, they walked on the Cordon with thin veils, or none at all, and in tight coats to show off their figure. In contrast to Constantinople, in Smyrna men and women sometimes travelled together on trams and boats, rather than in the separate sections for each sex.[39]

Smyrna was becoming a city of factories – although they could not be seen from the Cordon. Steam mills were set up in 1850 by McAndrew & Forbes, a firm which was also building factories in the Meander valley to process mastic and liquorice for export, and collecting taxes there for the Ottoman government. In 1854 a rich Greek called Dimo Issigonis, ancestor of Alec Issigonis, the designer of the Mini, founded one of the most modern factories in the Empire, making hydraulic pumps and other machines. There were also flour mills, and factories making paper, textiles, alcohol and soap. Large department stores like Orosdi Back opened branches in Smyrna, as they did throughout the Levant.[40] Even from Constantinople, brides came to buy their trousseaux in Smyrna, as its shops were better. Frank Street, the main shopping street, where shops had names like Bon Marché and Petit Louvre, was so crowded you could hardly move.[41]

In 1882 the French consul claimed that Smyrna was 'a city destined to an immense commercial development, its prosperity and cosmopolitan population are increasing more every day'.[42] An Ottoman chamber of commerce was established in 1885, under an Armenian president, with Turkish, Greek, Armenian and Jewish members; a British chamber of commerce followed in 1888; a French in 1889, Italian in 1900, and Dutch in 1902.[43]

Smyrna's trade boom was accompanied by a cultural renaissance. Like Alexandria and Beirut, Smyrna was a city of schools. They included

French schools run by Lazarist and Dominican monks, founded in 1787 and 1857 respectively, and a school run by Sœurs de Charité, where girls of all religions could be taught reading, writing, drawing and embroidery. An English Commercial School was founded at Bornova in 1848, Notre Dame de Sion for the daughters of the elite in 1875, and seven schools by the Frères des Ecoles Chrétiennes.[44] By 1911, in Smyrna and Anatolia 17,303 pupils were attending French-language schools.[45]

Boys' and girls' schools for Jews, founded in 1873 and 1878 respectively, by the Jewish educational organization called the Alliance Israélite Universelle, also provided a French education, based on French history and geography and the cult of Paris, the 'ville-lumière', where the Alliance had its headquarters. As a result, Jews as well as Catholics became transmitters of French culture in the Levant.[46] American missionaries opened girls' and boys' high schools in 1878 and 1879. In 1891 an International College for boys was founded, which moved outside the town to a modern campus at Paradiso in 1913. Like Victoria College in Alexandria, it was intended to welcome 'students of all nationalities'. English was obligatory. By 1912, 450 boys and 800 girls were attending. Most pupils were local Greeks and Armenians, many of whom subsequently became Protestant.[47]

The Ottoman government also opened schools for agriculture and for arts and crafts, and also for orphans;[48] however, wealthy Ottomans often preferred to send their children to 'foreign' schools. Adnan Menderes, for example, attended the International College in Smyrna. With more money to spend, foreign and minority schools − like private schools in most countries − had the reputation for being better than Ottoman schools, even at teaching the Ottoman language itself.[49]

One of the first Turkish novelists lived in Smyrna: Halid Ziya Uşakligil, born in 1866 into a wealthy family of carpet merchants, and author of the novel *Forbidden Love* (1900).[50] In his memoirs he wrote that, although he missed Constantinople, he slowly fell in love with Smyrna. He went to an Ottoman government school, but noticed how much bigger and better the nearby Alliance Israélite Universelle school was. In the Ottoman school, lessons were basic − Arabic, Persian, Turkish, the simplest geography − with a few hours of French added on, like an unwelcome guest at a dinner party; there was no homework. In the Alliance school, in contrast, pupils were taught (by teachers trained in Paris) subjects which helped them succeed in business: languages, mathematics and economics. The only thing they did not learn was Turkish: even if they knew a little, they pretended not to, as was fashionable for non-Muslims in Smyrna. For Turks, business in Smyrna seemed like a spider's web, almost impossible to penetrate. Their education made it difficult for them to compete with Christians and Jews.[51]

Halid Ziya also attended an Armenian Catholic school, claiming that he was the third Muslim in Smyrna to do so. Some Muslim Turks criticized him for being irreligious, an atheist, a lover of the Franks. One official would greet him on the Cordon with the words, 'Bonjur Mosyo' (the same official was laughed at by foreigners for wearing traditional dress). His first novels (five were published between 1889 and 1900) would be criticized for being contrary to Muslim tradition.[52]

Many Muslims regarded the Koran as an education in itself, and the greatest happiness, before family and work. In the years before 1908, among Turks, 'the necessity to study only just began to be awakened.'[53] Halid Ziya, in contrast, loved his Armenian school. Even the priests knew chemistry and biology, and they devoted all their time to the pupils, never trying to convert them. Every day was like a tornado. Learning French, loving the works of Voltaire, Hugo, Flaubert and Renan, helped make him a writer.[54]

The different communities were divided in sickness as well as in schooling. Separate hospitals catered for the French, British, Dutch, Greek, Armenian, Catholic, Jewish and Muslim populations, mainly treating patients from their own nationality or religion. The Greek community also had its own mental hospital – proof, in the opinion of the Greek newspaper *Amalthea*, of the superiority of the Greeks' civilizing mission in the East.[55]

Schools needed books and presses. By 1872 there were ten Greek, three Armenian, two French, one Ottoman and one Hebrew printing press in the city – a single statistic revealing Greek predominance in Smyrna (in 1910, fourteen of twenty-six presses were Greek).[56] By 1890 the city published four Greek, three Turkish, three French and three Ladino newspapers. Their names express the character of the city. *Amalthea*, founded in 1838, was named after the she-goat which had suckled Zeus, as 'magnificent Smyrna, the brain, the heart and the soul of Asia Minor' nourished the Greeks of the East. *Hizmet* ('Service' in Turkish) was founded in 1886 by Halid Ziya, who remembered that it was bought mostly for the commodity prices it published.[57] *Ahenk* ('Harmony' in Turkish and Armenian) was read by Armenians, *La Boz del Pueblo* ('The Voice of the People' in Ladino) by Jews. From 1892 to 1921 Joseph Nalpas, uncle of the French playwright Antonin Artaud, published the *Annuaire du Levant* in Smyrna.[58] Of the main French language newspaper, *Le Courrier de Smyrne*, it was said, 'If you want literature, buy the *Figaro* or the *Gaulois*. If you want politics, subscribe to the *Temps*; but if you want to know what people are saying in the salons and cafés of Smyrna, you must read the *Courrier de Smyrne*.'[59]

Schools and newspapers fostered cultural institutions. The 1859 *Shepherd's Oriental Yearbook* refers to the 'Smyrna Literary and Scientific Institution' at 19 Frank Street, with a reading room and library, stocking newspapers in many languages, and holding Monday philosophical classes and Thursday lectures. This may be the same as the Institut Scientifique Européen (motto 'Chacun pour tous, tous pour chacun'), founded in 1849, which moved to Paris in 1877.[60] The Academy of Anatolia for Archaeology and Geology and the Smyrna Jockey Club both met there. The Cercle Levantin, for local Catholics – a rival of the Frank Casino and the Greek club – was in Kraemer's Passage, the English Club on 158 Frank Street. Smyrna also encouraged the first archaeological expeditions in the area. From 1864 one of the engineers on the Smyrna–Aydin railway was also excavating Ephesus.[61] French, Italian and Greek companies regularly visited the 300-seat Theatre of Euterpe, which opened in Smyrna in 1841.[62] With 600 seats, the Sporting Club theatre on the Cordon welcomed visiting troupes – although the sound of bells on files of camels passing down the quay outside might interrupt performances.[63] The public was critical. A visiting Armenian troupe (Muslim custom forbidding women to appear on stage meant the first Ottoman plays were performed by Armenians) played in one of the first Ottoman operas, *Leblebici Horhor* ('Horhor the Chickpeas-Seller'). Halid Ziya wrote that, after a diet of Italian opera, an opera with a local theme like *Leblebici Horhor* drove the city mad: when he saw it, he thought he was dreaming.[64]

Smyrna was also a centre of sports. The first horse races in the Ottoman Empire began at Paradiso/Sirinyer, organized by Charlton Whittall from 1840 with horses provided by the Karaosmanoglu and Forbes families.[65] They appealed to Ottomans, with their long tradition of *cirit* or javelin-throwing tournaments on horseback. In 1850 and 1853 Sultan Abdulmecid himself – who, like his father, regularly travelled outside Constantinople – visited the races, one of which was called the Sultan's Cup in his honour. Thousands began to attend, Turks picnicking under trees, Christians drinking in the red-and-white marquee of Café Costi. A race card from 1915 for the 'courses de Paradiso', published by the historian of Smyrna Livio Amedeo Missir de Lusignan, shows a mixture of Turkish and Levantine names among riders or owners: Omer Lutfi Effendi, Aliotti, de Portu, Katib Suleyman Effendi, Kraemer.[66]

Most sports, however, emphasized the divisions in the city. Smyrna after 1880 is a lesson in destructive nationalism. In 1890 some Greeks founded the Panionian Gymnastic Association: the name came from Ionia, the classical Greek name for the area. It was a nationalist organization, for physical strength was regarded as a contribution to national greatness. In 1896, the year the first revived Olympic Games were held in Athens, the first Panionian Games were held at Bornova – there were competitions in swimming, track, gym, fencing and bicycle riding. Athletes came from Constantinople and Alexandria as well as Athens. Local Turkish schools also sent teams, and there was a special stand from which the governor would watch. Soon there was a sports stadium for 7,000 in Bornova, where another Greek sports association, the Apollonian, founded in 1892, also met. There were also English, Armenian and Turkish sports clubs.[67]

In 1893 a boat race from the Sporting Club to Alsancak was inaugurated by the governor Hassan Fehmi Pasha. Watched from the Cordon by 10,000 spectators, after a military band had played the Hamidiye march in honour of the Sultan, it too confirmed national divisions. There were three separate races: for Europeans, for locals, and for fishermen. The first was won by Monsieur Guiffray (a Guiffray was head of the port tramways); the second by Pastirmacioglu Bey; the third by Laz Ibrahim. The races became a popular annual event.[68] In 1894 the British community founded the Smyrna Football Club – thirteen years before the first Turkish club, Fenerbache, was founded in Constantinople, and nineteen years before the first Turkish team in Smyrna was established by Celal Bayar in 1913.[69]

Language also both united and divided the city. At home each group generally continued to speak its own language: Turkish, Spanish (in the case of Sephardi Jews),[70] Greek, Armenian or French. Owing to Greeks' numbers and wealth, some Turkish schools taught Greek as well as Turkish, in order to produce bilingual officials for government service. Ottoman officials in the konak were encouraged to know Greek.[71] Some Catholics wrote in Frango-chiotika – Greek written in Latin letters.[72]

From the 1840s, as in Alexandria and Beirut, French replaced Italian and lingua franca as the main common language. In 1863 the Italian consul-general complained that Italian had disappeared even among some Italians of the city. Smyrniot French was distinguished by a sing-song accent and rolled rs 'like stones in a torrent'.[73] In Jewish schools in Smyrna hours were spent on Turkish, but even more on French: 'You must learn French,' proclaimed the Grand Rabbi.[74] The great Greek poet George Seferis, born in Urla outside Smyrna in 1900, was brought up in French as well as Greek, and wrote to his father in French.[75] Halid Ziya's knowledge of French helped win him a post as teacher in the government secondary school and helped him become the first Turk to work in the Smyrna branch of the Ottoman Bank.[76]

Businessmen were often quadrilingual, using visiting cards in Ottoman, Greek, French and Hebrew, or just the first two.[77] Letterheads on invoices – for example of the carpet merchants Spartali Brothers & Co. or the Pol. Vidori paper and printing company – were printed in five languages and alphabets: Ottoman, French, Greek, Armenian and Hebrew. The bills were in French.[78] Among the 1,300 books published in Smyrna before 1922 were many translations of Molière, Chateaubriand, Balzac and George Sand.[79]

In 1895, at the age of nineteen, Andrew Ryan, later chief dragoman at the British embassy in Constantinople, visited Smyrna while studying for the Levant Consular Service.[80] He found the quay 'very picturesque, far cleaner than at home'. The cafés were 'in reality gambling places. Cards and backgammon prevail.' To his surprise, even in the British consulate, French was 'more useful far than English'. In the bazaars 'French again comes in.' He found 'everyone agreeable' in Smyrna, 'except in back parts where am jeered, shake my stick and depart'.[81]

The 'back parts' of Smyrna were a contrast to the splendours of the Cordon. In the mainly Turkish and Jewish areas on Mount Pagus, one consul wrote, 'Very numerous families are crowded into narrow and badly ventilated houses.' Smyrna had a reputation for attracting 'the dregs of all Europe'; 'vagabonds come from all the ports of Europe'. Thefts, 'stabbing cases' and murders were common.[82]

One of the richest families of Smyrna was, like the city itself, simultaneously Greek, Ottoman and European. According to family tradition, the first Baltazzi came from Venice via Chios to Smyrna in 1746. Some Baltazzis had Venetian passports. Greek wives soon made the family Orthodox. In 1782 a Baltazzi was one of the Smyrna Greeks who helped pay for the publication, by a Greek printing press in Venice, of Patriarch Gregory V's translation of St John Chrysostom's work *On the Priesthood*.[83] In the first half of the nineteenth century, like the Sursock family in Beirut, their role as tax collectors for the Ottoman government made them fortunes. With family members living in Athens, Vienna and Marseille, as well as Constantinople and Smyrna, they became bankers, entrepreneurs and landowners. The Sultan's banker Theodore Baltazzi administered the toll on the Galata bridge.[84] In 1850 his brother Emmanuel Baltazzi helped the great poet Lamartine – forced to leave France by his financial ruin after the revolution of 1848, which he had helped provoke – visit an estate given him by the Sultan at Tire, twenty-five miles outside Smyrna. He stayed there only a few weeks – long enough to attend receptions and poetry readings in Smyrna and to realize that he would never make money out of his new property.[85]

By 1862 the Baltazzis, having bought more land round Smyrna from the Karaosmanoglu family, were by far the biggest landowners in the area. As their estates expanded, so, it was said, did the number of peasants forced off them, thereby leading to a rise in brigandage.[86] Thanks to the fortune made in the Ottoman Empire, they were now ready, like the Sursocks in Beirut and the Zoghebs and Debbanes in Alexandria, for reincarnation as European nobles.

On his journey to Smyrna in June 1850, Sultan Abdulmecid had visited an Armenian Catholic banker called Jean Papasyan Effendi and the banker Georges Baltazzi in their villas in Bornova. The visit of his brother Sultan Abdulaziz to Smyrna from 21 to 24 April 1863, returning from a visit to Ismail Pasha in Egypt, was an apogee of Levantine and Ottoman Smyrna. The city was *en fête*, with fireworks, illuminations and crowds, from all communities, shouting 'Padishahim cok yaşa! [Long live the Sultan!] Vive le Sultan! Zito o Sultan!' Accompanied by the brilliant grand vizier Fouad Pasha, Abdulaziz visited the konak and the ruins of Ephesus, received the consuls and notables, and gave money to religious authorities, Muslim, Christian and Jewish. On 23 April (St George's Day) he visited the house of Charlton Whittall (who had come to Smyrna from Liverpool as a young man in 1809) in Bornova. He was presented with the keys of the house by two young Mrs Whittalls, wearing Turkish dress; held a reception for notables in large marquees in the garden (champagne was opened at a distance, so that pious Muslims should not be shocked by the sound of popping corks); then, at his own request, visited St Mary Magdalene church, which the Whittall family had built nearby six years earlier.

That evening the Kaptan Pasha gave a dinner on board his yacht at which Muslim guests alternated with non-Muslims round the table, and Turkish dishes with European ones. Throughout the meal, English was the main language. The next day, Friday, after going in state through Smyrna to pray in the Hisar Mosque, Abdulaziz attended races at Paradiso organized by the Smyrna Jockey Club. Later he visited the Baltazzis in their elegant verandahed mansion in Buca, outside Smyrna; the gate through which he entered was shut up afterwards as a sign of respect. By these receptions and ceremonies, the Ottoman dynasty advertised its approval not only of Smyrna, but also of Levantines' way of life. Some Muslims felt neglected.[87]

The Baltazzi were unstoppable. When Epaminondas Baltazzi died in 1887, his funeral brought much of Smyrna to a halt. The procession was escorted by Greek priests, kavasses in embroidered costumes, and Turkish soldiers carrying candles. Demosthenes Baltazzi was a talented archaeologist, who helped excavate Pergamon and became director of the Istanbul Archaeological Museum.[88]

Other members of the family left Smyrna. In 1864, in the British embassy chapel in Constantinople, Hélène Baltazzi, daughter of Theodore Baltazzi, married Albin Vetsera, Austrian consul-general in Smyrna and later Austrian representative on the Caisse de la Dette in Egypt. She was seventeen and had a dowry of 6 million francs; he was thirty-nine. The family moved to Austria. Hélène Vetsera's brothers Alexander and Aristide Baltazzi helped found the Vienna Jockey Club, and in 1876 one of the Baltazzis' horses won both the Derby and the Grand Prix in Paris. Their impact was explosive. The love affair of their niece Mary Vetsera with Crown Prince Rudolf of Austria led to the lovers' tragic deaths at Mayerling in 1889.[89]

The wealth of the Baltazzis confirmed the rise of the Greeks of Smyrna. While Alexandria was consciously cosmopolitan, Smyrna was dominated by a *danse macabre* between Greeks and Turks. Claiming to be both the most ancient and the most modern of the city's inhabitants, Greeks were everywhere, occupying past, present and future, creators of both the city's classical ruins and its modern industries.[90] Most banks – the Bank of Smyrna, the Bank of Athens, the Bank of Piraeus – and bank managers were Greek.[91] Half the top merchants, lawyers and doctors in Smyrna were Greek. They were so important in the life of the city that anti-Greek boycotts in 1909–11 affected Turks more than Greeks themselves, who merely switched to Austrian or Italian nationality.[92]

Many of the most prominent buildings, including the army barracks on Konak Square, were built by Greek architects. The tallest structure in the city – taller even than its minarets – was the bell tower of St Photeini Greek Orthodox church, built in 1856.[93] The buildings on the Cordon were mainly Greek-owned, including the Café de Paris and the Sporting Club. Some Greek houses resembled that of Mr Shaitanoglu at Karantina. No Pasha's house, it was said, was bigger; a garden of lemons and palm trees surrounded a house full of books and family portraits.[94]

Greeks' twenty-eight schools, with 8,600 pupils, were considered the best in the city, and grew larger with each rebuilding.[95] The Evangelical School, one of the most modern in the city, attracted French, Muslim,

Jewish as well as Greek students, and had a special business department.[96] Greek schoolchildren learned to consider Greece the origin of civilization, the fall of Constantinople in 1453 a catastrophe. The great Smyrna writer Kosmas Politis, in his novel *At Hadzifrangos* (1963), describes a party of Greek schoolchildren, having walked through the hostile Turkish quarter, being shown Smyrna from the castle on Mount Pagus and being told of the glories of Homer and Sophocles by a teacher who concludes, with tears in his eyes, 'All that was, is and will be Greek for ever more.'[97] Smyrna Greeks also had their own museum, founded in 1873, with 40,000 books, collections of sculpture, inscriptions and medals, and published monographs celebrating Ionia's Greek past.[98]

Some Greeks knew Turkish, the official language of the empire in which they lived. In the 1890s Aristotle Doctorides, for example, taught Turkish in Greek schools; and Greek in Turkish schools; he also published an Ottoman grammar in Greek. But, like Halid Ziya, Aristotle Onassis – then Onassoglou, son of a cotton exporter – remembered that his Greek fellow pupils in the Evangelical School despised him for knowing the language. Girls' schools did not teach pupils Turkish, in order to make it difficult for them to marry Turks.[99]

Charles de Scherzer, the Austrian consul-general, wrote, 'The Greeks are more intelligent, more active and more industrious than the Turks … occupied day and night with their businesses,' and they had the best schools. Turks were described as 'honest, good, sincere and hospitable', without ambition or activity for their women. He failed to mention the conscription which forced many Turkish men to serve in the Ottoman army trying to impose order on a restless Empire. He believed Smyrna contained 75,000 Greeks, 45,000 Turks, 15,000 Jews, 10,000 Catholics, 6,000 Armenians and 4,000 Europeans.[100] As the Greek population grew, the proportion of Turks sank: owing to Turks' relative poverty, Turkish rates of abortion and infant mortality were higher than other communities'. About 50 per cent of the population before 1850, by 1900 the Turks had shrunk to about 33 per cent.[101] The grand vizier Aali Pasha himself had warned the Sultan that the Muslim population was decreasing at a frightening rate, while Christians by their business activity were establishing 'an effective and fatal superiority over Your Majesty's Muslim subjects'. Muslims 'must like the Christians devote themselves to agriculture, trade, industry and crafts'.[102]

The Greek community was so rich and powerful that from 1878 the Smyrna municipality, created in 1868, was divided by the governor himself into two separate municipalities: one mainly for the Muslim and Jewish districts and the new quays; the other mainly for the Frank and Greek districts – although people of all communities could be elected to both. The division showed that, with the approval of the Ottoman government, the wealthier Christians did not want to pay for services for poor Muslim and Jewish districts.[103]

Without any military means, Greeks behaved as if they ran Smyrna. Greek cafés displayed portraits of King George and Queen Olga of the Hellenes on their walls.[104] Outside churches after Easter services, Greeks regularly fired guns in the air. At processions for Easter, or the feast of St Polycarp every 23 February – attended by the archbishop, the Greek consul, and community elders in full dress – blue-and-white Greek flags were everywhere. Crowds cheered for the Greek king as well as (and no doubt more than) the Ottoman sultan.[105]

In 1890, during a dispute betwen the patriarchate and the Ottoman government over the role of Greek law in matters of inheritance, the Archbishop ordered churches in the province and the city to shut. Twenty thousand Greeks gathered outside the konak in protest; a demonstrators' committee was received by the governor. In the end, at the governor's request, the Ottoman government backed down.[106]

Such was the restraint – or weakness, depending on the point of view – of the Ottoman authorities and population that in 1897 they allowed the departure of Greeks (of both Ottoman and Greek nationality), flags flying, bands playing the Greek national anthem, tickets and food provided by the Greek consul, to fight in the Greek army during the brief Turco-Greek war that year. Perhaps they realized that the volunteeers from Smyrna would make little difference: the Ottoman army easily won the war. Nevertheless, some date from this war the beginning of a break between Greeks and Turks in Smyrna. It was the spirit of the age. A similar break was happening at the same time between Germans and Czechs in Prague and Vienna. There were race riots in both cities; all immigrants to Vienna had to swear oaths to maintain its German character; the mayor declared, 'Vienna is and must remain German,' and banned Czech schools.[107]

The British consulate in Smyrna gave some Greeks British nationality to prevent their expulsion by Ottoman authorities trying to force them to assume Ottoman nationality. From 1898, 20,000 Muslims expelled from Crete, as a result of a Greek rising organized by a ruthless young politician called Eleftherios Venizelos, began to arrive as refugees in Smyrna, as did Tartars fleeing independent Bulgaria. Deliberately used by the Ottoman government as a counterbalance to the growing number of Greeks, many settled on the slopes leading up to the castle, covering them with vines and olive trees. Their expulsion gave them the ultra-nationalism of the frontier, and made them exaggeratedly anti-Christian. As in brawls on the Cordon, outsiders, rather than the people of the city themselves, were the biggest threat to the peace of Smyrna.[108]

Other disturbances came from brigands in the countryside, some of whom were also Cretan. The hinterland was hitting back at its port – especially after 1900, when there was a series of bad harvests. Like their victims, brigands were of all races: Captain Andreas, Arnavut Ahmed, Çerkes Sami, for example. Sometimes they claimed to be robbing the rich to help the poor. On 16 May 1907 a rich Dutch landowner and tobacco merchant called Baron van Heemstra was kidnapped by Greeks on his farm two hours from Smyrna. To save money, he had recently refused a police guard. After eight days in the mountains, and the payment of a ransom of 6,000 Turkish pounds, negotiated by his father-in-law, Richard Whittall, he was released. Some of his staff may have been involved. The Dutch government and community tried, unsuccessfully, to persuade the Ottoman government to reimburse the ransom.[109]

In the city itself, as in Alexandria before 1882, the main cause of violence was Greek anti-Semitism. Since Jews were generally pro-Turkish, attacking them may have been a covert way to attack Turks, when Greeks still dared not do so physically. Greeks accused Jews of ritually murdering a Christian child in 1868, 1872, 1888, 1890 and 1896. In 1868, so great was Jewish fear of Greeks that Smyrna Jews bought, from a Jewish merchant, the bells of a monastery tower dismantled by Turks during a Greek rising in Crete, in order to present them to the Archbishop of Smyrna. The gesture had little effect. In 1872 the Ottoman authorities could not, or would not, stop Greeks blockading Jewish districts of the city, until the Austrian consul intervened. Some Jews were murdered; others took refuge in Turkish houses. The bells of St Photeini rang against Jews in 1901, sparking off anti-Jewish riots.[110]

Nevertheless, new synagogues continued to be built – the finest, Beth Israel, in 1900. Greek anti-Semitism may also have been a reaction to the rapid Jewish advance since 1873, when a third had been living off charity. Jewish businesses and schools now flourished. Women began to go out and play cards. At this stage Zionism attracted only a minority: one Jewish newspaper wrote, 'These idealists are hastening to their ruin and are dragging us with them, we the faithful children of the Ottoman fatherland.'[111]

Smyrna was a law to itself – as it so often had been since its revival in the early seventeenth century. In 1895 and 1896 Constantinople was shaken by Armenian demonstrations and terrorist attacks; in retaliation, with the Sultan's encouragement, 30,000 Armenians were killed by Muslims on the streets of the capital, watched by Turkish soldiers and policemen. In Smyrna the governor-general organized patrols to prevent massacres. In Constantinople, in 1896 Armenians seized the headquarters of the Ottoman Bank; in Smyrna, Armenian plans to attack the Crédit Lyonnais in 1905 were foiled.[112] The peace of Smyrna was guaranteed, as in 1821, by foreign warships. Normally at least one British and one French warship were stationed nearby. Britain had the Mediterranean Fleet; Italy its Mediterranean Squadron; France the Division Permanente du Levant, established in 1892.[113]

From 1895 to 1907 the governor-general of Smyrna was called Kamil Pasha. A natural Levantine, born in Cyprus, he had held posts in Egypt and Beirut, and spoke Turkish, Greek, French and English. From his 'English predilections' he was known as 'ingiliz Kiamil', and he also attended the Greeks' Panionian Games.[114] Helped by his friend Eshref Pasha, leader of the municipality, schools, roads and tramlines were improved, and a hospital specializing in treatment of venereal disease – a problem in this pleasure-loving city – was opened.[115]

Dress revealed the city's European character. In 1894 the zeybek dress worn by mountain people – in particular their baggy trousers, both long and short – was proscribed. A new profession appeared in the city: by the stations of Alsancak and Basmahane (terminus of a second railway line, built in 1863–6, linking Smyrna and Afyonkarahsiar), shops sprang up where men arriving from the countryside could hire trousers by the day. The governor came in person to check that no one in baggy trousers walked through the centre of his city: decrees against them were repeated in 1904 and 1905.

Like Alexandria, Smyrna was a second city at least as dynamic as the capital. In 1907 exports were a third higher than in 1900. It too became a city of firsts: it had the Ottoman Empire's first newspaper (1828); first American schools (1833); first racecourse (1850); first electricity (1888); first football team (1890); first motor car (1905, owned by Richard Whittall); and first public cinema (1909).[116]

To Halid Ziya, coming from Constantinople, Smyrna seemed like another country, living under its own rules. As early as the 1880s the governor dared give an official ball in the konak – naturally Christians and Jews were the only women invited: Turkish women watched from behind lattices. Censorship was lighter than in Constantinople. Halid Ziya also enjoyed going to the theatre three times a week, being invited to the houses of the Greeks with whom he worked at the Ottoman Bank, and dancing with their sisters.[117]

In many areas the Ottoman Empire has left a reputation for backwardness and oppression. In Alexandria, Smyrna, Salonica and Beirut, by a mixture of choice and necessity, it created or permitted four dynamic cities. They show that, far from being incapable of reforms, the Empire could change very rapidly indeed. Many now consider the thirty years before 1914 in those cities a golden age.

Smyrna remained a city of pleasure. Different communities and clubs competed to hold the best annual festivals or balls, often in the Sporting Club. The anniversary of the Sultan's accession day, when all major buildings in the city were illuminated and notables visited the konak to congratulate the governor, was watched by crowds of up to 30,000. The arrival of the camel bearing the first figs of the season was another annual celebration.[118] Greeks visited Jewish districts when illuminated for Purim, Muslim districts when illuminated for Bairam.[119] In carnival season, reported a German visitor, you were 'showered with invitations to balls, dinners, and large and small soirées'.[120] Every class joined in: on Sundays in particular the noise from the processions was infernal, since 'the working class likes to wear masks a lot,' reported one lady.[121] Men dressed as women, 'with beautiful long dresses showing their big virile legs', or as zeybeks, Levantines or Arabs, imitating their accents as well as their dress. Some Smyrniots opened their houses to all visitors; shops stayed open all night.[122]

However, festivals – like schools and sports – also reflected rival nationalisms. If a Greek won the annual boat race from Konak (the city centre) to Alsancak, a Greek orchestra on the quay played the Greek national anthem. In the 1904 carnival the winning float, by the Apollonian Sporting Club, displayed the Greek athlete G. Issigonis dressed as Apollo playing his lyre, surrounded by Greek girls dressed as the nine Muses in classical tunics, singing Greek songs. Every 14 July, France celebrated the anniversary of the fall of the Bastille, with parties at the consulate and on board a French battleship anchored in the harbour; the Ottoman authorities often attended.[123]

During the 14 July celebrations of 1909, when a French squadron was in the harbour, *La Réforme* wrote, 'Since they are known for their grace and elegance we strongly advise our female friends to come there ready for war, armed with all their attractions. It is absolutely necessary that these noble foreigners are astonished and enthusiastic about our ladies.' By French accounts, on some 14 July celebrations the Cordon was more crowded than for the Sultan's birthday. Covered in tricolour flags, with singers especially hired to sing the Marseillaise in cafés, Smyrna looked and sounded like a French city. The authorities would censor newspaper reports to avoid angering the Sultan.[124]

In Smyrna, foreign consulates could act as havens for Turks as well as non-Turks. Scared for their lives, two governors of the province – in 1881 Midhat Pasha, a modernizer who had intended to make the Muslim and Jewish quarters as prosperous as the Christian ones; in 1906 Kamil Pasha – took refuge in the French and British consulates respectively. They did not leave until the foreign consuls guaranteed their personal safety – illusorily in the case of Midhat, who was later tried for allegedly organizing the murder of Sultan Abdulaziz, exiled to Yemen, and killed in prison.

Halil Menteşe, later a minister under the Turkish Republic, remembered that in Abdulhamid's reign 'everywhere freedom-loving people would meet each other and create their own spots ... In Izmir in the Kraemer Hotel, in the Patisserie Highlife, in the Frank quarter, we had our own corners.' The cosmopolitan topography of Smyrna helped Turks plot revolution. 'Freedom-loving people' – i.e. Turks opposed to the Sultan's absolutism – also met in a bookshop in the Yusufoglu *han* and in the military café by the main barracks in Kemeralti.[125]

In its atmosphere of freedom, innovation and commercial dynamism, Smyrna resembled another great multinational port with a vast hinterland, rapid population growth, and churches, synagogues and mosques side by side: Odessa. Inhabited by Ukrainians, Russians, Poles, Jews, Greeks, Turks and Italians, many of whom spoke to each other in French, Odessa inspired such sayings as 'Paris is not fit to shine Odessa's shoes.' There was so much music that beggars were said to be happier in Odessa than anywhere else. In Odessa, which had already helped incubate the Greek rising of 1821, revolution broke out in 1905; in Smyrna it came three years later.[126]

I I

Drifting Cities

Vive la constitution! Vive la liberté absolue! Vive la nation!
                                    Smyrna street slogans, August 1908

IN CONSTANTINOPLE THE Sultan was adding kiosks, schools and offices
to his palace city of Yildiz, overlooking the Bosphorus. However, even
some of his most senior officials, as well as his unpaid troops, had come
to distrust him. The Empire was on the edge of a precipice – or rebirth.
Finally, in 1908, revolution broke out not in Constantinople, nor in
Smyrna, but in Salonica.

From a distance the 'queen of the Aegean', as some called Salonica,
looked like Smyrna. Red-roofed white houses built in the Turkish style,
with protruding windows almost touching each other over the street,
climbed among minarets and cypress trees up the slopes of a hill to
a castle. As in Smyrna, they formed an amphitheatre around the bay.
Surrounded by orchards, the city appeared 'almost unreal in its perfec-
tion'.[1] Close up, however, according to an English soldier who served
there during the First World War, the filth and squalor 'and especially
the smells are indescribable'. The unpaved streets were full of begging
children.[2] Beyond the orchards were 'pestilential marshes'. Malaria was
rife. The cakes in Floca's, considered the chic café of the city, were
called *gâteaux mouches*, since they attracted so many flies, 'tickling, biting
and enraging us'.[3]

The harbour, like Smyrna's, was packed with caiques, sailing ships
and steamboats. The quay was lined with cafés and taverns called *musicos*.
According to Pierre Loti, they permitted 'a strange prostitution in the
cellars where mastic and raki are drunk to the point of complete intoxi-
cation'.[4] *Musicos* stayed open late, and their Greek and gypsy music were
the only sounds to be heard at night, apart from the tapping of the night-
watchman's club 'striking the hours on the cobbles of the pavement'.
Dominating the main square was the government konak, crowded with

petitioners, gendarmes and prisoners.[5] One of the main commercial streets, as in Smyrna and Alexandria, was called Frank Street.[6]

In 1850 the population had been about 70,000; by 1906 it had risen to 114,683, of whom 47,017 were Jewish, 33,756 Greek and 29,665 Muslim (of whom half may have been *dönme*, of Jewish origin). Whatever the census, Jews formed around half the population of the 'Madre de Israel', as they called Salonica. Jews were so dominant that until 1923 most shops closed on the Sabbath and other Jewish holidays and most people spoke some words of Spanish, known in the city as *Judezmo* – the language of Jews. Grocers and waiters were Greek, yoghurt sellers Albanian, clothes sellers Jewish, tram conductors Turkish, shoeshine boys gypsies.[7]

In offices, however, as in Smyrna and Alexandria, many people spoke French: Abdulmecid had spoken it to the city's Jewish and Levantine notables on his visit in 1859. Although many missed the subtlety of Ladino, French was so popular that all modern schools of whatever religion, even some German schools, taught it.[8] A French-language newspaper called the *Journal de Salonique* was founded in 1895; soon it had a circulation of about 1,000. France dominated culturally, Austria commercially. Austria had the largest share of the city's exports and imports. Notables' furniture and clothing came from Vienna, or was made in Salonica by Vienna-trained craftsmen.[9]

Salonica was duller than Smyrna: no bookshops, theatres or concerts; little social life except in cafés like Olympias and the White Tower. The consuls formed the aristocracy of the town, one of them recalled.[10] There was also a separate Jewish aristocracy. Entrepreneurs from the Allatini, de Botton and Modiano families – equally at home in Livorno and Salonica – helped bring Salonica, in a few years, out of the Middle Ages into the nineteenth century. Brick, soap and beer factories were opened. Dr Moise Allatini, Salonica's greatest modernizer, founded the first French-language school in 1858. He offered help and medical care to all, whatever their religion. The sea walls were demolished in 1866, and new boulevards were erected with villas more French and Austrian in style than the neoclassical mansions of Smyrna: Louis XIII and neo-Gothic appeared on the shores of the Aegean.[11] A quay constructed in the 1870s, at the same time as Smyrna's, also became the main meeting place of the city; streets were slowly paved, drains finally installed.[12] Sometimes, in his enthusiasm for urban improvement, the vali employed prisoners in chains to sweep the streets, under the gendarmes' watchful eyes.[13]

Railway links to Vienna in 1888 and to Constantinople in 1896 opened up the hinterland. In 1888 the Banque de Salonique was founded with

French and Austrian money. European fashions began to replace traditional dress.[14] Labour was cheap. When trams were installed in 1893, their Belgian manager remarked that he would not have bought horses to pull them if he had known how little workmen were paid in Salonica.[15]

There were no exclusively Jewish, Christian or Muslim quarters. Some chose not only employees but also wet nurses and spouses from other religions. Christians and Muslims visited each other's houses and made pilgrimages to the tombs of each other's holy men. Christians continued to pray in a section of the church of St Demetrius, although it had been turned into a mosque. Mustafa Kemal, a Muslim, born in Salonica in 1881, son of an official probably with Macedonian blood, lived in a two-storey house in the Ahmad Subachi district. After going to a traditional Koranic school, he switched, against his mother's advice, to the Fevziye school, much frequented by *dönme*. Then he enrolled in a government military school in order to join the army. Many attribute his later zeal for reforms, in part, to his Salonica background. At military college in Constantinople, he was at first known as Selanikli Mustafa.[16]

The variety of Salonica's population was celebrated in a series of postcards called 'Costumes à Salonique'. Whereas Smyrna postcards usually showed economic activities like fig-packing or transporting goods to the Cordon, in Salonica they showed Greek peasant women bedecked in gold coins; Macedonians with thick leggings, white tunics and embroidered aprons; Albanians in massive sheepskin cloaks; Turks in smart suits and a fez.[17] A French visitor, Captain Canudo, admired Salonica as 'a true crossroads of races ... You think you find there the power of life itself, growling, boiling, a human whirlpool in the centre of an ocean of European, African and Asiatic activity.'[18]

Salonica was also a battlefield. Sex could touch a nerve of race. On 7 May 1876 her relations tried to stop a Bulgarian girl called Stefana from converting to Islam. She wanted to marry Hairullah, a Muslim with whom she was in love. They appealed to the new power-brokers – the consuls. The French consul-general and the German vice-consul, a local millionaire called Mr Abbot, had the imprudence to enter a mosque during Friday prayers, without their kavasses. In front of the vali himself, they were murdered by a mob of 'mad wolves'. The terrified town shut up shop. In reprisal the great powers sent battleships to train their guns on the city. On 16 May six Muslims, some of whom had nothing to do with the murders, were hanged on the quay by the White Tower, watched by officials, consuls, a vast crowd, and British sailors in full dress. As in Alexandria in 1863, government authorities had been forced to advertise to the local population their humiliation by foreign powers.[19]

Many of Salonica's inhabitants rarely went outside the city. The bare, uncultivated mountains were ravaged by *comitacis*, *chetniks* and *cetes* – brigands who used nationalism (Greek, Albanian, Macedonian, Bulgarian or Turkish) as an excuse for pillage and murder. Bandits battled gendarmes in the mountains. Trains were held up, villages burnt, 'traitors' shot.[20]

The Internal Macedonian Revolutionary Organization (IMRO) was founded in 1893 in Salonica. Believing in 'Macedonia for the Macedonians' (though some wanted it to be part of greater Bulgaria), it soon developed its own shadow lawcourts, armed forces and taxes, like a state within a state.[21] Fanatically anti-Greek, it terrorized villages most of which would have preferred to remain neutral. On 29 April 1903 the Salonica office of the Ottoman Bank and the surrounding cafés, as well as a French boat in the harbour, were blown up by Bulgarians, led by a teacher called Delchev, hoping to shake Macedonia out of its lethargy and force European intervention. In reprisal, Bulgarians – recognizable by their dress – were killed in the street, until the governor, Fehmi Pasha, came to restore order in person, despite a bomb thrown at his carriage.[22]

In reaction, Greek bands became more aggressive, also establishing their own state within the state. They considered Macedonia 'the lung of Greece', without which Greece would die. On 12 August 1906 the inhabitants of the small Greek town of Anchilaos were massacred by Bulgarians; the Bulgarian agent in Constantinople resigned in shame.[23] Thousands of terrorized Macedonians emigrated to Constantinople or America.[24]

Only the Jews in Salonica had few national ambitions. Abdulhamid called them 'obedient, faithful, devoted'; the Alliance Israélite Universelle, in return, hailed him as 'a generous sovereign and protector of his Israelite subjects'. The Ottoman Empire allowed Jews greater freedom from government interference than did the new Balkan states. Many left Bulgaria for Salonica, contributing to the rise in its Jewish population from 28,000 in 1882–4 to 47,000 in 1905.[25] For once they had found a haven from anti-Semitism. Salonica charmed the young David Ben-Gurion, but, dismayed by its lack of enthusiasm for Zionism, he soon left.[26]

Salonica would soon stop being a haven. An organization of revolutionaries opposed to the Sultan, called the Committee of Union and Progress (CUP), had been established there in 1904. Its nucleus was two young officers, Enver and Cemal, and Talaat Bey, a telegraph employee. They were radicals, opposed to the Sultan's absolutism, who wanted to transform the Ottoman Empire into a modern constitutional monarchy and society. By 1907 there was a CUP branch in Smyrna, in touch with branches in Salonica and Paris. The main messenger between them was a Dr Nazim. In 1907 he met Halil Menteşe in a private room in the Sporting Club – they did not meet in public for fear of the Sultan's spies – warned him of an impending revolt in Macedonia, and asked him to spread propaganda among the troops in Smyrna. Dr Nazim did so, disguised as a tobacco merchant called Yakup Aga. New taxes and arrears of pay were more powerful arguments against the Sultan's government than Young Turk propaganda. In June 1907, demanding pay owed them, soldiers occupied the main Smyrna post office.[27] In November 1907, in much of Anatolia, peasants began to refuse to pay taxes.[28]

In addition to the IMRO and the Greeks, Young Turks also created a state within the state. The army was infiltrated; even the inspector-general Hussein Hilmi himself was sympathetic. Like Cretans, Young Turks had the ultra-nationalism of the frontier. Another Young Turk officer, Niyazi was of Albanian origin. Enver had a Christian Turk or Gagauz background, Talaat a Pomak or converted-Bulgarian one; Cemal came from the island of Mytilene in the Aegean; Cavid, head of the Salonica School of Arts and Crafts, was a *dönme*. Dr Nazim, born in Salonica, had studied in Paris. All were united in hatred of what Enver's uncle Halil called 'the imbecile rule of the palace'.[29]

In Salonica, Young Turks took advantage of a measure of freedom unparalleled anywhere else in the empire, due to a combination of geography and demography. The liberal character of the least Muslim large city in the Empire (Muslims comprised at most 30 per cent of the population), combined with the proximity of the largest army corps in the Ottoman Empire, based eighty miles away in Monastir (now Bitola), made Salonica an accelarator of political change more effective than Constantinople, Smyrna or Beirut.

Salonica had the further advantage of a large number of foreign consulates, post offices and Masonic lodges. Young Turks communicated with political exiles in Paris, and smuggled in subversive men and books, using Greek consuls as well as their own networks.[30] In Salonica they planned revolution in the cafés near the White Tower.[31]

Another meeting place for Young Turks was the house of a Greek called Dr Zannas, near the French consulate, on the smart new Boulevard Hamidiye: the number of the doctor's visitors could be attributed to the quality of his medical care. The vali himself, Hassan Fehmi Pasha, was one of the doctor's patients; the doctor also bribed Ottoman police officers to supply him with information.[32] Like Alexandria in 1882, Salonica was a time bomb waiting to explode.

Meetings between Edward VII and Nicholas II on their yachts in the Baltic on 9 and 10 June 1908, erroneously assumed by Young Turks to presage the partition of the Ottoman Empire, and fear of the imminent arrival of one of the Sultan's investigating commissions, precipitated the Young Turk revolution. Following a meeting in Salonica, on 4 July Young Turk officers took to the hills and sent manifestos to foreign consuls – proof of their importance in the local power structure, even for revolutionaries. Officers loyal to the Sultan were assassinated. The restoration of constitutional government (which had functioned briefly in 1876–7 until its suspension by Abdulhamid) was proclaimed in Monastir on 20 July.[33] Two regiments sent from Smyrna to suppress the mutiny refused to fire: they had not been paid for months, and had been infiltrated by agents of the CUP.[34]

On 24 July the Sultan capitulated and announced that elections to the Ottoman parliament would be held in the autumn. In front of the Salonica konak Hussein Hilmi Pasha read out the Sultan's decree. Three times he called for cheers for the Sultan; each time he was greeted by silence.[35] On the main square, Enver Bey, the handsome young leader of the revolution, proclaimed, 'We are no longer Turks, Greeks or Bulgarians but brothers. Long live the fatherland! – the nation! – liberty!' Speeches, ovations, flag-waving processions – one led by a virgin dressed in white, to symbolize the purity of the Ottoman constitution – succeeded each other.

In the following days, bristling with cartridges, pistols, and daggers, bloodstained brigands laid down their arms (or rather those too old to be useful) and proclaimed their love of Liberty, Fraternity and Justice, from the balconies of the Olympos Palace Hotel and the Cercle de Salonique. Men who had spent half their lives burning and killing embraced the Ottoman officers who had been trying to catch them. Even the most formidable brigand of all, Sandansky 'king of the mountains', joined in the frenzy of fraternization. Photographs of the brigands were turned by Salonica studios into postcards of 'brigand bands' or 'bandit chiefs', titled 'Hassan Cavus', 'Livanos' or 'Paulos with his companion'.[36] As in Constantinople, imams, priests and rabbis also embraced each other.[37] The number of murders in Macedonia fell from 1,768 in 1907 to 291 in 1909.[38]

The whole city – the whole Empire – wore cockades or 'liberty ribbons' in the white-and-red colours of the Young Turk revolution: white to show that Turkey must be pure – red to show willingness to shed blood to make it so. After thirty years of Abdulhamid's autocracy, modern Turkey had been reborn in Salonica. Until 1912 the ruling revolutionary party, the Committee of Union and Progress, held its congresses and published its newspaper *Yeni Felsefe* ('New Philosophy') in Salonica. Everything was discussed: the nature of society, the organization of labour, women's rights, the settlement of Bosnian Muslims in Macedonia, and, for the first time, the reform of the Turkish language. A group of Young Turk writers called Genç Kalemlar – 'Young Pens' – was formed there, including the Turkish Jewish nationalist Tekinalp (born Moise Cohen) in 1911.

Salonica had found its supreme moment, like Paris after the revolution of 1830. Like Paris, it was hailed as the holy city of the revolution, the crucible of liberty. The main square was renamed the Place de la Liberté; comparing it to the Kaaba or holy black stone in the centre of Mecca, there were plans to rename Salonica itself 'the Kaaba of Liberty'. No one considered it might soon be lost to the Empire.[39] In 1908 the ancient family of Evrenoszade, which had helped conquer the Balkans for the Ottomans in the early fifteenth century, decided to restore its ancestors' tombs, in what is now Giannitsa in Greece, twenty-five miles west of Salonica, as if they would be there for another five hundred years.[40]

On 13 April 1909 there was an attempt at counter-revolution in Constantinople by troops faithful to the Sultan and horrified by the CUP's alleged irreligion. The cry 'Long live Sheriat!' was heard in the streets of the capital. Salonica, in contrast, remained true to its role as 'the Kaaba of Liberty'; 30,000 demonstrators in the Place de la Liberté promised to protect the constitution. The 'operation army' under Shevket Pasha, Enver and Mustafa Kemal, with volunteers from Albanian, Greek and Bulgarian brigand bands, advanced by train to Constantinople. To win popular support they had to promise to protect the Sultan. Instead, on 23 April the troops surrounded Yildiz and deposed him. He was sent, again by train, to exile in Salonica, where he lived under house arrest in the Villa Allatini. He was replaced by a younger, more liberal brother, who reigned as Mehmed V.[41]

Like Salonica, Smyrna exploded with joy at news of the Young Turk revolution. The Sultan's spies disappeared overnight. National differences seemed forgotten. In the Café de Paris on the Cordon, Ottoman officers ordered the band to play the Sultan's Hamidiye march, the Marseillaise and the Greek national anthem. Students of the Sultan's secondary school paraded up and down the Cordon, wearing 'liberty ribbons'. Bands in the streets played the Hamidiye march and the Greek, French and British national anthems. Many of the Sultan's officials, including the governor, fled to Athens or were demoted and sent to Salonica.[42]

Different communities held separate parades in honour of the constitution. In the Kraemer Hotel, Armenians gave a banquet in honour of a CUP representative. Prince and Princess Andrew of Greece, on their way back from visiting relations in Russia, were cheered by crowds of Greeks at the archbishop's residence – who were then addressed by a CUP representative, presumably in Greek, about reconcilation and co-operation between peoples.[43] The postcards and ephemera of the revolution, republished in its centenary year, 2008, show the streets of Smyrna hung with Turkish, Greek and Italian flags, and banners proclaiming in Armenian, Greek, Ottoman and French, 'Liberté, Egalité, Justice, Fraternité; Vive la Constitution! Vive l'armée! Vive la nation!'[44]

In Constantinople the Sultan remained popular; in Smyrna his name was nowhere pronounced – further proof of what the city's historian Vangelis Kechriotis has called its 'insolent autonomy'. Some revolutionaries even attempted to tear down the decorative Islamo-Gothic clock tower built in front of the konak in 1901, out of money collected by public subscription to celebrate the twenty-fifth anniversary of the Sultan's accession.[45]

While most were euphoric, a few remained sceptical. The French consul in Smyrna, Paul Blanc, wrote, 'What liberty seemed to unify, religion could very well split at a critical moment . . . Muslims will always feel themselves the conquering race.' Fraternization was impossible: in reality, each group wanted not equality but more privileges. One Greek notable complained to him that the Greeks resembled heirs awaiting the death of a rich relation who have just been told that he is recovering. In October, pupils of Turkish, Armenian, Greek and Jewish schools in Smyrna went on mass demonstrations to all the consulates in the city, assuring them there was understanding between communities, and condemning those trying to spread discord.[46]

Soon, however, in both Salonica and Smyrna, revolutionary unity was fractured by national loyalties. Different national clubs had been allowed to open in 1908. Cries of 'Long live liberty!' would now be followed by 'Long live Albania!', or whatever the speaker's nation was.[47] People voted in part, though not entirely, in national blocks. A massive Greek demonstration of 30,000 ensured that Smyrna won the right to return two Greek deputies. In the autumn of 1908 all Smyrna's deputies were pro-CUP: two Turks, two Greeks, one Armenian and one Jew.[48]

After the revolution came strikes. Salonica became a centre of socialism and workers' meetings.[49] A newspaper called *La Solidaridad Ovradera*

('Workers' Solidarity') began to be published and unions to be formed.[50] Strikes in Smyrna by stevedores and porters, and in Salonica by employees of the Allatini mills, were settled on generous terms.[51] Greeks and Italians in Smyrna were more militant in their wage demands than Muslims. By October, striking railway workers had agreed to management terms, after pressure from the French consul (the Aydin railway was by then French owned) and the CUP: their working day was reduced from ten and a half to ten hours, instead of eight as they had hoped.[52] Strikers in the Levant were more supine than in Western cities. In France strikes led to confrontations with the army and shootings; in Liverpool the transport strike of 1911 led to gunboats on the Mersey.

Smyrna remained pro-CUP. Demonstrators in 1912 carried the urns containing the voting papers to the municipality to cries of 'Long live the Ottomans! Long live the Committee of Union and Progress!'[53] A sister of 'Gavur' Refik, Naciye Hanim, from the Katipzade family, stimulated by the atmosphere of freedom after 1908, was the first Muslim woman of Smyrna to write on women's issues. Believing that 'the status of women in society is the measure of the degree of its development', she complained that Smyrna women were behind their sisters in Salonica and Constantinople.[54]

Uşakizade Muammar Bey, a first cousin of Halid Ziya, was a modernizing mayor committed to good relations between the communities. The son of the leading Turkish businessman of the city, a wealthy carpet merchant called Haci Ali (who had won a gold medal at the 1867 Paris exhibition), and a member of the Sporting Club, he had employees from every community and was the first Turkish member of the New York Tobacco Exchange and the New Orleans Cotton Exchange. He also, exceptionally, treated his sons and daughters equally. His daughter Latife, born in 1899, was sent to school and, like her father, knew English and French.[55]

In these years Smyrna appeared to be, in the words of the Jewish newspaper Boz de Pueblo, 'a great commercial city destined for a brilliant future'. The Courrier de Smyrne wrote, 'Seeing Smyrna from afar you feel happy for, after all, in our souls we are all Smyrniots.' The main municipality was run by a council consisting of six Turks, four Greeks, one Jew and one Armenian.[56] The luxurious Théâtre de Smyrne, opened in 1911, had 'a variety of devices imported from Vienna which can reproduce the sound of rain, wind and thunder' and multicoloured lighting.[57] By 1914 Smyrna had 53 mosques, 53 masjids, 35 churches and 17 synagogues; among its schools, 11 were Turkish, 11 foreign, 12 Armenian, 19 Jewish and, showing their predominance, 76 Greek, in addition to 3 Greek teacher-training colleges.[58] In its last years as a cosmopolitan city, large numbers of Jews were beginning to live and work in Christian districts, and attend Christian schools.[59] In 1910 the first Jewish shop, Gran Bazar de Oryente, opened in the Rue Franque.[60] To the horror of the Grand Rabbi, Jewish girls began to go out at night, even on the Sabbath.[61]

The CUP continued to have Greek, Armenian and Jewish members. A new governor visiting the Archbishop could still proclaim that 'Greeks and Turks are children of the same fatherland.' Often Greeks with roots in Cappadocia – where Greeks were far from Greece, in a clear minority, and likely to speak Turkish – were more Ottoman in sentiment than Smyrniots.[62] Aristides Georgantzoglou Pasha, born in Cappadocia in 1850, worked in Smyrna for the government as deputy attorney between 1877 and 1894 and became famous for his efficiency and integrity. In 1908 he became one of the two Greek deputies for Smyrna. His services proved his loyalty to the Empire.[63]

The other Greek deputy from Smyrna, Karolidi Effendi, had been elected to the Ottoman parliament, although he had Hellenic nationality and was professor of history at Athens University. Speaking Turkish as well as Greek, he was determined to show that he could be a good Ottoman as well as representative of what he called 'Hellenic Smyrna and Hellenism and the Hellenic mind and science and the Hellenic national interest'. Speaking in the Ottoman parliament against the Law of Associations, which wanted to place all national and religious organizations under government supervision, he declared, 'I cannot be a good Ottoman without being a good Greek. I cannot love the Muslims without being a good Christian.'[64]

Some hoped that different nationalities in the Ottoman Empire would live together in peace as in Austria–Hungary – a model frequently mentioned in leaders' letters, although the bitterness of conflicts there was hardly reassuring.[65] Mehmed V, escorted by Enver Pasha, visited Salonica in June 1911, as his father had done in 1859. It was said that he returned with the keys not of conquered cities but of subjects' hearts. Salonica Greeks celebrated his arrival by the construction of a triumphal arch in Ottoman style.[66]

However, the city was disillusioned by the new regime's policy of Ottomanization, and the closure of national clubs and organizations in August 1909. As they had before 1908, Salonicans again began to feel they were 'sitting on a powder keg ... with a burning fuse licking its sides'. In the hills outside, brigandage revived.[67] Abdulhamid had divided and ruled; the Young Turks united all nationalities against them. In 1912 the Ottoman government began to try to impose a uniform school curriculum – threatening the heart of Greek self-esteem, a classical education. Cavid Bey, one of the deputies for Salonica, said in parliament that the state 'must have control over the ideas which pervade the schools otherwise it is impossible to have a constitution and Ottoman unity'.[68] Even Albanians turned against the Empire, and began to attack non-Albanian cities, such as Uskub (now known as Skopje).[69]

The outbreak of war in the Balkans, when Bulgaria, Serbia, Montenegro and Greece, encouraged by Russian diplomats, united to attack the Empire on 8 October 1912, was the beginning of the end of the Levant. A year earlier the Greek navy had acquired a 10,000-ton three-funnel battle-crusier built in Livorno, which the Ottoman Empire had wanted but been unable to afford. It was bought with a donation from the estate of George Averoff, president of the Alexandria Greek community in 1885–99.[70] In the autumn of 1912 the *Averoff*, as the ship was christened, sank Ottoman ships, liberated Chios, and stopped Ottoman soldiers being shipped across the Aegean to the Balkans. Alexandria financed Greek expansion.[71]

Helped by some of the brigands who had terrorized Macedonia before 1908, Balkan armies fought better than expected and the Ottoman army worse, perhaps because of over-promotion of inexperienced officers who supported the CUP. The great powers, except Germany, showed where their hearts lay. They had opposed frontier changes in favour of the Ottoman Empire in case of Ottoman victory – but not changes in favour of Balkan states when the Ottoman Empire was defeated. The Greek navy appeared off Salonica. The great powers sent battleships – apparently to guarantee order; in reality to protect their own nationals.

To protect Salonica and its inhabitants, and ensure a peaceful transition from Ottoman to Greek rule, the municipal council and the foreign consuls seized the initiative: with the Ottoman governor, they decided that the Ottoman police and gendarmes would remain in the city. On 5 November they told the Ottoman commander not to fight near Salonica; on 7 November the foreign consuls went to Greek army headquarters to negotiate the Greeks' entry into the city. Negotiations were in French. To avoid what he called 'unnecessary bloodshed', Hasan Tahsin Pasha, the Ottoman commander, agreed with the consuls not to defend Salonica; moreover, he knew the Greek army was stronger than his own.[72]

On 8 November Salonica was encircled by Greek and Bulgarian forces. Hasan Tahsin Pasha decided to surrender to the Greeks – in part to stop

Bulgarians entering Solon, as they called the city, which some considered rightfully Bulgarian. As in the brigand wars before 1908, Greeks and Turks preferred each other to Bulgarians. The surrender took place 'in a relaxed and friendly manner'. On 9 November Greek forces reached the outskirts of Salonica. Ottoman forces handed over their rifles; 26,000 Ottoman soldiers went into captivity.[73]

On 10 November, led by Crown Prince Constantine, Greek troops entered the city. Delirious Greeks sang their national anthem, shouted 'Christ is risen!' as if it were Easter, and trampled on the fezzes they had previously worn. Blue-and-white Greek flags covered the streets.[74] At a thanksgiving service the Archbishop cried, 'Hosannah to the glorious descendants of the fighters of Marathon and Salamis, to the valiant liberators of our beloved fatherland! ... The golden rays of liberty must illuminate all the corners of the unredeemed nation' – in other words Constantinople, Smyrna and beyond. Greek newspapers were printed in blue and ended articles with the cry 'To the city! To Constantinople!'[75]

So easy was the Greek victory that, at meetings in London with Lloyd George, Churchill (both at that time members of the Liberal government) and Sir John Stavridi, the Greek consul-general in London and a generous contributor to Liberal Party funds, Eleftherios Venizelos planned an Anglo-Greek alliance and the dissolution of the Ottoman Empire – assumed to be a matter of months.[76] Lloyd George considered the Greeks 'the people of the future in the Eastern Mediterranean' and an invaluable ally for the British Empire. As the Greek army entered Salonica, he drank a toast to the expulsion of the Ottoman Empire from Europe, including Constantinople. He developed a fatal veneration for Venizelos, a fellow Liberal, whom he considered the greatest Greek statesman since Pericles.[77]

Salonica was the first major city to be de-Levantinized. The Mausoleum of Galerius, which had first been transformed from a Roman temple into a church, then after 1430 into a mosque, in 1912, like many other mosques, became a church again.[78] Shop and street signs henceforth had to be in Greek. People talking French in the streets were sometimes assaulted for doing so – already in Constantinople since 1908 Greek diplomats had been trying to persuade local Greeks to leave French schools, stop speaking French, and Hellenize their shop signs.[79]

The assassination of King George of Greece while walking in Salonica on 13 March 1913 led to 'reprisals' against Muslims and Jews, often by Greek policemen and soldiers. Many died. After the Bulgarian school was attacked, and fighting broke out between Greek and Bulgarian soldiers on

1 June 1913, Bulgarians fled the city. Although they kept some privileges such as exemption from military service, and the right to keep accounts in Spanish, Jews regarded the Greek 'liberation' as far worse than Ottoman rule. Many left for France – like Haim Nahoum, father of the sociologist Edgar Morin. Already speaking French and feeling 'umbilically attached to Paris', he soon felt at home.[80] In the space of a year the population was transformed. Greek statistics for 1913 show a city of 157,889 inhabitants among whom 39 per cent were Jewish, 29 per cent Muslim, 25 per cent Greek, 4 per cent Bulgarian, and 3 per cent mixed. In 1905 the proportions of the first three had been 42 per cent, 24 per cent and 29 per cent respectively.[81]

Only Jews had supported British and Austrian proposals for Salonica and the surrounding area to become an autonomous city or province, on the model of Tangier or Mount Lebanon, protected by international guarantees and an internationally officered gendarmerie (as Macedonia had possessed since 1903). Joseph Nehamia, author of *Salonique la ville convoitée* (1913), believed Salonica should be a new Venice, 'the threshold of central Europe', the great port between Germany and Suez. Few, however, stepped out of their national skin to consider the rights of others or to put their city first.[82]

The city state had vanished with Napoleon's extinction of the independence of Venice in 1797 and of Genoa and Ragusa in 1806. No ideology of urban loyalty or cosmopolitanism existed to reflect the economic and cultural character of a mixed city. Not even religion could rival the seductive force of nationalism. Its appeal came from the feelings of pride, self-sacrifice and moral superiority with which it endowed its followers – and the physical protection which the armed forces of a nation state could provide. In Trieste, Italians preferred union with Italy to remaining in the Austrian Empire on which their prosperity depended. In Salonica and Smyrna, Greeks' nationalist zeal had become stronger than the material attractions of life in the Ottoman Empire – or they may have thought those attractions would increase in a new Greek empire. By 1914 Levantines no longer put deals before ideals. Zeal trumped self-preservation.

Once the brains, heart and commercial dynamo of Turkey in Europe, Salonica sank to being the second city of Greece, cut off from its former hinterland by the frontiers of Albania, Serbia and Bulgaria. Thousands of embittered Muslim refugees fleeing Bulgarian terrorism in the countryside – descendants of Christian converts to Islam, as well as Turks – arrived in Salonica. Many, including Mustafa Kemal's mother, moved to Constantinople. Some of the best schools in Istanbul today are continuations of schools founded in Salonica which moved, with staff, pupils and charitable foundation, in 1912. The famous Istanbul newspaper *Cumhuriyet* is the successor of the Salonica newspaper *Rumeli*.[83]

With the help of the Greek government, the Salonica Islamic Committee and the Khedive of Egypt – who, as a descendant of Muhammad Ali, still had properties nearby in Kavalla – many Muslims were also shipped from Salonica to Smyrna. Perhaps as many as 150,000 Muslim refugees arrived in the Aydin vilayet alone in 1912–14.[84] Among them were the publishers of the Salonica newspaper *Yeni Asir* ('New Century'), which is published in Izmir to this day.[85] Many were housed in Smyrna's schools and mosques, then sent to live on nearby farms.[86] In the bitter winter of 1912–13, Deedes Bey, an English officer in the Ottoman gendarmerie, head of the Smyrna Refugee Committee, was followed all over the city by women begging for blankets. He had to turn most away.[87] Beginning with Mustafa Kemal himself, Balkan refugees – living proof of Turkey's European roots – would provide much of the driving force behind its modernization in the twentieth century.

The Balkan wars – the first had been followed by another in June 1913, when its neighbours united against Bulgaria – embittered community relations in the Ottoman Empire. Turks resented defeat at the hands of Balkan states they called 'pig-herds and bandits'. 'For Europe Turkish blood is lawful,' one Muslim newspaper wrote. Great-power approval of Balkan states' expansion had shown diplomacy to be 'a masquerade which holds all the filth of hypocrisy and deceit'. For the patriotic Smyrna Jewish newspaper *La Boz del Pueblo*, 'European justice is zero ... All the fine words about the rights of man hide tigers and jackals.'[88]

Few considered that nations which had a demographic majority almost everywhere in 'Turkey in Europe' except Salonica were likely to conquer it, or that to lose provinces where the Empire had maintained 130,000 soldiers at vast cost might prove, in the words of the first great Turkish woman writer, Halide Edib, a blessing in disguise.[89] For decades Macedonia had been draining the Ottoman Empire of men and money.

Some Ottomans now believed that only Muslims could be loyal to the Empire. On 2 January 1914 a CUP newspaper in Smyrna wrote that Greeks were traitors who but for the commerce of Turkey would starve. To save 'the honour of our wives and daughters', Turks should not trade with Greeks, who were 'the enemies of our religion, our history, our honour, our homeland, in other words of our material and spiritual existence'. Celal Bayar believed that 'Gavur Izmir had to become Turkish Izmir.'[90] Mustafa Kemal, the man who would change Smyrna for ever, was more pessimistic. Seeing the Cordon 'full of members of a race which was our sworn enemy', he feared that Smyrna had 'slipped away from the hands of its true and noble Turkish inhabitants'.[91]

Indeed, below the Ottoman facade, Smyrna Greeks were increasingly nationalistic. An association of professors called Anatolia, founded in Athens in 1891, had established a seminary, a journal, and schools devoted to 'national reawakening'.[92] By 1907 nationalists financed and organized by the Hellenic government in Athens had taken over Greek community organizations in Smyrna, despite internal opposition. The Hellenic consul-general became as important in the Greek life of the city as its own archbishop and notables.[93] Like the Benakis from Alexandria, some Smyrniots went to live in Greece physically, as they already did in their hearts and minds. Although educated at the Evangelical School in Smyrna, George Baltazzi, son of Pericles Baltazzi, became a deputy in the parliament in Athens and, after serving in the Hellenic embassy in Constantinople, minister of foreign affairs.[94]

An ultra-nationalist called Chrysostomos, who had actively helped Greek brigand bands when bishop of Drama in Thrace, was appointed archbishop of Smyrna. He arrived on 10 May 1910, greeted by triumphal arches on the Cordon, flower-throwing crowds, and a newspaper article invoking the city's most famous Christian martyr: 'Hosannah! Our Polycarp is coming! Our new Paul is coming! New glory will exalt the throne of Polycarp and immortalize it for ever!'[95] *Amalthea* on 17 November 1910 wrote that it hoped that the Ottoman Empire would evolve not into Turkey, but into 'the Eastern empire': the Greek community had always 'lived and lives in this empire', 'on its own with no loss or intermingling'. No mention of the protection given by the Ottoman Empire to the patriarchate, or the economic and musical 'intermingling' in Smyrna.[96]

Dr Apostolos Psaltoff was a leading doctor of the city, operating in the Greek, Armenian, Jewish and British hospitals, as did many others. Yet he volunteered to fight with the Greek army against the Ottomans both in 1897 and in 1912: by his acts he showed himself to be an enemy of the cosmopolitan empire and city in which he worked. He was also a member of the Smyrna branch of a secret Panhellenic organization established to 'reinforce the patriotic sentiment' of the population and help defend it against the Young Turk government.[97]

So bad had relations become that in May and June 1914 the Ottoman and Greek governments – to the horror of Greek deputies in the Ottoman parliament – had begun to discuss 'transfer': the forced exchange of populations in order to homogenize the two countries. The wishes of the people concerned were not considered. Some Muslim refugees from Crete or the Balkans, and members of the Young Turk 'Special Organization', began to terrorize and kill Christians – not in Smyrna itself, but in small towns like Soke, Sevdiyekoy, Çeşme and Foça, even on Long Island in the Gulf of Smyrna.[98] In June 1914 Archbishop Chrysostomos prophesied a general massacre to chief dragomans visiting from the Constantinople embassies. Accused of encouraging Greeks to emigrate – the Ottoman government was still in theory committed to coexistence – the Archbishop was expelled on 20 August 1914. Celebrations of the feast day of the King of the Hellenes were, for the first time, forbidden, as were the Panionian Games. The Patriarch closed Greek schools and churches in protest at government policy.[99]

Prosperity, however, was growing at the same time as the nationalism which was destined to destroy it. The mansions of the Levantine merchants in Buca and Bornova, many now schools or university buildings, remain as testimonies to Smyrna's wealth in its last Levantine years – and to their builders' enjoyment of fiscal and legal privileges under the capitulations. The mansion built in Buca by the wealthy ship-owner Tommy Rees, founder of the Egypt & Levant Steamship Company, had fifteen bedrooms, a ballroom, a billiard room and a smoking room. The even larger Forbes mansion on the top of a nearby hill, now in a state of dereliction surrounded by the buildings of the Buca Social Insurance Hospital, has a commanding view of the city and the sea. Above a door in the splendid columned facade can still be read the inscription 'Built 1908, burnt 1909, rebuilt 1910.'

In her memoirs, one of the Whittalls remembered that her family were like 'a nation not a family ... In Turkey they were princes in their own right and their wealth and power, and to some extent their arrogance, had almost no limits.' A hundred members of the family would sit down to Christmas dinner at the 'big house' in Bornova, where Charlton Whittall had once entertained Sultan Abdulaziz.[100] Levantines ate well. At dinners in Smyrna, 'luxuriously decorated tables were festooned with roses and syringas and the unending dishes would have tired the most complaisant and best disposed stomachs.'[101]

A booklet published in 1912 to commemorate the centenary of the firm of C. Whittall & Co., which had used the same site on the Smyrna quay for a hundred years, looked forward to a prosperous future. It celebrated the 'marvellous expansion of imports and exports. Constitutional government is further stimulating trade and industry and the number of new factories which are being built afford striking evidence of the confidence in the future ... Smyrna is the commercial capital of the Ottoman empire.' The firm was especially proud of new machinery producing fifty tons of cleaned raisins a day, and of its profit-sharing scheme with staff.[102]

Their success in making Smyrna the carpet capital of the world was another sign of the confidence of Smyrna businessmen. No artefact linked East and West more visibly – as carpets' prominence in European portraits after 1400 testifies. After 1880, carpets became increasingly fashionable in the West.[103] In 1907 a group of Smyrna businessmen – from the same families which had been the dynamic force behind the creation of the Cordon – set up Oriental Carpet Manufacturers, soon known as OCM. They included Alberto Aliotti and Herman and Nelson d'Andria, whose families had come from Chios after the 1822 massacre; some British Levantines – James Baker, Sydney La Fontaine, Harold Giraud – and an Armenian, Takvor Spartali of Spartali Company – the biggest firm of carpet-weavers in Turkey, with over a thousand looms in Anatolia – whose daughter had married Alberto Aliotti.

OCM was established to improve the quality and designs of carpets, weaken local competition, and bring Eastern carpets to Western buyers in bulk. In effect they were cutting out the Turkish carpet merchants who had formerly dominated the trade, such as the Uşakligil family, who had previously employed thousands of looms in Anatolia. Enraged by their exclusion, the Uşakligils went into transport, soon owning so many camels they could undercut the Smyrna–Aydin railway. When one of their camels left Aydin, it was said, another was arriving at the same moment in Smyrna.[104]

By 1914 OCM was the largest business in the Ottoman Empire after the railway companies, employing carpet-makers throughout the country (usually Christians rather than Muslims, as they were more willing to let buyers and quality controllers into their houses). It had opened shops in Constantinople, Alexandria, Moscow, Vienna, Paris, London, Buenos Aires and Sydney. OCM controlled not only 90 per cent of Turkey's carpet exports, but also a third of Persia's carpet output. It could supply both Persia's 'bold simple colourings' and 'Smyrna's neutral tones'.[105] Similar cartels were being established by Smyrna businessmen for shipping and figs: the Smyrna Lightermen's and Barge Owners' Company in the early 1900s, Smyrna Fig Packers Ltd in 1910.[106]

Foreigners' economic domination in the city was, however, under challenge. The CUP representative in Smyrna, Celal Bayar, was helping Turkish businessmen establish their own local companies and banks.[107] Previously content with a fluid identity, even the most cosmopolitan Levantines determined to use, or invent, British, Italian, French or

Austrian roots to obtain a European passport. Above all, they wanted not to have Ottoman nationality, since they did not want to be at the mercy of the Ottoman government.[108]

The Levantine synthesis on which Smyrna had been built was breaking down. Some Levantine businessmen began to look forward to what Oscar van Lennep, member of a Dutch family resident in the city since 1731, called 'the natural liquidation of the Oriental Question' – in other words, European control of the region.[109]

Beirut after 1908 was also a drifting city. Always on opposing sides, while Damascus had remained loyal to Abdulhamid, Beirut had welcomed the Young Turk revolution. The governor took refuge in the British consulate, then fled. Beirut, like Smyrna and Salonica, believed it had entered a new era. The city still had Ottoman loyalties. After the Austrian annexation of the former Ottoman province of Bosnia in October 1908, angry crowds tried to stop an Austrian boat unloading and went to the Saray to volunteer in case war broke out.[110]

However, signs of hate between Arabs and Turks, as well as Muslims and Christians, were beginning to surface. Modern Arab nationalism was born not in Damascus or Baghdad, but in Beirut.[111] As early as 1880, British sources had talked of 'invincible antipathy' between the Turks and Arabs and of the latter's desire for the caliphate to be returned from Constantinople to the sherifs of Mecca. A few posters had appeared in the streets of Beirut denouncing Arabs as 'slaves to the degraded Turks', lamenting the hatred between Christians and Muslims, and calling for a revolt.[112] As in Smyrna between Greeks and Turks, the Levantine synthesis was breaking down.

Language was a key. Since the proclamation of the Ottoman constitution of 1876, Turkish had been the official language of government and parliament and in theory of government schools as well – although few non-Turks spoke it well. The Young Turks wanted to reimpose its use in lawcourts and schools where, by long usage in Arab provinces, Arabic had been allowed.[113] As in modern Belgium, language became the cutting edge of conflict between two peoples which had long coexisted in the same state. In 1910 there were protests over the spread of Turkish and the appointment of officials ignorant of Arabic. Ottoman officials were worried, and asked for the Ottoman navy to visit Beirut.

The memoirs of the Muslim notable Salim Salam show how one Beiruti was torn between Constantinople and Paris. Born in 1860, he learned French, attended both Christian and Muslim schools, and married a member of the

Muslim Barbir family. His sisters attended the British Syrian School for Girls; he sent his sons to the Syrian Protestant College and one son to England to study agriculture; his nephew Omar Onsi was one of Beirut's first modern painters. Christian teachers came to the house to teach French and Arabic to his sons and to his daughter Anbara. He was both an elegant man about town and a merchant with an office by the port, careful not to lose the common touch. He was head of the town council and the board of the Maqassid, the main Muslim charity, founded in 1878 mainly to help education. Like his Christian neighbours, he rejoiced at the fall of Abdulhamid.

He later wrote, 'The Turks were enemies to every project of development even if it cost the Treasury nothing . . . While they remain backward, we will remain backward.' After the Ottomans' defeats in the Balkan war in 1912, the British consul-general reported that 'on all sides' people were saying the Empire was doomed. Salam wrote, 'Some friends approached me with the suggestion that an annexation to Egypt under English protection be requested; others expressed a desire for a French occupation.'[114] Another sign of Ottoman weakness had been the shelling of the port of Beirut by two Italian warships on 24 February 1912, during the Italian attack on the Ottoman Empire in order to conquer what is now Libya. Ships were sunk, and about forty people were killed in the harbour.[115]

In January 1913 a Beirut Reform Committee of twenty-two Muslims and twenty-two non-Muslims, under Yussuf Sursock, Salim Salam and Ahmad Muhtar Bayhum, demanded decentralization and the introduction of Arabic as an official language of the province, with Turkish. Five Christian members secretly requested French intervention. On 9 April the Beirut Reform Committee and its club were closed down; journalists were arrested; there was a short strike. Flyers were posted urging Beirutis to flee to Mount Lebanon and refuse to pay taxes. The French consul-general claimed that the movement had won the people. In the end the government allowed – but did not impose – the use of Arabic in government offices, lawcourts and schools; there were even theoretical quotas for Arabic-speaking officials. Turkish, however, remained the sole official language of the Ottoman Empire.[116] Sursock and Bayhum were made senators – and later given the right to buy more government land in Galilee – but Arab demands had not been met.[117]

From 18 to 23 June 1913, with Muslims and Christians such as Ahmad Muhtar Bayhum and Albert Sursock, Salam attended a Syrian Arab Congress in Paris – the location itself was a snub to the Ottoman Empire. The congress passed resolutions favouring Armenian autonomy and the use of Arabic as an official language, and sent them both to the Ottoman

government and to the great powers.[118] Salam and Sursock told Pierre de
Margerie of the French Ministry of Foreign Affairs, 'We are not willing to
exchange our state for any other.' Margerie replied, 'We definitely have no
ambitions whatsoever in Syria and all that we hope for is that you live with
your state in peace.' Both sides were playing the Levantine mating game of
mutual seduction and exploitation, using words to hide their feelings. By
another account Salam lost his temper with two Christian delegates and
struck them with his cane. Salam and Sursock opposed the conscription law
and – revealing their priorities – wanted the Beirut province to have the
right to issue licences for new companies.[119] That year the small Arab secret
society al-Fatat moved its headquarters from Paris to Beirut.[120]

Alfred Sursock, cousin of Yussuf, also reflects the evolution in Beirutis attitudes. An Ottoman diplomat and businessman, regularly travelling between
Paris, Constantinople and Beirut, Sursock was profuse in assurances to the
Sultan of 'the inalterable attachment of his faithful Arab subjects'. At an audience, the Sultan promised him justice for the Arabs. In private, however,
even this privileged millionaire, whose career and fortune had benefited so
spectacularly from the Ottoman Empire, felt antagonism to it as an Arab. He
wrote, 'Everything is going from bad to worse for us. We remain subject to
injustice and violence. Equality between the Turks and us is a vain word.'
Some ministers, he believed, were animated by 'preconceived attitudes of
injustice' towards the few Arab officials.[121] One lady friend, Comtesse von
Studenitz, asking him not to laugh, predicted the break-up of the Empire
and the creation of Syria as an Arab kingdom by 1919. He would be king of
Syria, as he already was of 'my heart and my soul'.[122]

Like Smyrna and Alexandria, Beirut had become a city between
worlds. Some areas would seem to an Australian 'like a French port', with
women 'French in feature and deportment' and modern pharmacies and
bookshops.[123] Some Ottomans complained that it had forgotten its links
with the Empire. A vali is alleged to have felt that he was not Beirut's
governor but the Ottoman consul in a western city.[124] The city's variety
was its essence. It was at once the gate to Syria, an incubator and paci-
fier of nationalisms; Arab and European, Syrian and Lebanese, Western
and Eastern; peaceful and bellicose, looking to Rome and Boston, Paris
and Mecca, Constantinople and Cairo. Beirut was also a city ready to
revolt – but that revolt, like previous ones, might be a means to greater
autonomy, rather than independence: more Arab deputies in the Ottoman
parliament, and the expansion of Mount Lebanon to include Beirut as its
political as well as its economic capital.[125]

12

Catastrophe and Liberation

Soldiers! Your first goal is the Mediterranean! Forward!
Mustafa Kemal to the Fifth Army, 25 August 1922

A T FIRST, AS the First World War tore Europe apart, the Ottoman
Empire remained at peace. However, meeting in the grand vizier
Said Halim's home at Yeniköy on the Bosphorus between 18 and 23
July 1914, Enver, the minister of war, and his inner circle in the government – without telling the Sultan and the other ministers – had already
secretly decided to fight on Germany's side. Their motives were desire to
join what they believed would be the winning side; fear of partition – the
fate of Turkey in Europe after the Balkan Wars; and desire for Turkish
expansion in the Aegean, the Crimea and Central Asia. Moreover, Enver
Pasha loved action: in 1913 he had led both an attack on the Sublime
Porte itself and the Ottoman recapture of Edirne. On 2 August a secret
alliance with Germany was signed.[1]

On 8 September the Ottoman government took advantage of the
war to abolish the hated capitulations and foreign post offices, and
on 3 October Mount Lebanon's special status was ended.[2] Public
opinion was delighted. A Young Turk newspaper, *Tanin*, proclaimed
what most Turks believed: 'We were not the owners of the country. It was the foreigners.' A drum-beating, torch-bearing crowd
acclaimed the ministers. Said Halim gave a celebratory banquet in,
ironically, the 'very large and very European' Hotel Tokatliyan on
the Grande Rue de Péra, which belonged to an Armenian with a
Russian passport.[3]

The ambassadors of France and Britain – which had many subjects
protected by the capitulations – had refused even to discuss their abolition. Given their failure to defend the territorial integrity of the Ottoman
Empire in 1912, their offer to guarantee the rest of it in 1914, in return
for Ottoman neutrality, seemed worthless. Moreover, France and Britain

were allied to the traditional Ottoman enemy, Russia. Germany seemed the Ottoman's best safeguard against Russia.[4]

By mid-October, as Enver had requested, £2 million in gold had arrived from Germany. On 29 October the *Yavuz Sultan Selim* and other ships – the former in reality a German ship pretending to be under Ottoman command – steamed out of the Bosphorus to bombard Odessa and Sevastopol. On 2 November Russia declared war on the Ottoman Empire, followed by France and Britain. Four Ottoman ministers resigned; the Sultan was reputed to have declared, 'To make war on Russia! But its corpse alone would be enough to crush us.' Far from being dragged into the war, a victim of great-power machinations, the Ottoman Empire forced its way in by an act of unprovoked aggression, on the orders of the most popular man in the Empire, Enver Pasha.[5]

War was another blow to the cities of the Levant. Soon after the abolition of capitulations, Count Edmond de Hochepied, first dragoman of the Dutch consulate in Smyrna, a member of the city's oldest consular dynasty, was travelling to his country house at Sevdiyekoy. As was probably a Levantine habit, he had bought a third-class ticket, but sat in a first-class carriage. When a railway clerk complained, Hochepied boxed his ears. He was sentenced to six months in prison, later commuted by the Sultan. Ottoman officials were now prepared to punish those who had hitherto considered themselves above the law.[6] But, while the Ottoman Empire began to suffer the horrors of war, Smyrna remained an island of peace. Many French and British Levantines – Whittalls, Girauds, Pagys and Caporals – left to fight in the armies of France or Britain. The hyper-English neo-Gothic St John's church in Alsancak still contains a tablet dedicated by 'the British community of Smyrna in Honoured and Revered Memory of those of their members who volunteered for active service in defence of their country and lost their lives 1914–18'.

However, although they were enemy nationals, some of whose relations were fighting the Ottoman Empire, other French and British Smyrniots were allowed to stay. Perhaps the Ottoman government believed Smyrna could not survive economically without them. Rahmi Bey, the vali of Smyrna in 1913–18, came from the aristocratic Evrenos family, which, like other Muslims, had left Salonica for what remained of the Ottoman Empire in 1912. 'A gentleman of old family and large possessions', known as 'the Khedive of Smyrna', he had been considered pro-British by the British consul-general in Salonica in 1903–8, Sir Robert Graves.[7] In the houses of Smyrna merchants, where he was a frequent guest, he was said to drink any amount of alcohol without 'losing his wits or powers of locomotion'.[8] During the war, in the words of Grace Williamson, a nurse working in the English Nursing Home in Smyrna, Vali Rahmi Bey was 'quite sweet to all of us here ... Most of the English had absolute faith in him'.[9]

A symbol of Levantine flexibility, the OCM expanded into military supplies. In a triumph of profit over patriotism, it acquired the Ottoman Cloth Company, which supplied khaki for the uniforms worn by Ottoman soldiers fighting the countries from which OCM's directors came. A letter from Edmund Giraud expresses Levantines' equation of deals and ideals:

> The Turks have shown continually a great deal of good will towards us and have not only exempted all our workmen from military service but ... strangest of all – ever since the war broke out between Turkey and the Allies – have paid us in all TL 8,000 in gold ...
>
> Mr Guiffray, the French manager of the Compagnie Industrielle du Levant, also supplying cotton cloth to the Ottoman Government, holds the view that he is serving the interests of his country by continuing in business. Closing down would prejudice all foreign control of business after the war.[10]

At the end of December Harold Giraud sent a letter to London, in which he set out a Levantine dilemma: 'On the one hand, we have our nationality to consider, and the fear of acting in a way that might prejudice the same; on the other hand, we have our material interests and investments in this country to protect ... Personally, I am inclined to think that it is our duty to strain every effort in order to protect our assets.' In 1918 OCM even subscribed to an Ottoman war loan.[11]

As well as making money, Smyrna businessmen tried to make peace. British intelligence had identified Edwin Whittall as a useful intermediary. Again, money dominated. One officer wrote, 'If anyone could fix things up with the Turks on a financial basis he can. The Turks like and trust him.' Whittall tried to bribe Rahmi Bey, and Talaat Pasha himself, to take the Ottoman Empire out of the war; negotiations also involved Deedes Bey, formerly of the Ottoman gendarmerie in Smyrna. The terms discussed are under dispute: possibly Rahmi Bey's alleged asking price of £2 million was considered too high by the British government.[12]

Smyrna did not escape entirely unscathed. In March 1915 British ships began to bombard the forts defending the Gulf of Smyrna, recently strengthened by the installation of Austrian shore batteries: Rahmi Bey would watch the spectacle from the Cordon, sitting on the terrace of

Costi's café, as did 'all the men of Smyrna but very few of the women', according to Grace Williamson. Turks began to flee the city.[13] The British Admiral Peirse sent a message to Rahmi Bey through George Horton, the American consul at Smyrna, to demand the unconditional surrender and destruction of all coastal forts and batteries 'to spare your city and vilayet of Smyrna the horrors of war'.[14] There were also air raids on Smyrna. Both naval and aerial attacks stopped as a result of a combination of factors: effective Turkish defences (two British ships were sunk); protests from neutral Greek and Dutch businessmen; the realization of the wealth at stake in the city; and the fact that Allied bombs hit Christian schools and areas, into which Rahmi Bey had moved British and French citizens. If Allied bombs had hit Muslim areas, Muslims' retaliation might have been worse, for local Christians, than any bombardment. As in 1695 and 1770, when Smyrna had been threatened by Venice and Russia, in 1915 the city was saved by its cosmopolitanism.[15]

Smyrna avoided even worse horrors, owing to Rahmi Bey's refusal to obey Talaat's orders to deport the Armenians in his vilayet eastward, to face massacre and starvation, as happened to 900,000 Armenians living elsewhere in Anatolia. Rahmi Bey was a personal enemy of Enver, and enjoyed thwarting his policies.[16] A friend reported to Alfred Sursock in Beirut that Smyrna remained enjoyable: 'Social life is as intense as in the past. The theatre of Smyrna offers us very attractive cinematographic films as well as operettas in Greek. Theatres, cinemas, cafés, promenades are packed with people. Even the workers working in factories and the fields are at ease.'[17] Thanks to the government – and in particular the governor, Rahmi Bey – the Levantine synthesis survived.

Nevertheless, some of the expropriations and expulsions planned since 1912 did take place. In 1915, and again after Greece's entry into war on the Allied side in 1917, some Greeks were expelled from the coastline, sometimes being killed or forced to work in labour battalions. Their abandoned houses were distributed among Kurds and Laz from the East.[18]

Unlike Smyrna, Beirut had a bad war. The First World War further poisoned relations between Turks and Arabs in Lebanon. The Young Turk government had proclaimed martial law in 1914. Calling its officials traitors and valets of the European consuls, it suspended Mount Lebanon's autonomy. Mountain hotels were filled with Ottoman officers and courts martial rather than holidaying Beirutis. The chief of the Ottoman army in Syria, with almost unlimited powers, was Jemal Pasha. Still remembered as 'the butcher', he behaved like the commander of an occupying army rather than the defender of his country. In Beirut, inhabitants were given three days to leave their souks and houses before these were demolished and replaced by straight roads from the port to the Place de la Liberté, as the Place des Canons had been renamed after the Young Turk revolution of 1908 – 'planning' as domination.[19]

Ottoman authorities then discovered incriminating documents in the French consulate. It had been left in the care of the US consul by the departing French consul, François-Georges Picot, but the documents were revealed by a dragoman. They proved a death sentence for many prominent Lebanese and Syrians, who were shown to have been asking for French (or British, Russian or Greek) help and weapons to secure independence, possibly through armed revolt, before 1914.[20] Their trials for treason took place in Damascus, but many were hanged in Beirut, in order to overawe the city. On the mornings of 21 August 1915 and 6 May and 6 June 1916, gallows with corpses appeared among the trees and fountains of the Place de la Liberté. In all twenty-five Arab nationalists were hanged there, both Muslims and Christians, including Farid and Philippe el-Khazen, two former honorary dragomans at the French consulate.[21]

The hangings galvanized Arab nationalism, just as the British authorities' executions in Dublin of Irish rebels/freedom-fighters after the 1916 'Easter rising' poured oil on the flames of Irish nationalism. Blood called for blood. The last words on the scaffold of Omar Hamad, a Beiruti, were prophetic: 'Tell your oppressive government that this act will one day cause its ruin.' Abdel-Ghani Arayssi's were equally so: 'The glory of the Arabs will come ... Our skulls will form the foundation of Lebanese independence.'[22] The Hashemite dynasty of Mecca, and some Arab officers in the Ottoman army, many of whom had lost personal friends, were strengthened in their resolve to turn against the Ottoman Empire.[23] Salim Salam – himself briefly imprisoned – did not believe that Jemal Pasha was reacting to treason: 'His real intention was to cut off the intelligent heads so that, as he put it, the Arabs would never emerge again as a force.'[24] An Arab revolt, on the side of the Allies, was launched by the Hashemites in Mecca on 5 June 1916.

While Jemal Pasha was hanging people in Beirut, he was starving them in Mount Lebanon. Bad harvests, plagues of locusts, crop requisitions for the Ottoman army, conscription and speculators were among the causes of the famine. Above all, the Allied blockade of the coasts of the Ottoman empire – another factor driving the Hashemites to revolt – interrupted food supplies. Not even neutral ships, stocked with food bought by Lebanese and Jewish immigrants in America, were allowed by British authorities in Alexandria to sail to Lebanon. They feared supplies would feed the Ottoman army. Both sides used food as a political weapon, without regard for human life.

In the winter of 1917/18 Beirut streets were filled with starving beggars. 'The government seemed helpless to undertake any action to control speculators or to secure the grain they held,' writes the historian of the catastrophe, Linda Schilcher: probably, as some contemporaries alleged, government officials, from Jemal Pasha down, shared in the profits from the high price of bread.

The most prominent speculator, by his own family's admission, was Michel Sursock. Isabelle Bustros wrote to her brother Alfred Sursock, 'Is it true that Michel T has made millions and your brother Michel also, they tell me that he too has made a lot.' Michel Sursock refused to sell grain bought at 40 piastres a measure for less than 250 piastres, even at the request of the American Relief Committee in Beirut. A famous Beirut song of the time laments that the singer is not a horse in the Sursock stables – then he would be fed.[25] Other Sursocks were more generous. Michel's brother Alfred was called 'le père des pauvres'; in August 1918 fifty-eight camels loaded with wheat were on their way from 'his' villages to the city of Beirut. He was implored to use his influence with Jemal Pasha, who often stayed in his house, to release some of the many Beirutis sent into exile.[26]

All parties – Ottomans, Allies, Lebanese – contributed to the catastrophe. In all, perhaps 500,000 died in the whole of Syria, including a third of the population of Mount Lebanon. While staying in the Bassoul Hotel by the port, a young Turkish journalist working for Jemal Pasha called Falih Rifki Atay (who three years later witnessed the burning of Smyrna) heard 'waves of groans as if they came from the bottom of a well and so poignant they seemed to come from the depths of the soul'. They came from living skeletons in the surrounding streets: 'they were dragging themselves on to pavements to die, not having been able to find even the bark of a tree nor a piece of dried orange peel on which to gnaw.' Typhus, malaria and cholera accompanied the famine. Atay also claims that, while the poor were starving, he went to a party in a private house where 'Drink and pleasure flowed like water.'[27]

Salonica also had a bad war: its fate was decided by Eleftherios Venizelos. Half brigand, half bourgeois, Venizelos had become the dynamo of Greek politics. In 1915 he was dismissed as prime minister by King Constantine, who wanted to preserve Greece's neutrality. Initiating what became known as 'the national schism', Venizelos reacted by setting up a separate government in Salonica. The city was still sufficiently independent to be able to function as a rival to Athens. He greeted the British consul there with the words, 'Well, Mr Wratislaw, here I am again, in revolt as usual.'[28]

French troops arrived to support him. He was as keen to drag Greece into the war on the Allies' side as Enver had been to drag the Ottoman Empire into the war on Germany's. In both cases the sovereign and most politicians would have preferred to stay neutral. In 1917 King Constantine abdicated and went into exile. Venizelos became prime minister again. Greece entered the war.

In a final cosmopolitan paroxysm, Salonica became an allied military headquarters, its streets filled with Annamite, Indian and Senegalese troops, as well as French, British and Russian. Most of its Jewish inhabitants supported Germany and Austria, which they considered better for Jews than Russia and its allies.[29] The Place de la Liberté, once the focus of the Young Turk revolution, became, in the words of one British officer, 'the most crowded and cosmopolitan spot in the universe'. The buzz of conversation 'in half the languages in Europe rose like the noise of surf on the beach'.[30] Salonica's cafés and cabarets – the Odeon, the White Tower, the Skating Rink – 'did a roaring trade' among allied troops.[31] Floca's in particular became 'the forum of the allied armies'. Half a dozen languages could be heard coming from evzones, Orthodox priests, Turkish civilians, *demi-mondaines*, British intelligence officers, Russians, Serbians, boot-blacks and newspaper urchins as persistent as they were ubiquitous.[32]

On 5 August 1917 a fire broke out in the centre of the city. It was an abnormally hot summer and the fire spread quickly, as if directed by 'a diabolical intelligence'. Three-quarters of the old Ottoman and Jewish quarters were destroyed, including the Prefecture, the Cercle de Salonique, Flocas, the Olympus Hotel, banks, shops, warehouses, mosques and synagogues. Clouds of smoke hung over the city. The waterfront looked like a cliff of flame. British army lorries raced through the city picking up people and carrying them to safety. Perhaps 70,000 were left homeless: 'the air was filled with the shouts, cries and moans of a huge concourse of people, dishevelled in appearance, haggard of countenance and totally distraught.' Only a change in the direction of the wind made the fire die down the following day, and only prompt action by the Allies averted a famine. Venizelos, however, called this levelling of the old Ottoman city 'almost a gift of divine providence' – words which some twisted to mean he had directed it himself. Fire facilitated Hellenization.[33]

Retreating in the west in August 1918, the Central Powers collapsed on the Salonica front on 24 September. On 30 October – twelve days before the German armistice at Compiègne – the Ottoman Empire signed an armistice at Mudros. For the next five years, British, French and Italian forces occupied Constantinople. Henceforth, as Venizelos had calculated, the Ottoman Empire was the vanquished enemy to be dismembered, Greece the loyal ally to be rewarded. Venizelos aimed for a 'Greece on two continents and washed by five seas': Ionian, Mediterranean, Aegean, the Sea of Marmara and the Black Sea, possessing both Constantinople and Smyrna.[34] He overestimated the strength of Greece and of his own support in it. Greece was said to have the appetite of Russia with the resources of Switzerland.

The foundation of British power was the Royal Navy: its blockade of Germany had helped win the war. In Smyrna, the first sign of the end of the war was the arrival of a British warship on 6 November. Amid cheers from a waiting crowd, pealing church bells and whistling factory sirens, it moored by the Kraemer Hotel on the Cordon. Against his will, the manager was forced to hoist the Greek flag. 'The town is mad, quite Mafeking mad,' wrote an English prisoner of war called Lieutenant-Colonel Barker. The ship's commander was carried in triumph through the streets to cries of 'Vive l'Angleterre! Vive l'entente!' Cáfes played 'God Save the King' and the Marseillaise.[35]

The mask of loyalty to the Ottomans, maintained in the war, now fell. Smyrna Greeks displayed the Greek flag and portraits of Venizelos everywhere, even on their horses. Reading the newspapers of these years, with their catalogues of racial murders and insults, is a reminder of the destructive effects of nationalism – or, from another point of view, of coexistence. After four years' absence, on 18 December the ultra-nationalist Archbishop Chrysostomos returned to Smyrna in triumph. Hitherto Greeks and Armenians had been relatively unconcerned by each other's fate. Greeks had appeared as lethally indifferent to, and prepared to take advantage of, massacres of Armenians in 1895, 1896 and 1915–17 as Armenians had been during massacres of Greeks in 1821. On 19 January 1919, however, in the Armenian cathedral of St Stephen in Smyrna, there was a service, followed by a football match in the Panionian Stadium and a *vin d'honneur*, in honour of 'Greek–Armenian confraternity in Smyrna'. Chrysostomos claimed, 'The black centuries are over.' Freedom had come. There were cries of 'Long live Venizelos! Long live Boghos Nubar [Nubar Pasha's nephew]! Long live Greece! Long live Armenian independence!' The Armenian Philharmonic Orchestra of the city played the Greek and Armenian national anthems. Greek and Armenian athletes embraced each other.[36]

Nurettin, the violently nationalist commander of Aydin, a hero of the defeat of the British army at Kut in Mesopotamia in 1916, was dismissed by the Ottoman government on 11 March 1919.[37] On 16 March the Orthodox and Armenian patriarchs in Constantinople formally renounced their flocks' allegiance to the Ottoman Empire. Some Greeks tore up their Ottoman identity cards, and stamped on their Ottoman fezzes, in public. Chasms were widening. A Turkish journalist wrote of 'wounds that will bleed eternally in the heart of every Turk and Muslim'.[38] A conciliation committee sent from Constantinople under Abdurrahim Effendi, a son of Abdulhamid with a distinguished military record, stayed in Smyrna on 26–29 April 1919. A banquet brought together Chrysostomos, the consuls, Turks, Greeks and Armenians. Little was accomplished. Race hate now ran too deep. The Ottoman dynasty could no longer function as a unifying facade.[39]

Meanwhile the prospect of a Greek occupation of Smyrna was thought to threaten Turks' very existence in Anatolia. Resistance meetings – what pamphlets called 'an overwhelming mass repudiating Greek domination' – were held in Muslim cemeteries at night. Newspapers claimed 'the eternity of rule in Izmir is Muslim and Turkish'. The mayor, Haci Hasan Pasha, and religious leaders organized an anti-annexation congress which met in the theatre of the National Library on 17–19 March, to prepare resistance by both Turks and Jews. Crying 'They are giving Izmir to the Greeks!' they seized weapons from the police armoury. From Smyrna's minarets, muezzins shouted calls to resist in the middle of the call to prayer.[40] To forestall the Greeks, some Turks would have preferred an Italian occupation: Italy had been promised the area by France and Britain, in order to persuade it to enter the war.[41]

However, Greeks were also swept by a frenzy of nationalism – what, referring to the Turkish counterpart, Halide Edib would call 'a magnificent national madness'. They were convinced their country enjoyed a unique opportunity for expansion. On 1 May 1919 Chrysostomos made another inflammatory speech, in front of the Greek cathedral, ending 'Long live Greek Smyrna! Long live our union with our mother Greece!'[42] When the idolized Greek battleship *Averoff* arrived in Smyrna on 2 May, Greeks caressed its sides, kissed its sailors' feet, waved more flags.[43]

Finally, on 15 May 13,000 Greek troops arrived on battleships, again including the *Averoff*, escorted by HMS *Iron Duke* – sent by Britain to protect the Greek landing from a potential Italian attack. Church bells rang in triumph. Resplendent in embroidered robes and bejewelled tiara, decorated with a crowned double-headed Byzantine eagle, Chrysostomos blessed the troops. They then marched along the flag-draped Cordon under arches decorated with the slogan 'Zito o Venizelos!' Bands played the Greek national anthem. Crowds waved photographs of Venizelos, showered troops with flowers and kisses, and shouted, 'Long live Venizelos! Long live Greece! Long live Chrysostomos!' Men wearing the Ottoman fez were attacked or subjected to what Turks called 'obscene humiliations', including removal of the fez. The Ottoman vali was forced to cry, 'Zito o Venizelos!'

A shot rang out near the konak, possibly fired by a Salonica Turk called Hasan Tahsin: it went down in Turkish history as 'the first shot' – one of the first signs of active resistance to Allied occupation. Greek troops opened what Donald Whittall, an eyewitness, called 'a terrible fusillade at the barracks, the coffee houses and Government House [the konak].' By the end, about 100 Greeks and between 300 and 400 Turks had been killed, some on the Cordon itself. Revealingly, some Greeks had been killed since they still wore the fez and 'were thought to be Turks by Greek soldiers unacquainted with Smyrna customs'. Turkish soldiers in the barracks surrendered and received 'a good deal of knocking about'. Some prisoners were killed outside the Kraemer Hotel itself by Greek soldiers. 'Led by the roughs of the town [i.e. *qabadays*]', according to the Swedish consul Alfred van der Zee, Greek troops pillaged shops in the Turkish quarter and went on a rampage of rape and murder. A providential rainstorm at 4 p.m. ended the day's horrors.

Race hate replaced Levantine coexistence. The next day, according to George Perry of the American YMCA, 'morbidly curious Greek people were passing through the Turkish quarter gloating and priding themselves on their efficacy in pillaging and looting'. The occupation's baptism of blood helped ensure its failure.[44] It was the more revolting, wrote the British military representative, 'for having taken place in a great city which was completely at peace',[45] and for being accompanied by a promise from Venizelos, read out in St Photeini, that 'Greek freedom would bring equality and justice to everybody, irrespective of race and religions.'[46]

An inter-Allied commission of inquiry later concluded that the responsibility for the acts of 15 May fell on 'the Greek superior military commander and certain officers who failed in their duty'.[47] Although Greeks were in a majority only in the city of Smyrna, not in the surrounding area, Greek troops now began to spread out, reaching as far as Bergama, seventy miles to the north-east, by 12 June. Aydin changed hands seven times, finishing as little more than a ruin. Atrocities bred atrocities. Greeks who had fled or been deported before 1918 returned and were settled on lands from which Muslims had fled or been expelled. Some Turkish villages were burnt, for many local Greeks – usually more aggressive than soldiers from Greece itself – regarded the occupation as 'merely an opportunity to take revenge', in the words of the American consul George Horton.[48] Looking back, Greek writers acknowledged 'a nationalist current that was completely unrealistic but impossible to rein in'. An anti-Venizelist general called Joannis Metaxas prophesied a military disaster for Greece in Anatolia, like that experienced by the French Empire in Russia in 1812.[49] Venizelos, on the other hand, believed Turks were so impoverished that they would welcome Greeks as saviours, and that, in Anatolia, the latter would soon out-breed the former. Biology, he believed, was on the side of the Greeks.[50]

Smyrna Greeks entered a heaven of happiness, showering soldiers with flowers, cooking them special food 'as though it were Easter'.[51] The Hunters' Club on the Cordon became army headquarters; Greek soldiers were everywhere – on patrol, occupying the Ottoman barracks, vaccinating Turks, feeding Greek refugees from the interior. Celebrating Easter with a party on a field outside Cordelio, on the far side of the Gulf of Smyrna, they dreamed of taking the mother church of Orthodox Christianity in Constantinople itself:

> Now that the fustanella [a Greek uniform] has come to Smyrna,
> The fez will disappear and the blood of Turks will flow.
> Now that we have taken Smyrna, let us fly to St Sophia.[52]

The French consul, however, wrote a dispatch which is a model of lucidity. The Greek government, he said, 'has offended to the depths the national and religious dignity of the Muslims who will never forgive their former subjects for having dominated them so brutally ... Sooner or later the reaction which is hatching will become stronger and will organize itself into a real danger for all the Christian population without distinction.'[53]

On 16 May – the day after Greek troops landed in Smyrna – Mustafa Kemal Pasha sailed from Constantinople to Samsun, sent by the Sultan as inspector-general of troops in northern Anatolia. By July he had taken command not only of local troops but of a resistance movement independent of the Ottoman government. Although he rarely talked about it, his nationalism was no doubt sharpened by desire for revenge for the Greek occupation, seven years earlier, of his birthplace, Salonica, and for the fire there in 1917. On 6 June a mass meeting of men and – exceptionally – women in Sultanahmet in Constantinople was held in protest against the bloodstained Greek occupation of Smyrna. All swore to recover the city, which an Istanbul newspaper called 'our beloved Izmir, Anatolia's apple of our eye, our largest city, which is Turkish and Muslim from top to toe'. Like many Muslims, Halide Edib blamed Europe for Turkey's defeat: 'The European powers would have found a way of sending armies of conquest to the stars and the moon had they known that Muslims and Turks inhabited those heavenly bodies. Governments are our enemies. Peoples are our friends and the just revolt of our hearts our strength. The sublime emotion which we cherish in our hearts will last till the proclamation of the rights of the peoples.' That Greeks, and other nations, felt equally justified in their own 'sublime emotion' and desire for 'rights' was ignored.

Once an agent of cosmopolitanism, Smyrna was now – like Alexandria in 1882 – on the front line of nationalism. Even more than the arrival of Kemal in Anatolia, the Greek occupation of Smyrna kicked Turkish resistance into action. Kemal himself later said that, without it, the Turkish people might have gone on sleeping.[54] Allied representatives on the spot in 1919 wrote that it was the worst move Venizelos could have made for his own cause. Ottoman authorities, hitherto compliant, stopped co-operating with Allied armistice commissions and began to help the local resistance movements which, independent of the government in Constantinople, had begun all over western Anatolia.[55] The Turkish reaction on the ground showed the gap between decisions taken in great capitals in the West and local realities in the East. Drunk with power and ignorance, few Allied statesmen – least of all Venizelos himself – remembered his remark 'You cannot kick against geography.'

Nevertheless, driven by realism – commercialism – or dislike of Kemal, some Turks co-operated with the Greek occupation. They included the mayor, Haci Hasan Pasha; the muncipal administration and lawcourts, which continued to operate; and the newspapers *Koylu* and *Islahat* and their editors. Greeks also had support among some Muslim Circassians, although many supported Kemal: a pro-Greek Caucasian congress was held in Smyrna in October 1921. For a time some Muslims regarded the nationalist resistance in Anatolia as brigandage.[56]

The Jews of Smyrna were more hostile to the Greek occupation than some Turks. The Grand Rabbi never attended Greek ceremonies during the occupation. Many Jews lamented that the province of Smyrna had become a new Macedonia – though others privately enjoyed what they remembered as 'el tiempo del grego'.[57] Their distrust of Greeks was confirmed by Greeks' use of Jewish tombstones in the transformation of a Muslim school building, started by Rahmi Bey on the site of a Jewish cemetery, into the new Ionian University, planned by the Greek government to advertise its 'civilizing mission in the East'. Greece did not come to Asia Minor to conquer, it was said, but in 'the spirit of brotherhood', to bring to its peoples its 'superior civilization'.[58]

The Greek High Commissioner in Smyrna, Aristides Sterghiades, like his patron Venizelos, was a Cretan. 'Very authoritative, easily angered and not at all flexible', he was determined to ensure good relations with Muslims. His success in 1913 as the first Greek governor of the half-Muslim city of Janina in Epirus had helped get him appointed in Smyrna. He punished some of those who had killed Turks (executing three ring-leaders), established a special Department of Muslim Affairs, refused invitations from local Greeks, and interrupted sermons when they became too political. Turkish remained one of the two official languages of Smyrna, even after the Ottoman Empire had signed the Treaty of Sèvres with the Allies in August 1920. Greece then formally took over the administration, more civil servants arrived from Athens, and the last Ottoman vali left.[59] Despite all his efforts, however, there were many acts of repression. Some Turks were made to perform forced labour, or corvée, as in Ottoman times; to escape it they sometimes fled to join the national resistance. Their land was then given to Greek refugees.[60]

The years 1919–22 would be remembered as the golden sunset of 'sweet-smelling Smyrna': there were 500 cafés, 13 cinemas and many 'rag-time bars'. Young women wore dresses only two inches below the knee: 'Heavens what a place this is! ... As for the girls – oh lord!' wrote a British officer to his wife. Thirty-four newspapers were published: 11 Greek, 7 Turkish (the number increased during the Greek occupation), 5 Armenian, 5 Hebrew, 4 French.[61] The Girauds' fancy-dress ball for New Year 1921 was still talked about years later. Allied and Greek officers came to the house in Bornova: as the clock struck twelve, the party toasted Joyce Giraud, twenty-one like the century.[62]

Some Levantines, however, were lukewarm: the old Frankish–Ottoman alliance was not dead. Herbert Octavius Whittall wrote to the Allied peace conference to advocate the old Levantine dream of 'local government', guaranteed by Britain, France and America: he wanted neither Greeks nor Turks in power. A British representative wrote, 'The Levantines of Smyrna did not so much resent the doings of Sterghiades as the very presence of the Greeks whom they dislike, because they are accustomed to look upon the Greeks everywhere as an inferior class.' They also feared a diminution in their profits and privileges.[63] Fear of Greek competition led some families and companies to leave for France or Italy.[64]

International politics had provoked the Greek occupation; international politics helped end it. Greek troops had arrived in May 1919 in part due to the desire of Britain, France and Greece to prevent an Italian occupation: Italy had been promised the vilayet of Aydin in 1915 to lure it into the war, Italian troops were nearby, and some Italian ministers hoped to use Anatolia as a destination for Italian emigrants.[65] The first successes of Kemal in Anatolia brought him support among powers opposed to British hegemony in the region. In 1920 the Soviet Union signed a treaty with the Ankara government and began to supply it with much-needed weapons, for use against Greek armies. Italian representatives based in the Kraemer Hotel also gave help and encouragement to the Turks.[66]

The death from a monkey bite of King Alexander of the Hellenes on 25 October 1920, the defeat of Venizelos in general elections, and the restoration of King Constantine after three years' exile weakened even British enthusiasm for the Greek cause. On 19 December Constantine sailed into Piraeus, the port of Athens, on the *Averoff*, to scenes of hysterical enthusiasm. The powers began to talk of handing Smyrna back to Turkey.[67] Churchill, the British war minister, had been prophesying disaster for the Greeks – of whom he had once been a fervent supporter – since early 1920.[68]

The Greek commander General Leonidas Paraskevopoulos left Smyrna in November 1920, having been crowned by Archbishop Chrysostomos in St Photeini with a gold laurel wreath, on each leaf of which the name of one of the sixty Greek communities he had liberated in 'Ionia' had been inscribed: the wreath can be admired today in the National Historical Museum in Athens, beside Chrysostomos's bejewelled archiespiscopal tiara.[69]

On 11 June 1921 King Constantine landed in Smyrna, to encourage a final Greek campaign to destroy the Turkish army. He stayed in a villa in Cordelio, and issued a proclamation to his troops as hyper-nationalistic as any by Venizelos: 'You are fighting here for the Hellenic idea which produced in this very place that incomparable civilization which will never cease to merit the admiration of the whole world'.[70] Greek soldiers sang:

> With such a Constantine, with such a King,
> We will take Constantinople and St Sophia.
>
> . . . .
>
> We will send the Turks to the red apple tree.

Some substitued the name 'Venizelos' for 'Constantine'.[71] Impressed by
their morale, and finding even some Turks sympathetic, the King was
sure Greece would win – or so he wrote. The foreign minister George
Baltazzi, of the great Smyrna family, refused the great powers' offers of
mediation.[72]

Greek armies were more numerous and better armed than the Turks.
Soon they were sixty miles from Ankara – victory seemed close. On 7
July the Prime Minister of Greece announced that the enemy was 'in
a situation clearly approaching dissolution'.[73] Outside Ankara, however,
the Greeks were halted. Like invaders of Russia, they found victory in
the field had little effect in alien terrain with overstretched supply lines.
Greece had no general to match Kemal. In August 1921 – out of hostility
to Constantine – or desire to mollify the winning side – Britain, France
and Italy declared their neutrality. In September the Greek army fell back
to Eskişehir, in Western Anatolia. In October 1921 France signed a treaty
with Kemal's government and began to supply it with weapons, as Italy
already had. For its part, Britain stopped selling arms to Greece.[74] The
powers were abandoning it as a lost cause. King Constantine admitted
'the struggle is beyond our strength.'[75]

'The army will not withdraw from the occupied areas', there was
'no cause for alarm', according to Greek army bulletins. But that winter
Greek soldiers at the front, whose discipline had already begun to waver
in late 1920, were shouting for demobilization: they were demoralized
by exhaustion, defeat, bad food, low pay, desertions and the political
schism between pro- and anti-Venizelists.[76] Large numbers of competent
Venizelist officers were dismissed. Many soldiers wanted to get home
in time for the 1922 harvest.[77] The schism's bitterness can be judged by
Prince Andrew's astounding letter to the royalist General Metaxas in
January 1922: 'Something must be done quickly to remove us from the
nightmare of Asia Minor ... we must stop bluffing ... The people here
[in Asia Minor] are generally disgusting. A swollen Venizelism prevails ...
It would really be worth handing Smyrna to Kemal so as to kick all these
worthless characters who behave like this after we have poured out such
terrible blood here, blood of Old Greece ... My God when shall I get
away from this hell here?'[78] No one thought of withdrawing from central
Anatolia to make Smyrna and its surroundings into an urban redoubt.

By early 1922, from refugee accounts of expulsions and massacres,
Sterghiades knew the Greek government should evacuate Smyrna; no
one would listen. In Smyrna life continued as usual. Newspapers of these
months describe a lecture at the Alliance Française on the tricentenary

of Molière by Dr Varenne of the French Hospital, children's parties at Bornova, football matches, the arrival of an Italian operetta company, the movement of boats in the port. Members of a group known as Asia Minor Hellenic Defence addressed a petition to the Archbishop of Cambridge (*sic*) and the President of the USA asking them 'not to allow the return of thousands of Greeks under the Turkish yoke'.[79]

Sterghiades fell back – too late – on a plan for an autonomous non-national state of Ionia, under the Sultan's sovereignty. Some in Smyrna had been reported to be dreaming of it in the 1850s, but – like such plans for Salonica in 1912 – it demanded a sense of community – above all a city army – which did not exist. On 31 July 1922 only a few hundred municipal employees bothered to attend the proclamation ceremony. They included the mayor, Haci Hasan Pasha, and Cavid Bey, a professor of French. There were speeches in Greek, Turkish, Kurdish, Armenian and Ladino. Sterghiades said, 'Let the sufferings of the past be lessons for the future.'[80]

On 25 August, 400 miles east in Anatolia, the Greek front suddenly collapsed. In a last act of unreason, three of the best Greek regiments had just been sent to eastern Thrace to try to secure Constantinople (where the great powers' occupying armies upheld Turkish sovereignty in the city). Exhaustion did the rest – and the troops' knowledge that it would be difficult to return to Greece after September, when rains started to make the roads impassable.[81] Refugees began to pour into Smyrna, including Muslims. Trains arrived, packed with the dead as well as the living. News of the Greek retreat was posted in the Cercle Européen.

The life of the city continued. An Italian company was appearing in *Aida* at the Sporting Club. The Théâtre de Smyrne was showing a film called *Tango of Death*.[82] Ray Turrell, a relation of the Whittalls, remembered, 'The export season was just beginning, the warehouses were filling up, figs and raisins were being packed for the European markets' – many of the poor of Smyrna relied on the work they secured at this season to survive for the rest of the year.[83]

Hortense Woods of Bornova, a British admirer of Mustafa Kemal, had hitherto led a peaceful life, cosseted by servants and relations, painting in her garden, oblivious of the fighting in Anatolia. Politics obtrude on the pages of her journal for the first time on 29 August 1922. She wrote, 'All arabas [carts] have been requisitioned for the army. The Turks have taken Afion Kara Hissar [200 miles east]. A battle is raging.'

4 September: 'Smyrna is seized with panic and so is Bournabat and all the surrounding villages. People of every nationality are running away,

even English. People are afraid of the retreating army pillaging and burn-ing towns and houses, destroying everything they come across. They have more than once threatened to do this should they be forced to evacuate Smyrna ... Anyone coming from downtown Smyrna has some stories and you can see the fear in their eyes.'

5 September: 'A hundred thousand [refugees] have arrived in Smyrna and are gradually sent off to the islands.'

On 6 September she saw Greeks and Turks pouring through her village with carts loaded with belongings, and hundreds of sheep and camels: 'All Bournabat has fled.'[84]

No longer respecting officers' orders, the retreating Greek army commit-ted many atrocities. Even in 1921 Prince Andrew of Greece had witnessed what he called 'cruel reprisals against a peaceful and unarmed population in villages who had always received us with every demonstration of respect and submission'.[85] In 1922 parts of Eskişehir, Afyon, Cassaba, Ushak, Alaşehir and Manisa – towns the Greek army had occupied in Western Anatolia – were burnt. Jewish teachers in Smyrna wrote, on the basis of eyewit-ness accounts, 'Greeks as they retreat sack and burn everything on their path' – often including schools and mosques filled with Muslims. Women were raped, both sexes massacred, without pity.[86] Halide Edib wrote that neither side gave any quarter. Towns looked like hell on earth. The Grand National Assembly in Ankara issued a protest 'in the hope of preventing similar vandalisms in the cities of Bursa and Smyrna'.[87]

General Nicholas Trikoupis learned of his appointment as the new Greek commander only when he had been captured by the Turkish army, from Mustafa Kemal himself. Seeing them talking French together, Halide Edib remembered, was like seeing 'an amateur speaking to a professional'. Trikoupis looked 'sickly, overdressed and very theatrical'. Kemal tried to console him: 'War is a game of chance. The very best is sometimes worsted.'[88]

Sterghiades took better care of his papers than his people. The archives and employees of the Greek High Commission were evacuated on 5 September – in accordance with a secret plan drawn up a few days earlier. He asked for ships to evacuate refugees, but none were sent. A division sent to protect Smyrna mutinied on 5 September and was sent back to Greece.[89] On 7 September, having handed the keys of the High Commission to the French consul, amid the jeers of Greek onlookers, Sterghiades boarded a launch which took him to the *Iron Duke*. He settled in France, where he died in 1950. If he had returned to Greece, he would have been lynched.

The same day Professor Constantine Karatheodory evacuated the staff and equipment of the Ionian University, which had been due to open the following month – proof that, although they did not tell the general population so, Greek authorities knew that evacuation was necessary. Much of the equipment intended to serve Greece's 'superior civilization' in Smyrna was used in Salonica, in the university which opened in the Villa Allatini in 1926.[90] The building intended for the Ionian University is now the Anatolian Lycée.

The Cordon was lined not with strolling pleasure-seekers, but with refugees and their belongings and with haggard, unfed Greek troops and their equipment, sleeping everywhere, even in doorways. A British naval officer called Charles Howes called the Greek soldiers 'the most dilapidated, filthy, untidy, slouching lot of humans I have ever witnessed wearing uniform'.[91]

Shipping-line offices were besieged by people desperate to buy tickets on the earliest boat out.[92] Some Smyrniots thought it unnecessary to leave, as, in the words of a doctor in the Armenian National Hospital, Garabed Hatcherian, 'it seems very unlikely that brutalities would take place in Smyrna itself where so many Europeans live.' Moreover, 'fleets from every nation are in the harbour filling people with trust and reassurance' – as they so often had in the past. There were eleven British, five French, three American and two Italian naval vessels – including the same battleship, the *Iron Duke*, which had escorted the first Greek forces to Smyrna three years earlier. On 6 September, small forces of British, French, American and Italian marines had been landed to maintain order, protect their nationals, and guard their country's consulates, the fire station and other properties.[93] The Levantine synthesis appeared to be at work: foreign consuls, backed by their navies, had arranged a bloodless transition from Turkish to Greek rule in Salonica in 1912, and were now planning to arrange another, from Greek to Turkish rule, in Smyrna.

On 9 September Turkish troops entered the city, led by General Fahrettin Altay, riding a white horse which had belonged to General Trikoupis, followed by long files of baggage camels. In his memoirs Altay wrote how beautiful Smyrna appeared between the mountains and the sea in the morning light: the only black spot was the foreign warships in the harbour. The sound of the horses' hooves mixed with the waves from the sea like an anthem of glory.[94]

Despite two shots fired by Greeks, order was maintained as the troops rode down the cordon towards the konak, past the Greek refugees and abandoned Greek army equipment. The same Turkish soldiers had appeared to Hortense Woods in Bornova 'splendid men wearing new spotless uniforms and Circassian caps. Perfect discipline and perfect quiet.' Knowing, as did Lloyd George himself, that the British Prime Minister had staked his reputation on Greek victory in Anatolia, she could not resist adding, 'What will Lloyd George say? Now Kemal is greater than he.'[95] Grace Williamson in the English Nursing Home wrote, 'There was hardly any trouble! ... No shooting on the streets thank God. Such a relief; everyone is inwardly delighted to have the Turks back again.'[96] The Turkish entry into the city along the Cordon had gone better than the Greek one three years earlier. Turkish police began to reappear in their old Ottoman uniforms, British and Greek employees of the Oriental Railway Company to wear the Ottoman fez again.[97]

But – without a commander prepared to enforce order by summary executions – pillage and killings, by both Greeks and Turks, broke out in different spots in the afternoon, even including Frank Street. The supplies of the Greek army abandoned on the Cordon were removed 'on every imaginable little cart or pram or barrow'.[98]

Around 4 p.m. on 10 September Mustafa Kemal himself arrived, escorted by cavalry, in an open motor car presented to him by the Turks of Smyrna, which was covered in olive branches. He went to the konak, was cheered by a Turkish crowd, then spent several hours in consultation with Nurettin – the nationalist commander of Smyrna in 1918–19 – whom he had reappointed to command of the city. A proclamation was issued threatening with death Turkish soldiers who molested non-combatants. Then he went to the Kraemer Hotel. The following dialogue with a waiter took place: 'Did King Constantine come here to drink a glass of raki?' 'No.' 'In that case, why did he bother to take Izmir?'[99]

The Greek High Commissioner and generals had fled: the Archbishop was the only leader with the courage to stay – although he too had the foresight to dispatch his archives to Athens. In the evening of 10 September Chrysostomos was summoned by his old enemy Nurettin to the konak. After a brief interview, he was taken away to prison. The cross he had left at the konak entrance on arriving was not returned on his departure – a sign that his murder was planned, according to General Altay, who claimed in his memoirs that both Kemal and he deplored it.[100] A crowd was waiting outside. First they humiliated the Archbishop and cut off his beard; then they gouged his eyes out, before tearing him, and two accompanying Greek notables, to pieces. A French marine patrol nearby was forbidden to intervene. It is said that a Cretan soldier finally shot him dead to end his agony.[101] Some Turks who had collaborated with the Greek regime, and the Armenian director of the newspaper *La Réforme*, were also killed.[102] The city was turning from sanctuary to hunting-ground.

Despite the relative quiet in the city, on 10 September the British consul-general Sir Harry Lamb, of the Levant Consular Service, who had previously served in Salonica, told all British citizens to prepare to leave. Turkish irregulars – known as *cetes* – began to threaten people in the streets and demand money. Looting spread, by both Greeks and Turks. Captain Hepburn on the USS *Litchfield* wrote in his diary, 'Terror is in the air.'[103] The catastrophe had begun.

In the Armenian quarter in the north of the city, Turkish irregulars began to set buildings alight with petroleum. Pillage, rape and murder followed. The Armenian archbishop's offices were set on fire by soldiers with hand grenades; many who had taken refuge inside were killed. The city's restaurants and bakeries closed on 11 September, though some trams continued to run. That evening Nurettin told Major Davis of the American Red Cross, 'Take them [the Greeks] away, bring ships and take them out of the country, that is the only solution.'[104]

The French and Italian consuls had not appeared at a planned meeting with Kemal on 10 September. The days of the consuls had passed. Turkey and Greece had entered an era of generals and colonels. The next day, according to a telegram sent by Sir Harry Lamb, the Turkish civil governor 'to whom Mustapha Kemal then referred me, assured me that I need not be in an anxiety regarding their [British nationals'] safety until tomorrow night Wednesday' – 12 September. The precision about timing was chilling.[105]

On 12 September, having observed from the roof of the English Nursing home, Grace Williamson wrote that Smyrna looked 'dreadful; no end of dead and rubbish all together'.[106] On 13 September the wind changed direction, blowing north, away from the Turkish and Jewish quarters. Then Turkish soldiers in uniform, according to non-Turkish witnesses – Miss Minnie Mills of the American Collegiate Institute for Girls, and men of the Smyrna fire brigade – began to scatter petroleum on houses and set them alight. By the afternoon the Armenian quarter was ablaze.[107]

Smyrna had excellent modern fire brigades; they were prevented from reaching the fire by Turkish soldiers. More shops and houses began to be pillaged. Turks had already been told to leave Christian districts; some Jews saved their lives only by proving that they were circumcised.[108] During the war, the Armenians of Smyrna had been protected by Vali Rahmi Bey. A very large proportion indeed – up to 15,000 – were killed in 1922. Kemal finished in 1922 what Enver and Talaat had started in 1915: the elimination of Armenians from Anatolia.[109]

The fires started in different parts of the Christian districts soon merged, and by night became one all-engulfing wall of flame, two miles long and a hundred feet high. At first silhouetted against the flames, churches, theatres, the shops of Frank Street and the Kraemer Hotel then collapsed. A Dutch refugee, from the safety of the Dutch warship in the harbour, watched one quarter after another being reduced to rubble. 'Between midnight and one o'clock the fire reached the quays. The most beautiful part of the town now was caught by the flames. First the cinemas, the coffee houses, the clubs, then the Russian and French consulates ... It was not only the natural element that did its destructive work. By means of binoculars we could see arsonists performing their ominous work.'[110] It is said that the flames reached so high, that they could be seen by the monks on Mount Athos on the other side of the Aegean.[111] From her house in Bornova, Hortense Woods wrote, 'We can see the red glow and glowing smoke ascending ever higher. Bombs are constantly exploding. The sound reaches us very distinctly. All the beautiful houses and the quay gone.'[112]

The fire destoyed many factories and most of the warehouses, filled – in September – with the harvest of Anatolia. The entire carpet stock of OCM went up in flames. So many banks and banknotes were burnt that, for a long time in Smyrna, new notes had to be printed in very small sizes, as there was not enough bank paper to go round. Part of the Frank quarter at Alsancak and some large modern buildings survived: St Polycarp's, the Crédit Lyonnais, the National Bank of Greece; the New Evangelical Greek Girls School (now the Ataturk Lycée), which had just been expanded yet again; the Greek girls school (now the Namik Kemal Lycée); and the offices of an American charity called Near East Relief.[113]

By 16 September, however, when the fire was dying out, most of the Greek and Armenian quarters and much of the Frank quarter had been destroyed: 5 consulates, 5 hospitals, 21 churches and 32 schools – Catholic and Protestant, as well as Orthodox and Armenian. In 1923 an offical Turkish report estimated that 14,004 of 42,945 houses had been destroyed. For that time the fate of Smyrna was unprecedented – far worse than that of Alexandria in 1882 or Salonica in 1917: the world had not yet seen the charred cities of the Second World War. The French consul wrote, 'Nothing exists any more.'[114] *The Times* lamented, 'One of the richest cities in the Levant is like a skeleton.' The people of Smyrna would henceforth refer to before or after 'the fire' as, until recently, Europeans spoke of before or after 'the war'.[115]

The Turkish and Jewish quarters, however, had remained intact: it is said that trenches had been dug around them to prevent the fire spreading there. Italian soldiers also helped protect the Jewish quarter. In order to expand Italian influence, the Italian government had recently given many Smyrna Jews Italian citizenship. Smyrna's Muslims and Jews showed the same lethal indifference to the fate of other races that Greeks and Armenians had displayed towards each other during previous massacres.[116]

While Smyrna burned, those Christians who had not died hid in cemeteries, or other locations, or fled to the Cordon with what possessions they could carry. Terror replaced pleasure on the waterfront. At night, thieves came to rob and kill: Allied battleships in the harbour played their lights on the crowds to try to protect them. Both ends of the Cordon were blocked by Turkish forces.

Levantines' resolve to procure foreign passports proved their foresight. The cosmopolitan city was abandoned; nation states protected their own. From 13 September, through the burning city, British, French, Italian and American marines escorted convoys of their own nationals to their battleships. It took all the force of her personality for Alethea Whittall to be able to board, on a British ship, the patients and staff of all nationalites from the English Nursing Home, not merely those with British passports.[117]

Greece, however, abandoned its own. Fifty miles away in Çesme and Urla the last Greek troops were being evacuated on Greek ships back to Greece: the fate of Greek civilians was ignored.[118]

Once the foreigners had boarded their battleships, the Cordon was left packed with local Christians uttering what George Ward Price on the *Iron Duke* called 'such frantic screaming of sheer terror as can be heard miles away'. Pistol and rifle shots, and the occasional rattle of a machine gun, sounded above the roar of the fire and the crash of falling buildings. The smoke was so hot that people felt they were on fire.[119] Facing death by fire behind, death by water in front, and death by steel from soldiers and irregulars, the crowd was also tormented by animals: rats fleeing the burning buildings, and screaming horses and camels.[120] Garabed Hatcherian wrote in his diary, 'The fire, the shootings and the cudgel of the Turks have squeezed the Christian crowds from three sides. If there is a ray of hope it is the sea.'

On the Cordon, as foreign sailors could see through their binoculars, Smyrniots were robbed, set on fire, clubbed to death, or pushed into the sea by soldiers and irregulars. So many corpses clogged the sea that if you fell in you might not sink. Some sailors tried shooting at corpses to make them sink. Boys swam among them, scarves tied round their noses so they would not faint from the smell, and removed valuables, or cut off fingers for the sake of the rings on them. Some women gave birth on the quay and had to consign their stillborn babies to the water.[121] The stench from the bodies, blood and excrement on the Cordon, and in the sea, reached the ships.[122]

If they could not block the smell, some ships tried to drown the sound. In a refinement of pitilessness, bands on board played light music – or put on records like Caruso in *Pagliacci* – either out of naval routine or to drown the screams from the Cordon.[123] Films were made, and photographs taken, of the burning city. Such visual records were needed. All witnesses agreed that words alone could not convey the horror of Smyrna. 'No words can describe the awful effect of the city'; 'Whatever they say fails to express half the horror of that night'; it was 'too large and too fearful to be painted'.[124] The formality of one letter is especially eloquent. An English witness, Percy Hadkinson, wrote to the British High Commissioner in Constantinople, Sir Horace Rumbold, 'If Your Excellency could only have heard the cries for help and seen defenceless women and children unmercifully shot down or rushed into the sea to be drowned like rats or back into the flames to be burned to death, you would have fully realized the horror and extreme gravity of the situation.'[125]

Admirals and consuls waited for orders from London, Paris and Rome. In their turn, they urged Athens to take responsibility for evacuating the city. Finally, at midnight on 13/14 September humanity broke through. Facing near-mutiny by his horrified crew, Admiral Sir Osmond Brock of the *Iron Duke* ordered cutters to be lowered. George Ward Price of the *Daily Mail*, on board the *Iron Duke*, wrote, 'The bow touches the quay and a fighting shrieking terrified torrent of humanity pours over it.' It was hopeless to try to admit women and children only: 'The moment it is full they back out literally to overflowing.' Many boats capsized from the weight of the humans in them. Many individuals swam out to battleships; sometimes, but not always, they were allowed on board. The words 'Je suis français, j'ai perdu mes papiers' worked wonders on French ships. Perhaps 2,000 were removed on 14 September. Italian boats were the most welcoming.[126]

By 15 September the fire had burnt itself out; the centre of the city was reduced to rubble. The director of the Crédit Lyonnais, Jean Morin, who had been shamed into staying by his Turkish kavass, remembered that a pestilential smell continued to hang over the town. Flies were every-where. For weeks bales of tobacco from warehouses burnt slowly in the rubble, giving a strange red glow at night. The crowd moved into cellars in the town. People ate raw meat or ship's biscuit brought by American crews.[127]

After the massacres of 1821, Greeks had been considered indispensable. Smyrna had asked them to return to the city from their ships in the harbour. A hundred years later states and cities had changed: there had been too many wars. Nationalism trumped commercialism. Finishing what the fire had started, Kemal – in supreme command of the city – ordered the expulsion of the remaining Greeks and Armenians. On 16 September, under pressure from foreign admirals and consuls, he agreed to allow foreign powers to evacuate all surviving women and children, and men over the age of forty-five and below the age of eighteen. The excuse for the age restrictions on men was the continuing state of war with Greece. Men between eighteen and forty-five were to be deported inland to repair the damage inflicted by the retreating Greek armies. On 21 September the deadline was extended from that date to 1 October.[128]

Greece displayed no excess of 'Dunkirk spirit'. There were twenty-five empty passenger ships off the nearby Greek island of Mytilene and hundreds of boats on other islands; since Kemal would not guarantee their safety, none would sail to Smyrna. Moreover, Greek minds were on politics not human lives. A revolution broke out among troops on Mytilene on 21 September.[129] In the end, individual Americans and private charities, led by Dr Esther Lovejoy and Pastor Asa Jennings, began to organize relief flotillas, which sailed to Smyrna under the protection of the American flag. When the first ships were seen in the distance from the Cordon, 'agonizing, hopeless shrieks for help' were replaced by cries of joy.

As crowds moved towards the main pier to board the ships, through narrow barriers set up to control them, they were searched four times by Turkish soldiers, who relieved them of 'practically everything of value they have before their arrival at the ships'. To shrieks and tears, Turkish soldiers pulled away men and youths from their families, 'with a liberal allowance on each side of 18 and 45'; then, with the words 'Haydi, haydi' ('Come on, come on'), they pushed the men with their gun butts into columns of terrified prisoners.[130]

The commander of the USS *Edsall* considered Turkish methods of crowd control necessary. He wrote on 24 and 25 September: 'As soon as the gates were open the crowd became a mob. Women were knocked down, men walked over, children were torn from their arms by the crush and they were pushed through screaming and crying.' Turkish troops used rifle butts and bayonets to control the crowd. Fifteen thousand were loaded in four hours, 43,000 in one day. Women and children were taken to the Greek islands or Piraeus, while the men were taken out of the city to work in labour battalions on roads and reconstruction. Most died of hunger or mistreatment – which started in Smyrna, as they were marched with what the French consul, an eyewitness, called 'the most extreme brutality' through the poor Muslim suburbs. Even the gold fillings in their teeth were removed.[131] The deportations reflected desire not only for revenge but also, as in other ethnic cleansings, to remove the enemy's biological power base. A Turk said to one deportee, 'I'll see to it that your seed is wiped out!' Perhaps 15,000 of 125,000 deported Greek men returned.[132]

In all, between 16 September and 1 October, foreign ships and Greek ships flying the American flag took away about 200,000 (by the American estimate – by other estimates 300,000) Greeks and Armenians. With the largest fleet of the time, Britain took 60,000; Italy 10,000; France 7,000. The great majority was removed by ships chartered by charitable organizations. By 1 October the Cordon was 'perfectly empty', although the city was still full of refugees' abandoned barrels and bundles. Athens and Salonica were soon surrounded by cities of tents inhabited by refugees from Smyrna.[133]

In two weeks, the city changed identity from Greek-cosmopolitan to Turkish, as it changed its name from Smyrna to Izmir. The number of dead is difficult to calculate, since figures for the numbers of refugees who had arrived in the city, and of those who had already left it, before 12 September are unavailable. Estimates of the dead range from 80,000 to 180,000. Those who left before 12 September included relatively prosperous individuals such as the novelists Kosmas Politis and Dido Sotiriou and their families, and Dr Psaltoff, who had fought in the Greek army in 1897 and 1912.[134] Even privileged foreigners fled to Malta, Cyprus or Greece. Hortense Woods had her house occupied by Nurettin and – in the daytime – Kemal and Ismet Inönü, his chief of staff, used it as their headquarters; therefore she was protected. But she noticed in Bornova – despite the presence of her hero Kemal – 'the gates of the houses left wide open, the houses looted and deserted, the streets empty, the village abandoned by all former residents and our friends. Will they ever return?'[135]

Nationalism had created catastrophe. However, some Greeks and Armenians were helped by Turkish or Jewish neighbours, or by foreigners or their foreign nationality. While some of the Baltazzis fled to Athens, others had acquired Italian nationality and stayed in their villa in Buca protected by Italian troops.[136] Thanks to their British naturalization, the Issigonis family of wealthy businessmen had been escorted by marines on to a British battleship. The father died on board ship, the family arrived in London penniless. Alec Issigonis, born in Smyrna in 1906, inventor of the Mini car and the phrase 'less is more' (appropriate for a successful refugee), never mentioned the city again, like many Smyrna refugees. The manner of its loss was too painful: 'That part of the world is dead to us.'[137]

Another Greek family, the Onassoglou, enjoyed no such foreign protection. One uncle of Aristotle Onassoglou (Onassis) was hanged; two were deported east but returned alive. Some relations were burnt alive in a church. Seventeen female relations ended in refugee camps in Athens. Aristotle's grandmother Haci Nene, who spoke only Turkish, was murdered by a Greek thief on a boat from Smyrna to Lesbos. A cousin Antiope married – or was abducted by – a Turk and severed all links to her Greek family. Aristotle's father, Socrates Onassoglou, was imprisoned in Izmir, but was finally released, a broken man, thanks to his son's collection of Turkish and Jewish signatures on a plea for mercy. Aristotle, then eighteen, had used his Turkish to act as 'major-domo' to some Turkish officers who settled in the family villa in Kabataş. His friendship with the American vice-consul enabled him to leave on an American ship on 5 October; after a few months in Istanbul and Athens, he sailed for Buenos Aires, where he made his fortune – typically for a Levantine – in shipping. Smyrna, however, remained in his heart. He returned there on his yacht three times: in 1955, 1959 and 1963. On the first visit he found the same piano and furniture still in the family villa, which was occupied by Cretans.[138]

Who was to blame? Kemal, revealingly, was the first to point a finger. As early as 15 September, while the fire was still raging, he told Michel Graillet, the French consul, that armed Armenians and Greeks were responsible.[139] He repeated this claim in a telegram of 17 September to the Minister of Foreign Affairs, Yussuf Kemal Bey, in Ankara, marked 'Important and urgent':

> It is necesssary to comment on the fire in Izmir for future reference. Our army took all the necessary measures to protect Izmir from accidents, before entering the city. However, the Greeks and the Armenians, with their pre-arranged plans have decided to destroy Izmir. Speeches made by Chrysostomos at the churches have been heard by the Muslims, the burning of Izmir was defined as a religious duty. The destruction

was accomplished by this organization. To confirm this, there are many documents and eyewitness accounts. Our soldiers worked with everything that they have to put out the fires. Those who attribute this to our soldiers may come to Izmir personally and see the situation. However, for a job like this, an official investigation is out of the question. The newspaper correspondents of various nationalities presently in Izmir are already executing this duty. The Christian population is treated with good care and the refugees are being returned to their places.[140]

Interestingly, he assumes that the Turkish parliament considers it right to treat the city's Christians with 'good care' – rather than expel or deport them. Similarly, Falih Rifki Atay tried to reassure his readers – incorrectly – that Christians were still working in Smyrna and the harvest had not been destroyed. In reality that year Smyrna exported not figs but people.[141]

Others at the time, both Turkish and non-Turkish, also blamed Greeks – or Armenians dressed in Turkish uniforms – for starting the fires. They included the French admiral Dumesnil, the American admiral Mark Bristol, some journalists, and Alexander MacLachlan, president of the International College of Izmir. In *The Times* of 25 September 1922, for example, the last is quoted as saying that Turkish soldiers starting the fire were disguised Armenians.[142] In reality these apologists were usually people who had businesses, insurance claims, institutions, or national interests to protect. Wanting to continue to deal with the new Turkey, they feared to displease, and often admired, its leaders.[143] The chief argument in favour of Turkish responsibility for the fire is the preservation of the Turkish and Jewish quarters, while the Frank, Greek and Armenian quarters were destroyed: Greeks and Armenians are unlikely to have burnt only their own districts.

Moreover, the Turkish army was in command of the city during the fire, and so was responsible for events there. For the pyschologist, another argument might be the rapidity with which Kemal pointed the finger at others. In addition, he used the fire. The speed with which Greek and Armenian survivors were subsequently killed, expelled or deported – contrary to the assurances contained in Kemal's telegram of 17 September – suggests a plan. A further argument is that some favoured buildings were protected by Turkish soldiers, as if they anticipated catastrophe – for example, those of Near East Relief.[144]

The exact responsibility is hard to define. Events acquire their own momentum. War breeds madness, even in a political genius like Kemal, as well as in ordinary soldiers. Kemal was not in complete control of all sections of the Turkish army all the time. He often changed his mind, as the wind in Smyrna changed direction. On 13 September he declared that Turkey was in a state of war with Britain; on 14 September he denied it, claiming to have been misunderstood.[145] On 29 October foreigners were told that all their Greek servants had to leave; on 2 November Hortense Woods wrote, 'Kemal has ordered that no servants of European houses should be interfered with.'[146]

At the time, most Turks regarded the catastrophe as a liberation. While half the city burnt, the other half was putting out Turkish flags. Atay wrote, 'The fire had destroyed a great deal of the wealth of the Muslims of the city but the sections located on the mountains and various individual quarters within the city were spared. Although the burning of the city was a grievous loss, Muslim Izmir did not lose any of the joy of victory. Flags were hung everywhere in the streets.' But, despite deliberate patriotic amnesia, criticism of the fire surfaced later, among some Turks, in muted terms that imply Turkish responsibility.[147] In his memoirs, Ismet Inönü wrote that the young said they were following orders; the old complained of lack of discipline. Everyone blamed someone else. Nurettin has been a convenient scapegoat: Fevzi Cakmak, chief of the General Staff in 1922, said Kemal never forgave Nurettin. But Kemal had appointed him. What did they discuss in the konak on 10 September? Later Nurettin became a deputy; in his will he asked to be buried in Izmir on the Cordon.[148] Kemal was the supreme commander of the city during the fire. Smyrna was his responsibility. Perhaps his intention was to use the fire to expel the Greeks and to ensure that thereafter they had no city to which they might want to return.

Contradicting what he had written at the time in the newspaper *Akşam* about 'thousands of soldiers ... fighting fiercely to put out the fire', Falih Rifki Atay wrote in his memoirs, in the first, uncensored, version:

> Gavur Izmir burned and came to an end with its flames in the darkness and its smoke in daylight. Were those responsible for the fire really the Armenian arsonists as we were told in those days? ... As I have decided to write the truth as far as I know I want to quote a page from the notes I took in those days. 'The plunderers helped spread the fire ... Why were we burning down Izmir? Were we afraid that if waterfront konaks [offices], hotels and taverns stayed in place, we would never be able to get rid of the minorities? When the Armenians were being deported in the First World War, we had burnt down all the habitable districts and neighbourhoods in Anatolian towns and cities with this very same fear. This

does not solely derive from an urge for destruction. There is also some feeling of inferiority in it. It was as if anywhere that resembled Europe was destined to remain Christian and foreign and to be denied to us.

If there were another war and we were defeated, would it be sufficient guarantee of preserving the Turkishness of the city if we had left Izmir as a devastated expanse of vacant lots?[149] Were it not for Nurettin Pasha, whom I know to be a dyed-in-the-wool fanatic and rabble-rouser, I do not think this tragedy would have gone to the bitter end. He has doubtless been gaining added strength from the unforgiving vengeful feelings of the soldiers and officers who have seen the debris and the weeping and agonized population of the Turkish towns which the Greeks have burned to ashes all the way from Afyon.[150]

Kemal showed no regrets for the fire. After staying three nights in the Ipikcizade villa in Cordelio, on 14 September he drove through thousands of Greeks and Armenians, shouting 'Oh oh oh' – the exact route is unknown – to stay with the Uşakligil family in its villa in Göztepe, south of the city centre. His face was lit by the glow from the fire.[151]

The Uşakligils' stately classical mansion in Göztepe, now a museum, was on a hill three miles from and out of sight of the city centre, although the smoke rising from the centre must have been visible. From the colour the house was painted, it was known as the Beyaz Köşk, 'the White Kiosk'. There Kemal was received by the beautiful daughter of the house, Latife. Daringly, she had just returned alone to Smyrna after three years with her parents in France, to look after her ailing grandmother. Equally daringly, in her parents' absence, Latife, although a single woman, had the house prepared and greeted Kemal, whom she idolized, with the words, 'You honour Izmir and you achieve the dream of the Turkish nation and so do me and my house honour. Welcome pasha, welcome all pashas.' Kemal and his staff took the main house: Latife lived in servants' quarters; other houses in the garden were occupied by Kemal's staff.

Kemal and his entourage were overwhelmed by the house and the food. After the privations of Anatolia, dinner on the terrace with kalamari, meze, and plenty of wine and raki seemed like paradise. 'Your house is beautiful, very beautiful, Latife hanim,' said Kemal.

The nightmare on the Cordon, and the fire in the city, did not curtail their enjoyment. The following dialogue is reported by eyewitnesses:

'Did you own any property in the burnt area?'

'The most important part of our possessions are in the area. I don't care, it can all be burnt, I just want you to be alive. I don't care about my possessions since I saw these days of happiness. The state is safe, the country is safe. We can rebuild in a better way.'

'Yes, let it burn! Let it crash down! We can replace everything.'

Kemal's remark 'Let it burn! Let it crash down!' stuck in Latife's memory. She repeated it a month later in a letter to one of Kemal's aides, Bozok Bey. Kemal clearly wanted to make 'a clean sweep' in Izmir. He later praised 'the patriotic efforts of all members of the army to expel non-Muslims from western Anatolia'.[152]

Kemal was impressed by Latife's organization of the household. He spent his days at his headquarters in Hortense Woods's house in Bornova – where he charmed the old lady and her family – his evenings in Göztepe. He said he wished Latife ran army bases also. She should become his aide-de-camp. Their courtship had begun. Newspapers began to arrive in Kemal's room with flowers drawn by Latife round Kemal's photographs.[153] He gave her two pistols of General Trikoupis as a present: they can be admired in the Ataturk Salon of the Military Museum in Istanbul today. Thereafter she always carried one in her handbag – a souvenir both of the liberation of Izmir and of Kemal.[154]

Their courtship was observed with acid eyes by Halide Edib, who on 18 September came to dinner in the Beyaz Köşk with journalists from Constantinople, Kemal and his staff. To celebrate the liberation of Izmir, she and Latife drank champagne, Kemal raki. Sitting above what remained of the city, Kemal spoke of his childhood in Salonica, and sang songs from Rumeli. His chief of staff, Ismet, said, looking out at the bay, 'The people will shoot up into life and prosperity in no time, now that we have thrown off this nightmare from our lands.'[155] Like Kemal – reflecting the spirit of the age – he overestimated the power of the state, and underestimated the power of cities, as agents of modernization. On 2 October Kemal left the shattered city of Izmir for Ankara, soon to be the capital of the Turkish Republic.

The Levant had been made by the sea. Ships had brought merchants, teachers and immigrants to Smyrna, Alexandria and Beirut, turning them into wealthy cosmopolitan cities, linked to Europe as well as their own hinterlands. Ships had also brought British troops to Alexandria in 1807 and 1882, French troops to Beirut in 1860 and 1918, Greek troops to Smyrna in 1919.

By 1922, however, the tide had turned. Ships were losing power – as the Royal Navy, hitherto omnipotent, had found in March 1915, when it had failed to force the Dardanelles in the face of minefields and gunfire from Turkish shore batteries. Technology was being defeated by geography, navies by armies. The 'grey diplomatists' of the Royal Navy had been eager to bombard Alexandria in 1882; off Smyrna in 1922, in contrast, their guns were silent.

Falih Rifki Atay certainly saw the Turkish victory as a victory of the land over the sea. He wrote, when he saw Mustafa Kemal in his automobile – probably on the night of 13 September, going from Karşiyaka on the north of the Gulf of Smyrna to Göztepe on the south of the city – 'This automobile at the corner of the Mediterranean in Izmir and in contrast to the ships was like an apparition which suddenly gave light to every corner of the national struggle.' And for the routed Greek troops and abandoned Greek munitions and transports, 'the sea which they had thought to be an ally now proved to be a terrible barrier closing the road before them to Greece.'[156]

At the apogee of nationalism, cosmopolitan ports were under threat. After 1918, Trieste was Italianized, Odessa Sovietized. The capital of Russia was moved from St Petersburg to Moscow, as the capital of Turkey would be moved inland, five years later, from Constantinople to Ankara. In both cases one motive was to remove the government from an international port to 'the heart of the nation'. Both Odessa and St Petersburg lost their foreign communities and part of their educated elite, which fled to the West. St Petersburg also endured a form of city death, with starvation, grass in the streets, loss of half the population.[157]

The fire of Smyrna was the revenge of the poor on the rich as well as of the hinterland on its port. The Turkish army was joined by what Andrew Mango calls 'Muslim irregulars, many of them outlaws of long standing': their presence with Kemal's troops may explain why Muslim, as well as Greek, refugees had poured into Smyrna before 9 September.[158]

The Smyrna catastrophe is a lesson in the dangers of ignoring geography and relying on foreign powers. A teacher for the Alliance Israélite Universelle wrote words which could apply to any nation in its hour of triumph. He attributed the Greek defeat to 'the blindness of the Greek people, its fatuity and self-importance ... To be too proud, too disdainful of others, too imbued with yourself, your race, its great value, that creates an arrogant mentality, presuming too much of yourself, despising those who surround you.'[159]

Yet the great powers did protect Constantinople from the fate of Smyrna.[160] The Turkish government wanted all Greeks, including the Ecumenical Patriarchate, to leave Constantinople.[161] In November 1922

Refet Pasha, Kemal's representative, told a British diplomat that 'the Greeks, if they were not actually expelled, would be well advised to leave as in future in a new Turkey they would be unable to make a living here. The Turks were going to take the commerce into their own hands: he had already started to organize for that purpose.'[162] However, Allied troops remained in occupation of Constantinople. As a further argument to be used in the peace negotiations taking place with Turkey at Lausanne, in February 1923, ignoring Turkish protests, a British fleet steamed into Izmir harbour, watched by a crowd on the Cordon.[163]

Backed by the threat of force, by the treaty signed with Turkey at Lausanne in 1923, Britain, France and Italy guaranteed minorities' rights to live in Istanbul, and the continuation of the Ecumenical Patriarchate there. These rights were further safeguarded by allowing Turks to continue to live under Greek rule in western Thrace. Over 100,000 Turks still live in Thrace; all but 2,000/3,000 Greeks have left or been expelled from Istanbul – 150,000 in 1922–4 alone. Accelerated by a capital tax on minorities in 1942, anti-Greek riots in 1955, and expulsions of Greeks during a worsening of the Cyprus crisis in 1964, Istanbul has, in accordance with Refet's prediction, been Turkified by the Turkish government. However, in contrast to Smyrna, there has been no bloodbath.[164]

After Kemal left for Ankara on 2 October 1922, the great Smyrna dispersal continued. At first some Jews had welcomed the Turkish victory, hoping that Jewish schools would benefit from the destruction of their Greek and Armenian rivals. Most soon changed their minds. Municipal services, including the electricity supply and drains, had broken down. On 8 January 1923 a teacher called E. Benaroya wrote to Alliance Israélite Universelle headquarters in Paris:

> Life in Smyrna has become worse than that we experienced in Morocco before the French occupation, a dull life, monotonous, without any material or moral distraction. Theatres, cinemas, cafés, the clubs where newspapers from the entire world were available, where we found every kind of instructive and agreeable distraction, all have disappeareed, annihilated by the fire ... We live here like hermits, inflicted by every possible and imaginable kind of interdiction, impossible customs tariffs, in brief charged with expiating we longer know what sin of humanity.

The Turkish newspaper *Hizmet*, now known as *Yanik Yurt*, or 'Burnt Earth', also complained of the moroseness of life in Izmir.[165] The number of Jews in Izmir fell from about 10,000 in 1932 to 5,383 in 1955 and 4,067 in 1965.[166]

At this stage, Izmir Jews did not regard Palestine as their promised land. They preferred Istanbul, Egypt, France or – since Spanish was their mother tongue – South America. To this day there is an 'Izmirliler Mahallesi' ('Izmirlis's District') in Buenos Aires. Born in Smyrna in 1889, the famous singer Algazi Izak, known as Bulbul Salomon ('Solomon the Nightingale'), whose classical Turkish singing soothed the dying Ataturk in 1938, died in Montevideo in 1950.[167]

Cosmopolitanism had failed in Smyrna. By its very success, by Christians' use of foreign contacts and powers to strengthen their institutions and raise their profits, it had made a Turkish reaction almost inevitable. Nationalism, however, also at first proved a failure.

In March 1923 Hortense Woods called Izmir 'A most melancholy sight, sad as sad could be.'[168] Blackened ruins, heaps of stone and weed-choked rubble, the haunt of wandering goats, continued to disfigure the heart of the city into the 1950s. Greeks could be expelled from Smyrna, but not the Greek language. Boys from Alsancak, where many Catholic families still spoke Greek, called the district where they played 'ta kamena' – 'the burned places'.[169]

The modernization of Turkey was not helped by the destruction of its most modern city, and of some of its most modern schools, hospitals and businesses. Even if the need to expel Greeks and Armenians for the creation of a national economy is accepted, gentler methods not only would have saved lives, but also might have quickened the creation of a strong Turkish economy.

On 26 January 1923 Kemal was received with joy and awe when he returned to Izmir to hold an economic congress. At the congress, however, there was criticism both of the emancipation of women and of the economic effect of the disappearance of Greeks and Armenians.[170] Ruralization and poverty stalked Turkey. In 1913 about 27 per cent of the population of present-day Turkey had been urban; by 1927 the figure had sunk to 17 per cent.[171] The population of Izmir itself sank from 225,000 in 1914 to 154,000 in 1927. Like St Petersburg, it has never recovered its former importance: '1922 killed the city,' says the journalist Engin Ardiç.[172]

During the congress in Izmir Kemal married Latife. His mother, Zubeyde hanim, had preceded him from Ankara to demand Latife's hand in marriage; her parents had arrived from France for the equivalent reason. The wedding – the exchange of contracts – took place in Izmir on 29 January: Kemal turned a victory dinner given by Latife's father, Muammar Uşakligil, in the White Kiosk into a wedding banquet. Latife later boasted that it may have been the first wedding dinner in Turkey where bride and groom sat at the same table. Kemal gave Latife the miniature Koran in a gold case which he had worn around his neck throughout the war of independence. The governor of Izmir kissed her hand, calling her the conqueror of the conqueror of the city. Muammar Bey, who normally never interfered, had begged her on his knees to reconsider, saying, 'Think again: an army base is not a home.' She insisted. She and Kemal divorced two years later. Neither remarried.[173]

The year 1923 in Izmir and Salonica was dominated by the compulsory exchange of populations between Greece and Turkey, agreed at Lausanne by the Greek and Turkish governments. For some it was a catastrophe, for others a liberation from feared and hated neighbours. Thirty-two thousand Muslims from Greece settled in and around Izmir. Many brought with them the Greek language, and an almost unassuageable nostalgia for the skies and mountains of Macedonia.[174] Balkan Muslims would be seen using lace-edged parasols left behind by Greek ladies to shield themselves from the Anatolian sun as they worked in the fields.[175]

The 1922 harvest had been burnt. The 1923 harvest was not even picked, since the new immigrants – accustomed to cereals and tobacco – did not know how to cultivate figs, vines and olives. Exports declined by half.[176] Foreign importers had lost their old connections and complained that they now knew no one in Izmir to sell them figs or sultanas.[177] In 1924 the French consul wrote, 'Disorder and incapacity rule in the administration. The government of Angora seems to have achieved the economic ruin of Turkey. The military dictatorship of Angora is exercised in such a pitiless way that no one dares raise their voice.' There was no business left for foreign banks to do. He was, however, reflecting the foreigners' point of view. That year in Ankara the Iş Bankasi was founded, with the help of Muammar Uşakligil, to help create a national economy. Today it is one of the largest banks in Turkey.[178] No objective assessment of the Turkification of the economy has yet been made: Turkish businessmen, perhaps to please their government, argued that pre-war production levels had been reached by 1925. Foreign diplomats were probably overcontemptuous of new Turkish firms.[179]

Smyrna was no longer a great Levantine port 'with business relations with the entire world', as the *Annuaire oriental* of 1922 had described it.[180] Many Smyrna firms relocated to Athens, Alexandria, Trieste or Marseille.[181]

Even Muslims left. Muammar Uşakligil was mayor from 1923 until 1924, when he resigned in a dispute over whether the city's streets should be lit by gas or electricity. He had lost much property near the Armenian quarter, but received some compensations in shares. Halide Edib cryptically remarked that the Uşakligil family enriched itself by Latife's marriage more than Kemal did. Others think Latife's dowry – perhaps $660,000 – helped pay for the construction of Ankara. The Uşakligil family, including Latife, settled in Istanbul after the divorce in 1925: the departure of its richest family was a sign of the eclipse of Izmir.[182]

Of other Izmir families, the Keuns and Forbeses moved to Athens, the van Lenneps – whose group portrait by Antoine de Favray in Turkish dress is an icon of Smyrna's cosmopolitan past – to the USA. Of the forty members of the de Jongh family, which had arrived in Smyrna in 1812, and founded the newspaper *L'Impartial*, some moved to Athens, others stayed in Smyrna. Oscar and Cléophe de Jongh had been shot dead on 12 September in their villa in Buca, while trying to protect a Greek maid.[183] As the fire spread, the young Fred de Jongh had leapt directly from the window of the Rees building on the Cordon on to a waiting yacht, clutching the company ledgers under his arm – a leap as famous, for Smyrna Levantines, as Nijinsky's leap in *Le spectre de la rose* for modern ballet-lovers. The yacht took him to Mytilene; he later worked in Alexandria, where he died around 1965. The de Jongh house in Buca is now a school for government health officials.[184]

Edmond de Hochepied had buried his family portraits and silver, and titles of nobility, in the gardens of the old family house in Sevdiyekoy, then moved to the Dutch consulate in Smyrna. In October 1922 he returned with a kavass, but found everything taken – even the beehives. Refugees from Crete and Macedonia had moved in. He stayed as vice-consul until his death in 1929. That was the end of the Hochepieds in Smyrna, after a residence of 245 years – longer than almost any other Smyrna family. The Dutch consulate, in which the Hochepieds had so often served, closed in 1933.[185]

Enjoying French protection since 1793, 'devoto del nationalismo francese' according to an Italian report in 1920, the Balladur family finally left physically for France, as it already had culturally, in 1935. Edouard Balladur was born in Smyrna in 1929, but has spent all his life since the age of six in France, where in 1993–5 he was prime minister. He has compensated for his mixed background by becoming ultra-French, as other citizens of the Levant became ultra-British or ultra-Italian – and Balkan Muslims, including Kemal himself, ultra-Turkish.[186]

The harbour was nationalized in 1934 – the same year that a new law, restricting many professions such as doctor to Turkish nationals, led to a further Levantine exodus. In 1936, for example, the International College in Paradiso, often attacked in the radical anti-foreign press, moved to Beirut, where it remains to this day.[187] That year in Istanbul, Catholic processions in the street were banned for the first time since the sixteenth century, and forced to take place in church courtyards.[188]

Nevertheless, while many left, other Smyrniots, once the ashes had settled, returned. They were 'Smyrniots at heart' as *L'Impartial* had said in 1910 – and still hoped to make a living there. Many believed, and still do, like many Turks, that the fire was started and spread by Armenians.[189]

Once so pro-Turkish, Hortense Woods had been devastated – as any wealthy woman of her time would have been – to learn that she might lose her Greek maids. On 29 October 1922 she wrote, 'What upsets me more than I can say is Calliope is leaving for good ... and now we remain without servants!! What shall we do?' On 1 November, 'I miss Calliope more than I can say ... Doing my room tires me.' In the end Europeans were allowed to retain their Greek servants: Calliope and Sophia stayed in Izmir.[190]

In late 1922 Jean Morin of the Crédit Lyonnais saw the first Levantines come back 'to contemplate what remained of their houses'. He helped them recover some of their money and jewels – while knowing that something always had to be left in bank safes to satisfy Turkish officials ordered by their government to seize all Greeks' and Armenians' property. By the time of his departure in April 1923 a form of life had returned to what remained of the European quarters. Walking in the streets could be dangerous while engineers were dynamiting the city's ruined buildings.[191] Charles Wilkinson, born in Izmir in 1933, remembers that his grandfather was one of the first to return in 1923, repurchasing looted Whittall and Lafontaine family silver for 'next to nothing' in the bazaar. He remembers, 'They got over it. Grandfather had factories in Turkey and talked Turkish and Greek and liked the people. It was a good life.'[192]

In 1923 OCM registered as a Turkish, rather than British, company, and in 1924 it rewarded Rahmi Bey for his services by making him a director. In the long term, despite a temporary recovery in 1925–9, the killing or expulsion of Greek and Armenian weavers meant that most carpet production moved to Iran, India and Greece. In 1986 the company was finally taken over by Ralli Brothers of London – a firm with roots in the area, since the Rallis first came to London from Chios after 1822.[193]

Izmir experienced the political, as well as the demographic and economic, effects of Kemalism. Kemal liked the city, visiting it ten times, more often than Istanbul. One reason was the need to fortify the region against Italian aggression: Mussolini did not finally abandon Italian ambitions in south-west Anatolia until after Turkey's defeat of the Sheikh Said rebellion in eastern Anatolia in 1925 proved the Republic's durability.[194] Although Ankara had replaced it as the driving force of modernization in Turkey, Izmir retained a subsidiary role. In 1925 Kemal opened the first public ball for Muslim men and women in Turkey with a foxtrot in Izmir.

Izmir experienced not only the first city destruction of the twentieth century, but also some of its first show trials. In June 1926 there was a plot by discontented bodyguards to kill Kemal in Izmir. Kemal used it to eliminate some of his most loyal colleagues, who opposed the pace of his reforms. Twenty-five deputies were arrested. The trials took place in the Alhambra cinema, before an 'independence court': defendants had neither lawyers nor the right to appeal. To display confidence, Kemal gave a ball in Çeşme. Among the fourteen men hanged, in front of the konak, with, as in Ottoman times, the verdict written on pieces of paper attached to their corpses, were Dr Nazim, who had once organized Young Turk congresses in Salonica, and Cavid Bey the former finance minister. Those spared included Kemal's most admired collaborators, Refet, Rauf, Rahmi Bey and Kazim Karabekir. Kemal remained a god, but his dictatorial methods were unpopular. A crowd in Izmir dared to welcome the spared men with 'Thank god, who has returned our pashas to us.' In 1930 Izmir would support the opposition party of Fethi Bey Okyar.[195]

Like the rest of Turkey, Izmir also experienced a process of Turkification, in reaction to its previous multilingualism. All official documents had to be in Turkish, and street names were Turkified. In accordance with the 'Citizen, speak Turkish!' policy, begun in 1928, students sometimes attacked people in their own doorways, as well as in the street, if they spoke French or Spanish, rather than Turkish. Non-Muslims were dismissed from the municipality.[196] The last French-language newspaper, *L'Echo d'Izmir*, formerly *Le Levant*, closed in 1940.[197]

Slowly, however, a new Izmir rose from the ashes of Smyrna. An energetic new mayor called Şukru Kaya went on a study tour of Europe in 1924. French cultural influence still predominated. René Danger, a pupil of the urban planner Henri Prost who had drawn up plans for Casablanca, Rabat and Fez for the French government, also drew up plans for Izmir, which were approved in 1925.[198] Behcet Salih Uz, mayor from 1931 to 1940, also helped the revival of the city, which he loved as if it were his own child.[199] From 1934 a hundred acres of the former Armenian quarter were transformed into the Kültürpark, modelled on Gorky Park in Moscow. Turkey's greatest open-air exhibition centre, welcoming from 1938 the Izmir International Fair, is built on rubble and bones. Dominating the huge Republic Square in the middle of the Cordon, on the site of the Kraemer Hotel, is a statue of Kemal on horseback facing the Mediterranean, by his favourite sculptor, Pietro Canonica. It is decorated with bas-reliefs of the War of Independence and the inscription 'Soldiers! Your first goal is the Mediterranean.' When the statue was unveiled in 1932, it was surrounded by ruins.[200]

In the Second World War, thanks to Turkey's neutrality, Izmir was spared the bombing experienced by its old trading partners Livorno and Marseille – and Berlin, Hamburg and Dresden – which made the great fire of Smyrna appear, in retrospect, a trial run for future 'city deaths'. Turkish neutrality in practice favoured the Allies: Girauds, Whittalls and de Jonghs worked for British intelligence in Alsancak, running a small force known as the Levant Schooner Flotilla. It looked after escaped British service-men, dropped saboteurs, and provided intelligence on Axis shipping in the Aegean.[201]

The great Greek poet George Seferis had grown up nearby, and had childhood memories of the city, although he and his father had left in 1914. He returned to 'the city so well known to memory and so strange now' as a diplomat, in 1950 – when Greece and Turkey were allies united by hostility to the USSR. He found stumps of masonry and herbs grow-ing on the site of St Photeini. His Smyrna, he felt, had more in common with ancient Ephesus than with modern Izmir. It was a city that had lost its shadow. Letters to relations – for example 'Madame Desp Seferiades Quais 134 Smyrne Asie Mineure' – had been returned marked 'Retour à l'envoyeur parti',[202] though he found an aunt married to a Turk in Buca. 'I don't feel hatred,' he wrote. 'What I feel inside me is the opposite of hatred: an attempt to accommodate in my mind the mechanism of catas-trophe.' Again, he wrote, 'The evil thing happened. What matters is to redeem the evil of everything.'[203]

While Turkey was Turkified, Greece was Hellenized. The country's population rose by 25 per cent thanks to the arrival of Orthodox refugees from Turkey. Of the 1,221,849 refugees counted in 1928, 66 per cent were women or children under ten – a sinister statistic revealing how many Greek men had been killed, or marched to their death. At first they lived in huts around Athens: the walls of the royal palace acted as message boards for families trying to find lost relations. Their grim unsmiling faces – of people who have seen hell – can be seen in the photographs in the Centre for Asia Minor Studies, set up in Athens in 1933, which to this day functions as principal custodian of their cultural memory.[204]

Eventually the refugees built villages on cheap land outside Athens made available by the government. Some settlements were called New Smyrna or New Ionia. The first schools and orphanages opened in 1929. Some refugees continued to wear the fez, speak Turkish, drink raki rather than retsina and despise mainland Greeks as peasants without manners – feeling more alienated in Greece than they had in Smyrna under the Ottoman Empire. In Greece they were dependent; in Smyrna they had felt themselves their own masters.[205] Greeks mocked them as 'turkospouroi' – children of Turkish seed. One newspaper ran a column on 'the follies of Eftalia', an imaginary refugee from Smyrna. Frivolous and unstable, she gossiped, avoided paying taxes, and her behaviour was scandalously free. Within living memory young women were silenced by their mothers, when talking too freely, by the word 'Smyrnia!'[206]

Having seen their capital wiped out overnight, many refugees from Anatolia joined the Communist Party, which almost won control of Greece in 1944–9. Most were anti-monarchist.[207] The father of Dido Sotiriou, for example, who had once owned a soap factory in Aydin, worked as a docker in Piraeus. His daughter, born in Aydin in 1909, became a Communist activist and journalist, author of the best-selling Smyrna novel *Farewell Anatolia* (1969). Like Elias Venezis, from Ayvalik, author of *Number 31328* (1931, about his experiences as a deportee in Anatolia) and *Aeolia* (1943), she advanced the myth, born of nostalgia rather than accuracy, of Greek–Turkish harmony in the blessed land of Anatolia, a paradise destroyed by others – Germans, British, Levantines – not by Greeks or Turks.[208] She wrote, 'The same earth nurtured our two peoples. Deep down we neither hated them nor they us' – although she also acknowledged, 'Love for our Greek motherland burned like an eternal flame in our hearts.' She described the fire and massacre of 1922: 'Terror lurked like a killer in the dark alleys waiting for the darkest dawn the Greek people had ever known.'[209] Kosmas Politis also described the fire, in his novel *In the Hadjifranco Quarter* (1962), being especially bitter about the abandonment of the Greeks by their own government. He wrote that many survivors avoided speaking about the past, 'as if they had a secret pact of silence'.[210]

Other writers devoted themselves to recording in books and articles the manners and customs of their lost city. Like Cubans introducing salsa and rumba from Havana to the cabarets of New York after 1959,[211] refugees from Smyrna brought the music of Asia to the streets of Athens. Rebetiko songs were sung – sometimes in Turkish – in taverns in Piraeus and Salonica, often by Smyrna bands reformed in Greece. Refugees also opened restaurants called 'Sweet-smelling Smyrna', 'Smyrna Betrayed', 'Lost Asia Minor'.[212] Musicians such as Panagiotis Toundas and Spyros Peristeris – both born in Smyrna – became living legends, recorded by foreign record companies.

Like Jewish laments for Jerusalem, or Spain, Greek songs ached for the lost paradise:

> Anyone hearing me sing says I have no pain.
> But I soothe my pain with my songs.
> Mother, Smyrna is burning, and my people are burning;
> Neither spoken nor written words can describe our sorrow.

> Greece, Greece, you will never know peace again.
> You live one year in peace and thirty in flames.

> Smyrna, now I am leaving you,
> My poor heart is departing from you.
> Cruel fate is dragging me to foreign lands.
> Nothing in the world resembled Smyrna's holocaust.
> It got burned and turned to ashes. Kemal had his way.
> And a school got burnt as well, which was a maidens' school,
> And a tender maiden burnt also, who was oh as white as milk![213]

As Cavafy had written, the city would always follow you. Smyrna Greeks did not, however, dream of returning. In late 1922 Kemal had refused to listen to siren voices urging him to march his victorious army on his birthplace, Salonica.[214] In a similar act of statesmanship – unlike French and German politicians after 1918 – Venizelos put the past behind him. He visited Ankara in 1930, and signed a treaty of friendship and commerce with Kemal which settled rival property claims by the two countries.[215]

The catastrophe was for some a liberation. The Greek economy benefited from Levantine dynamism. As Syros had boomed thanks to refugees from the massacre of Chios after 1822, so Athens boomed thanks to refugees from the massacre of Smyrna a hundred years later. OCM moved part of its operations to Greece. In March 1923 H. Sykes wrote from Athens to Richard Huffner in London that Smyrna Greeks were doing well in

Athens and were taking businesses over. Some called the catastrophe a blessing in disguise for Greece. Piraeus became a port of the first rank.[216]

The population of Nea Smyrna rose from 6,500 in 1934 to 15,000 in 1940, and is now over 80,000. Formerly slums, parts of Nea Smyrna, with gleaming modern flats, now look more prosperous than many districts of Izmir. To this day, however, it retains features of a city in exile. Since 1965 a lifesize statue of Archbishop Chrysostomos stands outside a new version of St Photeini church, containing a throne, altar and screen saved from the fire of Smyrna. Outside is a reproduction of the old five-storey bell tower of St Photeini, paid for by Aristotle Onassis.

The largest building in Nea Smyrna is the majestic Estia Nea Smyrna ('New Smyrna Hearth'), begun in the 1930s and finished in 1975, beside the athletics grounds of the Panionian Sports Club, which had reformed in Athens. Decorated outside with a frieze showing scenes from Smyrna's Greek and Roman history and the exodus in 1922, it contains a large library, and a museum with relics from the lost city: icons, photographs, costumes; the cross and pen of Chrysostomos. On the first floor is a lecture hall. One wall is filled by a gigantic canvas of Smyrna in flames, beneath a smoke-filled sky. The librarian, Mrs Themis Papadopoulos, considers that the destruction of Smyrna was not only a catastrophe for Greeks, but 'a kind of suicide' for Turks.[217]

In contrast to Smyrna, Salonica had a relatively peaceful transition from cosmopolitan metropolis to provincial city. For once, a national government behaved well. There were almost no reprisals against Muslims in Greece for the destruction of Smyrna – either because the Greek authorities opposed them, as Necat Cumali writes, or because the authorities were afraid of the Turkish army.[218] A Muslim, Osman Said, was elected mayor of Salonica in 1923.

In 1923 those Muslims and *dönme* who had not already left were, against their will, compulsorily exchanged with, and their properties allotted to, Greeks from Anatolia. Salonicans' protest against 'a disgraceful bartering of bodies to the detriment of modern civilization' had no effect, since both the Greek and the Turkish governments were determined to enforce the exchange.[219] The deportees' departure was orderly: Muslims camped on the Salonica quay before sailing away from their homeland on ships owned by the Turkish government, which had refused cheaper and more modern foreign boats.[220] Greek families in Salonica bought the second-hand Viennese furniture of departed Muslims. Once the glory of the Salonica skyline, in 1925 twenty-six minarets were pulled down by the Greek authorities as symbols of 'frightful slavery'. 'Their threatening height will no longer intimidate us nor remind us of the former misfortunes of our race,' wrote a journalist: 'The red fezzes are leaving, the yashmaks vanish.' Greeks were 24 per cent of the city's population in 1914, 75 per cent in 1928.[221]

Departing Muslims are said to have told Salonica Jews that their turn would be next. After the return to power of Venizelos in 1928, the Greek government began to turn against the Jews. After a pogrom in 1932 and attacks on people keeping the Sabbath as the weekly holiday in 1934, many Salonica Jews moved to Palestine: the port of Haifa was modernized with the help of fishermen and stevedores from Salonica.[222] The Jewish population declined from 65,000 in 1920 to 52,000 in 1935. A blanket of political insignificance settled on the city. Few men from Salonica obtained jobs in the Greek civil service.[223]

The ultimate barbarism was the deportation of 43,000 Jews to their death at Auschwitz by Salonica's German occupiers in 1943. In the streets of Salonica, eyewitnesses saw people fall on each other, in order to steal, 'like hyenas on a dead horse'. In contrast to courageous protests made in Athens, in Salonica the Greek elite was, in Mark Mazower's words, 'frostily detached'. 'We felt pity but we never suspected the evil that was soon to befall them,' wrote Yorgis Ioannou, who also claimed that Jews in Salonica – intensely devoted to their families – had always held themselves aloof from other people.[224] The municipality seized and destroyed the long-coveted Jewish cemetery, one of the oldest and largest in Europe: it is now part of Thessaloniki University. Jewish shops and offices were pillaged. Cut off from its past, although no longer from its hinterland, modern Thessaloniki is dominated by ghosts and immigrants. The best minds, it is said, always go to Athens. There they 'breathe easier'.[225]

13

Alexandria: Queen of the Mediterranean

Will Alexandria remain the Proteus of the west or turn to Cairo?
Turn its back on the sea?

Fernand Leprette, *L'Egypte, terre du Nil*, 1939

ALEXANDRIA WAS ONE of the few cities in the Levant not to have a catastrophic twentieth century. That is one reason why it has inspired such golden memories. No massacres; no fires; no deportations. Several thousand Greeks, and others (for example the Pastroudis family, founders of a famous restaurant, and the Rees family and its shipping line), moved from Smyrna to Alexandria after 1922: 'Despo' Lascaris burnt her shoes on arrival, as they had stepped on so many corpses. Most Alexandrians, however, were unaffected by 'the Catastrophe'.[1] Cavafy's sole recorded reaction was to lament the loss of a market for Greek books.[2]

At first, however, Alexandria, too, had seemed destined to explode. The British proclamation of a protectorate and deposition of Khedive Abbas Hilmi in November 1914, and the British army's demands for Egyptian labour during the First World War, exasperated Egyptian nationalists. At the same time, US president Woodrow Wilson's promises of democracy and national rights raised expectations. At a tea party at Ras el-Tin on 9 October 1918, Prince Omar Toussoun suggested to Saad Zaghloul, a promising Egyptian politician, that he form a delegation or *wafd* to the forthcoming peace conference in Paris.[3]

The Wafd became the first mass party in the Middle East. It demanded independence for Egypt, though it was prepared to concede Britain special rights in the Suez Canal Zone. Trade unions had recently become stronger. In 1919 there were tram strikes in Alexandria, riots and uprisings elsewhere. British authorities were intransigent. In March 1919 Saad Zaghloul, and other nationalists, like their Turkish counterparts, were sent to prison in Malta. All schools except Victoria College closed, as students refused to attend classes. Even women joined demonstrations.[4] On 23

May 1920 – 'Red Monday' – 30 Egyptians and 15 Europeans died in riots in Alexandria.[5] Returning to Alexandria from Malta in April 1921, Saad Zaghloul was welcomed by delirious crowds. Ships sailed out from the harbour to greet him. Streets were lined with triumphal arches. A similar popular triumph in Alexandria was organized on 17 September 1923, when he returned from another spell in a British prison, and in July 1924 when leaving for discussions with the British prime minister Ramsay MacDonald in France.[6]

Despite the dissolution of the Ottoman Empire, Egypt still felt connected to Turkey. On 22–24 May 1921 there were fights between Greeks and Egyptians in Alexandria, in part inspired by the war between Greeks and Turks in Anatolia: some Alexandrian Greeks fought in the Greek army.[7] Although a Greek newspaper blamed 'the wild passions and rapacious instincts of a native mob', as in 1882 it may have been a Greek or Italian who opened fire. More Egyptians than foreigners died: in all, forty-three Egyptians, twelve Greeks and two Italians. Greek shops were sacked by crowds shouting, 'Long live Saad Zaghloul!' On occasion Egyptian police joined the rioters. Europeans – distinguishable by their dress and hats – were attacked in Place Muhammad Ali. The rest of Egypt was also swept by violence.[8]

E. M. Forster was blind to write, in *Alexandria: A History and a Guide*, published in Alexandria in 1922, that Alexandria 'has never taken national susceptibilities too seriously', or that Alexandrians had never been 'truly Egyptians'.[9] He was judging the city by his Levantine friends. As their ovations to Saad Zaghloul – and their acts in 1882 – showed, the 75 per cent of the city who were Muslims or Copts – and some of those of Syrian or Jewish origin – felt very Egyptian indeed. They wanted independence, and had a reputation for rebelliousness. 'Obsessional like all Alexandrians,' remarks a character in Youssef Chahine's film *Alexandria Again and Again* (1990).

The poems of Bayram al-Tunsi, an Alexandrian of Tunisian origin (hence his name, 'the Tunisian'), born in 1893, reflect the views of many Alexandrians. Protected as a Tunisian by the French consulate, al-Tunsi published them in a nationalist newspaper *Al-Ahali*. One poem attacking the municipal council, symbol of European and government control, is still remembered in Alexandria today:

> The heart has been plunged into grief and distress,
> By passion for a lover named the Muncipal Council.
>
>   · · · · · ·

> Should the loaf come, half I eat,
> And half I leave for the muncipal council.
> O vendor of radishes, one for a penny,
> How much goes to the children,
> How much to the municipal council?

In another poem we hear the resentment of the poor:

> You live in proud houses,
> But it is I who build them.
> You sleep in silken sheets,
> But it is I who wove them.
>
> .   .   .   .   .
>
> I house you, clothe you, feed you
> and then you treat me so!¹⁰

Most rich Alexandrians probably never read these poems. But they were a sign that, however cosmopolitan Alexandria might appear, the city was also, as Smyrna had been, on the front line of national and class conflicts.

Finally, in March 1922, Britain granted Egypt a form of independence, reserving authority over the Suez Canal, over Egypt's relations with minorities, the capitulations and the Sudan, and over Egyptian defence. Britain also retained influence through the continued presence of British troops in Cairo and Alexandria, and of British officials in Egyptian service. Until the 1940s, for example, the director-general of the ports of Egypt, the commander of the Alexandria City Police and the Alexandria harbour-master were British.

Thrones had disappeared in Russia, Austria, Germany and Turkey. Egypt, however, experienced a revival of monarchy. Fouad I, son of Khedive Ismail and uncle of the former khedive Abbas Hilmi, had been Britain's choice as sultan in 1917 – thanks in part to his friend Ronald Storrs, oriental secretary at the British residency. Other princes, out of loyalty to the Khedive or the Ottoman Empire, refused the throne. A former playboy, Fouad spoke with a 'high spasmodic bark': a bullet had remained stuck in his throat after his brother-in-law had shot him during a quarrel over his first wife's money. At times the bark sounded like a gun being fired.¹¹

Having shuttled in his youth between Turin (where he was educated), Vienna (where he had served as Ottoman military attaché), Paris and Constantinople, as well as Cairo and Alexandria, even more than most of his family he was a natural cosmopolitan. King Fouad, as he became after the proclamation of the constitution in 1922, had also acquired a taste for grandeur and cultural patronage. He helped found Cairo University – importing Italian and French professors – and commissioned magnificent editions of foreign documents on nineteenth-century Egypt, for which historians will always be grateful. He also founded the Arab Language Academy, modelled on the Académie Française, to guard the purity of Arabic, and the Arab Music Academy, which established a system of notation.

In Alexandria, Fouad commissioned the transformation of Ras el-Tin Palace, and the creation of a throne room in 'Islamic baroque', by the architect of the royal palaces, his friend Ernesto Verrucci Bey. Verrucci Bey was also the architect of the neo-baroque arcade erected on the corniche around a statue of Khedive Ismail by Pietro Canonica (sculptor of the statue of Kemal on the Smyrna Cordon), inscribed in Italian and Arabic 'a Ismail il magnifico la communità italiana' and unveiled in 1938.[12] The names of the streets were royalized: Rue de la Porte de Rosette became Rue Fouad; Promenade Reine Nazli, along the eastern harbour, was named after his wayward second wife, Nazli Sabry, a pupil of Alexandria's smartest girls' school, Notre Dame de Sion, and a descendant of Soliman Pasha – Fouad had sworn to marry her after he saw her unveiled one evening at the Cairo opera. Alexandria also had the Rue Prince Abdul Moneim, Rue Sultan Hussein, and many others.[13]

Bayram al-Tunsi was sent into exile in France for twenty years, after denouncing Fouad's marriage to Nazli in May 1919 – when the country was near revolution – as 'besmirching the honour of the nation and its martyrs'. Fouad was 'the traitor for whom blood is squeezed from your hearts in order that he may drink it with his bride amid his Ministers and parasites, then dance to the sound of British guns'.[14]

From this low point in national esteem, however, King Fouad slowly recovered. He became a major political force, able to keep Saad Zaghloul out of office for most of his reign. In Alexandria he held a monthly levee, which British naval officers were required to attend; the King, 'most affable and civil', spoke to them in French.[15] To diplomats, bankers and politicians, he gave what the British diplomat David Kelly called 'astonishing' audiences, analysing men and events with embarrassing frankness, and complaining of the limits placed on his power by the new – in his opinion far too democratic – 1922 constitution, based on that of Belgium. Egyptians 'were completely unsuited for parliamentary government on those lines ... Why had we not left him to run the country as he well knew how to do, if we would only cease interfering?'[16]

Sir Richard Vaux, president of the *tribunaux mixtes* in Alexandria, found King Fouad 'the ablest man in his own dominions ... [with] an almost encyclopedic knowledge of the men and affairs of his country ... A prodigious worker, he easily mastered the details of administration and it is safe to say that his ministers were in truth his ministers and not his masters.'[17] Another official praised the King's 'perception of world affairs, common sense judgements and humane interest in all aspects of contemporary Egyptian life'.[18] Fouad's friends included two wealthy Egyptian ladies from prominent Jewish families, Madame Rolo and Madame Cattaui Pasha (born Alice Suares), chief lady-in-waiting to the Queen. Like most Egyptian Jews at the time, they felt Egyptian and, if they thought of it, regarded Zionism as 'terribly unchic'. A few years later a Zionist official reported of the 25,000 Jews living in Alexandria, 'A decided animosity and antipathy to Zionist aims has sprung up. They look upon it as something that threatens their own peace and must be discouraged.'[19]

The Egyptian government and the foreign embassies continued to move to Alexandria every summer. The British residency alone required a special train.[20] Egyptians idolized Saad Zaghloul, the peasants' son; the King preferred an Alexandrian called Ismail Sidqi. Born in Alexandria in 1875, clever and charming, Sidqi went to the Collège des Frères and the Khedivial Law School and was secretary-general of the municipality from 1899 to 1914. From his Christian education, this Muslim remained devoted to St Theresa of Lisieux. In 1930–33 and again in 1946 he was prime minister. To considerable public criticism, he authorized the construction of a new corniche road running from the eastern harbour further east to King Fouad's other palace at Montazah, which the Egyptian government had bought for Fouad from the exiled Khedive Abbas Hilmi in 1924 and which he had had remodelled by Verrucci Bey.[21] Soon the corniche was lined with beaches, restaurants and nightclubs.

A relic of Alexandria's years as a court city is the Royal Jewellery Museum, housed in the suburb of Rushdi, in a villa built in 1919 for a cousin of King Fouad called Princess Zeyneb Fazil. It is European in style, with stained-glass windows depicting scenes from European history. Sales and thefts from the royal family's collections since 1952 have been extensive. Nevertheless the selection of royal jewellery in the museum is awesome: a platinum sceptre inlaid with diamonds, sapphires and pearls; gold and silver chess sets; tiaras, necklaces, medals.

The revival of Egyptian nationalism did not at first harm cosmopolitanism. During King Fouad's reign a new nationality law, more liberal than in other successor states, allowed all former subjects of the Ottoman Empire – Christian or Muslim, Turkish or Arab – resident in Egypt in 1914 to become Egyptian. Believing that 'religion belongs to God, the homeland to everyone', the Wafd attracted many Copts. A favourite phrase was 'masters in our house, generous to our guests'. As Nahas Pasha, Zaghloul's sucessor as leader of the Wafd, said in a speech to community leaders in Alexandria in 1937, 'Nothing can divide us any more. You love Egypt and Egypt loves you.'[22]

Refugees from the Russian and Ottoman empires, as well as immigrants from Europe and the Levant, were added to the Alexandrian cauldron. The architect of the handsome neoclassical Stade d'Alexandrie, built by public subscription for the first Mediterranean and African Games in 1927, was a Russian called Alexander Nicohossov Bey.[23] The Orthodox patriarchate moved to Alexandria from Cairo, with its ancient library, in 1927.[24] Continuing its role as a radicals' haven, the city also welcomed refugees from Italian Fascism, such as Sayyid Idris al-Senussi, leader of the Libyan resistance, and the writer, painter and composer Enrico Terni and his wife, the novelist Fausta Cialente. They found in Egypt an 'absolute liberty' which Italy no longer enjoyed.[25]

Alexandria's cultural life also reflected its mix of races. In 1919 the Association des Amis de l'Art was started by Prince Youssef Kemal and Max Debbane; it organized the third exhibition of Islamic art ever held (after those in Paris in 1903 and Munich in 1910): the Exposition d'Art Mussulman of 1925 – showing objects mainly from the Benaki and Lagonicos collections. L'Atelier d'Alexandrie (Association d'Artistes et d'Ecrivains) was founded in 1934 by Gaston Zananiri, Muhammad Naghi and Enrico Terni, eventually settling in the stately Palais Tamvaco in the *quartier grec*, where it still is. It provided artists with studios, and organized lectures and exhibitions, showing the work of local painters such as Clea Badaro, the surrealist Enrico Brandani, Thalia Flora Caravia from Smyrna, Seif Wanly and Ezzat Ibrahim.[26] The British Boys School, for those who could not afford Victoria College, opened in 1929; the English Girls College in 1935. Despite, or because of, the latter school's hyper-Englishness (forms were called Shakespeare, Byron, Lamb and Masefield), girls – 'of every race and religion', from all over the Middle East, including Saudi Arabia – took to the school 'like moths to a candle'. They loved the freedom and the sports, unknown in French schools, and soon spoke 'impeccable' English.[27]

The golden age of cosmopolitanism in Alexandria was the twenty-year period between 1936 and 1956. Tensions decreased after Nahas negotiated a new treaty of friendship with Britain in 1936, giving Egypt greater independence, and a timetable for evacuation of British forces from Cairo and Alexandria to the Canal Zone and the removal of British advisers from Egyptian ministries.[28] In 1937, after 400 years, the hated capitulations – denounced as 'a form of slavery and reaction from whose evils the Egyptians from the Pasha to the fellah suffer' – were finally abolished. The *tribunaux mixtes* began to be wound down, and closed in 1949. Their headquarters on the Place Muhammad Ali became an Egyptian law court, as it still is. The consular courts also closed in 1948. Henceforth Egyptian law reigned supreme in Egypt.[29]

The great Cairo novelist Naguib Mahfouz, who like many Cairenes spent the summer in Alexandria, noted the change. Before 1936, he remembered, Egyptians had regarded Alexandria as a

> European city where Italian, French, Greek or English were heard far more often than Arabic. The city was beautiful and so clean that one could have eaten off the streeets ... But all that was for the foreigners. We could only observe from the outside ... until the Treaty of 1936 which subjected foreigners to the same law as Egyptians ... When the Capitulations were abolished, foreigners in Alexandria were forced to change their attitude. They no longer owned the country; we Egyptians were no longer second-class citizens. They realized they and we would be appearing before the same magistrates so we began to feel more at ease. The characteristics of European life were still very present; but once the capitulations were abolished they became accessible to us as well.

Egyptians no longer felt outsiders. Mahfouz went to smart Greek restaurants like Athineos, famous for its classical orchestra and *thés dansants*: 'in short Alexandria was a European city but belonged to us – Egyptians.'[30] He remembered Alexandria as a city where 'popular joy radiated everywhere.'[31]

Many Greeks, and others, began to speak Arabic fluently – better than they read or wrote it. In mixed areas, Alexandrians remember visiting, going to school, and eating with their neighbours and staying in their houses, whatever their religion. Like Beirutis talking of the years before their civil war, the novelist Edwar al-Kharrat remembered, 'It was not important: we never inquired about each other's religion or even thought about it.' 'They would eat our food and we would eat theirs,' remembers Mohammed Ibrahim abd el-Samad. 'All lived together as one family without any difference between Muslim, Christian or Jew,' claims Hajj Mustafa al-Mulla.[32]

Many Egyptians loved Alexandria because it was both Egyptian and different – and an agreeable place to spend the summer. 'Even the way Alexandrians spoke Arabic was different,' remembers Samira N., descended from an Alexandrian family with roots in Morocco and the Aegean. She still feels more Alexandrian than Egyptian.[33]

After 1936, Egypt began to experience a form of parliamentary government. As a result of general elections, governments sometimes changed. Ministers could be criticized in parliament, and might subsequently resign. The director-general of the Alexandria municipality Chakour Pasha, who had been appointed by the government, had resigned after attacks in *La Réforme*.[34] At the same time the economy boomed. Factories making cigarettes, beer, soap, paper and cement were built on the outskirts of the city. Alexandria harbour welcomed the seaplanes of Imperial Airways as well as warships, merchant ships, yachts and fishing boats.[35]

Some of the richest capitalists in Alexandria were now Egyptians. Amin Pasha Yahya, for example, owned part of central Alexandria, including the Trianon café, and founded the Alexandria Produce and Trading company, the Alexandria Navigation Company, the Alexandria Chamber of Commerce, housed in a neoclassical building facing Saad Zaghloul Square, and in 1934 the Union Alexandrine to link foreign and Egyptian business interests. Like Farghaly Pasha, 'Far from being suspicious of foreign economic influences, Yahya celebrated a close working relationship with foreigners,' in the words of Robert Tignor.[36]

Smyrna had been burnt, Constantinople Turkified, and Salonica Hellenized. Alexandria – still officially bilingual in French and Arabic – now had no rivals as a Levantine metropolis. In 1930 the city awarded itself the title 'Queen of the Mediterranean'.[37]

French, the language of the Levant, was more than ever 'sovereignly established' as the language of Alexandria: 'We are loved, read, listened to like nowhere else,' wrote a French visitor, Claude Avelin, in 1934. On arriving as a young bride in 1937, an American called Josie Brinton, who had married the son of a judge in the *tribunaux mixtes*, found that 'it is really necessary to know how to speak French out here.' The French language played a greater role in Egypt than French commerce.[38]

In 1927 a massive neo-Romanesque French school, the Collège Saint-Marc, was built near Chatby. French schools in Alexandria in 1929 educated over 10,000 pupils, and French was also used as a medium of instruction in some Egyptian and Jewish schools. Special French books for use in French-language schools, such as *Morceaux choisis sur l'Egypte*, by Raoul Canivet (1925), were published in Egypt. There were plans for a French-language university in Alexandria. After 1922 French and other foreign schools also began to teach Arabic a few hours a week 'by respect for Egyptian nationalism'.[39]

French was not Alexandria's only language. In these years, a Swiss Alexandrian remembered, 'it was quite usual to give orders to ones's domestic staff in Arabic in the morning, to address one's hairdresser in Greek, to speak Italian in the shoe shops and then to speak in English in the afternoons over a game of bridge, five o'clock tea or a game of pool and finally in the evenings to receive and entertain one's friends in French.'[40] Yvette (Eve) Cohen, later Lawrence Durrell's second wife, spoke Spanish, French, Italian, Greek and Arabic, and learned English at the Scottish School for Girls. Durrell's third wife, Claude Vincendon, spoke French, English, Italian, German, Greek, Arabic and Hebrew.[41] Many Alexandrians switched from French to Greek to Italian to English in the same sentence, throwing in a few words in Arabic.[42] The Smouhas, rich Jews from Baghdad who had settled in Alexandria, called the 'polyglot broth' of Arabic, Italian, English and French which they spoke at home 'farabish'.[43] Ahmed Rassim, an Alexandrian who worked in the Foreign Ministry, wrote stories and poems in both Arabic and French; Sayid Darwish, the national poet and author of the national anthem, wrote sketches in the Arabized Greek of Alexandria waiters. Even films were multilingual, with subtitles in French, English, Greek and/or Arabic, depending on the original soundtrack.[44]

A portent of Egyptianization, however, was that from 1930, in the growing Egyptian film industry, actors and actresses were often given Arabic, Islamic-sounding names, although they and the film producers and directors who invented the names might be Christians or Jews whose first language was French. Outside the film industry, too, many Christians who had hitherto called themselves Pierre or Robert began to baptize their sons Samir or Fouad. They believed that Christian names sounded European, and would be a handicap in the future. Thus Michel Chalhoub, born in Alexandria, writes in his memoirs, 'I am a son of Alexandria ... I am French in culture.' He detests racism and fanaticism but renamed himself Omar Sharif. In addition to French, he speaks Arabic, English and Greek, with a working knowledge of Italian and Turkish.[45]

Alexandria did not, like Paris or New York, develop one overriding identity which, after two or three generations, cancelled prior loyalties. Alexandrians remained attached to their original national and religious community, as well as developing loyalties to their city, and in some cases to Egypt. Every year parts of Alexandria were decorated with Greek, British, French or Italian flags, during processions and festivals commemorating Easter, Empire Day, the fall of the Bastille, or Mussolini's 'March on Rome'. Foreign communities fought in their respective country's wars. The names of Alexandrian Greeks inscribed on the walls of the courtyard of the Orthodox patriarchate commemorate their deaths as Greeks in Greece's wars of 1912–13, 1916–22 or 1940–45.[46]

The Salvago family for example, among the wealthiest inhabitants of Alexandria – they put up 25 per cent of the original capital of the National Bank of Egypt – remained Greek, not Egyptian. Born in Syros, Nicholas Salvago paid for Alexandria Greeks to be educated outside Egypt, in Europe or the USA. His son Michel Salvago was both head of the Greek community and president of the Cercle Muhammad Ali – although he had been forced to resign as a member of the municipal council in 1923, owing to accusations that, as a leading shareholder in the tram, gas and water companies serving the city, he had enriched himself at the city's expense.[47]

His wife Argine, née Benaki – sister of the novelist Penelope Delta – was one of the 'uncrowned queens of Alexandria', famous for her taste and her lovers of both sexes, seduced by her purple-blue eyes. The couple lived in a palatial classical-style villa (now the Russian cultural centre), packed with porcelain and antiquities, on the corner of the Rue des Pharaons and the Rue des Ptolémées in the *quartier grec*. When the King of Greece came to stay in the Second World War, he said he would be embarrassed to return her hospitality in Athens: his palace was less impressive than her house. One of his officers was so unaccustomed to Alexandrian luxuries that he thought the butler, muttering in his ear the name and vintage of the wine he was serving, was making improper suggestions. The charities the Salvagos supported were mainly Greek.[48]

A sense of separation from Egyptians is also conveyed in the newspapers of the time. Long before Egyptians began to consider themselves Arabs, non-Egyptians often referred to them as 'natives' or 'Arabs', not Egyptians – as Fausta Cialente complained in her novel *Ballata Levantina* (1961). Rich Egyptians themselves called poor Egyptians 'fellaheen'.[49] In 1929 Michel Salvago said, 'Greeks continue to work there in perfect accord with native elements.' That year a newspaper wrote that 'a native was knocked over by a car in the district of Minet el-bassal.'[50]

For some these golden years were dominated by money. Both Lawrence Durrell and Fausta Cialente complained that Alexandrians had no subject of conversation except money. Alexandrians had money instead of blood in their veins – although Cialente also admitted that they were 'fairly cultivated'.[51] A judge in the *tribunaux mixtes*, Baron Firmin van den Bosch, remembered that conversation on the terrace of the Cercle Muhammad Ali switched at once from passing cars and women, and the latest scandals, when a boy brought a typed bulletin from the bourse with the day's cotton prices. When the price was high, Alexandrians gave more parties. Like the Salvagos', many Alexandria villas had superb collections, combining Ptolemaic antiquities, pictures by Van Dongen or Vlaminck, Ottoman tiles, Chinese porcelain, and the latest book by Proust or Paul Morand.[52] By the late 1930s Alexandrians could also enjoy a 'nightly round of cocktail parties'. Some boasted that they never dined at home.[53]

Maison Jansen, the fashionable interior decorator of Paris, opened a shop on the Rue Fouad. At 3 Rolo Street, Victor Lehmann from Jansen transformed the house of the richest Briton in Alexandria, a cotton trader and member of the muncipal council called Oswald Finney (also president of the Alexandria Commercial Company, the Alexandria Insurance Company, the Filature Nationale d'Egypte and the Minet al-Bassal Stock Exchange) into a Gobelins-lined Venetian-style palace, with Dresden china and Romney portraits. A marble staircase rose through four floors to a parquet-floored ballroom. The rooftop terrace had views of the entire city. Every year during the carnival season he and his Austrian wife, Josa, gave a fancy-dress ball for a thousand.[54]

Love affairs as well as money dominated Alexandria conversations. For Fernand Leprette, 'modern to the tip of their delicate little feet with painted toe nails, Alexandrians have a furious desire to break with all prejudices, to taste every sensation. They hold bourgeois morality in horror. All are afraid to seem dupes even of their own hearts. And in fact their heart is fairly practical ... They are free beings ... the living ornament of the city.' Some Europeans wintered there for the sake of the women.[55] Van den Bosch agreed. He called the women 'pretty little beasts of prey'. 'Their beauty, charm and frenetic joie de vivre let them permit themselves everything.' Edwar al-Kharratt would write a novel called *Girls of Alexandria*. A Frenchman commented on Alexandria, 'What do you expect, my friends, we are in the East?' – a sentiment expressed in English as 'This would never happen in England!'[56] In their attitude to sex and race, and religious differences, their readiness to select what and whom they wanted from different cultures, Alexandrians were more modern than many Parisians or Londoners.

In their attitude to poverty, however, they were antediluvian. Robin Fedden, an English writer who married an Alexandrian Greek-Italian called Renée Catsaflikis, found, 'The parquet floors quake over an abyss of poverty; the black satin and pearls are complementary to rags and tatters. Nothing but their labours link the peasant to the cotton kings. Even their diseases are different.'[57] Foreigners were shocked; many Alexandrians took poverty for granted. Robert Levesque, a Frenchman living in Alexandria, noted that, in this city of huge fortunes, pickpockets and beggars grabbed your money on the street.[58]

In 1936, the year that Britain and Egypt signed their treaty, King Fouad died. The arrivals of his son, King Farouk I, in Alexandria harbour in May 1936, returning from his education in England, and in July 1937, after a holiday in Europe, were government-organized popular triumphs. In 1936, showered with rose petals, Farouk drove from the harbour to the train station in an open Rolls-Royce. In 1937, crowds of Girl Guides, Boy Scouts, schoolchildren and workers and religious students shouted, 'Long live Farouk!', 'Long live the king of the Nile!' Handsome and well-intentioned, he was admired as 'Farouk the Pious', who regularly went to mosque in public.[59]

In 1938 his marriage made him even more popular. Both he and his bride, Farida, were only seventeen. She came from Alexandria's modernizing elite, and had been educated at Notre Dame de Sion. Her father, Yussef Zulficar Pasha, was the first Egyptian vice-president of the *tribunaux mixtes*. Her uncle Mahmud Said, who had also worked in the *tribunaux mixtes*, was a superb sensual painter, educated at Victoria College, L'Atelier, in Cairo and Paris. His passion for women was reflected in paintings such as *Women of Bahriye* (1937), showing girls with anklets and diaphanous veils looking at men on the corniche, and *In the Dance Club* (1936), with couples dancing in tight embrace. His nude models were mainly servants girls, whom he paid and seduced.[60] Another Alexandrian painter, Mohammed Naghi, was chosen by the municipality to paint a picture of the 'School of Alexandria' – the famous men and women of the city, of all nationalities and religions, including Archimedes and Averroes, St Catherine the Martyr and Cavafy, Alexander the Great and the writer Taha Hussein: a visual affirmation of Alexandria's role as a cosmopolis.[61]

King Farouk was a natural Alexandrian. It would be his idea to revive the Egyptian navy, with headquarters in Alexandria, and ships bought from Britain. In 1940, during celebrations of the fiftieth anniversary of the municipality, Ahmed Kamel Pasha, the director-general, expressed the official view. Alexandria's future was assured not only by 'this spirit of confraternity and solidarity between the Egyptian and foreign elements'

– and the municipality's 'particular benevolence for the working class and the poor' – but also by 'the High sollictitude of His Majesty the King ... who has made of our beautiful city not only the second capital of the Kingdom but also His Residence of predilection'; Farouk's first child, a daughter, was born there.[62] The newspaper *La Réforme*, founded in 1895, also prophesied the 'finest destiny' for Alexandria as a crossroads of East and West, 'a furnace of different races, religions and customs ... under the aegis of His Majesty King Farouk'.[63]

By then, however, Alexandria was under threat from outside. After 1935, Fascist Italy began to expand its navy. Mussolini made threatening speeches about 'Mare Nostrum' ('Our Sea') – his term for the Mediterranean. In 1936 Italy conquered Ethiopia; in March 1937 Mussolini was offered by conquered Libyans what he called 'the sword of Islam', which he brandished in the direction of Egypt. He told Hitler that Italy was 'shackled' by Britain in the Mediterranean: 'We must have Egypt, we shall only be great if we have Egypt.' Groups of Italians shouted 'L'Egitto sara a noi!' – 'Egypt will be ours!' – in the streets of Alexandria.

For Britain, however, Egypt had become 'the key to Asia' and 'the connecting link that holds together the eastern and the western world' – in particular the different pieces of the British Empire.[64] By its location near the frontier between Egypt and Italian-occupied Libya, in the path of an Italian invasion, Alexandria had become a military and naval base vital for Britain's control of the Mediterranean.

Four times, when war seemed imminent – August 1935, September 1938, April and August 1939 – the Mediterranean Fleet was ordered from its base in Malta to the relative safety of Alexandria.[65] The first sight for passengers arriving in Alexandria harbour was now Britain's 'grey diplomatists', the warships of the Mediterranean Fleet, constantly exercising in order to be ready 'to strike at the Italians on their very doorstep', in the words of their commander the great Admiral Andrew Cunningham. Beside them merchant vessels looked like intruders. More resolute than London politicians, British officers in Alexandria longed for action against 'Gassolini', as they called 'Il Duce'.[66] A system of trenches and barbed-wire defences was set up between Alexandria and Mersa Matruh on the Libyan frontier. The navy began to acquire larger docks and more storehouses. The RAF also came to Alexandria, and installed bases at Aboukir and Amriya: on the beaches of Alexandria, Egyptian boys became experts at identifying Blenheims, Hampdens and Gloster Gauntlets practising ascents and loops in the sky.[67]

One officer in the expanding British garrison was called 'Boy' Browning; on the King's Birthday on 23 June 1936 he commanded the Trooping the Colour parade, held in Alexandria Sporting Club, with music by the massed bands of the Mediterranean Fleet and the drums of the Grenadier Guards. His wife, Daphne du Maurier, began the most English of novels, *Rebecca* (1938), while living in Alexandria – the passion for Cornwall which drives the book may have been heightened by hatred of Egypt. She expressed views held by many foreigners: 'I can't help thinking the natives are filthy and never really clean'; 'It is entirely lacking in charm'; 'I did not know it was possible to hate a country with such intensity.'[68]

The British in Alexandria remained aloof from other nationalities. Most shared the conviction that, as Olivia Manning remembered in *The Levant Trilogy* (1975–80), set in wartime Egypt, 'Britain was supreme in the world and the British the most fortunate of people.'[69] British officers' social life – revolving round golf, tennis, polo and racing at the Sporting Club, and cocktail parties – was insular, but energetic: the commander-in-chief of the Mediterranean Fleet once broke a tooth during a dinner party.[70] As for the other ranks, Admiral Cunningham wrote, they 'found ample amusement ashore'. In addition to the Alexandria Fleet Club, which provided beds, a restaurant, a library, a concert hall, a cinema and shops, there were the bars of the Rue des Sœurs.[71] Soldiers and sailors also had access to 'clean brothels', regularly inspected: 'Our VD rate was extremely low,' remembered one officer.[72]

Alexandria harbour was relatively small and often congested. From 1937 the British ambassador Sir Miles Lampson – who on his previous post in China had been known as 'Let 'em have it Lampson', since he favoured the return of the 'treaty ports' like Shanghai to Chinese jurisdiction – urged the Egyptian government, under cover of improving the harbour for commercial purposes, to pay for it to be dredged and enlarged, and to buy a boom net and shore guns to defend it in a future war. Nahas Pasha, the popular prime minister and successor of Saad Zaghloul as leader of the Wafd party – who, like most Egyptians, hated the Italian Empire for its brutality in Ethiopia and Libya – said he would agree 'at once with the greatest joy'.[73] The need in a future war to use Alexandria as a naval base, and to rely on a co-operative Egyptian government, had been one reason for Britain's signature of the liberal 1936 treaty with Egypt. A new dock was brought out from Portsmouth to the improved port of Alexandria in August 1939.[74]

In 1939, despite British reassertion of control of transport, censorship and food supplies, and the proclamation of martial law, Egypt was sufficiently independent to resist British pressure to declare war on Germany. It remained neutral. Egyptian governments, however, co-operated with the British war effort, even after Italy's declaration of war on France and Britain on 15 June 1940. Soon British prisoners of war in Italy asked for food parcels from Pastroudis, in view of 'the vast amount of money he has had out of our pockets already'.[75]

The Mediterranean Fleet moved its HQ from Malta to Alexandria, to escape Italian air raids. Under Admiral Cunningham, Britain kept four battleships, nine cruisers, an aircraft carrier, twenty-five destroyers and twelve submarines based in Alexandria – the greatest concentration of sea power outside home waters.[76] The spectacle of the British Empire going to war, 'slow to start but always sure of itself and one would search in vain for one slip, one sign of decrepitude', impresssed Fernand Leprette, a French teacher in Egypt, more than all the speeches by Hitler and Mussolini prophesying the Empire's downfall. Soon there were 20,000 Allied soldiers in Egypt – Poles, Indians, Australians and New Zealanders, as well as British.[77] In addition to its role as a base in the war against Italy, the port of Alexandria became essential for the supply of stores, munitions, tanks and airplanes for Allied forces throughout the Middle East, including Malta. Cunnningham and Wavell, the army commander-in-chief in the Middle East, agreed that, if the navy withdrew from Alexandria, Egypt was lost.[78]

As capital of a neutral country, Cairo blazed with lights at night. As a British base, Alexandria was the only city outside Britain and Germany to be bombed in 1940–41.[79] It became the city of bombing raids, panic and mass exodus brilliantly evoked by Ibrahim Abdel Meguid in his novel *No One Sleeps in Alexandria* (1999) and by Youssef Chahine in his film *Alexandria Why?* (1978). Until July 1944 there was a blackout every night. The night sky was lit by searchlights and anti-aircraft fire. Exploding bombs and the rattle of anti-aircraft guns made a noise like the London Blitz. Hellenistic cisterns served as air raid shelters. The boats of the Alexandria Volunteer Inshore Patrol took the bearings of falling bombs and mines in the harbour, so they could be retrieved and defused. The Alexandria Volunteer Ambulance Unit helped the British Red Cross ambulances.[80]

British troops' search for sex and drink might have been expected to alienate Egyptians. In the words of Alan Moorehead, 'nightly thousands of sailors and soldiers roamed around the blue-black streets in search of company in a land where white women were outnumbered a hundred to one and even that remaining one was on the point of being evacuated.' The Rue des Sœurs – the street where riots had started in 1882 – lined with bars and brothels, with half-naked women in the doorways beckoning 'Kombakir' ('Come back here'), was a favourite destination.[81]

A sailor called Michael Croft wrote in 'Sailor song back to the Andrew [his ship] (after a rough night in Sister Street Alex)':

> There are seven ways to heaven,
> And I've slipped on every one.
> Now the pearly gates are closing
> And I haven't strength to run.[82]

John Nahman remembers, 'The Australians were terrifying ... they killed quite a few local tarts. The New Zealanders were hardly any better.'[83] An Alexandrian Armenian called Anahide Merametdjian told Michael Haag, 'Some women had a wonderful time. They went to bed every night with a different officer or man. The Greek, Italian and Lebanese women [she excludes Armenians] gave themselves to the troops.'[84]

Despite Axis victories, the popularity of Hitler ('Hajj Muhammad') among many Muslims and the unpopularity of the British, there were no anti-British riots. Egyptian men took their families and belongings to safety in the Delta, then returned to their work despite the air raids.[85] Other Alexandrians, however, remember the war as a period when they would loot British lorries and attack or kill British soldiers, stripping off their uniforms to be sold.[86]

Lampson, an imperial dinosaur of six foot five inches and eighteen stone, whom British generals considered 'always the headmaster wielding the big stick', complained that King Farouk was flashing signals to Italian submarines from his palace.[87] He was probably wrong. Yet Lampson secretly hoped to force the King's abdication and arrange Egypt's 'incorporation in some form or other in the British Empire'. He was convinced that Farouk sympathized with the Axis; British planes had orders to force his plane down if it turned west for Libya when flying between Cairo and Alexandria.[88]

As the Italian army advanced from Libya, a second city sprang up outside Alexandria: barbed wire; army camps; oil tanks; tanks, tank-carriers and armoured cars. Both on land and on sea the congestion was incredible.[89] The war did not, however, stop Greek tradesmen sending boats as far as Algiers to get supplies of cheese and condoms, nylons and spaghetti.[90] While Europe suffered rationing and starvation, Egypt remained a land of plenty. On his way to the Crete campaign, Evelyn Waugh wrote, 'The food in Alexandria is delicious. We live on quails and prawns and wood strawberries.'[91]

Alexandria was on the front line of the struggle between Vichy and Free France, as well as between Axis and Allies. In June 1940 France had sent a battleship, four cruisers and three destroyers to the safety of Alexandria harbour.[92] After the Franco-German armistice, Vice-Admiral Godefroy, in command of the French fleet, found his British counterpart, the commander-in-chief of the Mediterranean Fleet Admiral Cunningham, 'a completely exceptional personage with a perspicacious and profound viewpoint'.[93] The combined arguments of Cunningham and his own captains persuaded him not to scuttle, but to disarm his ships, even after Britain sank much of the French navy in Mers el-Kebir on the Algerian coast in August 1940 and a battle between the two fleets nearly started in Alexandria harbour. The French ships remained, enigmatically neutral, in Alexandria harbour until they sailed away to Dakar in 1943.[94] Their real enemy was neither the British nor the Axis, but the Gaullists: there were frequent fights between their sailors and Free French soldiers in the streets of Alexandria.[95]

The British war effort gave the British community in Alexandria its finest hour. One of the most prominent families, with contacts at every level of the city, was the Barkers, descended from William Barker of Derbyshire, who had arrived to trade in Smyrna in 1760. He had twenty children by two wives. His son John had been British consul-general in Alexandria in 1827–30 and a confidant of Muhammad Ali and Ibrahim. John Barker's son Frederick had settled in Alexandria. His shipping agency, Barker & Company, founded in 1850 – telegraphic address 'Barker, Alexandria' – had prospered. Frederick's nephew Sir Harry Barker KCMG became director of the National Bank of Egypt, vice-president of the Alexandria Sporting Club, president of the British Chamber of Commerce and the British community of Alexandria, chairman of the board of governors of Victoria College, and a member of the municipal council. He also led what his grandson called 'a small committee of the British community of Alexandria' which was sometimes 'called on by the embassy for advice'.[96]

The Barkers' photograph albums show the pleasures of life at the top of British Alexandria: sailing expeditions; the ambassador's duck shoot in the Delta; hunting ibex and gazelle in the desert; polo matches in the Alexandria Sporting Club; the British Benevolent Fund ball; palatial villas surrounded by well-kept gardens.[97] Despite marriages to Greek or Levantine ladies, British Alexandrians were prevented from 'going native' by four protective barriers: English nannies and governesses; education in England or at English schools in Alexandria; summers in England; and service in the British army. Although they had lived in Alexandria since the 1850s, and considered 'they would probably continue to reside in Alexandria', in 1940, in a further assertion of Britishness, the Barkers had successfully petitioned in 'His Britannic Majesty's Consular Court for Egypt' to remain 'natural-born subjects of His Majesty'.[98]

Three generations of the Barker family served the war effort. Michael Barker was an officer in the Rifle Brigade; his father, Henry Alwyn Barker, was Staff Captain Alexandria Area; Henry Alwyn Barker's father, Sir Henry Barker, as in the First World War, worked for the Ministry of War Transport, helping civilian ships to be loaded and unloaded as quickly as possible in Alexandria harbour.[99]

Sir Henry Barker's sister-in-law Gabriella Barker, who worked for the Maternité Internationale hospital and the Alliance of Social Workers of Alexandria, organized revues by Alexandria ladies – called the 'Desert Angels' – to entertain British troops and wounded.[100] They wore smart blue uniforms with 'Mrs Barker's Concert Party' embroidered on the epaulettes: Jacqueline Klat's parody of the balcony scene in *Romeo and Juliet*, in kitchen Arabic and broken English, regularly brought the house down.[101]

Despite its long preparation, Admiral Cunningham found Alexandria 'a most unsatisfactory base in every respect'. Docking and repair facilities were inadequate, and the harbour was shallow, with a difficult entrance, and had almost no net defences, minesweeping and patrol forces, or anti-aircraft guns and radar. There was no base for the Fleet Air Arm. In September 1940 he wrote, 'I don't mean to be driven out of Alex unless we have to go', but admitted having prepared 'our organization for retiring to Port Said and Haifa'.[102] Churchill would not consider withdrawal to Gibraltar, as the First Sea Lord Sir Dudley Pound proposed, to concentrate on the defence of Atlantic trade and the United Kingdom.[103]

From Alexandria, Cunningham was able to organize the sinking of half the Italian fleet at Taranto on 11 November 1940, and five more ships at Cape Matapan in March 1941. To the fury of the army and air commander-in-chiefs, who considered it 'sheer lunacy' for him to stay in Alexandria, he refused to live in Cairo, but flew there once a week for meetings. He spent every night on board his flagship in the harbour, in order to share the dangers and difficulties of his men; his days were spent at headquarters in the Gabbari docks or at the British summer embassy in Rushdi, 'invariably' making time for golf or tennis in the afternoon.[104] Years later, in his war memoirs, Marshal of the RAF Lord Tedder was still complaining that, because Cunningham remained in Alexandria, 'vital decisions affecting all three services had to be made over an unreliable public telephone.'[105]

After Greece's conquest by the Axis in May 1941, the King, the government, thousands of soldiers and the Greek fleet, including the *Averoff*, arrived in Alexandria – along with, among the refugees, five British writers who would find inspiration in the wartime city: Robin Fedden, Elizabeth David, Robert Liddell, Olivia Manning and Lawrence Durrell.[106] For a time Alexandria was the capital of the exiled Greek government, which lived on the corniche, in the Windsor Hotel; the King stayed at Argine Salvago's. George Seferis, by then a diplomat, felt that Alexandria was a corner of the Greek world; but the back streets looked like Blake's illustrations of hell.[107]

On 26 May 1941, at a conference with other C-in-Cs and the Prime Minister of New Zealand after the German attack on Crete, Wavell advised against trying to evacuate the remaining British troops from the island. If sunk, the fleet would take three years to be replaced. Cunningham, however, like Churchill, was empowered by a sense of history. He replied, 'You have said, general, that it will take three years to build a new fleet. I will tell you, gentlemen, that it will take three hundred years to build a new tradition.' Appealing to emotion over reason, he feared that ever afterwards 'when soldiers go overseas they will tend to look over their shoulders instead of relying on the navy. It was impossible to abandon the troops in Crete.'[108] Sending every spare ship he had – although many were in urgent need of repair – under constant bombardment from the Luftwaffe, the navy took off 18,000 of 32,000 troops. However, it suffered the loss of three cruisers, six destroyers and 2,000 sailors.[109] In addition, one aircraft carrier, seven cruisers and six destroyers were badly damaged.[110]

In 1941/2 Italy and Germany temporarily established naval and air superiority in the Mediterranean. Italian submarines and German U-boats even mined the entrance of Alexandria harbour. At times Cunningham considered his ships safer out at sea than in harbour. On 19 December 1941 two Italian 'human torpedoes', divers in submersible 'chariots', launched from a submarine outside the harbour, crippled two battleships moored at Alexandria: HMS *Queen Elizabeth* – on which Admiral Cunningham lived – and HMS *Valiant*. Underwater detection at Alexandria was difficult owing to the vast amount of Nile water pouring into the sea, causing varying densities of sea water.[111]

The war on land was also going badly. On 21 June 1942 the Allied base at Tobruk, in Libya, fell. Soon Axis forces were only sixty miles from Alexandria. Rommel's motorcycle outriders were said to have reached the western suburbs. British anti-aircraft guns were evacuated from the deserted corniche.[112]

On 26 June the Australian novelist Patrick White, stationed at Alexandria in the Australian air force, wrote, 'These are gloomy days out here with the Germans advancing and nobody knowing much about the real state of affairs. My faith in armies deteriorates as the machines encroach. We still seem to go out to war as if to a picnic, however many times we are upset.' He had fallen in love with an Alexandrian Greek, called Manoly Lascaris, from a wealthy cosmopolitan family of Constantinople and Smyrna; they would live together for the next fifty years. They had met in the house of Baron Charles de Menasce, a piano-playing porcelain-collector from a famous Alexandrian family, who lived, White wrote, 'in a Proustian atmosphere surrounded by Gobelins tapestries, objets de virtu and portraits of his mother. They are a large and cosmopolitan family and I was asked to many large and cosmopolitan parties, where I indulged in three languages and rubbed shoulders with Greeks, French, Egyptians, Armenians and Syrians. That is Alexandria, a babel of the middle east.' He was happy with his Alexandrian friends: he saw enough of the English on active service.[113]

On 28 June German radio announced that German troops would be in Alexandria by 6 July, in Cairo by 9 July. Another radio message said, 'Ladies of Alexandria get out your party frocks. We are on our way.' The same day the Mediterranean Fleet suddenly left for Beirut and Haifa. The British commander-in-chief, General Sir Claude Auchinleck, prepared to withdraw east, although Churchill had told him to defend Egypt 'just as drastically as if it were Kent or Sussex, without any regard to any other consideration than destruction of the enemy'.[114]

A private letter by a British officer called Myles Hildyard confirms Allied forces' despondency, and admiration for the enemy commander General Erwin Rommel as a genius of the battlefield. Hildyard wrote on 6 July 1942, 'There is no feeling of all-out effort and none of the confidence in a general which the Germans have in Rommel.'[115] In Alexandria's restaur-ants, it was said, officers of the interned French fleet toasted Rommel's victories. British soldiers began to look over their shoulders, to make sure of a place on a lorry out.[116]

A Greek remembers her Italian neighbours showing her with glee the cakes they had baked for arriving Italian troops. Some were said to have been so eager to be the first to cheer the victorious Italian army that they had booked places on balconies on the Rue Sherif Pasha. They had plenty of Italian flags, left over from the state visit of King Victor Emanuel

III in 1933.[117] Many Alexandrians left for Palestine or South Africa. To the horror of their friends, the Finneys had already left, in 1940.[118] The Barkers stayed. When old Sir Henry Barker died, on 20 July 1942 at seventy, perhaps worn out by the strain, Prince Omar Toussoun came to his funeral. Although a nationalist, he was the one member of the royal family to be resolutely pro-Ally – perhaps because he knew, through his Senussi friends, the nature of Italian rule in Libya.[119]

The side of the Alexandria–Cairo road for cars going to the capital was packed. The side for cars going into Alexandria was full of military traffic. Trains for Cairo were so crowded that passengers had to be pushed through the windows.[120] Alan Moorehead found on the outskirts that 'all those entrenchments, those salt flats that had once swarmed with soldiers were now barren of human life. Even the bedouin seemed to have fled.' A silver barrage balloon still floated above the city, but nearly all ships had left the harbour. Shops were shut. The streets were half empty; even the bar of the Hotel Cecil, the favourite of Allied officers, was deserted.[121] Cecil Beaton wrote that Alexandria was 'a dead city; all Wrens and sailors evacuated; roads without traffic; windows open on to empty rooms; telephone bells ringing unanswered'. He too found British soldiers 'tired and discouraged', rightly considering their equipment inferior to that of the Germans.[122]

A run on the banks began on 24 June. The National Bank of Egypt was about to reissue old notes that had been overprinted with the inscription 'cancelled pending incineration', until the arrival of a stock of unused notes from England restored confidence.[123] Some shops were said to have put welcome notices in German and Italian in their windows, and to be selling postcards with the face of Hitler pasted on the statue of Muhammad Ali.[124] Lawrence Durrell, then a press attaché in Cairo, made a list of them, and they were put out of bounds to British troops. Egyptian families who had let rooms to British officers began to burn the uniforms they had left behind, for fear of being compromised. Wells Pasha, director general of ports and lighthouses of Egypt, went absent without leave from Alexandria, and was later dismissed.[125]

In contrast to Moscow when the German army approached in October 1941, however, there was no breakdown of law and order, no closure of factories and bakeries, no looting, no mass flight of terrified officials. The cosmopolitan city of Alexandria stood the test of war better than the capital of the Soviet Union.[126]

The diary of Mary de Zogheb is one record of Alexandria's war years. She was born Mary Debbane in 1893, into a wealthy Greek Catholic family which had come from from Sidon in 1820 as wood merchants. Having served as consuls of Brazil, they had been made counts by its emperor in 1857. The Debbane chapel in a side street off Rue Sherif Pasha still displays the coat of arms of Brazil as well as the Debbanes', above their motto 'Fides et Honor ante omnia' ('Faith and Honour above all'). Educated at Notre Dame de Sion, Mary married Georges 'Ziquet' de Zogheb. The Zoghebs remained one of the richest and most international families in the city. Ziquet ran through two fortunes; but he and Mary continued to keep servants in their flat on the Rue Fouad, and led a strenuous social life, with love affairs on both sides. 'Old Mary', as she was called, played golf and bridge and sunbathed; Ziquet organized revues at Casino San Stefano, celebrating and mocking Alexandrians of the day, and later had a job as a steward at the racecourse. French was her first language; she had no nationality. The only reason she later became Egyptian was to inherit from her sister Maggy. From 1924 until her death in 1985 she wrote a brief record of her day in small pocket diaries, sometimes also describing her thoughts and public events. It says more, in fewer words, than many more personal journals.

Tea and bridge parties went on, despite air raids, but she also served meals to British troops at the United Forces and Britannia clubs, with friends like Linda Rolo, Gabriella Barker and Haydee Rees. On 26 June she wrote, 'English rather depressed events.' Then

> [29 June] Panic in town. Fleet and admiralty Wrens etc evacuate clubs and military hostels shut.
> [30 June] Panic. Many departures ... Kiki Salvago and colleagues ... the Vincendon, the M Rolo ... most to Cairo, Luxor. Roads and trains packed.
> [3 July] Hospitals evacuated. Many Jewish departures.

However, she also noted, of the troops going to and returning from the war in the desert, 'Lorries troops desert, all waving and cheers V [for victory]. A few days ago all downcast'.

[4 July] 'No siren'. By 6 July people were returning from Cairo, although the thud of artillery fire from the desert could still, for many more months, be heard in Alexandria.[127]

At the first battle at el-Alamein, sixty-six miles west of Alexandria, in June 1942, Auchinleck had held the German advance. But he refused to go on the offensive. The army had little faith in him.[128]

Churchill arrived in August, dismissed Auchinleck, and appointed in his place General Bernard Montgomery – who knew Egypt well, having been stationed in Alexandria in 1931–3. During lunch at Eighth Army headquarters at Burg el-Arab, twenty-five miles south-west of Alexandria, Egyptian brandy had to be brought from Alexandria and poured into French bottles for the Prime Minister – 'We were very deception-minded in those days,' remembered Montgomery's chief of staff, General Francis de Guingand.[129] At 7.30 am on 13 August Montgomery arrived, two days early, at a crossroads outside Alexandria. He soon transformed the Eighth Army and its Polish, Greek, Indian, Australian and New Zealand allies from a defensive force into an aggressive fighting machine. Montgomery was implacable. He ordered, 'In the event of enemy attack there would be no withdrawal.'[130]

Alexandria began to relax. The beaches filled up with troops on leave as well as the usual 'huge indolent population of smart women'. But for the sound of artillery fire from the desert, wrote de Guingand, in Alexandria 'one might have been at Deauville or Cannes.'[131]

On the night of 23 October, under a full moon and with the benefit of overwhelming superiority in armaments and intelligence, the Eighth Army took the offensive. During the second Battle of el-Alamein Alexandrians could hear what Lampson called the 'solid unceasing roar' of the barrage from the battlefield. The sea was thick with torpedo craft, the air 'literally filled with planes'. Alexandrians would go out on their balconies at night to listen and try to work out what was happening.[132] Outnumbered and outgunned – while Rommel was on sick leave – the Germans and Italians were defeated. Before Alamein, Churchill later wrote, we never had a victory; after Alamein we never had a defeat.[133] Within three months the Eighth Army was in Tripoli.

In September 1942 the Egyptian government had shown its confidence in Alexandria by starting a university there. It was called the Université Farouk Ier – Cairo University was the Université Fouad Ier – and it was opened by the King in person on 8 February 1943. He was still handsome and popular: people were disappointed that he drove through the streets, decorated with triumphal arches, in a closed rather than an open car.[134] The event was commemorated by a gold medal which can be seen today in the National Museum in the Villa Bassili on the Rue Fouad, former residence of a dynasty of wood and cotton merchants. Revealing the servile adulation and royal luxury surrounding the young king, its Arabic inscription reads, 'King Farouk's university – Alexander the Great who established Alexandria – and King Farouk the first is the King 1361/1943.' On one side are superimposed effigies of Alexander and Farouk, as equals.[135]

The first president of the university was a blind writer called Taha Hussein. Like many Alexandrians, he believed that Egypt was part of the Mediterranean rather than the Islamic world, and that Arabic and Islam formed only two of many elements composing the country. In a famous early work, *Pre-Islamic Poetry* (1926), which had raised a storm of criticism, and forced him to resign from Cairo University, he had pointed out post-Muhammad elements in the Koran and attacked traditional methods of interpretation. For him modernity came not through Islamic revival, nor through nationalism, but through Paris. He had been educated there, married a Frenchwoman, and translated Gide into Arabic. 'Only by eagerly welcoming modern civilization can we have true peace of mind and a wholesome attitude to the realities of life,' he wrote.[136] The vast Faculty of Engineering built for the university in 1951 was in the neo-pharaonic style beloved of the Wafd party – maintaining a distance from Egypt's Muslim heritage.

As one war receded from Alexandria, another began. The first battle of the Cold War between Communism and its enemies, which would dominate world politics until 1989, took place near Alexandria in April 1944. Greek troops and sailors mutinied in support of a larger role for Communists in a future Greek government. They were suppressed by British forces with about ten dead; 20,000 were disarmed and interned in camps. Lawrence Durrell, by then working in the British Information Office in the Rue Toussoun, wrote to the Alexandrian intellectual Henri el-Kayem that he was 'almost mad with all the political crises'.[137] In the 1940s for a left-wing Greek Alexandrian called George Pierides, author of a novel *The Cotton Dealers* (1945) and editor of a Greek periodical, *Ellyny*, Alexandria was 'the great metropolis of Hellenism': 'All our intellectual activity concentrated almost exclusively on Greek matters and problems.' Like all Alexandrians in their memoirs, he protested – perhaps a little too much – that this was not a sign of 'a negative attitude towards Egypt. It was due to the self-sufficiency of the community with which our whole social, national, family, professional and intellectual existence was identified.'[138]

Alexandria also witnessed another beginning. Encouraged by the British Foreign Secretary, Antony Eden, the Arab League, intended to unite the countries of the Arab world, was founded in Alexandria by the Alexandria Protocol, signed in the Villa Antoniadis on 7 October 1944.[139]

Alexandria appeared stable and welcoming enough to assume a new role, as an asylum for fallen royalty.[140] The Ottoman princes already established in Alexandria since 1924 (including Ali Vasib Efendi, great-grandson of

Murad V, director of the Villa Antoniadis, used by the municipality as a house in which to entertain guests and hold flower shows)[141] were joined in 1944–6 by Crown Prince Paul and Crown Princess Frederica of the Hellenes and their children. In 1946 ex-King Victor Emanuel of Italy and his grandson ex-King Simeon of Bulgaria, and ex-king Zog of Albania, came at King Farouk's invitation, with many relations and servants.[142]

For a time Alexandria was the capital of 'free Albania', a base from which expeditions were sent to try to liberate the country from Communism. The self-made king, Zog I, lived in a 'pretty regal' villa in Ramleh, in greater state than the head of the ancient House of Savoy, Victor Emanuel. The latter lived with his wife in the small Villa Jela in a new area called Smouha City: a marshy district which had been drained and laid out as a garden city, with its own sports club and racecourse, by a friend of King Fouad called Joseph Smouha.[143] The attractions of Alexandria were educational as well as political. Prince Leka, son of King Zog, and Simeon of Bulgaria attended Victoria College; the present Queen of Spain, daughter of Paul and Frederica of the Hellenes, went to the English Girls College.

At Montazah on 16 July 1947 King Farouk held a hallucinatory royal tea party, to reconcile the kings of Albania and Italy, the latter having invaded the former's kingdom in 1938. Guests included the kings of Italy, Albania and Bulgaria and members of their dynasties and of the Ottoman and Russian imperial families.[144] Out of politeness, Jewish coin collectors of Alexandria would let Victor Emanuel – a keen numismatist – inspect their collections; out of revulsion at the anti-Jewish laws which he had signed in 1938, they absented themselves during his visits. When Victor Emanuel was buried at St Catherine's church in 1948, the funeral procession was organized by King Farouk.

On the surface Alexandria retained the character of a royal capital. On 11 February 1945, to celebrate the King's birthday, a relay race was run from Ras el-Tin Palace to Abdine Palace in Cairo, followed by a military review.[145] In other years, palaces, offices and villas, and ships in the harbour were illuminated. 'The whole town' came to the corniche to watch the firework display, as the King was driven past cheering crowds in a procession of red Rolls-Royces from Montazah to Ras el-Tin: red was the colour reserved for palace cars.[146] From 1945 the director-general of the municipality was a trusted servant of the King, the chief architect of the royal palaces, Mustafa Fahmy Pasha.

However, Farouk had begun his transformation from handsome young hero into obese buffoon. There were two triggers: a head-on car crash in November 1943, followed by long and painful recuperation, and the failure of his marriage to Queen Farida. Addicted to gambling and women, he became an embarrassment, then a scandal, to many Egyptians. In 1943 Noël Coward, like many British friends, had found him charming and courteous, 'a big fine-looking young man'. Sholto Douglas, the commander-in-chief of the RAF in the Middle East, called him well informed and well read and 'unquestionably very popular'.[147] A year later an English officer was shocked by the King's 'ravenous appetite' and the 'marked coarseness' in his conversation; his entourage – including his favourite servant/companion Antonio Pulli, later Pulli Bey – was 'very third class'.[148] Farouk began to frequent nightclubs and parties. Mary de Zogheb noted after a party at Alice Zervudachi's on 6 September 1944, 'King Farouk came late, goes often to parties.'[149]

The King's love of Alexandria was reflected in his mistresses. Three were Alexandrians: Princess Fatma Toussoun, widow of a son of Prince Omar Toussoun, and two Jewish women: Irene Guinle, whom he met at the orange-juice bar of the Alexandria Red Cross ball in 1941, and an actress called Liliane Cohen, known as Camellia, who later died in a car crash.[150] The first was the most serious. She installed a special lift and a gambling room for the King in her block of flats in Alexandria, and had a child by him. In the end, however, she fell in love with a Brazilian prince, Juan de Orléans Bragance, who had come to Egypt to inaugurate the first flight between the two countries, and left for Brazil.

Alexandria remained cosmopolitan to the core. Zionist officials, hoping to find immigrants for Palestine there, admitted that, because of the low level of religious tensions, there were very few. Only a few millionaires like barons Felix and Georges de Menasce contributed to Zionist funds.[151] While marriages outside one's religious group remained exceptional elsewhere – marriages between Protestants and Catholics or Christians and Jews could seem shocking in England in the 1960s – they were beginning in Alexandria: between Eve Cohen and Lawrence Durrell in 1947, for example, despite difficulties made by her parents.[152] Films were made about inter-community relations, such as *Hassan, Markos wa Cohen* or *Marika, Fatima wa Rachel*. Marriages were also beginning between Muslims and non-Muslims: the Egyptian actor Rushdi Abaza, for example, born in 1929, was the son of an Egyptian police officer and an Italian mother.[153] A member of a wealthy Jewish family, Marcelle Adès married Prince Ibrahim Fazil (himself half French through his mother) in 1950. Omar Sharif married Faten Hamama in 1955 – being obliged to become Muslim in order to do so. British women who married Egyptians later worked in Alexandria's British schools – for example Ann Khalfallah, wife of a university professor.[154]

Alexandria cultural life also remained cosmopolitan, under the unifying umbrella of the French language. To this day in Alexandria French is the second language of street signs and car number plates (preceded by 'Privé Alx', or 'Private Alexandria'). In April 1945 the French writer Etiemble, then teaching at the university, began to edit a review called *Valeurs* ('cahiers trimestriels de critique et de littérature, publiés avec la collaboration des écrivains de France et du Proche Orient'). Fifteen hundred copies were published of each issue, with articles such as 'La structure de l'image chez Sartre' by Naguib Baladi. It was financed by a local businessman called Alfred Cohen.[155] The Alexandria Music Conservatoire – the first in Egypt, which gave many Alexandrians a first-rate musical education – was started by a group of wealthy backers in 1947, a cultural association called Egypte–Europe in 1949.[156] There were exhibitions of French contemporary art at the Galerie Lehmann in the Rue Fouad. During the winter season the Comédie Française and the Ballets de Monte Carlo performed in the Theatre Muhammad Ali.[157]

The British Boys School taught pupils of thirty-nine different nationalities.[158] At the university, teachers included Mohammed Mandour, who in 1946 was arrested for writing articles attacking capitalist pashas like Ismail Sidqi and Ahmad Abboud;[159] the historian of the later crusades A. S. Atiya; Hilde Zaloscer, a refugee from Vienna and expert on Coptic art; the great classical archaeologist Alan Wace, who worked for British intelligence; and Robert Liddell, author of an Alexandria novel, *Unreal City* (1952), which describes the excitement caused by the appearance of British soldiers and sailors in Alexandria bars. D. J. Enright published his first volume of poems, *Season Ticket*, 'aux éditions du Scarabée Alexandria Egypt 1948', while teaching at the university, about which he later wrote a novel called *Academic Year* (1955).

For Enright, Alexandria was not the history-drenched city of Cavafy, but 'this bright new city Arabi–Amerikani with its heavy swinging doors and its glassy smile'. His students, he wrote, had a horror of anything old. His widow, Madeleine, who was teaching at the Mission Laique Française, remembers that he loved the city's liveliness, openness, and mix of languages and races: 'We felt at home without difficulty.'[160] 'The students were lively and responsive and, considering that the whole of their course was conducted in a language which was not their first, quite able,' remembered John Heath-Stubbs, one of the teachers of English literature.[161] Jean Cocteau came with a theatre company in 1949. After a reception at the French consul's, he wrote, 'Women are of great beauty and great elegance. Between Cairo and Alexandria there is a sort of battle of flowers.'[162]

At a time when the capitals of Europe were struggling with strikes, shortages and socialism, Alexandria became a city of nightclubs. 'Romance', in the Hôtel Méditerrannée, advertised itself as 'the most select nightclub in Alexandria', 'the rendez-vous of the elite'; scented jasmine plants climbed up pillars in the dining room. 'It was divine, a very cosy place,' remembers one habituée. Other nightclubs included L'Auberge bleue, Le Scarabée, The Ship, and Monseigneur, which had a Brazilian band and hosted the election of Miss Egypt.[163]

At most of them King Farouk had a table for six permanently reserved. He was not the only Muslim to enjoy the clubs. Prince Omar Toussoun had been a conservative Muslim, but his sons Said and Hassan, who continued to live in Alexandria, gave cocktail parties, organized horse races, and lived surrounded by liveried servants.[164] The wife of Prince Said Toussoun, Princess Mahivesh Toussoun – sometimes called 'la première dame d'Alexandrie' – was a trained nurse. Every morning she went to help the Muhammad Ali Charity for the governorate of Alexandria, of which she was head. She said, 'We had to start almost from nothing. There is so much to do.'[165]

Two political earthquakes, however, transformed Egypt and Alexandria. The 1945 celebrations of Empire Day, in the Sporting Club in the presence of Lord Killearn (as Sir Miles Lampson had become), with a fly-past, the singing of the national anthems of the different countries of the Empire, and 'Rule, Britannia', had been Alexandria's swansong as a British base. In March 1946 twenty-four students (some estimates are higher) died on 'Martyrs' Day' in clashes on the corniche with Egyptian police and British troops, while protesting against the British presence. Protests were more violent in Alexandria than in Cairo: 'Out English! Out foreign soldiers! Out, out, out!' Seeing two British soldiers torn to pieces by Egyptians near the Ramleh bus station convinced Catherine Bereketti that one day she would leave Egypt. Post-war lack of money and energy, as well as Egyptian protests, made Britain quit. Moreover, the independence of India and the elimination of Italian imperialism lessened Alexandria's strategic importance. In 1946 and 1947 British forces evacuated Cairo and Alexandria, retreating to the Suez Canal Zone.[166]

By May 1947, for the first time since 1882, there were no British warships moored in Alexandria harbour. No British troops stood on sentry duty outside Ras el-Tin or Mustafa Pasha Barracks; no RAF planes flew from Aboukir. The headquarters of the Mediterranean Fleet returned to Malta.[167] The monarchy and the minorities had lost their protector and manipulator.

A year later the humiliation of defeat in the first Arab war with Israel caused another earthquake in Egypt. The first small anti-Jewish riots by Egyptians had already taken place in Alexandria in 1936, to cries – heard previously only from Christians – of 'Down with the Jews! Jews get out of Egypt and Palestine!' During the 1948 war, the Israeli air force dropped bombs on Alexandria.[168] Although less humiliating than the defeats of 1956 and 1967 were to be, Egypt's defeat in 1948 caused a change of mood. The King was a convenient scapegoat. After 1948, discontented 'Free Officers', led by Gamal Abdul Nasser, began to plan his overthrow.[169]

14

Egyptianization

'Under those uniforms, they are mad for luxury ... we are at the
mercy of the Uniforms.
  I tell you, all the old class barriers have been wiped out.
  No, they have only given place to other ones. You'll see.'
                                   Naguib Mahfouz, *Miramar*, 1967

INDIVIDUALS TRANSFORM CITIES. The fate of Smyrna had been
in part decided by Venizelos and by Mustafa Kemal – as well as by
the clash of Greek and Turkish nationalism. Modern Alexandria had
been made by Muhammad Ali and his dynasty, as well as by the need
of Egypt and Europe for a great modern port to link their economies.
After 1945, Alexandria's future was decided by its inhabitants as well as by
governments.

Alexandria after 1945 was at its most alluring. Money, sex and food
were available in abundance. In *The Levantine*, published in early 1952,
the novelist John Sykes compared the city to 'a luxury liner cruising for
... pleasure about the Levant', whose inhabitants – 'tedious monkeys'
with 'an unslakeable appetite for being smart and in the swim' – were
happy, after summering in Europe, to return every year, to 'a winter of
good weather and bridge and gossip'.[1] Europe was at its most vulnerable.
The Red Army was poised to attack. Communists were close to power in
France, Italy and Greece. Yet many young Alexandrians decided to leave
their city for the ruined and rationed continent.

The city had long boasted that it was as closely connected to Europe
as to Egypt. As Alexandrians frequently remark, Alexandria was 'like a
little bit of Europe: 'almost the same thing ... at least on a par with
Spain'.[2] Cosmopolitanism took what it had given. Europe had sent people
to Alexandria; now it began to draw them back.

Many young Alexandrians found Alexandria stifling. What you did in
the evening was common knowledge next morning. Servants could be

spies.[3] Some may also have decided that, as D. J. Enright wrote in *Academic Year*, Alexandria was 'a conspiracy of pretence ... a colossal lie'.[4] The hero in Youssef Chahine's *Alexandria Why?*, set in 1945, longs to leave 'this tomb that is Alexandria' for the United States, to find a good job.

Patrick White felt he could 'easily settle down' in Egypt. He loved Manoly Lascaris and his flat in the Rue Safiye Zaghloul with its courtyard of banana and mulberry trees.[5] But they left in 1946, as they could not live together in Alexandria as easily as in Sydney. Alexandria could tolerate bachelors like Cavafy; it could not, and cannot, accept a homosexual couple.[6]

Some, moreover, felt threatened by the rise of nationalism, the end of the *tribunaux mixtes*, the departure of the British army. New laws were passed in 1947 imposing quotas of Egyptian staff in companies and the use of Arabic in official documents: Michael Barker claimed that Copts were sometimes, as Christians, counted as foreigners. The percentage of company directors in Egypt who were foreigners fell from 90 per cent in 1931 to 83.6 per cent in 1937 and 65 per cent in 1951.[7]

Alexandria became a city of farewells. Already in 1937, perhaps in reaction to the end of capitulations, the Greek businessman Stefanos Lagonikos had left for Switzerland with a collection of Ottoman ceramics and textiles.[8] Togo Mizrahi was an Italian Jew, born in Alexandria in 1901. Founder of the Egyptian Films Company, he was the epitome of cosmopolitanism – both educated in Europe and Arabic-speaking. He made thirty-two films in sixteen years, including *Cocaine* (1930), made in Alexandria; films on racial interaction such as *The Two Delegates* (1934) and *Seven o'Clock* (1937); four Greek-language films between 1937 and 1943; and many others about Egyptian life, or based on folk tales – like *Salama* (1945), which starred the adored Egyptian singer Oum Kulthoum, with lyrics by Bayram al-Tunsi (pardoned in 1938, he said he would like to kiss the dust at the King's feet, and thenceforth worked in films). In accordance with the fashion for cinematic Arabization, Mizrahi often acted in his own films under the name Ahmed al-Mishriqi. He also helped launch the career of two Egyptian Jews, the actress Leila Mourad and a comic actor called Shalom. Nevertheless, accused of Zionism after the first Arab–Israeli War, in 1948 this apparently integrated Alexandrian moved to Italy. He died in Rome in 1986, cut off from Egypt, but still using writing paper with an Egyptian address.[9]

Another Alexandrian who left his native city was Gaston Zananiri. He came from a Greek Catholic family which had moved from Syria to Alexandria in the eighteenth century. His grandfather Arturo had played an important role in 1882 as dragoman at the British consulate. His father, Georges Zananiri Pasha, was secretary-general of the Conseil Sanitaire Maritime – with a nose so large that he was called a nose with a man, rather than a man with a nose. Gaston, born in 1904, educated at Victoria College, was a possible model for Balthazar in *The Alexandria Quartet*.[10] Like Taha Hussein, he believed in Egypt's Mediterranean identity, on which in 1939 he published *L'Esprit méditerranéen dans le Proche Orient*; from 1940 to 1950 he worked in the Ministry of Foreign Affairs.[11]

In his memoirs, *Entre mer et désert*, Zananiri remembered Alexandria as 'brilliant, rich and superficial, open to the Mediterranean while closed to Egypt', and 'far too inclined to frivolity'. Yet his own life reflected its vivid culture. He helped start L'Atelier d'Alexandrie and to run an annual salon of paintings and sculpture in the Palais Zogheb.[12] His memoirs reveal the city's ambiguous relationship – of attraction as well as fear – to Egypt and Islam. He claims that Christians in Egypt felt both superior and over-whelmed. He resigned from the Foreign Ministry in 1950 when accused of making Christian propaganda – though the 'fussiness, excitability and fundamental incompetence' of which his headmaster at Victoria College had complained may also have contributed.[13] He moved to Paris in 1951 and became a Dominican priest. Like his friend Louis Massignon, who became a Greek Catholic priest since Greek Catholics held services in Arabic, he appreciated the Koran, in part because of the prominence in it, second only to the Prophet Muhammad, of the Prophet Jesus.[14] His life's work was the *Dictionnaire de la Francophonie*, listing foreign writers in French, and his memoirs, finished in Paris in 1982. His definition of a Levantine was 'a rootless individual who takes root wherever he finds himself'.[15]

Georges Moustaki was another young man who both loved and left Alexandria. In his memoirs he praised the city: 'Arab, Greek, cosmopoli-tan and polyglot, refuge of the nomads of the Mediterranean and the five continents, at the heart of human history and out of time, Alexandria my childhood and my youth'. It was so cheerfully cosmopolitan that he never subsequently felt out of place anywhere in the world. He wrote a 'hymn to the rootless' called 'le métèque'. In reality he left for Paris at the age of seventeen. He found the concierges unpleasant and the city grey, but he did not go back to Alexandria until his seventieth birthday. Alexandria he found sterile and suffocating. It was in Paris, not in his native city, that, as a singer, he found fame, fortune and fulfilment.[16]

Many others also got out. 'I felt I was witnessing the end of an era. I realized I was getting nowhere. A life without a future,' says Prince

Nicholas Romanov, a great-nephew of King Victor Emanuel III. In 1950, four years after he had arrived, he left.[17] Paolo Terni, a grandson of Fausta Cialente, loved being greeted in the streets of Alexandria by the Greek grocer, the Egyptian cigarette-seller, the Lebanese florist and the Viennese baker – 'It was like a film.' Nevertheless, he wanted to see Sartre and Paris. Moreover, he felt a change in atmosphere, and a rise in police hostility, after the 1948 war.[18] Another young man, John Nahman, says, 'Egypt was stifling, I was so happy to get out,' to study theatre in Dublin. He remembers with horror the sycophantic atmosphere at Alexandria dinners: 'Oh Yvonne, comme c'est amusant! C'est drôle!' screeched by her court of sycophants at every remark uttered by a wealthy hostess.[19] These individual examples reflected general trends. In particular, Armenians began to leave for the Soviet Union and, after 1948, Jews for Israel.[20]

The most dramatic departure was King Farouk's. By 1948 he had been weakened by defeat, a sense of personal impotence, and widely believed accusations of corruption. Like most rich Alexandrians, he resumed the pre-war habit of summering in Europe: Deauville and Capri knew him well.

His unpopularity grew with abuses such as using soldiers of the Frontier Corps to build himself yet another Mediterranean residence, on government land at Ras el-Hikma, between Mersa Matruh and Alexandria.[21] There was public criticism when the royal yacht *Mahroussa* was refitted for him at government expense. When returning from Europe, he was advised to land in Alexandria at night, for fear of a hostile crowd. By January 1952 the wife of Russell Pasha, former head of the Cairo police, reported of the army, 'A large part is said to be anti king.'[22]

Egyptians resented the vast British bases still in the Canal Zone. On 25 January 1952 British troops killed fifty Egyptian auxiliary policemen during fighting in Ismailia. The next day – Black Saturday – Cairo, but not Alexandria, erupted. In the words of Naguib Mahfouz, 'Concealed anger, suppressed despair, unreleased tension, all the things people had been nursing inside them had suddenly burst their bottle, exploding like a hurricane of demons.' Four hundred buildings in the centre of the city were set on fire by young men 'shrieking, howling like dogs'.[23] Many died. The glow from the blaze could be seen on the face of King Farouk as he entertained relations and officers in Abdine Palace to celebrate the birth of a son and heir, Ahmad Fouad, by his second wife, Narriman. The riots were probably started by socialists and members of the extremist Islamist organization the Muslim Brothers. The Wafd government may have let

them get out of control in order to try to intimidate the British government. The King sacked Nahas Pasha as prime minister.

From Alexandria on 3 April 1952, Colonel Sir Edward Peel MC, of
Peel & Company, which had been in the city over a hundred years, tried
to instil sense in the British government. He wrote, 'Security and British
interests in the Middle East are being jeopardized for an unattainable
objective – a secure base on the canal.'[24] That year five prime ministers
came and went in as many months: by the summer Ahmad Abboud Pasha,
the richest man in Egypt, was said to be paying the King to appoint the
prime minister of his choice. The American ambassador Jefferson Caffery
reported a feeling of 'impending revolution'. 'The factors of instability
in Egypt outbalance by far the factors of stability.'[25] The failure of negotiations for a British withdrawal of all military personnel from the Canal
Zone was the single most important factor of instability. The King himself
felt time was running out, and warned the American ambassador, 'You
will all be sorry if I get turned out.'[26]

Nevertheless, as usual the King went by special royal train to Alexandria
for the summer. As usual the beaches were packed with sweating Cairenes,
and the corniche with the latest Packards and Chryslers. The King was
aware of opposition in the officer corps and for once did not plan to go
to Europe that summer. It was a race for time between him and the 'Free
Officers' led by Nasser. One prime minister, Hussein Sirry, failed to get
the King to give orders to arrest the officers. The King thought he could
control the army by suspending the Officers' Club board of directors,
and appointing a new government under the reformist Neguib el-Hilali –
arranged in Alexandria by Hafez Afifi, the King's *chef de cabinet* – with the
King's brother-in-law Ismail Shirin as minister of war. At 4 p.m. on 22
July the new cabinet was sworn in by the King in the throne room of Ras
el-Tin. At 9 p.m. the King finally ordered the arrest of the Free Officers.[27]
That night the King's beautiful sister Princess Faiza danced in Romance
with the American ambassador's secretary Robert Simpson, watched by
a crowd of hypnotized journalists. Later, Princess Faiza and her friends
went fishing. Returning early in the morning, they noticed all the lights
in Montazah Palace were blazing.

For that night, warned of the King's move, the Free Officers' units had
occupied key installations in Cairo: palaces, ministries, Farouk Airport,
and army headquarters. Casualties were limited to two soldiers defending
the last of these. From Cairo at 7 a.m. on the morning of 23 July came a
radio announcement by Colonel Anwar el-Sadat: 'People of Egypt, the
country has just passed the most troubled period of its history.' Appealing

for calm, he blamed the defeat of 1948 on 'the agents of dissolution'. There was no mention of revolution or republic.[28]

Foreign diplomats and Egyptian politicians were caught off guard. The CIA and MI6, however, were not: they considered Nasser and the Free Officers more likely than the King to be an effective barrier against Communism, and had been encouraging them since May 1952, or earlier.[29]

On 23 July there were phone calls and messengers between Alexandria and Cairo. At 2 a.m. the Minister of the Interior, Mortada el-Maraghy, intelligent and energetic, spoke to the officers' figurehead leader, the popular General Muhammad Neguib: 'I appeal to you as a soldier and as a patriot to put a stop to this affair.' Ali Maher, the King's former *chef de cabinet* and prime minister, known as 'the fox', was imposed by the army as a new prime minister; he and Farouk had a meeting on 24 July. The King's detested coterie of Pulli Bey, his valet Mohammed Hassan, two pashas of Lebanese origin, Elias Andraos and Karim Thabet, and six others were dismissed.[30]

The American embassy refused to intervene. As for Britain, Anthony Eden later said, 'I had frequently indicated to our Embassy that British forces would not intervene to keep King Farouk on his throne.' This policy was confirmed to General Neguib in person by John Hamilton of the British embassy.[31] In 1882 the monarchy was a useful instrument of control for Britain in Egypt. In 1952 it was not.

It soon became clear that the Free Officers wanted more than a change of ministry. The King prepared to leave. He had often enjoyed driving himself very fast through Alexandria in a red car. On his last drive through his favourite city, from Montazah to Ras el-Tin – where the *Mahroussa* was moored – early on the morning of 25 July, Farouk was driven by a chauffeur in a black car, to try to escape notice. His wife, his son and their nanny, Miss Anne Chermside, sat behind. A photograph shows him sitting by the nervous chauffeur, shielding his face. He was followed by another car containing his daughters by his first wife.[32] By 7 a.m. on 25 July the palaces were surrounded by tanks, and buzzed by aircraft from Cairo.

The same day Neguib and Colonel Sadat flew to Alexandria from Cairo. Temporary headquarters were established in Mustafa Pasha Barracks. They had discussions with Ali Maher at Wizara, the government's summer office in the Rue d'Aboukir in Bulkeley. Crowds cheered. Farouk may have wanted to leave Egypt on the evening of 25 July but had to wait for the *Mahroussa*'s batteries to be recharged.[33]

On 26 July at 9.20 a.m. the officers' ultimatum demanding the King's abdication and exile was presented to Ali Maher. He had believed that the officers – as they had first proclaimed – wanted to expel only the King's cronies, not the King. When told the news, Ali Maher went 'pale as death' according to Sadat. The fox had been outfoxed. The ultimatum – by 'the army representing the power of the People' – accused the King of responsibility for 'shameful fortunes'; violations of the constitution; contempt for the will of the people; complete anarchy – 'no citizen now feels his life, his dignity or his goods in security'; defeat in the war with Israel; and 'traffic in defective arms and munitions'.[34]

On 26 July Montazah surrendered. The Sudanese guards at Ras el-Tin put up a token resistance: seven were wounded, probably by mistake. There had been more resistance from army headquarters in Cairo than from the palace in Alexandria. Compared to the bloodbaths which have stained other cities in the twentieth century, it was a civilized coup. Nasser is reported to have said, 'Let us spare Farouk and send him into exile. History will sentence him to death.'[35] Neguib boasted – describing his military coup, incorrectly, as a 'revolution' – 'Few if any revolutions I think have accomplished more with the loss of fewer lives.'

Perhaps the lack of bloodshed was partly to impress the American and British governments. On 23 July the officers had reassured 'our friends the foreign nationals in Egypt that the army considers itself entirely responsible for the protection of their persons and property'. In other words, the army would not allow a repetition of the violence in Cairo six months earlier. Nor would it give British forces in the Canal Zone a pretext for intervention – as 'our friends the foreign nationals in Egypt' had provided in 1882.[36]

Ras el-Tin, the supreme architectural expression of the Muhammad Ali dynasty's love of Alexandria, now witnessed its downfall. When he presented the ultimatum to the King at 10.42 a.m., Ali Maher, who knew him well, said, 'I am sorry, Your Majesty.' The guards in the palace still wanted to fight or kill any Free Officers who entered. The King ordered them not to. His last gamble was to offer to make Neguib a field marshal. The offer was refused.[37] At noon in the marble hall, appearing calm, but coughing and shuffling his feet, the King signed his abdication in favour of his one-year-old son, Ahmad Fouad; his hand was shaking so much that he signed twice.[38] Most of the royal collections, including his beloved books, stamps and coins, were in Cairo; nevertheless, a large number of trunks were loaded on the yacht. To his amazement, the one person he asked to accompany him into exile – Pulli Bey, the servant whom he had known since he was a boy – refused; the King was abandoned by his sycophants.[39]

At 5.30 his sisters Fawzia and Faiza – whose husbands had urged them to stay at home – came to say goodbye in the grand salon. In keeping with the character of the coup and the city, the crowd outside Ras el-Tin and lining the corniche was silent. No insults or bloodshed as in other countries.[40]

Sixteen years earlier King Farouk had arrived in Alexandria as a handsome youth showered with rose petals. Now he left for ever, bloated and despised. Egyptians' principal reaction was surprise at the speed and ease of his overthrow. At 5.45 the King descended the staircase to the landing stage, then went by launch to the boat.

Robert Simpson and the ambassador Jefferson Caffery were present – perhaps to show American approval, or to ensure lack of bloodshed. As Farouk and Narriman, carrying the new young King Ahmad Fouad 'of Egypt and the Sudan' in her arms, passed the royal guards, the royal anthem was played and the royal standard was lowered for the last time. Then, according to Neguib, 'the palace servants in accordance with Egyptian custom set up a wail of lament that could be heard a quarter of a mile away.' It was punctuated by the rhythmic booming of a twenty-one-gun salute – in honour of the new young king, not of Prince Farouk, as he now was.

At 6 p.m. General Neguib came on board the *Mahroussa* to say good-bye to the ex-King. Both were, by Neguib's account, close to tears. He reminded Farouk that he had been the only officer to resign in 1942, in protest at the British imposition of Nahas Pasha as prime minister: 'It was you, Effendim, who forced us to do what we have done.'

'You've done what I always intended to do myself,' replied the King, who wanted to appear less foolish than he felt. Other versions of his reply are 'I should have done the same thing myself if you hadn't' (Sadat) – perhaps meaning that he had planned to leave Egypt after ensuring his son's succession. Another version is 'What you did to me I was going to do to you' – he would have arrested the officers if they had not expelled him.

They saluted and shook hands. The conversation continued:

'I hope you will take good care of the army. My grandfather, you know, created it.'

'The Egyptian army is in good hands.'

'Your task will be difficult. It isn't easy, you know, to govern Egypt.'

'Such', according to Neguib, 'were Farouk's last words. I felt sorry for him as we disembarked. Farouk I knew would fail as an exile even as he had failed as king. But he was such an unhappy man in every way that I could take no pleasure in his destruction, necessary though it was.'[41]

The *Mahroussa* sailed for Naples – 'It was a good departure,' remembers Rear-Admiral Rashidy, who was on an escort ship and, like most officers in the Egyptian navy, loved its protector King Farouk.[42] Every ship in the harbour hoisted its flags in farewell.[43] The King's departure was watched by a vast crowd on shore – including, through binoculars, his friend ex-King Zog of Albania.[44]

For King Farouk, as for other Alexandrians, leaving Egypt was not difficult. He merely exchanged one Mediterranean city for another. For Alexandria, however, the King's departure was ominous. Whatever his failings, he represented a monarchy which was cosmopolitan, multilingual and favourable to minorities. Whatever the Free Officers' ideals, they were first and foremost nationalists.

In 1952 Alexandria itself was deposed, as well as the King. The coup expressed one of those hidden contests of cities, which can drive events as much as class or international wars – like those between Istanbul and Ankara, or Beirut and Damascus. In 1882 – by the presence of foreign nationals and Khedive Tewfik – Alexandria had provided an excuse and a base for the British invasion of Egypt. It had acted as a Trojan horse in Egypt. In 1952 the coup was Cairo's revenge on Alexandria. The presence in Alexandria of the King and the ministers facilitated the success of the coup in Cairo. The tanks as well as the orders for the coup came from Cairo.

On 28 July one of the first decisions made by the new government was to order to Cairo the civil servants and ministers summering in Alexandria. The Wizara government office building was handed over to Alexandria University. It was the end of Alexandria's role as a summer capital and of Egypt's assertion of a Mediterranean identity. Neguib wrote, 'It was time we thought for the politicians and bureaucrats to realize that they were the servants not the masters of the Egyptian people.'[45] In 1952, for the first summer in peacetime, Egypt was governed from Cairo: the opposition festered in Alexandria. Outside the villa of Nahas Pasha – a convinced constitutional monarchist – cars lined up day and night, and visitors waited hours to see him; but the geography of power had shifted. The Wafd's days were over.[46] In Naguib Mahfouz's novel *Autumn Quail* (1962) the hero, a senior civil servant, makes the fatal mistake of spending the summer of 1952 in Alexandria, instead of returning to Cairo where the power is.[47] Like Russia in 1918, when the capital was moved from St Petersburg back to Moscow, Egypt had turned inland, both literally and metaphorically.

The coup did not interrupt the city's social life: 'Beach cabin, dinner casino' is Mary de Zogheb's entry in her diary for 24 July. On 25 July, 'Neguib and army corps Alex. Calm.' Her sole comment on 26 July is 'Abdication of King Farouk. A sixteen years' reign. Palace surrounded, port shut. M. Neguib ultimatum to the King on behalf of the army because of his breaking the constitution etc.' Newspapers hailed a new era of social justice and economic co-operation. On 31 July all titles were, in theory, abolished. Mary de Zogheb was not deceived: on 8 August she wrote, 'Lewa Neguib declares he does not interfere in politics but directs everything. Military dictatorship. Increase of various taxes.' On 12 August: 'Everyone depressed. New laws in preparation. Augmentation of different taxes, limitation of landed property to 200 feddans [roughly 200 acres]. To give to the fellahs. Not practicable. Will ruin country?' On 9 September: 'Agrarian law passed. Everyone has right to only 200 feddans. The division should be made in 5 years. Very great malaise.'[48]

At the time these views might have seemed those of a selfish clique. Now, when Egypt imports much of its food, many Egyptians would agree with them. Many say of Nasser, 'He ruined the country.'

For a time there was a honeymoon between the new government and the non-Muslim communities: on 1 August the president of the Hellenic Community of Alexandria congratulated General Neguib on his patriotic work and expressed his 'warmest good wishes for the grandeur, the happiness and the prosperity of the Egyptian nation'.[49] At this stage the Free Officers wanted to make Egypt safe for capitalism. In early September, after workers' attacks on some Alexandria weaving factories, two of those involved were hanged, seven condemned to hard labour for life.[50] On 15 September, at the height of his popularity, General Neguib, surrounded by officers, visited the Kozzikion Greek hospital in the city. He said, 'Greece and Egypt are in essence one nation. There is no difference between Muslim, Christian or Jew. Everyone is a child of the same country if they all work for its benefit.'[51]

One reform was the closure of the bars and brothels of the port district. Lined with chemists and workshops, the Rue des Sœurs is now filthy but apparently respectable. However, a warning that, below its smiling face, the military regime might have a hidden agenda was its arrest of rival officers and politicians in August and September 1952. Within three months all political parties had been dissolved and many newspapers shut. Within six months the Free Officers had abolished the constitution which they had accused King Farouk of violating. Egypt is still waiting for the free elections promised in 1952.

In November the government distributed among primary schools a children's story *The Little Chiefs*, by Mahmoud Ahrane and two other Muslims, attacking people in Egypt of foreign origin as 'a scourge' to 'the best nation in the world'. Such people had come to Egypt 'to suck our blood and steal our goods'. Pressure from the Greek community secured its withdrawal; before 1952, its appearance would have been unthinkable.[52]

However, Alexandria remained itself. 'During this time,' Michael Barker later remembered, 'Alexandria remained a substantially cosmopolitan city. Business generally prospered, bringing many visitors'. In June 1953 the Free Officers held a reception at the Villa Antoniadis for the foreign communities: Michael Barker talked to Gamal Abdul Nasser. The family's business interests in the city still included the Alexandria Water Company, the Société Egyptienne de Bonneterie and Alexandria Engineering Works (Marine), in addition to Barker & Company. They also helped run charities such as the British Services Club, the British Community Council of Alexandria, and the Victoria House and Nurses' Home. On 27 July 1954 Britain signed an agreement to withdraw troops from the Suez Canal by 1956.

The Royal Navy called at the harbour. Edith Piaf sang 'La Vie en rose' at Romance, and there were international tennis tournaments at the Sporting Club. Alexandria's social life could still be compared to that depicted by Proust.[53] The city's businessmen thought they could win over the Free Officers by appointing them to company boards.

Nasser himself was Alexandrian. He had been born in Bacos in 1918 (the family home, 12 Kannawatty Street, is now a museum, rarely visited). His mother was Alexandrian, his father a postmaster from Upper Egypt. He and his officers resumed the previous regime's habit of spending summer holidays in Alexandria: some of them built villas in the park of Montazah; Nasser and General Abdulhakim Amer preferred Ma'amoura.[54] Nasser often visited the city. In Alexandria on 26 October 1954, as he – having replaced Neguib as president of Egypt – spoke to workers from the 'Liberation Province' along the Suez Canal, an attempted assassination by an outraged member of the Muslim Brothers turned into an ovation. Nasser shouted, 'My life is yours, my blood a sacrifice to Egypt ... I have lived for you and will do so until I die.' The attempt led to mass trials of Muslim Brothers by special 'people's courts', and may have been organized by Nasser's police. Many supporters of the Muslim Brothers were executed or imprisoned.[55]

In 1955 a great exhibition of 127 portraits from the city's private collections was held in L'Atelier and the Amitiés Françaises. It included works by Effat Naghi, Clea Badaro, Amelia Ambron and Adrien de Menasce. In the preface to the catalogue, in French and Arabic, Max Debbane, a brother of Mary de Zogheb who worked for the municipality, wrote the last paean to Alexandria as a living cosmopolis. It was 'since its foundation until our days perhaps the city in the world where the human face offers the most diversity'. Only Alexandria could provide such 'varied fusions' of 'all the races of three continents'.[56]

The worst blow against Alexandria came not from within but from foreign governments: from Britain, France and Israel. Its fate in the next twenty years resembles the looting of a treasure house, by thieves who do not know what they are looking for and damage themselves in the process. In 1954 the Israeli government had revealed its attitude by 'Operation Suzanna'. Israeli agents – mainly local Jews – placed firebombs in cinemas and post offices in Cairo and Alexandria. The intention was to sow discord between the Egyptian government and its Western allies, and no doubt to encourage more Egyptian Jews to emigrate to Israel. In reality most preferred to stay in Egypt: a new wing of the famous Hôpital Israélite of Alexandria was opened in March 1956.[57]

The British government – which had withdrawn the last British troops from the Canal Zone on 13 June 1956 – turned against Egypt after Nasser announced the nationalization of the Suez Canal on 26 July 1956. It was the supreme moment in the history of modern Alexandria, a rejection of cosmopolitanism, an assertion of Egyptianization. Nasser was reacting to the withdrawal of World Bank funding for the Aswan Dam, intended to transform Egyptian agriculture, for which he blamed the American and British governments. Summoned by the government, Egyptians had been pouring into the city all day, by bus, train and donkey cart. In the Place Muhammad Ali there was a sea of men in white galabiyas and turbans, among them a few skullcaps and fezzes. No women or Europeans were visible. From the balcony of the bourse – the commercial heart of the city – from 7.30 in the evening Nasser, formerly timid and morose, spoke in total confidence, with outstretched arms. Giving Egyptians a sense of intimacy, Nasser addressed the crowd in popular, rather than literary Arabic. Those who did not listen in the square did so on radios.

It was the fourth anniversary of the departure of King Farouk, and the choice of time and place may reflect Nasser's desire both to assert his power in the city of his birth, semi-European Alexandria, and to commemorate its role as a site of Egypt's struggle with oppressors, in 1882, 1921, 1946 and 1952. Blaming Mr Black, president of the World Bank, for having a soul 'as black as his name' and refusing Egypt its chance of prosperity, Nasser attacked imperialism in general, and the Suez Canal Company in particular as an imperialist 'state within a state'. One hundred and twenty thousand Egyptians had died to construct it. Arab nationalism had now been set on fire 'from the Atlantic Ocean to the Arabian Gulf'. He then shouted, in a gale of defiant laughter, 'We are realizing our glory and our grandeur ... I proclaim the nationalization of the Suez canal. The canal belongs to us. From its revenues we will construct the dam. Four years ago hour for hour, on this spot, Farouk left Egypt. I today in the name of the people take the Company. This evening our Egyptian canal will be directed by Egyptians. Egyptians! Egyptians!' 'Gamal! Gamal!' cried the delirious crowd. It felt it was living history – indeed, during the speech, at a pre-arranged signal, Egyptians had occupied the offices of the Canal Company. After Nasser left, police vehicles had to use water hoses to calm down the crowd.[58]

More than the 1952 coup or land reform, the Egyptianization of the canal made Nasser a hero in Egypt and the Arab world. At last Egypt had asserted its sovereignty over all its territory. Contrary to French and British predictions, the canal ran efficiently with the help of Greek and Egyptian pilots. Shareholders were compensated. Soon, however, the situation deteriorated. In London and Paris madness descended. Though the British and French governments applied in their own countries the nationalization policies for which they condemned Nasser in Egypt, yet they determined to overthow him. 'I want this man destroyed,' shouted Eden.[59]

Like many Alexandrians, Mary de Zogheb began to feel more Egyptian. On 12 August she praised Nasser's 'calm and reasonable tone'. In contrast she found 'Eden Mollet [the French prime minister] very violent'. On 21 August she wrote, 'Stagnation business in town.' On 16 September, 'Commerce business here very bad. But very calm. Newspapers Europe sow panic but also Consulates. Many English French Italians are leaving definitively.' Lying to the rest of the world, the British and French governments secretly encouraged an Israeli attack, in order to provide a pretext for their own. She was not fooled. On 29 October she wrote, 'Very grave tension. Plot with Israel to provide an excuse for Anglo-French intervention?'[60]

Although Eden knew Alexandria, in their desire to destroy the Egyptian government he and his ministers wanted to launch a full-scale land, sea and air attack on it. Fearing the effect of civilian casualties on British public opinion, the chiefs of staff dissuaded him; moreover, they considered

Alexandria 'a tough job', 'fairly risky'.⁶¹ Port Said, 150 miles to the east, at the entrance to the canal, suffered instead. However, during the Allied air raids, from 31 October until ceasefire on 7 November, Alexandria's airport and radio station, a post office, a Protestant church, a synagogue and the harbour were hit. There was a blackout.⁶² Eden claimed Britain was not at war with Egypt, merely in a 'state of armed conflict'. In reality Britain was doing in Egypt what it had waged two world wars to stop Germany doing in Europe: bombing, invading, occupying.

The papers gathered by Michael Barker show how the Suez crisis affected one British family in Alexandria. So good were the police, so gentle the city's temper, that during the Anglo-French attack Michael Barker 'walked round the city streets without interference, although clearly an Englishman'. Josa Finney continued to be driven through the city in her Rolls-Royce.⁶³ Nevertheless, 'Suez' ended British, French and Jewish Alexandria – and Anthony Eden: his obsession with Egypt destroyed him, as Lloyd George's obsession with Turkey had destroyed him.

On 6 November 15,000 British – two-thirds of them from Cyprus and Malta – 10,000 French and many thousands of Jewish residents were told to leave Egypt: only the very old and those married to Egyptians or with Egyptian nationality could stay. Bank accounts and properties were sequestrated. Throughout their lives these people had been protected by their nationality. Suddenly it turned against them, depriving them of homes, money and businesses, transforming many from bourgeois to beggars.⁶⁴ On 9 November Mary de Zogheb noted, 'Business country stagnation. Sequestrations almost *everywhere* English French Jews other nationalities.'⁶⁵

Soon her diary reads like the finale of an opera. The cast was leaving for London, Paris, Rome, Athens. Many were too frightened not to agree to Egyptian authorities' requests to sign documents saying they were leaving voluntarily. Friends helped save each other's possessions; many found that servants dispatched abroad with suitcases bulging with their master's property were never seen again.⁶⁶ The lobby of the Cecil Hotel looked like Piccadilly Circus Underground station at rush hour: people milling around waiting to leave. Few wanted to go. One lady, informed that she must travel on a boat leaving the next morning, replied, 'Je ne suis pas une femme de matin.'⁶⁷

[10 December] Adieux to Margot Adler. Crowds at the Max Rolos.
[11 December] Adieux to the Max Rolos. Max very depressed Yvonne courageous. All of us devastated.

[13 December] Adieux to the Joseph Tuby, Madame Sisi Ahmed. Adieu to Rose tired [she had been kept for hours in the passport office]. Adieux en passant to the Ray Erzi.

[14 December] Adieux to the Benj Tuby. Winnie [Khayyat] accompanied Rose on board everything fine. Took her pearls which she wanted to leave me.

Michael Barker described the mechanics of expulsion: 'a plain clothes gallabieh policeman' arrived with a written order to his family to present themselves to the governorate. There they were told to go to the passport office and apply for an exit visa: the visa was valid for two weeks, and included the words 'never to return'. The sequestrator of enemy bank accounts issued a cheque to a travel company to pay for the fare. Barker kept one document (in English under Arabic text):

> Ministry of Interior 25A
> To Mr Henry Alwyn Barker
> Owing to the existing situation the Ministry of Interior gives you an advice to leave the country as soon as possible. The passport department will give all necessary facilites to you. Kindly do the needful to execute the same.
> General Investigation Inspectorate Alexandria.[68]

In contrast to Smyrna, departure was usually peaceful: no violence, little looting. Nor were there mob attacks, as happened in Istanbul in September 1955, when, with government encouragement, in order to persuade 'minority' businesses to leave, over 5,000 Christian-owned properties and 80 churches were attacked, the Grande Rue de Péra was covered in broken glass and looted textiles, and martial law was proclaimed.[69] In Alexandria the process was carried out by government officials, and baggage allowances were generous. Even in the government there was dispproval of the expulsions. The governor of Alexandria told Henry Alwyn Barker he would be back in a few months. Other officials would have preferred the foreigners to be interned – as in the Second World War – rather than expelled. Policemen wept on the quay.[70]

Henry and Michael Barker found that the money in their bank accounts now belonged to the Egyptian government. Charles de Zogheb, son of Mary, helped arrange the sale of gun cartridges and drink from their houses, to enable them to pay their servants' severance pay. Having said goodbye to their staff on 14 December, the Barkers left their city the following day, on board SS *Esperia* of the Adriatica Line – the ship once used to take Alexandrians on holiday now took them into exile. At 9 a.m. on 19 December 1956 they arrived in Venice with ten Egyptian pounds and twenty-five trunks and pieces of luggage. A cousin was waiting on the snow-covered quay with money and sleeper tickets for London.

'This was the end of life for the Barker family as they had known it for nearly 200 years in Turkey and Egypt: nearly five generations had lived in Alexandria,' wrote Michael Barker. Most British Alexandrians' patriotism was so profound that they never, in writing, blamed Britain for their expulsion – although Michael Barker did complain that the Foreign Office, by manipulating the exchange rates, made a profit out of later compensation payments (out of Egyptian funds held in London, as the British of Smyrna had been compensated for their losses in 1922 out of Turkish funds held in London). Many British Alexandrians were shocked by arrival in what the playwright Christopher Hampton, whose father worked for the Cable & Wireless Company, called 'the bizarre wet country called England': a land where people spoke in whispers in public places and the rule of law barely compensated for the prevailing drabness, puritanism and Philistinism.[71]

Others who left Alexandria that year included Theodore Horowitz, former jeweller to the King; Sistovaris the furrier, who moved to Geneva; and Victor Lehmann of Jansen, who had decorated so many Alexandrian houses.[72]

Thanks to their languages, Alexandrians abroad did well in tourism, shipping, fashion and diplomacy. Michael Barker worked in shipping. He and his father returned often to Egypt to wind up their properties and businesses. Barker & Company was finally closed in 1978 'after protracted negotiations with the Egyptian Maritime Organization and the payment of all staff redundancy requirements'. The Barkers' three properties in Alexandria – in Rue des Abbasides, Rue Rouchdi in Ramleh and Rue Fenderl – were sold cheap, as was the case with other expellees' Alexandria properties, to Egypt's new rulers, the police, the secret police and the army respectively.[73] Those possessions which Michael Barker had managed to take, or persuade a friendly Soviet diplomat to smuggle, out of Alexandria (including one of King Farouk's gold snuffboxes, bought at the 1954 sale of the royal collections) were stolen by burglars in London in 1977. After Barker died, in 1999, there was a service in London; but his ashes were cremated where his heart lay, in Alexandria, in the family grave in the old Protestant cemetery in Chatby.[74]

In 1956 Victoria College was renamed Victory College. New Egyptian teachers – often old pupils 'more British than the British' – tried to keep the school as it was before the British staff left, but it is now entirely Egyptian.[75] The Ottoman Bank in Egypt became the Bank of the Republic. Some jewels and cash remained untouched in London bank safes for decades, after their owners' accounts had been frozen by the Egyptian government in 1956.[76] The last surviving institution of British Alexandria is the Alexandria Schools Trust, founded in 1972. Out of some of the compensation money paid by the British government, it continues to help pay for English teachers in former British schools in Egypt and the Sudan.

Departing Alexandrians did not necessarily choose to go to the country of their co-religionists. Race or religion was not as fundamental in their lives as has been claimed. Many preferred Canada, France or Britain to the lands of their 'roots', Israel, Greece or Lebanon.[77] 'The natural thing was to be French, we only spoke French at home,' remembers André Levy, of a Jewish family from Smyrna and Alexandria, who moved to Paris in 1954 – he changed his Levantine accent in three days, to avoid mockery by other pupils at his college.[78] If Egyptian Jews went to Israel, some found, as they now write in their memoirs, their new country 'squalid' or 'not very Alexandrian', and their new compatriots less friendly than Muslim and Christian neighbours had been in Egypt. Some advocated 'Levantinism' as an alternative to Zionism.[79] Even New York could seem less glamorous and magnetic than Cairo or Alexandria.[80] And many Alexandrian Greeks were dismayed by modern Greece – 'one big lie' according to one; Greeks were 'not very pleasant' according to another. Some Alexandrians had similar reactions in Lebanon.[81]

Alexandria was losing its human, its economic and its cultural capital. After 1956 it contained villas like abandoned ships: shuttered, empty, family photographs left on the table. The young Mohammed Fayed, for example, born in the poor district of Anfushi in Alexandria in 1929, lived in an abandoned British villa; he started his business career through deals with a Saudi neighbour, Adnan Khashoggi, and Leon Carasso, a Jew with British nationality who needed an Egyptian frontman. However, he too decided to leave Alexandria.[82]

The collections of Alexandria were sold for knock-down prices. In July and September 1959, for example, in a hall on the Rue Fouad, Georges Vassilopoulos auctioned the contents of the villas of César Aghion and Madame Lina Gabriel Aghion in the Rue des Pharaons. They included signed pieces of French eighteenth-century furniture; 'a very important collection of Ming china' as well as Dresden and Wedgwood; and Gobelins and Savonnerie carpets from the grand and petit salons. A 108-piece Berlin dinner service went for 850 Egyptian pounds.[83]

In 1958 the elected municipality – which had begun to lose its autonomy in the 1920s – was absorbed into the Ministry of the Interior. In
1961 the final blow came with sequestrations or expropriations of most
remaining private businesses, properties and bank accounts, Egyptian
or foreign. The state's appetite had been sharpened by its gains in 1956.
Possibly Nasser was also encouraged by his new ally the Soviet Union,
or by fury at the collapse of the United Arab Republic uniting Syria
and Egypt: one of the Sursocks was said to have given a celebration
party when this happened. Possibly a sudden enthusiasm for nationalization came from books Nasser had been reading. His policy was erratic.
Sometimes there were desequestrations, and some British had got their
houses back in 1959.

Despite Nasser's record and speeches denouncing the rich, most
Egyptians, Syrians and Greeks had convinced themselves they would be
spared. Daphne Benaki says, 'We thought it was paradise, it would never
end.'[84] On 19 July 1961, however, the bourse was shut. On 23 July news
of a list of sequestrations arrived during the interval of a performance
of *Bells are Ringing* at the Théâtre Muhammad Ali. The stunned audience began to leave. At the Automobile Club that evening there was an
unnatural hush: 'People were talking in whispers, nobody was laughing,
nobody getting drunk. We did not know who to talk to, so we did not
talk to anyone,' says an eyewitness.[85] This is how Alexandria ended: not
with a bang or a whimper, but by presidential decree.

Events in the diary of Mary de Zogheb for 1961 now read like the
blows of a demolition gang:

[1 April] You realize the Italians etc. are leaving by the lack of people in
the churches. Many people are leaving. Jews very pessimistic.
[21 July] Nationalisation all factories – companies – wood – cigarettes –
machines – banks – shares – insurance companies. Panic.
[22 July] President's speech: all to level fortunes to the advantage of
workers and peasants. Arcs de triomphe, illuminations!
[23 July] Lunch Agami. Sylvie Alice Paul all pessimistic.

On 26 July a new limit on land holdings, 100 feddans (104 acres) a head,
was imposed.

[31 July] Dismissed Suffragi. Everyone is dismissing servants chauffeur.
[29 September] Syria declares secession new government named. Nasser
radio: still for Arab unity. The people is for me. It is a small group of
capitalists who are against my laws.

On 17 October alone 422 more people were sequestrated and 37 imprisoned.

> [18 October] Talk of shutting the Mohammed Aly Club. Too few members and not enough money. Z. [her husband] often alone there in the afternoon.
> [26 October] People more and more scared. Many leave. Jews above all sequestrated.[86]

Thus even after the Israeli invasion in 1956, many Jews, with Egyptian or another nationality, had been able to stay.

The total number of people to suffer sequestration or nationalization is unknown. Many businessmen never recovered from the shock of arriving at their office one morning in 1961 to find an army officer sitting at their desk, telling them to remove their personal possessions, hand over the office keys, and leave at once: 'You have nothing more to do here.' Henceforth the officer had the power to sign cheques from the company chequebook.[87] The day Charles Boulad, founder of the Alexandria Import and Export Company, was dismissed from his own company was the only time his son Jo saw him cry.[88] Comte Aziz de Saab, proprietor of *La Réforme*, died in 1962, six months after his newspaper and extensive urban and agricultural properties had been sequestrated. The cruellest blow was to receive a letter expelling him from the Syrian Club, of which he had been president. Alexandria clubs often expelled members whom they thought had displeased the regime. *La Réforme* closed in 1964.[89]

One elite had been replaced by another: businessmen by officers. Those whose businesses were sequestrated or nationalized felt that the officers appointed to run them were governed by indifference, ignorance or timidity. Companies were ruined. The dynamic Egyptian economy of the 1940s and early 1950s was destroyed by the state. 'As a result almost all foreigners found themselves with no alternative but to leave Egypt,' in the words of Michael Barker – in particular the tradesmen and craftsmen. Others are blunter: 'They only knew how to fill their pockets,' says one Alexandrian.[90]

Every day Mary de Zogheb wrote the names of more people who had left the city 'definitively': Choremi, Benaki, Sevastopoulo, Catzeflis, Colucci, Salama.[91] Businessmen arrested included Ahmad Abboud, Khalil Sursock, Farghali Pasha, and members of the Smouha and Adès families. Many had their Egyptian passports taken away. In all, by Robert Tignor's calculation, the Egyptian government paid about £321 million for assets worth £681 million. Tignor thinks that, rather than being a sudden whim of the President, the state's assault on private property (like the national-ization of the Suez Canal) may in reality have been long in preparation.[92]

Under Nasser, Egypt became a police state. It was less cruel than others. Executions were rare; baggage allowances could be generous. Nevertheless, there were travel and export restrictions, censorship, tapped telephones, denunciations, night-time arrests, bulging prisons, concentration camps for Communists and Muslim Brothers. 'The maid, the porter, the street vendor – anyone could be spying,' remembers one Egyptian.[93] Alexandrians dreaded having to travel to Cairo to deal with their papers in the massive Mugamma government building on Tahrir Square. Emigration could be difficult, even for those who employed a 'broker' to help passage through customs by bribes in the right places. Many were allowed to take vast quantities of luggage. Some, however, had valuables taken from them even once they were on board ship.[94] Some Egyptians, long after they had arrived abroad, continued to speak in hushed voices, so ingrained was their dread of spies.[95]

Four national leaders – Eden, Mollet, Ben-Gurion (Israeli prime minis-ter in 1956) and Nasser – helped destroy Alexandria. By attacking Egypt, Eden and Mollet helped destroy British and French 'soft power' there – schools and businesses. Ben-Gurion helped end what one Egyptian Jew remembered as 'one of the most cosseted and privileged Jewish commun-ities in the world'[96]. By removing most of the rich and many non-Muslims, Nasser increased state power, but in the long term he left a vacuum for the Islamist movement which he detested and which threatens to bury the modern Egypt he wanted to create.

Alexandria's diminution reflects a general as well as a particular pattern. States like to subdue cities, as jailers like to recapture prisoners. Alexandria suffered in milder form the fate of Florence, extinguished as a city state by the Pope and the Emperor Charles V in 1530; of Paris, punished for decades of radicalism by the French army in 1871; and of Smyrna in 1922. The hinterland bites back.

Alexandria had once been a symbol of modernity. A guidebook of 1938 described it as 'improving rapidly and continuously in hygiene, comfort and all modern progress'.[97] In 1956–63 it lost its freedom and elegance – at the same time that it achieved a worldwide reputation for them, thanks to the popularity of Lawrence Durrell's *Alexandria Quartet*, published in 1957–60, but set in the cosmopolitan heyday before 1945. It is not only a love letter to Alexandria and its women, but also a political novel. A central theme is minorities' determination, as the 'grasp' of France and Britain weakens, not to be 'engulfed by the Arab tide, by the Muslim tide'.[98]

The city's fall increased its fascination. It was now, like Naples after the fall of the Kingdom of the Two Sicilies in 1860, a city which had lost its role. In 1963 the journalist David Holden wrote, 'European Alexandria has been washed into history . . . like Algiers and Tunis – or Leptis Magna and Cyrene . . . The Alexandria telephone book reads like a Levantine requiem.' Farewell parties for departing Alexandrians were frequent. The bourse became offices of the government political party; the Cercle Muhammad Ali a government cultural centre.

Comte Patrice de Zogheb had once organized the annual Old Etonian dinner at the Union Club, and concerts and plays in a theatre in his flat. Now he was reduced to playing records of *The Messiah* on Sunday afternoon. Pastroudis was 'still a source of bitter solace'; but one Greek friend screamed, 'Gone! All gone! Tonight we are historians. We speak now only of history.'[99]

Alexandria's Greeks had supported Nasser in 1956, but not his subsequent economic policies. The Greek hospital became Gamal Abdul Nasser Hospital. The singer Demis Roussos and his parents left in 1961; Stratis Tsirkas, author of another Levantine novel, *Drifting Cities*, went in 1963, despite his socialism. The great international cotton firm of Choremi & Benaki, founded in 1875, closed in 1962. A grandson of one of the founders, Jean Choremi, had to stow away on a ship in order to leave. From his life in Alexandria he has retained, above all, what he calls, sitting in the family house on Chios, a living museum of an Alexandrian dynasty, 'a terrible aversion for Arabs'.[100]

Some Alexandrian Greeks moved to Athens. Below the inevitable portrait of Cavafy, the Association of Greeks from Egypt in Athens still employs Egyptians to cook and serve Egyptian food like ful and falafel to Greeks from Egypt. The exiles had been Greeks in Egypt; in Greece and Cyprus they were often called Egyptiotes.[101] Manos Haritatis established the Elia Hellenic Literary and Historical Archive in St Andrew Street in Athens in 1980. Not only private archives like that of Cavafy, but also those of Alexandria institutions like the Orthodox patriarchate and the Hellenic Community, have now been taken there.[102] Alexandria's history, like Alexandrians' businesses, has been nationalized.

The old Muslim elite, which frightened Nasser more than any other, also began to leave. The street names were deroyalized, although most Alexandrians still refer to Sharia Fouad rather than Freedom Street. Most of the royal family departed for Europe. Prince Said Toussoun never returned from his 1952 summer holiday in France: he was replaced as president of the Sporting Club by the governor of the city. The tombs of his father, Prince Omar Toussoun, and their ancestor Said Pasha were expelled by the government from the mosque on Nabi Danwil Street. In 1966 the statue of Khedive Ismail on the corniche was removed from its arcade and replaced by a 'Tomb of the Unknown Sailor' – still the site of a public celebration every 26 July.[103] It is said that Nasser's government also intended to remove the statue of Muhammad Ali from what was, under Nasser's dictatorship, renamed Midan al-Hurriya, or Freedom Square.

Ali Pasha Yahya, son of Amin Pasha Yahya, like other business-men, had tried to win over the officers. One of these, Salah Salem, was invited to dinner in the grand dining room in the family house in Zizinia, reserved for special occasions. The major threw his chicken bones over his shoulder on to the floor – a gesture his hostess politely imitated. Ali Yahya, however, left Egypt in 1959; the family business empire has been reduced to properties from which it is difficult to extract rents. The house in Zizinia was sold and, as usual in such cases, demolished – to be replaced by three blocks of flats. His son lives in California.[104]

In 1965 a departure and a death signalled the end of an era. On 6 July Argine Salvago, aged seventy-eight, tried to leave with thirty-five pieces of luggage. She was stopped at customs when they found a gold bracelet in her maid's suitcase, and was kept for sixteen hours on the quay without food, not being allowed to return home until three the next morning. Finally – no doubt through bribery – she secured permission to leave with most of her collection of Islamic antiquities. Her friend Mary de Zogheb wrote in her diary:

[24 August] Argine telephones. Adieux.
[26 August] Argine left. Telephones. I was out.[105]

Argine Salvago's house became the consulate of the USSR: photographs of Lenin and Stalin replaced signed photographs of European royalty. If it had not been bought by a foreign government, it might now be as close to ruin as other mansions in the *quartier grec*. She died in 1977, leaving much of her collection to the Benaki Museum.[106] Other great Alexandria collections of antiquities and porcelain also ended in museums outside Egypt: the Fitzwilliam Museum (Menasce), the Victoria & Albert (Finney), the British Museum (Ralph Harari). Others were dispersed at sales like the Aghions', enabling astute antique dealers or tourists to buy Sèvres and Lalique at knock-down prices.[107]

In the year that Argine Salvago left, Max Debbane, the arch-priest of Alexandrinology – the study of Alexandria, which he considered as important as Egyptology – had died at the age of seventy-two. He had once lived in the Villa Ambron – later occupied by Lawrence Durrell – in the Moharrem Bey district, surrounded by a garden of banyan trees. His step-children considered him 'a silly scented Syrian'.[108] In his last years he would be seen walking through the streets of the city he loved, wearing a bow tie and a large black felt hat, the image of 'shadowy solitude'. For years he ran the *Bulletin* of the Société Archéologique d'Alexandrie. He wrote only a few monographs, but assembled, among the objects and souvenirs in his flat, thousands of files and dossiers on Alexandria, filled with notes in his small cursive handwriting. Seeing them, 'all arranged, noted, divided in an order of which only he knew the key', wrote his obituarist, in words which could apply to many other historians, 'we had the appalling sentiment of a second death, more cruel perhaps than the first: the death of this universe, object of so much effort, which he had patiently constructed in his own image.' Three thousand three hundred of his books were bought by the library of the American University of Cairo. The files and dossiers have gone.[109]

The physical condition of the people improved, through better diet and health care. The physical condition of the city deteriorated. James Morris in 1966 found that 'all over the Levantine city an air of seedy neglect lies like a blight.' The concierge of the Cecil Hotel told him water would come on 'maybe after two hours'.[110] Walls were covered in political slogans. Photios Photaros, maître d'hôtel in the Union Restaurant, which used to fly in frogs' legs from France, now came in every day only to feed the cats which kept out the rats.[111] There was little maintenance. The city looked so run-down that a visitor asked Azza Heikal, professor at the university, if it had just been attacked in a war.[112]

Conversation in Alexandria had once been deplored for its frivolity. To a survivor's account of Auschwitz, her cousin had replied, 'We had a terrible time with sugar shortages.'[113]

Other remarks were less heartless:

You will soon notice how easy it is to do nothing.
The women, like the painters, of Alexandria have too much technique but too little temperament.[114]
You see those two bald Syrians over there? One of them likes sailors, the other likes shoes.

After 1961 the tone changed:

> Nasser taught Egyptians to think they were something and they are nothing, nothing, nothing!
> We have lost everything, everything, everything![115]
> We live in a jungle. Beasts of prey are fighting over the loot.[116]
> What can I do, how could I leave my mother when she stubbornly refused to leave Alexandria?
> Before the war now, this was the happiest city in the world.
> And look at us now!
> What have we done to deserve it?
> What will become of us?'[117]
> All my friends have gone, it is like a village now.

The exodus of up to 100,000 Alexandrians in 1956–66 – Nasser's greatest gift to the West – took them to São Paulo or Sydney, Montreal or Milan, Athens or Tel Aviv, London or Paris. They generally prospered. However, they formed groups – 'les Bahharines [Beach-Lovers] de Montréal', 'the Skandarani from Down Under', 'les métèques de São Paulo' – meeting, under an alien sun, for cards, dinner and exchanges of memories. Many never got over Alexandria. 'No one ever leaves Alexandria,' wrote Jacqueline Cooper, the daughter of a prominent businessman called Jules Klat, who now lives in Geneva.[118]

To the cult of the city's Hellenistic and Roman past was now added another, of 'the golden age' of 1860–1960. Smyrniots preferred not to speak of the past. Alexandrians talked – still talk – of little else. Many have written memoirs or novels, with titles like *Farewell to Alexandria*, *Losing Alexandria* or *Leaving Alexandria*. Such is the impact of *The Alexandria Quartet* that they often reproduce, as their own memories, scenes and phrases inspired by Durrell.[119] Food has the same importance in their memories as music in Smyrniots'. Alexandria had had no equivalent to the cafés of the Cordon, blending different musical traditions: popular music was more Western. In the magazine *AAHA* (*Amicale Alexandrie Hier et Aujourd'hui*), they talk with fervour about honeycakes, *loups de mer*, falafel. 'Everything has changed, but the smell has remained in our nostrils, the taste on our lips and the memory in our hearts,' in the words of a Brazilian website, in French, on 'les pâtissiers d'Alexandrie'.[120]

The great Alexandria dispersion was not inevitable. Race relations were better than in 1882 or 1921. Egyptians were participating in the economic, social and cultural advantages of the city. There was no lethal territorial dispute between states, as in Smyrna; nor, as in India in 1947, an explosion of religious hatred such as led to the panic-stricken exodus of Hindus and Muslims from formerly mixed cities. Nor did Egypt resemble Algeria, a colony founded on conquest and expropriation. In 1962, at the end of the war of independence, most Algerians wanted the French to leave: over a million Frenchmen were ferried across the Mediterranean to settle in France. In Alexandria, however, the main causes of Egyptianization were accidental: Suez and socialism.

Many members of the old elite stayed in Alexandria because of age, poverty or good relations with the regime (the Cordahi and Sursock families, for example, were not sequestrated). Princess Fawzia, the last surviving sister of King Farouk, still (2010) lives in a villa in Alexandria. Farghaly Pasha continued to be driven to the Sporting Club every day in his dark-green Rolls-Royce, wearing the tarboosh, symbol of the old regime; he lived long enough to attend Nasser's children's weddings and to be consulted on Sadat's open-door economic policy. Another survivor, Alexander Benaki, known to his family as Bobos, gave John Carswell an English lunch in 1964 in 'his [Tudor-style] mansion dressed in tweed plus-fours, smoking a pipe', accompanied by a pair of bounding cocker spaniels. He stayed in Alexandria partly out of love for horses.[121]

The most cheerful survivor from the old elite was Bernard de Zogheb, son of Ziquet and Mary de Zogheb, known to his family and friends as Binta or Little Binta (*bint* means 'daughter' in Arabic). Hit by a car at thirteen while chasing butterflies, he had retained a childlike side to his nature. Friends adored his humour and kindness: 'the kindest man I ever knew'; 'the only person who will cry at my funeral'.[122] As a young man working as a secretary for the RAF during the war, he had made friends with soldiers and airmen, some of whom he later visited in England; but there were no permanent attachments. His mother's efforts to marry him off were in vain.

After the war he had spent much of his time painting, playing Scrabble, writing his diary and articles about parties for *La Réforme illustrée*. He invented characters like Hazel Halloub and Farfalina Piha (who hid her enormous behind by wearing bows on it), so that none of the real people mentioned at the parties came last. Like many Alexandrians of his milieu, Muslims as well as Christians, he spoke and wrote perfect French and English, good Italian, some Greek, but only 'three words of Arabic' – the Arabic of the kitchen or bars by the port.

He combined a passion for self-commemoration with what his

biographer Hala Halim called 'a totally individual and very playful way of doing things'. He made his books of crossword puzzles into illuminated manuscripts: filling in each letter in a puzzle in a different colour of felt-tip pen, then recording the place where he had solved it – 'having dinner with Sam and Adrian in Chelsea' for example – and covering the top and bottom of each page with drawings.

Zogheb's frivolity was expressed in comic operas written in the pidgin Italian of Alexandria maids from Istria. They are the last bow of a form of lingua franca. The music is modern; the characters are played by puppets. *Le Sorelle Brontë* satirized the cult of the Brontë sisters, showing them as wild women hungry for sex, fame and money. *Le Vacanze a Parigi* described diners at Prunier's who hide in the toilet as they cannot pay their bill; Madame Lavabo is a Russian princess. *La Vita Alessandrina* was a fantasy about Cavafy, 'timido e furtivo', meeting the three archangels Mochele, Gaby and Raff in a bar, where they drink 'bladimeri'. The opera opens with a scene 'Waiting for the Zervudachis' – a parody of Cavafy's poem 'Waiting for the Barbarians' – about a tea party given by Cavafy's mother, which this rich Alexandrian family does not deign to attend. *Copts and Robbers* is an account of a dinner party which shows what Alexandrians thought of the writers they inspired: Claudia Roden's recipes are wrong; Olivia Manning was 'a vicious namby-pamby little witch with a whiny voice'. Zogheb said of Durrell – inaccurately – 'He knew nobody, he was just a little teacher.'[123] However, he liked Robert Liddell, who dedicated his life of Cavafy (1977) 'to Bernard de Zogheb and other Alexandrian friends'.

In order to escape his family, Bernard de Zogheb spent years abroad, working in Paris for Agence France Presse writing photograph captions, or as a tour guide in Greece and Morocco. Like his friend the painter Adrien de Menasce, he had difficulty in securing an European passport. The RAF had turned him down because he said he was Egyptian.[124] Although born in Paris in 1921, he could not obtain a French passport. In the end, since he was of Lebanese descent, he was able to acquire a Lebanese passport.

In the early 1980s he returned to Alexandria to look after his mother. The city was at the height of Egyptianization: the shops were empty; the galabiya of the Egyptian peasant had replaced European suits on the city's streets. After his mother's death in 1985, he moved to a flat on the Rue Jabarti. It had an L-shaped living room with a Greek wall with watercolours of Greece and photographs of wild flowers; an Egyptian wall with an engraving of Alexandria and his collections of butterflies, stones and fossils; and a gift wall with sketches of a performance of his version of

Phaedra. Every morning he had breakfast with Lucette de Saab. While she did gym, he read her his diary – though some aspects of his life, his visits to the port, he tried to keep secret, like the friends of Gaston Zananiri who 'hid with care a secret life about which everyone talked in private'.[125] He held exhibitions of his paintings and gave parties, often wearing a sailor suit or tight-fitting jeans. At times he was the life and soul of a party, making devastating impersonations; at others he could sit for hours in silence 'like a great camel'.[126]

He was interviewed by Hala Halim and Michael Haag. Speaking in his warm, ironical Levantine voice, he joked that the golden age of Alexandria had been 'more gilt bronze than golden'. At least when walking along the corniche he could avoid seeing how the city had changed. 'I can look out to the sea, that has not changed.' He died on 14 July 1999, saying, 'How sad it is to die on a 14 July' – he would miss the annual party of the French consul-general.[127] One of his last admirers was Suzanne Mubarak, wife of the President of Egypt.

Meanwhile Egyptianization has helped turn Alexandria into its opposite. The bourse survived British and Axis bombardments, but not Egyptian independence. As seat of the ruling National Democratic Party, it was burnt during bread riots on 18 January 1977. The site is now a car park.

A concrete jungle has engulfed villas and gardens; blocks of flats resemble ruins painted by Monsu Desiderio. The Villa Ambron is being allowed to fall down, in order to facilitate demolition and the erection of more blocks of flats. The upper floors of the Palais Zogheb look close to collapse; the New Elite School and a sandwich shop squat uneasily on the ground floor. The cotton bourse of Minat al-Bassal resembles a ghost town of silent warehouses. Egyptian cotton is no longer the most prized in the world.[128] Many of the great nineteenth-century buildings on the Place Muhammad Ali – like the Monferrato building and the Passage Menasce – are now filled with clothes shops, cafés, advertisements, temporary mosques, and squatters' huts. The streets are as dilapidated as the buildings. On some days the city appears engulfed in an ocean of rubbish. Cafés preserve the names, but not the standards, of the past. The corniche is a twelve-lane highway; round the city stretch miles of blocks of flats which look ready to collapse even before they are finished. The San Stefano Hotel has been pulled down and rebuilt as a towering mall complex for tourists from the Gulf.

Eighteenth-century books from the university library have been sold for nothing: no library in the city has room for them. In 1966 James Morris had written that Egyptians' 'irresistible vigour' would one day revive Alexandria.[129] But it is precisely that vigour which is destroying the Egyptianized city. The population rose from 573,063 in 1927 to 919,024 in 1947 to 1,801,100 in 1966 and 2,855,627 in 1986, and in 2009 was over 4 million. The Queen of the Mediterranean has become the capital of the Nile delta. Industrial cities and huge steel, cement, paper and textile factories have been built on the outskirts. Thirty-eight per cent of the population works in industry. As the Egyptian economy began to rejoin the rest of the world, traffic in the port of Alexandria between 1975 and 1993 doubled – but the main port of Cairo is now Sokha, on the Red Sea, not Alexandria.[130] Alexandria is of diminishing importance in the Egyptian economy. The governor is still, fifty years after the military coup, a general. One businessman says, 'The city is run by a group of businessmen with access to the inner circle round His Majesty and the new royal family ... Everything stops if a Mubarak comes to town.'[131]

Once Egyptianization was complete, Islamization gathered pace, as some had foretold. Saudi money, Egyptian tradition and Sadat's fears of the Left have contributed, in proportions difficult to determine, to the new religiosity. More Islamic and less cosmopolitan now than Cairo, Alexandria has become a stronghold of the Muslim Brothers. What Youssef Chahine calls 'a black wave coming from the Gulf' – which led to censorship of some of his films – has turned Alexandria pious. Temporary or *urfi* marriage is spreading. During Friday prayers many mosques now put out prayer mats on pavements and in the street, and roads are closed to traffic, to accommodate the crowds of men who need room to pray; women are invisible. Piped Koran readings in shops and taxis are common, as are black bumps on men's foreheads, known as *zabeeba*, or 'raisins', advertising the frequency of their religious prostrations. The bigger the *zabeeba*, it is said, the bigger the hypocrite. Horse racing has stopped at the Sporting Club, as betting is considered 'un-Islamic'. Spectator stands are falling down; a members' mosque has been erected. Once Alexandria had been 'solid with bars'. Now there are three. Alcohol was banned in the Sporting Club in 1990, in the Yacht Club in 2004. Some Muslims stop visiting even their closest relations if there is alcohol in the house.[132]

In 1963 David Holden had found 'not a veil to be seen'.[133] Now almost all Alexandrian women cover their hair with scarves; the niqab, or face veil, and black gloves are also beginning to appear. Saad Zaghloul and his wife, Safiye Zaghloul, one of the first Egyptian women to unveil her face, are commemorated in Alexandria in the names of a street and a square, with a statue of Saad Zaghloul staring out to sea above female figures in pharaonic dress representing Egypt, by the Egyptian sculptor Mahmoud Mukhtar. Their secular attitudes, however, have been forgotten.

With every year Egypt becomes more religious. Many Alexandrians feel they are living on a volcano. It could 'explode any time'. 'There is no hope in this country.' 'The city is being trashed.' 'Anyone who can gets out.'[134]

After making peace with Israel in 1978, President Sadat had twinned Alexandria with Haifa and sent the *Mahroussa* there on a goodwill visit. There is still an Israeli consul, but little trade or tourism between the two countries; Alexandria is twinned with Odessa and St Petersburg, but no longer with Haifa.[135] The last synagogue on the Rue Nabi Danwil, lined with boards proclaiming the generosity of the Mosseri, Adès and Menasce families, is well kept but empty. There are not enough Jews left in Alexandria to form a quorum to keep the Sabbath.

Founded in 1992 by the Hellenic Foundation for Culture, the Cavafy museum in his eight-room flat on the Rue Lepsius (now Rue Sharm el-Sheikh, as decayed as other streets in the district) is visited by more Greeks than Egyptians. The loudspeakers of a nearby mosque project the call to prayer into Cavafy's icon-hung bedroom. The museum's curator, Mahmud Said, says, 'Alexandria is not much interested in Cavafy any more. We're not even interested in the Alexandria he lived in.' For the novelist Ibrahim Abdel Meguid, 'It is enough to put Cavafy out of favour that he was Greek and wrote in Greek. Cosmopolitan Alexandria is finished.' An Alexandria deputy representing the Muslim Brothers, Sobhi Saleh, says, 'Cavafy was a one-time event in Alexandria; his poems are sinful.' Today he would be driven out of the city.[136]

15

Beirut: Birth of a Capital

PHILIPPE BERTHELOT: Mais Beyrouth fait partie du Liban.
EMIR FAISAL: Beyrouth n'est pas compris dans les frontières du Liban actuel.

Conversation at the Quai d'Orsay, Paris, 21 October 1919

ALEXANDRIA AND SMYRNA had been homogenized. Beirut was the last Levantine city to remain diverse in character, the last in which foreign states continued to interfere as if by right, and often by invitation. Beirut was also the first Levantine city to be a capital since Alexandria under Muhammad Ali and Said. It became a centre of Arab nationalism throughout the Middle East.

After the Ottoman defeat in September 1918, Beirut began to assume a new identity. On 30 September that year the 'republic of merchants' took control. Alfred Sursock, Salim Salam and Ahmad Bayhum arranged the departure of the Ottoman vali Ismail Hakki (to whom Sursock continued to send money). Omar Daouk, head of the municipality, headed an interim administration. On 5 October, five days after the entry into Damascus of British and Arab forces, confirming the nationalist 'martyrs'' prophecies, Fatma Mahassani, sister of two of them, hoisted the Hashemite flag above the Petit Saray in Beirut.[1]

French sailors occupied the port on 7 October. They were cheered as liberators by Christian crowds – although the liberators of Beirut itself had in fact been Arabs. The sons of Salim Salam saw their Greek Catholic tutor among the cheering crowd; but he would not meet their eyes. On 8 October the Hashemite flag was replaced on government buildings by the French tricolour. French officials took control of the old Ottoman administration and began to take measures to end the famine.[2]

Public soup kitchens were set up. French officials requisitioned speculators' wheat supplies, and imported more from Egypt. Price controls were established, and 50,000 people were placed on a rationing system. But on 2 November an Australian soldier noticed large numbers of naked, begging children: 'The wail of starvation pursued you down the alleys of the city.'[3]

After 1918 the old Levantine game was played with new participants. Emir Faisal, son of Sherif Hussein of Mecca, hoped to rule a united inde-pendent Syria from Damascus 'with the aid of a great civilized nation' – i.e. France.[4] He often visited Beirut, on his way to and from the Paris peace conference. Muslims drew his carriage in triumph through the city on 22 November 1918 to the Place de la Liberté, to which he gave its present name of Sahat al-Shuhada or Place des Martyrs. Later the Place des Martyrs was given a massive central sculpture showing one veiled and one unveiled woman (i.e. a Muslim and a Christian), united in grief.

Faisal was the only leader who tried to conciliate all communities and opinions. He had many Christian and Jewish friends, and on 1 May 1919 he spoke on the Place des Martyrs of the necessity of union 'with all elements of the Syrian fatherland'.[5] Mount Lebanon should be enlarged, but it should not include Beirut. Beirut was 'the door to Syria ... a house cannot be without its door'.[6] Beirut was a bone of contention. Because of its size, and commercial importance, Faisal, and many others, wanted Beirut to be an autonomous free port, distinct from both Lebanon and Syria.[7]

Maronites, however, wanted to expand Mount Lebanon to include Beirut, the Bekaa valley and the coast in a 'new Phoenicia' in its 'natural and historic frontiers' – which were neither natural nor historic. Maronites shocked even their French protectors by claiming to speak for Lebanon; they felt their culture and their Christanity entitled them to independ-ence from Syria. Waging propaganda campaigns in Paris, which their patriarch visited in 1919, they took French policy hostage, weakening France's influence over other groups, as some French officials complained. They even threatened to make a mass immigration to France if it did not support their policy – or turn to Britain.[8]

Alfred Sursock had survived the horrors of the war and the fall of the Ottoman Empire as dynamic as ever – his sister Isabelle congratulated him at the end of the war, 'At last your dreams are realized. I imagine the joy you felt on seeing the Anglo-French troops enter Beyrouth. I imagine the joy of the whole country. At last you are delivered from all your suffer-ings.'[9] French officers replaced Jemal Pasha and his staff as guests in the Sursock palace.

A member of the Beirut municipal commission, president of 'the Committee of the Christians of Beyrouth', Alfred Sursock, the former

Ottoman diplomat, now turned to the Maronites. In late 1918 and early 1919, at meetings and receptions in his palace, representatives of 'the Christian masses' decided to ask for a greater Lebanon including Beirut, 'under the aegis and with the assistance of their traditional protector France'. The only links they wanted with Syria were economic. Sursock refused to join the congress in Damascus which demanded total independence for Syria, without French control.[10]

Determined to enforce its 'inalienable rights', which it considered to date back to François I and which had recently been confirmed under the Sykes–Picot Agreement dividing the Ottoman Empire between France and Britain in 1916, the French government wanted to control both Lebanon and Syria, using whichever factions were malleable. Their expectations and investments in Lebanon were so high that the French were bound to dominate the country. Moreover, the Lebanese silk industry was already necessary to Lyon silk firms.[11]

From a family of Jesuit-educated priests and professors, Emile Edde, a Beirut politician who spoke better French than Arabic, said that the Christians wanted France, while the Muslims wanted independence. In reality the inhabitants shifted between identities, emphasizing whichever suited them at the time: French, Lebanese, Syrian or Arab. Many Orthodox and Greek Catholics had reservations about the French connection. Najib Sursock, unlike his cousin Alfred, favoured union with Syria.[12] Many Muslims were ready to co-operate with France, especially when it seemed strong. But no Lebanese wanted to be treated as a colony like Algeria, source of the regiments of Chasseurs d'Afrique landing in Beirut. Answered prayers cause more unhappiness than unanswered ones. Already Beirut newspapers were asking if their French 'liberators' did not in reality resemble a private company preparing to exploit the country.[13]

By September 1919 British troops had left. General Henri Gouraud, a devout Catholic who had spent years in French North Africa, arrived as High Commissioner. The number of French troops in Syria rose from 15,000 in October 1919 to 66,000 a year later. The High Commissioner moved into the Résidence des Pins, a large, elaborately decorated neo-Moorish residence which Alfred Sursock had built in 1915–17 in a pine forest near the Damascus road and had hoped to turn into a club and cinema.[14] French administrative advisers assumed greater power. In March 1920 a new currency, the Syrian pound, was created, based on the franc and issued by the French-owned Bank of Syria.

On 7 March 1920 Faisal was proclaimed king of Syria (including Lebanon and Palestine) by the congress in Damascus. On 24 July his minuscule army was routed by French forces at Maysaloun on the Beirut–Damascus road. He and his followers were sent into exile. France was now in control.[15]

Against the wishes of much of its non-Maronite population, the frontiers of Lebanon were expanded by France to include the Muslim cities of Sidon and Tripoli and their surrounding coastline, as well as Beirut and the Bekaa valley. At a grandiose ceremony on 1 September 1920 on the steps of the Résidence des Pins, General Gouraud proclaimed the new state of 'Grand Liban', flanked by the Maronite Patriarch, and the Mufti (who later claimed he had been obliged to attend), as well as French officers and officials 'en grande tenue'.

Gouraud stated, with more optimism than honesty, that the new Lebanon was for everyone, against no one. 'Union will make your grandeur, as rivalries of race and religions created your weakness.' The speech of thanks of the governor of Beirut, Neguib Bey Aboussouan, was an extreme expression of Lebanese Francomania:

> And it is no mean source of pride for Lebanon – this prolongation overseas of France – to be delivered by the liberator of Champagne [Gouraud]. In the shade of the flag whose sublime and immaculate glory makes France eternal, imperishable and necessary, Greater Lebanon will live. Now definitively placed under the powerful and beneficent aegis of France ... Beyrouth, flower of Syria, capital of Lebanon, recovering its freedom, acclaims in you its benefactor.

He also referred to the realization of medieval dreams – i.e. the crusades. In Beirut the past could be as toxic as in Smyrna.[16]

Lebanon was born, but, as Georges Fayyad wrote to Alfred Sursock – one Christian to another – 'it is a monster as its head [Beirut] is bigger than its body.' For Fayyad, alarmed by the 'contradictory interests of the communities', Lebanon was essentially Christian: its frontiers should be reduced to those of its Christian population – roughly pre-1915 Mount Lebanon – and Beirut should be a free city. The addition of Muslims, and Lebanon's separation from Syria without the latter's consent, had increased Lebanon's innate combustibility.[17]

After 1920 Beirut acquired some outward aspects of a capital. The Grand Saray, the Ottoman barracks on the hill above the old city, became the seat of the French High Commission for 'the states of the Levant' – Lebanon and Syria. Thereby, for the only time in its history, Damascus was subordinated to Beirut, the inland capital to the Levantine port.

French troops from Senegal – what an enthusiastic French officer called 'la force noire' – were housed in barracks ringing the city.[18] The French High Commissioners, whether soldiers like General Maxime Weygand or civilians like Henri de Jouvenel, had ultimate power in Lebanon until 1943. As a sign of French power, France created, to try cases involving French citizens or other Europeans, *tribunaux mixtes* on the model of those which Egyptians were so eager to abolish. French was their sole language, and the magistrates – although paid from the Syrian and Lebanese budgets – were French. Beirutis greeted their inauguration in 1923 with riots and closed bazaars.[19]

The Petit Saray, the former seat of the Ottoman governor, was occupied by a French-controlled Lebanese government. In 1925 Lebanese nationality was created as a legal category. That year a constitution was proclaimed and a parliament built near the Place des Martyrs on what became the Place des Etoiles, round which a series of straight streets were laid out, replacing ancient souks, *hans*, churches and mosques. The parliament is in the 'Art Deco Phoenician' style preferred by the French mandate.[20] The clock tower outside it, finished in 1932, was a present from a Lebanese emigrant in Mexico, Miguel Abed.[21]

In 1927 the municipality of Beirut moved into another elegant neo-Phoenician building near the Place des Martyrs. It was designed by Youssef Bey Aftimos, who in another century had built the clock tower in honour of Abdulhamid by the Grand Saray.

Confessionalism reigned in the Beirut municipality, as throughout Lebanon. In accordance with article 95 of the constitution, religious affiliation determined the allocation of official posts both in ministries and in municipalities.[22] The president of the Beirut council was always Sunni, the first being the wealthy landowner and merchant Omar Bayhum. Every religious group was represented in proportion to its number of votes, as is still the case: five Muslims, two Maronites, two Orthodox, one Greek Catholic, one representing all other minorities. Municipal officials – of whom there were about 550 – were approximately half Muslim and half Christian. The police were mainly Muslim. The budget of the Beirut municipality at this time was about a third that of the state, like the number of its officials.[23]

By apportioning municipal appointments strictly by religion, Beirut enforced a sense of difference, instead of encouraging integration. In the equally diverse city of New York, some groups did dominate some jobs – the Irish the Police Department for example – but there were no official quotas. The French mandatory authorities also encouraged differences by subsidizing religious schools. More tolerant in this domain than the Ottoman Empire, France recognized the Shia, for the first time, as a distinct religious group with its own courts. Maronites emphasized their difference from other communities by speaking French and giving free French lessons.[24]

In addition to its birth as a capital, Beirut was becoming a modern business city. Businessmen there wanted it to be the economic capital of Asia and France's gateway to the East. Even in the political uncertainty of 1919, hotels and houses in the city were packed. 'From all sides people are coming to Beirut' and were hoping to make it 'a little Paris'.[25] That year Gouraud established a bourse. In 1921 the first international fair of Beirut attracted 1,200 participants.[26] Georges Fayyad wrote to Alfred Sursock on 7 September 1922, 'Economically my dear Alfred it will be the general entrepot of the eastern Mediterranean, it will be the industrial city of the Levant with its workshops, its docks, its fairs, its exhibitions. Thanks to the commercial genius of its inhabitants, their capacity and their capital, the countries of Asia will come to restock themselves there.'[27]

After a dispute with the French government over ownership of the Résidence des Pins, Sursock resigned his official positions and returned to business.[28] The names of the companies of which he was owner or president suggest Beirut's economic boom: Société Syrienne d'Essences; Compagnie Syrienne d'Eau et d'Electricité; Société Française Générale d'Entreprises et de Travaux Publics, Section d'Orient; Parc de Beyrouth – Champ de Courses; Société des Hôtels et Casinos de Syrie. He served on official commissions for tourism, the silk industry and the government of greater Lebanon, and believed that French capital and technical knowledge would help develop Syria.[29] The vast programme he had in view, however, was cut short by his early death, in 1924.

Beirut also resumed its role as a force for political and social change. Already in 1909 a women's magazine published in Beirut had compared the despotism of the husband to the despotism of the Sultan. In London in 1927 with her father, Salim Salam, to discuss his land concession around Lake Huleh in Palestine, Anbara Salam had experienced the pleasures of unveiling. 'What', she said to their friend Faisal I (who a year after his expulsion from Syria had been appointed king of Iraq by the British government), walking in Richmond Park, 'has the English woman done to deserve such independence,' and what 'terrible sin' had Arab women committed to deserve 'a life full of repression and denial'? A woman in a veil resembled a prisoner on parole. When Anbara Salam returned, she lectured at the American University in Beirut (as the Syrian Protestant college had been renamed in 1921) on 'An Oriental Woman in England'. She wore no veil. The storm from Muslims was such that she went into hiding and never did anything so daring again in public for the rest of her life. Her younger sister Rasha, however, rode to school on a bicycle.[30] By the 1930s Beirut women could go shopping without asking their husband's permission. Many Muslim women unveiled in the city centre, but veiled again before returning to their own district.[31]

New political parties revealed Lebanon's close links with Europe. The Parti Populaire Syrien (or PPS), dedicated to creating a 'greater Syria' from the Red Sea to Cilicia, including Cyprus, was founded in 1932 by Antun Saad, instructor in German in the American University of Beirut. Followers called him 'the leader', and the party had a swastika-like symbol. The Phalange, as its name and uniforms revealed, was based on the Spanish Fascist party. Dedicated to Maronite power, with the slogan 'God, Family, Fatherland', it had been founded by Pierre Gemayel in 1936 on his return from the Berlin Olympics. Early members came mainly from the Université Saint-Joseph, but the party mentality, like the Gemayels themselves, came from Christian Mount Lebanon, more extreme than the cities of the coast.[32]

As Beirut expanded west, south and east from its ancient core, rich landowners benefited from 'favourable expropriations' by the municipality. Streets were enlarged, lost their Ottoman names, and acquired French ones, often commemorating the war just won (Foch, Weygand, Verdun). Part of the corniche was called Avenue des Français.[33] The area of the city rose from 1,400 acres in 1922 to 3,000 in 1936; the number of cars from 100 in 1919 to 11,000 in 1939.[34]

In 1930 the *Revue du Liban*, reflecting the desires of its mainly Christian and Francophile readers, called Beirut 'a capital worthy of the name, a great Mediterranean city'.[35] It was the only city in the Levant to have an attractive modern centre and infrastructure – apart from Tel Aviv, founded down the coast in 1909, which had become the capital of the Zionist 'state within a state' in British-ruled Palestine. By 1932 Beirut's population had risen to some 159,000: 53,530 Sunni, 29,477 Maronite, 23,060 Armenian, 20,072 Orthodox, 11,657 Shia, 8,450 Catholics, 5,056 Druze, 3,697 Protestants, 2,246 Syriac Catholics and 1,759 Syriacs. The equal balance between Muslims and non-Muslims confirmed the city's mixed Levantine character – in contrast to Tel Aviv, which was planned as a city without 'goys'.[36]

Moreover, Beirut was a bilingual city: many Lebanese – including Pierre Gemayel, who had lived in Alexandria – spoke and wrote better French than Arabic. Of daily newspapers published in Beirut, three were in French and twelve in Arabic, with a total circulation of 7,450 and 18,000 respectively.[37]

Haifa, the main port of British-mandated Palestine, was seen as a commercial rival. Omar Daouk, president of the chamber of commerce, petitioned the High Commissioner: 'Beirut is threatened by the large modern port of Haifa – Iraq and Persia are both looking for an outlet on the Mediterranean and transdesert traffic is increasing.' In competition, a new port and airport were opened in Beirut in 1938, confirming its role as a central transport hub.[38] Already in 1928 the first airload of pilgrims had flown from Beirut to Mecca.[39] Soon the airport was connected by regular flights to Marseille, Cairo and Warsaw. On 7 January 1939 Gabriel Puaux was the first French High Commissioner to arrive in Beirut by air.[40]

Beirut was also modernizing politically. In 1936 a treaty would have given the Lebanese government more power and French authorities less; however, it was shelved by the French government. Riots by Muslims in the streets of Beirut, in favour of union with Syria, could be controlled only by the deployment of Senegalese troops, the imposition of martial law, and, as in 1903, the pleas of the notables of the 'republic of merchants'.

The riots revealed the persistence of Muslim hostility to a state that many regarded as a French invention. Many at first refused Lebanese identity cards, since they considered themselves Syrian. In 1925 Muslim revolts in the south of Lebanon, as well as in Syria, had been suppressed with difficulty.[41] The constitution was suspended from 1932 to 1937. Many Muslims, including Salim Salam and some Shia, participated with Orthodox Christians in 'conferences of the coast' at Salam's house, which as late as 1936 called for Lebanon's inclusion in Syria.[42] They boycotted elections and claimed that, while the cities of the coast contributed 82 per cent of government income, Mount Lebanon received 80 per cent of government expenditure. Also complaining of systematic discrimination over jobs, they demanded that half of government posts and the presidency itself be reserved for Muslims.[43] The Salams remained powerful Sunni merchants and politicians, as they still are; this did not, however, stop them from selling land in Palestine to the Jewish Agency like other Beirut notables such as the Sursocks and Shihabs. They received a good price; their Palestinian tenants were replaced by Jewish immigrants.[44]

The new Lebanon developed a new philosophy and foundation myth. While some Lebanese were ready to 'live and die for Arabism', others looked towards the Mediterranean. They hoped to make Lebanon a 'new Phoenicia'. Their leaders were three brilliant brothers-in law: Bsharra al-Khoury, a skilful politician; Michel Chiha, the architect of the confessional system and editor of *Le Jour*, who had helped draft the 1926 constitution; and Henri Pharaon. Like many Lebanese to this day, Chiha knew, but never wrote in, Arabic. He had married the sister of Henri Pharaon, his partner in the Banque Pharaon et Chiha, who was a Greek Catholic – a member of the most successful of all communities in business and the arts, and in maintaining good relations both with local nationalists and European powers.

These 'neo-Phoenicians' saw themselves as heirs to a distinct historical entity, 3,000 years old, based on the ancient trading cities of Tyre and Sidon – the earliest city states in the world, which were, and are, as inspiring for some Lebanese as ancient Alexandria and Smyrna had been for some of their modern Greek inhabitants.[45]

Some considered Phoenicianism a Christian conspiracy; but, like the Wafd in Egypt, or Mustafa Kemal with his cult of Hittites in modern Turkey, some Muslims also desired a pre-Islamic identity. From this time Phoenician references like ships, the cedar and the first alphabet began to appear in Lebanon on coins and pictures, in books and slogans, as they still do. The National Museum, opened on 27 May 1942, directed by Emir Maurice Shihab, a member of the ancient ruling dynasty, devoted more rooms to the country's Phoenician than its Islamic past. Like history, archaeology was a political issue.[46]

The 'neo-Phoenicians' thought that Lebanon was destined by history and geography to be a crossroads of civilizations and a link between East and West. 'Europa', carried across the sea on the back of a bull, had been daughter of the King of Tyre; Lebanon could reconnect to Europe through their common Mediterranean identity. Michel Chiha believed that Lebanon's identity was based on variety: 'Lebanese identity is Mediterranean. Lebanon is simply Lebanese; it is not more Phoenician than it is Egyptian, Aegean, Assyrian, Median, Greek, Roman, Byzantine, Arab.'[47] 'Luminous Lebanon', where the first alphabet had been devised, should again be a source of light for West and East. It would be 'the chosen land, the land of mutual understanding, tolerance and freedom' (Bsharra al-Khoury); 'a fountainhead of philosophy and culture' (a future Lebanese president, Camille Chamoun).[48]

★

In 1941 Beirut added war between Vichy France and Britain to its stock of conflicts. The fall of France in June 1940 had shattered Lebanese Christians, many of whom had based their lives on French power and culture. Many Arabs, however, believing that your enemy's enemy was your friend, supported Germany. They were delighted that, after their twenty years of humiliation by France, it was now France's turn.[49] 'No more Monsieur, / No more mister. / All of them out. / Praise to Allah and to Lord Hitler' was the song on the streets of Damascus and Beirut.[50] The French administration tried to remain neutral, but in April and May 1941 it allowed German planes to use Syrian airfields, and itself sent military supplies, in order to support an Iraqi conflict with Britain.[51]

At Churchill's insistence, Britain and the Free French decided to invade on 21 May and launched 'Operation Exporter' on 8 June 1941. Thus Allied troops were diverted to a sideshow, although Iraq had by then been subdued, most German aeroplanes had left, and Wavell needed all available troops for the war in Egypt. The motives were fear of German infiltration and the need to show fighting spirit when the Allies had just lost Greece. Some French, however, would later suspect that Britain had invaded Syria to get them out. The Free French commander General Georges Catroux – the most senior French officer to rally to de Gaulle – printed thousands of tracts promising Syria and Lebanon full independence.[52]

Vichy troops, ships and aeroplanes fought better than expected – above all against the Free French; it was said that, if French troops had fought against the Germans in 1940 with the ardour they displayed against the Allies in 1941, the war might have taken a very different course.[53] But by early July, thanks in part to Australians' fighting prowess, Allied forces had won. Beirut suffered little damage, except from night raids by the RAF, since the Lebanese president Alfred Naccache had insisted on declaring it an 'open city'.[54] Through the intermediary of the American consul, an armistice was signed on 14 July. On 15 July Allied forces made a public entry into Beirut. The city relaxed. Around the Place des Martyrs pavements, windows and rooftops were packed with people waving Free French flags. The Lebanese thought they were obtaining independence.[55] Ninety per cent of French troops in Syria and Lebanon chose to sail for Vichy France, rather than stay in the Levant to fight for Free France. The immense majority of Frenchmen preferred Pétain to de Gaulle – perhaps spurred by the apparently successful German invasion of the Soviet Union, launched on 22 June 1941. French officials, however, remained.[56]

★

After causing a war between Britain and Vichy France, the Levant nearly caused another between Britain and Free France – as well as driving de Gaulle, in the opinion of some witnesses, to the edge of insanity.[57] The key figure was General Sir Edward Spears. Between 1941 and 1944 he had two conflicting roles: as head of Franco-British liaison in Syria and Lebanon and as British minister to those states. As Churchill's Francophile liaison officer with the French government, on 17 June 1940 he had flown in the same plane with de Gaulle from Bordeaux to Britain. From late June 1941, however, appalled by de Gaulle's remark that he was not interested in British victory – and his determination, reiterated on a second visit in August 1942, not to grant the promised independence to Syria and Lebanon for many years – Spears switched roles. From de Gaulle's protector, he turned into an enemy, determined, as he said, not to hold down Syria and Lebanon 'to be raped by Free France' – the only reward for which would be 'a kick in the pants'. Visitors to the Levant could switch identities as easily as its inhabitants. Without any previous interest in Syria and Lebanon, Spears adopted them as causes – sometimes acting as their ambassador to the British government.[58]

Spears may also have been influenced by private passions. In his memoirs he wrote that Levantines 'sprang from a civilization far older and higher' than the French. Maud Farghallah was one Beirut lady who knew him well. Another was Emira Amal al-Atrash, a Druze princess from Syria, who had won fame as a singer and actress in Cairo under the name Asmahan. In May 1941 she had been employed as a British propaganda agent in Damascus, to convince Syrians – with the help of gold sovereigns – that Britain would win the war against Vichy France. Thereafter she lived in Beirut, often singing at parties in the Bustros and Tueni palaces. A true Levantine, she combined many different roles: Druze princess, Egyptian film star, Arab singer, British agent and *grande horizontale*. Like many British officers – including General Jack Evetts, commander of British troops in Syria – Spears was smitten. He wrote one of the most romantic passages in a British general's memoirs: 'She was and will always be to me one of the most beautiful women I have ever seen. Her eyes were immense, green as the colour of the sea you cross on the way to paradise ... Later I was to learn that she had a glorious voice ... She bowled over British officers with the speed and accuracy of a machine gun. Naturally enough she needed money and spent it as a rain cloud scatters water.'[59]

A French friend says of this period, 'She was all woman. She knew how to manipulate men. *Elle était diabolique avec les hommes.*'[60] General Evetts's infatuation became so public that he was sent back to England.

In mid-September she suddenly left Beirut, with a jovial American journalist called Mr Violet, who was also a German agent. They drove by car to Aleppo to catch the Taurus Express (known as *le bordel ambulant*), running between Baghdad and Istanbul, into neutral Turkey. Asmahan intended to sell to the German embassy in Ankara the military plans she had had the foresight to steal from her British lovers. Just before the train reached the Turkish frontier, she was arrested by a British officer. He remembers, 'She bit me on the arm, she kicked for quite a long time.'

Back in Beirut, under *résidence surveillée*, she exploited the hostility between the British and the Free French, and received a villa, a salary and a cavalry bodyguard from the latter.[61] It was said that in her bedroom you would find Air Commodore Kenneth Buss under the bed, General Evetts in the bed, and Spears hanging from the chandelier: you did not feel alone.[62] The engagement book of Lady Spears contains many entries reading: 'Cocktail prolongé Emira'; 'Dine Emira.'

After the Free French stopped her salary, she moved to Jerusalem, then Cairo. In 1944, having just finished a film named *Love and Vengeance*, she died in a car crash in a canal in the Nile Delta. Spears later took the trouble to travel out of Cairo into the Egyptian countryside to visit the scene of her death.[63]

Meanwhile the 'Spears Mission' in Syria and Lebanon, with its headquarters in Beirut, developed into a parallel government, divided into military, naval and economic sections, with 100 political officers. One of Spears's achievements was, in 1942, to defeat landlords' and peasants' desire to raise bread prices by hiding their wheat. They were as ready to starve their own people as Jemal Pasha and Michel Sursock had been in the First World War. Donkeys used to carry sacks of wheat to secret hiding places were loaded with sacks so that they set off on their own accord, leading the staff of the Wheat Commission to the caches.[64]

Also, Lebanese politicians, sinking religious differences in what was then the moderating atmosphere of Beirut, had been drawing up the 'National Pact'. The outstanding figure was Riad al-Solh. Son and grandson of Ottoman officials, a Muslim educated at the Lazarist school and the Ottoman college in Beirut, he had at first supported union with an independent Syria. During the French mandate, he had been condemned to death *in absentia*. Even after the lifting of his sentence, he never entered the Grand Saray.[65] After 1937, however, he rallied to the idea of an independent Lebanon. Other supporters included Bsharra al-Khoury, Michel Chiha and Henri Pharaon, and also the Maronite Patriarch, who had wanted France to leave since a dispute over the tobacco monopoly in 1935. He said that France was like the sun: it illuminated from afar but burnt close up.

In August 1943 elections brought nationalist governments to power in both Syria and Lebanon. Of the eighty-one *qabadays* in Beirut – key figures in delivering votes – fifty-one supported their friend Riad al-Solh.[66] Spears admitted in his diary – but not in the memoirs he wrote later – that he secretly encouraged nationalists' demands for independence.[67] To his staff he boasted that Riad al-Solh did nothing without his advice, and he compared the situation to the outbreak of the French Revolution in 1789; some of his staff, as well as the Foreign Office, were shocked by his desire to bully and browbeat French officials 'on every possible occasion'.[68]

Lebanese nationalism had been growing stronger since 1870, and also reflected a worldwide desire for emancipation from Europe. The national pact between Bsharra al-Khoury and Riad al-Solh was finalized in Aley, in the mountains above Beirut, on 19 September 1943. It renounced ideals of Maronite hegemony or Syrian unity in favour of a Levantine deal, based on balance. Using the 1932 census as the basis for job allocations, there were to be thirty Christian and twenty-five Muslim deputies in the parliament. The president would be Maronite, the prime minister Sunni Muslim, and (after 1947) the speaker of the Chamber of Deputies Shia. The minister of defence would be Druze, the chief of staff Maronite. Constituencies were to be multi-member, with seats in them reserved for each confession, in order to make deputies of each religion need votes from other groups. Confessionalism as a safety valve: the National Pact, it was hoped, would make Muslims feel Lebanese, and Christians feel Arab. In practice, however, because they were better educated and organized, Maronites obtained more jobs, and Shia fewer, than their numbers warranted.[69]

At the opening of the Chamber of Deputies on 7 October, Riad al-Solh, the prime minister, declared his determination to win 'total national sovereignty' and to end the mandate and the use of French as an official language – attacking France's cultural as well as its political hegemony. (Henceforth Arabic was the sole official language of the government: French remained widely used as a language of culture, and commerce. The many Lebanese who read or write Arabic with difficulty have to employ professional translators for official documents.) Believing that Lebanon should have 'an Arab face', he supported revision of the 1926 constitution and closer links with Arab neighbours.[70]

The French authorities – most of whom had served Vichy – reacted with a botched putsch. De Gaulle was less realistic in the Levant than he would be in Algeria. On 11 November 1943, despite, the night before, having given Spears his word of honour not to do so, the French delegate-general Jean Helleu suspended the constitution, closed the Chamber of Deputies, imposed a curfew, and had the ministers and President al-Khoury dragged from their beds and sent to prison in north Lebanon. Al-Khoury's blood-spattered son rushed to wake Spears with the news. The streets of Beirut were filled with Senegalese troops 'laughing as they fired inaccurately at passers-by', in Spears's words. On 15 November Spears himself had his car stopped and a loaded revolver thrust in his face. Outside the American University of Beirut a student demonstration was fired on. Many were wounded.[71]

The French coup achieved the miracle of uniting almost all Lebanese against it. On 12 November a protesting crowd of mainly Christian women gathered in the centre of Beirut. In a Muslim district, they were joined by Muslim women who suddenly 'with one gesture as if obeying an unvoiced command, threw their veils back over their heads'. Spears felt that he was in presence of a 'great wave of sentiment . . . like a genie released from a cave'. The crowd presented him with a petition asking Churchill to intervene: 'We Lebanese Ladies of different creeds strongly protest against the hideous aggression and treachery committed against the officials of our Independent government . . . an insult to our honour and liberty.' Dr Bayard Dodge of the American University told Spears that the French had thrown away their remaining prestige, even with Christians. The Maronite Archbishop of Beirut said 'with great heat' that there was complete accord between Christians and Muslims: after years of exploitation, the French must go. The Mufti agreed. A general strike was proclaimed. However, many shops in the Christian area of Jemayze, beyond the Place des Martyrs, refused to close.[72]

On 22 November, under British pressure – there were more British than French troops in the region – Helleu ordered the release of the President and the ministers. Bsharra al-Khoury and Riad al-Solh made a triumphant re-entry into Beirut. Helleu was recalled. The joy of the crowds on the Place des Martyrs reminded Spears of Paris on 11 November 1918, the day the First World War ended.[73] In January 1944 the Lebanese took control of the administration from the French.[74]

For most Lebanese, Spears was a liberator. In December 1944, however, he was dismissed. The Foreign Office considered him responsible for 75 per cent of the trouble in Lebanon and 'definitely Francophobe'.[75] He left with honours: he was made a citizen of Beirut and Damascus, and had a street named after him. The 'Salon Spiro for men' barber's shop on the

Rue Spears today is an appropriate memorial to a man who was always pleased with his own appearance.[76]

His departure changed little, however. Lebanon wanted independence, France control. Remaining bones of contention were control of the gendarmerie and economic affairs, and French desire for military and naval bases. On 6 May 1945 French troops – many of them Senegalese – disembarked from battlecruisers in Beirut harbour. Lebanon and Syria refused to negotiate. A general strike was proclaimed. French forces bombarded Damascus, including the parliament building, causing what Spears's successor, Terence Shone, called 'a reign of terror' and 800 deaths. Finally, on 31 May, Churchill reluctantly ordered British forces to confine the French to barracks.[77]

De Gaulle declared that he would not forget that Britain had 'insulted France and betrayed the West'. However, on 1 August full control of the armed forces in Lebanon and Syria passed to the national governments. On 31 December 1946 Riad al-Solh was able to inform the Chamber of Deputies that the last French troops had left Lebanon. His diary recorded the ecstasy of liberation: 'My hand shook as I held the text of my speech and my voice trembled with emotion. I could hardly pronounce words which I had been rehearsing all my life ... I would have wished our martyred companions to have been with me here today. I see the ghost of my father happy and smiling. I am filled with joy at being lucky enough to be alive on this day.'[78]

Sir Anthony Eden and Gamal Abdul Nasser, Cairo, 21 February 1955. Nasser had come to the British embassy to dine with Eden, at that time a supporter of the Egyptian government, who was passing through on his way to a conference in the Far East.

Katie Sursock and Bernard de Zogheb at the opening of an exhibition of his paintings at Casa Bella, Alexandria, 8 December 1959. Zogheb recorded the twilight of cosmopolitan Alexandria until his death there in 1999.

Ras el-Tin Palace, Alexandria, c.1930. Originally built in 1811–17 in traditional Ottoman style for Muhammad Ali, who used it as his main residence in his second capital, Ras el-Tin was expanded and modernized by his descendants. It was from the palace quay, on the royal yacht *Mahroussa*, that King Farouk left Egypt after his dethronement in 1952.

View of Beirut, *c.*1880. In the distance is Mount Lebanon, then semi-autonomous under a Christian governor. Beirut, the only port in the region with a population equally balanced between Muslims and Christians, enjoyed a golden age in the last decades of the Ottoman Empire.

The Place Hamidiye (now the Place des Martyrs), Beirut, *c.*1895. At the end is the Ottoman governor's palace, now demolished. This is still the main square of the city, beside which Rafic Hariri built his mosque and was buried in 2005.

Proclamation of 'Grand Liban' by the French high commissioner General Gouraud at the Résidence des Pins, 1 September 1920. Many citizens wanted to remain part of Syria rather than be included in a Christian-dominated Lebanon under a French mandate. Gouraud sits between the Mufti on his left (who later claimed he had been forced to attend) and the Maronite Patriarch on his right.

General de Gaulle and Emira Amal al-Atrash at a reception in Beirut, 1941. Amal al-Atrash, a Druze princess from Syria, also known as the singer Asmahan, had been a British agent in Syria, but subsequently transferred her loyalties to France. She died in a car crash in 1944, but her songs are still admired in the Arab world today.

By 1968 Beirut had become the main tourist resort for the
Middle East and a city of concrete.

Refugee camp on the edge of Beirut, 1974. Palestinian camps, run by the PLO and
UNRWA, formed a belt of misery round Beirut. Some were bulldozed during the
civil war; others are still there.

Israeli bombing of west Beirut during 'Operation Peace in Galilee', July 1982.
Thousands of Lebanese and Palestinians died during the 1982 war. In the foreground
is the Ramlet al-Beida beach, which in peacetime is packed with bathers.

Grass grows by the martyrs' statue in the Place des Martyrs, which had once been
busier than Piccadilly Circus, 1991.

The green line, 1982. The 'green line' separating 'Muslim' west and 'Christian' east Beirut in the Lebanese civil war derived its name from the green lines marking the Israeli–Jordanian armistice of 1948, and the Greek–Turkish armistice of 1963 in Cyprus, rather than from the plants growing along it.

A sniper resting by a vantage point along the green line, 1985. Many Beirut snipers claimed they were fighting for their country; others were paid by the number of people they killed.

Swimmers in front of the ruins of the Hôtel Saint-Georges, 1987. In the intervals between fighting, Beirutis were able to go out to work and to places of amusement.

Troops supervise the removal of barricades and rubble from a street on the green line separating west and east Beirut at the end of the civil war, December 1990.

Jacques Chirac and Rafic Hariri in the Place des Martyrs, Beirut, June 1993. Behind them is a 1960 statue commemorating nationalist 'martyrs' hanged by the Ottoman authorities in 1915–16. In a modern version of the traditional connection between France and the Levant, Chirac and Hariri remained political and financial allies until the latter's assassination in 2005.

16

The Paris of the Middle East

We handed you a dagger instead of a rose.

Nizar Kabbani, 1990

AFTER 1946, INDEPENDENT Beirut, Lebanon and the National Pact survived threats which might have sunk many stronger countries. In 1948 the Arab defeat in the first Arab–Israeli war led to the arrival in Lebanon of 120,000 embittered and impoverished Palestinian refugees, many of whom settled in a 'belt of misery' of temporary camps around Beirut; many richer Palestinians had already moved to Beirut in order to avoid the conflict, thereby weakening Palestinian chances of defeating Israel.

Despite Syrian opposition, the economic union with Syria ended in 1950. In 1951 Riad al-Solh was assassinated during a visit to Amman, in revenge for the execution of Antun Saad two years earlier for launching Parti Populaire Syrien attacks on Lebanese government buildings. He was commemorated by the Beirut municipality with a statue in a square near the parliament, now called Place Riad al-Solh.[1] In 1956 the British–French–Israeli attack on Egypt destabilized the Middle East and helped lead to the Egyptian–Syrian union in the 'United Arab Republic' of 1958–61, under the siren of Arab nationalism Gamal Abdul Nasser. In 1961 there was another attempted military coup by the PPS.[2]

The main threat to Lebanon was military. The Lebanese army and gendarmerie had only a few thousand men; but, as in the nineteenth century, Beirut remained a city of guns. Many Lebanese kept a gun in the house; taxi drivers kept a gun under the driving seat, although it was rarely fired.[3] Fathers had sons photographed holding a gun, even when they were babies.[4] All political leaders, even Riad al-Solh, employed armed bodyguards. When the Druze leader Kemal Jumblatt, a socialist aristocrat, was expelled from parliament for brandishing a revolver, he shouted, 'I am leaving now but will return by force of arms.'[5] The amount of firing and shooting during the election of 1950 reminded a British diplomat of the London Blitz.[6]

A journalist called Georges Naccache, editor of *L'Orient*, was imprisoned for calling the Lebanese parliament an arrogant alliance of money and feudalism, threatened by two fifth columns, Muslim and Christian;[7] but he was right. Some Muslims felt marginalized by the Christian-dominated state. In 1951, according to a police report, 'all Muslims in Lebanon, the educated and uneducated among them, feel they are not given their due and that extremist Maronite elements are working through the instititutions of power to make them a totally neglected and worthless minority.' Christians dominated senior positions in companies, the presidency and ministries – including the Census Department, which never published a census for fear of revealing the rise in the proportion of Muslims. Some Muslims feared Lebanon would become a 'national home' for Arab Christians and an ally of Israel, as some Maronites occasionally said they wished.[8] The president from 1952, Camille Chamoun, was openly pro-Western, even wanting to take Lebanon into the British-dominated 'Baghdad Pact' uniting Turkey, Iraq, Iran and Pakistan. Muslims put photographs of Nasser rather than Chamoun on their walls.

In 1958 more guns started pouring into the country. Many statesmen such as Saeb Salam (son of Salim), and also the Maronite Patriarch, opposed President Chamoun, who was trying, against the terms of the constitution, for a second term. The Patriarch believed that Maronites were a drop in the ocean and must live in peace with Muslims.[9] Salam was the natural leader of Muslims through the patronage he could dispense as chairman of Middle East Airlines – at that time the largest airline in the region – and his family's control of the Maqassad charities for Sunni Muslims.[10] In May a general strike was proclaimed. Cinemas and nightclubs closed. The house and garden of Saeb Salam, and those of other leaders, filled with armed young men, 'raising their guns at the buzz of a cicada'. Barricades were built in Beirut streets. Some roads resembled 'empty canyons', crossed only by cats and the occasional army patrol: families watched from their balconies.[11]

The commander-in-chief of the army was General Fouad Shihab, who came from a poor branch of the great feudal dynasty. He refused to let the army intervene in politics. President Chamoun, in contrast, asked for American intervention to maintain law and order. American marines and tanks landed from the ships of the Sixth Fleet on the beach of Ramlet al-Beida below Ras Beirut, to the astonishment of bikini-clad sunbathers, although the American ambassador Robert Murphy remembered, 'No nuclear weapons were unloaded.' For a time the Lebanese army blocked their advance into the middle of the city.[12]

That summer throughout the country around 2,500 died in inter-community warfare. Chamoun resigned in July and was replaced as president by Shihab, with the slogan 'No victors, no vanquished'. The last American marines withdrew in October that year. The English writer Desmond Stewart called the events of 1958 in Lebanon the first fully sustained popular revolution in the Arab world (as opposed to a military coup like that of July 1952 in Egypt). Maintaining good relations with the Muslims and their hero Nasser, Shihab raised the size of the Lebanese army to 15,000 and strengthened military intelligence, the Deuxième Bureau.[13] One of his qabadays, Ibrahim Koleilat, an influential gang leader in the port district, helped deliver votes, as well as running drug and arms-smuggling businesses, and protection rackets; his acquittal in 1966 for the assassination of an anti-Nasser newspaper editor called Kemal Mrouwi was greeted in his district with volleys of gunfire, and many slaughtered sheep.[14]

Proof of Lebanon's viability as a state of many races and religions, as desired by Chiha and Pharaon, was the continued presence of a small Jewish community, despite the state of war with Israel. Jews remember Lebanon as a paradise of security and prosperity. 'I have everything to be happy. Farewell 1947. Long live 1948,' wrote one of them, Désiré Liniado. After the creation of Israel and the Suez war, Jews fled or were expelled from its Arab neighbours; in Beirut, however, numbers rose from 5,000 to 7,000.[15]

At the same time, in a major transformation, Shia were beginning to move from the countryside into Beirut's southern suburbs. Their community structures were recognized by the Lebanese state in 1967; their first official leader was Imam Musa Sadr, whose disappearance in August 1978, during an official visit to Libya, has never been explained. Some Shia still believe in his imminent return.[16]

As competition between religions helped give Beirut better schools and universities, so regional conflicts for a time benefited its economy. The third Arab–Israeli war, in 1967, boosted Beirut as a transit port by closing the Suez Canal for eight years, as the 1948 war had eliminated Haifa as a rival for the transit trade with the Levant and Iraq. A third basin for the port of Beirut was constructed in 1967; a fourth was approved just before the outbreak of civil war in 1975.[17] Coups and nationalizations in Syria drove many Syrians to move to Lebanon, with their skills and capital. Similarly, Nasser's nationalizations in Egypt after 1961 drove many Syro-Lebanese back to Beirut (where some were shocked by the sight of richer boys at school paying others to polish their shoes).[18]

As Chiha and Pharaon had planned, capitalism became part of Beirut's identity. By 1951 30 per cent of the world's gold traffic was passing through the city.[19] Economic growth averaged 7 per cent a year. In contrast to the state socialism imposed in Syria and Egypt, a law of 1956 introducing secrecy in banking transactions, at the suggestion of Michel Chiha, helped turn Lebanon into 'the Switzerland of the Middle East' – an epithet of which many Lebanese were proud. In other Arab countries, regimes rose and fell; Beirut prospered. The street of banks below the Grand Saray and adjoining the parliament and the Place de l'Etoile is a monument to Lebanese capitalism.[20] Beirut contained both Jewish banks (the Zilkha and Safra banks) and Palestinian (the Arab Bank and the Intra Bank, which crashed in 1966). When Theo Larsson, son of the Swedish consul in Jerusalem, arrived in Beirut, President Chamoun told him that in Lebanon 'nothing is forbidden except an empty pocket, in which case nothing is forgiven.' Beirut had once been considered provincial; now it was a global city, hailed by *Time* in 1964 as 'the Suez of money'.[21] For the first time emigration almost ceased.[22]

As peasants poured in in search of work – especially Shia from the south – the population of Beirut rose from 300,000 in 1950 to 1.2 million in 1975. By then the city had reached the unique position of being a capital containing half the population of its country.[23] As the economy boomed, Paul van Zeelandt, economic adviser to the government, was reported to have said; 'I don't know what makes the economy work, but it is doing very well and I wouldn't advise you to touch it.'[24]

James Morris wrote a vibrant tribute in 1957: 'When I first went to Beirut I disliked this deep-rooted sense of the mercenary.' However, he grew to prefer the city to the rest of the Middle East, 'embroiled in a ceaseless quest for power and revenge' – 'for I know that the passions animating this little State threaten no lives, insult no ancient dignities, tamper with no ideologies but are concerned only with ... profit'.[25] In 1962 Wladimir d'Ormesson wrote in *Le Figaro* that Beirut was an intellectual, spiritual and religious capital, an island of peace in a region burning with fever: 'In Lebanon everything reflects calm, equilibrium, order, work, peace' – and, supreme honour – 'intimate familiarity' with France. Except in Rome, he had never seen so many different religious establishments.[26]

Beirut became the Monte Carlo, as well as the Switzerland, of the Middle East. On 17 December 1959 the Casino du Liban, overlooking the sea outside the city, was inaugurated with bars, restaurants, forty foreign croupiers and a floor show from Paris. Crowds meant that it took two hours for a car to make the short journey from Beirut for the gala open-ing.[27] In these years the Bolshoi Ballet, the Berlin Philharmonic Orchestra, and the Comédie Française performed at the Baalbec Festival, started in the Roman ruins in 1955, as well as popular Lebanese singers like Fairouz (born Nuhad Haddad in 1935 in Beirut). The festival was both inter-national and Lebanese.[28]

Beirut's brilliance between 1958 and 1975 has been overshadowed by later horrors. Some, however, remember it as a golden age, the city's defining historic moment – like 1922–56 for Alexandria and 1908–22 for Smyrna. Tony Besse, who moved to Beirut from Aden, considers this time 'the best years of my life ... a real salon of conversation as in the eighteenth century'. Many others who lived there in these years would agree: 'Paradise! Absolute paradise!'; 'A fantastic city ... it humanized me'; 'The best part of my life.' Some preferred it to Paris or Rome. As in Alexandria, no one talked about religion.[29] Tourism increased by 25 per cent between 1962 and 1963, and by 400 per cent from 1968 to 1974.[30] Films appeared in Beirut before London; it was, and is, easier to buy French magazines there than in London.

A Canadian student at the American University (AUB) in these years remembers, 'In Beirut you could have a great social life very quickly; it was not an expat ghetto' (unlike, at that time, the Tangier of Paul Bowles). Thereafter she would compare other cities to Beirut – always to their disadvantage.[31]

A focus of this golden age of Beirut was the five-storey, 110-room Hôtel Saint-Georges, overlooking the Bay of St George, where British ships had landed weapons for Maronites in 1840. It had opened in 1934 as the city's first luxury hotel.[32] A favourite of British officers and their girlfriends in the 1940s, it had become the place where 'everyone' – jour-nalists, politicians, businessmen – went in search of news, excitement or romance. Habitués included deputies such as Raymond Edde and Emir Majid Arslan (a Druze notable who sat in twenty-four different cabinets); Mai Jumblatt, wife of Kemal Jumblatt; the Iraqi singer Afifa Iskander; and, every morning around midday, Kim Philby.

Beirut, indeed, had become the spy and press capital of the Middle East. In 1952, after Nasser's coup in Egypt and the consequent increase in govern-ment control, an agent reported to the Sûreté Générale in Beirut, 'Most foreign agencies that maintained main offices in Cairo have moved to Lebanon and opened offices under assumed names such as commercial companies and the like to cover their operations and their Egypt offices have become secondary.'[33] MECAS (the Middle East Centre for Arab Studies), a school for teaching British diplomats Arabic, had already moved from Jerusalem to Shemlan, a village in the hills above Beirut, in 1947. It was denounced in the Egyptian press as a school for British spies, although the quality of the instruction attracted many non-British businessmen and diplomats.[34] From 1956 until his flight, probably by boat, from Beirut to the Soviet Union on 23 January 1963 as a British investigation was closing in, Philby worked in Beirut as a correspondent for *The Economist* and *The Observer*. Despite or because of his reputations as a drunk and a bottom-pincher, he had many friends, Lebanese and British. The British diplomat Glen Balfour-Paul found him the best informed journalist in the town, 'infinitely entertaining – and indeed helpful': for, in this city of multiple identities, he was still working for British intelligence (SIS) as well as the USSR.[35]

Philby's father, the great explorer St John Philby, had moved to Beirut from Saudi Arabia in 1955. He died in Beirut in 1960, and, as a convert to Islam, is buried in a Muslim cemetery. Both Philbys received the news of the death of their first wives by telegram to the Hôtel Saint-Georges: it was the easiest place to find them.[36]

It was also in the bar of the Saint-Georges that Eleanor Brewer first met Philby, and that she later told her husband, Sam Brewer, correspondent of the *New York Times*, 'Kim and I want to get married.' He is said to have replied, 'I hope I am not in your way.' The barman Ali Bitar worked for the Deuxième Bureau. The part owner was Myrna Bustani, the first woman deputy in the Lebanese parliament and head of one of the growing number of international Lebanese businesses, CAT (Contracting and Trading Company Ltd), founded by her father, Emile Bustani, in Haifa in 1937. The fish for the hotel restaurant was caught locally; the meat was flown in from Paris.[37]

With its mixture of hotels, cafés and nightclubs, the corniche west of the Hôtel Saint-Georges reminded Alec Waugh of Cannes or Monte Carlo. The names of the hotels, reflecting owners' cultural preferences, would soon become familiar to the world's newspaper readers: Normandy, Phoenicia, Riviera, Commodore, Carlton.[38]

In the high noon of nationalism, when Greeks were being expelled from Istanbul, Alexandria was losing its minorities, the French were leaving North Africa, and the Israeli prime minister David Ben-Gurion proclaimed, 'It is our duty to fight against the spirit of the Levant that ruins individuals and societies,' Lebanon was a triumphant exception. In

1960 in the Chamber of Deputies in Beirut there were, for Christians, 30 Maronite deputies, 11 Orthodox, 6 Greek Catholic, 5 Armenians and 2 for minorities; for Muslims, 20 Sunni, 19 Shia and 6 Druze.[39]

Despite being based on confessionalism, the Lebanese state was and is officially multi-faith. The Christian president invited the Mufti of Beirut to a meal after one of the daily fasts during Ramadan. Both Christian and Muslim religious festivals are national holidays. Muslim deputies and ministers attend official Christian services with the president, such as the feast day of Mar Maroun, patron saint of the Maronites, every 6 February at the Mar Maroun church in Ashrafiyeh; Christians, however, do ·not attend mosques, on the grounds that they do not know the required prostrations.[40] Many parents gave their children neutral names – Karim, Samir, Mona, Randa – used by both Muslims and Christians.[41]

Lebanon was dominated by a generation of 'new Levantines'. Among them, in addition to President Fouad Chehab and Emile Bustani, was Emir Farid Hares Shihab. Head of the Sûréte Générale from 1948 to 1958, he was described by his friend Professor John Munro of AUB as one who 'wore his Levantine identity lightly. He was completely at ease moving betwen East and West, shifting effortlessly from Arabic to French to English and adopting the rhetoric and gestures appropriate to each.' He had an 'instinctive empathy for all kinds of people'. His was a world 'in which a combination of refined manners, intellect and conduct were prized; where passion was regarded with suspicion and ideology was seen as a crutch for the unthinking'.[42]

Another was the head of the Greek Catholic community, Henri Pharaon. Pharaon devoted his career to mediation between Christians and Muslims. In 1943 he helped design a new national flag, keeping the Cedar of Lebanon in the centre, but replacing the French tricolour by two horizontal red lines with a white band in the middle.[43] As foreign minister in 1945, he helped finalize the charter of the Arab League, challenging any clauses which might threaten Lebanese independence.[44] Fearful of what he considered the worst divisions in his country in his lifetime, he had held a meeting in his villa in 1957 to oppose Chamoun's re-election.[45] Short and ugly, with a prominent purple birthmark, he was rich enough to indulge his many interests, such as improving Arab racing stock. He helped run the Beirut port and the Beirut hippodrome, and won many horse races.[46] He was also an international tennis champion, and, like Anthony Benaki in Alexandria, an obsessive collector – 'the greatest collector in the Arab world, far ahead of his time', in the opinion of his friend John Carswell.[47]

In the family villa – built in 1892 by his father, Raphael Pharaon, behind the Grand Saray; since 2004 a museum – he assembled a collection epitomizing his Levant. The garden contains classical columns. Palmyra statues and Hellenistic sarcophaguses, Chinese jade and porcelain, Greek icons and Persian carpets fill the rooms, which are lined with panels from twenty-seven eighteenth-century panelled rooms from houses in Syria. There are golden, blue and red rooms, dating from 1623, 1775 and 1778; they come from the Basil house in Aleppo or the Kuwatli house in Damascus. He claimed to have saved them from 'certain ruin'.[48] Some said that he did not simply remove rooms from houses being demolished, but arranged for the demolitions himself, specifically for that purpose.[49]

These golden years also, however, saw Beirut turn from a paradise of beauty into a visual nightmare – as was beginning to happen in other cities, such as Istanbul and Alexandria. Hitherto the Beirut house of the elite had been an attractive stone building with iron balustrades, balconies, verandahs, arched windows and a surrounding garden. Many details were imported from France, Italy or England; the wood often came from Romania. A spectacular example was the curved Barakat building, erected in 1924–36 on the corner of the Rue de Damas and the Rue de l'Indépendence by the architect Youssef Aftimos for Nicholas and Victoria Barakat. Its elevated site and curving windows gave it commanding views over the city.[50]

However, factories making cement and concrete – for which Palestinians provided cheap labour – had begun to appear in the suburbs. In 1945, 390 building permits were issued; in 1955 there were 1,261.[51] In the late 1950s a group of architects changed Lebanese planning laws requiring apartments to be sold together, which had favoured blocks of four or five. They could henceforth be sold separately. In violation of zoning laws, apartment towers such as the Interdesign Centre and the Murr Tower (34 floors, 510 windows) began to be built. Some were by Khalil Khoury, 'the Le Corbusier of Lebanon'. If there is an argument in favour of 1960s architecture, Beirut is not it.[52]

In 1960, two years after the foundation of the Irish Georgian Group in Dublin, the daughter and heir of Alfred Sursock, Yvonne Cochrane (she had married an Irish baronet, Sir Desmond Cochrane, who became Irish consul in Beirut) founded an organization to protect old houses: she lamented that they were being sacked, 'abandoned to scorn and neglect'. When young, Yvonne Sursock had gasped every morning at the beauty of her view of Beirut. Grown up, she gasped every morning at its ugliness.

But hers was a voice crying in the wilderness – or rather in the urban jungle – against the sound of demolition squads and builders' drills.[53] In 1968 the writer John Gunther complained of the craze for skyscrapers. Beirut was committing treason against itself and the 'unmatched' surrounding beauty. The streets and the sea were filthier than in 'any other city of consequence that I have ever seen'.[54]

Symbol of Beirut's self-destruction was the replacement in 1960 of the attractive stone Petit Saray of 1884 on the Place des Martyrs by the concrete Rivoli cinema. The Place des Martyrs became a vast public space for taxis, buses, public celebrations and political demonstrations. Lined with cafés, barbers and the Gemayel pharmacy – livelihood of the founder of the Phalange – it was the heart of Beirut and Lebanon, the beginning and end of thousands of daily journeys.[55]

On the far side was the Beirut brothel district, kingdom of Madame Marika. She had arrived in 1912 as a young Greek girl. First Ottoman, then French officers 'protected' her. In time her beauty and force of character made her the leading procuress of Beirut. Her three-storey villa, with 'zoned' rooms filled with different types of girl, was a home from home for government ministers. An army of ruthless and resourceful pimps kept it well stocked.[56]

Yet Beirut was not just a city of capitalism and construction. In those days, wrote Mai Ghoussoub, 'Beirut exuded optimism and the most disadvantaged believed in its promises.'[57] In addition to AUB and Saint-Joseph, new universities opened: the Lebanese University in 1950; the Haigazian Armenian University in 1955; the Arab University – affiliated to Alexandria University, and at first part-financed by the Egyptian government – in 1960. At the Ecole Nationale des Lettres, run by the University of Lyon, the French critic Gabriel Bounoure, former director of public instruction under the French mandate, initiated generations of students into 'the life of the spirit'. Through him, remembers the writer Effet Adnan, 'I entered literature by the grand door' – although her early French education also taught her to think the world was French and the Catholic Church infallible. At some schools pupils were punished for speaking Arabic outside Arabic class.[58] The press and parliament were freer than in any country in the region, with the possible exception of Israel. In 1965 a form of social security was introduced.[59]

Beirut could be called the Paris of the Middle East not only because it was a city of pleasure, but also because of its cultural hegemony as the intellectual, publishing and entertainment capital of the Arabs. Its position was reinforced, as Paris's had been, by the repression prevalent in neighbouring capitals. Beirut was both Arab and Westernizing at the same time – each aspect benefiting from the other. In 1956 the first Arab book fair was held at AUB. Banned in Egypt, Naguib Mahfouz's novel *Children of Our Quarter* was published in Beirut in 1965. Taha Hussein announced that Beirut had dethroned Cairo as cultural centre of the Arabs. First Syrian and Palestinian publishers, later Iraqis, Libyans and Tunisians, moved to Beirut. It was there that Arab politicians and officers published their memoirs. In 1970, 1,358 periodicals were published in Lebanon, compared to a total of 2,714 in the whole Arab world, from Morocco to Oman. Newspapers published in Beirut – like *Al-Nahar*, edited by Ghassan Tueni – began to be read in the rest of the Arab world, as Egyptian newspapers had once been.[60]

Beirut became a city of writers. The poet Adonis, an Alawi from Syria, was stimulated by the varied groups of Marxists, neo-Phoenicians and Arab nationalists he met when he arrived in 1956.[61] In 1966 another Syrian poet, Nizar Kabbani, whose love poems mesmerized the Arab world, also moved to Beirut, where he founded a radical publishing company. He later wrote the words to a civil-war hit, 'Beirut, Lady of the World', sung by Magda Roumi, which shows the hold that Beirut had acquired over Arabs' imagination. For once, a poet blamed people, not the city:

> We were envious of you and your beauty.
> It was harming us.
> We burdened you, O Beirut, with our sins.
> We ignored you, we made you weep.
>
> .   .   .   .   .   .
>
> Rise from the rubble!
> We now know your roots are deep within us.

At a meeting in AUB, Kabbani urged Arab women to rise in revolt 'against this Orient of slave-prisoners ... which sees you as a delicacy to be relished in bed ... Rise to the level of humanity ... We want to give woman back her body.'[62] The great Palestinian poet Mahmoud Darwish, whose family came from one of the villages 'abolished' (i.e. emptied and razed to the ground) after 1948 by Israel, also moved to Beirut in 1972. He wrote a poem of gratitude to the city as Arabs' 'only tent' and 'only star'.[63]

Another Palestinian writer, Edward Said, hated Alexandria – which he called 'Levantine, cosmopolitan, devious and capricious' – in contrast to Cairo – 'Arab, Islamic, serious, international, intellectual'. In Alexandria, he found, 'So forlorn is the city without its great foreign communities, so apparently without a mission, so reduced to minimal existence as a cut-rate resort, that it filled me with sadness.'[64] He far preferred Beirut: 'Everything seemed possible in Beirut then [before 1975], every kind of person, every idea and identity, every extreme of wealth and poverty.' Especially in the Ras Beirut area – near the American University, the sea and Rue Hamra – which dazzled foreigners and rural Lebanese with its life and colour, he found 'a nonsectarian pluralistic and open community of scholars, political activists, business people and artists unlike anything else in the Arab world.' However, he noticed that 'everyone' knew everyone else's religion or ethnic origin, and he heard Christian relations denouncing Muslims for their alleged lechery, hypocrisy, corruption and degeneration.[65]

Beirut was also becoming – as Alexandria had once been – a city of exiles: Armenian, Palestinian, Kurdish, Syrian. Exiles in Beirut revealed the essence of the Lebanese state. Armenians remained Armenian, with their own rival revolutionary parties of Hunchaks and Tashnaks (who sometimes fought each other in the Beirut streets) and their own schools and university.[66] They had not at first been welcome, as they were accused of taking Lebanese jobs: cheap Armenian labour had been used by the French authorities on construction projects in the 1920s.[67] Yet, because they were Christian, they were given Lebanese citizenship and allocated seats in parliament.

In 1930 the supreme head of the Armenian Church established his Catholicosate in Beirut, in the district of Antelias; visitors to the Armenian museum attached to the church can admire icons and embroideries, jewelled reliquaries, and silver chandeliers, visible evidence of Armenian prosperity in Ottoman Anatolia (and of Armenians' success in saving valuables despite the horrors of 1915). The treasures recall some of those in Topkapi Palace.

Most Palestinians, in contrast, lived in refugee camps outside Beirut, without Lebanese citizenship; they were the responsibility not of the Lebanese authorities, but of the United Nations (whose refugee organization, UNRWA, was founded for this purpose). After their determination to return to Palestine – Armenians had no desire to return to Turkey – their religion is the principal explanation for their exclusion from much of Lebanese life. Christian Palestinians – for example Youssef Beidas, founder of the Intra Bank – found it easier than Muslims (who had to prove wealth or a Lebanese ancestor) to get Lebanese passports. Most Muslim Palestinians found it difficult even to obtain work permits.[68]

Palestinian camps – like Chatila, in a pine grove south of Beirut – remained more isolated from Beirut than the Armenian districts of Burj Hammoud and Qarantina. They had their own systems of schools, factories, lawcourts and hospitals (named after the lost cities of Acre, Gaza and Haifa), organized and financed by UNRWA. The camps were and are dense masses of buildings, like prison blocks; at first, in order to stress the temporary nature of their stay in Lebanon, Palestinians were not even allowed to dig individual latrines, and had to share communal ones. In 1951 the Lebanese government refused a United Nations proposal to build permanent housing for them. Bad as their conditions were, however, Palestinians were freer in Lebanon than in Syria or Jordan.[69]

Below the glittering surface, Lebanon was a volcano waiting to erupt. A Lebanese Egyptian novelist settled in Paris called Andrée Chedid wrote, 'Their little land was seriously ill but noone would admit it. Still sparkling under the balm of prosperity it concealed its fevers, its crises, its torpor. The contrasts were part of the magic. Foreigners and tourists considered it generous and grasping, loved its joie de vivre, took offence at its display of wealth, went into raptures over its warmheartedness and welcome and made fun of its bragging.' In this 'strange mixture of sectarianism and freedom', where 'everything could be negotiated', she noted that the name of God was 'involved in the most trivial incident, in every quarrel, in every reconciliation'.[70]

Michel Chiha had written in 1947 that the creation of the state of Israel was one of the greatest errors in contemporary politics: however small an event it appeared at the time, it would help 'shake the world to its foundations'. It certainly shook Lebanon.[71] Lebanon was not only a vulnerable state with a weak army and too many guns in private hands. By 1975 there were two armies on the same soil, Lebanese and Palestinian – in addition to many private forces. It is this – as much as confessionalism and the presence of sixteen religions in one state – which shows that people were wrong to say Lebanon was a state like any other.

After the 1967 Arab–Israeli war the Palestine Liberation Organization increased the number of its 'operations' (attacks) from Lebanon into Israel, from two in 1967 to twenty-nine in 1968. Its leader, Yassir Arafat, began to speak of Lebanon as if he owned it. He called it 'strategically essential for our action ... We are a revolution and we are fighting on our territory. Lebanon is an Arab land which should protect us and not fight us.' In retaliation, Israel destroyed thirteen Middle East Airlines planes in Beirut airport on 28 December 1968.[72]

Beirut became the capital of the Arab Left and the 'Palestinian revolution' as well as of Lebanon and Arab capitalism. The radical Palestinian doctor George Habash, educated in Beirut, founded the Arab Nationalists Movement and the Popular Front for the Liberation of Palestine there, in 1950 and 1967 respectively. On Bliss Street, near the American University, the League of Arabian Gulf Students denounced American imperialism. 'Long live the unity of revolutionary forces' was their cry. They swore to support the struggle for independence and national liberation, against police torture and colonialists' hegemony.[73]

In April 1969 the suppression of a pro-Palestinian demonstration left eleven dead and eighty-two wounded. The government resigned. There were more clashes, and Palestinians occupied police stations in Beirut.[74] On 3 November 1969 the Cairo Accords, approved even by Gemayel and the Phalange, gave Palestinians complete freedom in their camps and in some areas freedom to carry weapons outside them – freedoms negotiated by Nasser, which he would never have allowed in his own country. The agents of the Lebanese Deuxième Bureau were expelled from the camps. Like Greek refugees from Asia Minor in Greece, but to a far greater degree, Palestinians helped destabilize Lebanon.[75]

In retrospect, the election of Suleyman Frangieh as president in 1970 was the critical moment, when the lunatics began to take over the asylum. Unlike his predecessors, Frangieh had blood on his hands. In 1957 he and his followers had been involved in a battle in a church, during which twenty-three people died: he had been forced to flee to Syria for a year. He was also the first president to come from a purely Christian, rather than a mixed, area. His election – which he won by one vote, beating a moderate Shihabist rival called Elias Sarkis – was greeted by overjoyed Christians in Beirut firing their rifles in the air.[76]

The authority of the state declined. Palestinians' roadblocks outside their camps, even on the road between Beirut and its airport, led to harassment and kidnappings. The vulnerability of the city was shown on 9 April 1973. Israeli commandos landed by sea near the famous Pigeons' Grotto at Ras Beirut, killed three PLO leaders in the fashionable Verdun district, and fled – without meeting opposition.[77]

Far from being self-centred, Lebanese were more passionately affected by Palestine than any other Arab people. The leaders' funeral was escorted by the largest demonstration in the city's history – perhaps a quarter of a million people. Many Lebanese felt, as the novelist Elias Khoury wrote, 'Palestine is not a country. Palestine is a condition. Every Arab is a Palestinian. Palestine is the condition of us all.' Others, however, were ready to prove their hate of Palestinians by acts. In 1970–71 King Hussein crushed the PLO in Jordan; Arafat and around 100,000 Palestinians moved to Lebanon. Because of their popularity, the Lebanese state was powerless or unwilling to stop them. Beirut became the capital of the PLO.[78] By 1975 the total number of Palestinians on Lebanese soil may have reached 400,000 – 15 per cent of the population.

Palestinians became almost as aggressive to Lebanon as to Israel itself. Moreover, thanks to subventions from Arab governments, they were rich and well armed (often with Soviet weapons paid for by Libyan money). Camps had their own munitions factories. With stores of weapons and ammunition hidden in underground galleries and passages, the PLO could field 20,000 armed men and could at times, military intelligence reported, outgun the Lebanese army. Part of Beirut, literally as well as figuratively, was a powder keg.[79]

On 3 May 1973 Palestinians kidnapped three Lebanese soldiers. The Lebanese air force bombed the camps. Palestinians fired cannon at Beirut airport from the nearby camp of Borj al-Barajneh. They began to domi-nate west Beirut, sending soldiers into cafés to demand money. Strikes became common. In retaliation, the army began to arm the Phalange and other Maronite forces in secret; Christians began to buy 'klashens', as Arabs called Kalashnikovs, directly from dealers in Palestinian camps.[80] The novel *Death in Beirut* by Tawfiq Yusuf Awwad, published there in 1975, contains warnings of catastrophe: 'Beirut is boiling like a cooking-pot.' It ends with Beirut in flames 'from one end of the city to the other'.[81]

In much of Beirut business continued as usual. The historian Michael Johnson, despite warnings of rape and burglary from Christian friends, felt his wife was safer walking alone at night in west Beirut than in London.[82] In 1974 the twenty-seven-storey Holiday Inn opened near the Place des Martyrs. Topped by a revolving restaurant, its construction had caused the destruction of some of Beirut's last sixteenth-century buildings.

On Sunday 13 April 1975 Palestinians killed four people, including one of Pierre Gemayel's bodyguards, outside a church in the Christian suburb of Ain el-Romaneh during its consecration; in retaliation a bus-load of Palestinians was attacked. Twenty-seven died; nineteen were wounded.[83] Having massacred the city, Lebanese began to massacre each other. War had begun. The Holiday Inn would prove a bad investment.

17

The Dance of Death

O love of Beirut

. . . .

is it true you may forget me,
my defeated love?
I went back to my house,
my house I did not find.
Only smoke and twisted beams,
no rose and no fence.

Fairuz

Dehors ça tuait.

Michel Fani

IN APRIL 1975 Beirut switched identities. It became its opposite: a city
of death not profit. Zeal replaced deals – on the surface. As in a period
of revolution – Paris in 1830 or 1848, eastern Europe in 1989 – time
accelerated. Beirut in 1975 is a lesson in how quickly a city unravels.
Smyrna had been destroyed by governments and armies. Alexandria had
been diminished by Suez and socialism. In Beirut, the last great Levantine
port, the city was the prey of Beirutis themselves.

The soundtrack of the city changed. In parts of the city centre, voices
became sharper and quicker, like car doors being slammed or guns being
cocked. The bullet's whistle, the bark of the Kalashnikov, the drone of
the missile and the explosion of the hand grenade became familiar sounds,
as did the roar of private electricity generators when power cuts became
more frequent.[1] Many Beirutis' eardrums were permanently damaged.

The key to the civil war is that, even more than in 1958, Lebanon had
an army and no army. Its generals feared that, if the Lebanese army was
used against militias, it would disintegrate, as soldiers would refuse to fight
their co-religionists. No military genius was present to give the army a

sense of purpose and of separation from society – as in Austria, another state composed of rival groups, which the army ('You can do anything with bayonets except sit on them,' boasted the prime minister Prince Schwarzenberg) had saved from disintegration in 1848–9; or as Fouad Shihab had done, to a lesser degree, in Lebanon from 1958 to 1964.

In Istanbul in the 1970s, political conflict began to pit street against street, moustache against moustache: the Left wore thick moustaches; the nationalist Right thin ones; the religious Right Islamist beards. However, the Turkish army – 800,000 strong and absorbing 25 per cent of the national budget – was the strongest institution in the country; it had an officer corps ready to give orders to fire on civilians. By the military coup of 12 September 1980, it prevented an incipient civil war.[2] The Lebanese army, however, stayed prudently in its barracks, 'waiting for orders'. It was Maronite-dominated, although a Muslim section calling itself the Lebanese Arab Army broke away in January 1976.[3] The Phalange began to fight the PLO and its Sunni allies.

As Andrée Chedid recounts in *The Return to Beirut* (1985), at first people said, 'Nobody wants a catastrophe, we enjoy life … you have nothing to fear.' However:

> An evil circle gradually surrounded the city. The walls were covered in graffiti. There was talk of more murders, more kidnapping. Arms of all sizes began to appear. Weapons of war, tanks and jeeps with cannon rose from the bowels of the earth. A few shells were fired. Children went up to the top floors of the tall buildings to follow the tracer bullets and see the flashes of gunfire. It looked like a firework display; fear had not yet made its presence felt.

Kidnaps, murders, massacres that no one tried to stop and ceasefires that nobody intended to observe were part of daily life.[4] Radio stations warned listeners of snipers not traffic jams. Cars became potential deathtraps, ready to explode; buildings turned into military positions. No one knew where checkpoints, or barricades made of sandbags, cement and vehicles, would spring up next. The friend of the morning could be the executioner of the evening. The condolence visit became the principal form of social life. Even outside the parliament building, bodies were left in the street like empty beer cans. They became such a common sight that some people turned vegetarian. The 'Lebanese miracle' had become a nightmare.[5]

In the country once celebrated for tolerance, you could be dragged from your car, robbed, kidnapped or killed if you were of a religion different from that of the gunmen at the roadblock; some tried to erase the religious identity inscribed, by Lebanese law, on their identity cards. Confessionalism – the foundation of the country – was literally killing its people. At this stage the civil war was a religious war. By November 1976 40,000 had been killed and perhaps 400,000 or more Lebanese had fled to work in Europe, North America or the Gulf. The country which had once welcomed exiles now generated them. The famous nightclub Les Caves du Roy closed its doors and moved to Saint-Tropez.[6]

The Murr Tower and Holiday Inn skyscrapers of Beirut, with their commanding views, became militia redoubts, concrete versions of the crusader castles which seven hundred years earlier had dominated Beirut and the surrounding countryside.[7] The location of the main hotels along the corniche in west Beirut, intended to give tourists better views, ensured that they could be easily supplied from the sea by Christian militias, such as the 'Tigers', as the Chamoun family militia was called, or the Phalange led by the Gemayels.

In the 'war of the hotels' in the autumn of 1975 they were taken by Sunni Muslims led by Ibrahim Koleilat, the *qabaday* leader of the Sunni Murabitoun militia allied to the PLO. He told a press conference that 'the existing regime with its decayed institutions based on political confessionalism which has made Lebanon a country of privileges for the Maronite community is utterly unacceptable.' Kheffiyeh-wearing gunmen looking like hippies were photographed smoking joints at the Hôtel Saint-Georges bar. Photographs of Nasser (whose death in 1970 had inspired mass grief in Lebanon – woe to those who did not wear a black armband or tie a black ribbon to their car aerial) surveyed the rubble of the Phoenicia Hotel.

The Holiday Inn held out longest. Phalange gunmen threw bodies from the windows as they retreated from floor to floor. Its fall, on 21 March 1976, was commemorated in a Murabitoun poster showing a fighter demolishing the hotel with the butt of his gun above the inscription in Arabic 'On 21 March the Murabitoun destroyed the symbol of Fascist treason and took the oath to continue the journey whatever the cost – Ibrahim Koleilat.' The Beirut Hilton was gutted before it opened.[8]

The war was about loot as well as religion: it was not a war between haves and have-nots, but between rival gangs of want-mores. Beirut became a paradise for robbers. Some militias claimed to be 'the vanguard of the revolution', the 'tip of the spear of the Lebanese working class'. But they too, Rashid al-Daif points out in his Lebanese *Animal Farm, Dear Mr. Kawabata* (1995), murdered or burgled on the basis of greed or religion, not class or ideology.[9] There was no socialist agenda. Even though the economy, which had been growing at about 4 per cent a year, contracted by about 19 per cent in 1975 and 57 per cent in 1976,[10] Lebanon's economic *ancien régime* survived: many of the rich carried on their businesses from the safety of London, Paris or New York.

The souks in the centre of the city were blown up, partly to hide the looting which had emptied their shops. Electrical goods were especially popular. Looters worked methodically through the fighting. Police head-quarters were pillaged. Nor were banks safe. From the Capuchin church, thieves drilled their way into the headquarters of the British Bank of the Middle East and stole the contents of all the safes.[11] When the supermarket Spinneys was pillaged, looters were dismayed to find that, in their excite-ment, they had taken tins of catfood.[12] Sometimes eight-year-olds would ring doorbells with sacks of stolen objects for sale. It was possible to buy a Persian rug for the price of a loaf of bread.[13]

One hotel overlooking the corniche in west Beirut, the Carlton, had a more peaceful role than its rivals. The parliament had been looted, the Grand Saray burnt. Therefore the Carlton was the scene of the presidential election of 1976, when on 8 May the banker and moderate Elias Sarkis was chosen by deputies to replace Suleyman Frangieh: Lebanese depu-ties were guarded by soldiers of the PLO. Sarkis passed part of his presidency in the basement of the presidential palace at Baabda outside Beirut, without water or electricity, playing cards with his bodyguards while his country destroyed itself.[14]

Beirut became synonymous with chaos. Like Smyrna in 1922, and Alexandria under Nasser, it shows the vulnerability of wealth. However rich a city is, it needs an army to protect it. No army, no profits.

Meanwhile, on both sides, religious enclaves were being eliminated. In revenge for the murder of four Phalange gunmen, on 'Black Saturday', 6 December 1975, and again on 19 January 1976, Phalange gunmen killed hundreds of Muslims working in the port area in Qarantina, verifying their religion by checking their identity cards. On 20 January 1976 the Christian village of Damour in the south was overrun by the PLO; 500 Maronites were killed.

On 12 August 1976 Phalange and Tigers razed the Palestinian refugee camp at Tell al-Zaatar near Christian east Beirut, massacring perhaps as many as 3,000 Palestinians, including children. Champagne was drunk in celebration, not only at parties that night in east Beirut, but in Regine's and other clubs in Paris, which had become home to many Lebanese.[15] James Morris had admired Camille Chamoun for his 'smooth and know-ing cosmopolitanism'. He had looked elegant in white tie and tails next to his beautiful wife, welcoming heads of state to Lebanon; but he had as much blood on his hands as other leaders.[16]

Beirut became a divided city – no longer the Paris of the Middle East, but a new Nicosia or Belfast. Between the Muslim west and the Christian east was a twilight zone known as the green line, after the green line separating Greek and Turkish Cyprus since 1963, itself named after the armistice line between Israeli and Jordanian forces, drawn on the map of Palestine with a green wax pencil by Lieutenant-Colonel Moshe Dayan in 1948.[17]

The green line, five and a half miles long and between twenty and a hundred yards wide, stretched from the port to the Place des Martyrs – now, more than ever, living up to its name – down the Damascus road to the airport. There were three crossing points: at the port, the National Museum and the airport. Soon it was literally a green line. As in the Yucatán after the collapse of Maya civilization, nature began to reclaim the city. The green line and its adjoining houses were filled by a green stream of grass, weeds, bushes and creepers. Once the country's transport hub, the Places des Martyrs became a waste of weeds and ruins.

The green line attracted animals as well as plants. During ceasefires, dogs and rats came out to scavenge. It is said that they devoured those corpses which no one had had the time or courage to bury, and at times they attacked women and children. As weeds and grasses grew thicker, flocks of sheep replaced cars and buses on the Place des Martyrs; cows appeared on the Rue Clemenceau. A horse escaped from the racing stables was photo-graphed wandering through a deserted airport waiting lounge. Never had so many birds of so many species been seen in the city. Lebanese no longer had time to shoot birds, since they were shooting each other.[18]

The green line was a snipers' paradise. Like tree trunks devoured by ants, buildings were eaten away by bullet holes; snipers blasted holes through the walls of adjoining properties so they could walk from house to house for miles without appearing in the street.[19]

Beirut produced a synergy between sniping and architecture. Fortified sniper positions were created in buildings, often with special 'view-sheds' added to give snipers a better sight of their prey. They were decorated with the heraldry of violence: stencilled emblems of different militias – the cedar or cross of the Phalange; the Arabic monograms of the PLO or the Shia militia Amal, founded in 1976.[20]

With its curving windows and graceful colonnade, the Barakat house was so well designed that it became a fortress for Phalange snipers. They reinforced doors and walls with concrete supports. Their sandbags and mattresses, plates and rubbish still lay discarded behind favoured shooting points in the pockmarked facade when I visited it in 2002, twelve years after the guns had fallen silent. Crosses were still painted on the walls.[21]

In Beirut the cross – a symbol of war, not love – appeared on walls, on uniforms, round necks and wrists, tattooed on Christian flesh, and in some cases cut into Muslim. In the Christian areas of Jemayze and Ashrafiyeh in east Beirut, crosses of all shapes and colours are still visible: white on black on white; green on brown; red on white. Some are profession-ally stencilled; others are barely visible. Most crosses are symbols of the Lebanese Forces (as different Christian militias were called after their amalgamation by Bashir Gemayel in 1980) and the Maronites.[22]

Crosses were not the only wall decoration. Throughout the city, post-ers and slogans appeared praising war and 'martryrdom', often below the image of a 'martyr'. Many commemorated particular heroes – Nasser, Kemal Jumblatt, Bashir Gemayel or Ayatollah Khomeini – or events like the Palestinian catastrophe of 1948. Some slogans could have been used by any group: 'Oh mother of the martyrs, sing the song of joy! All of us here are your children'; 'We will cross a sea of blood to reach God's blessed victory'; 'Immortal in the consciousness of people and the nation'; 'Together until victory'; 'Our Lebanon needs you.'[23]

Photographs show the fighters generally to have been young men (and at the beginning women) between seventeen and twenty-seven, like 'area boys' anywhere in the world, standing at street corners to show their power, holding their beloved 'klashens'. Sometimes they were wreathed in smiles from the joints of hashish they were smoking.[24]

Militia offices sprang up on the ground floors of blocks of flats. They were lined with photos of dead 'martyrs', and filled with young men going in and out. Guns were worn not only on the street, but during prayers (Christian or Muslim), while fishing, in bars; they could be checked into cloakrooms like umbrellas.[25]

Beirut shows how easily humans become monsters, and how quickly the social and economic ties holding a city together can disintegrate. In her story 'The Tranformation of Said', Mai Ghoussoub, who left Beirut to found Al Saqi, the best Arab bookshop in London, describes how a young man begins to rejoice in the fear that his Kalashnikov puts into the eyes of passers-by; people step aside for him in shops and begin to ask him favours; cigarettes suddenly become plentiful. He learns to leap in and out of cars 'in a manly fashion'. His face becomes bright and hopeful.[26]

Throughout the civil war Beirut remained, heroically, a city of books, newspapers, publishers and printing workers, analysing, describing and memorializing the war. Thanks to its writers, we know what Beirut killers thought, or said they thought, at the time. Their comments reveal not only some of the city's particular character, but a general desire for war similar to that felt in Europe in 1914. 'War is my only friend. It's like my wife. I love it; in peace I feel afraid.' 'I think I liquidated in one day all my problems of identity. At the very moment I got behind the barricade ... I became perfectly integrated.'[27]

In 1979 Maroun Baghdadi and Nayla de Freige published in *Al-Nahar* interviews they had conducted with what they called 'the Kalashnikov generation', a sample of 900 university students aged between sixteen and twenty-two fighting in the civil war. Seventy-six per cent of men and 21 per cent of women had had sexual intercourse; there was no difference in ratios between Muslims and Christians. Thirty-two per cent had carried arms: 43 per cent of the men, 13 per cent of the women. They were highly politicized, disproving the cliché that Lebanese think only of profit and pleasure. Their desire was to 'become more and more involved with reality'. They did not fight because of family pressures, but for themselves and 'this melange of cultures, this sweet life, the Mediterranean, the blue sea'. Here are some quotations from men:

> I learned everything all of a sudden. Before we did not understand anything about it, there were too many combinations, the war clarified everything.
>
> It was behind my doushka that I found my independence.
>
> I found my father pitiful, really pitiful. And me I was so powerful, yes powerful. Do you understand this sensation of force, of sudden power, to have in your own hand your own life, your own death?

After massacres at Tell al-Zaatar and Damour, with memories of blood and mud, some felt, or denied, guilt. Samir and Jihad recalled: 'when you fire a rocket and you hear the cries of children afterward. I'm sure it was in my head, an illusion. Yes an illusion ... I could not get by without the strength of pills.' 'Today when I think about it, it's a nightmare.'

Lebanese women had won the right to fight since their enforced abstention from the civil war in 1860. Joumana said, 'Finally I went into the streets carrying weapons and I fought. I'm not ashamed to admit that my femininity blossomed during the war ... I was only concerned with having the same rights as any man ... My charm, my only attraction was in my Kalashnikov, the rest was secondary.'

For some the war was a party: 'We were suddenly the masters of a city that had frequently scorned us ... we were everywhere, we were the kings.

I suddenly felt that everything could belong to me, we went into marvellous houses, places like you see in the cinema. Beirut was at our feet.'

Here are a few of the answers given when they were asked why they fought:

FARID: 'We want to live with respect.'
JIHAD: 'For the disinherited, it is our war, the war of the poor.'
SAMIR: 'For the country and my family and for Lebanese sovereignty.'
MARCEL: 'For the country against feudalism, corruption and foreigners.'
MARWAN: 'For democracy, for the unity of Lebanon.'
NAGI: 'For secularism, unity and democracy.'
JAMAL: 'For the Arabism of Lebanon and its unity.'
NAYLA: 'For socialism and women.'
FADIA: 'For honour.'
KHALIL: 'For me.'[28]

The interviewed were all university students. They did not include mercenaries or poorer combatants. Some observers think that, for them, 60 per cent of sniping was done for pleasure. It was a game like marbles or tric-trac.[29] The historian of photography in Lebanon Michel Fani heard a friend boasting about putting a loaded hand grenade in a prisoner's mouth: in the end the victim's mouth muscles forced him to let it drop, thereby killing himself. Many snipers were paid by the number of people they killed; since they were 'honourable men', they claimed never to lie about the head count. Most casualties were civilians rather than fighters. The streets of Beirut today are full of killers. Some became nightclub bouncers, others ministers. There have been cases of, for example, a man meeting, as the electrician come to work in his flat, the person who had tortured or kidnapped him several years earlier. Both freeze. Nothing is said.[30]

Each period invents a new horror. Ottoman governors had expressed their zeal by the number of salted heads they sent the sultan. In the Balkans, 'nose-taking' had been common; in the Lebanese civil war, ears were a speciality – gunmen were said to make garlands of them.[31] One reason why snipers took drugs was not only to alleviate boredom, but to try to drown the memories which could torment even the most hardened killers.[32]

By the end of 1976 Palestinians and their allies controlled 80 per cent of the country. The Maronite enclave north of Beirut – roughly the area of pre-1918 Mount Lebanon – with 1 million almost entirely Christian people, may have been small, but it was efficient. Through the port of Jounieh, Israeli boats brought modern weapons for the Phalange. The Maronite Church and the Phalange looked after Christian refugees from the rest of Lebanon: during the civil war, most Christians left Sidon and Tripoli. Soon 'Marounistan' contained most of the Lebanese army, ministries and industry. The great experiment of coexistence had collapsed.[33]

East and west Beirut resembled different countries. In the former were bursting supermarkets, bustling marinas, cinemas smelling of perfume not garbage. In the latter, people queued in potholed streets for bread and water. Sometimes they not only washed in the street but, as photographs show, drank water lying in it. Refuse piled up on the streets of 'the Paris of the Middle East', attracting cats and rats. There were thirty different militias under the National Front in West Beirut, many of them – including the PLO – linked to organized crime, like the IRA and the INLA in Belfast. Streets and pavements were crowded with carts and trestle tables, selling goods looted from shops and the warehouses of the port. Curfew started at 8 p.m.

The arms and drugs trades, reconstruction (refitting new window panes was best done by the gangs which had shattered them) and remittances from Lebanese abroad at first helped keep the economy buoyant. Special quays for smugglers sprang up along the coast. Arms dealers' ships hovered offshore, waiting for the right moment to land their weapons. Whisky became cheaper than anywhere else in the world. The Levant, wrote Jonathan Randal, the *New York Times* correspondent, expired in Lebanon in 1975, referring to the old synthesis of deals between notables and religious groups; but economically the Levant was thriving.[34]

Evenings in west Beirut were spent listening to the radio news, knitting, playing cards, or watching from balconies as flares and rockets lit the night sky. Hosts laid out extra binoculars and telescopes if guests were expected for dinner. After one dinner, having quarrelled with her Christian best friend, Lina Tabbara, a Muslim working for the Ministry of Foreign Affairs, remembered thinking, 'I feel the seeds of hatred and the desire for revenge taking roots in my very depths ... An end has got to be put to this cowardly indifference.' She wanted Muslims to give back 'at least twice as good as we got'. Korans and crosses in shops sold out.[35] Edward Said noticed, 'Children speak interchangeably of computer games, football scores and massacres and their easy way of pointing out differences between grads, rpgs and katyushas is chilling.[36]

The Lebanese civil war had so many facets that it could be explained however you wished: it could be seen as essentially religious, political, military or international. It also had a dynastic aspect. The Middle East in the late twentieth century saw a resurgence of political dynasties, masking their power behind republican slogans and constitutions. Egypt is controlled by the Mubaraks, Yemen by Ali Abdullah Salah and his family. The Assads, from the Alawi minority, have been in power in Syria since 1970. Fearing Syria's simmering Sunni majority, they had close links with Lebanon's Shia (Imam Musa Sadr issued a convenient fatwa stating that Alawis were Muslims) and, due to a family friendship, the Maronite Frangieh dynasty.[37]

Dynasties were kept alive from below as well as above. Dynasties in Lebanon could act as social-security and employment agencies. Like consuls in the past, notables or *zaims* from prominent families could bypass the inefficient state system. With one phone call, a *zaim* could arrange a phone line or a visa. Some considered notables more effective, and more durable, than revolutionaries.[38]

By personal inclination Kemal Jumblatt, founder of the Progressive Socialist Party, was a socialist, interested in Gandhi. He won the Lenin Peace Prize, and gave away much of his land. Nevertheless, he was also a hereditary leader of the Druze community, as his ancestors had been since the seventeenth century. To try to solve their problems, he received his followers on Tuesday and Thursday in his Beirut mansion, and on Saturday and Sunday in his castle in Moukhtara in the Chouf valley.[39]

Hitherto, like the Salams in 1958, *zaims* had acted as a restraining force. Michel Chiha had felt that Lebanon's crises could always in the end be fixed between notables. After 1975, however, zeal replaced deals. Perhaps due to pressure from below, new notables were more ruthless than old, and less willing to share political office and commercial opportunities with their rivals. In the struggle for domination of the Maronites, the Gemayels' followers murdered rival Maronites, sparing neither women nor children: some of the Frangieh family in 1978, the bodyguards of Camille Chamoun in 1980, Dany Chamoun, his wife and two young sons on 21 October 1989. Dany Chamoun reflects the 'Beirut switch', from pleasure to murder (and in some cases back again). Before he had started leading the Tigers militia, and participating in massacres, he had appeared to be a 'sweet person', the 'last person in the world you would have thought could become a fighter' according to one friend.[40] In the case of the Shia, however, old feudal families like the Osseiran and al-Asaad were replaced not by new dynasties but by new parties: the 'left-wing' Amal, founded in 1976, and its more religious rival Hezbollah, dating from 1982.[41]

Whatever their religion, the notables shared one habit. With the exception of the PLO and Hezbollah, no matter how bloodstained their policies, Lebanese leaders wore well-cut, well-ironed suits: dark in winter, shining white in summer. Violence did not kill vanity.

★

1982 was a year of especial horror. Since the 1940s the Phalange had been intermittently allied to Israel, since both disliked Muslim Arabs. During crises, Phalange soldiers had often protected the Jewish quarter of Beirut. Nevertheless, wiser voices in the Israeli Foreign Ministry warned what later governments forgot: that the Maronites did not really control Lebanon; moreover, they were disunited.[42]

From 1980 the baby-faced warlord Bashir Gemayel and his 'young wolves' – some of whom called themselves, after the American film, 'the Dirty Dozen' – determined to take power in Lebanon and expel the PLO and ultimately all Palestinians. Gemayel had united all Christian militias in the 20,000 strong Lebanese Forces, which still exist today, with an office near the Place des Martyrs. He believed, 'Our only problem is the Syrian and Palestinian presence.' Regular meetings took place in Lebanon and Israel between him and the Israeli defence minister Ariel Sharon. Israel offered training and weapons, and shared the same goals. On many occasions it showed its hostility to the cosmopolitan Levantine city whose ethos was so different from its own. On 17 July 1981 it attacked west Beirut in an aerial apocalypse.[43]

Uncontested mistress of the skies, Israel began more air raids in June 1982, its planes making silver streaks in the sky as they dive-bombed the city. Seventy-six thousand Israeli soldiers invaded Lebanon, reaching Beirut in August 1982. The Israeli government told civilians to leave the city – 'We do not want to hurt you' – although the population had already been swelled by refugees from the Israeli invasion of southern Lebanon. Merciless bombardments from air and sea hit apartment buildings, newspaper and ministerial offices (including the Prime Minister's), embassies, hospitals and the main Beirut synagogue, while it was full of sleeping refugees.[44] The American ambassador called it 'a blitz against west Beirut'.[45]

During breaks in bombardments there were stampedes of cars and people, through the green line at the museum crossing, to reach the haven of Christian east Beirut which, since it was allied to Israel, was safe. There even a militant Marxist like Hazim Saghie was impressed by the peace and 'long periods without gun battles'.[46] To Jean Said Makdisi, sister of Edward Said and wife of Professor Usama Makdisi of AUB, the battle sounded like devils beating drums under the earth. The bombings revealed, in her opinion, 'a lunatic destructive urge to kill, to root out every living thing, to leave nothing standing, to eradicate the city'. Against her will, she too moved to east Beirut. By August 35,000 Israeli troops were outside Beirut.[47]

Finally the PLO agreed to leave Beirut, the city which it had helped to ruin. On 12 August, as Israeli bombings continued, the Prime Minister exploded, 'Agreement has been hard to come by but we have achieved it. What do they want? There is only one thing left and that is for them to kill us all. Let them kill us all ... Enough, enough.'[48] Photographs confirm the extent of the death and destruction. Michael Johnson estimates that in all, excluding Palestinians, 15,000 Lebanese were killed, 40,000 wounded and 300,000 made homeless that summer.[49]

By international agreement, American, French and Italian troops landed to keep order during the PLO withdrawal. Arafat had been living in a series of interchangeable dark-green Range Rovers, driving around the city so as not to be in one place for long and present a target to Israeli agents. When he left with the honours of a head of state on 30 August, accompanied to the port by the Prime Minister, defying reality by flashing the V for Victory sign, he paid Beirut a compliment many Beirutis would have preferred to forgo: 'I am leaving this city but my heart will always be in Beirut.' Since all sides were in agreement, for once the Lebanese army acted effectively, taking over west Beirut to the relief of the inhabitants. The Prime Minister declared on 1 September, 'As of today there is no more east and west Beirut.'[50]

As Palestinian and Syrian troops withdrew, deputies were helicoptered into the city to provide a quorum to elect a new president. Bashir Gemayel was careful to follow constitutional forms, rather than launch a military coup. Deputies met in the Villa Mansour at the museum crossing, so that they could come from both sides of the city. Some ruffled their hair, or had themselves photographed besides armed guards of the Lebanese Forces, to prove that they had been 'forced' to vote. On 2 September Bashir Gemayel was elected president: the Christian east, which idolized him, exploded with joy. Kalashnikovs were fired; church bells pealed.[51] Foreign troops left ahead of schedule – whether intentionally or not – leaving the city in the power of Israel and the Lebanese Forces.

One rule of Lebanese politics, however, is that whoever emerges strongest unites other factions against him. On 14 September, as on every Tuesday afternoon, Bashir Gemayel went to his Ashrafiyeh office to speak to his followers. He and his entourage were blown up by a landmine – almost certainly organized by Syrian agents posing as members of the Parti Populaire Syrien. The perpetrators were later released from Lebanese jails by Syrian pressure. Bashir inspired such adoration that experienced journalists, as well as loyal Maronites, swore that they had seen him emerge from the rubble alive.[52]

Next morning, using his murder as a pretext, massacres started in the camps of Palestinians on the southern edge of the city at Sabra and Chatila.

They were organized by the Israeli army – which guarded the camps' perimeters and had a headquarters overlooking them on top of a six-storey Lebanese army building – and by the Lebanese Forces. The Israeli army, in particular the Minister of Defence, Ariel Sharon, knew the camps well from aerial reconnaissance, agents on the ground, and the evidence of their own binoculars. The chief perpetrators, in successive waves, were Israeli special forces, specially flown-in Shia soldiers of the Israeli-funded South Lebanese Army, and the 'apaches' of the Lebanese Forces under Elie Hobeika. It was a carefully planned operation. Killing continued through the night of 15/16 September, with the help of Israeli flares. No mercy was shown: after the first question about what to do with women and children, Hobeika said that he never wanted to hear that question again.[53]

The guarantee of the safety of civilians in the Palestinian camps given by the US and Israeli governments was an illusion. Many victims were found clutching their identity cards, as if trying to prove their legitimacy. By some corpses beer cans and syringes were found, showing that soldiers had needed stimulants to help them kill. The 'terrorist' targets were in reality any Palestinians. There was a total of 1,326 victims.[54]

On the afternoon of 15 September, while the massacres were taking place, in another world – the Christian village of Bekfaya, residence of the Maronite Patriarch – Bashir Gemayel was buried with the pomp of the Lebanese state and the Maronite Church: processions of chanting girls; sermons; military bands; a fly-past by two Israeli planes. A Maronite monk compared him to Jesus Christ.[55]

The Lebanese game continued. When a survivor of the massacres told the Sunni politician Saeb Salam that she knew Phalange fighters had been involved from the markings on their uniforms, he replied, with a notable's contempt for the poor, 'Since when do you know how to read?'[56]

In 'The Diary of Beirut under Siege', the poet Adonis wrote:

> The cities break up,
> The land is a train of dust.
>
> . . . . . .
>
> They found people in sacks:
> One without a head,
> One without a tongue or hands.
> One strangled.
> The rest without shape or names.
> Have you gone mad?
> Please do not write about these things.[57]

In a classic example of dynasticism, Bashir's brother Amin Gemayel was voted next president of Lebanon. He began to install extreme Maronites in key positions. Israel withdrew its troops to the south without its longed-for peace treaty, concluding from this 'Beirut summer', as one general said, that Lebanese were vermin, snakes and scorpions.[58]

The invasion had one unexpected long-term consequence. Like many Arabs, the bin Laden family had often visited Beirut on holiday. Television ensured that they saw the Israeli bombardments of the city. They blamed Israel's ally, fund-raiser and weapons-supplier, the United States. August 1982 contributed to September 2001. Osama bin Laden later claimed, 'As I looked at those demolished towers in Lebanon, it entered my mind that we should punish the oppressors in kind and that we should destroy towers in America so that they taste some of what we tasted and so that they be deterred from killing our women and children.'[59]

The principal beneficiaries of the Israeli invasion were Syria and the Shia, now one-third of the population of Beirut. The Shia of Lebanon had long had close links with Iran, which in the sixteenth century they had helped transform from a Sunni into a Shia country. After 1979, Lebanese Shia were armed and funded by the new revolutionary government of Iran. Amin Gemayel went to visit President Assad in Damascus in February 1984. Reflecting the Assads' fears of Syria's Sunni majority, which they had recently suppressed in assaults on Aleppo and Hama, the Syrian government preferred the Shia, the Druze and even the Lebanese Forces to Lebanese Sunni.[60]

In 1984 Amal took over west Beirut. Like the Phalange in east Beirut, it was not just a military machine, but also a social-welfare organization, help-ing, more effectively than the Lebanese state, to provide poorer followers with food, housing, electricity and water: for some it replaced the family as their main means of support.[61] The Shia, some of whom were even poorer than Palestinians, soon showed that Israel and the Phalange had no monopoly of brutality. In what was called 'the war of the camps', Amal forces shelled their Palestinian neighbours unremittingly. In the words of their leader Nabih Berri, today speaker of the Lebanese parliament, their motive was 'to avenge ancient battles', probably referring to the murders of the prophet Muhammad's grandsons Hussein and Hassan in AD 680, which began the Sunni–Shia schism.[62] Under fire, refugees queued in sewage for their rations. In all about 2,100 died. By 1988 not one building was left standing in Chatila. The 1969 Cairo Accords, legalizing the PLO's armed presence in Lebanon, were formally abrogated in 1987. Although about 300,000 Palestinians continue to live in camps there, many fled to Europe: Arab countries would no longer receive them.[63]

The Syrian government and Hezbollah, adopting the *nom de guerre* Islamic Jihad, used murder and kidnapping as political instruments. Syria's aim was, and is, 'privileged relations' and 'co-ordination' with Lebanon in every sphere – including 'joint ministerial committees': in other words, hegemony.[64] The Iraqi embassy was attacked in 1981, the French in 1982, the US embassy in 1983, US marines' headquarters and a French barracks in 1983: at the last two, 241 and 58 respectively were killed, and the two countries soon withdrew their remaining troops. One CIA officer claims that his agency never recovered from the loss of so many agents in Beirut.[65]

No one was safe. The US ambassador was assassinated in 1976, Kemal Jumblatt in 1977, the French ambassador in 1981, the President of the AUB in 1984, the Prime Minister in 1987, the Mufti of Beirut by a car bomb (22 dead, 150 wounded) in 1989, and in another car bomb the same year, as he was driving down Hamra, the President of Lebanon himself, René Mouawad. The last two had offended the Syrian government since they wanted to negotiate with its enemies, General Aoun and Walid Jumblatt, who had succeeded his father, Kemal, as Druze leader. When the Mufti was killed, the Maronite Patriarch received condolence visits, and ordered church bells rung, as for a Christian dignitary.[66]

Finally, after 1988 the army began to intervene in politics under the man whom his followers considered the de Gaulle of Lebanon, General Michel Aoun: he believed that 'only the army can release our captive country from the prison of foreign interests.' More fighting led to more incomprehensible realignments. Syria besieged Christian east Beirut, which in 1976 it had intervened to protect. In a final paroxysm, in 1988–90 the state split in two, under two prime ministers: Michel Aoun in east Beirut, Selim al-Hoss in west. As if battles between communities were not enough, battles within them broke out: Maronites fought Maronites, Shia Shia (Amal vs Hezbollah, with Syria supporting the former), Palestinians Palestinians. There were five separate military zones: Israeli in the south, Druze, Syrian, Maronite and Aounist.[67]

Both Syrian forces and General Aoun's bombed different sections of the city. Streets were covered in garbage, broken glass and abandoned cars; sagging buildings, draped in broken signs and dangling wires, and covered in bullet holes, appeared to have performed a dance of death.[68] The Commodore Hotel, haunt of foreign journalists covering the war, with a parrot at the bar which imitated the sound of falling missiles, was looted and closed in 1987.[69]

Smyrna had been one of the first cities in the twentieth century to experience partial city death. Beirut was one of the first to experience city chaos, like parts of Lagos and Mexico City today. Beirut seemed an experiment in how long a city can function without effective government or municipality. The word *libanisation* entered the *Grand Dictionnaire Larousse*, to describe 'the process of fragmentation of a country resulting from confrontation between different communities'.[70]

By 1990, even more Lebanese had fled – a third of the population, perhaps more. They kept houses in Lebanon but worked abroad, forming, as a result of civil war, the first global generation, living between several countries at once. So much has been written about the Westernization of the Middle East that the Levantinization of Europe has been overlooked. Confirming the persistence of the soft power of Paris and London long after the departure of French and British troops from the Middle East, in these years the two capitals, which had already welcomed thousands of émigrés from Egypt, attracted Lebanese writers like Hanan al-Shaykh and Amin Maalouf; bankers, architects, fast food proprietors and chemists – hence the Bliss pharmacies (named after a street named after the American missionary who helped found AUB) – and the Maaroush restaurants spreading in London today.

Raymond Edde, son of Emile Edde, was a long-serving deputy and leader of the National Front. Known as 'the conscience of Lebanon', he had been the one politician who had opposed the Cairo Accords of 1969. The only major Christian politician to live in west Beirut, he made his flat there a news centre to try to locate the kidnapped, offering coffee to streams of visitors, including 'armed elements' and Arafat himself. (Even he lost his temper, however, when he was brought the decomposing body of an old woman, which no one knew what to do with. The more he shouted, the more his assistant Lina Tabbara laughed.) In 1976, after the third attempt on his life, he moved to Paris. He never came back. He died in the Hôtel Prince de Galles in 2000 – unconvinced that, under Syrian occupation, Lebanon had recovered its sovereignty.[71]

However, despite the chaos, killing and emigration, Beirut survived. The heroes of the war were the civilian drivers, nurses, doctors, workers who carried on their jobs at the risk of their lives, sometimes crossing the green line to get to the office. For example, in the Swissair office in west Beirut alone, three employees made the journey across the green line every day in order to get to work.[72] When there was no fighting, people could be seen going to offices, restaurants and the cinema. The state structure and national frontiers survived.

For the novelist Rabih Alamedine, even in war 'Beirut is probably the greatest city in the world.' There more than anywhere in the Arab world you could smell 'the fragrance of freedom'. Syrians idolized Beirut for that reason. Braving the civil war, some came simply to enjoy the legendary Beirut corniche, among women in chadors or miniskirts, workers and joggers – to breathe an atmosphere less stifling than their own country, or to shop for goods unavailable there.[73]

As in London during the Blitz, danger increased the appetite for pleasure. Like French nobles remembering the *douceur de vivre* of the *ancien régime*, some Beirut homosexuals speak of the war as a golden age: militia men arrived in their flats hot from battle. Women too found love 'under fire' exciting. 'To get rid of the last remnant of their mother's moral teaching', according to the novelist Hoda Barakat, some women went to newspaper offices at night, to meet young journalists when they were at their most emotional.[74]

Beirutis became used to living on the edge. Even after the explosion of a nearby car bomb, amid sirens and screams, the Summerland Hotel held a fashion parade of wedding dresses. Sunbathers would say 'that was close', readjust their sunglasses, and continue sunning themselves.[75] Even during fighting, some would hire ambulances – the best form of transport in civil-war Beirut – to get to a party. Many of the old refused to leave, such as Marguerite Chiha and Yvonne Cochrane. The latter said later, 'You cannot abandon your country when it's on its knees. I could not leave the servants.' The Palais Sursock survived the war almost unscathed.[76]

Ugliest and most hospitable of men, Henri Pharaon continued to try to mediate between Muslims and Christians, to inspect his horses at the race-course – during ceasefires there were races – and to give surrealist dinner parties, despite the shooting outside: foie gras, truffles, a tour of the collection before dessert. After the collapse of the Lebanese pound in 1983–4, when Beirut became 'dollarized', he was ruined. Dealers began to buy back from him, cheap, the treasures which they had sold to him expensively before the war. Two Muslim militiamen who had taken refuge in his house were killed by Christian gunmen in front of him, as they were drinking his coffee: Camille Chamoun, to whom he had telephoned, had personally guaranteed their safety.

In the end he was persuaded to hand over his house to his son, who still runs the family bank. The son sold it to the jeweller Robert Mouawad and, to the horror of Henri Pharaon's friends, moved his father, by then almost blind, into the Carlton Hotel. One reason for their bad relations was the son's disgust with his father's preference for men – a preference, known to contemporaries in Beirut, which would have ruined his political career in Europe or other Arab countries. There was a scene about money, or jealousy, with one of them. At the age of ninety-two, one of the fathers of Lebanese independence was murdered in his hotel bedroom by a former lover. The circumstances were not mentioned when his death was announced on Lebanese radio.[77]

In 1977 and 1983–4, when there were lulls in the fighting, the city had begun to recover. In 1983 Amin Gemayel drove his car from east to west, proclaiming, with more optimism than realism, 'There is no more west or east Beirut.'[78] In 1984, writes the CIA agent Robert Baer, 'hardly a building was not being painted, patched up or torn down to put up another one'. The city had become 'one vast construction site'. The airport reopened.[79] Indeed, the war was accompanied by a building boom on the Beirut outskirts, caused by refugees fleeing Israeli occupation in the south, or the fighting in the city centre. Orchards were replaced by blocks of flats, often equipped with special war-time amenities: generators, wells, underground shelters. The urban geographer Michael Davie writes that nearly all the agricultural land between the city and the airport 'disappeared in a matter of months'.[80]

Finally in 1989, as in 1860, the great powers intervened. After being shelled in the presidential palace by Syrian planes, Aoun was evacuated to Paris via the French embassy. The US, Saudi Arabia and Syria – all bitten by the 'scorpions' in Beirut – agreed on the need for a settlement. A meeting of deputies was held at Taif in Saudi Arabia – they did not feel safe in Beirut. As Syria had originally proposed in 1975, a new rule imposed parity between Christian and Muslim deputies rather than the earlier 6:5 ratio – a major concession for Maronites, although the proportion of all Christians in the national population had long been nearer 30 than 50 per cent. A new president was elected. The Shia speaker of parliament was given more power.

The continued presence of the Syrian army was felt to be a guarantee of law and order – although the choice of the cruellest of Christian warlords, Elie Hobeika, by then a deputy for Beirut, as minister of state for displaced persons showed a warped sense of humour: he had 'displaced' many persons himself. He was blown up with his bodyguards by a car bomb in Beirut in 2002, just before he was due to attend a trial in Brussels concerning Ariel Sharon's responsibility for the massacres of 1982.[81] A new obsession with Lebanon's Arab identity, to the exclusion of others, was shown by the phrase in the Taif Accord that 'Lebanon is Arabic in belonging and identity, tied to all the Arab countries by true fraternal relations' – as if it were closer to Yemen than to France, now a second home for hundreds of thousands of Lebanese.[82] Neo-Phoenicianism appeared to be dead.

Lebanon resumed the reconstruction process which it had tried to start in 1976 and 1982. Like other countries after similar horrors, it wanted to forget – a law of amnesty was passed in 26 August 1991. Looking like sullen schoolboys caught misbehaving, the militiamen were lined up, with their bags, made to hand in their weapons, and given jobs in the army, security or the police. Their party was over.[83]

18

New Levants for Old

I want to reassure the Christians that we are one. Parity will stay for ever.

Saad Hariri, prime minister of Lebanon, 21 February 2010

A s in 1975, Lebanon did another switch – this time from the dance of death to the pursuit of profit. Despite the horrors of the war, no other city – neither Athens nor Amman nor Dubai – had replaced Beirut as the regional capital. Its combination of brains, pleasure and freedom was unrivalled. A Levantine synthesis was reborn. In 1992 there was a grand reopening of the Beirut racecourse: leaders of different factions, who had been fighting each other for fifteen years, embraced as if there had been no war.[1] In 1996, after thirteen years, the bourse reopened.

The Haussmann of Beirut was called Rafic Hariri. He was a natural Levantine, at ease in different worlds; his website refers to Lebanon's Phoenician past.[2] Born in Sidon in 1944, he studied at the Beirut Arab University, then moved to the Lebanese eldorado, Saudi Arabia. There his construction business made him, by 1982, one of the richest men in the world, a friend both of the Saudi royal family and, through shared business interests, of Jacques Chirac, with houses in Paris and dual Lebanese and Saudi citizenship. Chirac and Hariri frequently visited each other. In one sign of the Levantinization of Paris, Hariri is said to have helped finance Chirac's campaign to become president of France in 1995. He also became the conduit for Saudi money in Lebanese politics, including at one time $500,000 a month to stop Lebanese soldiers deserting to militias.[3] For most of 1992–2004 he was prime minister. Attempting to make Beirut compete with Dubai and Hong Kong, he showed that it possessed one criterion of a great city: the ability to reinvent itself.

From 1994 with his company Solidere he started a huge programme of demolition and rebuilding in 450 acres in the city centre and on land reclaimed from the sea. For many years the city centre was dominated by the sight of builders' cranes and the sound of the demolition drill – louder even than the muezzin's call or church bells, both of which had become more strident since the civil war.[4] Although streets around the parliament kept their original facades, Robert Fisk, a journalist who had remained in the city throughout the civil war, author of the classic history *Pity the Nation* (2001), was appalled by the 'orgy of destruction' of old buildings which he saw and heard: 'The buildings slithered into themselves.'[5] Archaeologists were in despair at the lost opportunities for excavation.

Tower blocks fifty storeys high – even taller than those which had horrified visitors in the 1960s – were built. In parts they obstruct the legendary view of the snows of Mount Lebanon from the corniche. However, Solidere gave many Lebanese and tourists what they wanted: marinas, modern shops and cafés in pedestrian areas, a 'Levantine Saint-Tropez'. Without one master plan, the area might have remained in ruins for decades. The 'before' and 'after' photographs of Foch and Allenby streets are a convincing argument. If Solidere did not exist, some Beirutis say, nothing might have happened. However artificial, the city centre has become, after the corniche, one of the main meeting places of the city, a focus for that conviviality which some Lebanese consider their main characteristic.[6]

On the other hand, redevelopment was carried out, as many Beirutis complain, by the rich for the rich. Some call it 'an urban catastrophe', 'the urban form of neo-liberalism'. Under Hariri, Lebanon incurred a massive government debt. Many of the new tower blocks (Platinum Tower, Beirut Tower, Marina Tower and the Four Seasons) are unlit at night – their duplexes and penthouses used only a few weeks a year.[7] Many poor owners or tenants who did not buy shares in Solidere at the agreed price lost money, were threatened, or moved to the fringes of the city. Because its owners opposed the plan, the Hôtel Saint-Georges was never rebuilt. The Lebanese state, as usual, was the biggest loser, selling at low prices land which is now worth far more.[8]

Hariri also built, on the west of the Place des Martyrs, the neo-Mameluke and neo-Ottoman blue-domed Muhammad al-Amine Mosque, in part financed by Walid bin Talal, a Saudi prince with Lebanese ambitions, since through his mother he was a grandson of Riad al-Solh. On the site of a former Muslim prayer hall, it is a grandiose assertion of Muslim power and piety in the main public space of the city, dwarfing the nearby Maronite, Catholic, Orthodox and Armenian cathedrals. It is the largest mosque in Beirut, and has four minarets – an honour once reserved in

Constantinople for the sultan alone: Hariri had to be persuaded not to add a fifth.[9]

It is not only the city which has been reconstructed. A visitor can see, from the number of bulbous lips and bandaged noses, that Beirut has become one of the plastic-surgery capitals of the world. In a particularly visible sign of flexible identity, there are said to be one and a half million operations a year in what in Beirut is called 'aesthétique'. 'I try my best,' says one resculpted woman.[10]

The revival of the city centre was accompanied, after 1997, by a night-club boom on the other side of the Place des Martyrs, off the former green line, in what have become the legendary Rue Monot (named after the Jesuit who founded the Université Saint-Joseph) and Rue Gouraud, with around 100 bars and nightclubs. Pacifico, with Cuban music, is the oldest. BO18 (on the site of the Qarantina massacre of Palestinians), designed as a bunker sunk in the ground, with a retractable roof, is intended by its architect, Bernard Khoury, to resemble a mass grave. With seats shaped like coffins, it is a protest against 'naive amnesia'. Tables used to be shrines to the murdered; their photos were hidden among the bottles.[11]

For some visitors these bars, far more than the city's businesses or universities, are Beirut. A grandson of Yvonne Sursock, Paddy Cochrane, co-owner of The Alleyway and Gauche Caviare, calls them 'the main lifeblood of Beirut'. Some visitors book tickets in New York before their plane lands in Beirut; others travel from Amman or Damascus to spend one night at Acid, the first openly gay nightclub in the Middle East. At summer weekends perhaps 20,000 young people go clubbing.[12]

At the beginning, some were trying to dance the past away. In her memoir *Beirut I Love You* (2009), Zeena el-Khalil wrote, 'People were so humiliated and broken from war, the only thing they could do was to forget ... all they wanted to do was party ... Beirut is total and absolute freedom ... Love and sex and drugs and alcohol were our new law and order ... After you have killed people you don't care what you drink, as long as you get drunk.'[13]

The frenzy for pleasure has been heightened by the preceding night-mare, as well as by the contrast with life in what Ghassan Tueni, former editor of *Al-Nahar*, calls the Great Arab Prison – the other Arab countries – and Lebanon's other cities, like increasingly puritan Sidon and Tripoli. All communities meet in the bars, including Shia from the southern suburbs, who supply some of Beirut's best DJs. Pop culture is non-denominational. If there are fights, they are about women.[14]

★

However, as in 1975, Beirut also shows the vulnerability of wealth. Thirty thousand Syrian troops continued to occupy parts of Lebanon and Beirut. President Emile Lahoud, elected in 1998, was a Syrian protégé who, in the interests of Syrian hegemony, strengthened the pro-Syrian security apparatus in the police and army. Hariri's task was to promote growth, secure the inflow of foreign money, and, in the words of William Harris, 'sustain the Lebanese banking system so that Syria could keep its ramshackle financial affairs afloat and the Syrian/Lebanese security elite could cream off tens of millions of dollars for its private comforts'.[15] The Syrian security chief in Lebanon, Rustum Ghazzale, who looked like a character from a 1970s thriller, and the Lebanese deputy chief of military intelligence, Jamil Sayyid, were considered by many the real rulers of the country. Syrian hegemony was a multi-billion-dollar operation, funded by a share of revenues from drugs, customs, construction and the Casino du Liban.[16]

As Beirut and Damascus again entered into conflict, Hariri began to try to limit Syrian hegemony. On 27 August 2004 he was summoned to Damascus, given a fifteen-minute interview by President Assad, and threatened; he later told a friend that, to the Syrian government, 'we are all ants.' Points at dispute were the division of spoils and Assad's insistence that President Lahoud obtain an unconstitutional extension of his term of office. Hariri resigned as prime minister in protest.

Hariri employed the most modern security techniques. His mansions were fortresses. He went nowhere without a phalanx of well-trained bodyguards. Nevertheless, on 14 February 2005 – St Valentine's Day – after attending parliament and drinking a cup of coffee in the Café de l'Etoile, he was driving near the icon of Beirut tourism, the Phoenicia Hotel, in a convoy of armoured Mercedes when it was blown up by a car bomb. Hariri and eighteen guards and passers-by were killed. The crater from the blast was so wide that it looked as if a meteorite had hit the city. The sound was like the thunderclap made by Israeli planes breaking the sound barrier over the city. The blast not only blew out the windows of the Phoenicia Hotel, but also shook the walls of the AUB hospital.[17]

For a few weeks, as all who were there remember, Beirut seemed to glow with grief. Whatever his faults, Hariri had revitalized the economy and, unlike most other Lebanese leaders, he had no blood on his hands. A wave of emotion and indignation brought communities together. On 16 February, at his funeral by his uncompleted mosque, rich and poor, Muslim, Christian and Druze came from all areas of the city, holding candles and flags, some of which showed a crescent and a cross intertwined.

For the first time there were Muslim women in a funeral cortège. Church bells tolled at the same time as the muezzin called to prayer. Some mourners had a Koran in one hand and a cross in another. The grave became a shrine surrounded by candles, some with images of the Virgin Mary and the Maronite St Charbal. The Place des Martyrs was submerged in a sea of photographs of Hariri and red-and-white Lebanese flags.

Many thought that this was Beirut's supreme moment, like Alexandria in 1956, or Salonica in 1908: the 'Cedar Revolution', the 'Beirut Spring', the 'springtime of the Arabs', when Lebanon said no to dictatorship and murder. The Mufti declared the assassination an attack on all Sunnis. Cardinal Sfeir, the Maronite patriarch, attended the funeral to show his solidarity. President Chirac and his wife flew in from Paris to attend their friend's funeral – the presence of President Lahoud and all representatives of the Lebanese government had been refused by the Hariri family: as so often in the Levant, a foreign government was trusted more than the local one.[18]

In the following weeks a tent city of protesters demanding 'Independence 05' sprang up in the square. More graffiti appeared – in Arabic, French and English – on special canvas walls erected by the grave, among hearts and entwined crosses and crescents: 'Syria out!' 'Liban aux Libanais!' 'Freedom or death!' 'Wanted Syrial killer!' 'We'll always remember you.' 'We love you.'[19]

Nevertheless – in an unconscious admission of Syrian guilt in the murder, and an open assertion of confessionalism – putting sect before country, the Shia parties Amal and Hezbollah separated themselves from the rest of Lebanon and sided with their patron, Syria. On 8 March there was a huge demonstration on the Place Riad al-Solh beside the Place des Martyrs, with many Shia bussed in from the southern suburbs of the city, to express gratitude for Syria's role in the country.[20] On 14 March there was an even bigger counter-demonstration, of Sunni, Druze and Christians holding banners saying 'Independence 05', 'Freedom', 'Hey Syria who's next?' 'Leave Now,' 'Syria out!' and similar slogans. (One Ashrafiyeh lady is said to have been accompanied by a Filipina maid holding a board saying, 'Madame wants Syria out.') Lebanon appeared to be two countries again.

On 26 April 2005, thanks to Lebanese and international pressure, the last Syrian troops left Lebanon. Many Syrian workers fled for fear of public hostility. Again showing a Levantine preference for foreign institutions, there has been no Lebanese investigation of the crime. Four pro-Syrian generals, including Jamil Sayyid, have been indicted by an international tribunal; at the time of writing, no one has been tried.[21]

The army left; the agents remain. Over the next five years there were random bombings in Christian areas of Beirut and eight anti-Syrian writers and deputies were murdered – as their equivalents had been in 1915–16 by the Ottomans – in order to intimidate Beirut and the Lebanese. They included the great Samir Kassir, son of a Palestinian, author of a history of Beirut, who taught at the Université Saint-Joseph, wrote equally well in French and Arabic, and had accused the Syrian government of Hariri's death in *Al-Nahar*; his colleague Gibran Tueni; and Pierre Gemayel, son of Amin Gemayel. At the funeral of Pierre Gemayel, crowds shouted anti-Hezbollah slogans.[22]

The Syrian regime was not the only challenge facing Lebanon. Rich, well-armed and well-organized, Hezbollah, with its headquarters in the southern district of Beirut, had become a state within the state, like the PLO before 1982, but less corrupt, stronger and Lebanese. It had thirty-three seats in the parliament (less than the 40 per cent of Shia in the population would warrant), ministers in the government, and a social-security system as effective as its militia.

Moreover, it had foreign backers and weapons suppliers in Syria and Iran. Its revered secretary-general is Sheikh Hassan Nasrallah, born the son of a Beirut grocer in 1960. Claiming to represent the 'national resistance', its prestige had been raised by its contribution to the Israeli withdrawal from south Lebanon in 2000. Its ubiquitous posters (of a green fighter on a yellow background, or Iranian or Lebanese imams) and armed guards made the south of the city seem like a suburb of Tehran, with miniskirts. Even the new Rafic Hariri International Airport, which appeared to be a hub of global travel, was in reality, because it was near the Hezbollah area, staffed and watched by Hezbollah supporters.

Hezbollah rallies its faithful at the great annual Shia festival of Ashura. To mournful music and rhythmic drumbeats, commemorating the murders of Muhammad's two grandsons Hussein and Hassan in AD 680, massive crowds of all ages, like a river of black and green, segregated in groups of men and women, march through the Shia districts, beating their chests and shouting, 'Ya Hassan!', 'Ya Hussein!', 'Death to Israel! Death to America!'

Despite warnings, Hezbollah continued to launch attacks on Israel from its redoubts in the south of the country. After it kidnapped two Israeli soldiers and killed eight more in 2006, Israel, as in 1982, launched a massive retaliation: hammer blows for pinpricks. It showed Israel's desire not only to weaken Hezbollah, but also, in the words of the Israeli chief of

staff Dan Halutz, to 'turn back the clock in Lebanon by twenty years ...
The Lebanese government is responsible. Lebanon will pay the price.'[23]

For three weeks in July–August 2006, from land, sea and air, Israel again
devastated Lebanon. Again clouds of smoke rose above Beirut. From the
cafés of Hamra you could hear missiles hitting the south of the city, whence
most inhabitants had fled. Although much of the attack targeted only
Hezbollah supporters, showing the effectiveness of Israeli intelligence, the
scale of destruction was startling. Blocks of flats, shops and offices reduced
to a mass of blasted concrete, twisted metal and rubble made parts of the
city look like an earthquake zone.[24]

Israel also targeted the infrastructure of reconstruction: bridges, roads,
oil refineries, factories. Lebanon had the worst of both worlds, blamed by
Hezbollah for not giving it more power, by Israel for giving it too much.

Like the PLO before it, Hezbollah inflicted proportionately little
damage in Israel: its missiles often killed Palestinians rather than Israelis.
One million Lebanese were temporarily displaced, 500,000 Israelis. From
Paris, where he had resettled, the poet Adonis said what many felt: that
Beirut was dying a second time.[25]

Well funded by Iran, after the ceasefire Hezbollah at first proved more
effective than the Lebanese government in providing money and relief,
water and electricity, to the inhabitants of the southern suburbs as they
returned to their shattered homes. On 23 September, at a massive parade
in honour of what he called Hezbollah's 'divine, historic and strategic
victory' over the US and Israel, Nasrallah claimed that 'no army in the
world is strong enough to disarm us' and called for a government of
national unity. He also said that, if he had anticipated the Israeli reaction – no excess of imagination required – he would not have ordered
the soldiers' kidnapping. When told that the tourist season – one of the
economic strengths of Lebanon – had been ruined, a Hezbollah spokes-
man replied that tourism was merely 'hummous and prostitution'.[26]

An unintended consequence of the Israeli attack was the demise of
Tony Blair. The Middle East bites back at bellicose British premiers:
Turkey helped destroy Lloyd George; Egypt Eden; Lebanon Blair. When
only the US, UK and Israel – for some Lebanese a new 'axis of evil' –
opposed a ceasefire in 2006, the Labour Party was 'nauseated'. Brown
replaced Blair a year later.[27]

Having suffered onslaughts from Syria and Israel in 2005 and 2006,
Lebanon then endured attack from another quarter: Hezbollah tried to
topple the government of Fouad Siniora, or to gain more power and
ministers in it. For seventeen months from December 2006 Hezbollah

supporters established an armed tent city near the parliament and on the Place des Martyrs. The cafés and businesses of the city centre had to close, depriving thousands of their livelihoods. In January 2007 Sunni and Shia – the latter recognizable by their discipline and the black clothes worn for Ashura – fought and killed each other and plunged sections of west Beirut into chaos. Masked men and burning tyres blocked the airport road. Photographs of Hariri were also burnt. Again smoke clouds rose above the city. The army – now 60,000 men and better armed than before (but mainly Shia in composition) – imposed a curfew. A Hezbollah deputy declared that it had been 'a democratic protest as in any country'. Robert Fisk wrote, 'I never believed I would see Lebanon become a sectarian battleground again.' Many felt the country was heading for civil war, and that Hezbollah would win.[28]

As if Lebanon had not endured enough catastrophes, in 2007 a new fanatic Sunni group, called Fatah al-Islam, gained power in some Palestinian refugee camps, until it was crushed by the Lebanese army. Its leader, Abu Salim, declared, 'Our goals are beyond Lebanon; we want the Levant to be governed by Islam again and then the whole world.'[29]

In May 2008 there was another Sunni–Shia mini-conflict. To show its power, Hezbollah briefly took over west Beirut. There were around 100 dead and 200 wounded; offices and charitable institutions were attacked and destroyed. Many businesses closed. The Sunni Dar al-Futwa radio station and three Hariri-owned television channels were forced off air. For a time it seemed that Shia might overthrow the state, as Shia crowds had overthrown the Shah in Tehran in 1978–9. To some these short conflicts, added to the recent Israeli war and Syrian assassination spree, were more disturbing than the civil war itself. They suggested that no one had learned its lessons. A regular contributor to *L'Orient–Le Jour*, a passionate believer in Levantine cosmopolitanism, Dr Antoine Courban wrote, 'It is the end, I know it is the end. Like the Kingdom of Camelot, once upon a time there was a dolce-vita country called Lebanon.'[30]

He is not the only prophet of doom. Other comments were: 'There is no hope for such mentalities. Lebanon is doomed'; 'Without international protection, Lebanon will not survive';[31] 'Ils vont nous massacrer tous!'; 'What Lebanon needs is a Khomeini.'[32]

However, the system goes on. Confessionalism has not changed, although the balance of demographic power now favours the Shia. Although religious confession is no longer written on identity cards, it remains a crucial factor in jobs and education. Posts in the government and the Beirut municipality, from the mayor down, are still 'sectarianized'.

The municipal council is equally divided between twelve Muslims and twelve Christians; despite their massive presence in the suburbs, the Shia are under-represented.[33] There is still no civil marriage. The great Lebanese novelist Amin Maalouf, who has lived in Paris since 1976, laments, 'Lebanon is addicted to confessionalism. It is subversive, a poison destroying the state, a drug to which the whole country is addicted.' He advocates removing mention of religious identity from all records.[34]

Despite its deceptive surface of modernity, Beirut remains subject to the geography of fear. Many people prefer to live in the same area or street as members of their own confession. There are few estate agents, since the residential property market is governed by religion as well as money. There are now nineteen religious communities recognized by the state, and fifteen different religious legal codes working in Lebanon. The thousands of Iraqi refugees who have settled in Beirut since the Anglo-American invasion of their country in 2003 reside according to religion, not nationality: Shia Iraqis choose Shia districts; Sunni Sunni districts; Christians Christian districts.

Dynasticism maintains its grip, as in Syria under the Assads. Thus Saad Hariri, due to popular demand more than personal taste, inherited his father's political power base. Mustafa Berri, Taymur Jumblatt and Nadim Gemayel are being groomed for their father's succession. Khazens and Salams are still ministers and deputies. There is still a catastrophic security situation. In the autumn of 2007 some deputies felt they had to meet and sleep in the Phoenicia Hotel, in rooms with permanently drawn curtains, for fear of assassination.[35] The houses of prominent politicians are guarded first by sniffer dogs, then by Lebanese soldiers, then by concrete blocks, and finally by guards from their own militias.

Beirut faces a choice: between retribalization and re-Levantinization. It could resemble other divided and retribalized cities. Baghdad is now zoned between Sunni and Shia areas. In Jerusalem, too, Palestinians and Israelis are increasingly segregated: the city itself remains one of the principal obstacles to peace between Israel and Palestine.

In 1992–5 Sarajevo, which once had a 'unique character' as 'a multi-cultural, multi-ethnic and pluri-religious centre', in the words of UN Resolution 824, with mosques, synagogues and churches side by side, endured a civil war in which 100,000 were killed, often with weapons left over from the Lebanese civil war. As they watched it on television, Lebanese said that, in comparison, they were angels.[36] Soon Sarajevo looked like a city with its guts hanging out. Before the war it was half

Muslim; now it is 90 per cent Muslim. Saudi-funded mosques are being built. The language as well as the city itself has been divided, into Serbian, Croatian and increasingly Islamicized Bosniak.[37] The capital of Europe, Brussels, the last area of Walloon–Flemish cohabitation, is not a bilingual city but a city inhabited by two rival groups, speaking rival languages. Mixed offices and mixed marriages are less and less common: 'everything is ruled by language'. The country is on the brink of partition. Some Flemish hope that Brussels, 'our Jerusalem', will eventually become a Flemish city.[38]

On the other hand, the late twentieth and early twenty-first centuries have seen, in other cities, a process of re-Levantinization or globalization. The long Levantine farewell is over. Geography is biting back at history. Cities like Shanghai, Odessa and St Petersburg are again becoming the great cosmopolitan ports they once were.

Perhaps the hyper-nationalism of the twentieth century will prove to have been an interlude. In a global age, international cities are no longer – can no longer be – the slaves of the nation state which they once were. Mayor of Delhi Sheila Dikshit thinks they are beginning to resemble the city states of the past.[39]

With 350 languages, and a population one-third of which was born outside the United Kingdom, London has become a world city, hailed by some New Yorkers and Parisians as the capital of the twenty-first century.[40] Like Paris, it provides more spaces for diversity of opinion, religion and habits for people from the Middle East than any Middle Eastern city, with the possible exception of Beirut. Teachers and an absence of confessionalisation or quotas have helped lessen racial conflicts. In Southfields Community School in Wandsworth – and in many others – there are pupils speaking over seventy languages.[41] London's cosmopolitan character was confirmed by the diversity of those who died in the July 2005 bombs on the Underground.

Istanbul too is becoming a great international city again, an economic centre for the Balkans and the Black Sea. With 22 per cent of Turkey's population (16 million of 73 million), it now, according to one set of statistics, generates 43 per cent of Turkey's international trade. The consular corps in Istanbul is now larger than the diplomatic corps in Ankara. In 2009, for the first time since it was banned in 1943, carnival was celebrated in the street again, near the last Greek taverna, Madame Despina's.[42]

Izmir has shrunk in importance economically. It provided 33 per cent of Turkey's exports in 1977, 13 per cent in 2001. Faced with the attractions of Istanbul, big business and the young are leaving. However, it retains some of its old character. It is the largest city in Turkey not to vote for the religious party (AKP) and not to have an AKP mayor: hence Prime Minister Recep Tayyip Erdogan calls it Gavur Izmir – Infidel Izmir. The mayor wants to make Izmir 'a global brand'. It now has direct flights to Athens, and a Greek café called The Island of Mastic on the Cordon – the first Greek-owned business in the city since 1922. Nicos, the owner, speaks for many when he says, 'In our hearts we just want to get on as neighbours. We are like two branches from the same tree.'[43]

Alexandria also is reconnecting to the outside world. A French-language university for future government officials, dedicated 'au développement africain' and named after the poet president of Senegal Léopold Senghor, opened on 4 November 1990, in the presence of presidents Mubarak and Mitterrand, the presidents of Senegal and the Democratic Republic of Congo, and Senghor himself. On the opening day a lift carrying the five presidents broke down. Mubarak passed the time by speaking about the renaissance of Alexandria – in English. An Arab Maritime University at Aboukir and a Japanese University are planned; the private Pharos University opened in 2006.[44]

Below ground and underwater – in the window of opportunity between demolition and construction – 'Alexandrinology' is reviving. Since 1990 Franck Godidio and Jean-Yves Empereur, founder of the Centre d'Etudes Alexandrines, have begun to excavate the world's first cosmopolis, both on land and underwater. The archaeological and touristic potential are enormous.[45] However the scene in Youssef Chahine's film *Alexandria Again and Again* where a builder's drill smashes into the tomb of Alexander the Great is entirely plausible.

Alexandria again has an international institution. Inspired by its ancient predecessor, the Biblioteca Alexandrina opened in 2002 on the corniche, near the site of the palace city of the Ptolemies. A colossus of Ptolemy II, raised from the sea, and a modern bust of Alexander the Great stand by the entrance to this glass-and-aluminium library. It is the first library to be founded from the start as an international institution, with international as well as Egyptian sponsors and funding, and is directly dependent on the presidency, not on the Ministry of Education or Culture.

The Biblioteca Alexandrina is intended, as the foundation plaque states, to be 'a beacon of knowledge and a place for encounters and dialogue between peoples and cultures', linking Alexandria to both the outside world and its own past. In 2009 it hosted an international conference on Darwin – an audacious move in a Muslim city.[46] The Biblioteca also performs a vital human function: it is one of the few public spaces where young men and women meet, far from parents' and neighbours' eyes. Almost every chair in the enormous reading room is occupied.[47] As one Alexandrian, Jo Boulad, says, 'In a Mediterranean city you never lose hope. The sea always brings something.'[48]

In spite of some inhabitants' prophecies of doom, Beirut may have a chance of rejoining other global cities. The President, Michel Sleiman, is determined to defend what he optimistically calls 'the beautiful dynamic of interaction among Lebanese groups … We reject political sectarianism in all its forms.'[49] It remains true to its role as a window on the world. Every year there are Arabic and French book fairs. Agenda Culturel (www.agendaculturel.com) lists an impressive number of new films, plays, exhibitions, publications, in Arabic, French and English, every week in Beirut – more than in any other Arab city. Novels about the civil war and histories of Lebanon are staples of Beirut publishers' lists. The cultural organization Umam organizes meetings and films about the war in a programme called Confronting Memories. A few killers have apologized in public for their acts. The Barakat house has been saved from demolition by the municipality and is being transformed into Beit Beirut – a museum of the war.[50] Rather than being a city of two hostile languages, like Brussels, three languages – Arabic, French and English – are in constant use at the same time, even in the same sentence: 'Yallah, bye-bye, mon vieux.'

The last taboos are being challenged, as is shown by the publication of the first novel in Arabic with a gay hero, *The Stones of Laughter* (1990), by Hoda Barakat; the foundation of gay-rights groups, discussed in the film *Beirut Apartment* (2007); and the establishment in 2009 by Joumana Haddad of an erotic magazine for women, called *Jasad*.[51] On 20 April 2010, with the slogan 'civil marriage not civil war', there was a march for secularism in the city.

Far from Lebanon being put back twenty years, as the Israeli chief of staff had hoped, in 2009 the *New York Times* put Lebanon at the top of places to go – to the amazement of one Beiruti, for whom a foreign passport and a packed suitcase are necessities of life.[52] Beirut's charm, like that of Levantine cities in the past, comes from its combination of *joie de vivre*, vulnerability and diversity. It is an escape from the prison of nationalism. Warren Singh-Bartlett, who works on the Lebanon *Daily Star*, admires its 'ferocious edge', combined with 'wildly different visions of life'. It is a mixture of Paris, Tehran, Damascus, Erevan and Saint-Tropez in one city. Ghassan Salhab, director of films on the war, like *Le Dernier Homme* (2006), returned to Beirut from Paris in 2003. For him Paris was too comfortable: 'Beirut inspires me. It constantly places us on the borderline. We are constantly forced to question ourselves.'[53]

'I'm in Lebanon now because I have to live in a civilized country,' says Saudi-born novelist Mohammad Rashid. For a Libyan shopkeeper, 'Beirut is civilized! Women and men mix freely in Lebanon.' Peter Grimsditch, the British-born managing editor of the *Daily Star*, said in 2005 that there was nowhere he would rather live: 'I haven't been anywhere in the world where I feel the power of the state bearing down on me less. Europe is absolutely intolerable.' Beirut has the advantages of its weaknesses. The weakness of the state almost destroyed it in 1975–90; but you feel freer from state surveillance in Beirut than in Cairo, Istanbul or London.[54]

The last great Levantine port with the 'fragrance of freedom', and a demographic balance between its communities, is threatened by the hyper-nationalist governments of Tehran, Damascus and Jerusalem, and the discontented counter-state of Hezbollah. Whether they will inflict new catastrophes is impossible to predict. With its conflicts and conjunctions, universities and refugee camps, on the fault lines between East and West, clericalism and secularism, city and state, coast and hinterland, at once vulnerable and resilient, Beirut remains at the heart of 'the world's debate', and an experimental laboratory for the future of the Middle East. On this city depends the security of all its neighbours.

The Beirut dilemma goes to the heart of the Levant. At certain times – Smyrna in the nineteenth century, Alexandria and Beirut for periods of the twentieth – Levantine cities could find the elixir of coexistence, putting deals before ideals, the needs of the city before the demands of nationalism. Like all cities, however, Levantine cities needed an armed force for protection. This could be provided by the Ottoman, British or French armies, but not by the cities' own citizens, since they were unwilling to shoot co-religionists. No Levantine city produced an effective police force or national guard of its own. The very qualities that gave these cities their energy – freedom and diversity – also threatened their existence. No army, no city.

The true heirs of the Levant are some of the richest cities of today: London, Paris and New York – Dubai, Bombay and Singapore. Their mixed populations (now including many people originally from the Levant) make them increasingly different from their hinterlands, but they are protected by national armies and police forces. Ben-Gurion was blind to denounce 'the spirit of the Levant that ruins individuals and societies'. Levantine cities are the future, as well as the past. Globalisation means we are all Levantines now.

Acknowledgements

I am grateful to all those who have helped with the research and writing of this book, particularly the staff of the British Library, the Centre d'Etudes Alexandrines, ELIA, the Institut Français d'Etudes Anatoliennes, the Istanbul Library, the Koç Library and the London Library. For their time and patience in answering questions, I am especially grateful to Bassem Abdallah, Aouni Abdulrahim, Guy Abela, Sally Adès, Tom Adès, Princess Catherine Aga Khan, Oner Akgerman, Daphne Aliberti, Enrico Aliotti, Engin Ardiç, Paul Auchterlonie, Mohammed Awad, Josiane Ayoub, Alex Baltazzi, Mona Bassili, Nayla Bassili, Alex Benaki, Micky Benaki, Andrew Board, Jo Boulad, Hilary Bowker, Toby Buchan, Willy Buttigieg, Ipek Çalislar, John Carswell, Jean Chammas, Jean Charaf, Peter Clark, Colin Clement, Francesco Colucci, Jean Choremi, Marc and Hala Cochrane, Paddy Cochrane, Yvonne Cochrane, Antoine Courban, Leslie Croxford, Medhat Dakakni, Robert Debbas, Zeki Dogan, Marcos Dragoumis, Jean-Yves Empereur, Craig Encer, Madeleine Enright, Başar Eryoner, Richard Fattorini, Caroline Finkel, Derek Flower, Kadriya Foda, Eleni Frangakis-Syrett, Malte Fuhrmann, Reggie Gallia, Marcos Galounis, Brian Giraud, Gwynneth Giraud, Dominique Gogny, Solomon Green, Michael Haag, Ahmad Hamade, Sahar Hamouda, Rita Hani, Will Hanley, Azza Heikal, Cecil Hourani, Ahmad Husseini, Dwan and Nur Kaoukgi, M. and Mme Max Karkagi, Vangelis Kechriotis, Tarif Khalidi, Fayza al-Khazen, Paschalis Kitromilides, Omer Koc, Mr and Mrs Kostas Konstantinidis, Daphne Krambs, Germaine Labarthe, George and Natasha Lemos, Andre Levy, Giovanni Licciardello, Sam Lock, Christopher Long, Peter Mackridge, Charles Manoli, Basil Marcou, Sophia Mooney, Metin Munir, Hoda el-Naggar, Leila Naguib, Fouad Nahas, John and Denise Nahman, Tony Naufal, Fernande Nissaire, Anke and Lienke van Nugteren, Osman Vassib Osmanoglou, Bahattin Oztuncay, Guy Pagy, Themis Papadopoulo, Jacques Perot, Nicholas Philippakis, Rear Admiral S. A. Rashidy, Samir Rebees, John Rodenbeck, Jackie Rolo, Prince Nicholas Romanov, Alan de Lacy Rush, Lucette de Saab, Ibrahim and Marie-Hélène Saad, Mahmud Sabit, Evangelos Sahperoglou, Dyala Salam, Robert Saliba, Giovanni Salmeri, Antony Santilli, Ferdinand Scherzer, John Scott, Cecile Shaalan, Hanan al-Shaykh, Albert Simes, Rodney Simes, Kostas Stamatopoulos, John Stefanidis, Norman Stone, Mme Tawil, Martin Taylor, Paolo Terni, Rev. Leighton Thomas, Professor Zafer Toprak, Princess Nesrine Toussoun, Molly Tuby, Pelin Uysal, Yolande Whittall, Charles Wilkinson, Antony Wynn, Emir Yaner, Alex Zannas, Virginia Zervudachi. Particular thanks to Juliet Brightmore for her help with illustrations, and to Edward Chaney, Roger Hudson, Caroline Knox, Charles Manoli, Metin Munir and Roland Philipps for advice on the manuscript. Deepest thanks to Douglas Matthews for his index and to Caro Westmore for her work on the typescript.

Quotations from the translations of C. P. Cavafy's poems by Edmund Kelly and Philip Sherrard are made by kind permission of Princeton University Press. Every reasonable effort has been made to trace copyright holders, but if there are any errors or omissions, the publisher will be pleased to insert the appropriate acknowledgement in any subsequent printings or editions.

Notes

Unless otherwise stated, all books in English are published in London, all books in French in Paris.

Introduction

1. Edward Gibbon, *The Decline and Fall of the Roman Empire*, 6 vols. (1776–88), vol. 6, ch. 59.
2. Nezar Alsayad, *Cities and Caliphs: On the Genesis of Arab Muslim Urbanism* (1991), p. 151.
3. Patrick Leigh Fermor, *Roumeli: Travels in Northern Greece* (1966), pp. 100, 107; Alexander de Groot, 'The dragomans of the embassies in Istanbul', in Geert Jan Van Gelder and Ed de Moor, eds., *Eastward Bound: Dutch Ventures and Adventures in the Middle East* (Amsterdam, 1994), p. 131.
4. William Makepeace Thackeray, *Notes of a Journey from Cornhill to Grand Cairo* (2nd edn, 1846), p. 62.
5. Irad Malkin and Robert L. Hohlfelder, *Mediterranean Cities: Historical Perspectives* (1988), p. 186.

Chapter 1: The Vineyards of Pera

1. Philip Mansel, *Constantinople: City of the World's Desire* (1995), pp. 7, 16.
2. Colin Imber, *Ebu's-su'ud: The Islamic Legal Tradition* (Edinburgh, 1997), pp. 75, 104.
3. J. Ursu, *La Politique orientale de François Ier 1515–1547* (1908), p. 18; Gérard Poumarède, *Pour en finir avec la croisade. Mythes et réalitiés de la lutte contre les Turcs aux XVIe et XVIIe siècles* (2004), p. 107.
4. See, for example, the Venetian ambassadors' reports quoted in Virginia Aksan and Daniel Goffman, eds., *The Early Modern Ottomans: Remapping the State* (Cambridge, 2007), pp. 40–41.
5. Deno J. Genakopoulos, 'The Diaspora Greeks', in Nikiforos P. Diamandouros et al., eds., *Hellenism and the First Greek War of Liberation: Continuity and Change* (Thessaloniki, 1976), pp. 70–71.

6. Ursu, pp. 28–9.
7. Rudolph Peters, *Islam and Colonialism: The Doctrine of Jihad in Modern History* (The Hague, 1979), p. 3; Virginia Aksan, *Ottoman Wars 1700–1800: An Empire Besieged* (2007), p. 27.
8. Jean-Louis Bacqué-Gramont, Sinan Kuneralp and Frédéric Hitzel, *Représentants permanents de la France en Turquie et de la Turquie en France* (Istanbul, 1991), pp. 2–4.
9. Ernest Charrière, *Négociations de la France dans le Levant*, 4 vols. (1848), I, 118; Ursu, pp. 35, 37.
10. A. Hamilton et al., eds., *Friends and Rivals in the East: Studies in Anglo-Dutch Relations in the Levant from the Seventeenth to the Early Nineteenth Century* (Leiden, 2000), p. 191.
11. Abbé Antoine Degert, 'Une ambassade périlleuse de François de Noailles en Turquie', *Revue historique*, 159 (Nov. 1928), 225–60, pp. 230, 233, 237.
12. Pierre Duparc, *Recueil des instructions données aux ambassadeurs et ministres de France ... Turquie* (1969), pp. 202, 448.
13. Antoine Galland, *Voyage à Constantinople 1672–1673*, 2 vols. (2002), I, 261, II, 167, 261.
14. Christiane Villain Gandossi, 'Les attributions du Baile de Constantinople dans le fonctionnnement des echelles du Levant au xvie siècle', in *Les Grandes Escales*, vol. 11 (Brussels, 1974), pp. 227–44; Marie F. Viallon, *Venise et la porte ottomane 1453–1566* (1995), p. 90.
15. Gérard Poumarède, 'Négocier près la Sublime Porte: jalons pour une nouvelle histoire des capitulations ottomanes', in Lucien Bély, *L'Invention de la diplomatie* (1998), pp. 71–5, 79.
16. Niels Steensgaard, 'Consuls and nations in the Levant from 1570 to 1650', *Scandinavian Economic History Review*, 15, 1–2 (1967), p. 18.
17. See the reproduction, and translation, of the 1740 capitulations in *Napoléon III et l'Europe* (2006), pp. 24–6.
18. Eric R. Dursteler, *Venetians in Constantinople: Nation, Identity and Coexistence in the Early Modern Mediterranean* (Baltimore, 2006), p. 25; Dariusz Kolodziejczyk, *Ottoman–Polish Diplomatic Relations 15th–18th Century: An Annotated Edition of Ahdnames and other Documents* (Leiden, 2000), pp. 123–5.
19. Ari Bulent, 'Early Ottoman diplomacy', in Nuri Yurdusev, ed., *Ottoman Diplomacy: Conventional or Unconventional?* (Basingstoke, 2004), p. 40. Capitulations were also granted to Poland in 1533, the Holy Roman Empire in 1719, Sweden in 1736, Naples in 1740, Denmark in 1756, Prussia in 1761, Spain in 1782.
20. Susan A. Skilliter, 'An ambassador's *tayin*: Edward Barton's ration on the Egri campaign 1596', *Turcica*, 25 (1993), pp. 153, 158.
21. Zeki Celikkol, Alexander de Groot and Ben. J. Slot, *It Began with the Tulip: Turkey and the Netherlands in Pictures* (Ankara, 2000), pp. 18, 27, 31, 39; Marlies Honekamp-Mazgon, *Palais de Hollande in Istanbul* (Istanbul, 2002), *passim*; cf. Duparc, p. 294 for the French ambassador visiting the Mufti in 1728.
22. F. W. Boal, 'Ethnic residential segregation, ethnic mixing and resource conflict: a study in Belfast, Northern Ireland', in Ceri Peach, Vaughan Robinson and Susan Smith, *Ethnic Segregation in Cities* (1981), pp. 243, 245.

23. Jon Calame and Esther Charlesworth, *Divided Cities: Belfast, Beirut, Jerusalem, Mostar and Nicosia* (Philadelphia, 2009), pp. 30–32; Annie Sacerdoti, *The Guide to Jewish Italy* (Venice, 2004), p. 80.
24. Dursteler, pp. 29, 39.
25. Steensgaard, p. 19, Haga to States General, 7 Mar. 1614.
26. Dursteler, p. 155.
27. Aksan and Goffman, pp. 7, 71, 73, 86.
28. Roe to Sir Isaac Wake 1626, quoted in G. R. Berridge, 'Notes on the origins of the diplomatic corps: Constantinople in the 1620s', in *Discussion Papers in Diplomacy* (Clingandael, 2004), p. 7.
29. Dursteler, p. 66.
30. George Sandys, *Travels: Containing an History of the Original and Present State of the Turkish Empire* ... (6th edn, 1670), p. 67.
31. Dursteler, pp. 93, 95; Alexander de Groot, *The Ottoman Empire and the Dutch Republic: A History of the Earliest Diplomatic Relations* (Leiden and Istanbul, 1978), pp. 222f; Ronald C. Jennings, *Christians and Muslims in Ottoman Cyprus and the Mediterranean World 1571–1640* (New York, 1993), p. 133; Youssef Courbage, 'Situation démographique comparée du Bilad al cham au xviie et xixie siècles', in *Les Relations entre musulmans et chrétiens dans le bilad al cham. Actes du colloque de 2004* (Beirut, 2004), pp. 35, 46.
32. Steensgaard, pp. 22–4.
33. Michael Rogers, 'To and fro: aspects of Mediterranean trade and consumption in the 15th and 16th centuries', in *Villes au Levant. Hommage à André Raymond* (1990), pp. 57, 59, 64.
34. See Marie de Testa and Antoine Gautier, *Drogmans et diplomates européens auprès de la Porte Ottomane* (Istanbul, 2003), pp. 35, 45 and *passim*; Groot, 'Dragomans', pp. 130–58.
35. In the early years of Islam, in conquered Christian areas, it had been customary for Muslims to pray in churches, since mosques had not yet been built.
36. Dursteler, pp. 178–81; cf. Daniel Goffman, *Britons in the Ottoman Empire 1642–1660* (Seattle, 1998), pp. 25–7.
37. Dursteler, p. 9.
38. Author of *Les quatre premiers livres des navigations et peregrinations orientales* (Lyon, 1567–8), with the first semi-accurate illustrations of the Empire.
39. Author of *Observations de plusieurs singularitez* (1553).
40. Richard Fletcher, *Moorish Spain* (1992), pp. 8, 94, 138, 148; personal communication re cleaning utensils, Suraiya Faroqhi, 8 Dec. 2007.
41. P. Harvey, *Muslims in Spain 1500–1614* (Chicago, 2005), pp. viii, 1, 14, 339; Sakina Missouma, *Alger à l'époque ottomane* (Aix-en-Provence, 2003), p. 165.
42. Selim Deringil, 'There is no compulsion in religion; on conversion and apostasy in the late Ottoman Empire 1839–1856', in id., *The Ottomans, the Turks and World Power Politics* (2000), pp. 109, 130.
43. Gilles Veinstein, 'Retour sur la question de la tolérance ottomane', in Bartolome Bennassar and Robert Sauzet, eds., *Chrétiens et musulmans à la renaissance* (1998), pp. 419, 420.
44. Nabil Matar, *In the Lands of the Christians: Arab Travel Writing in the Seventeenth Century* (2003), pp. xxv–xxvii.

45. Dursteler, pp. 59, 160–63, 166–9.
46. Jocelyne Dakhlia, *Lingua Franca: Histoire d'une langue métisse en Méditerranée* (2008), pp. 64, 70, 75, 199, 252–3, 297.
47. Ibid., pp. 105, 148, 169, 193, 262.
48. Ibid., pp. 81, 96–7, 100, 493.
49. Ibid., p. 137. Many Greeks also spoke 'the Franck language which they call the Frank': W.V. Harris, ed., *Rethinking the Mediterranean* (2005), p. 274.
50. Dakhlia, pp. 82, 124, 174, 269, 308–9, 363–4; Lord Byron, *Letters and Journals*, 12 vols. (1972–82), II, 37, to Francis Hodgson, 20 Jan. 1810.
51. Fermanel Stochove, *Le Voyage d'Italie et du Levant* (Rouen, 1664), quoting passport issued 4 Mar. 1631, 'notre souverain volonté est que vous les receviez avec respect et bon accueil'; cf. Stephen Olin, *Greece and the Golden Horn* (New York, 1854), p. 312, 29 June 1853.
52. John Bramsen, *Letters of a Prussian Traveller*, 2 vols. (1818), II, 46, 397, '17 zuldadir 1229'.
53. William Turner, *Journal of a Tour in the Levant*, 3 vols. (1820), II, 60.
54. Byron, II, 262, letter of 26 Dec. 1812.
55. Philip Mansel, 'The grand tour in the Ottoman Empire', in Paul Starkey and Janet Starkey, eds., *Interpreting the Orient: Travellers in Egypt and the Near East* (Reading, 2001).

Chapter 2: Smyrna: The Eye of Asia

1. Thomas MacGill, *Travels in Turkey, Italy and Russia*, 2 vols (1808), I, 69.
2. Sandys, p. 23.
3. Antoine Galland, *Le Voyage à Smyrne*, ed. Frédéric Bauden (2000), p. 79.
4. Léon Kontente, *Smyrne et l'Occident, de l'Antiquité au XXIe siècle* (Montigny, 2005), pp. 251, 279; Daniel Goffman, *Izmir and the Levantine World 1550–1650* (Seattle, 1990), pp. 13, 14.
5. Apostolos E. Vacalopoulos, *The Greek Nation 1453–1669* (New Brunswick, 1976), p. 287.
6. Ibid., p. 146; Goffman, *Britons*, p. 82.
7. Goffman, *Izmir*, pp. 21, 36, 43.
8. Andrew C. Hess, *The Forgotten Frontier: A History of the Sixteenth Century Ibero-African Frontier* (Chicago, 1978), pp. 208–9.
9. Stelios A. Papadopoulos, ed., *The Greek Merchant Marine, 1453–1850* (Athens, 1972), p. 19.
10. Goffman, *Izmir*, p. 67.
11. Ibid., pp. 36–7, 40.
12. Ibid., pp. 43, 44.
13. Ibid., pp. 61–2.
14. M. Dapper, *Description exacte des isles de l'Archipel et de quelques autres adjacentes* (Amsterdam, 1703), p. 224.
15. Sandys, p. 11.
16. Michael Strachan, *The Life and Adventures of Thomas Coryate* (Oxford 1962), p. 196, 14 Feb. 1613.

17. M. Pitton de Tournefort, *Relation d'un voyage du Levant, fait par ordre du Roy*, 2 vols. (1717), I, 370, 386.
18. MacGill, I, 50.
19. Tournefort, I, 375, 379; 'Relation de l'île de Chio' (1747), in Antoine Galland, *Recueil des rites et cérémonies du pélerinage de la Mecque* (Amsterdam, 1754), pp. 104, 115.
20. Tournefort, I, 381; Richard Pococke, *A Description of the East*, 2 vols (1743), II, ii, 3, 11.
21. Goffman, *Izmir*, p. 58.
22. Caroline Finkel, *Osman's Dream: The Story of the Ottoman Empire 1300–1923* (2005), pp. 180–81, 185; Sandys, p. 12; Sonia Anderson, *An English Consul in Turkey: Paul Rycaut at Smyrna 1667–1678* (Oxford, 2001 edn), p. 165.
23. R. R. Madden, *Travels*, 2 vols. (1827), I, 147.
24. William Knight, *Oriental Outlines, or, a Rambler's Recollections of a Tour in Turkey, Greece and Tuscany in 1838* (1839), pp. 256, 299.
25. Goffman, *Izmir*, pp. 41, 55.
26. Julien Pillaut, *Les Consulats du Levant*, 2 vols. (Nancy, 1902), II, 16; Groot, *The Ottoman Empire and the Dutch Republic*, p. 216.
27. M. Du Mont, *Voyages*, 4 vols. (The Hague, 1699), II, 364.
28. Johan van Droffelaar, '"Flemish Fathers" in the Levant', in Geert Jan Van Gelder and Ed de Moor, eds., *Eastward Bound: Dutch Ventures and Adventures in the Middle East* (Amsterdam, 1994), p. 100n; Kontente, p. 295; Kamal S. Salibi, *A House of Many Mansions: The History of Lebanon Reconsidered* (2009 edn), p. 98.
29. M. Courmenin, *Voyage de Levant* (1629), p. 52.
30. Sir Charles Fellows, *Travels and Researches in Asia Minor, More Particularly in the Province of Lycia* (1852), p. 10n, states that he uses ancient place names 'as being the best known to English readers'; cf. *Antiquitates Asiaticae*, about classical antiquities, published in 1728 by Edmund Chishull, Anglican chaplain in Smyrna in 1698–1701.
31. Sir Thomas Roe, *Negotiations of Sir Thomas Roe, in his Embassy to the Ottoman Porte, from the Year 1621 to 1628 Inclusive*, 2 vols. (1740), I, 186, 189; Tournefort, II, 491, 498, 501, 513.
32. Roe, I, 433, 445, 647, 818: Roe to Buckingham 26 Aug. 1625, to Arundel 20 Oct. 1625, to Buckingham 12 May 1627, to Buckingham 27 June 1628.
33. François-René, Vicomte de Chateaubriand, *Itinéraire de Paris à Jérusalem et de Jérusalem à Paris*, 2 vols. (1846 edn), I, 270.
34. Alexander Drummond, *Travels through Different Cities of Germany, Italy, Greece and several parts of Asia as far as the Banks of the Euphrates* (1754), p. 119; Richard Chandler, *Travels in Asia Minor and Greece*, 2 vols. (3rd edn, 1817), I, 63; James Dallaway, *Constantinople: Ancient and Modern* (1797), p. 205.
35. Finkel, pp. 225–7, 247; M. Poullet, *Nouvelles relations du Levant*, 2 vols. (1667), II, 23; Galland, *Voyage à Smyrne*, p. 260; MacGill, I, 76.
36. Robert Dankoff, *An Ottoman Mentality: The World of Evliya Çelebi* (Leiden, 2004), pp. 31, 36, 64, 68, 85, 91, 109, 111, 142.
37. I am grateful for translations of Evliya Çelebi to Caroline Finkel.
38. Corneille Le Bruyn, *Voyages au Levant*, 6 vols. (The Hague, 1732), I, 87; Anderson, *An English Consul*, p. 160.

39. Anderson, *An English Consul*, p. 59.
40. Evliya Çelebi, *Seyahatnamesi*, 10 vols. (Istanbul, 1999–2007), ix, 49, 52, 53.
41. Drummond, p. 119; Chandler, I, 64; Paul Calligas, *Voyage à Syros, Smyrne et Constantinople* (2004 edn), p. 59, 20 July 1844.
42. C. B. Elliott, *Travels in the Three Great Empires of Austria, Russia and Turkey*, 2 vols. (1838), I, 33.
43. Still a feature of houses in the side streets of the districts of Beyoglu in Istanbul and Sancak in Izmir.
44. Charles Texier, *Description de l'Asie mineure faite par ordre du gouvernement Français*, 3 vols. (1849), III, 49.
45. Le Bruyn, I, 76; Chandler, I, 72; Galland, *Voyage à Smyrne*, pp. 90, 106–7.
46. M. Merlijn Olnon, 'Köprülü imperial policy and the refashioning of Izmir', in Maurits van den Boogert, ed., *Ottoman Izmir* (Istanbul, 2007), pp. 45, 48–9; Galland, *Voyage à Smyrne*, pp. 105–6.
47. E. Frangakis-Syrett, 'Commercial practices and competition in the Levant: the British and the Dutch in eighteenth-century Izmir', in A. Hamilton et al., eds., *Friends and Rivals in the East: Studies in Anglo-Dutch Relations in the Levant from the Seventeenth to the Early Nineteenth Century* (Leiden, 2000), pp. 145, 147; Kontente, p. 299.
48. Goffman, *Izmir*, p. 22. Camels can still be seen in the region outside the city; they are now used for tournaments, rather than transport.
49. Galland, *Voyage à Smyrne*, p. 182; Tournefort, II, 497; Elena Frangakis-Syrett, *The Commerce of Smyrna in the Eighteenth Century* (Athens, 1992), p. 29.
50. Goffman, *Izmir*, pp. 52–3; Drummond, pp. 114, 122–3.
51. Le Bruyn, I, 83.
52. Goffman, *Izmir*, p. 136.
53. F. W. Hasluck, *Christianity and Islam under the Sultans*, 2 vols. (New York, 1973 edn), II, 407–10, 414, 423.
54. Anderson, *An English Consul*, p. 9.
55. Ibid., p. 7; Tournefort, II, 495.
56. Samuel Woodruff, *Journal of a Tour to Malta, Greece . . . and Spain in 1828* (Hartford, 1831), p. 155, 5 Oct. 1828.
57. Tournefort, II, 497.
58. Goffman, *Izmir*, pp. 82, 87.
59. Kontente, p. 314.
60. Anderson, *An English Consul*, p. 30.
61. John Freely, *The Lost Messiah* (2002 edn), pp. 31, 66, 68.
62. Ibid., p. 83; Daniel Goffman, 'Izmir, from village to colonial port city', in Edhem Eldem, Daniel Goffman and Bruce Masters, *The Ottoman City between East and West: Aleppo, Izmir and Istanbul* (Cambridge, 1999), p. 101.
63. Freely, pp. 91, 93, 193.
64. Ibid., pp. 136, 143, 219, 222, 239.
65. A word also applied, in modern Turkey, to transsexuals and transvestites.
66. Evliya, IX, 49, 51–2.
67. Anderson, *An English Consul*, p. 17; Le Bruyn, I, 81.
68. Galland, *Voyage à Smyrne*, pp. 92–3.
69. Thanks for this translation to Caroline Finkel.

70. Pococke, II, i, 51.

71. Celikkol, de Groot and Slot, pp. 141, 222; Groot, *The Ottoman Empire and the Dutch Republic*, p. 335. A Dutch consul was established in Izmir in 1656.

72. Anderson, *An English Consul*, pp. 41, 44, 49, 223, 235, 237, 291–2, 294–7.

73. Ibid., pp. 30, 234n, 244.

74. Frédéric Hitzel, *Relations interculturelles et scientifiques entre l'Empire Ottoman et les pays de l'Europe occidentale* (thesis, Paris IV, 1995), pp. 434, 346, 349.

75. Frédéric Hitzel, ed., *Livres et lecture dans le monde ottoman* (1999), *passim*.

76. Richard Clogg, *Studies in Ottoman Greek History* (Istanbul, 2004), p. 211n.

77. More precisely in 1644, 1648, 1650, 1660, 1681, 1688, 1698 and 1794: Vera Tchentsova, 'Le fonds des documents grecs (F. 52. "Relations de la Russie avec la Grèce") de la collection des archives nationales des actes anciens de la Russie et leur valeur pour l'histoire de l'Empire Ottoman', *Turcica*, 30 (1998), 383–96.

78. Galland, *Voyage à Smyrne*, pp. 114–28; A. de La Motraye, *Voyages du Sr. A. de La Motraye en Europe, Asie et Afrique*, 2 vols. (La Haye, 1727), I, 184–5.

79. Galland, *Voyage à Smyrne*, p. 183.

80. Ibid., p. 119; La Motraye, I, 185.

81. Jonathan I. Israel, 'Trade politics and strategy: the Anglo-Dutch Wars in the Levant', in A. Hamilton et al., eds., *Friends and Rivals in the East: Studies in Anglo-Dutch Relations in the Levant from the Seventeenth to the Early Nineteenth Century* (Leiden, 2000), pp. 17, 18.

82. van Droffelaar, pp. 109, 113.

83. Honekamp-Mazgon, pp. 48, 61.

84. van Droffelaar, p. 110n.

85. Anderson, *An English Consul*, pp. 86, 89, 135.

86. Goffman, 'From village to colonial port city', p. 97.

87. T. Simpson Evans, ed., *The Life of Robert Frampton, Bishop of Gloucester* (1876), p. 40.

88. MacGill, I, 70; British Library (henceforward referred to as BL) Add. MSS 38591, J. O. Hanson, 'Recollections of Smyrna and Greece 1813', f2.

89. La Motraye, I, 185.

90. Galland, *Voyage à Smyrne*, pp. 150–51; cf. John Murray, *Handbook for Travellers in the Ionian Islands, Greece, Turkey, Asia Minor and Constantinople* (1840), p. iv: 'Next to the language of the country Italian will be found the most useful language both in Greece and Turkey.' In 1820 the British consul issued a British passport to a British subject, beginning 'Noi Francesco Werry, Console di Sua Majesta Britannica in Smirne e sue dipendenze'.

91. Tournefort, II, 498.

92. Anderson, *An English Consul*, pp. 129, 234; if no presents were given the officials felt defrauded: see Henry Maundrell, *A Journey from Aleppo to Jerusalem at Easter, A.D. 1697* (1810 edn), p. 35, 11 Mar. 1697.

93. Francis Hervé, *A Residence in Greece and Turkey*, 2 vols. (1837), I, 377.

94. Diary of Rev. John Covel, Nov. 1670, in J. Theodore Bent, ed., *Early Voyages and Travels in the Levant* (1893), p. 140.

95. Goffman, 'From village to colonial port city', p. 119; Ismail Hakki Kadi, 'A silence of the guilds? Some characteristics of Izmir's craftsmen organizations

in the 18th and early 19th century', in van den Boogert, ed., *Ottoman Izmir* , pp. 82, 84, 88.

96. Tournefort, II, 498; Martha Nicol, *Ismeer; or Smyrna and its British Hospital in 1855* (1856), p. 198; Dallaway, p. 206.
97. Leon Caignart de Saulcy, *Carnets de voyage* (1955 edn), p. 70, 2 May 1845.
98. John E. Emerson, *Letters from the East*, 2 vols. (3rd edn, 1830), I, 65.
99. Knight, p. 271; James Emerson, *Letters from the Aegean*, 2 vols. (1829), I, 76.
100. Alexis de Valon, *Une année dans le Levant: voyage en Sicile, en Grèce et en Turquie*, 2 vols. (2nd edn, 1850), II, 64; A. W. Kinglake, *Eothen* (1919 edn), p. 60.
101. BL, Hanson, 'Recollections', f. 443; Valon, II, 62–3.
102. Le Bruyn, I, 87; personal information, Costas Dimitri, 20 Feb. 2009.
103. Carlo Goldoni, *Four Comedies* (1922 edn), p. 151. Another play, *Le Marchand de Smyrne* by S. Chamfort (1785), ends with an old Turkish slave-owner liberating his slaves.
104. Poullet, II, 30.
105. Galland, *Voyage à Smyrne*, pp. 119, 131, 133.
106. Poullet, II, 27; Kontente, p. 309.
107. Marie-Carmen Smyrnelis, *Une ville ottomane plurielle: Smyrne aux xviie et xviiie siècles* (Istanbul, 2006), p. 47, consul to Choiseul-Gouffier, 3 June 1785.
108. Goffman, *Izmir*, p. 115.
109. Ibid., p. 139; cf. for other estimates Kontente, p. 337.
110. Evliya, IX, 54.
111. Kontente, p. 299; Tournefort, II, 496.
112. Anderson, *An English Consul*, pp. 57n, 80; id., 'The Anglo-Dutch "Smyrna fleet" of 1693', in A. Hamilton et al., eds., *Friends and Rivals in the East: Studies in Anglo-Dutch Relations in the Levant from the Seventeenth to the Early Nineteenth Century* (Leiden, 2000), pp. 96, 105–7.
113. Frangakis-Syrett, *Commerce*, pp. 253–4; Goffman, 'From village to colonial port city', p. 129.
114. Frangakis-Syrett, *Commerce*, p. 47.
115. Le Bruyn, I, 70–72; MacGill, I, 121; Kontente, p. 380.
116. Frangakis-Syrett, *Commerce*, pp. 53–8; Kontente, pp. 378–9.
117. Galland, *Voyage à Smyrne*, p. 135.
118. Goffman, *Izmir*, p. 134; id., 'From village to colonial port city', pp. 95, 118.
119. Svat Soucek, 'The strait of Chios and the Kaptanpaşa's navy', in Elizabeth Zachariadou, ed., *The Kapudan Pasha, His Office and His Domain* (Rethymnon, 2002), p. 145.
120. Kontente, p. 343; Tournefort, I, 366.
121. Tournefort, I, 366.
122. Frangakis-Syrett, *Commerce*, pp. 119–21; Kontente, p. 393; Pococke, II, i, 37.
123. Whose family, of Greek origin, had fled Crete at the time of the Ottoman conquest in 1669.
124. Tom Rees, *Merchant Adventurers in the Levant* (Stawell, 2003), p. 37.
125. Abdul-Karim Rafeq, *The Province of Damascus 1723–1783* (Beirut, 1966), pp. 243, 293, 300.
126. Joseph de Bauffremont, *Journal de campagne de l'amiral de Bauffremont, prince de Listenois, dans les pays barbaresques (1766)* (1981), p. 66; Kontente, p. 383.

127. Aksan, *Ottoman Wars*, p. 153.

128. François Charles-Roux, *Le Projet français de conquête de l'Egypte sous le règne de Louis XVI* (Cairo, 1929), p. 15, note by M. Saint-Didier, May 1774; Aksan, *Ottoman Wars*, p. 154.

129. Clogg, *Studies*, pp. 197, 203.

130. Frangakis-Syrett, *Commerce*, pp. 59–60; Kontente, p. 384.

131. *An Authentic Narrative of the Russian Expedition against the Turks by Sea and Land* (1772), pp. 107, 113.

132. Frangakis-Syrett, *Commerce*, p. 60, letter of 15 Mar. 1773.

133. François Charles-Roux, *La Syrie et Palestine au xviiie siècle* (1925), pp. 106, 110.

134. Daniel Panzac, *La Caravane maritime – marins européens et marchands ottomans en Méditerranée (1680–1830)* (2004), p. 204; Kontente, p. 385.

135. Roderick H. Davison, *Essays in Ottoman and Turkish History 1774–1923* (1990), pp. 31, 33, 37, 43, 55.

136. Christoph K. Neumann, 'Decision-making without decision-makers: Ottoman foreign policy circa 1780', in Caesar E. Farah, ed., *Decision-Making and Change in the Ottoman Empire* (Kirksville, 1993), pp. 29–38.

137. Charles-Roux, *Le Projet français*, p. 50.

138. See Bibliotheca Alexandrina, *Alex-Med Newsletter*, 12 Aug. 2008, p. 12 and *passim*.

139. Charles-Roux, *Le Projet français*, pp. 39, 42, 43, 60, 74, 82, 85.

140. Claude Charles de Peyssonnel, *Examen du livre intitulé Considérations sur la guerre actuelle des Turcs* (Amsterdam, 1788), pp. 22, 29, 154–5, 166–75, 239.

141. Henry Laurens, *Les Origines intellectuelles de l'expédition d'Egypte. L'Orient islamisant en France* (Istanbul, 1987), p. 182.

Chapter 3: Smyrna: Massacres and Merriment

1. Celikkol, de Groot and Slot, pp. 171, 175; Clogg, *Studies*, p. 244n; Finkel, p. 469.

2. Clogg, *Studies*, p. 93, declaration by British consul and merchants, 25 Mar. 1797.

3. Clogg, *Studies*, pp. 12, 67 (Francis Werry to Spencer Smith, 17 Mar. 1797), 69, 78, 84 (id. to Levant Company, 2 Apr. 1797, 8 Apr., 12 Apr.), 85–7 (dispatch of Mr de Cramer, imperial consul-general, 17 Mar.), 93 (declaration by British merchants, 25 Mar.); Kontente, pp. 404–5.

4. In Constantinople, before an execution, a man was often forced to sign a confession of his crimes. It was later stuffed in the mouth of his decapitated head for the public to read.

5. Kontente, p. 389; MacGill, I, 131.

6. Clogg, *Studies*, p. 242n; Gilles Veinstein, 'Ayan de la region d'Izmir et le commerce du levant', in id., *Etat et société dans l'Empire Ottoman, xviie–xviiie siècles* (Aldershot, 1994), pp. 132–44; Frangakis-Syrett, *Commerce*, pp. 37–40; Kontente, pp. 350, 411.

7. Kontente, pp. 362, 395, 416; Hyde Clarke, *History of the British Community*

at Smyrna (1862), passim. In 1809 British merchants voted to send a gift to Husseyin Karaosmanoglu, in thanks for his affection and protection during the absence of the British consul: Frangakis-Syrett, *Commerce*, p. 116.

8. Clogg, *Studies*, pp. 87–9, letter of Joseph Franceschi and declaration of Russian captains, 17 Mar. 1797.
9. Ibid., pp. 104–5, order of 15 May, Werry to Spencer Smith, 2 June 1797.
10. Constantino Oikonomos, *Etude sur Smyrne*, tr. and ed. Bonanventure F. Slaars (Smyrna, 1868), pp. 128–9; MacGill, I, 186, cf. Woodruff, p. 153; Clogg, *Studies*, p. 202n.
11. BL, Hanson, 'Recollections', ff. 51, 54, 55, 65.
12. Suryaiya Faroqhi, *Subjects of the Sultan: Culture and Daily Life in the Ottoman Empire* (2000), pp. 237–9.
13. Chateaubriand, I, 270, 271, 274.
14. J. M. Tancoigne, *Voyage à Smyrne, dans l'archipel et l'île de Candie en 1811, 1812, 1813 et 1814*, 2 vols. (1817), I, 33.
15. Rev. R. Walsh, *A Residence at Constantinople, during a Period including the Commencement, Progress, and Termination of the Greek and Turkish Revolutions*, 2 vols. (1836), I, 43; cf. Duc de Raguse, *Voyage de M. le Maréchal Duc de Raguse*, 5 vols. (1837), II, 193.
16. BL, Hanson, 'Recollections', ff. 51, 54, 55, 65.
17. MacGill, I, 78; Hervé, I, 313, 315; Earl of Carlisle, *Diary in Turkish and Greek Waters* (1854), pp. 127, 128.
18. Maxime du Camp, *Souvenirs et paysages d'Orient* (1848), p. 46.
19. MacGill, I, 98. By some accounts the casino was founded in 1778.
20. John Cam Hobhouse, diary of 1810, at http://www.hobby-o.com, 8 Mar. 1810.
21. MacGill, I, 183; Knight, p. 274; Rev. Charles Swan, *Journal of a Voyage up the Mediterranean; Principally among the Islands of the Archipelago, and in Asia Minor*, 2 vols. (1826), I, 141, diary 10 Jan. 1825; Oliver Jens Schmitt, *Les Levantins: cadres de vie et identités d'un groupe ethno-confessional de l'Empire Ottoman au 'long' 19e siècle* (Istanbul, 2007), pp. 452–3, quoting diary of Pierre Deval, 1826.
22. Fellows, pp. 4–5, 13 Feb. 1838.
23. William Turner, III, 139.
24. MacGill, I, 99.
25. Hervé, I, 323, 343, 344.
26. Clogg, *Studies*, p. 136; Kontente, p. 360.
27. Tancoigne, I, 38.
28. BL, Hanson, 'Recollections', f. 12; MacGill, I, 86; *Smyrna, Metropolis of the Asia Minor Greeks* (Athens, 2001), p. 127.
29. Rees, p. 150.
30. Clogg, *Studies*, p. 9.
31. Elena Frangakis-Syrett, 'The Raya communities of Smyrna in the eighteenth century', *International Journal of Maritime History* (1998), *passim*.
32. A. Korais, *Mémoire sur l'état actuel de la civilisation en Grèce* (1803), pp. 37, 41, 45, 53n, 57, 66.
33. Andreas G. Lemos, *The Greeks and the Sea* (1976), pp. 66, 70.

34. Papadopoulos, pp. 17, 30, 102.
35. Petros Mengous, *Narrative of a Greek Soldier* (New York, 1830), pp. 65–6.
36. Frangakis-Syrett, *Commerce*, pp. 101–2.
37. Oikonomos, pp. 16, 17, 23, 57, 59, 61, 69; Clogg, *Studies*, p. 163, journal of Charles Williamson, Sept. 1819; Marie-Carmen Smyrnelis, ed., *Smyrne, la ville oubliée?* (2006), p. 68.
38. Kontente, pp. 381, 408.
39. Smrynelis, *Une ville ottomane plurielle*, pp. 105n, 111.
40. Finkel, p. 412.
41. Vernon J. Puryear, *Napoleon and the Dardanelles* (Berkeley, 1951), p. 302, letter of Alexander I, 12 Mar. 1808.
42. Richard Clogg, *The Movement for Greek Independence 1770–1821* (1976), p. 115.
43. Hobhouse diary at http://www.hobby-o.com, 9 Dec. 1809; Mengous, p. 77.
44. Papadopoulos, p. 42; Aksan, *Ottoman Wars*, p. 289.
45. See for example Theophilus C. Prousis, *British Consular Reports from the Ottoman Levant in an Age of Upheaval* (Istanbul, 2008), pp. 57–9, 61, William Meyer to Lord Maitland, 13 Dec. 1820, 15 Mar. 1821.
46. John A. Petropoulos, *Forms of Collaboration with the Enemy: Memoirs of Kanellos Delegiannes* (n.d.), pp. 134–5.
47. Christine Philou, 'To be or not to be Roum in the 1820s', paper given at Ecole Française d'Athenes, Feb. 2006.
48. Hakan Erdem, 'Ottoman responses to the Greek War of Independence', in Faruk Birtek and Thalia Dragonas, eds., *Citizenship and the Nation-State in Greece and Turkey* (2005), pp. 69, 70, 74.
49. Clogg, *Studies*, pp. 205, 207, dispatches of Werry to Levant Company 11 Apr., 3 May 1821; cf. Alvan Bond, *Memoir of Rev. Pliny Fisk* (Edinburgh, 1828), pp. 142–54, letters lamenting 'the most tragical and bloody scenes', June–Nov. 1821.
50. Theodophilus C. Prousis, 'Smyrna 1821: a Russian view', quoting the diary of the Russian consul, Apr. 1821, in *Modern Greek Studies Yearbook*, 7 (1991), pp. 150, 152.
51. Clogg, *Studies*, pp. 208, 220–21, 224, dispatches by Werry, 3 May, 16 July, 17 Aug. 1821.
52. Ibid., pp. 208–18, 223, 226, dispatches of 12 May, 17 May, 18 June, 2 July, 2 Aug., 17 Sept. 1821; Prousis, 'Smyrna 1821', p. 156, diary for 16 June 1821.
53. Clogg, *Studies*, pp. 230, 231, 232–3, dispatches of 15, 30 Nov. 1821.
54. Personal communication, H. Şukru Ilicak, 16 May 2008.
55. Aksan, *Ottoman Wars*, p. 292; Walsh, II, 69, 70; David Brewer, *The Greek War of Independence* (New York, 2001), pp. 160–66; Prousis, *Consular Reports*, p. 146, report of 1 June, 2 July 1822.
56. Allan Cunningham, *Anglo-Ottoman Encounters in the Age of Revolution*, 2 vols. (1993), I, 290.
57. Peter Calvocoressi, *Threading My Way* (1994), *passim*.
58. Lemos, pp. 88, 91; John Travelos and Angelike Kokkou, *Hermoupolis* (Athens 1984), *passim*.
59. Papadopoulos, pp. 408, 410.

60. Allan Cunningham, *Anglo-Ottoman Encounters*, I, 300.

61. Kontente, p. 443.

62. Allan Cunningham, *Anglo-Ottoman Encounters*, I, 218.

63. Georges Douin, *Navarin 6 juillet–20 octobre 1827* (Cairo, 1927), pp. 98, 169.

64. Erdem, p. 77; Douin, *Navarin*, p. 28, declaration of June 1827.

65. Allan Cunningham, *Anglo-Ottoman Encounters*, I, 294, 315; Groot, 'Dragomans', p. 155.

66. David H. Finnie, *Pioneers East: The Early American Experience in the Middle East* (Cambridge, Mass., 1967), p. 24.

67. Kontente, pp. 438–9; Nathalie Clayer et al., eds., *Presse turque et presse de Turquie* (1992), pp. 4–6.

68. Kontente, pp. 458, 470; Jan Schmidt, *From Anatolia to Indonesia: Opium Trade and the Dutch Community of Izmir 1820–1940* (Istanbul, 1998), pp. 73–4.

69. F. V. J. Arundell, *Discoveries in Asia Minor*, 2 vols. (1834), II, 418, 364–5; John Murray, *Handbook* (1840), p. 261.

70. E. C. Wines, *Two Years and a Half in the Navy; or, Journal of a Cruise in the Mediterranean and the Levant*, 2 vols. (Philadelphia, 1832), II, 134; Gerasimos Augustinos, *The Greeks of Asia Minor: Confession, Community and Ethnicity in the Nineteenth Century* (1992), p. 92.

71. Bond, p. 104, letter of 30 Jan. 1820.

72. Woodruff, p. 167; cf. Chandler, I, 74.

73. Wines, II, 137.

74. Woodruff, p. 153; MacGill, I, 102; Clogg, *Studies*, p. 107, dispatch of 17 July 1797.

75. Patricia Crimmin, 'The Royal Navy and the Levant trade c.1795–c.1805', in Jeremy Black and Philip Woodfine, eds., *The British Navy and the Use of Naval Power in the Eighteenth Century* (Leicester, 1988), pp. 226, 227, 233.

76. Woodruff, p. 158.

77. George Hawthorn journal, sold by Sotheby's, 18 May 2004; I am grateful for this reference to Sophia Mooney.

78. Thomas Hope, *Anastasius*, 2 vols. (1819), I, 184.

79. James Emerson, I, 85.

80. Hervé, I, 379.

81. Knight, pp. 292–3.

82. Anderson, *An English Consul*, p. 14; Valon, II, 434; Knight, p. 293n.

83. Woodruff, p. 166.

84. James Emerson, I, 36–7.

85. Philip Mansel, *Dressed to Rule: Royal and Court Costume from Louis XIV to Elizabeth II* (2005), pp. 104–5.

86. Aksan, *Ottoman Wars*, p. 360.

87. Sybil Zandi Sayek, 'Fêtes et processions', in Marie-Carmen Smyrnelis, ed., *Smyrne, la ville oubliée?*, pp. 157–68; Vangelis Kechriotis, 'The Greeks of Izmir at the end of the empire: a non-Muslim community between autonomy and patriotism', DPhil thesis (Leiden University, 2005), pp. 157, 161; Schmitt, pp. 354–5.

88. Hervé II, 44; James Emerson, I, 238.

89. Kinglake, p. 54.
90. Kontente, p. 469.

Chapter 4: Alexandria: The Key to Egypt

1. Chateaubriand, II, 141.
2. W. Birch, *Journal of a Voyage up the Mediterranean* (Poulton, 1818), pp. 160–61; T. R. Jolliffe, *Letters from Palestine* (2nd edn, 1820), p. 318, Oct. 1817.
3. Daniel Panzac, *Les Corsaires barbaresques* (1999), p. 132n.
4. Desmond Gregory, *Malta, Britain and the European Powers 1793–1815* (1996), pp. 137, 192, 216; Aksan, *Ottoman Wars*, p. 236.
5. Ronald T. Ridley, *Napoleon's Proconsul in Egypt: The Life and Times of Bernardino Drovetti* (1998), p. 33; Sylvie Guichard, ed., *Lettres de Bernardino Drovetti, Consul de France à Alexandrie 1803–1830* (2003), p. 103, letter to Pierre Balthalon, 1 June 1804.
6. Jack A. Crabbs, *The Writing of History in Nineteenth-Century Egypt: A Study in National Transformation* (Cairo, 1984), pp. 44, 46; Cheikh Abd-el-Rahman el Jabarti, *Merveilles biographiques et historiques ou chroniques du Cheikh Abd-El-Rahman El Djabarti*, 10 vols. (Cairo, 1896), VIII, 111.
7. Henry Dodwell, *The Founder of Modern Egypt: A Study of Muhammad Ali* (Cambridge, 1931), pp. 19–20; Jabarti, VIII, 36.
8. Muhammad H. Kutluoglu, *The Egyptian Question (1831–1840)* (Istanbul, 1998), p. 36.
9. Vice-Amiral Durand-Viel, *Les Campagnes navales de Mohammed Aly et d'Ibrahim*, 2 vols. (1935), I, 41, 60–63, 77.
10. Jabarti, VIII, 47, 148, 204; Deborah Manley and Peta Ree, *Henry Salt: Artist, Traveller, Diplomat, Egyptologist* (2001), p. 76.
11. Khaled Fahmy, *All the Pasha's Men: Mehmed Ali, his Army and the Making of Modern Egypt* (Cambridge, 1997), p. 84.
12. F. Robert Hunter, *Egypt under the Khedives 1805–1879* (1984), pp. 20–21, 48; Amédée Sacré and Louis Outrebon, *L'Egypte et Ismail Pacha* (1865), pp. 65–6.
13. René Cattaui, ed., *Le Règne de Mohamed Aly d'après les archives russes en Egypte*, 2 vols. (1931), I, 3, Boghos to consuls, 22 May 1819.
14. Georges Douin, ed., *La Mission du Baron de Boislecomte: l'Egypte et la Syrie en 1833* (Cairo, 1927), p. 62, report of 19 June 1833.
15. Edouard Driault, *Mohamed Ali et Napoléon (1807–1814): correspondance des consuls de France en Egypte* (Cairo, 1925), p. 201, Drovetti bulletin, 26 Nov. 1812.
16. M. Sabry, *L'Empire Egyptien sous Mohammed Ali et la question d'Orient (1811–1849)* (1930), p. 80.
17. Robert Ilbert, *Alexandrie 1830–1930*, 2 vols. (Cairo, 1996), I, 67; Durand-Viel, I, 149–50; Raguse, III, 131–2.
18. Guichard, p. 437, 6 Feb. 1823.
19. Ridley, p. 44; Manley and Ree, p. 241.

20. Ridley, pp. 207–8.

21. Jabarti, VIII, 279, 300, 322, 344 (1810–13); Driault, p. 93, dispatch of Drovetti, 28 Nov. 1810.

22. Driault, p. 77, dispatch of Drovetti, 17 July 1810; Ridley, p. 232; Afaf Lutfi al-Sayyid Marsot, *Egypt in the Reign of Muhammad Ali* (Cambridge, 1984), p. 147.

23. Jabarti, IX, 196; Dodwell, p. 58; Marsot, pp. 147, 166–7; Sabry, p. 31, dispatch of Drovetti, 28 Nov. 1812.

24. Robert Richardson, *Travels Along the Mediterranean and Parts Adjacent, in Company with the Earl of Belmore, during the years 1816–1817–1818*, 2 vols. (1822), I, 22, 25.

25. Stephen Olin, *Travels in Egypt, Arabia Petraea and the Holy Land*, 2 vols. (New York, 1843), I, 19; Baroness von Minutoli, *Recollections of Egypt* (1827), p. 2.

26. W. R. Polk and R. Chambers, *The Beginnings of Modernization in the Middle East* (Chicago, 1968), pp. 156–7.

27. Prousis, *Consular Reports*, p. 206, Salt to Londonderry, 6 Nov. 1821; Gaston Wiet, *Mohammed Ali et les beaux-arts* (Cairo, 1949), p. 25; Brian Fagan, *The Rape of the Nile* (Boulder, 2004 edn), pp. 57, 59, 170; Manley and Ree, pp. 81, 98, 204.

28. Ridley, p. 220.

29. Jabarti, IX, 237, 239–40, 293–4, 305; Fahmy, *All the Pasha's Men*, p. 10; Michael J. Reimer, *Colonial Bridgehead: Government and Society in Alexandria 1807–1882* (Boulder, 1997), p. 59.

30. Driault, pp. 178, 188, bulletins of Drovetti, May, 2 July 1812; Ilbert, I, 25; Manley and Ree, p. 69.

31. Cattaui, I, 377, dispatch of 24 June 1830.

32. Reimer, pp. 60–61; A. B. Clot Bey, *Aperçu général sur l'Egypte*, 2 vols. (1840), I, 195.

33. Wiet, pp. 195–9, 209–13; Sir Gardner Wilkinson, *Handbook for Travellers in Egypt* (1847), p. 101.

34. C. Rochfort Scott, *Rambles in Egypt and Candia*, 2 vols. (1837), I, 43.

35. J. Millie, *Alexandrie d'Egypte et le Caire* (Milan, 1868), p. 23.

36. Alfred J. Butler, *Court Life in Egypt* (1887), p. 121.

37. H. Noel Williams, *The Life and Letters of Admiral Sir Charles Napier KCB* (1917), p. 204.

38. Comte Benedetti, *Essais diplomatiques* (nouvelle série), 2 vols. (1897), II, 178.

39. E. B. Barker, *Syria and Egypt under the Last Five Sultans*, 2 vols. (1876), II, 8, 151.

40. By this author's estimate, at least thirty on Egypt alone, excluding those mentioning Egypt as part of a longer journey.

41. M. Goupil-Fesquet, *Voyage en orient fait avec Horace Vernet en 1839 et 1840* (1840), p. 33.

42. Nubar Pacha, *Mémoires* (Beirut, 1983), p. 67; James Augustus St John, *Egypt and Mohammed Ali; or, Travels in the Valley of the Nile*, 2 vols. (1834), I, 61.

43. Francis Schroeder, *Shores of the Mediterranean*, 2 vols. (1846), II, 6–7; Olin, *Travels*, I, pp. 32–3; Benedetti, II, 177–8.

44. Hon. Sir Charles Augustus Murray KCB, *A Short Memoir of Mohammed Ali* (1898), pp. 58–9; Scott, *Rambles*, I, 178–9.

45. Wiet, pp. 289–300; Prince Pückler-Muskau, *Egypt under Mohammed Ali*, 2 vols. (1845), I, 72.
46. Sir Charles Murray, p. 50.
47. Manley and Ree, p. 252, 16 Sept. 1826.
48. Ibid., p. 246.
49. Ibid., pp. 250–51, audience of 16 Sept. 1826; Dodwell, p. 195, quoting Bowring.
50. Manley and Ree, p. 263, 16 Aug. 1827.
51. Benedetti, II, 184.
52. Jabarti, IX, 196.
53. James Augustus St John, II, 441.
54. Ibid., I, 41–2; Reimer, p. 148; Jabarti, IX, 326. The sheikh was wrong: as long as the butcher killed the animal in the 'halal' way, and said 'Bismillah al rahman al rahim' when doing so, his religion was immaterial – as I was informed in a discussion in the Bibliotheca Alexandrina on 7 Dec. 2008.
55. Fahmy, *All the Pasha's Men*, p. 95.
56. Driault, p. 160, report by Mengin, 20 Jan. 1812.
57. Eliza Fay, *Original Letters from India* (1925), pp. 72–3, letter of 25 July 1779.
58. Jabarti, IX, 225, 325 (1813).
59. Georges Douin, *Une mission militaire française auprès de Mohamed Aly: correspondance des généraux Belliard et Boyer* (1923), p. 39, Belliard to Boyer, 29 Oct. 1824, 30 Nov. 1824.
60. Guichard, p. 452, letters to Pierre Balthalon, 22 Dec. 1823.
61. Fahmy, *All the Pasha's Men*, p. 94, letter of 20 Jan. 1824.
62. Gerald de Gaury, *Rulers of Mecca* (1951), p. 228. I am grateful for this reference to Alan de Lacy Rush.
63. Durand-Viel, II, 127; cf. Benedetti, II, 185: 'La vie humaine n'avait à ses yeux qu'une valeur relative.'
64. Driault, p. 79, dispatch by Saint-Marcel, 21 July 1810.
65. Manley and Ree, pp. 191–2, audience of 20 Nov. 1820.
66. Fahmy, *All the Pasha's Men*, pp. 87–9, letter of 18 Feb. 1822; Dodwell, p. 232.
67. Fahmy, *All the Pasha's Men*, pp. 99, 102, 111; Douin, *Une mission militaire française*, p. 48.
68. Fahmy, *All the Pasha's Men*, pp. 100–2, 260–1.
69. Dodwell, p. 227, quoting Muhammad Ali's letters and circulars to officials.
70. R. Garreau, *Un angoumois homme de mer: Besson Bey* (Antibes, 1949), *passim*; Pückler-Muskau, I, 53, 60; Dodwell, p. 225.
71. Georges Douin, *L'Egypte de 1828 à 1830: correspondance des Consuls de France en Egypte* (Rome, 1935), p. 160, dispatch of Baron d'Haussez, 25 June 1829; Durand-Viel, II, 20; Fahmy, *All the Pasha's Men*, pp. 135–7.
72. Bayle St John, *Two Years' Residence in a Levantine Family* (1856), p. 38.
73. Scott, I, 30–31; Edward Hogg, *A Visit to Alexandria, Damascus and Jerusalem during the Successful Campaign of Ibrahim Pasha*, 2 vols. (1835), I, 89; Schroeder, II, 67.
74. Wiet, p. 200; Durand-Viel, II, 47, dispatch of Aug. 1830; Scott, I, 43; Reimer, pp. 55, 56.
75. Driault, p. 120, dispatch from Saint-Marcel, 6 May 1811.

76. Pückler-Muskau, I, 6.
77. Bramsen, I, 172, 177; William Turner, II, 315, 341.
78. Reimer, p. 81; Cattaui, I, 263, 336, 356, dispatches of 8 July 1828, 5 Mar. 1829, 25 Aug. 1829, Pezzoni to Heyden; Dodwell, p. 229.
79. Ilbert, I, 108.
80. Ridley, p. 113, letter of Sept. 1822.
81. Edmund Spencer, *Travels in European Turkey*, 2 vols. (1851), II, 297.
82. Pierre Deval had also served in Alexandria and Baghdad, and as consul in Algiers since 1814.
83. J. C. Hurewitz, *The Middle East and North Africa in World Politics*, 2 vols. (New Haven, 1975), I, 227–9, dispatch from Deval, 30 Apr. 1827, Husseyin Pasha to Grand Vizier, 19 Dec. 1827; Panzac, *Les Corsaires barbaresques*, pp. 197–9, 273.
84. Mohamed Awad, 'The metamorphoses of Mansheyeh', *Mediterraneans* (2006), p. 42; Mrs Charles Lushington, *Narrative of a Journey from Calcutta to Europe, by Way of Egypt, in the years 1827 and 1828* (1829), p. 185.
85. Reimer, p. 73; Ilbert, I, 110–11; Mohamed Awad, *Italy in Alexandria: Influences on the Built Environment* (Alexandria, 2008), p. 79; Ezio Godolli and Milva Giacomelli, eds., *Italian Architects and Engineers in Egypt from the Nineteenth to the Twenty-first Centuries* (Florence, 2008), pp. 13–14.
86. Scott, I, 20; Schroeder, II, 70.
87. Schroeder, I, 70; Ilbert, I, 80; Major and Mrs George Darby Griffith, *A Journey Across the Desert from Ceylon to Marseilles*, 2 vols. (1845), II, 38; M. Gisquet, *L'Egypte, les Turcs et les Arabes*, 2 vols. (1846), I, 58; Wilkinson, p. 73.
88. M. Mengin, *Histoire de l'Egypte sous le règne de Mohammed Aly* (1823), pp. 52, 413.
89. Pascal Coste, *Toutes les Egyptes* (Marseille, 1998), pp. 40, 55, 57, 143, 155.
90. Driault, p. 132, dispatch by Saint-Marcel, 3 July 1811; Cattaui, I, 67, 85, dispatches of Drovetti to Russian government, 26 May 1826, 5 Aug. 1827; James Augustus St John, II, 532.
91. Reimer, p. 84; Ilbert, I, 193.
92. Guichard, pp. 432, 448, 487, letters of 14 Aug. 1823, 26 Sept. 1824; Giovanni d'Athanasi, *A Brief Account of the Researches and Discoveries in Upper Egypt made under the direction of Henry Salt Esq.* (1836), p. 2.
93. Ilbert, I, 22.
94. Thomas Philipp, *The Syrians in Egypt 1725–1975* (Stuttgart, 1985), p. 64; Guichard, pp. 432, 448 (14 Aug. 1823).
95. Prousis, *Consular Reports*, p. 188.
96. Reimer, pp. 68–70, 72; Fahmy, *All the Pasha's Men*, p. 211.
97. Reimer, pp. 60, 62, 66; Ilbert, I, 113.
98. Awad, *Italy in Alexandria*, p. 94.
99. Ilbert, I, 22; James Augustus St John, I, 2–3.
100. Ilbert, I, 22; Marsot, pp. 187, 191.
101. Clot Bey, *Aperçu général*, II, 328.
102. Baron d'Armagnac, *Nezib et Beyrout: souvenirs d'Orient de 1833 à 1841* (1844), p. 6; David S. Landes, *Bankers and Pashas: International Finance and Economic Imperialism in Egypt* (1979 edn), p. 196n.
103. Minutoli, p. 6; Hogg, I, 90, 101n; William A. Bromfield, *Letters from Egypt and Syria* (1856), p. 21, 22 Oct. 1850.

104. Bayle St John, p. 17.
105. Philipp, *The Syrians in Egypt*, p. 63n.
106. Durand-Viel, II, 140.
107. Ilbert, I, 167.
108. Dodwell, p. 194, dispatch of Murray, 8 July 1847.
109. See Comte Joseph d'Estourmel, *Journal d'un voyage en Orient*, 2 vols. (1844), II, 495–7.
110. Philip Sadgrove, 'Travellers' rendezvous and cultural institutions in Mohammed Ali's Egypt', in Paul Starkey and Janet Starkey, eds., *Interpreting the Orient: Travellers in Egypt and the Near East* (Reading, 2001), p. 259.
111. James Augustus St John, II, 358; Ilbert, I, 134.
112. Minutoli, pp. 154–7; A. Clot, *Aperçu général sur L'Egypte*, II, 156–7.
113. Scott, I, 46–7; Manley and Ree, p. 254; Wilkinson, p. 101.
114. Philip Sadgrove, *The Egyptian Theatre in the Nineteenth Century 1799–1882* (Reading, 1996), pp. 35, 39, 40.
115. Cf. Baron de Kusel Bey, *An Englishman's Reminiscences of Egypt* (1915), p. 38: 'Alexandria and its European suburb Ramleh are hard to beat for open-handed and open-hearted hospitality.'
116. Raguse, III, 216n, 218.
117. Bayle St John, p. 131.
118. H. R. Ross, *Letters from the East* (1902), p. 199n.
119. Florence Nightingale, *Letters from Egypt* (1998 edn), p. 24.
120. David Millard, *Journal of Travels in Egypt, Arabia Petraea and the Holy Land during 1841–2* (Rochester, NY, 1843), pp. 30, 34.
121. James Augustus St John, II, 358, 376.
122. Ed. de Cadalvène and J. de Breuvery, *L'Egypte et la Turquie de 1829 à 1836*, 2 vols. (1836), I, 27; Hogg, I, 145; cf. for a similar account A. B. Clot Bey, *Mémoires* (Cairo, 1949), p. 38.
123. Wilkinson, p. 72; Nassau William Senior, *A Journal Kept in Turkey and Greece in the Autumn of 1857 and the Beginning of 1858* (1859), p. 18, 19 Nov. 1855.

Chapter 5: Alexandria: Bid for Empire

1. Manley and Ree, pp. 226, 256; Dodwell, p. 73.
2. Durand-Viel, I, 314, 316, 367; Cattaui, I, 150, dispatch of 13 Dec. 1827; Manley and Ree, pp. 238, 266, 273.
3. Fahmy, *All the Pasha's Men*, pp. 38, 48; Sabry, p. 44, dispatch of 7 July 1813.
4. Durand-Viel, I, 163.
5. Fahmy, *All the Pasha's Men*, p. 52.
6. Kate Fleet, *The Muslim Bonaparte: Diplomacy and Orientalism in Ali Pasha's Greece* (Princeton, 1999), pp. 23–4, 31, 51, 79, 105–7, 116.
7. Fahmy, *All the Pasha's Men*, pp. 53–5, letter of 23 Jan. 1822. In 1832 he complained that the Ottomans had been tyrannical and treacherous for five hundred years: ibid., p. 71.
8. Ibid., pp. 56–9, letters of 24 Dec. 1825, 28 Oct. 1827.

9. Cattaui, II, 11, 21, 45, Lavison to Bouteneff, 24 Apr., 26 May 1836.
10. Landes, p. 331.
11. James Augustus St John, II, 363; Bromfield, p. 20, letter of 22 Oct. 1850; Wiet, p. 249.
12. Douin, *Boislecomte*, pp. 85, 98, report of 29 June 1833.
13. Fahmy, *All the Pasha's Men*, pp. 61–6; Cattaui, I, 448, Lavision to Bouteneff, 11 Nov. 1831.
14. Fahmy, *All the Pasha's Men*, pp. 67, 161.
15. Ibid., pp. 270–6.
16. Douin, *Boislecomte*, pp. 286, 287, 292, report of 19 Sept. 1833; Kontente, p. 457.
17. Kutluoglu, p. 73.
18. Ibid., p. 91; Douin, *Boislecomte*, pp. xxvii, xxxiv to Admiral Roussin, 8 Sept. 1832.
19. Kutluoglu, pp. 98–104.
20. Ibid., pp. 109, 113; Sabry, pp. 377, 379, report of Campbell, 1836.
21. Dominque Chevallier, *La Société du Mont Liban à l'époque de la révolution industrielle en Europe* (1971), pp. 14, 96, 99, 102.
22. Cattaui, I, 463, 532, 542, dispatches of 1 Feb. and 12, 31 Aug. 1832.
23. Sabry, p. 182.
24. Henry Laurens, 'La France et le califat', *Turcica*, 31 (1999), pp. 152–3.
25. Fahmy, *All the Pasha's Men*, p. 71, to Ibrahim, 3 June 1832.
26. Sabry, pp. 219, 227, letters of 28 Dec. 1832, 3 Feb. 1833.
27. E. B. Barker, II, 118, letter of John Barker to James Calvert, 1 Apr. 1830.
28. Manley and Ree, p. 239; Dodwell, p. 86; Driault, p. 209, circular of 13 Cemma al-Awal 1255.
29. Fahmy, *All the Pasha's Men*, pp. 285–9.
30. Ehud R. Toledano, *State and Society in Mid-Nineteenth-Century Egypt* (Cambridge, 2003 edn), pp. 158–60.
31. Fahmy, *All the Pasha's Men*, pp. 89, 282, letters of 1822, 30 June 1833.
32. Byron, who travelled in the Ottoman Empire in 1809–11, wrote that 'The Turks abhor the Arabs (who return the compliment a hundred fold) even more than they hate the Christians.'
33. Cattaui, II, ii, 352, Duhamel to Nesselrode, 6 July 1837.
34. Jabarti, VIII, 204, IX, 53, 153.
35. Fahmy, *All the Pasha's Men*, pp. 91, 245–6, 252–4, 269.
36. Ibid., pp. 253, 256, 245, 5 Sept. 1832.
37. Sabry, p. 153, letter of 12 Dec. 1827.
38. Ibid., p. 550.
39. Ibid., p. 473, Ibrahim to Muhammad Ali, 4 Sept. 1839.
40. Zeynep Çelik, *Urban Forms and Colonial Confrontations: Algiers under French Rule* (1997), pp. 27, 30; Missouma, pp. 34, 46.
41. Kutluoglu, pp. 191–2.
42. Toledano, p. 98.
43. Fahmy, *All the Pasha's Men*, p. 283.
44. Manley and Ree, p. 251.
45. Kutluoglu, pp. 119–20.

46. Athanase G. Politis, ed., *Le Conflit turco-égyptien de 1838–1841 et les dernières années du règne de Mohamed Aly d'après les documents diplomatiques grecs* (Cairo, 1931), pp. xv, xxxii.
47. Kutluoglu, p. 94, letter of 4 Feb. 1833.
48. Sabry, p. 292, report of Farren, British consul in Damascus, 29 May 1834.
49. Dodwell, pp. 171, 408, reports of Medem, 20 Mar. 1838, 2 May 1838.
50. Athanase Politis, pp. xiv, 41, dispatches of 4 May and 6 Apr. 1838.
51. Fahmy, *All the Pasha's Men*, p. 284.
52. Douin, *Boislecomte*, pp. 141, 239, 249, reports of 3 July, 30, 31 Aug. 1833; Dodwell, p. 156.
53. A. J. Rustum, *The Royal Archives of Egypt and the Disturbances in Palestine, 1834* (Beirut, 1938), pp. 13, 17.
54. Kutluoglu, p. 140.
55. Ibid., pp. 26–7.
56. Commodore Sir Charles Napier, *The War in Syria*, 2 vols. (1842), I, xlivn, account by the dragoman of the British consul.
57. Sabry, pp. 454–5.
58. Dodwell, p. 105, dispatch by consul Barker, 8 Mar. 1830.
59. Ibid., p. 189; Durand-Viel, II, 210, 223.
60. Sabry, p. 499, dispatch from Hodges, 23 Aug. 1840.
61. François Charles-Roux, *Thiers et Mehemet Ali* (1951), pp. 167, 171 (9 Sept. 1840), 201 (17 Sept. 1840), 231 (9 Oct. 1840).
62. Durand-Viel, II, 228, 239, 244.
63. Gabriel Dardaud, 'Un officier français du génie: Gallice Bey', *Revue des Conférences Françaises en Orient*, Dec. 1947, 657–70.
64. Charles-Roux, *Thiers*, p. 243.
65. W. P. Hunter, *Narrative of the Late Expedition to Syria Under the Command of Admiral the Hon. Sir Robert Stopford GCB, GCMG*, 2 vols. (1842), I, 7, 70.
66. Charles-Roux, *Thiers*, pp. 239, 243.
67. Philip Mansel, *Paris between Empires* (2001), pp. 362–3.
68. Charles-Roux, *Thiers*, p. 242.
69. W. P. Hunter, I, 272, 293, II, 309.
70. Sir Charles Napier, I, 255; Williams, p. 205.
71. Sir Charles Napier, I, 260, II, 168; Charles-Roux, *Thiers*, pp. 245–6.
72. Mansel, *Paris between Empires*, p. 364.
73. Toledano, p. 2; Charles-Roux, *Thiers*, pp. 243–5, 250, letter of 24 Oct. 1840.
74. Durand-Viel, II, 200; Charles-Roux, *Thiers*, p. 252.
75. Kutluoglu, pp. 178–87, 195; Charles-Roux, *Thiers*, p. 255; Sabry, pp. 533–4; Toledano, pp. 1–2.
76. Charles-Roux, *Thiers*, p. 315.
77. Ibid., pp. 257, 260.
78. Bayle St John, p. 11.
79. Reimer, pp. 90–93; Wilkinson, p. 97.
80. Gabriel Baer, *Studies*, p. 137.
81. Nubar Pacha, p. 86.
82. Ilbert, I, 47; Sabry, p. 578, Stoddart dispatch, 29 Aug. 1846.

83. Juan Cole, *Colonialism and Revolution in the Middle East: Social and Cultural Origins of Egypt's Urabi Movement* (Princeton, 1993), p. 84; Rosemay Said Zahlan, 'George Baldwin', in Paul Starkey and Janet Starkey, eds., *Interpreting the Orient: Travellers in Egypt and the Near East* (Reading, 2001), p. 32.

84. Dodwell, p. 179.

85. Gustave Flaubert, *Correspondance générale* (1973–), I, 565, to Dr Clocquet, 15 Jan. 1850.

86. Wiet, pp. 387–8.

87. Angelo Sammarco, *Les Règnes d'Abbas, de Said et d'Ismail* (Rome, 1935), p. 56; cf. Dardaud, p. 668.

88. Reimer, pp. 86–7.

89. Bayle St John, pp. 290, 292.

90. Driault, pp. 34, 199, letters of Drovetti 9 Apr. 1809, 4 Nov. 1812.

91. Jabarti, IX, 142, 170 (July 1813).

92. Fahmy, *All the Pasha's Men*, p. 131.

93. Jabarti, IX, 199 (1816).

94. Dodwell, p. 194.

95. Ibid., pp. 262–3, dispatch by Murray, 5 Aug. 1849.

Chapter 6: Beirut: The Republic of Merchants

1. Lt-Col. Edward Napier, *Reminiscences of Syria and Fragments of a Journal and Letters from the Holy Land*, 2 vols. (1843), I, 94, 96.

2. Gustave Flaubert, *Voyage en Orient 1849–1851* (2006 edn), p. 230.

3. Muhammad Adnan Bakhit, 'The Christian population of Damascus in the sixteenth century', in Benjamin Braude and Bernard Lewis, *Christians and Jews in the Ottoman Empire*, 2 vols. (1982), II, 39.

4. Chevalier d'Arvieux, *Mémoires*, 6 vols. (1735), II, 337, 345, 360–61.

5. May Davie, 'Les chrétiens dans l'espace et la société de Beyrouth', in *Les Relations entre musulmans et chrétiens dans le bilad al cham. Actes du colloque de 2004* (Beirut, 2004), p. 179.

6. Kamal Salibi, 'Maronite historians of Lebanon', in P. M. Holt and B. Lewis, eds., *Historians of the Middle East* (1962), pp. 212, 221, 238.

7. Abdul Rhhim Abu Husayn, *The View from Istanbul: Lebanon and the Druze Emirate in the Ottoman Chancery Documents* (2004), p. 52.

8. Allan Cunningham, ed., *The Early Correspondence of Richard Wood, 1831–1841* (1966), p. 45, to Mr Ongly, 5 Apr. 1832.

9. Hurewitz, I, 28, 34; René R. Ristelhuber, *Les Traditions françaises au Liban* (2nd edn, 1925), pp. 121, 130, 273, 276, letter of 1 Nov. 1715.

10. Douin, Boislecomte, p. 258, 1 Sept. 1833; Charles Issawi, *The Fertile Crescent 1800–1914: A Documentary Economic History* (Oxford, 1988), p. 160.

11. Henri Guys, *Relation d'un séjour de plusieurs années à Beyrout et dans le Liban*, 2 vols. (1847), I, 20, 225.

12. Thomas Philipp, *Acre: The Rise and Fall of a Palestinian City* (2001), pp. 128, 130, 133.

13. Leila Kamel, *Un quartier de Beyrouth: Saint Nicolas. Structures familiales et structures foncières*, 2 vols. (Beirut, 1998), *passim*.

14. Alphonse-Marie-Louis de Prat de Lamartine, *Correspondance Générale de 1830 à 1848*, 2 vols. (1943), I, 305, letters to Edmond de Cazales, 24 July and 6 Sept. 1832.

15. Leila Fawaz, *Merchants and Migrants in Nineteenth-Century Beirut* (2000 edn), p. 46; Samir Kassir, *Histoire de Beyrouth* (2003), p. 128.

16. Charles Issawi, 'British trade and the rise of Beirut 1830–1860', *International Journal of Middle East Studies* (Aug. 1977), 91–101, pp. 92, 93, 94, 98, dispatch of 16 Nov. 1835.

17. Fawaz, *Merchants*, pp. 81–2.

18. Kassir, *Beyrouth*, p. 133.

19. Derek Hopwood, *The Russian Presence in Syria and Palestine 1843–1914: Church and Politics in the Near East* (Oxford, 1969), p. 15.

20. Allan Cunningham, *Early Correspondence*, p. 137, Wood to Ponsonby, 14 Oct. 1839; C. E. Farah, *Arabs and Ottomans: A Chequered Relationship* (Istanbul, 2002), p. 228.

21. Ristelhuber, pp. 147, 148; Salibi, *A House of Many Mansions*, p. 113; Chevallier, p. 249.

22. C. B. Elliott, II, 217, 218, 222; Guys, II, 17; Farah, *Arabs and Ottomans*, p. 214.

23. Joseph Hajjar, *L'Europe et les destinées du Proche Orient*, 4 vols. (Damascus, 1988), I, 160, 164–5, dispatch of French consul Duhamel, 11 Nov. 1835.

24. Fawaz, *Merchants*, p. 37.

25. Kassir, *Beyrouth*, p. 135.

26. William Turner, II, 55; Olin, *Travels*, II, 460–62.

27. Edward Napier, I, 86; Schroeder, II, 159–60.

28. E. B. Barker, II, 2–3; Issawi, *Fertile Crescent*, p. 87.

29. Chevallier, p. 204.

30. Farah, *Arabs and Ottomans*, p. 153; Ussama Makdisi, *The Culture of Sectarianism: Community, History and Violence in Nineteenth-Century Ottoman Lebanon* (Berkeley, 2000), pp. 54–5, 193.

31. Sir Charles Napier, II, 303, 306, 308.

32. Farah, *Arabs and Ottomans*, pp. 140–42; Allan Cunningham, *Early Correspondence*, pp. 143, 147.

33. Edward Napier, I, 87n, 88.

34. Ibid., I, 93.

35. Durand-Viel, II, 232.

36. Williams, pp. 159, 182–90; Farah, *Arabs and Ottomans*, p. 150.

37. Sir Charles Napier, I, 119, report of 7 Oct. 1840; W. P. Hunter, I, 175, 218, II, 306–7; Durand-Viel, II, 232, 235.

38. Chevallier, p. 52.

39. C. W. M. van de Velde, *Narrative of a Journey through Syria and Palestine in 1851 and 1852*, 2 vols. (1854), I, 62.

40. Carlisle, p. 220, 19 Dec. 1853.

41. Flaubert, *Voyage*, pp. 328–9; Patrick Cabanel, ed., *Une France en Méditerranée: écoles, langue et culture française* (2006), pp. 67, 90, 208–11 and *passim*.

42. Fouad C. Debbas, *Beirut our Memory* (2nd rev. edn, Beirut, 1986), pp. 143–4.
43. F. A. Neale, *Eight Years in Syria, Palestine and Asia Minor from 1842 to 1850*, 2 vols. (1851), I, 209, 211; Kassir, *Beyrouth*, p. 195.
44. Kamel, p. 141.
45. Neale, I, 220–1, 225, 249.
46. Ibid., I, 214.
47. A. P. Terhune, *Syria from the Saddle* (1897), p. 19.
48. Gregory M. Wortabet, *Syria, and the Syrians: or, Turkey in the Dependencies*, 2 vols. (1856), I, 35–7, 40, 43; Neale, I, 209, 247.
49. Chevallier, p. 196.
50. Allan Cunningham, *Early Correspondence*, p. 243, to Ponsonby, 17 May 1841.
51. Ussama Makdisi, pp. 37–8.
52. Hurewitz, I, 284; Engin Akarli, *The Long Peace: Ottoman Lebanon 1861–1920* (Berkeley, 1993), pp. 19, 20, 21, 28; Ussama Makdisi, pp. 79–80.
53. Ussama Makdisi, pp. 91–2, 224.
54. Ibid., pp. 115, 118, 135, 138–9; Leila Fawaz, *An Occasion for War: Civil Conflict in Lebanon and Damascus in 1860* (1994), pp. 54, 62.
55. Akarli, p. 30; Fawaz, *Merchants*, p. 24.
56. Debbas Archives, Beirut (henceforward referred to as DA), journal of Madame de Perthuis, 27 Apr., 27, 29 May, 1, 2 June 1860. I am grateful to Robert Debbas for permission to consult the journal.
57. Fawaz, *Occasion*, p. 75; DA, Perthuis journal, 23, 25 June 1860.
58. Fawaz, *Occasion*, pp. 132–4.
59. DA, 'Autobiographie de Dimitri Youssef Debbas', f. 56, consulted by kind permission of Robert Debbas.
60. Fawaz, *Occasion*, pp. 48–9, 51, 131.
61. Antoine Hokayem, *Les Provinces arabes de l'Empire Ottoman aux archives du Ministère des Affaires Etrangères de France 1793–1918* (Beirut, 1988), pp. 337, 386, 388.
62. Ussama Makdisi, pp. 150, 153, 157; Fawaz, *Occasion*, p. 205.
63. Fawaz, *Merchants*, pp. 112–13; DA, Perthuis journal, 9 May, 9 July 1861.
64. Akarli, pp. 40–41, 45, 58, 71; John P. Spagnolo, *France and Ottoman Lebanon 1861–1914* (1977), pp. 46, 74, 66; Fawaz, *Occasion*, pp. 107, 118, 194, 203, 205.

Chapter 7: Alexandria: Khedives and Consuls

1. Sammarco, pp. 133–5; Sabry, pp. 208, 221; Ilbert, I, 142
2. Anouar Louca, *Voyageurs et écrivains français en Egypte* (Cairo, 1956), p. 282; cf. Reimer, p. 143; Eustace Murray, *The Roving Englishman in Turkey: Sketches from Life* (1855), pp. 39 (claiming that British consuls can cause 'almost any amount of mischief unchecked'), 42, 50–51.
3. Nubar Pacha, pp. 171, 343.
4. Ilbert, I, 115.

5. Reimer, p. 115.
6. Ibid., p. 146; Khaled Fahmy, 'Towards a social history of modern Alexandria', in Anthony Hirst and Michael Silk, eds., *Alexandria, Real and Imagined* (Aldershot, 2009), p. 294.
7. Sabry, pp. 147, 218.
8. Mansel, *Constantinople*, pp. 283, 286–7.
9. Reimer, pp. 130–31.
10. Middle East Centre, St Antony's College, Oxford (henceforward referred to as MEC), GB 165 0246, petition of 8 Feb. 1864.
11. Gabriel Baer, *Studies in the Social History of Modern Egypt* (Chicago, 1969), pp. 192–9 (similar schemes had already been aborted in 1861); Sabry, pp. 39, 231.
12. Toledano, pp. 34, 127, 145, 147, 198; Benedetti, II, 208.
13. Toledano, pp. 52, 83–8, 131.
14. Ross, p. 172, 7 May 1852.
15. Toledano, pp. 59, 63, 121, 280.
16. Sabry, p. 37, dispatch of French consul, 2 Oct. 1854; Sammarco, p. 21, dispatch of Austrian consul, 31 July 1854.
17. Ilbert, I, 39; Nubar Pacha, p. 66.
18. Toledano, p. 133.
19. Landes, p. 135, Dervieu to André, 27 Mar. 1863.
20. Sabry, pp. 20, 43–44, 223, Bulwer letter, 9 Aug. 1864.
21. Ghislain de Diesbach, *Ferdinand de Lesseps* (2004), pp. 41, 43, 119, 124.
22. Landes, pp. 224, 315; Diesbach, pp. 143, 154, 241.
23. Landes, p. 88n.
24. Sacré and Outrebon, p. 70.
25. John Ninet, *Lettres d'Egypte 1879–1882*, ed. Anouar Louca (1979), p. 163, letter of 18 Sept. 1881.
26. Lucien Basch, 'Les jardins des morts', *Mediterraneans*, 8 (2006), p. 366.
27. Sabry, p. 221, dispatch of French consul, 19 Nov. 1865.
28. Daniel J. Grange, *L'Italie et la Méditerranée 1896–1911*, 2 vols. (Rome, 1994), I, 516, 521n.
29. Laurence Grafftey-Smith, *Bright Levant* (1970), pp. 32–3.
30. Ilbert, I, 117.
31. François Charles-Roux, *Souvenirs diplomatiques* (1956), p. 220.
32. Mohamed Awad and Sahar Hamouda, *The Zoghebs: An Alexandrian Saga* (Alexandria, 2005), pp. 9, 37, 59, 75, 122 and *passim*.
33. Ilbert, I, 158.
34. Landes, p. 125; Reimer, p. 114.
35. Ilbert, I, 37; Landes, p. 85.
36. Ilbert, I, 45–6.
37. Stephen Halliday, *The Great Stink of London* (1998), *passim*.
38. Ilbert, I, 126, 186; Sacré and Outrebon, pp. 69, 74, 77.
39. E. de Kay, *Sketches of Turkey in 1831 and 1832* (New York, 1833), p. 287.
40. Cole, pp. 198, 199, 202; Kusel Bey, pp. 61–3.
41. Reimer, pp. 143–4.
42. Ilbert, I, 114.

43. Achille Biovès, *Français et Anglais en Egypte 1881–1882* (1910), pp. 130, 150; Laurent Dornel, 'Cosmopolitisme et xenophobie: Français et Italiens à Marseille 1870–1914', in *Cahiers de la Méditerranée*, 67 (Dec. 2003), p. 249n.
44. Ilbert, I, 183, 206.
45. Charles Royle, *The Egyptian Campaigns 1882 to 1885* (rev. edn, 1900), p. 7.
46. Sabry, p. 210; Reimer, p. 128.
47. Nubar Pacha, p. 354.
48. Landes, p. 242.
49. Nubar Pacha, p. 251.
50. Landes, pp. 157–8, 299.
51. Ibid., pp. 189, 286.
52. Ibid., pp. 311, 312.
53. Edwin de Leon, *Egypt under its Khedives* (1882), pp. 222–4; Ilbert, I, 176.
54. Ilbert, I, 180, 196; Marie-Cécile Navet-Grenillet, *Penelope Delta et Alexandrie: une femme grecque à la confluence des langues et des cultures* (unpublished thesis, Montpellier University, 1998), p. 309; *Cahiers d'Alexandrie*, série II, fasc 2, 1964, p. 87n; Charles-Roux, *Souvenirs*, pp. 218–19.
55. Godolli and Giacomelli, p. 16; Gaston Zananiri, *Entre mer et désert: mémoires* (1996), p. 51.
56. Personal communication, John Nahman, 20 Sept. 2008.
57. Ilbert, I, 56–7; Zananiri, p. 52; E. M. Forster, 'Cotton from the outside', in id., *Alexandria: A History and a Guide: And Pharos and Pharillon* (2004 edn), pp. 234–6.
58. Reimer, p. 127.
59. Pierre Giffard, *Les Français en Egypte* (1883), p. 59.
60. Gabriel Charmes, *Cinq mois au Caire et dans la basse Egypte* (1880), pp. 23–4; A. B. de Guerville, *La Nouvelle Egypte* (1905), p. 10.
61. Ilbert, I, 82; Mira el-Azhary Sonbol, ed., *Beyond the Exotic: Women's Histories in Islamic Societies* (Syracuse, NY, 2005), p. 203.
62. Alexander Scholch, *Egypt for the Egyptians! The Socio-Political Crisis in Egypt 1878–1882* (Oxford, 1981), p. 74; W. S. Blunt, *Secret History of the English Occupation of Egypt* (1907), p. 46.
63. Godolli and Giacomelli, p. 34.
64. Sabry, p. 197.
65. Ilbert, I, 208.
66. MEC, GB 165 0293, Sir Richard Vaux, 'Egyptian and other episodes, personal, political and legal' (1941), f. 111.
67. Ilbert, I, 139; Reimer, p. 153.
68. Godolli and Giacomelli, p. 21.
69. Sadgrove, *Egyptian Theatre*, pp. 43, 68–70, 129, 139, 143.
70. Landes, p. 128; Polk and Chambers, p. 287n.
71. Blunt, *Secret History*, p. 178.
72. Ninet, pp. 58, 60, 1 July 1879; Scholch, pp. 96–8; cf. Sir Charles Rivers Wilson, GCMG, CB, *Chapters from My Official Life* (1916), p. 137, letter of 22 June 1878 on 'the Prince Hereditaire': 'This one is an immense improvement in every way on his august father, and I am gradually coming to the opinion that the substitute of the one for the other is the only way out of the Egyptian difficulty.'

73. Flaubert, *Correspondance*, I, 528, letter of 17 Nov. 1849 to Madame Flaubert; Ninet, pp. 52, 97, 15 June 1879, 1 Dec. 1880.
74. *Mediterraneans*, 8 (2006), p. 83.
75. Scholch, p. 341; Blunt, *Secret History*, pp. 131, 139.
76. Cole, pp. 204–5; Scholch, pp. 23, 44, 62.
77. Blunt, *Secret History*, pp. 47–8.
78. Ninet, pp. 184–5, 23 May 1882.
79. Michael Llewellyn Smith, *Athens: A Cultural and Literary History* (2004), p. 143.
80. Navet-Grenillet, p. 649; Jacques Hassoun, *Alexandrie et autres récits* (2001), pp. 223–7; Ninet, p. 122, 25 Mar. 1881; one of the Menasce had already paid off the Greek colony in 1880.
81. Robert Ilbert and Ilias Yannakakis, *Alexandrie 1860–1960: un modèle éphémère de convivialité: communautés et identité cosmopolite* (1992), p. 245.
82. Cole, p. 244; Sabry, p. 208; Ilbert, I, 143, 425.
83. Scholch, p. 159.
84. Ibid., p. 193.
85. Ibid., p. 203.
86. Ibid., pp. 231–2.
87. David Nicholls, *The Lost Prime Minister: A Life of Sir Charles Dilke* (1995), pp. 101–2.
88. Paul Auchterlonie, 'A Turk of the West. Sir Edgar Vincent's career in Egypt and the Ottoman Empire', *British Journal of Middle Eastern Studies*, 27, 1 (2000), p. 51; Roy Jenkins, *Gladstone* (1995), p. 507; Richard Shannon, *Gladstone: Heroic Minister 1865–1898* (2000 edn), pp. 298, 303.
89. Shannon, p. 302.
90. Major-General Sir Alexander Bruce Tulloch, *Recollections of Forty Years' Service* (1903), pp. 250–52.
91. Dardaud, p. 670.
92. Royle, pp. 36, 38.
93. Cole, p. 245.
94. Blunt, *Secret History*, p. 286.
95. Royle, p. 40.
96. Sir Edward Malet, *Egypt 1879–1883* (1907), pp. 365, 371, 372, 29 May 1882.
97. Malet, pp. 434, 437, 8 June 1882; Ninet, p. 188, 11 June 1882; Royle, p. 42.
98. Blunt, *Secret History*, pp. 257, 260, Ahmed Ratib to Arabi, 22 Feb. 1882, Mohammed Zafir to Arabi, 22 Feb. 1882; Royle, p. 57.
99. Blunt, *Secret History*, p. 306; Scholch, p. 286.
100. John Philip, *Reminiscences of Gibraltar, Egypt and the Egyptian War* (Aberdeen, 1893), p. 130.
101. Ninet, p. 187, 12 June 1882; Royle, p. 45.
102. Cole, pp. 254–5, 258; Reimer, pp. 177–8.
103. Blunt, *Secret History*, p. 326, letter from Sabunji, 11 June 1882.
104. Ibid., p. 311.
105. Ibid., p. 314; W. S. Blunt, *Gordon at Khartoum* (1911), pp. 551, 552 (letter of July 1883 to Lady Anne Blunt), 556, 557.
106. Royle, pp. 46–52, 55.

107. Ninet, pp. 187–8, 12 June 1882; Malet, p. 402, 11 June 1882; Kusel Bey, pp. 72, 74, 176; Cole, pp. 254–5, 281; Reimer, p. 172; E. E. Farman, *Egypt and its Betrayal* (1908), pp. 304, 306.

108. Malet, p. 404, 12 June 1882; Royle, p. 56; Scholch, p. 250.

109. Royle, p. 56; B. Girard, *Souvenirs maritimes 1881–1883: journal de bord* (1895), pp. 150–52, 10, 11, 13 June 1882.

110. Malet, p. 422, 17 June; Kusel Bey, p. 76; Scholch, p. 335.

111. Scholch, pp. 246, 254.

112. Sir Walter Frederick Miéville, KCMG, *Under Queen and Khedive: The Autobiography of an Anglo-Egyptian Official* (1899), p. 89, 9 July; Royle, p. 59.

113. Royle, p. 58.

114. Blunt, *Secret History*, p. 317: from his smart dress and genial personality, the Admiral was known as 'the swell of the ocean'.

115. Ibid., p. 379; Scholch, pp. 261, 264.

116. Girard, pp. 152–3, 10–14 July 1882; Diesbach, p. 330.

117. Royle, p. 63.

118. Kusel Bey, pp. 199–201; Tulloch, p. 276; Ilbert, I, 226; Royle, p. 85.

119. Ninet, p. 189, 15 July; Royle, p. 87.

120. Royle, p. 94.

121. Royle, p. 131.

122. Ilbert, I, 228–9; Royle, p. 102; MEC, 'Plan croquis indiquant les maisons qui ont été brulées après le bombardement du 11 juillet, dressé par l'ingénieur Ulisse Calvi, Alexandrie le 11 août 1882'.

123. Royle, p. 95.

124. A. G. Hulme Beaman, *Twenty Years in the Near East* (1898), p. 46.

125. Admiral Lord Charles Beresford, *Memoirs*, 2 vols. (1914), I, 191, letter of 25 July 1882.

126. Philip, p. 34.

127. Kusel Bey, pp. 209–10; Charles Chaille-Long, *My Life in Four Continents*, 2 vols. (1912), I, 265.

128. Ilbert, I, 231.

129. Royle, p. 69n. Visitors to Athineos on the Alexandria corniche – a survival of Alexandria art deco of the 1930s – can admire some of these photographs: they have been hung on the walls as a nationalist statement by the Nassar family, who acquired the restaurant from the Egyptian government in 1970, after the departure of its Greek founders, the Athineos family.

130. Ibid., pp. 89, 104–5; cf. Admiral Sir Dudley de Chair, *The Sea is Strong* (1961), pp. 37–9.

131. Colonel J. F. Maurice, *Military History of the Campaign of 1882 in Egypt* (1887), pp. 20, 22; Royle, p. 105.

132. Kusel Bey, p. 216; Arnold Wright, *Twentieth Century Impressions of Egypt* (1909), p. 459; Beresford, I, 191–2, letter of 25 July 1882.

133. Ilbert, I, 232n; Tulloch, p. 286.

134. Blunt, *Secret History*, pp. 379–81, 387–8.

135. Chaille-Long, I, 263; Ninet, p. 190, 13 July 1882.

136. Jack Fisher, *Fear God and Dread Nought: The Correspondance of Admiral of the*

Fleet Lord Fisher of Kilverstone, 3 vols. (1952–6), I, 107, letters of 20, 31 July 1882; Beresford, I, 180; Royle, p. 100.
137. Royle, p. 111; Blunt, *Secret History*, p. 389.
138. Royle, p. 109.
139. Shannon, p. 304.
140. Royle, p. 132.
141. Gilbert Delanoue, *Moralistes et politiques musulmans dans l'Egypte du xixe siècle*, 2 vols. (Cairo, 1982), II, 504, 515, 526, 517.
142. Royle, p. 132.
143. Ibid., p. 187.
144. Maurice, p. 22; Beresford, I, 182; Royle, p. 198.
145. Malet, p. 455, letter to Lord Granville, 18 Sept. 1882.
146. Esther Zimmerli Hardman, *From Camp de César to Cleopatra's Pool* (Alexandria, 2008), p. xxx; Coles Pasha, *Recollections and Reflections* (1918), p. 21.
147. ELIA, Cavafy Archive, John to Constantine Cavafy, 12 Aug., 17 Sept. 1882.
148. Philip, pp. 122–4.
149. ELIA, Cavafy Archive, John to Constantine Cavafy, 30 Oct. 1882.
150. ELIA, Cavafy Archive.
151. Shannon, p. 306; Miéville, pp. 90, 95.
152. E. H. D. Moberly Bell, *The Life and Letters of C. F. Moberly Bell* (1927), pp. 25, 32.
153. Joseph Lehmann, *All Sir Garnett* (1964), p. 319.
154. Ninet, p. 109, 14 July 1882.
155. Ilbert, I, 247–8, 295; Coles Pasha, pp. 24, 41.

Chapter 8: Alexandria: British Years

1. Roger Owen, *Lord Cromer* (2002), pp. 177, 216, 224, 241, 251; Shannon, p. 317.
2. Eça de Queiros, *Les Anglais en Egypte* (2008), pp. 8, 9, 11, 36, 42, 47, 83, 91.
3. Guerville, p. 134; Queiros, p. 91; Michael Haag, *Alexandria: City of Memory* (2004), p. 103.
4. Ilbert, I, 258.
5. Butler, p. 184.
6. Ilbert, II, 686; *Le Phare d'Alexandrie*, 11 Dec. 1898.
7. Guerville, p. 127.
8. Abbas Hilmi II, *The Last Khedive of Egypt: Memoirs*, ed. Amira Sonbol (Cairo, 2006), p. 89.
9. Ibid., p. 103.
10. Ilbert and Yannakakis, pp. 17, 34, presents the case for a cosmopolitan city; cf. E. Breccia, *Alexandria ad Aegyptum* (Bergamo, 1914), p. 22, and John Murray, *Handbook for Travellers in Turkey in Asia*, 2 vols. (4th rev. edn, 1878), I, 60: 'The races have nothing that joins them; with the exception of commerce there are no relations between them; everyone lives in a state of permanent trepidation of each other.'

11. S. E. Poffandi, *Indicateur égyptien* (Alexandria, 1892), pp. 4–5; Abbas Hilmi, p. 177.

12. Ilbert, I, 472, 480.

13. Sahar Hamouda, *Omar Toussoun: Prince of Alexandria* (Alexandria, 2005), pp. 11, 23, 38, 50, 56, 89 and *passim*.

14. Coles Pasha, p. 43.

15. Rees, pp. 191–3.

16. Ilbert, I, 423–4.

17. *Mediterraneans*, 8 (2006), p. 132.

18. J. K. L. Goddard, *48!* (Tunbridge Wells, 2003), pp. 166–7, 171, 220–21, 310 and *passim*. He also had four night watchmen, ten watchdogs, and guards for special occasions, 'supplied by the security department of the Alexandria governorate'.

19. Gabriel Baer, *Studies*, p. 202.

20. *La Bourse égyptienne*, commemorative articles 6 Jan. 1940, and personal information supplied by Chakhour's granddaughter Madame Fernande Nissaire, Alexandria, 10 Dec. 2008; Poffandi, pp. 160–61; Ilbert, I, 469n.

21. Ilbert, I, 282, 286.

22. Ibid., I, 288; Gabriel Baer, *Studies*, pp. 206–8.

23. Wright, pp. 427, 443.

24. *Mediterraneans*, 8 (2006), p. 29. Of 84 members elected to the administrative council between 1912 and 1956, 49 per cent were English, 19 per cent Muslim Egyptians.

25. Zananiri, p. 49; Union Club, Alexandria, jubilee brochure, Alexandria, 1954, *passim*.

26. Poffandi, pp. 170–81.

27. Ilbert, I, 260, 482.

28. Ibid., I, 361.

29. Guerville, pp. 8–10.

30. Godolli and Giacomelli, p. 34; Wright, pp. 424, 436.

31. Ilbert, I, 326, 335–6, 339, 353; Wright, p. 436.

32. Basch, pp. 364–373; cf. the life-size statue of George Averoff, surrounded by four goddesses, erected in 1896 in the courtyard of the Orthodox patriarchate by the Greek community, whose president he was in 1885–99.

33. R. Storrs, *Orientations* (def. edn, 1943), p. 43.

34. Henri el-Kayem, *Par grand vent d'est avec rafles: mémoires d'un Alexandrin* (1999), pp. 66–7.

35. Samir W. Raafat, *Cairo, the Glory Years: Who Built What, When, Why and for Whom* (Alexandria, 2003), pp. 22–3.

36. Zimmerli Hardman, pp. 56–8.

37. Haag, *Alexandria*, pp. 90, 92, 111.

38. Jacques Hassoun, *Juifs d'Egypte: images et textes* (1984), pp. 161, 196.

39. Ilbert, II, 697.

40. Magda Wassef, ed., *Egypte: cent ans de cinéma* (1995), pp. 18–20, 62–3. Later, Alexandria had the Institut Cinématographique Egyptien, started in 1932 by Mohammed Bayoumi.

41. Ilbert, I, 446, 455; Haag, *Alexandria*, p. 158.

42. Ilbert, II, 682–3.
43. Sahar Hamouda and Colin Clement, *Victoria College: A History Revealed* (Cairo, 2004), pp. 15–17, 35.
44. Ibid., pp. 39, 43.
45. Ibid., pp. 17, 28, 51, 55, 56–7.
46. Hamouda and Clement, pp. 55–7; *La Réforme illustrée*, 29 Feb. 1948.
47. Hamouda and Clement, pp. 11–12.
48. Ilbert, I, 458, 466.
49. Breccia, p. 2.
50. MEC, 165 0246, letter of 31 Jan. 1906 from Mr Rowlatt.
51. Names taken from a petition against a revision of the Treaty of Sèvres in 1921: ELIA, MSS 124.
52. Grafftey-Smith, pp. 34–5.
53. Wright, p. 321.
54. Navet-Grenillet, p. 500.
55. Ibid., pp. 473–4.
56. Ibid., p. 337.
57. Ibid., pp. 353, 474, 867–71.
58. Michael Haag, *Vintage Alexandria: Photographs of the City 1860–1960* (Cairo, 2008), p. 51; *Le Livre d'or du journal La Réforme* (Alexandria, 1945), pp. 121, 184.
59. Navet-Grenillet, pp. 525, 595.
60. Katerina Trimi, 'La famille Benakis: un paradigme de la bourgeoisie grecque alexandrine', in Meropi Anastassiadou and Bernard Heyberger, eds., *Figures anonymes, figures d'élite: pour une anatomie de l'Homo ottomanicus* (Istanbul, 1999), pp. 83–102; Navet-Grenillet, pp. 614–15; *Mediterraneans*, 8 (2006), p. 93.
61. Herwig Maehler, 'The Mouseion and Cultural Identity', in Anthony Hirst and Michael Silk, eds., *Alexandria, Real and Imagined* (Aldershot, 2009), pp. 3, 7.
62. Navet-Grenillet, pp. 627, 633, 637–8, 661.
63. Information kindly communicated by Alex Zannas, 20 Feb. 2009.
64. Navet-Grenillet, pp. 565–6, 798, 846; Marc Terrades, *Le Drame de l'Héllenisme: Ion Dragoumis (1878–1920) et la question nationale en Grèce au début du xxe siècle* (2005), pp. 128–9.
65. Ilbert, II, 615; John Carswell, 'The Greeks in the East. Alexandria and Islam', in Stephen Vernoit, ed., *Discovering Islamic Art: Scholars, Collectors and Collections 1850–1950* (1999), p. 139. Other Alexandria Greeks, such as the Glymenopoulo family and Helena and Anthony Stathiotis, left their Egyptian antiquities to the National Archaeological Museum in Athens.
66. George Savidis, ed., *C. P. Cavafy: Collected Poems* (rev. edn, 1992), p. 275; Haag, *Alexandria*, p. 66; Robert Liddell, *Cavafy* (2002 edn), p. 37.
67. Liddell, *Cavafy*, pp. 19, 21, 27, 33.
68. Savidis, pp. 28, 44, 102.
69. Ibid., pp. 76, 144, 157, 193, 199
70. *Mediterraneans*, 8 (2006), p. 101.
71. I am grateful for this point to Cavafy's latest translator, Evangelos Sahpeyroglou.
72. Savidis, pp. 19, 107.

73. Ilbert, II, 614, 631.
74. Ibid., II, 633; Arthur Goldschmidt Jr, *The Egyptian Nationalist Party 1892–1919* (1968), pp. 315, 321.
75. Schmitt, p. 177, report of 15 Sept. 1806.
76. Sir Charles Napier, II, 15n.
77. Prisse d'Avennes, *Mémoires secrets sur la cour d'Egypte* (1930), pp. 29, 30.
78. Jabarti, IX, 162–3, 260; Walter G. Andrews and Mehmet Kalpakli, *The Age of Beloveds: Love and the Beloved in Early Modern Ottoman and European Culture and Society* (2005), p. 237 and *passim*.
79. Savidis, pp. 38, 122; Haag, *Alexandria*, pp. 41–2, 50.
80. E. M. Forster, *Selected Letters*, ed. Mary Lago, 2 vols. (1983), I, 269, to Syed Ross Masood, 8 Sept. 1917.
81. Savidis, pp. 57, 171.
82. C. P. Cavafy, *Collected Poems* (Oxford, 2007), pp. xxix–xx, xxxii.
83. Coles Pasha, p. 41. Twenty years later, in a letter to Henry Miller, Durrell would call them 'certainly the loveliest and most world-weary women in the world'.
84. Charmes, *Cinq mois*, p. 25.
85. Hector Dinning, *By-Ways on Service: Notes from an Australian Journal* (1918), pp. 140–43.
86. Butler, p. 152.
87. Ilbert, I, 459n.
88. Gabriel Baer, *Studies*, p. 176.
89. Judith E. Tucker, *Women in Nineteenth Century Egypt* (1985), pp. 151, 154, 191.
90. Zananiri, p. 50.
91. John Murray, *Handbook* (1840), p. 19.
92. Shadia el-Sousssi, 'Borrowed words from Italian in Alexandrian Arabic', in Bibliotheca Alexandrina, *Alex-Med Newsletter*, 7 (July 2007), p. 9.
93. Edgar Morin, *Vidal et les siens* (1989), p. 28.
94. Maurice Pernot, *Rapport sur un voyage d'étude à Constantinople, en Egypte et en Turquie d'Asie (janvier–août 1912)* (1912), p. 334.
95. Ibid., pp. 48, 283.
96. Jean Riffier, 'Les Œuvres françaises et l'invention de la Syrie', in Bernard Delpal et al., eds., *France–Levant, de la fin du xviie siècle à la Première Guerre mondiale* (2005), p. 234.
97. Gaston Deschamps, *A Constantinople* (1913), p. 5; Leyla Duran to the author, Istanbul, 1996; Gilles Veinstein, ed., *Salonique 1850–1918: la ville des juifs et le réveil des Balkans* (1992), p. 83.
98. Valentin Chirol, *Fifty Years in a Changing World* (1927), pp. 25, 29.
99. Interview with Marcienne de Zogheb, 6 Feb. 2006.
100. Iri M. Kupferschmidt, 'Who needed department stores in Egypt? From Orosdi Back to Omar effendi', *International Journal of Middle East Studies*, 43, 2 (Mar. 2007), 175–92, pp. 177, 180.
101. Henri Nahum, *Juifs de Smyrne, xixe–xxe siècle* (1997), pp. 97, 104, 106–12, 124; Joel Beinin, *The Dispersion of Egyptian Jewry: Culture, Politics and the Formation of a Modern Diaspora* (Cairo, 2005), pp. 46, 50.

102. Quoted in a brochure on the exhibition 'The Ottomans in Paris', Ottoman Bank Museum, Istanbul, Oct.–Dec. 2008, *passim*.
103. Ilbert, I, 96, 465; Grange, I, 507, 531, 691, dispatch of Bottesini, 9 Jan. 1898; Marc Kober, *Entre Nil et sable: écrivains d'Egypte d'expression française* (1999), *passim*.
104. Abbas Hilmi, pp. 276–7.

Chapter 9: Beirut: The Jewel in the Crown of the Padishah

1. Akarli, pp. 43, 44, 51, 78; Spagnolo, *France and Ottoman Lebanon*, pp. 163, 290.
2. Akarli, pp. 60, 99, 152, 194; Spagnolo, *France and Ottoman Lebanon*, pp. 114, 210.
3. Chevallier, pp. 127 (dispatch of the French consul, 20 Nov. 1869), 289–90; Spagnolo, *France and Ottoman Lebanon*, p. 141.
4. Schmitt, p. 442.
5. Bernard Heyberger, 'Livres et pratique de la lecture chez les chrétiens (Syrie Liban) xviie–xviiie siècles', in Frédéric Hitzel, ed., *Livres et lecture dans le monde ottoman* (1999), pp. 211, 214, 216.
6. Farah, *Arabs and Ottomans*, p. 53.
7. Dagmar Glass and Geoffrey Roper, 'The printing of Arabic books in the Arab world', in Geoffrey Roper, ed., *Middle Eastern Languages and the Print Revolution* (Westhofen, 2002), pp. 193–4; Franck Mermier, *Le Livre et la ville: Beyrouth et l'édition arabe* (2005), 32.
8. George N. Atiyeh, 'The book in the modern Arab world', in id., ed., *The Book in the Islamic World* (Albany, 1995), p. 42.
9. James A. Field Jr, *America and the Mediterranean World 1776–1882* (Princeton, 1969), pp. 97, 286.
10. Finnie, p. 199; Field, p. 179.
11. Kassir, *Beyrouth*, p. 223.
12. Jens Hanssen, *Fin de Siècle Beirut: The Making of an Ottoman Provincial Capital* (New York, 2005), pp. 171, 185.
13. Ibid., p. 138; Issawi, *Fertile Crescent*, p. 231.
14. Mermier, p. 28; Louis Bertrand, *Le Mirage oriental* (1913), pp. 238, 318.
15. Hanssen, *Fin de Siècle Beirut*, p. 185; Kassir, *Beyrouth*, pp. 210, 213, 238.
16. Chantal Verdeil, 'Les écoles d'orient: le réseau scolaire congréganiste en Syrie', in Bernard Delpal et al., eds., *France–Levant, de la fin du xviie siècle à la Première Guerre mondiale* (2005), pp. 145–66; Riffier, p. 234.
17. Kassir, *Beyrouth*, p. 255.
18. Anne Mollenhauer, 'The Central Hall House: regional commonalities and local specificities: a comparison between Beirut and al-Salt', in Jens Hanssen, Thomas Philipp and Stefan Weber, eds., *The Empire in the City: Arab Provincial Capitals in the Late Ottoman Empire* (Beirut, 2002), pp. 275–96; Nada Sehnaoui, *L'Occidentalisation de la vie quotidienne à Beyrouth 1860–1914* (Beirut, 2002), pp. 95, 102, 119, 135, 152; Kassir, *Beyrouth*, pp. 248–52.

19. Hanssen, *Fin de Siècle Beirut*, pp. 41, 88; Hasan Kayali, *Arabs and Young Turks: Ottomanism, Arabism and Islamism in the Ottoman Empire 1908–1918* (1997), p. 28.

20. Chevallier, p. 292.

21. Jens Hanssen, 'Practices of Integration', in Jens Hanssen, Thomas Philipp and Stefan Weber, eds., *The Empire in the City: Arab Provincial Capitals in the Late Ottoman Empire* (Beirut, 2002), p. 69.

22. John P. Spagnolo, ed., *Problems of the Modern Middle East in Historical Perspective* (Reading, 1992), pp. 12–13, 14, 21, 24.

23. Jens Hanssen, 'Your Beirut is on my desk: Ottomanizing Beirut under Sultan Abdulhamid II 1876–1909', in H. Sarkis and P. Rowe, eds., *Projecting Beirut* (Munich, 1998), pp. 47–9, 55–6.

24. Kassir, *Beyrouth*, pp. 172–3.

25. May Davie, *Beyrouth 1825–1975: un siècle et demi d'urbanisme* (Beirut, 2001), p. 59.

26. Samir Khalaf, *Heart of Beirut: Reclaiming the Bourj* (2006), p. 68.

27. Hanssen, *Fin de Siècle Beirut*, p. 246; Sawsan Agha Kassab and Khaled Omar Tadmouri, *Beirut and the Sultan: 200 Photographs from the Albums of Sultan Abdul Hamid II* (Beirut, 2003), pp. 41, 59, 69, 161.

28. Hanssen, *Fin de Siècle Beirut*, pp. 87–92, 101; Fawaz, *Merchants*, p. 72; photographs in Debbas, pp. 18–40.

29. Albert Hourani and Nadim Shehadi, eds., *The Lebanese in the World: A Century of Emigration* (1992), pp. 7, 31, 116, 125, 129 and *passim*; Alixa Naff, *Becoming American: The Early Arab Immigrant Experience* (Carbondale, 1985), pp. 78–100; I am grateful for these references to Richard Davenport-Hines.

30. Sawsan and Tadmouri, p. 147.

31. Hanssen, *Fin de Siècle Beirut*, pp. 106, 110, 125.

32. Robert Saliba, *Beirut 1920–1940: Domestic Architecture between Tradition and Modernity* (Beirut, 1998), p. 31.

33. Hanssen, *Fin de Siècle Beirut*, p. 192; DA, Perthuis journal, 20 Sept., 1 Oct. 1860, 1 Jan., 6 Feb. 1861.

34. See for example MEC, GB 0132, diary of Mr Hallward, 9 June 1890: 'At 4 started with to make a round of calls on natives – Soursoks, Twanys and Bustros; they occupy a quarter at the other end of the town we saw mostly only the ladies, some of whom are pleasant enough, they have fine large houses.'

35. Gabriel Charmes, *Voyage en Syrie: impressions et souvenirs* (1891), p. 137.

36. Sehnaoui, p. 174.

37. Kassir, *Beyrouth*, p. 256; Sehnaoui, pp. 31–2.

38. Fawaz, *Merchants*, p. 115.

39. Ohannes Pacha Kouyoumdjian, *Le Liban à la veille et au début de la guerre: mémoires d'un gouverneur 1913–1915* (2003), pp. 48–50; Spagnolo, *France and Ottoman Lebanon*, pp. 211, 240.

40. Michael Johnson, *Class and Client in Beirut* (1986), p. 19.

41. Edward Atiyah, *An Arab Tells his Story: A Study in Loyalties* (1946), p. 5; Fawaz, *Merchants*, p. 42.

42. Atiyah, pp. 3–5, 10–12.

43. Johnson, *Class and Client*, pp. 20–21, 82; Kayali, p. 120; Kassir, *Beyrouth*, pp. 280–81.
44. Atiyah, pp. 28, 41, 48, 51, 63, 132.

Chapter 10: Smyrna: Greeks and Turks

1. Hervé Georgelin, *La Fin de Smyrne: du cosmopolitisme aux nationalismes* (2005), p. 38; Smyrnelis, *Smyrne*, pp. 129–33.
2. Vasilis Colonas, *Greek Architects in the Ottoman Empire (19th–20th Centuries)* (Athens, 2005), p. 95.
3. Eleni Frangakis-Syrett, 'The making of an Ottoman port: the quay of Izmir in the nineteenth century', *Journal of Transport History*, 22, 1 (2001), pp. 23–46.
4. Colonas, p. 98; Kontente, pp. 623–4; Schmidt, *From Anatolia to Indonesia*, p. 73.
5. Paul Eudel, *Constantinople, Smyrne et Athènes: journal de voyage* (1885), pp. 303, 319, 318.
6. Akgerman Collection, Izmir, consulted by kind permission of Mr Onur Akgerman, 31 July 2006.
7. Smyrnelis, *Smyrne*, p. 120; cf. Eudel, p. 302: 'Elle n'a rien de turc à première vue; sa physionomie est plutôt celle d'une ville occidentale.'
8. Schmitt, p. 447.
9. Smyrnelis, *Une ville ottomane plurielle*, p. 137, dispatch of French consul, 27 Mar. 1880.
10. Lt-Col. R. L. Playfair, *Handbook to the Mediterranean: Its Cities, Coast and Islands* (1881), p. 85.
11. Smyrnelis, *Smyrne*, pp. 145, 150–56.
12. George Horton, *The Blight of Asia* (Indianapolis, 1926), p. 105; Elias Petropoulos and Ed Emery, *Songs of the Greek Underworld: The Rebetika Tradition* (2000), pp. 23, 29, 38, 43; cf. *Smyrna before the Catastrophe* (Athens, 1992), p. 70.
13. *Smyrne: Estudiantina nea ionia* (compact disc: Athens, 2003); Petropoulos and Emery, p. 23.
14. Petropoulos and Emery, pp. 16–17; Markos Dragoumis, 'The music of the rebetes', in id., ed., *From Byzantium to Rembetiko* (Kerkyra, 2007), pp. 239–49.
15. Stathis Gauntlett, 'Between orientalism and occidentalism', in Renée Hirschon, ed., *Crossing the Aegean* (Oxford, 2004), p. 251.
16. *Smyrna, Metropolis*, pp. 192–9; Terrades, p. 183n.
17. John Murray, *Handbook* (1878), I, 247.
18. Schmitt, pp. 454–5.
19. Kontente, p. 580.
20. Georgelin, p. 114; Kontente, p. 616.
21. Norman Douglas, *Looking Back* (1934), p. 167.
22. Colonas, pp. 109–10.
23. Kontente, pp. 610–11.
24. *Smyrna, Metropolis*, pp. 67, 75.
25. Kontente, p. 592 and n.

26. *Smyrna, Metropolis*, pp. 84–6.
27. Ibid., pp. 46, 101, 113.
28. Schmitt, p. 351, quoting issue of 26 June 1850.
29. Başar Eryoner Collection, consulted Nov. 2008 by kind permission of Başar Eryoner: cards dated 27 Oct. 1910 and 27 Feb. (unknown year).
30. Charles de Scherzer, *La Province de Smyrne considérée au point de vue géographique, économique et intellectuelle* (Vienne, 1873), p. 77; Kontente, p. 471.
31. *Smyrna before the Catastrophe*, p. 80.
32. Schmidt, *From Anatolia to Indonesia*, p. 45 and *passim*.
33. Scherzer, pp. 125–7.
34. Smyrnelis, *Smyrne*, pp. 126–7.
35. *Shepherd's Oriental Yearbook for 1860* (Smyrna, 1859), pp. 134–44.
36. Schmitt, p. 103.
37. Pinar M. Yarmakli Parmaksiz, 'A Muslim family in infidel Izmir at the turn of the century: the Evliyazades', in Maurits van den Boogert, ed., *Ottoman Izmir* (Istanbul, 2007), pp. 151, 153, 155, 162; Kontente, p. 410.
38. Kontente, pp. 582, 583, 604.
39. Ipek Çalislar, *Latife Hanim* (Istanbul, 2006), pp. 43–5.
40. Schmitt, p. 259; Kontente, pp. 492, 513; Ilhan Tekeli and Selim Ilkin, 'The public works program and the development of technology in the Ottoman Empire in the second half of the nineteenth century', *Turcica*, 28 (1996), p. 214–16.
41. Kontente, p. 610; Horton, p. 104.
42. Georgelin, p. 39, dispatch of 13 Feb. 1882.
43. *Smyrna, Metropolis*, p. 91; Kontente, p. 577.
44. Georgelin, pp. 64–5; Du Camp, p. 38; Kontente, p. 483.
45. Pernot, p. 334.
46. Nahum, *Juifs de Smyrne*, pp. 114, 115, 119.
47. Rev. Joseph K. Greene, *Leavening the Levant* (Boston, 1916), pp. 224–5; Kontente, pp. 591, 593; Georgelin, p. 67; Pernot, p. 265.
48. William Cochran, *Pen and Pencil in Asia Minor; or, Notes from the Levant* (1887), pp. 139, 173.
49. Feroz Ahmad, *From Empire to Republic: Essays on the Late Ottoman Empire and Modern Turkey*, 2 vols. (Istanbul, 2008), I, 108.
50. Kontente, p. 577.
51. Halid Ziya Uşakligil, *Kirk yil. Anilar* (Istanbul, 1987 edn), pp. 99–104, 110, 165; thanks for the translation to Pelin Uysal.
52. Ibid., pp. 125, 127, 226, 259–60.
53. Necati Cumali, *Macédoine 1900 nouvelles*, ed. Faruk Bilici (2007), pp. 34, 192.
54. Uşakligil, pp. 110, 116, 117, 120, 166.
55. Kechriotis, 'The Greeks of Izmir', pp. 66–7, 71; Scherzer, p. 51.
56. Scherzer, p. 67; *Smyrna, Metropolis*, pp. 168–9.
57. Uşakligil, pp. 212–13.
58. Kontente, pp. 603, 619; Livio Missir de Lusignan, *Vie latine de l'Empire Ottoman* (Istanbul, 2004), p. 62.
59. Alessandro Pannuti, *Les Italiens d'Istanbul au xxe siècle* (Istanbul, 2008), p. 232; another French-language weekly, *L'Impartial*, lasted from 1841 to 1915.

60. Schmitt, p. 456.
61. Ibid., p. 453; Kontente, p. 595.
62. Kontente, p. 480.
63. Smyrnelis, *Smyrne*, p. 146.
64. Kontente, pp. 570, 581.
65. Williams, p. 163.
66. Smyrnelis, *Smyrne*, p. 61; *Smyrna, Metropolis*, p. 157; http://www.levantine-heritage.com.
67. Georgelin, pp. 88, 135–7; *Smyrna, Metropolis*, p. 156; Ugur Yeğin, ed., *Once Upon a Time ... Izmir from the Collection of Ugur Goktaş* (Izmir, 2009), pp. 188–9.
68. Kontente, p. 599.
69. A. C. Wratislaw, *A Consul in the East* (1924), p. 85.
70. Nahum, *Juifs de Smyrne*, p. 46.
71. Kontente, p. 613.
72. Schmitt, pp. 344, 346.
73. Ibid., p. 340, dispatch of 8 June 1863; cf. pp. 310, 342.
74. Nahum, *Juifs de Smyrne*, pp. 104, 106, 107, 109.
75. Roderick Beaton, *George Seferis: Waiting for the Angel* (2003), p. 14.
76. Uşakligil, pp. 200, 203, 323.
77. *Smyrna, Metropolis*, pp. 97, 101, 105.
78. See the invoice dated 25 Aug. 1901 reproduced in Kechriotis, 'The Greeks of Izmir', p. 327; Bulent Senoçak, *Levant'in yildizi Izmir* (Izmir, 2003), p. 54.
79. *Smyrna, Metropolis*, pp. 145, 147, 164–5, 168–9.
80. A section of the consular service, functioning from 1875 to 1933. Among its officials were James Elroy Flecker, Reader Bullard and Walter Smart; its jurisdiction was wider than the normal definition of Levant, extending from Meshed to Mogador.
81. MEC, GB 165/0248, diary of Andrew Ryan, 3 Aug. 1895.
82. Smyrnelis, *Smyrne*, p. 172, report of 15 Feb. 1881; Schmitt, pp. 111 (report of Italian consul, 1862), 375 (24 Oct. 1846, report of archbishop); John Murray, *Handbook* (1978), I, 254.
83. *Smyrna, Metropolis*, p. 35.
84. Mihail-Dimitri Sturdza, *Dictionnaire historique et généalogique des grandes familles de Grèce, d'Albanie et de Constantinople* (1983), pp. 224–6; Kontente, p. 463.
85. Willy Sperco, 'Lamartine et son domaine en Asie Mineure', *Revue de France*, 15 Oct. 1938, pp. 1–22.
86. Kontente, pp. 600–601.
87. Louis Gardey, *Voyage du sultan Abd-ul-aziz de Stamboul au Caire* (1865), pp. 219–53; Schmitt, pp. 483–4, based on *Smyrna Mail*, 28 Apr. 1863; Exeter University, Special Collections (henceforward referred to as EUSC), Barker MSS 259, letter of 8 Aug. 1863; Senior, p. 204.
88. Kontente, p. 595.
89. Sturdza, pp. 224–5.
90. Georgelin, pp. 21–2.

91. *Smyrna, Metropolis*, pp. 31, 93–4.
92. Elena Frangakis-Syrett, 'The economic activities of the Greek community of Izmir in the second half of the nineteenth and early twentieth centuries', in D. Gondicas and C. Issawi, eds., *Ottoman Greeks in the Age of Nationalism* (Princeton, 1999), pp. 19, 22, 33, 26.
93. *Smyrna, Metropolis*, p. 120.
94. Colonas, pp. 99, 100, 121.
95. Kontente, p. 621.
96. Elia Mss, 'Report on intellectual and artistic activity', *c.*1921.
97. Georgelin, pp. 91, 94; Kechriotis, 'The Greeks of Izmir', p. 257.
98. Giovanni Salmeri, 'The contribution of Greeks to the local historiography of Smyrna' (unpublished typescript, 2006).
99. Georgelin, pp. 57, 80.
100. Scherzer, pp. 17, 40–41, 43, 44.
101. Georgelin, pp. 25, 30; Kontente, pp. 516, 542.
102. Finkel, p. 471.
103. Kontente, p. 558.
104. Georgelin, p. 102.
105. Kechriotis, 'The Greeks of Izmir', pp. 262–3; *Smyrna, Metropolis*, p. 118.
106. Georgelin, p. 155.
107. Kontente, pp. 605–6; Gary B. Cohen, *The Politics of Ethnic Survival: Germans in Prague 1861–1914* (Princeton, 1981), p. 3; Brigitte Hamann, *Hitler's Vienna* (1999 edn), pp. 105, 178, 247, 264, 275, 298, 316.
108. Georgelin, p. 169; Kechriotis, 'The Greeks of Izmir', p. 240.
109. Kontente, pp. 567, 591n, 629, 635; Jan Schmidt, *Through the Legation Window: Four Essays on Dutch, Dutch Indian and Ottoman History* (Istanbul, 1992), pp. 2–6, 10, 14.
110. Kontente, pp. 525, 531, 539, 549, 631; Nahum, *Juifs de Smyrne*, p. 81; Smyrnelis, *Smyrne*, p. 100.
111. Kontente, p. 620; Nahum, *Juifs de Smyrne*, pp. 137, 139, 155, 234.
112. Georgelin, pp. 158, 161–6.
113. Kontente, p. 592.
114. Unpublished memoirs of R. Lang of the Ottoman Bank (n.d.), consulted by kind permission of Peter Clark, ff. 62, 64.
115. Kontente, pp. 602, 625; Georgelin, p. 127.
116. Kontente, pp. 467, 557, 598–9, 602, 637; Yeğin, p. 143.
117. Uşakligil, pp. 205, 235, 238–9, 281.
118. Kontente, p. 626.
119. Smyrnelis, *Une ville ottomane plurielle*, p. 136.
120. Schmitt, pp. 274–6, 279.
121. Osman Koker, ed., *Bir zamanlar Izmir* (2009), p. 126, postcard of 24 Feb. 1905 from 'Léontine' to 'Georges'.
122. Schmitt, p. 449; Georgelin, pp. 103–5.
123. Georgelin, pp. 103, 108–9, 156–7.
124. Schmitt, p. 371; Vangelis Kechriotis, 'Allons, enfants de la ville! National celebrations and political mobilisation and urban space in Izmir at the turn of the 20th century' (unpublished typescript, *c.*2008), pp. 129–32.

125. Smyrnelis, *Smyrne*, p. 133; Kontente, pp. 560, 640.
126. Nicolas V. Iljine, ed., *Odessa Memories* (Seattle, 2003), pp. xxxiv, 11, 14, 17, 25, 29, 66, 102, 302.

Chapter 11: Drifting Cities

1. A. Goff and Hugh A. Fawcett, *Macedonia: A Plea for the Primitive* (1921), p. 128.
2. A. Griffin Tapp, *Stories of Salonica and the New Crusade* (1922), p. 14.
3. H. Collinson Owen, *Salonica and After: The Sideshow that Ended the War* (1919), pp. 1, 22; Mary A. Walker, *Through Macedonia to the Albanian Lakes* (1864), pp. 34–5.
4. Pierre Loti, *Aziyade* (Livre de Poche, 1970), p. 21.
5. Elias Petropoulos, *La Présence ottomane à Salonique* (Athens, 1980), *passim*; Victor Bérard, *La Macédoine* (1897), pp. 164, 169; G. F. Abbott, *The Tale of a Tour in Macedonia* (1903), p. 29.
6. Paul Risal, *La Ville convoitée: Salonique* (1914), p. 143.
7. Veinstein, *Salonique*, pp. 28–32; Risal, p. 347.
8. Veinstein, *Salonique*, pp. 71, 211, 217; Rena Molho, *Salonica and Istanbul: Social, Political and Cultural Aspects of Jewish Life* (Istanbul, 2005), p. 135.
9. Antoine Scheikevitch, *Hellas? ... Hélas! Souvenirs de Salonique* (1922), p. 12; Edgar Morin, p. 47n; Leon Sciacky, *Farewell to Ottoman Salonica* (Istanbul, 2000), p. 91. Ferdinand Schirza in Istanbul still has some of the Viennese furniture of his father, an Austrian who worked for the Ottoman railways in Salonica before 1912.
10. Wratislaw, p. 212.
11. Veinstein, *Salonique*, pp. 34–5, 171–4; Hélène Desmet-Grégoire, *Cafés d'orient revisités* (1997), pp. 83, 86.
12. Veinstein, *Salonique*, p. 107.
13. Risal, p. 247.
14. Veinstein, *Salonique*, pp. 187, 189; Sam Levy, *Salonique à la fin du xixe siècle* (Istanbul, 2000), pp. 26–8.
15. Mark Mazower, *Salonica, City of Ghosts: Christians, Muslims and Jews 1430–1950* (2004), p. 250.
16. Veinstein, *Salonique*, pp. 105, 116.
17. Elias Petropoulos, *Old Salonica* (Athens, 1980), pp. 66–8.
18. I. Canudo, *Combats d'Orient* (1917), p. 78.
19. Sciacky, p. 37–8; Risal, pp. 251–3; Apostolos E. Vacalopoulos, *A History of Thessaloniki* (Thessaloniki, 1972), p. 116; the execution provides the opening scene of Pierre Loti's novel *Aziyade*.
20. Bérard, pp. 151, 153, 162; H. Collinson Owen, p. 19.
21. Veinstein, *Salonique*, pp. 132, 135; Sciacky, p. 72.
22. Sciacky, p. 81.
23. Allen Upward, *The East End of Europe* (1908), p. 63.
24. Douglas Dakin, *The Greek Struggle in Macedonia 1897–1913* (Thessaloniki, 1966), p. 336.

25. Mark Levene, 'Port Jewry of Salonika between neo-colonialism and the nation state', in David Cesarani, ed., *Port Jews: Jewish Communities in Cosmopolitan Maritime Trading Centres 1550–1950* (2002), pp. 123, 128, 133, 141, 158.

26. Mazower, p. 283.

27. Aykut Kansu, *The Revolution of 1908 in Turkey* (Leiden, 1997), p. 82; Kechriotis, 'The Greeks of Izmir', pp. 169–72.

28. *Smyrna, Metropolis*, p. 104.

29. Kansu, *The Revolution of 1908*, p. 89.

30. Mehmet Hacisalihoglu, 'The negotiations for the solution of the Macedonian question', *Turcica*, 36 (2004), pp. 168–9; Sciacky, p. 120; A. J. Panayotopoulos, 'Early relations between the Greeks and the Young Turks', *Balkan Studies*, 21 (1980), 87–95, p. 88.

31. Desmet-Grégoire, pp. 88, 89.

32. Dakin, pp. 211–12, 377.

33. Veinstein, *Salonique*, pp. 232–3; Osman Koker, *Souvenir of Liberty: Postcards and Medals from the Collection of Orlando Carlo Calumeno* (Istanbul, 2008), pp. 18–19.

34. Kansu, *The Revolution of 1908*, p. 95.

35. Veinstein, *Salonique*, p. 236.

36. Mert Sandalci, *Max Fuchtermann Kartpostallari*, 3 vols. (Istanbul, 2000), III, 853–70.

37. Koker, *Souvenir*, pp. 20, 46–7; Edgar Morin, p. 59.

38. Cumali, p. 274.

39. Veinstein, *Salonique*, pp. 114, 238; Cumali, p. 271, report of Louis Steeg, Uskup, 20 July 1908.

40. Heath Lowry, 'The Evrenos dynasty of Yenice Vardar', *Journal of Ottoman Studies*, 32 (2008), p. 147.

41. Aykut Kansu, *Politics in Post-Revolutionary Turkey 1908–1913* (Leiden, 2000), pp. 71, 90, 118.

42. Kansu, *The Revolution of 1908*, pp. 108–9.

43. Kechriotis, 'The Greeks of Izmir', pp. 176, 180, 181; Koker, *Souvenir*, pp. 27–8; Bahattin Oztuncay, ed., *100th Anniversary of the Restoration of the Constitution* (Istanbul, 2008), p. 23.

44. Koker, *Souvenir*, pp. 68, 106–7.

45. Kechriotis, 'The Greeks of Izmir', p. 177.

46. Ibid., pp. 184, 198, 200; Georgelin, p. 173.

47. Kansu, *The Revolution of 1908*, pp. 170, 177, 223.

48. Ibid., p. 213.

49. Molho, p. 249.

50. Veinstein, *Salonique*, p. 204.

51. Ibid., p. 193.

52. Kechriotis, 'The Greeks of Izmir', pp. 187–91.

53. Kansu, *Politics*, pp. 349, 366.

54. Parmaksiz, pp. 157, 158, 161.

55. Çalislar, pp. 27, 29, 32, 34, 45.

56. Kontente, p. 653; Pannuti, p. 229, quoting *Courrier de Smyrne*, 6 Aug. 1910.

57. Colonas, p. 114.

58. Çalislar, pp. 31, 35.

59. Georgelin, p. 205, Benaroya to Alliance Israélite Universelle, 18 Sept. 1922, complaining of the destructions of Jewish shops and houses in Christian districts of the city.

60. Nahum, *Juifs de Smyrne*, p. 145: *La Boz del Pueblo*, 1911.

61. Kontente, p. 584.

62. Kechriotis, 'The Greeks of Izmir', pp. 149n (*Amalthea*, 17 Nov. 1910), 151, 159, 274–5.

63. Ibid., pp. 204–5, 216.

64. Ahmad, I, 112; Karabiber Bey, director of political affairs in the vilayet, was another Greek opposed to Greek nationalism.

65. Vangelis Kechriotis, 'Greek Orthodox, Ottoman Greek or just Greek? Theories of coexistence in the aftermath of the Young Turk Revolution', *Etudes balkaniques*, 1 (2005), 51–72.

66. Elias Petropoulos, *Old Salonica*, p. 178.

67. Oztuncay, *100th Anniversary*, p. 28; Sciacky, p. 149.

68. Kechriotis, 'The Greeks of Izmir', pp. 274–5; Ahmad, I, 110.

69. Dakin, pp. 407, 441.

70. Ilbert, I, 427–32; Floresca Karanasou, 'The Greeks in Egypt from Mohammed Ali to Nasser 1805–1961', in Richard Clogg, ed., *The Greek Diaspora in the Twentieth Century* (1999), pp. 30, 35, 36; Sturdza, p. 174. I am grateful for further information to Emir Yaner. Averoff, Tossizza's brother-in-law, also gave Greece an Olympic stadium and helped finance schools, a conservatory and a polytechnic insititute; Alexandria, where he had lived from 1865 until his death in 1899, received a Greek school and hospital.

71. Visit to *Averoff* battleship, now a museum ship moored at Piraeus, 20 Feb. 2009.

72. Jean Leune, *Une revanche, une étape* (1914), pp. 338–9, 344.

73. Edward J. Erickson, *Defeat in Detail: The Ottoman Army in the Balkans 1912–1913* (Westport, 2003), pp. 223–5; Leune, p. 363.

74. Veinstein, *Salonique*, pp. 250–53.

75. Leune, pp. 311, 316–17.

76. Paschalis M. Kitromilides, ed., *Eleftherios Venizelos: The Trials of Statesmanship* (Edinburgh, 2006), p. 148.

77. Winston Churchill, *The World Crisis: The Aftermath* (1929), p. 391; Giles Milton, *Paradise Lost: Smyrna 1922* (2008), pp. 43, 45, quoting Stavrides's diary, Nov. 1912.

78. Machiel Kiel, *Studies on the Ottoman Architecture of the Balkans* (Aldershot, 1990), p. 145.

79. Oztuncay, *100th Anniversary*, pp. 26–7.

80. Edgar Morin, pp. 90, 115, 120; Sciacky, p. 157; Molho, p. 46.

81. René Darques, *Salonique au vingtième siècle* (2000), pp. 61, 69.

82. Risal, p. 365; Molho, pp. 175–7, 190, 365.

83. I am grateful for this point to Professor Zafer Toprak.

84. Justin McCarthy, *Death and Exile: The Ethnic Cleansing of Ottoman Muslims 1821–1922* (Princeton, 1995), pp. 141–2, 145, 156, 159, 261.

85. Kontente, p. 600.

86. Ibid., pp. 668–70.

87. John Presland, *Deedes Bey* (1941), p. 102.

88. Nahum, *Juifs de Smyrne*, pp. 67, 240.
89. Ebru Boyar, *Ottoman Turks and the Balkans: Empire Lost, Relations Altered* (2007), pp. 118, 143; Dakin, p. 244.
90. Ugur U. Ugur, 'A reign of terror: CUP rule in Diyarbekir province 1913–1919', MA thesis (University of Amsterdam, 2005), p. 18.
91. Andrew Mango, *Ataturk* (2000), p. 217.
92. Paschalis M. Kitromilides, *Enlightenment, Nationalism, Orthodoxy: Studies in the Culture and Political Thought of South-Eastern Europe* (1994), XIII, 8.
93. Kontente, p. 606.
94. Victoria Solominidis, 'Greece in Asia Minor: the Greek administration of the vilayet of Aydin, 1919–1922', PhD thesis (University of London, 1984), pp. 16, 20.
95. *Smyrna, Metropolis*, p. 122; Dakin, pp. 142, 328.
96. Kechriotis, 'The Greeks of Izmir', pp. 165, 251, 259, 274–5; Ahmad, I, 110.
97. Vangelis Kechriotis, 'Between professional duty and national fulfillment: the Smyrniot medical doctor Apostolos Psaltoff 1862–1923', in Merope Anastassiadou and Paul Dumont, eds., *Médecins et ingénieurs ottomans à l'âge des nationalismes* (1998), pp. 338, 340–42, 346.
98. Milton, pp. 57–9.
99. Georgelin, pp. 184, 190n, 194, 195; Solominidis, pp. 20–21.
100. Ray Turrell, *Scrap Book 1809–1922* (Englefield Green, 1987), pp. 7, 9, 16.
101. Paul Jeancard, *L'Anatolie* (1919), pp. 24, 26, 102.
102. *Trading in the Levant* (Manchester, 1912), unpaginated.
103. Scherzer, p. 170.
104. Çalislar, p. 29.
105. Antony Wynn, *Three Camels to Smyrna: The Story of the Oriental Carpet Manufacturers Company* (2008), pp. 27–30, 48, 86, letter of Jan. 1914 from Mr Edwards; Çalislar, pp. 27–8.
106. Smyrnelis, *Smyrne*, p. 206.
107. I am grateful for this point to Professor Zafer Toprak.
108. Schmitt, pp. 383, 388, 414–18.
109. Schmidt, *Through the Legation Window*, p. 16n, Oscar van Lennep, 5 Apr. 1914; cf. Senior, pp. 207–8, 219 (8, 11 Nov. 1857), for a previous van Lennep's belief in a future Greek takeover, shared by Mr Whittall and the British and Prussian consuls.
110. Sursock Archives (henceforward referred to as SA: consulted by kind permission of Yvonne Lady Cochrane), Ibrahim Kfouri to Alfred Sursock, 11, 16 Oct. 1908.
111. George Antonius, *The Arab Awakening* (1938), pp. 54, 79, 89–90.
112. Kayali, pp. 33–4; National Archives, London, FO 195/1306, G. Dickson to J. Goschen MP – I am grateful for this reference to Alan Rush.
113. Kayali, p. 91.
114. Kamal S. Salibi, 'Beirut under the Young Turks as depicted by the political memoirs of Salim Ali Salam 1868–1938', in Jacques Berque, ed., *Les Arabes par leurs archives* (1976), pp. 193–211, *passim*.
115. Eliezer Tauber, *The Emergence of the Arab Movement* (1993), p. 275; Geraldine Hodgson, *The Life of James Elroy Flecker* (Oxford, 1925), p. 174, letter of Feb. 1912; Debbas, pp. 219–23 for photographs.

116. William W. Haddad and William Ochsenwald, *Nationalism in a Non-National State: The Dissolution of the Ottoman Empire* (Columbus, Ohio, 1977), pp. 215–16, 226–7; Kayali, pp. 106, 111–18, 128, 132, 135, 138; Tauber, pp. 135–9.

117. Kayali, p. 176.

118. Ibid., pp. 127, 185; Hurewitz, I, 566.

119. Salibi, 'Beirut under the Young Turks', pp. 193–211, *passim*; Johnson, *Class and Client*, p. 64; Kassir, *Beyrouth*, p. 244.

120. James L. Gelvin, *Divided Loyalties: Nationalism and Mass Politics in Syria at the Close of Empire* (Berkeley, 1998).

121. SA, Alfred Sursock to Mehmed V, 17 Sept. 1912 and drafts in Alfred Sursock's hand.

122. SA, letter of Amélie Comtesse Studenitz, 5 Mar. 1912.

123. Hector Dinning, *Nile to Aleppo with the Light-Horse in the Middle East* (1920), pp. 115, 118.

124. Kouyoumdjian, p. 25.

125. Cf. Carla Edde, *Beyrouth: naissance d'une capitale 1918–1924* (2009), p. 25.

Chapter 12: Catastrophe and Liberation

1. Y. T. Kurat, 'How Turkey drifted into World War I', in Kenneth Bourne and D. C. Watt, eds., *Studies in International History* (1960), pp. 297, 300, 303.

2. Schmitt, p. 227.

3. Mansel, *Constantinople*, pp. 354, 371.

4. Olivier Bouquet, 'Du haut de Péra: étude du jeu diplomatique de l'Europe dans l'Empire Ottoman 1909–1914', thesis (Paris, 1993), pp. 153, 155, 157, 162, 164, 174.

5. Mansel, *Constantinople*, pp. 371–3.

6. Schmidt, *From Anatolia to Indonesia*, pp. 170–71.

7. Sir Robert Graves, *Storm Centres of the Near East* (1933), p. 295; Lowry, p. 159.

8. Milton, p. 53.

9. http://www.levantineheritage.com/, Grace Williamson diary, 9 Mar., 28 Apr. 1915.

10. Wynn, p. 122.

11. Ibid., p. 123.

12. EUSC, MSS 259, Whittall Papers, Captain W. R. Hall, director of naval intelligence, to Commodore Roger Keyes, chief of staff Dardanelles (copy, n.d.).

13. Horton, p. 92; http://www.levantineheritage.com/, Grace Williamson diary, 5 Mar., 11 Apr. 1915.

14. Wynn, pp. 127–8.

15. Presland, p. 153, diary for 13 Mar. 1915; Wynn, p. 127; Milton, pp. 103–4; http://www.levantineheritage.com/, Grace Williamson diary, 9 Mar. 1915.

16. Milton, p. 97.

17. SA, Albert Bassoul to Alfred Sursock, 12, 17 Nov. 1917.

18. Nahum, *Juifs de Smyrne*, p. 159; Solominidis, p. 18.

19. Gérard D. Khoury, *La France et l'Orient arabe: naissance du Liban moderne* (2009 edn), pp. 77, 117, 283; Debbas, p. 66.

20. Khoury, *La France et l'Orient arabe*, pp. 66, 68; Kouyoumdjian, pp. 15, 68, 135.

21. Antonius, pp. 187, 189; photograph of the hanged men in Michel Fani, *Une histoire de la photographie au Liban* (Beirut, 2005), p. 317.

22. Joseph G. Chami, *Du Mont Liban à l'indépendance* (Beirut, 2002), p. 59.

23. Kouyoumdjian, p. 145; Jafar al-Askari, *A Soldier's Story: From Ottoman Rule to Independent Iraq* (2003), p. 105.

24. Salibi, 'Beirut Under the Young Turks', p. 214.

25. Linda Schatkowski Schilcher, 'The famine of 1915–1918 in Greater Syria', in John P. Spagnolo, ed., *Problems of the Modern Middle East in Historical Perspective* (Reading, 1992), pp. 234, 249; Kouyoumdjian, pp. 123, 136; SA, Isabelle Bustros to Alfred Sursock, Nov. 1918.

26. SA, letters to Alfred Sursock from Jemal Pasha, 2 Apr. 1915; from Madame Saoud Chehab, 7 Feb. 1917; from Michel Bustros, in Sivas, 22 Mar. 1917.

27. Falih Rifki Atay, *Le Mont des oliviers* (2009), p. 118; Khoury, *La France et l'Orient arabe*, pp. 79–81; H. E. Chehabi, 'An Iranian in the First World War', in id. ed., *Distant Relations: Iran and Lebanon in the Last 500 Years* (2006), pp. 126–31.

28. Wratislaw, p. 332.

29. Scheikevitch, pp. 10, 174.

30. H. Collinson Owen, pp. 1, 13, 19, 21.

31. Ibid., p. 29.

32. Ibid., p. 23; Goff and Fawcett, pp. 141–3.

33. Darques, p. 149; Goff and Fawcett, pp. 161, 163; Wratislaw, p. 343; Mazower, pp. 320, 324.

34. Kitromilides, *Eleftherios Venizelos*, pp. 158, 187.

35. Milton, p. 127.

36. *L'Indépendant* (Smyrna), 20, 27 Jan. 1919.

37. Kontente, pp. 696, 701; Bahattin Oztuncay, *Hatira-i uhuvvet Portre Fotoğraflarin Cazibesi 1846–1950* (Istanbul, 2005), p. 63.

38. Mansel, *Constantinople*, p. 385.

39. Kontente, p. 707.

40. Stanford J. Shaw, *From Empire to Republic: The Turkish War of National Liberation 1918–1923. A Documentary Study*, 5 vols. (Ankara, 2000), I, 501, 505–6, 508.

41. Ibid., I, 478, 482; Kontente, pp. 705, 709.

42. *Smyrna, Metropolis*, p. 126.

43. Nahum, *Juifs de Smyrne*, p. 162.

44. Boogert, p. 144; Kontente, pp. 720–21; Solominidis, pp. 50–59, 60–69, 73–5; Milton, pp. 153–9; Shaw, I, 516.

45. McCarthy, p. 266, dispatch of 17 May 1919; he also referred to 'constant shooting, looting and hunting down of Turks'.

46. Solominidis, p. 57.

47. *Les Atrocités grecques en Asie mineure: rapport de la commission interalliée d'enquête sur l'ocupation grecque de Smyrne et des territoires adjacents 12 octobre 1919* (Constantinople, 1922), signed Bristol, Bunoust, Hare, Dallolio.

48. Shaw, I, 539, 522, dispatch of 21 July 1919; Nahum, *Juifs de Smyrne*, p. 164; Michael Llewellyn Smith, *Ionian Vision: Greece in Asia Minor 1919–1922* (2nd edn, 1998), p. 91.
49. Solominidis, pp. 235, 264; Llewellyn Smith, *Ionian Vision*, p. 51.
50. Llewellyn Smith, *Ionian Vision*, p. 133.
51. *Smyrna, Metropolis*, pp. 217, 219.
52. *Smyrna before the Catastrophe*, pp. 89, 137, 170; Milton, pp. 179, 182.
53. Nahum, *Juifs de Smyrne*, p. 256.
54. Shaw, II, 559; Halide Edib, *The Turkish Ordeal* (1928), pp. 25–34; Mango, p. 217.
55. Llewellyn Smith, *Ionian Vision*, p. 107; Shaw, II, 582 (reports of admirals Calthorpe and Webb, 31 July, 17 Aug. 1919), 649, 651, 667, 671.
56. Kontente, pp. 719, 732, 739, 745.
57. Ibid., pp. 711, 735, 748; Nahum, *Juifs de Smyrne*, pp. 116–18.
58. Henri Nahum, *La Grande Guerre et la guerre greco-turque vues par les instituteurs de l'Alliance Israélite Universelle d'Izmir* (Istanbul, 2003), p. 52; *Smyrna, Metropolis*, p. 229.
59. Solominidis, pp. 134, 152–7, 222–3; Milton, p. 173.
60. Dakin, p. 225.
61. Solominidis, p. 144; Milton, p. 123.
62. Milton, pp. 195, 201, quoting Eldon Giraud's memoirs.
63. Ibid., p. 144; Solominidis, p. 205; cf. Shaw, II, 565, report of 17 June 1919, for British 'hostility and apprehension' towards the Greek occupation.
64. Schmitt, pp. 230–32.
65. Solominidis, pp. 39, 44; Milton, p. 145.
66. Shaw, II, 581.
67. Dakin, pp. 229, 231, 237.
68. Letter of 24 Mar. 1920, 'private and secret', to Lloyd George, in Martin Gilbert, ed., *Winston Churchill*, vol. 4: *1917–1922. Companion Documents*, 3 vols. (1977), III, 1053, 1324; Shaw, III, 1317, Churchill letter of 25 June 1921.
69. *Smyrna, Metropolis*, p. 234.
70. Kontente, p. 747.
71. Turrell, p. 204.
72. King Constantine, *A King's Letters to a Friend* (1927), pp. 190–93, letters of 18 June, 9 Aug. 1921; HRH Prince Andrew of Greece, *Towards Disaster: The Greek Army in Asia Minor in 1921* (1930), p. 107.
73. Ibid., p. 107.
74. Solominidis, pp. 100, 106, 128; *Smyrna, Metropolis*, p. 237.
75. Milton, p. 231.
76. Jean Morin, *Souvenirs d'un banquier français* (1983), p. 254.
77. Llewellyn Smith, *Ionian Vision*, pp. 175, 177.
78. Shaw, III, 1641, Prince Andrew to Metaxas, Jan. 1922.
79. Kontente, p. 752; *L'Indépendant* (Smyrna), 6 Apr. 1922; *L'Echo de France* 3, 5, 14 Mar. 1922.
80. *Smyrna, Metropolis*, p. 240–44; Kontente, p. 754; Solominidis, p. 237.
81. Llewellyn Smith, *Ionian Vision*, pp. 275, 277.

82. Brian Giraud Archives, Izmir (henceforward referred to as BGA: consulted by kind permission of Brian Giraud), diary of Hortense Woods, 2 Sept. 1922; Milton, p. 257.

83. Turrell, p. 211; Nahum, *La Grande Guerre*, p. 8, letter of E. Nabon, 5 Oct. 1914.

84. BGA, Woods diary.

85. Andrew, p. 41.

86. Nahum, *La Grande Guerre*, pp. 65, 66, 70, letters of 7, 8, 29 Sept. 1922.

87. Edib, pp. 365, 367; Bilal N. Şimşir, ed., *British Documents on Ataturk*, 8 vols. (Ankara, 1984–2006), IV, 391, protest of 7 Sept. 1922.

88. Edib, p. 363.

89. Llewellyn Smith, *Ionian Vision*, pp. 299–305.

90. *Smyrna, Metropolis*, pp. 229, 246; Solominidis, pp. 188, 216; Dakin, p. 256n.

91. Milton, p. 245; http://www.levantineheritage.com/, Grace Williamson diary, 6 Sept. 1922.

92. Nahum, *La Grande Guerre*, p. 65, letter of 7 Sept. 1922; Lord Kinross, *Ataturk: The Rebirth of a Nation* (Nicosia, 1981 edn), p. 322.

93. Solominidis, pp. 216–23, 246, 248; Kontente, p. 758; Milton, pp. 240, 254, 261.

94. Fahrettin Altay, *10 Yil Savaş Ve Sonrasi 1912–1922* (Istanbul, 1970), p. 351.

95. Kinross, p. 321; Milton, p. 268; BGA, Woods diary, 10 Sept. 1922.

96. http://www.levantineheritage.com/, Grace Williamson diary, 9 Sept. 1922.

97. Ibid., 11 Sept. 1922.

98. Kontente, p. 762; Milton, p. 265.

99. Mango, pp. 344, 349; Kinross, p. 322; Edib, p. 381.

100. Altay, pp. 360–61.

101. Georgelin, p. 217; Kontente, p. 764.

102. Kontente, p. 765.

103. Edib, p. 385; Milton, pp. 273, 276.

104. Milton, pp. 277–80, 295, 301–2.

105. Şimşir, IV, 403, consul to Curzon, 11 Sept. 1922.

106. Milton, p. 313.

107. Ibid., pp. 321–4.

108. Kontente, p. 770n; Georgelin, pp. 209, 212–14.

109. Kontente, pp. 777–8.

110. Boogert, p. 226, quoting Nieuws van den Dag; Milton, p. 340, quoting George Ward Price on HMS *Iron Duke*.

111. Lawrence Durrell, preface to Ilias Venezis, *Aeolia* (1949), p. v.

112. BGA, Woods diary, 14 Sept. 1922.

113. Georgelin, pp. 215, 222.

114. Ibid., p. 222, dispatch of 15 Sept. 1922; *Smyrna, Metropolis*, p. 269.

115. Smyrnelis, *Smyrne*, p. 199; Kontente, p. 771.

116. Kontente, p. 761.

117. Smyrnelis, *Smyrne*, p. 197; http://www.levantineheritage.com/, Wallace account.

118. Mango, p. 344.

119. Kinross, p. 325, Captain Thesiger on HMS *George V* on 'the most awful

scream one could ever imagine'; Kenneth Edwards, *The Grey Diplomatists* (1938), pp. 47–53.

120. Milton Chater, 'History's greatest trek', *National Geographic* (Mar. 1923), p. 538.
121. Milton, pp. 338, 349, 354, 381.
122. Ibid., p. 366.
123. Kinross, p. 326; Milton, pp. 333, 337.
124. Milton, pp. 333, 342, 381, 389.
125. Ibid., p. 336.
126. Georgelin, p. 223; Kontente, p. 769; Milton, pp. 340, 351, 354.
127. Milton, p. 355; Morin, *Souvenirs*, pp. 259, 272.
128. Şimşir, IV, 427, 437, telegrams of 17, 18 Sept. 1922; Milton, p. 357.
129. Milton, pp. 367, 374, 376, 386.
130. Ibid., pp. 358, 367–78, 381; Shaw, IV, 1736–8, reports of 24–28 Sept. 1922.
131. Alexander and Helen Karnikas, *Elias Venezis* (New York, 1969), p. 14; cf. Schmidt, *Ottoman Izmir*, p. 146, for the account of Panyotis Marselis; Georgelin, p. 220, dispatch of Graillet, 16 Sept. 1922.
132. Dimitir Pentzopoulos, *The Balkan Exchange of Minorities and its Impact on Greece* (2002 edn), pp. 47, 100; Stratis Doukas, *A Prisoner of War's Story* (Birmingham, 1991), p. 2.
133. Milton, p. 387; Kontente, p. 780; BGA, Woods diary, 1, 2 Oct. 1922.
134. Kontente, p. 781.
135. Milton, p. 392.
136. Personal communication, Alex Baltazzi, 13 May 2009.
137. Gillian Bardsley, *Issigonis: The Official Biography* (Thriplow, 2005), pp. 12, 28, 42, 51.
138. Nicholas Gage, *Greek Fire* (2001), pp. 117–51, 236.
139. Georgelin, p. 207.
140. http://en.wikipedia.org/wiki/Great_Fire_of_Smyrna.
141. Shaw, III, 1739–40.
142. Georgelin, p. 203.
143. Wynn, pp. 154–6.
144. Georgelin, p. 210.
145. Şimşir, IV, 404, 410, notes and telegrams of 13, 14 Sept. 1922.
146. BGA, Woods diary, 29 Oct., 2 Nov. 1922.
147. Kahri Dikkaya et al., *Avrupali mi, Levanten mi?* (Istanbul, 2006), p. 148, on Huseyin Kurnaz, who, by his account, burnt his own house while trying to burn down a neighbour's.
148. Çalislar, pp. 57, 64.
149. That is, would the destruction of Christians' buildings help keep Izmir Turkish?
150. http://en.wikipedia.org/wiki/Great_Fire_of_Smyrna.
151. Kinross, pp. 326–7.
152. Çalislar, pp. 18, 54, 80, letter of 26 Oct. 1922.
153. Ibid., pp. 53–8, 64; Mango, p. 346.
154. Çalislar, p. 98.
155. Edib, pp. 387–8.

156. http://en.wikipedia.org/wiki/Great_Fire_of_Smyrna.
157. W. Bruce Lincoln, *Sunlight at Midnight: St Petersburg and the Making of Modern Russia* (2001), pp. 233, 245, 252–3.
158. Mango, p. 345; BGA, Woods diary, 6 Sept.: 'More refugees are coming in, both Greek and Turkish, with thousands of camels and sheep, with no idea of where they are going to go.'
159. Nahum, *La Grande Guerre*, pp. 95–9, undated letter of Mr Canetti.
160. Churchill later called 'Mustafa Kemal's army having celebrated their triumph by the burning of Smyrna to ashes and by a vast massacre of its Christian population' a 'foretaste of what the fate of Constantinople might be': *The World Crisis: The Aftermath* (1929), p. 419.
161. Harry J. Psomiades, *The Eastern Question: The Last Phase* (Thessaloniki, 1968), p. 89.
162. National Archives, London, FO 371/7917, Henderson to Curzon, 28 Nov. 1922.
163. Schmidt, *Through the Legation Window*, pp. 216–17.
164. Mansel, *Constantinople*, pp. 407, 410.
165. Nahum, *Juifs de Smyrne*, p. 167; Nahum, *La Grande Guerre*, p. 85; Smyrnelis *Smyrne*, p. 222.
166. *Smyrna, Metropolis*, p. 295.
167. *Turkish Daily News*, 19 Mar. 2007, p. 5.
168. BGA, Woods diary, 27 Mar. 1923.
169. Nahum, *Juifs de Smyrne*, p. 183; cf. Kontente, pp. 816–17; personal communications, Ergun Cagatay, Istanbul, 14 May 2009, Guy Pagy, 21 May 2009.
170. Nahum, *La Grande Guerre*, p. 79, 28 Jan. 1923.
171. Kontente, p. 810.
172. Personal communication, 3 May 2010.
173. Çalislar, pp. 95, 99, 106–13.
174. Cumali, pp. 12, 40–41.
175. Ayhan Aktar, 'Turkifying the economy', in Renée Hirschon, ed., *Crossing the Aegean* (Oxford, 2004), p. 84.
176. Kontente, p. 800.
177. Aktar, p. 80.
178. Nahum, *Juifs de Smyrne*, p. 259, letter of 17 Sept. 1924; Çalislar, p. 292.
179. Aktar, p. 91.
180. *Annuaire oriental* (Constantinople, 1922), pp. 1392–1418, for lists of businesess and institutions in Smyrna. Before the fire, there were many firms selling 'assurances contre l'incendie'.
181. Caglar Keyder, *The Definition of a Peripheral Economy: Turkey 1923–1929* (Cambridge, 1981), pp. 89–90.
182. Çalislar, pp. 288–91; Edib, p. 387.
183. Milton, pp. 286–9; http://www.levantineheritage.com/, de Jongh testimony and Grace Williamson diary, 12 Sept. 1922.
184. http://www.levantineheritage.com/, de Jongh testimony.
185. Schmidt, *Through the Legation Window*, pp. 153, 207, 214, 219; Jean Morin, pp. 255–6.
186. Schmitt, pp. 153, 207, 406, 410.

187. *Smyrna, Metropolis*, p. 275; Kontente, p. 825.
188. Pannuti, p. 489.
189. Turrell, pp. 137, 157; Dikkaya, p. 147.
190. BGA, Woods diary, 29 Oct., 1, 15 Nov., 9 Dec. 1922, 14 Feb. 1923.
191. Jean Morin, pp. 277-80.
192. Interview, 9 Feb. 2006.
193. Wynn, pp. 278, 281.
194. I am grateful for this point to Emir Yaner.
195. Kinross, pp. 420, 431; Mango, pp. 445-7, 451; Kontente, p. 814.
196. *Smyrna, Metropolis*, p. 275; Nahum, *Juifs de Smyrne*, pp. 197-9.
197. Nahum, *Juifs de Smyrne*, p. 238.
198. Smyrnelis, *Smyrne*, pp. 208-9.
199. Kontente, p. 815.
200. *Smyrna, Metropolis*, p. 275; Kontente, p. 819.
201. Michael Woodbine Parish, *Aegean Adventures 1940-1943* (Lewes, 1993), pp. 172, 177.
202. George Seferis, *A Poet's Journal: Days of 1945-1951* (Cambridge, Mass., 1974), pp. 164-5, 1, 2 July 1950; Roderick Beaton, p. 50.
203. Roderick Beaton, pp. 288-91.
204. Georgios A. Yiannakopoulos, ed., *Refugee Greece: Photographs from the Archive of the Centre for Asia Minor Studies* (Athens, 1992), pp. 19, 32, 53, 59.
205. Pentzopoulos, p. 206.
206. Ibid., p. 210.
207. Renée Hirschon, *Heirs of the Greek Catastrophe* (1988), p. 30; Pentzopoulos, p. 193.
208. Peter Mackridge, 'The myth of Asia Minor in Greek fiction', in Renée Hirschon, ed., *Crossing the Aegean* (Oxford, 2003), pp. 235-46.
209. Dido Sotiriou, *Farewell Anatolia* (Athens, 1991), pp. 21, 58, 61, 265.
210. Kosmas Politis, 'At Hadzifrangos', *The Charioteer*, 11 (1969-70), pp. 75, 85.
211. Cf. Andy Garcia's film *The Lost City* (2005), with its haunting pre-Castro music.
212. Mazower, pp. 3, 370.
213. Gauntlett, pp. 250-55; *Smyrna, Metropolis*, p. 251.
214. Kinross, p. 336.
215. Pentzopoulos, p. 119.
216. Ibid., p. 115, 166.
217. *Nea Smyrna* (map with history) (Athens, 1999), *passim*; interview, 24 Feb. 2009.
218. Cumali, pp. 183, 221-4.
219. Mazower, p. 344.
220. Bruce Clark, *Twice a Stranger: How Mass Expulsion Forged Modern Greece and Turkey* (2006), pp. 158-9, 162-5, 178.
221. Mazower, p. 351.
222. Molho, p. 26; Mazower, pp. 412, 428.
223. Yorgos Ioannou, *Refugee Capital: Thessaloniki Chronicles* (Athens, 1997), pp. 105, 116.
224. Ibid., pp. 85, 87, 93; Mazower, p. 440.
225. Mazower, p. 428; Ioannou, pp. 131, 137.

Chapter 13: Alexandria: Queen of the Mediterranean

1. Karanasou, pp. 24–57; David Marr, *Patrick White: A Life* (1991), p. 217.

2. Haag, *Alexandria*, p. 110; thus Durrell exaggerated when he wrote, in the preface to Elias Venezis's *Aeolia* (1948), 'The flames of Smyrna illuminated the whole Levant': in reality they were soon forgotten.

3. Janice J. Terry, *The Wafd* (Beirut, 1981), pp. 75, 76.

4. Ibid., pp. 79, 102–3; Ilbert, II, 653.

5. C. W. R. Long, *British Pro-Consuls in Egypt 1914–1929: The Challenge of Nationalism* (2005), p. 118.

6. Ibid., pp. 157, 164.

7. As can be seen from the names of those fallen in the '1916–1922' war, on tablets in the courtyard of St Mark's Orthodox cathedral.

8. Ilbert, II, 641, 647, 652–3; Malak Badrawi, *Political Violence in Egypt 1910–1924* (2000), p. 194; Haag, *Alexandria*, pp. 112–13.

9. E. M. Forster, *Alexandria*, pp. 6, 191.

10. Marilyn L. Booth, *Bayram al-Tunisi's Egypt: Social Criticism and Narrative Strategies* (Exeter, 1990), pp. 33–7, 41, 50, 59, 69, 589; *Mediterraneans*, 8 (2006), pp. 125–6.

11. Grafftey-Smith, p. 47; Sholto Douglas, *Years of Command* (1966), p. 190.

12. Awad, *Italy in Alexandria*, pp. 38–40, 142, 181, 254.

13. See the map in Haag, *Alexandria*, p. xiv.

14. Booth, p. 59.

15. Lionel Dawson, *Mediterranean Medley* (1933), p. 189.

16. Sir David Kelly, *The Ruling Few* (1952), p. 226; Morin, *Souvenirs*, p. 308.

17. MEC, Vaux, 'Egyptian and other episodes'.

18. Sir Stewart Symes, *Tour of Duty* (1946), p. 28.

19. Gudrun Kramer, *The Jews in Modern Egypt 1914–1952* (1989), p. 194; these sentiments have been reiterated to me in interviews by Molly Tuby, 14 May 2004, and Solomon Greene, 1 May 2006: 'We thought it would all end in tears.'

20. Sir Miles Lampson, *Politics and Diplomacy in Egypt: The Diaries of Sir Miles Lampson 1935–1937* (Oxford, 1991), pp. 290–91, 16, 19 July 1935.

21. Malak Badrawi, *Ismail Sidqi 1875–1950* (1996), pp. 61, 100, 113; Vice-Amiral Godefroy, *L'Aventure de la Force X à Alexandrie, 1940–1943* (1953), p. 126; Ilbert, II, 587.

22. Jacques Berque, *L'Egypte: impérialisme et révolution* (1967), pp. 262, 553.

23. Mohamed Awad and Sahar Hamouda, eds., *Voices from Cosmopolitan Alexandria* (Alexandria, 2006), p. 71; cf. the inscription in the Orthodox cemetery: 'Ci-gît Ivan Oumno né le 15 mars 1883 à Kazan, décédé le 7 mars 1961 à Alexandrie, priez pour lui.' Another Russian Alexandrian, who lived by giving piano lessons, was Evkodia Kutuzov, descendant of the conqueror of Napoleon and subject of a film by Asma al-Bakri.

24. Zananiri, p. 37.

25. Ilbert et Yannakakis, p. 171.

26. el-Kayem, p. 54; Zananiri, pp. 247, 256.

27. Jacqueline Carol, *Cocktails and Camels* (Alexandria, 2008), pp. 92–4; id., *Scribbles* (Geneva, 2004), p. 21.

28. Terry, p. 234.

29. Nathan J. Brown, 'The precarious life and slow death of the mixed courts of Egypt', *International Journal of Middle East Studies*, 25 (1993), p. 46.

30. *Mediterraneans*, 8 (2006), pp. 128–9, Mahfouz interview of 1996.

31. Daniel Rondeau, *Alexandrie* (1997), p. 29.

32. Lutfi A. W. Yehya, 'Alexandria reminiscences of an old historian', *Mediterraneans*, 8 (2006), pp. 365–7; G. Philippou Pieridis, *Memories and Stories from Egypt* (Nicosia, 1992), p. 84; Awad and Hamouda, *Voices*, pp. 34, 58, 99, 103, 108–9.

33. Interviews, 19, 26 Aug. 2007.

34. Zananiri, p. 298.

35. Fernand Leprette, *Egypte: terre du Nil* (1939), pp. 11, 108.

36. Robert L. Tignor, *State, Private Enterprise and Economic Change in Egypt 1918–1952* (Princeton, 1984), pp. 136–7.

37. Ilbert, I, 537.

38. Claude Avelin, *La Promenade égyptienne* (1934), p. 42; Haag, *Alexandria*, p. 163; Charles-Roux, *Souvenirs*, p. 158.

39. Frédéric Abécassis, 'Alexandrie, 1929', *Cahiers de la Méditerranée*, 67 (2003).

40. Zimmerli Hardmann, pp. 16, 30, 78.

41. Haag, *Alexandria*, pp. 235, 324.

42. Jacqueline Cooper, *Tales from Alexandria* (Geneva, 1994), p. 6.

43. Jean Naggar, *Sipping from the Nile: My Exodus from Egypt* (New York, 2008), pp. 31, 122.

44. *Mediterraneans*, 8 (2006), pp. 115–18; Haag, *Alexandria*, p. 164.

45. Omar Sharif, *L'Eternel masculin* (1977), pp. 57, 76, 102; Mohamed Awad and Sahar Hamouda, *The Birth of the Seventh Art in Alexandria* (Alexandria, 2007), pp. xii, 223.

46. Leprette, *Egypte*, p. 106.

47. *Le Mondain égyptien* (Cairo, 1939), p. 66; Jean François Bouvier, *L'Ordre du Nil: vie et combats d'Antoine Arache Bey* (n.d.), unpaginated.

48. Haag, *Alexandria*, p. 132.

49. Fausta Cialente, *The Levantines* (1963), p. 116.

50. Haag, *Vintage Alexandria*, p. 50; interview of Mr Salvago, *La Patrie: journal des héllènes*, 20 Oct., 10 Dec. 1929.

51. Ian S. MacNiven, ed., *The Durrell–Miller Letters 1935–1980* (1988), p. 168, Durrell to Miller, May 1944; Cialente, pp. 58, 81.

52. Baron Firmin van den Bosch, *Vingt années d'Egypte* (1932), pp. 161–6.

53. Carol, *Cocktails and Camels*, p. 26.

54. Shirley Johnston with Sherif Sonbol, *Egyptian Palaces and Villas* (2006), pp. 106, 135; Haag, *Vintage Alexandria*, pp. 54–5; *Le Livre d'or du journal La Réforme*, pp. 292–3.

55. Leprette, *Egypte*, p. 122.

56. Bosch, p. 166; cf. D. J. Enright, *Academic Year* (1984 edn), p. 89.

57. Robin Fedden, ed., *Personal Landscape: An Anthology of Exile* (1945), p. 11.

58. *Mediterraneans*, 8 (2006), p. 227.

59. William Stadiem, *Too Rich* (1992), p. 126; Barrie St Clair McBride, *Farouk of Egypt* (1967), pp. 63, 85; Hugh McLeave, *The Last Pharaoh: The Ten Faces of Farouk* (1969), pp. 16, 99.
60. Interview with Alex el-Kayem, 14 Feb. 2010.
61. Haag, *Alexandria*, p. 154.
62. *La Bourse égyptienne*, 6 Jan. 1940, consulted thanks to Madame Fernande Nissaire.
63. *Le Livre d'or du journal La Réforme*, p. 5.
64. Steven Morewood, *The British Defence of Egypt 1935–1940: Conflict and Crisis in the Eastern Mediterranean* (2005), pp. 21, 25, 27, 53, 98; Artemis Cooper, *Cairo in the War 1939–1945* (1989), p. 48.
65. Lawrence R. Pratt, *East of Malta, West of Suez* (1975), pp. 121–2.
66. Margret Boveri, *Mediterranean Cross-Currents*, tr. Louisa Marie Sieveking (1938), p. 417; Admiral of the Fleet Viscount Cunningham of Hyndhope, *A Sailor's Odyssey* (1951), p. 176.
67. Adel Sabit, 'Life in Alexandria in the 1940s', unpublished typescript (Cairo, c.2000), consulted by kind permission of Mahmud Sabit.
68. Margaret Forster, *Daphne du Maurier* (1993), pp. 123–8, 133–4.
69. Olivia Manning, *The Levant Trilogy* (2003 edn), p. 71.
70. Henry Colyton, *Occasion, Chance and Change: A Memoir 1902–1946* (Wimborne, 1993), p. 112; John Winton, *Cunningham* (1998), p. 74.
71. Viscount Cunningham, p. 207; Haag, *Vintage Alexandria*, p. 122.
72. Nigel Hamilton, *Monty: The Making of a General 1887–1942* (1981), p. 234.
73. Sir Miles Lampson, *Politics and Diplomacy in Egypt*, pp. 301, 877, 931, 2 Nov. 1935, 21 July 1936, 22 Nov. 1937; Morewood, p. 87.
74. Morewood, pp. 158, 169.
75. Count Patrice de Zogheb, *Red Cross and Red Crescent: Work in Alexandria under the Patronage of HRH Prince Mohammed Ali* (Alexandria, 1943), pp. 74, 88, 95, 158.
76. Winton, p. 79.
77. Fernand Leprette, *La Muraille de silence: notes d'un français d'Egypte pendant la guerre* (Cairo, 1942), p. 65.
78. Viscount Cunningham, pp. 233, 241.
79. Morewood, pp. 140, 169–70.
80. Haag, *Alexandria*, pp. 178, 190; Hanna F. Wissa, *Assiout: The Saga of an Egyptian Family* (Lewes, 1994), p. 340.
81. Alan Moorehead, *African Trilogy* (1944), p. 121; Georges Moustaki remembers a 'derisory and deceptive coitus' with a prostitute who called to him 'come to mix your white skin with my brown skin': Georges Moustaki, *Les Filles de la mémoire* (1989), pp. 21–2.
82. Victor Selwyn et al., eds., *Return to Oasis: War Poems and Recollections from the Middle East 1940–1946* (1980 edn).
83. Interview with John Nahman, 23 Sept. 2008.
84. Haag, *Alexandria*, pp. 212–14.
85. Viscount Cunningham, pp. 399–400.
86. Awad and Hamouda, *Voices*, pp. 99, 103, 107.
87. Field Marshal Lord Wilson, *Eight Years Overseas* (1948), pp. 19, 25, 31, 33, 34; Morewood, pp. 176, 211.

88. Terry, pp. 240, 247.
89. Eve Curie, *Journey among Warriors* (1943), p. 68.
90. Artemis Cooper, p. 192.
91. Evelyn Waugh, *The Letters of Evelyn Waugh*, ed. Mark Amory (1980), p. 152, 7 May 1941.
92. Winton, pp. 79.
93. Godefroy, p. 6.
94. Winton, pp. 82, 88; Colyton, p. 211.
95. Artemis Cooper, p. 53.
96. EUSC, Barker MSS, 'Historical notes on Egypt'.
97. Auchterlonie, 'A British family'; Barker photograph albums consulted by kind permission of Mrs Michael Barker and Craig Encer, Aug. 2009.
98. *Egyptian Gazette*, 30 Apr. 1940.
99. EUSC, MSS 238/1/2.
100. Gabriella Barker, *Desert Angels* (1956), pp. xiii, 3, 5, 16, 18, 41, 80; Zananiri, p. 276.
101. Jacqueline Cooper, pp. 88-9.
102. Michael Simpson, ed., *The Cunningham Papers*, 2 vols. (Aldershot, 1999-2006), I, 17, 152, Cunningham to Pound, 22 Sept. 1940; Winton, p. 74.
103. Douglas Austin, *Malta and British Strategic Policy 1925-1943* (2004), p. 94.
104. Winton, pp. 99, 105, 227; Viscount Cunningham, p. 281; Marshal of the RAF Lord Tedder, *With Prejudice: War Memoirs* (1966), pp. 99, 104.
105. Tedder, p. 151.
106. Haag, *Alexandria*, p. 191.
107. Roderick Beaton, pp. 198-201.
108. Winton, p. 211.
109. John Connell, *Wavell: Soldier and Scholar* (1964), pp. 474-5; Viscount Cunningham, p. 389.
110. Winton, p. 221.
111. Ibid., p. 248; Viscount Cunningham, p. 176.
112. Zananiri, p. 41.
113. David Marr, ed., *Patrick White Letters* (1994), pp. 47, 49, 57, letters of 15 Aug., 13 Nov. 1941 to Jean Scott Rogers; a more negative portrait is in White's autobiography, *Flaws in the Glass: A Self-Portrait* (1983 edn), pp. 98-9.
114. Nigel Hamilton, pp. 608-9; John Connell, *Auchinleck* (1959), p. 653, Churchill to Auchinleck, 3 July 1942.
115. Myles Hildyard, *It is Bliss Here: Letters Home 1939-1945* (2005), p. 179, letter of 6 July 1942.
116. Sir Edward Spears, *Fulfillment of a Mission: The Spears Mission to Syria and Lebanon, 1941-1944* (1977), p. 22; Michael Carver, *Dilemmas of the Desert War* (1986), pp. 133, 137.
117. Personal communication, Princess Catherine Aga Khan, 19 Dec. 2009.
118. Haag, *Alexandria*, p. 175.
119. Personal communication, Princess Nesrine Toussoun, 22 Dec. 2009.
120. Personal communication, Yolande Whittall, 9 Mar. 2010.
121. Moorehead, pp. 357-8.
122. Cecil Beaton, *The Years Between* (1965), pp. 183-6, June 1942.

NOTES TO PAGES 258–264

123. Haag, *Alexandria*, p. 197; EUSC, Barker MSS, 'Historical notes on Egypt', 2 July 1942.
124. François Sureau, *Les Alexandrins* (2003), p. 26.
125. Haag, *Alexandria*, p. 197; Artemis Cooper, pp. 193–5.
126. Simon Sebag Montefiore, *Stalin: The Court of the Red Tsar* (2003), pp. 349–52.
127. Centre d'Etudes Alexandrines, Alexandria (henceforward referred to as CEA), diary of Mary de Zogheb, consulted thanks to Jean-Yves Empereur and Dominique Gogny.
128. Nigel Hamilton, p. 577, note of 6 Aug. 1942.
129. F.W. de Guingand, *Operation Victory* (1978), p. 151.
130. Ibid., pp. 5, 8; Viscount Montgomery, *The Memoirs of Field-Marshal the Viscount Montgomery of Alamein, KG* (1958), p. 1.
131. Keith Douglas, *Alamein to Zem Zem* (1966 edn), p. 76; Guingand, p. 162.
132. Haag, *Alexandria*, pp. 212–14.
133. Winston Churchill, *The Second World War*, vol. 4: *The Hinge of Fate* (1951), p. 541.
134. *The Sphinx*, 13 Feb. 1943.
135. Zananiri, p. 277.
136. Ibrahim Ibrahim, 'Taha Husayn: the critical spirit', in John P. Spagnolo, ed., *Problems of the Modern Middle East in Historical Perspective* (Reading, 1992), pp. 105–18; Gordon Waterfield, *Egypt* (1967), pp. 129–30, 136.
137. Haag, *Alexandria*, p. 291; el-Kayem, p. 70, letter of Durrell, 10 Apr. 1944.
138. Pieridis, pp. 30, 46, 54, 63, 78.
139. Berque, p. 603.
140. Cf. Eve Cohen: 'We thought it would go on for ever and ever . . . Egypt seemed so solid', in Haag, *Alexandria*, p. 239.
141. Godefroy, p. 206.
142. Stelios Hormouzios, *No Ordinary Crown* (1972), p. 149.
143. C. L. Sulzberger, *A Long Row of Candles: Memoirs and Diaries 1934–1952* (1969), p. 441.
144. Ali Vasib Efendi, *Bir Şehzadenin Hatirati* (Istanbul, 2004), p. 369.
145. *Le Livre d'or du journal La Réforme*, p. 387.
146. Wissa, p. 322.
147. Noël Coward, *Middle East Diary* (1944), pp. 53, 58; cf. Sholto Douglas, p. 199.
148. McBride, p. 135.
149. CEA, Zogheb diary.
150. Stadiem, pp. 55–6, 213; McLeave, pp. 145, 165, 180.
151. Haag, *Alexandria*, pp. 140, 145–6, 257.
152. Cooper, *Cocktails and Camels*, pp. 256–8.
153. Awad and Hamouda, *Seventh Art*, p. 199.
154. The parents of John Nahman – Jewish and Greek Orthodox – became Swiss in order to marry.
155. *Valeurs*, 1 (Apr. 1945).
156. *Mediterraneans*, 8 (2006), p. 27; Awad and Hamouda, *Voices*, p. 40.
157. Rees, p. 207.
158. Interview with Rev. Leighton Thomas, 6 Dec. 2004.

159. Tignor, *State*, p. 228.
160. D. J. Enright, *Season Ticket* (Alexandria, 1948), p. 13; interview with Madeleine Enright, 30 Sept. 2006.
161. John Heath-Stubbs, *Hindsights* (1993), p. 210; el-Kayem, pp. 93, 99, 101, 109, 112.
162. Jean Cocteau, *Maalesh* (1949), pp. 125, 126.
163. Haag, *Alexandria*, p. 236; interview with Princess Catherine Aga Khan, 19 Dec. 2009; *Le Phare égyptien*, 18 Feb. 1950, lists nightclubs.
164. Cf. CEA, Zogheb diary, 30 Sept. 1944: 'cocktail chez le prince Said Toussoun. assez de monde.'
165. Personal communication, Princess Nesrine Toussoun, 22 Dec. 2009; *Journal d'Egypte du dimanche*, Jan. 1949.
166. Harry F. Tzalas, *Farewell to Alexandria* (Cairo, 2003 edn), p. 28; Selma Botman, *Egypt from Independence to Revolution 1919–1952* (Syracuse, NY, 1991), pp. 47–9; interview with Princess Catherine Aga Khan, 19 Dec. 2009. Bryan Hornsby also witnessed the incident: interview, 13 Feb. 2010.
167. Peter Elliott, *The Cross and the Ensign: A Naval History of Malta 1798–1979* (Cambridge, 1980), p. 175.
168. Kramer, pp. 146, 162, 215.
169. P. J. Vatikiotis, *Nasser and his Generation* (1978), pp. 55, 102, 105.

Chapter 14: Egyptianization

1. John Sykes, *The Levantine* (1952), pp. 5, 11, 14.
2. Interviews with Kadriya Foda, 13 Feb. 2007, and Abdel Kader el-Naggar, 14 June 2009.
3. Interview with Jackie Rolo, 29 Aug. 2009: 'Any escapade caused gossip.'
4. Enright, *Academic Year*, pp. 157, 207.
5. Marr, *Letters*, p. 51, letter of 26 June 1942.
6. Marr, *Patrick White*, pp. 239, 241.
7. Marius Deeb, 'The socio-economic role of the foreign minorities in Egypt 1805–1961', *International Journal of Middle East Studies*, 19 (1978), p. 22; Kramer, p. 207.
8. Auctioned by Sotheby's Monaco, 7 Dec. 1991.
9. Awad and Hamouda, *Seventh Art*, pp. 33–46.
10. Zananiri, pp. 23, 327, 329.
11. Ibid., p. 67.
12. Ibid., pp. 15, 24, 212, 247, 256.
13. Hamouda and Clement, p. 97.
14. Zananiri, pp. 55, 98–100.
15. Ibid., p. 342.
16. Moustaki, pp. 19, 26, 38, 80; Cécile Barthélémy, *Georges Moustaki* (Paris, 1970), p. 18.
17. Interview with Prince Nicholas Romanov, 2 Oct. 2008.
18. Interview, 17 Sept. 2008.

19. Interviews, 20, 23 Sept. 2008.
20. Ilbert and Yannakakis, p. 141.
21. Mohammed Neguib, *Egypt's Destiny* (1955), p. 97.
22. Berque, p. 694; Vatikiotis, p. 122.
23. Naguib Mahfouz, *Autumn Quail* (1990), p. 19.
24. Robert Tignor, *Capitalism and Nationalism at the End of Empire* (Princeton, 1998), p. 60.
25. Joel Gordon, *Nasser's Blessed Movement: Egypt's Free Officers and the July Revolution* (New York, 1992), pp. 27, 35.
26. *Foreign Relations of the United States 1952–1954*, IX, 2 (Washington, 1986), p. 1800, dispatch from Caffery, 8 May 1952.
27. McLeave, p. 266; McBride, p. 189.
28. Jean Lacouture and Simone Lacouture, *L'Egypte en mouvement* (1957), pp. 124, 143–4; Anwar el-Sadat, *Revolt on the Nile* (1957), pp. 102, 111.
29. Vatikiotis, pp. 108, 122.
30. Neguib, p. 115; Lacouture and Lacouture, p. 148.
31. McLeave, pp. 271–2.
32. Jean-Yves Empereur, *Alexandrie: hier et demain* (2001), p. 118.
33. McBride, p. 193.
34. el-Sadat, p. 125; G. Vaucher, *Gamal Abdel Nasser et son équipe*, 2 vols. (1959), I, 289.
35. Nasser spoke too soon. At the time of writing (2010), Nasser's popularity has waned. Thanks in part to a recent television serial, many now consider Farouk's reign a golden age.
36. Neguib, pp. 129–33; el-Sadat, p. 119.
37. McBride, pp. 195–7.
38. McLeave, p. 276.
39. Gilbert Sinoué, *Le Colonel et l'enfant roi* (2006), pp. 144–5.
40. Hassan Hassan, *In the House of Mohammed Ali: A Family Album 1805–1952* (Cairo, 2000), p. 132; Adel M. Sabit, *A King Betrayed* (1989), pp. 218, 219.
41. Neguib, p. 145.
42. Interview with Rear Admiral Rashidy, 16 Nov. 2008.
43. McLeave, p. 279.
44. Jason Tomes, *King Zog: Self-Made Monarch of Albania* (2003), pp. 277, 279.
45. Neguib, p. 140.
46. Roger Vailland, *Choses vues en Egypte* (1982 edn), pp. 170, 172.
47. Mahfouz, *Autumn Quail*, pp. 83, 85, 88.
48. CEA, Zoghreb diary.
49. Elia Mss, letters of 1 Aug. 1952.
50. Tignor, *Capitalism*, pp. 65–6.
51. *Takydromos* (Alexandria), 16 Sept. 1952, translated by Matilda Pyrli, to whom many thanks.
52. Elia Mss, letters from the president of the Communauté Hellénique d'Alexandrie to Minister of Education, 29 Nov. 1952, to Mahmoud el-Sisy, secretary-general of the press department of the Ministry of the Interior, 2 Jan. 1953.
53. EUSC, Barker MSS; el-Kayem, p. 119.

54. Personal communication, Mimi Awad, 5 Jan. 2010.
55. Vatikiotis, p. 144.
56. *Le Portrait à Alexandrie dans les collections particulières* (Alexandria, 1955).
57. Beinin, p. 19.
58. Leila Ahmed, *Border Passage* (1999), pp. 149–50; Tzalas, pp. 132–7; Barry Turner, *Suez 1956* (2007 edn), p. 180; Lacouture and Lacouture, p. 450.
59. James Morris, *Farewell the Trumpets: An Imperial Retreat* (1998 edn), p. 526.
60. CEA, Zogheb diary.
61. Hugh Thomas, *The Suez Affair* (1986 edn), pp. 82, 92; Barry Turner, pp. 203, 255.
62. CEA, Zogheb diary, 31 Oct., 4 Nov. 1956.
63. EUSC, Barker MSS; Tignor, *Capitalism*, pp. 131–2.
64. Lucette Lagnado, *The Man in the White Sharkskin Suit* (New York, 2007), p. 173.
65. CEA, Zogheb diary.
66. Naggar, p. 262.
67. Carol, *Cocktails and Camels* (1960 edn), pp. 31, 232, 234, 239, 243–4.
68. EUSC, Barker Mss 238/1/2.
69. Munevver Eminoglu, *A Beyoglu Photo-Romance* (Istanbul, 2000 edn), p. 57; Pannuti, pp. 488–9.
70. Tignor, *Capitalism*, pp. 130–31.
71. EUSC Barker MSS; Christopher Hampton, *White Chameleon* (1991), p. 17; Gabriel Josipovici, *A Life* (2001), p. 140.
72. Horowitz's 100-volume library on jewellery was sold on 18 Nov. 1997 in Geneva.
73. EUSC, MSS 238/1/2.
74. Ibid. and Marina Barker interview at http://www.levantineheritage.com/.
75. Hamouda and Clement, pp. 194–5.
76. Personal information, George Warren, former director of the Ottoman Bank, 24 Nov. 2009.
77. Beinin, pp. 19, 21, 27.
78. Interview with A. Levy, 16 June 2009; cf. the same sentiment expressed by Christian Ayoub in his talk 'Le français comme langue au moyen orient' (unpublished typescript, Montreal, 1971): 'My fatherland is the language I speak.'
79. Kramer, p. 195; Tziana Carlino, 'The Levant: A Transmediterranean Literary Category?' (online, 2006), *passim*.
80. Lagnado, p. 227.
81. Interviews with Micky Benaki, Daphne Krambs, Feb. 2009.
82. François Sureau, *Les Alexandrins* (2003), p. 432; Tom Bower, *Fayed* (1998), pp. 7, 9, 16–17.
83. Catalogues des collections de Madame Lina Gabriel Aghion, 15 Rue des Pharaons, 18 Sept. 1959, de feu César Aghion, 28 Rue des Pharaons, 10–11 July 1959; consulted by kind permission of Max Karkagi.
84. Interview with Daphne Krambs, 22 Feb. 2009.
85. Interview with M.H.S., 12 Dec. 2008.
86. CEA, Zogheb diary.

87. Interview with Alex Benaki, 6 Aug. 2009.
88. Personal communication, 7 Feb. 2007.
89. Interview with Lucette de Saab, 10 Dec. 2008.
90. Interview, 10 Dec. 2008.
91. CEA, Zogheb diary, 25 Sept., 23 Oct., 20 Nov., 3 Dec. 1961 and *passim*.
92. Tignor, *Capitalism*, pp. 135, 165–6, 174.
93. Lagnado, p. 106.
94. Personal information, André Aciman and Leslie Croxford, 7 Jan. 2010.
95. Interview with Azza Heikal, 15 June 2009.
96. Lagnado, p. 93.
97. Hugh H. Walker, *The Anglo-American Guide Book to Alexandria* (Cairo, 1938), p. 127.
98. Lawrence Durrell, *The Alexandria Quartet* (1968 edn), pp. 484, 552.
99. David Holden, 'Letter from Alexandria 1963', in Christopher Pick, ed., *Egypt: A Travellers' Anthology* (1991), pp. 27–31.
100. Interview, Chios, 24 July 2007.
101. Visited 24 Feb. 2009: info@synaige.gr.
102. http://www.elia.org.gr.
103. Deborah Starr, *Remembering Cosmopolitan Egypt: Literature, Culture and Empire* (2009), p. 33.
104. Personal information, Leila Naguib, Cairo, 31 Dec. 2009; cf. Gina Alhadeff, *The Sun at Midday* (New York, 1997), p. 189: 'Where the garden once was three apartment blocks and a mosque have been built.'
105. CEA, Zogheb diary.
106. Interview with Micky Benaki, Athens, 21 Feb. 2009.
107. Azza Heikal, *L'Education Alexandrine* (Alexandria, 1996), p. 41.
108. Josipovici, p. 25.
109. *Cahiers d'Alexandrie* (1965), p. 39; ibid. (1966), p. 58.
110. James Morris, *Among the Cities* (1985), pp. 18–19.
111. Anthony Sattin, *Lifting the Veil: British Society in Egypt 1768–1956* (1988), pp. 55, 151.
112. Interview, Azza Heikal, 15 June 2009.
113. Personal communication, John Stefanidis, 2 Oct. 2009.
114. Zananiri, p. 85; MacNiven, p. 159, Durrell to Miller, 8 Feb. 1944.
115. Personal communications, Madame Arcache, Jean Choremi; Robert Liddell, *Unreal City* (1993 edn), p. 99.
116. Naguib Mahfouz, *Miramar* (2000 edn), pp. 8, 67, 95.
117. Morris, *Among the Cities*, p. 18.
118. Jacqueline Cooper, p. 145.
119. Robert Mabro, 'Nostalgic literature on Alexandria', in Jill Edwards, ed., *Historians in Cairo* (Cairo, 2002), p. 240.
120. *Alexandrie Info*, 21 (Dec. 2003); cf., for more food nostalgia, Victoria Thompson, *Losing Alexandria* (Sydney, 1998), pp. 28, 53, 174.
121. John Carswell, 'Kutahya ware', *Hali*, 121 (Mar./Apr. 2002), 78–9, p. 79.
122. Interview with John Nahman, 14 Oct. 2008.
123. Interview with Michael Haag, 10 Aug. 2007.
124. CEA, Zogheb diary, 10 Sept. 1942.

125. Zananiri, p. 319.
126. Interview with Sam Lock, 20 Jan. 2010.
127. Hala Halim, 'Waiting for the Zervudachis', *Mediterraneans*, 8 (1996), pp. 374–9; interview with Jo Boulad, 10 Dec. 2008.
128. Visit, 16 Dec. 2008.
129. Morris, *Among the Cities*, p. 21.
130. Eric Denis, 'Alexandrie: seconde ville d'Egypte ou métropole méditer-ranéenne', *Revue géographique de l'Est*, 2–3 (1997), pp. 173, 182, 183.
131. Interview with B.M., 8 Dec. 2008.
132. Personal information, Colin Clement, 9 Feb. 2007, Lucette de Saab, Mimi Awad, Jan. 2010.
133. Holden, p. 27.
134. Interviews with Nisha Sursock, 11 Feb. 2007, Colin Clement, 16 Feb. 2007, Dr Tadros, 24 July 2008.
135. David Hirst and Irene Beeson, *Sadat* (1981), p. 328.
136. *International Herald Tribune*, 14 Oct. 2009, p. 2.

Chapter 15: Beirut: Birth of a Capital

1. Chami, *Du Mont Liban*, pp. 46–7.
2. Salibi, *A House of Many Mansions*, p. 168; Edde, p. 45; Khoury, *La France et l'Orient arabe*, pp. 133, 137.
3. Dinning, *Nile to Aleppo*, p. 122; Khoury, *La France et l'Orient arabe*, pp. 132, 136; Edde, pp. 64–6.
4. Edde, pp. 75, 79.
5. Khoury, *La France et l'Orient arabe*, p. 224; Kassir, *Beyrouth*, p. 339.
6. Edde, p. 79.
7. Ibid., pp. 91, 181, 340.
8. Ibid., pp. 31, 80, 82, 85; Khoury, *La France et l'Orient arabe*, pp. 267, 268.
9. SA, Isabelle Bustros to 'Alfred Chéri', Nov. 1918.
10. Edde, pp. 41, 57, 83.
11. Patrick Seale, *The Struggle for Arab Independence: Riad al-Solh and the Makers of the Modern Middle East* (Cambridge, 2010), p. 129.
12. Edde, pp. 264–5.
13. Ibid., pp. 49, 99.
14. Chami, *Du Mont Liban*, p. 65.
15. Edde, p. 89, 90, 94.
16. Chami, *Du Mont Liban*, p. 63; Khoury, *La France et l'Orient arabe*, p. 397.
17. SA, Fayyad to Sursock, 7 Sept. 1922.
18. Kassir, *Beyrouth*, pp. 307, 315.
19. Pierre Fournié and Jean-Louis Riccioli, *La France et le Proche-Orient 1916–1946* (1996), p. 104; Edde, p. 237.
20. Debbas, p. 66; Kassir, *Beyrouth*, p. 345.
21. Chami, *Du Mont Liban*, p. 123.
22. Seale, *Struggle*, p. 329.

23. Edde, pp. 118, 120, 132, 134, 141; Kassir, *Beyrouth*, p. 261.
24. Edde, pp. 62, 225, 226, 230.
25. SA, letters to Alfred Sursock from Vlado, 6 January 1919, from Georges Fayyad, 15 Dec. 1919.
26. Chami, *Du Mont Liban*, p. 81; Edde, p. 176.
27. SA, Georges Fayyad to Sursock, 7 Sept. 1922.
28. Edde, p. 124.
29. SA, Alfred Sursock to Louis Garchey, 18 Mar. 1924, and 'Résultats du voyage de M. Sursock à Paris, 15 janvier au 22 fevrier 1924'.
30. Tarif Khalidi, 'Unveiled: Anbara Salam in England 1925–1927', in *The Arabs and Britain: Changes and Exchanges* (Cairo, 1999); Kassir, *Beyrouth*, p. 378.
31. Khalaf, p. 210.
32. Kassir, *Beyrouth*, pp. 406–7; Asher Kaufman, *Reviving Phoenica: In Search of Identity in Lebanon* (2004), pp. 128, 181.
33. Edde, pp. 149, 164, 171.
34. Gerard Khoury, ed., *Selim Takla 1895–1945: une contribution à l'indépendance du Liban* (Beirut, 2004), p. 216.
35. Khoury, *Selim Takla*, p. 253.
36. Mark LeVine, *Overthrowing Geography: Jaffa, Tel Aviv and the Struggle for Palestine* (2005), p. 206.
37. Kassir, *Beyrouth*, pp. 387, 392; Kaufman, p. 192.
38. Marwan Buheiry, *Beirut's Role in the Political Economy of the French Mandate 1919–39* (Oxford, 1990), pp. 18–19.
39. Khoury, *Selim Takla*, p. 216.
40. Fournié and Riccioli, p. 225; Kassir, *Beyrouth*, pp. 331–2.
41. Chami, *Du Mont Liban*, p. 94; Kassir, *Beyrouth*, p. 308.
42. Chami, *Du Mont Liban*, p. 159; cf. Seale, *Struggle*, p. 321.
43. Buheiry, pp. 18–19; Kassir, *Beyrouth*, p. 401; Chami, *Du Mont Liban*, p. 163.
44. Johnson, *Class and Client*, p. 72; May Seikaly, *Haifa: The Transformation of an Arab Society 1918–1939* (1998 edn), p. 219.
45. Kaufman, pp. 159, 167, 195.
46. Salibi, *A House of Many Mansions*, p. 179; Kaufman, p. 236.
47. Kaufman, pp. 39, 109, 131, 132, 163.
48. Farid el-Khazen, *The Making and Politics of the 1943 National Pact* (Oxford, 1991), *passim*; Kaufman, p. 176.
49. Mai Ghoussoub, *Leaving Beirut: Women and the Wars Within* (1998), p. 126.
50. Curie, pp. 79, 85.
51. Seale, *Struggle*, pp. 424–5.
52. Chami, *Du Mont Liban*, p. 187; Max Egremont, *Under Two Flags* (1997 edn), p. 225.
53. Mary Borden, *Journey Down a Blind Alley* (1946), p. 143; Henri de Wailly, *Syrie 1941: la guerre occultée* (2006), p. 389.
54. Spears, p. 169.
55. Moorehead, pp. 172–3; Wailly, p. 385.
56. Simpson, I, 487, 491; Egremont, pp. 228–9, 232.
57. A. B. Gaunson, *The Anglo-French Clash in Lebanon and Syria 1940–45* (1987), p. 62.

58. Ibid., pp. 67, 82, 96; Eyal Zisser, *Lebanon: The Challenge of Independence* (2000), p. 89.
59. Spears, p. 171.
60. Philip Mansel, 'The Siren of the Nile' (unpublished typescript, 1998).
61. Charles Mott-Radclyff, *Foreign Body in the Eye: A Memoir of the Foreign Service, Old and New* (1975), p. 96.
62. Colyton, p. 196.
63. Mansel, 'The Siren of the Nile'; Egremont, p. 234.
64. Gaunson, p. 90; Spears, pp. 174–89, 193; Egremont, pp. 238–9.
65. Chami, *Du Mont Liban*, p. 151; Zisser, p. 15; Seale, *Struggle, passim.*
66. Seale, *Struggle*, pp. 387, 651; Igor Timofeev, *Kamal Joumblatt et le tragique destin du Liban* (Beirut, 2000), p. 54.
67. Gaunson, p. 125.
68. Egremont, pp. 239, 241, 248, 251.
69. Zisser, pp. 57, 66; Salibi, *A House of Many Mansions*, p. 186; Seale, *Struggle*, pp. 504–6.
70. Gaunson, pp. 120–21; Selim Abou, *Le Bilinguisme Arabe–Français au Liban* (1962), pp. 119, 132n.
71. Spears, pp. 226, 227, 230, 240, 256; Gaunson, pp. 123, 132.
72. Spears, pp. 236–7, 245; Borden, pp. 225–6.
73. Gaunson, p. 139; Spears, p. 274.
74. Zisser, p. 88.
75. Gaunson, pp. 124, 147, 153; Egremont, p. 254.
76. Buheiry, p. 23; Spears, pp. 297–8; Zisser, p. 94.
77. Gaunson, pp. 171–6.
78. Ibid., pp. 178, 180; Seale, *Struggle*, pp. 597–8.

Chapter 16: The Paris of the Middle East

1. Zisser, pp. 159, 183, 187, 202; Seale, *Struggle*, pp. 680–82, 730.
2. Joseph G. Chami, *Le Mandat Fouad Chehab* (Beirut, 2003), p. 168.
3. Andrée Chedid, *The Return to Beirut* (1989), pp. 10, 126.
4. See the photograph in Michael Gilsenan, *Lords of the Lebanese Marches: Violence and Narrative in an Arab Society* (1996).
5. Timofeev, pp. 80–83.
6. Zisser, p. 197.
7. Jonathan Randal, *The Tragedy of Lebanon* (1990 edn), p. 50.
8. Youmna Asseily and Ahmad Asfahani, *A Face in the Crowd: The Secret Papers of Emir Farid Chehab OBE 1942–1972* (2007), p. 150; Desmond Stewart, *Turmoil in Beirut: A Personal Account* (1958), p. 57, 25 May 1958; Salibi, *Many Mansions*, p. 198; Timofeev, p. 93.
9. Timofeev, p. 194.
10. Johnson, *Class and Client*, pp. 68, 75–6.
11. Stewart, *Turmoil*, pp. 30–31, 35, 38, 39.
12. Ibid., pp. 46, 87, 117; Robert Murphy, *Diplomat among Warriors* (1964), p. 486.

13. Zisser, p. 239.
14. Johnson, *Class and Client*, pp. 84, 141.
15. Kirsten E. Schulze, *The Jews of Lebanon: Between Coexistence and Conflict* (Brighton, 2001), pp. 6, 71, 76, 87, 96; I am grateful for this reference to Cecil Hourani.
16. Chami, *Du Mont Liban*, p. 157; Rosemary Sayigh, *Too Many Enemies: The Palestinian Experience in Lebanon* (1994), p. 163.
17. Kassir, *Beyrouth*, pp. 425, 431, 432.
18. Personal communication, Fouad Nahas, February 2010.
19. Khalaf, p. 233.
20. Kassir, *Beyrouth*, pp. 494, 501.
21. Theo Larsson, *Seven Passports for Palestine: Sixty Years in the Levant* (Pulborough, 1995), p. 111.
22. Chami, *Du Mont Liban*, p. 206.
23. Kassir, *Beyrouth*, p. 515.
24. Carolyn Gates, *The Merchant Republic of Lebanon: Rise of an Open Economy* (1998), p. xv.
25. James Morris, *The Market of Seleukia* (1957), pp. 109, 112, 113.
26. Chami, *Le Mandat Fouad Chehab*, p. 237.
27. Ibid., p. 72.
28. Ibid., p. 298.
29. Personal communications, 12 June 2009; Peter de Roos, 24 Jan. 2006, Alex Sursock, 18 Apr. 2005, Rose Issa, 10 Apr. 2009; Albert Manguel, 'Once again Troy', in Anna Wilson, ed., *Lebanon, Lebanon* (2006), p. 118.
30. Khalaf, p. 237.
31. Personal communication, H.B., 24 June 2009.
32. Fournié and Riccioli, p. 149.
33. Asseily and Asfahani, p. 48.
34. James Craig, *Shemlaan: A History of the Middle East Centre for Arab Studies* (1998), *passim*.
35. Bruce Page, David Leitch and Phillip Knightley, *Philby: The Spy who Betrayed a Generation* (1968), pp. 271, 274; Glencairn Balfour-Paul, *Bagpipes in Babylon: A Lifetime in the Arab World and Beyond* (2006), p. 183; Patrick Seale and Maureen McConville, *Philby: The Long Road to Moscow* (rev. edn, 1978), p. 284.
36. Elizabeth Monroe, *Philby of Arabia* (1973), pp. 292, 295.
37. Desmond Stewart, *Orphan with a Hoop: The Life of Emile Bustani* (1967), p. 83; Said K. Aberish, *The St George Hotel Bar* (1989), pp. 9, 11, 21, 22, 77, 78, 182, 192.
38. Alec Waugh, *The Mule on the Minaret* (1964), p. 88; Kassir, *Beyrouth*, p. 513.
39. Chami, *Le Mandat Fouad Chehab*, p. 100.
40. Asma Freiha and Viviane Ghanem, *Les Libanais et la vie au Liban, de l'indépendance à la guerre 1943–1975*, 2 vols. (Beirut, 1992), I, 172.
41. Kassir, *Beyrouth*, p. 533.
42. Asseily and Asfahani, pp. 191–2.
43. Salibi, *A House of Many Mansions*, p. 169. Red and white were also the colours of Austria, the former protecting power of Pharaon's community, the Greek Catholics.

44. Zisser, p. 101.
45. Caroline Attie, *Struggle in the Levant: Lebanon in the 1950s* (2004), pp. 145, 160.
46. Freiha and Ghanem, II, 426–8, 430–31.
47. John Carswell, 'Henri Pharaon', obituary, *The Independent*, 8 Aug. 1993; Chami, *Du Mont Liban*, p. 219.
48. Debbas, p. 138; Dorothea Duda, *Innenarchitektur syrischer Stadthäuser des 16 bis 18 Jahrhunderts: Die sammlung Henri Pharaon in Beirut* (Beirut, 1971), pp. 173–4.
49. Personal communication, M.R., 15 Oct. 2005.
50. Saliba, pp. 21, 39, 45, 53.
51. Kassir, *Beyrouth*, p. 499.
52. Kaelen Wilson Goldie, 'City limits', *Daily Star* (Beirut), 23 Apr. 2009.
53. Chami, *Le Mandat Fouad Chehab*, p. 93.
54. John Gunther, *Twelve Cities* (1968), pp. 281–2.
55. Kassir, *Beyrouth*, p. 521; Khalaf, pp. 171–8; Charles Glass, *Tribes with Flags* (1999), p. 402.
56. Khalaf, pp. 212, 215.
57. Ghoussoub, p. 34.
58. Margot Badran and Miriam Cooke, eds., *An Anthology of Arab Feminist Writing* (2nd edn, Bloomington, 2004), pp. 7, 15, 17; Timofeev, p. 34.
59. Chami, *Le Mandat Fouad Chehab*, p. 21.
60. Mermier, pp. 46–7, 49, 56–7, 72–4.
61. Kaufman, p. 232.
62. Nizar Kabbani, *Republic of Love* (2003), p. 18; Tawfiq Yusuf Awwad, *Death in Beirut* (1992 edn), pp. 80–81.
63. Nizar Kabbani, *Sand and Other Poems*, tr. Rana Kabbani (1986), pp.19, 58; Kassir, *Beyrouth*, p. 597.
64. Edward Said, 'Cairo and Alexandria', in id., *Reflections on Exile* (2001), pp. 337, 343, 339.
65. Awwad, p. 5; Edward Said, *After the Last Sky: Palestinian Lives* (1986), pp. 171, 173–4; Jean Said Makdisi, *Beirut Fragments: A War Memoir* (New York, 1990), p. 79.
66. Chami, *Le Mandat Fouad Chehab*, p. 22.
67. Seale, *Struggle*, p. 191.
68. Christopher Stone, *Popular Culture and Nationalism in Lebanon: Fairuz and the Rahbani Nation* (2008), p. 80.
69. Zisser, p. 229; Sayigh, pp. 23, 30, 37.
70. Chedid, pp. 10, 75.
71. He also said, as early as 1954, that the US and the UK were in part the prisoners of Israel: Michel Chiha, *Palestine* (Beirut, 1957), pp. 1 (5 Dec. 1947), 282 (6 Nov. 1954).
72. Joseph G. Chami, *Le Mandat Charles Helou* (Beirut, 2004), pp. 111, 168, 202, 219; Kassir, *Beyrouth*, pp. 563, 569.
73. Asseily and Asfahani, pp. 95–6.
74. Joseph G. Chami, *Chronicle of a War 1975–1990* (Beirut, 2005), p. 15.
75. Kassir, *Beyrouth*, pp. 573–4.
76. Ibid., pp. 575, 608; Glass, p. 339.

77. Alain Menargues, *Les Secrets de la Guerre du Liban* (2004), p. 464.
78. Amiel Alcalay, *After Jews and Arabs: Remaking Levantine Culture* (Minneapolis, 1993), p. 95; Kassir, *Beyrouth*, p. 578.
79. Chami, *Chronicle*, pp. 228–9.
80. Farid el-Khazen, *The Breakdown of the State in Lebanon 1967–1976* (2000), pp. 189–192, 203, 211; Timofeev, pp. 271–6.
81. Awwad, pp. 66, 182.
82. Michael Johnson, *All Honourable Men* (2001), p. 53.
83. Timofeev, p. 287; Chami, *Chronicle*, p. 24.

Chapter 17: The Dance of Death

1. Tony Hanania, *Unreal City* (2000), p. 140; Michel Fani, *Alphabet de Beyrouth* (2000), p. 140.
2. See Mehmet Ali Birand, *Shirts of Steel: An Anatomy of the Turkish Armed Forces* (1991), *passim*.
3. Chami, *Chronicle*, p. 68.
4. Chedid, pp. 123, 131.
5. Chami, *Chronicle*, pp. 26, 27, 39, 41; Rashid al-Daif, *Dear Mr Kawabata* (1995), p. 132.
6. Chami, *Chronicle*, p. 43.
7. Sayigh, p. 268.
8. Johnson, *Class and Client*, pp. 183, 185–6; Lina Mikdadi Tabbara, *Survival in Beirut: A Diary of Civil War* (1979), p. 104; poster reproduced in Zeina Maasri, *Off the Wall: Political Posters of the Lebanese Civil War* (2009), 5:4.
9. al-Daif, pp. 106, 141.
10. Calame and Charlesworth, p. 60.
11. Tabbara, p. 72; Chami, *Chronicle*, pp. 35, 61.
12. Jean Said Makdisi, p. 29.
13. Tabbara, pp. 46, 76.
14. Menargues, pp. 36, 62; Chami, *Chronicle*, p. 175.
15. Tabbara, p. 145; el-Khazen, *Breakdown*, pp. 306, 325.
16. Morris, *Seleukia*, p. 112.
17. Calame and Charlesworth, pp. 93, 123.
18. al-Daif, pp. 127, 132; Hanania, p. 199; Glass, p. 404; Chami, *Chronicle*, p. 92.
19. Calame and Charlesworth, pp. 38–40, 217; Larry Pintak, *Beirut Outtakes* (Lexington, 1988), p. 60.
20. Calame and Charlesworth, pp. 38, 50–51.
21. Visited 1 Oct. 2002.
22. Photographs of crosses taken by Ahmad al-Husseini, Aug. 2004.
23. Ghoussoub, pp. 105–6; Maasri, *passim*.
24. Tabbara, p. 138.
25. Jean Said Makdisi, p. 59; Chami, *Chronicle*, pp. 132, 141; Maasri, 5:2.
26. Ghoussou, pp. 81–3.

27. James M. Malarkey, 'Notes on the psychology of war in Lebanon', in Halim M. Barakat, ed., *Towards a Viable Lebanon* (1988), pp. 291, 296.
28. Maroun Baghdadi and Nayla de Freige, 'The Kalashnikov generation', in Elizabeth Warnock Fernea, ed., *Women and the Family in the Middle East: New Voices of Change* (Austin, 1985), pp. 169–82.
29. Pintak, p. 67.
30. Michel Fani, *Alphabet de Beyrouth* (2000), p. 142; Jean Said Makdisi, p. 57; personal communication, Nur Kaoukgi, 28 Jan. 2010.
31. Tabbara, p. 101; Hanania, p. 142.
32. Hanan al-Shaykh, *The Story of Zahra* (1993 edn), pp. 139, 143.
33. William Harris, *The New Face of Lebanon* (2006), pp. 222–4.
34. Johnson, *Class and Client*, pp. 197, 201; Pintak, pp. 52, 54, 56; Jean Said Makdisi, pp. 139; Tabbara, p. 128; Randal, p. 65.
35. Alexandre Najjar, *The School of War* (2006), pp. 61, 99, 102; Tabbara, pp. 6, 8, 27, 54.
36. Said, *After the Last Sky*, p. 170.
37. Sayigh, p. 168.
38. Johnson, *Class and Client*, p. 97; Sayigh, p. 41.
39. Timofeev, p. 132.
40. Pintak, p. 46; personal communication, H.B., 24 June 2008; cf. Glass, pp. 377–80.
41. However, Charles Glass saw the eighty-two-year-old infirm former speaker Adel Bek Osseiran, minister of defence and agriculture, receiving followers and tenants 'day and night' in Beirut in 1984: Glass, p. 445.
42. Zisser, pp. 162–3.
43. Menargues, pp. 77, 180, 192, 217, 225.
44. Robert Fisk, *Pity the Nation: Lebanon at War* (2001 edn), pp. 282, 286, 315; *Daily Star* (Beirut), 29 Aug. 2003; Schulze, p. 137.
45. David Gilmour, *Lebanon: The Fractured Country* (Oxford, 1983), p. 166.
46. Hazim Saghie, 'Crossings: Beirut in the eighties', in Malu Halas and Roseanne Saad Khalaf, eds., *Transit Beirut: New Writings and Images* (2004), p. 112.
47. Jean Said Makdisi, pp. 162, 184.
48. Menargues, p. 387; Jean Said Makdisi, p. 185.
49. Johnson, *Class and Client*, p. 204n.
50. Menargues, pp. 297–8, 412, 421.
51. Ibid., pp. 374, 405, 409, 411.
52. Patrick Seale, *Assad of Syria* (1988), p. 391; Menargues, pp. 451, 457.
53. Menargues, pp. 437, 469, 473–481. See also the 2005 film *Massacre* by Lokman Slim.
54. Sayigh, pp. 114–22.
55. Menargues, pp. 469–71; Fisk, p. 464.
56. Menargues, p. 493.
57. Abdallah al-Udhari, tr. and ed., *Modern Poetry of the Arab World* (1986); Adonis, *The Desert: The Diary of Beirut under Siege* (1982), pp. 64–5.
58. Sayigh, pp. 131–2.
59. Interview in *Daily Star* (Beirut), 4 Nov. 2004, p. 11.
60. Sayigh, pp. 142, 149, 164; Seale, *Assad*, pp. 334, 328.

61. Michael Davie and Elaine Gebrane, *Beyrouth, regards croisés* (1997), pp. 130–40.
62. Sayigh, p. 200; Johnson, *Class and Client*, pp. 213, 222.
63. Sayigh, pp. 191, 197, 222, 317, 322, 324.
64. William Harris, p. 200; Menargues, p. 148.
65. Robert Baer, *See No Evil* (2002 edn), pp. 100, 188.
66. Chami, *Chronicle*, pp. 90, 284, 288, 298, 300; Johnson, *All Honourable Men*, p. 241.
67. Sayigh, p. 194; William Harris, pp. 231, 244, 254, 269.
68. Jean Said Makdisi, pp. 48, 211; Fisk, p. 633; Chami, *Chronicle*, *passim*, for photographs.
69. Fisk, pp. 217, 433–4.
70. William Harris, p. 1.
71. Tabbara, pp. 88, 99, 106, 125, 161; Fani, *La Photographie au Liban*, pp. 392, 394.
72. Cf. for one such case Jean Said Makdisi, p. 183n.
73. Rabih Alameddine, *Koolaids* (1999 edn), p. 201; Najjar, p. 60; Elizabeth Picard, 'Les Syriens, l'envers du décor', in Jad Thabet, ed., *Beyrouth: la brûlure des rêves* (2001), p. 95.
74. Hoda Barakat, *The Stones of Laughter* (Northampton, Mass., 2006), pp. 38, 85.
75. Jean Said Makdisi, p. 30.
76. Personal communication, 25 Jan. 2008.
77. Carswell, 'Henri Pharaon'; interviews with John Carswell, 9 Aug. 2006, Jean de Freige, 23 Feb. 2005, and others who prefer anonymity.
78. Chami, *Chronicle*, p. 240.
79. Robert Baer, p. 98.
80. Michael F. Davie, *A Post-War Urban Geography of Beirut* (1993), *passim*.
81. *Daily Star* (Beirut), 25 Jan. 2002.
82. Kaufman, p. 248.
83. Nawaf Salam and Fares Sassine, *Lebanon: A Century in Pictures* (Beirut, 2003), p. 280.

Chapter 18: New Levants for Old

1. Personal communication, Nabil Saidi, an eyewitness, 20 Apr. 2010.
2. Kaufman, pp. 2, 24.
3. Nicholas Blanford, *Killing Mr Lebanon: The Assassination of Rafik Hariri and its Impact on the Middle East* (2006), pp. 31–2.
4. Kassir, *Beyrouth*, p. 526n.
5. Fisk, p. 665.
6. Khalaf, pp. 138–9, 236.
7. Associated Press, 22 Jan. 2010, quoting Iman Haidar; thanks for this reference to Aouni Abdul Rahim.
8. Blanford, pp. 44–6.
9. Khalaf, p. 31.
10. Algerina video, 11 Apr. 2010.

11. Suzanne Cotter et al., *Out of Beirut* (Oxford, 2006), pp. 29, 97; Kassir, *Beyrouth*, p. 627.
12. Interviews with Paddy Cochrane, 8 Feb. 2008, 7 May 2010.
13. Zeena el-Khalil, *Beirut I Love You* (2009), pp. 55, 79, 105.
14. Interview with Paddy Cochrane, 7 May 2010.
15. William Harris, pp. 289, 292.
16. Blanford, pp. 63, 68.
17. William Harris, pp. 293, 298, 302–5; Blanford, pp. 6–12, 128.
18. *Daily Star* (Beirut), 16, 25 Feb. 2005.
19. Blanford, p. 147; Philip Mansel diary, 16 Feb. 2005.
20. Blanford, p. 160.
21. Ibid., pp. 162, 165, 177; Nicholas Blanford (p. 158) quotes Bashar al-Assad attributing responsibility to 'probably one of those intelligence pockets we have'.
22. Ibid., p. 176; *The Independent*, 15 June 2007.
23. *Montreal Gazette*, 13 July 2006; I am grateful for this reference to Charles Bland.
24. Laleh Khalili, 'Beirut's southern suburbs in the aftermath of the July War', *Middle East in London* (Oct. 2006), 6–10, p. 12.
25. *Courrier International*, 9 Aug. 2006.
26. *International Herald Tribune*, 23 Sept. 2006.
27. Andrew Rawnsley, *The Party is Over* (2010), pp. 382–5.
28. Blanford, p. 51; *Daily Star* (Beirut), 25, 26 Jan., 1 Feb. 2007; *The Independent*, 24, 25 Jan. 2007; *Courrier International*, 7 Dec. 2006, pp. 45–6.
29. *International Herald Tribune*, 30 May 2007.
30. Personal communication, 23 May 2008; *Daily Star* (Beirut), 10, 21 May 2008.
31. Personal comments, Samir Rebees, 16 Jan. 2008, Tony Naufal, 2 Feb. 2008.
32. Personal comments by Lebanese who prefer to remain anonymous, 10 June 2005, 5 Jan. 2003.
33. Personal communications, Mona Harb, Sami Nasr, 12 Feb. 2008.
34. *Daily Star* (Beirut), 22 Feb. 2010.
35. Ibid., 24 Oct. 2007.
36. Robert Donia, *Sarajevo: A Biography* (2006), p. 3; Samir Kassir, 'Entre chien et loups', in Jad Thabet, ed., *Beyrouth: la brûlure des rêves* (2001), p. 140.
37. *Courrier International*, 2 Oct. 2008, p. 20.
38. Anke van Nugteren and Lienke van Nugteren, 'The Belgian language question' (unpublished typescript, Brussels, 2009); N. Eliot, Y. Mansfield and J. Kotek, *Divided Cities* (1999), pp. 232–3.
39. Stefan Hertmans, *Intercities* (2001), pp. 4, 12; interview with Mayor Dikshit, *International Herald Tribune*, 26 Sept. 2005.
40. See 'Londres capitale du xxi siècle', *Courrier International*, 16 May 2007.
41. *The Times*, 11 July 2005, 2 Sept. 2006.
42. *Hurriyet Weekend*, 14 Mar. 2009, p. 11.
43. *Turkish Daily News*, Izmir issue, July 2007; *The Guardian*, 20 Oct. 2009.
44. Olivier Poivre d'Arvor, *Alexandrie Bazar: le roman d'une ville* (2009), p. 60.

45. Nicholas Woodsworth, *The Liquid Continent*, 3 vols. (2008), I (*Alexandria*), 106–7.
46. *International Herald Tribune*, 27 Nov. 2009, p. 5.
47. Arvor, pp. 80–83, 86; Woodsworth, I, 75.
48. Interview with Jo Boulad, 8 Dec. 2008.
49. *Daily Star* (Beirut), 14 July 2009, 6 Mar. 2010.
50. *International Herald Tribune*, 17 Apr. 2010, re Asad Shaftari of the Phalange.
51. *Courrier International*, 30 Apr. 2009, p. 58; http://www.asadmag.com.
52. *Courrier International*, 29 Jan. 2009, p. 25.
53. *Daily Star* (Beirut), 28 Dec. 2003; Warren Singh-Bartlett, *Financial Times*, 5 Aug. 2006.
54. Michael J. Totten, 'From Baghdad to Beirut', *City Journal*, 10 Jan. 2010 (online).

Bibliography

Manuscript sources

BGA: Brian Giraud Archives, Izmir: diary of Hortense Woods, June 1922–May 1923

BL: British Library Add. MSS 38591, J. O. Hanson, 'Recollections of Smyrna and Greece 1813'

CEA: Centre d'Etudes Alexandrines, Alexandria: diary of Mary de Zogheb

DA: Debbas Archives, Beirut: journal of Madame de Perthuis 1854–61; 'Autobiographie de Dimitri Youssef Debbas'

ELIA (Hellenic Literary and Historical Archive), Athens: Cavafy Archive (consulted online at http://www.elia.org.gr)

EUSC: Exeter University, Special Collections: Barker and Whittall family papers

George Hawthorn journal (sold by Sotheby's, 18 May 2004)

John Cam Hobhouse, diary of 1810, at http://www.hobby-o.com

R. Lang of the Ottoman Bank, unpublished memoirs (n.d.)

MEC: Middle East Centre, St Antony's College, Oxford: diary of Andrew Ryan, 1895; Sir Richard Vaux, 'Egyptian and other episodes, personal, political and legal' (1941)

National Archives, London, documents FO 195/1306 and FO 371/7917

SA: Sursock Archives, Beirut: papers of Alfred Sursock

Unpublished typescripts

Auchterlonie, Paul, 'A British family in the Middle East: the Barkers of Smyrna, Aleppo and Alexandria' (c.2009)

Ayoub, Christian, 'Le français comme langue au moyen orient' (Montreal, 1971)

Kechriotis, Vangelis, 'Allons, enfants de la ville! National celebrations and political mobilisation and urban space in Izmir at the turn of the 20th century' (c.2008)

Mansel, Philip, 'The Siren of the Nile' (c.1998)

Nugteren, Anke van, and Nugteren, Lienke van, 'The Belgian language question' (typescript, Brussels, 2009)

Sabit, Adel, 'Life in Alexandria in the 1940s' (Cairo, c.2000)

Salmeri, Giovanni, 'The contribution of Greeks to the local historiography of Smyrna' (2006)

Books

Unless otherwise stated, all books in English are published in London, all books in French in Paris.

Abbas Hilmi II, *The Last Khedive of Egypt: Memoirs*, ed. Amira Sonbol (Cairo, 2006)

Abbott, G. F., *The Tale of a Tour in Macedonia* (1903)

Abécassis, Frédéric, 'Alexandrie, 1929', *Cahiers de la Méditerranée*, 67 (2003)

Abou, Selim, *Le Bilinguisme arabe–français au Liban* (1962)

Aburish, Said K., *The St George Hotel Bar* (1989)

Adonis, *The Desert: The Diary of Beirut under Siege* (1982)

Ahmad, Feroz, *From Empire to Republic: Essays on the Late Ottoman Empire and Modern Turkey*, 2 vols. (Istanbul, 2008)

Ahmed, Leila, *Border Passage* (1999)

Akarli, Engin, *The Long Peace: Ottoman Lebanon 1861–1920* (Berkeley, 1993)

Aksan, Virginia, *Ottoman Wars 1700–1800: An Empire Besieged* (2007)

—— and Goffman, Daniel, eds., *The Early Modern Ottomans: Remapping the State* (Cambridge, 2007)

Aktar, Ayhan, 'Turkifying the economy', in Renée Hirschon, ed., *Crossing the Aegean* (Oxford, 2004)

Alameddine, Rabih, *Koolaids* (1999 edn)

Alcalay, Amiel, *After Jews and Arabs: Remaking Levantine Culture* (Minneapolis, 1993)

Alhadeff, Gina, *The Sun at Midday* (New York, 1997)

Ali Vasib Efendi, *Bir Sehzadenin Hatirati* (Istanbul, 2004)

Alsayad, Nezar, *Cities and Caliphs: On the Genesis of Arab Muslim Urbanism* (1991)

Altay, Fahrettin, *10 Yil Savas Ve Sonrasi 1912–1922* (Istanbul, 1970)

Anderson, Sonia, 'The Anglo-Dutch "Smyrna fleet" of 1693', in A. Hamilton et al., eds., *Friends and Rivals in the East: Studies in Anglo-Dutch Relations in the Levant from the Seventeenth to the Early Nineteenth Century* (Leiden, 2000)

—— *An English Consul in Turkey: Paul Rycaut at Smyrna 1667–1678* (Oxford, 2001 edn)

Andrew, of Greece, HRH Prince, *Towards Disaster: The Greek Army in Asia Minor in 1921* (1930)

Andrews, Walter G., and Kalpakli, Mehmet, *The Age of Beloveds: Love and the Beloved in Early Modern Ottoman and European Culture and Society* (2005)

Annuaire oriental (Constantinople, 1922)

Antonius, George, *The Arab Awakening* (1938)

Armagnac, Baron d', *Nezib et Beyrout: souvenirs d'Orient de 1833 à 1841* (1844)

Arundell, F. V. J., *Discoveries in Asia Minor*, 2 vols. (1834)

Arvieux, Chevalier d', *Mémoires*, 6 vols. (1735)

Arvor, Olivier Poivre d', *Alexandrie Bazar: le roman d'une ville* (2009)

al-Askari, Jafar, *A Soldier's Story: From Ottoman Rule to Independent Iraq* (2003)

Asseily, Youmna, and Asfahani, Ahmad, *A Face in the Crowd: The Secret Papers of Emir Farid Chehab OBE 1942–1972* (2007)

Atay, Falih Rifki, *Le Mont des oliviers* (2009)

Athanasi, Giovanni d', *A Brief Account of the Researches and Discoveries in Upper Egypt made under the direction of Henry Salt Esq.* (1836)

Atiyah, Edward, *An Arab tells his Story: A Study in Loyalties* (1946)

Atiyeh, George N., 'The book in the modern Arab world', in id., ed. *The Book in the Islamic World* (Albany, 1995)

Les Atrocités grecques en Asie mineure (Constantinople, 1922)

Attie, Caroline, *Struggle in the Levant: Lebanon in the 1950s* (2004)

Auchterlonie, Paul, 'A Turk of the West. Sir Edgar Vincent's career in Egypt and the Ottoman Empire', *British Journal of Middle Eastern Studies*, 27, 1 (2000), 49–67

Augustinos, Gerasimos, *The Greeks of Asia Minor: Confession, Community and Ethnicity in the Nineteenth Century* (1992)

Austin, Douglas, *Malta and British Strategic Policy 1925–1943* (2004)

An Authentic Narrative of the Russian Expedition against the Turks by Sea and Land (1772)

Avelin, Claude, *La Promenade égyptienne* (1934)

Avennes, Prisse d', *Mémoires secrets sur la cour d'Egypte* (1930)

Awad, Mohamed, *Italy in Alexandria: Influences on the Built Environment* (Alexandria, 2008)

—— 'The metamorphoses of Mansheyeh', *Mediterraneans*, 8 (2006)

—— and Hamouda, Sahar, *The Birth of the Seventh Art in Alexandria* (Alexandria, 2007)

—— *The Zoghebs: An Alexandrian Saga* (Alexandria, 2005)

—— eds., *Voices from Cosmopolitan Alexandria* (Alexandria, 2006)

Awwad, Tawfiq Yusuf, *Death in Beirut* (1992 edn)

Bacqué-Gramont, Jean-Louis, Kuneralp, Sinan, and Hitzel, Frédéric, *Représentants permanents de la France en Turquie et de la Turquie en France* (Istanbul, 1991)

Badran, Margot, and Cooke, Miriam, eds., *An Anthology of Arab Feminist Writing* (2nd edn, Bloomington, 2004)

Badrawi, Malak, *Ismail Sidqi 1875–1950* (1996)

—— *Political Violence in Egypt 1910–1924* (2000)

Baer, Gabriel, *Fellah and Townsman in the Middle East* (1982)

—— *Studies in the Social History of Modern Egypt* (Chicago, 1969)

Baer, Robert, *See No Evil* (2002 edn)

Baghdadi, Maroun, and de Freige, Nayla, 'The Kalashnikov generation', in Elizabeth Warnock Fernea, ed., *Women and the Family in the Middle East: New Voices of Change* (Austin, 1985)

Bakhit, Muhammad Adnan, 'The Christian population of Damascus in the sixteenth century', in Benjamin Braude and Bernard Lewis, *Christians and Jews in the Ottoman Empire*, 2 vols. (1982), II

Balfour-Paul, Glencairn, *Bagpipes in Babylon: A Lifetime in the Arab World and Beyond* (2006)

Barakat, Hoda, *The Stones of Laughter* (Northampton, Mass., 2006)

Bardsley, Gillian, *Issigonis: The Official Biography* (Thriplow, 2005)

Barker, E. B., *Syria and Egypt under the Last Five Sultans*, 2 vols. (1876)

Barker, Gabriella, *Desert Angels* (1956)

Barthélémy, Cécile, *Georges Moustaki* (Paris, 1970)

Basch, Lucien, 'Les jardins des morts', *Mediterraneans*, 8 (2006), 364–73

Bauffremont, Joseph de, *Journal de campagne de l'amiral de Bauffremont, prince de Listenois, dans les pays barbaresques (1766)* (1981)

Beaman, A. G. Hulme, *Twenty Years in the Near East* (1898)

Beaton, Cecil, *The Years Between* (1965)

Beaton, Roderick, *George Seferis: Waiting for the Angel* (2003)

Beinin, Joel, *The Dispersion of Egyptian Jewry: Culture, Politics and the Formation of a Modern Diaspora* (Cairo, 2005)

Bell, E. H. D. Moberly, *The Life and Letters of C. F. Moberly Bell* (1927)

Benedetti, Comte, *Essais diplomatiques* (nouvelle série), 2 vols. (1897)

Bent, J. Theodore, ed., *Early Voyages and Travels in the Levant* (1893)

Bérard, Victor, *La Macédoine* (1897)

Beresford, Admiral Lord Charles, *Memoirs*, 2 vols. (1914)

Berque, Jacques, *L'Egypte: impérialisme et révolution* (1967)

Berridge, G. R., 'Notes on the origins of the diplomatic corps: Constantinople in the 1620s', in *Discussion Papers in Diplomacy* (Clingandael, 2004)

Bertrand, Louis, *Le Mirage oriental* (1913)

Bibliotheca Alexandrina, *Alex-Med Newsletter*, 2004–

Biovès, Achille, *Français et Anglais en Egypte 1881–1882* (1910)

Birand, Mehmet Ali, *Shirts of Steel: An Anatomy of the Turkish Armed Forces* (1991)

Birch, W., *Journal of a Voyage up the Mediterranean* (Poulton, 1818)

Blanford, Nicholas, *Killing Mr Lebanon: The Assassination of Rafik Hariri and its Impact on the Middle East* (2006)

Blunt, W. S., *Gordon at Khartoum* (1911)

—— *Secret History of the English Occupation of Egypt* (1907)

Boal, F. W., 'Ethnic residential segregation, ethnic mixing and resource conflict: a study in Belfast, Northern Ireland', in Ceri Peach, Vaughan Robinson and Susan Smith, eds., *Ethnic Segregation in Cities* (1981)

Bond, Alvan, *Memoir of Rev. Pliny Fisk* (Edinburgh, 1828)

Boogert, Maurits van den, ed., *Ottoman Izmir* (Istanbul, 2007)

Booth, Marilyn L., *Bayram al-Tunisi's Egypt: Social Criticism and Narrative Strategies* (Exeter, 1990)

Borden, Mary, *Journey Down a Blind Alley* (1946)

Bosch, Baron Firmin van den, *Vingt années d'Egypte* (1932)

Botman, Selma, *Egypt from Independence to Revolution 1919–1952* (Syracuse, NY, 1991)

Bouquet, Olivier, 'Du haut de Péra: étude du jeu diplomatique de l'Europe dans l'Empire Ottoman 1909–1914', thesis (Paris, 1993)

Bouvier, Jean François, *L'Ordre du Nil: vie et combats d'Antoine Arcache Bey* (n.d.)

Boveri, Margret, *Mediterranean Cross-Currents*, tr. Louisa Marie Sieveking (1938)

Bower, Tom, *Fayed* (1998)

Boyar, Ebru, *Ottoman Turks and the Balkans: Empire Lost, Relations Altered* (2007)

Bramsen, John, *Letters of a Prussian Traveller*, 2 vols. (1818)

Braude, Benjamin, and Lewis, Bernard, *Christians and Jews in the Ottoman Empire*, 2 vols. (1982)

Breccia, E., *Alexandria ad Aegyptum* (Bergamo, 1914)

Brewer, David, *The Greek War of Independence* (New York, 2001)

Bromfield, William A., *Letters from Egypt and Syria* (1856)

Brown, Nathan J., 'The precarious life and slow death of the mixed courts of Egypt', *International Journal of Middle East Studies*, 25 (1993), 33–52

Buheiry, Marwan, *Beirut's Role in the Political Economy of the French Mandate 1919–39* (Oxford, 1990)

Bulent, Ari, 'Early Ottoman diplomacy', in Nuri Yurdusev, ed., *Ottoman Diplomacy: Conventional or Unconventional?* (Basingstoke, 2004)

Butler, Alfred J., *Court Life in Egypt* (1887)

Byron, Lord, *Letters and Journals*, 12 vols. (1972–82)

Cabanel, Patrick, ed., *Une France en Méditerranée: écoles, langue et culture française* (2006)

Cadalvène, Ed. de, and de Breuvery, J., *L'Egypte et la Turquie de 1829 à 1836*, 2 vols. (1836)

Cavafy, C. P., *Collected Poems* (Oxford, 2007)

Calame, Jon, and Charlesworth, Esther, *Divided Cities: Belfast, Beirut, Jerusalem, Mostar and Nicosia* (Philadelphia, 2009)

Çalislar, Ipek, *Latife Hanim* (Istanbul, 2006)

Calligas, Paul, *Voyage à Syros, Smyrne et Constantinople* (2004 edn)

Calvocoressi, Peter, *Threading My Way* (1994)

Camp, Maxime du, *Souvenirs et paysages d'Orient* (1848)

Canudo, I., *Combats d'Orient* (1917)

Carlino, Tziana, 'The Levant: A Transmediterranean Literary Category?' (online, 2006)

Carlisle, Earl of, *Diary in Turkish and Greek Waters* (1854)

Carol, Jacqueline, *Cocktails and Camels* (Alexandria, 2008)

—— *Scribbles* (Geneva, 2004)

Carswell, John, 'The Greeks in the East. Alexandria and Islam', in Stephen Vernoit, ed., *Discovering Islamic Art: Scholars, Collectors and Collections 1850–1950* (1999)

—— 'Henri Pharaon', obituary, *Independent*, 8 Aug. 1993

—— 'Kutahya ware', *Hali*, 121 (Mar./Apr. 2002), 78–9

Carver, Michael, *Dilemmas of the Desert War* (1986)

Cattaui, René, ed., *Le Règne de Mohamed Aly d'après les archive russes en Egypte*, 2 vols. (1931)

Çelebi, Evliya, *Seyahatnamesi*, 10 vols. (Istanbul, 1999–2007)

Çelik, Zeynep, *Urban Forms and Colonial Confrontations: Algiers under French Rule* (1997)

Celikkol, Zeki, de Groot, Alexander, and Slot, Ben. J., *It Began with the Tulip: Turkey and the Netherlands in Pictures* (Ankara, 2000)

Chaille-Long, Charles, *My Life in Four Continents*, 2 vols. (1912)

Chair, Admiral Sir Dudley de, *The Sea is Strong* (1961)

Chami, Joseph G., *Chronicle of a War 1975–1990* (Beirut, 2005)

—— *Le Mandat Charles Helou* (Beirut, 2004)

—— *Le Mandat Fouad Chehab* (Beirut, 2003)

—— *Le Mémorial du Liban* (Beirut, 2002)

—— *Du Mont Liban à l'indépendance* (Beirut, 2002)

Chandler, Richard, *Travels in Asia Minor and Greece*, 2 vols. (3rd edn, 1817)

Charles-Roux, François, *Le Projet français de conquête de l'Egypte sous le règne de Louis XVI* (Cairo, 1929)

—— *Souvenirs diplomatiques* (1956)

——— *La Syrie et Palestine au XVIIIe siècle* (1925)

——— *Thiers et Mehemet Ali* (1951)

Charmes, Gabriel, *Cinq mois au Caire et dans la basse Egypte* (1880)

——— *Voyage en Syrie: impressions et souvenirs* (1891)

Charrière, Ernest, *Négociations de la France dans le Levant*, 4 vols. (1848)

Chateaubriand, François-René, Vicomte de, *Itinéraire de Paris à Jérusalem et de Jérusalem à Paris*, 2 vols. (1846 edn)

Chater, Melville, 'History's greatest trek', *National Geographic* (Mar. 1923)

Chedid, Andrée, *The Return to Beirut* (1989)

Chehabi, H. E., 'An Iranian in the First World War', in id., ed., *Distant Relations: Iran and Lebanon in the Last 500 Years* (2006)

Chevallier, Dominique, *La Société du Mont Liban à l'époque de la révolution industrielle en Europe* (1971)

Chiha, Michel, *Palestine* (Beirut, 1957)

Chirol, Valentin, *Fifty Years in a Changing World* (1927)

Chishull, Edmund, *Antiquitates Asiaticae* (1728)

Churchill, Winston, *The Second World War*, vol. 4: *The Hinge of Fate* (1951)

——— *The World Crisis: The Aftermath* (1929)

Cialente, Fausta, *The Levantines* (1963)

Clark, Bruce, *Twice a Stranger: How Mass Expulsion Forged Modern Greece and Turkey* (2006)

Clarke, Hyde, *History of the British Community at Smyrna* (1862)

Clayer, Nathalie, et al., eds., *Presse turque et presse de Turquie* (1992)

Clogg, Richard, *The Movement for Greek Independence 1770–1821* (1976)

——— *Studies in Ottoman Greek History* (Istanbul, 2004)

Clot Bey, A. B., *Aperçu général sur l'Egypte*, 2 vols. (1840)

——— *Mémoires* (Cairo, 1949)

Cochran, William, *Pen and Pencil in Asia Minor; or, Notes from the Levant* (1887)

Cocteau, Jean, *Maalesh* (1949)

Cohen, Gary B., *The Politics of Ethnic Survival: Germans in Prague 1861–1914* (Princeton, 1981)

Cole, Juan, *Colonialism and Revolution in the Middle East: Social and Cultural Origins of Egypt's Urabi Movement* (Princeton, 1993)

Coles Pasha, *Recollections and Reflections* (1918)

Colonas, Vasilis, *Greek Architects in the Ottoman Empire (19th–20th Centuries)* (Athens, 2005)

Colyton, Henry, *Occasion, Chance and Change: A Memoir 1902–1946* (Wimborne, 1993)

Connell, John, *Auchinleck* (1959)

——— *Wavell: Soldier and Scholar* (1964)

Constantine, King, *A King's Letters to a Friend* (1927)

Cooper, Artemis, *Cairo in the War 1939–1945* (1989)

Cooper, Jacqueline, *Tales from Alexandria* (Geneva, 1994)

Coste, Pascal, *Toutes les Egyptes* (Marseille, 1998)

Cotter, Suzanne, et al., *Out of Beirut* (Oxford, 2006)

Courbage, Youssef, 'Situation démographique comparée du Bilad al cham au xviie et xixie siècles', in *Les Relations entre musulmans et chrétiens dans le bilad al cham. Actes du colloque de 2004* (Beirut, 2004)

Courmenin, M., *Voyage de Levant* (1629)

Coward, Noël, *Middle East Diary* (1944)

Crabbs, Jack A., *The Writing of History in Ninetenth-Century Egypt: A Study in National Transformation* (Cairo, 1984)

Craig, James, *Shemlaan: A History of the Middle East Centre for Arab Studies* (1998)

Crimmin, Patricia, 'The Royal Navy and the Levant trade *c.*1795–*c.*1805', in Jeremy Black and Philip Woodfine, eds., *The British Navy and the Use of Naval Power in the Eighteenth Century* (Leicester, 1988)

Cumali, Necati, *Macédoine 1900 nouvelles*, ed. Faruk Bilici (2007)

Cunningham, Allan, *Anglo-Ottoman Encounters in the Age of Revolution*, 2 vols. (1993)

—— ed., *The Early Correspondence of Richard Wood, 1831–1841* (1966)

Cunningham of Hyndhope, Admiral of the Fleet Viscount, *A Sailor's Odyssey* (1951)

Curie, Eve, *Journey among Warriors* (1943)

al-Daif, Rashid, *Dear Mr Kawabata* (1995)

Dakhlia, Jocelyne, *Lingua franca: Histoire d'une langue métisse en Méditerranée* (2008)

Dakin, Douglas, *The Greek Struggle in Macedonia 1897–1913* (Thessaloniki, 1966)

Dallaway, James, *Constantinople: Ancient and Modern* (1797)

Dankoff, Robert, *An Ottoman Mentality: The World of Evliya Çelebi* (Leiden, 2004)

Dapper, M., *Description exacte des isles de l'Archipel et de quelques autres adjacentes* (Amsterdam, 1703)

Dardaud, Gabriel, 'Un officier français du génie: Gallice Bey', *Revue des Conférences Françaises en Orient*, Dec. 1947, 657–70

Darques, René, *Salonique au vingtième siècle* (2000)

Davie, May, *Beyrouth 1825–1975: un siècle et demi d'urbanisme* (Beirut, 2001)

—— 'Les chrétiens dans l'espace et la société de Beyrouth', in *Les Relations entre musulmans et chrétiens dans le bilad al cham. Actes du colloque de 2004* (Beirut, 2004)

Davie, Michael F., *A Post-War Urban Geography of Beirut* (1993)

—— and Elaine Gebrane, *Beyrouth, regards croisés* (1997)

Davison, Roderick H., *Essays in Ottoman and Turkish History 1774–1923* (1990)

Dawson, Lionel, *Mediterranean Medley* (1933)

Debbas, Fouad C., *Beirut our Memory* (2nd rev. edn, Beirut, 1986)

Deeb, Marius, 'The socio-economic role of the foreign minorities in Egypt 1805–1961', *International Journal of Middle East Studies*, 19 (1978), 11–22

Degert, Abbé Antoine, 'Une ambassade périlleuse de François de Noailles en Turquie', *Revue Historique*, 159 (Nov. 1928), 225–60

Delanoue, Gilbert, *Moralistes et politiques musulmans dans l'Egypte du xixe siècle*, 2 vols. (Cairo, 1982)

Denis, Eric, 'Alexandrie: seconde ville d'Egypte ou métropole méditerranéenne', *Revue géographique de l'Est*, 2–3 (1997), 163–88

Deringil, Selim, 'There is no compulsion in religion; on conversion and apostasy in the late Ottoman Empire 1839–1856', in id., *The Ottomans, the Turks and World Power Politics* (2000)

Deschamps, Gaston, *A Constantinople* (1913)

Desmet-Grégoire, Hélène, *Cafés d'orient revisités* (1997)

Diamandouros, Nikiforos P., et. al., eds., *Hellenism and the First Greek War of Liberation: Continuity and Change* (Thessaloniki, 1976)

Diesbach, Ghislain de, *Ferdinand de Lesseps* (2004)

Dikkaya, Kahri, et al., *Avrupali mi, Levanten mi?* (Istanbul, 2006)

Dinning, Hector, *By-Ways on Service: Notes from an Australian Journal* (1918)

—— *Nile to Aleppo with the Light-Horse in the Middle East* (1920)

Dodwell, Henry, *The Founder of Modern Egypt: A Study of Muhammad Ali* (Cambridge, 1931)

Donia, Robert, *Sarajevo: A Biography* (2006)

Dornel, Laurent, 'Cosmopolitisme et xenophobie: Français et Italiens à Marseille 1870–1914', *Cahiers de la Méditerranée*, 67 (Dec. 2003)

Douglas, Keith, *Alamein to Zem Zem* (1966 edn)

Douglas, Norman, *Looking Back* (1934)

Douglas, Sholto, *Years of Command* (1966)

Douin, Georges, *L'Egypte de 1828 à 1830: correspondance des consuls de France en Egypte* (Rome, 1935)

—— *La Mission du Baron de Boislecomte: l'Egypte et la Syrie en 1833* (Cairo, 1927)

—— *Une mission militaire française auprès de Mohamed Aly: correspondance des généraux Belliard et Boyer* (1923)

—— *Navarin 6 juillet–20 octobre 1827* (Cairo, 1927)

Doukas, Stratis, *A Prisoner of War's Story* (Birmingham, 1991)

Dragoumis, Markos, 'The music of the rebetes', in id., ed., *From Byzantium to Rembetiko* (Kerkyra, 2007)

Driault, Edouard, *Mohamed Ali et Napoléon (1807–1814): correspondance des consuls de France en Egypte* (Cairo, 1925)

Drummond, Alexander, *Travels through Different Cities of Germany, Italy, Greece and Several Parts of Asia as far as the Banks of the Euphrates* (1754)

Du Mont, M., *Voyages*, 4 vols. (The Hague, 1699)

Duda, Dorothea, *Innenarchitektur Syrischer Stadthäuser des 16 bis 18 Jahrhunderts: Die Sammlung Henri Pharaon in Beirut* (Beirut, 1971)

Duparc, Pierre, *Recueil des instructions données aux ambassadeurs et ministres de France . . . Turquie* (1969)

Durand-Viel, Vice-Amiral, *Les Campagnes navales de Mohammed Aly et d'Ibrahim*, 2 vols. (1935)

Durrell, Lawrence, *The Alexandria Quartet* (1968 edn)

Dursteler, Eric R., *Venetians in Constantinople: Nation, Identity and Coexistence in the Early Modern Mediterranean* (Baltimore, 2006)

Edde, Carla, *Beyrouth: Naissance d'une capitale 1918–1924* (2009)

Edib, Halide, *The Turkish Ordeal* (1928)

Edwards, Kenneth, *The Grey Diplomatists* (1938)

Egremont, Max, *Under Two Flags* (1997 edn)

Eliot, N., Mansfield, Y., and Kotek, J., *Divided Cities* (1999)

Elliott, C. B., *Travels in the Three Great Empires of Austria, Russia and Turkey*, 2 vols. (1838)

Elliott, Peter, *The Cross and the Ensign: A Naval History of Malta 1798–1979* (Cambridge, 1980)

Emerson, James, *Letters from the Aegean*, 2 vols. (1829)

Emerson, John E., *Letters from the East*, 2 vols. (3rd edn, 1830)

Eminoglu, Munevver, *A Beyoglu Photo-Romance* (Istanbul, 2000 edn)

Empereur, Jean-Yves, *Alexandrie: Hier et demain* (2001)

Enright, D. J., *Academic Year* (1984 edn)

—— *Season Ticket* (Alexandria, 1948)

Erdem, Hakan, 'Ottoman responses to the Greek war of independence', in Faruk Birtek and Thalia Dragonas, eds., *Citizenship and the nation-state in Greece and Turkey* (2005)

Erickson, Edward J., *Defeat in Detail: The Ottoman Army in the Balkans 1912–1913* (Westport, 2003)

Estourmel, Comte Joseph d', *Journal d'un voyage en Orient*, 2 vols. (1844)

Eudel, Paul, *Constantinople, Smyrne et Athènes: Journal de Voyage* (1885)

Evans, T. Simpson, ed., *The Life of Robert Frampton, Bishop of Gloucester* (1876)

Fagan, Brian, *The Rape of the Nile* (Boulder, 2004 edn)

Fahmy, Khaled, *All the Pasha's Men: Mehmed Ali, His Army and the Making of Modern Egypt* (Cambridge, 1997)

—— 'Towards a social history of modern Alexandria', in Anthony Hirst and Michael Silk, eds., *Alexandria, Real and Imagined* (Aldershot, 2009)

Fani, Michel, *Alphabet de Beyrouth* (2000)

—— *Une histoire de la photographie au Liban* (Beirut, 2005)

Farah, C. E., *Arabs and Ottomans: A Chequered Relationship* (Istanbul, 2002)

Farman, E. E., *Egypt and its Betrayal* (1908)

Faroqhi, Suryaiya, *Subjects of the Sultan: Culture and Daily Life in the Ottoman Empire* (2000)

Fawaz, Leila, *Merchants and Migrants in Nineteenth-Century Beirut* (2000 edn)

—— *An Occasion for War: Civil Conflict in Lebanon and Damascus in 1860* (1994)

Fay, Eliza, *Original Letters from India* (1925)

Fedden, Robin, ed., *Personal Landscape: An Anthology of Exile* (1945)

Fellows, Sir Charles, *Travels and Researches in Asia Minor, More Particularly in the Province of Lycia* (1852)

Fermor, Patrick Leigh, *Roumeli: Travels in Northern Greece* (1966)

Field, James A., Jr, *America and the Mediterranean World 1776–1882* (Princeton, 1969)

Finkel, Caroline, *Osman's Dream: The Story of the Ottoman Empire 1300–1923* (2005)

Finnie, David H., *Pioneers East: The Early American Experience in the Middle East* (Cambridge, Mass., 1967)

Fisher, Jack, *Fear God and Dread Nought: The Correspondance of Admiral of the Fleet Lord Fisher of Kilverstone*, 3 vols. (1952–9)

Fisk, Robert, *Pity the Nation: Lebanon at War* (2001 edn)

Flaubert, Gustave, *Correspondance générale* (1973–)

—— *Voyage en Orient 1849–1851* (2006 edn)

Fleet, Kate, *The Muslim Bonaparte: Diplomacy and Orientalism in Ali Pasha's Greece* (Princeton, 1999)

Fletcher, Richard, *Moorish Spain* (1992)

Foreign Relations of the United States 1952–1954, IX, 2 (Washington, 1986)

Forster, E. M., *Alexandria: A History and a Guide: And Pharos and Pharillon* (2004 edn)

—— *Selected Letters*, ed. Mary Lago, 2 vols. (1983)

Forster, Margaret, *Daphne du Maurier* (1993)

Fournié, Pierre, and Riccioli, Jean-Louis, *La France et le Proche-Orient 1916–1946* (1996)

Frangakis-Syrett, Elena, *The Commerce of Smyrna in the Eighteenth Century* (Athens, 1992)

—— 'Commercial practices and competition in the Levant: the British and the Dutch in eighteenth-century Izmir', in A. Hamilton et al., eds., *Friends and Rivals in the East: Studies in Anglo-Dutch Relations in the Levant from the Seventeenth to the Early Nineteenth Century* (Leiden, 2000)

—— 'The economic activities of the Greek community of Izmir in the second half of the nineteenth and early twentieth centuries', in D. Gondicas and C. Issawi, eds., *Ottoman Greeks in the Age of Nationalism* (Princeton, 1999)

—— 'The making of an Ottoman port: the quay of Izmir in the nineteenth century', *Journal of Transport History*, 22, 1 (2001), 23–46

—— 'The Raya communities of Smyrna in the eighteenth century', *International Journal of Maritime History* (1998)

Freely, John, *The Lost Messiah* (2002 edn)

Freiha, Asma, and Ghanem, Viviane, *Les Libanais et la vie au Liban, de l'indépendance à la guerre 1943–1975*, 2 vols. (Beirut, 1992)

Gage, Nicholas, *Greek Fire* (2001)

Galland, Antoine, *Voyage à Constantinople 1672–1673*, 2 vols. (2002)

—— *Le Voyage à Smyrne*, ed. Frédéric Bauden (2000)

Gandossi, Christiane Villain, 'Les attributions du Baile de Constantinople dans le fonctionnnement des echelles du Levant au xvie siècle', in *Les Grandes Escales*, vol. 11 (Brussels, 1974)

Gardey, Louis, *Voyage du sultan Abd-ul-aziz de Stamboul au Caire* (1865)

Garreau, R., *Un angoumois homme de mer: Besson Bey* (Antibes, 1949)

Gates, Carolyn, *The Merchant Republic of Lebanon: Rise of an Open Economy* (1998)

Gaunson, A. B., *The Anglo-French Clash in Lebanon and Syria 1940–45* (1987)

Gauntlett, Stathis, 'Between orientalism and occidentalism', in Renée Hirschon, ed., *Crossing the Aegean* (Oxford, 2004)

Gaury, Gerald de, *Rulers of Mecca* (1951)

Gelvin, James L., *Divided Loyalties: Nationalism and Mass Politics in Syria at the Close of Empire* (Berkeley, 1998)

Genakopoulos, Deno J., 'The Diaspora Greeks', in Nikiforos P. Diamandouros et al., eds., *Hellenism and the First Greek War of Liberation: Continuity and Change* (Thessaloniki, 1976)

Georgelin, Hervé, *La Fin de Smyrne: du cosmopolitisme aux nationalismes* (2005)

Ghoussoub, Mai, *Leaving Beirut: Women and the Wars Within* (1998)

Gibbon, Edward, *The Decline and Fall of the Roman Empire*, 6 vols. (1776–88)

Giffard, Pierre, *Les Français en Egypte* (1883)

Gilbert, Martin, ed., *Winston Churchill*, vol. 4: 1917–1922. *Companion Documents*, 3 vols. (1977)

Gilmour, David, *Lebanon: The Fractured Country* (Oxford, 1983)

Gilsenan, Michael, *Lords of the Lebanese Marches: Violence and Narrative in an Arab Society* (1996)

Girard, B., *Souvenirs maritimes 1881–1883: journal de bord* (1895)

Gisquet, M., *L'Egypte, les Turcs et les Arabes*, 2 vols. (1846)

Glass, Charles, *Tribes with Flags* (1999)

Glass, Dagmar, and Roper, Geoffrey, 'The printing of Arabic Books in the Arab world', in Geoffrey Roper, ed., *Middle Eastern Languages and the Print Revolution* (Westhofen, 2002)

Goddard, J. K. L., *48!* (Tunbridge Wells, 2003)

Godefroy, Vice-Amiral, *L'Aventure de la Force X à Alexandrie, 1940–1943* (1953)

Godolli, Ezio, and Giacomelli, Milva, eds., *Italian Architects and Engineers in Egypt from the Nineteenth to the Twenty-first Centuries* (Florence, 2008)

Goff, A., and Fawcett, Hugh A., *Macedonia: A Plea for the Primitive* (1921)

Goffman, Daniel, *Britons in the Ottoman Empire 1642–1660* (Seattle, 1998)

—— *Izmir and the Levantine World 1550–1650* (Seattle, 1990)

—— 'Izmir, from village to colonial port city', in Edhem Eldem, Daniel Goffman and Bruce Masters, *The Ottoman City between East and West: Aleppo, Izmir and Istanbul* (Cambridge, 1999)

Goldoni, Carlo, *Four Comedies* (1922 edn)

Goldschmidt, Arthur, Jr, *The Egyptian Nationalist Party 1892–1919* (1968)

Gordon, Joel, *Nasser's Blessed Movement: Egypt's Free Officers and the July Revolution* (New York, 1992)

Goupil-Fesquet, M., *Voyage en orient fait avec Horace Vernet en 1839 et 1840* (1840)

Grafftey-Smith, Laurence, *Bright Levant* (1970)

Grange, Daniel J., *L'Italie et la Méditerranée 1896–1911*, 2 vols. (Rome, 1994)

Graves, Sir Robert, *Storm Centres of the Near East* (1933)

Greene, Rev. Joseph K., *Leavening the Levant* (Boston, 1916)

Gregory, Desmond, *Malta, Britain and the European Powers 1793–1815* (1996)

Griffith, Major and Mrs George Darby, *A Journey across the Desert from Ceylon to Marseilles*, 2 vols. (1845)

Groot, Alexander de, 'The dragomans of the embassies in Istanbul', in Geert Jan Van Gelder and Ed de Moor, eds., *Eastward Bound: Dutch Ventures and Adventures in the Middle East* (Amsterdam, 1994)

—— *The Ottoman Empire and the Dutch Republic: A History of the Earliest Diplomatic Relations* (Leiden and Istanbul, 1978)

Guerville, A. B. de, *La Nouvelle Egypte* (1905)

Guichard, Sylvie, ed., *Lettres de Bernardino Drovetti, consul de France à Alexandrie 1803–1830* (2003)

Guingand, F. W. de, *Operation Victory* (1978)

Gunther, John, *Twelve Cities* (1968)

Guys, Henri, *Relation d'un séjour de plusieurs années à Beyrout et dans le Liban*, 2 vols. (1847)

Haag, Michael, *Alexandria: City of Memory* (2004)

—— *Vintage Alexandria: Photographs of the City 1860–1960* (Cairo, 2008)

Hacisalihoglu, Mehmet, 'The negotiations for the solution of the Macedonian question', *Turcica*, 36 (2004)

Haddad, William W., and Ochsenwald, William, *Nationalism in a Non-National State: The Dissolution of the Ottoman Empire* (Columbus, Ohio, 1977)

Hajjar, Joseph, *L'Europe et les destinées du Proche Orient*, 4 vols. (Damascus, 1988)

Halas, Malu, and Khalaf, Roseanne Saad, eds., *Transit Beirut: New Writings and Images* (2004)

Halim, Hala, 'Waiting for the Zervudachis', *Mediterraneans*, 8 (1996)

Halliday, Stephen, *The Great Stink of London* (1998)

Hamann, Brigitte, *Hitler's Vienna* (1999 edn)

Hamilton, A., et al., eds., *Friends and Rivals in the East: Studies in Anglo-Dutch Relations in the Levant from the Seventeenth to the Early Nineteenth Century* (Leiden, 2000)

Hamilton, Nigel, *Monty: The Making of a General 1887–1942* (1981)

Hamouda, Sahar, *Omar Toussoun: Prince of Alexandria* (Alexandria, 2005)

—— and Clement, Colin, *Victoria College: A History Revealed* (Cairo, 2004)

Hampton, Christopher, *White Chameleon* (1991)

Hanania, Tony, *Unreal City* (2000)

Hanssen, Jens, *Fin de Siècle Beirut: The Making of an Ottoman Provincial Capital* (New York, 2005)

—— 'Practices of integration', in Jens Hanssen, Thomas Philipp and Stefan Weber, eds., *The Empire in the City: Arab Provincial Capitals in the Late Ottoman Empire* (Beirut, 2002)

—— 'Your Beirut is on my desk: Ottomanizing Beirut under Sultan Abdulhamid II 1876–1909', in H. Sarkis and P. Rowe, eds., *Projecting Beirut* (Munich, 1998)

Harris, W.V., ed., *Rethinking the Mediterranean* (2005)

Harris, William, *The New Face of Lebanon* (2006)

Harvey, P., *Muslims in Spain 1500–1614* (Chicago, 2005)

Hasluck, F.W., *Christianity and Islam under the Sultans*, 2 vols. (New York, 1973 edn)

Hassan, Hassan, *In the House of Mohammed Ali: A Family Album 1805–1952* (Cairo, 2000)

Hassoun, Jacques, *Alexandrie et autres récits* (2001)

—— *Juifs d'Egypte: Images et textes* (1984)

Heath-Stubbs, John, *Hindsights* (1993)

Heikal, Azza, *L'Education Alexandrine* (Alexandria, 1996)

Hertmans, Stefan, *Intercities* (2001)

Hervé, Francis, *A Residence in Greece and Turkey*, 2 vols. (1837)

Hess, Andrew C., *The Forgotten Frontier: A History of the Sixteenth Century Ibero-African Frontier* (Chicago, 1978)

Heyberger, Bernard, *Les Européens vus par les Libanais à l'époque ottomane* (Beirut, 2004)

—— 'Livres et pratique de la lecture chez les chrétiens (Syrie Liban) xviie–xviiie siècles', in Frédéric Hitzel, ed., *Livres et lecture dans le monde ottoman* (1999)

Hildyard, Myles, *It is Bliss Here: Letters Home 1939–1945* (2005)

Hirschon, Renée, *Heirs of the Greek Catastrophe* (1998)

Hirst, Anthony, and Silk, Michael, eds., *Alexandria, Real and Imagined* (Aldershot, 2009)

Hirst, David, and Beeson, Irene, *Sadat* (1981)

Hitzel, Frédéric, *Relations interculturelles et scientifiques entre l'Empire Ottoman et les pays de l'Europe occidentale* (thesis, Paris-IV, 1995)

—— ed., *Livres et lecture dans le monde ottoman* (1999)

Hodgson, Geraldine, *The Life of James Elroy Flecker* (Oxford, 1925)

Hogg, Edward, *A Visit to Alexandria, Damascus and Jerusalem during the Successful Campaign of Ibrahim Pasha*, 2 vols. (1835)

Hokayem, Antoine, *Les Provinces arabes de l'Empire Ottoman aux archives du Ministère des Affaires Etrangères de France 1793–1918* (Beirut, 1988)

Holden, David, 'Letter from Alexandria 1963', in Christopher Pick, ed., *Egypt: A Travellers' Anthology* (1991)

Honekamp-Mazgon, Marlies, *Palais de Hollande in Istanbul* (Istanbul, 2002)

Hope, Thomas, *Anastasius*, 2 vols. (1819)

Hopwood, Derek, *The Russian Presence in Syria and Palestine 1843–1914: Church and Politics in the Near East* (Oxford, 1969)

Hormouzios, Stelios, *No Ordinary Crown* (1972)

Horton, George, *The Blight of Asia* (Indianapolis, 1926)

Hourani, Albert, and Shehadi, Nadim, eds., *The Lebanese in the World: A Century of Emigration* (1992)

Hunter, F. Robert, *Egypt under the Khedives 1805–1879* (1984)

Hunter, W. P., *Narrative of the late Expedition to Syria under the Command of Admiral the Hon. Sir Robert Stopford GCB, GCMG*, 2 vols. (1842)

Hurewitz, J. C., *The Middle East and North Africa in World Politics*, 2 vols. (New Haven, 1975)

Husayn, Abdul Rahim Abu, *The View from Istanbul: Lebanon and the Druze Emirate in the Ottoman Chancery Documents* (2004)

Ibrahim, Ibrahim, 'Taha Husayn: the critical spirit', in John P. Spagnolo, ed., *Problems of the Modern Middle East in Historical Perspective* (Reading, 1992)

Ilbert, Robert, *Alexandrie 1830–1930*, 2 vols. (Cairo, 1996)

—— and Yannakakis, Ilias, *Alexandrie 1860–1960: un modèle éphémère de convivialité: communautés et identité cosmopolite* (1992)

Iljine, Nicolas V., ed., *Odessa Memories* (Seattle, 2003)

Imber, Colin, *Ebu's-su'ud and the Islamic Legal Tradition* (Stanford, 1997)

Ioannou, Yorgos, *Refugee Capital: Thessaloniki Chronicles* (Athens, 1997)

Israel, Jonathan I., 'Trade politics and strategy: the Anglo-Dutch Wars in the Levant', in A. Hamilton et al., eds., *Friends and Rivals in the East: Studies in Anglo-Dutch Relations in the Levant from the Seventeenth to the Early Nineteenth Century* (Leiden, 2000)

Issawi, Charles, 'British trade and the rise of Beirut 1830–1860', *International Journal of Middle East Studies* (Aug. 1977), 91–101

—— *The Fertile Crescent 1800–1914: A Documentary Economic History* (Oxford, 1988)

Jabarti, Abd al-Rahman, *Merveilles biographiques et historiques ou chroniques du Cheikh Abd-El-Rahman El Djabarti*, 10 vols. (Cairo, 1896)

Jeancard, Paul, *L'Anatolie* (1919)

Jenkins, Roy, *Gladstone* (1995)

Jennings, Ronald C., *Christians and Muslims in Ottoman Cyprus and the Mediterranean World 1571–1640* (New York, 1993)

Johnson, Michael, *All Honourable Men* (2001)

—— *Class and Client in Beirut* (1986)

Johnston, Shirley, with Sonbol, Sherif, *Egyptian Palaces and Villas* (2006)

Jolliffe, T. R., *Letters from Palestine* (2nd edn, 1820)

Josipovici, Gabriel, *A Life* (2001)

Kabbani, Nizar, *Republic of Love* (2003)

...

...

...

...

...

Kadi, Ismail Hakki, 'A silence of the guilds? Some characteristics of Izmir's craftsmen organizations in the 18th and early 19th century', in Maurits van den Boogert, ed., *Ottoman Izmir* (Istanbul, 2007)

Kamel, Leila, *Un quartier de Beyrouth: Saint Nicolas. Structures familiales et structures foncières*, 2 vols. (Beirut, 1998)

Kansu, Aykut, *Politics in Post-Revolutionary Turkey 1908–1913* (Leiden, 2000)

—— *The Revolution of 1908 in Turkey* (Leiden, 1997)

Karanasou, Floresca, 'The Greeks in Egypt from Mohammed Ali to Nasser 1805–1961', in Richard Clogg, ed., *The Greek Diaspora in the Twentieth Century* (1999)

Karnikas, Alexander and Helen, *Elias Venezis* (New York, 1969)

Kassab, Sawsan Agha, and Tadmouri, Khaled Omar, *Beirut and the Sultan: 200 Photographs from the Albums of Sultan Abdul Hamid II* (Beirut, 2003)

Kassir, Samir, 'Entre chien et loups', in Jad Thabet, ed., *Beyrouth: la brûlure des rêves* (2001)

—— *Histoire de Beyrouth* (2003)

Kaufman, Asher, *Reviving Phoenica: In Search of Identity in Lebanon* (2004)

Kay, E. de, *Sketches of Turkey in 1831 and 1832* (New York, 1833)

Kayali, Hasan, *Arabs and Young Turks: Ottomanism, Arabism and Islamism in the Ottoman Empire 1908–1918* (1997)

el-Kayem, Henri, *Par grand vent d'est avec rafles: mémoires d'un Alexandrin* (1999)

Kechriotis, Vangelis, 'Between professional duty and national fulfillment: the Smyrniot medical doctor Apostolos Psaltoff 1862–1923', in Merope Anastassiadou and Paul Dumont, eds., *Médecins et ingenieurs ottomans à l'âge des nationalismes* (1998)

—— 'Greek Orthodox, Ottoman Greek or just Greek? Theories of coexistence in the aftermath of the Young Turk Revolution', *Etudes balkaniques*, 1 (2005), 51–72

—— 'The Greeks of Izmir at the end of the empire: a non-Muslim community between autonomy and patriotism', DPhil thesis (Leiden University, 2005)

Kelly, Sir David, *The Ruling Few* (1952)

Keyder, Caglar, *The Definition of a Peripheral Economy: Turkey 1923–1929* (Cambridge, 1981)

Khalaf, Samir, *Heart of Beirut: Reclaiming the Bourj* (2006)

Khalidi, Tarif, 'Unveiled: Anbara Salam in England 1925–1927', in *The Arabs and Britain: Changes and Exchanges* (Cairo, 1999)

el-Khalil, Zeena, *Beirut I Love You* (2009)

Khalili, Laleh, 'Beirut's southern suburbs in the aftermath of the July War', *Middle East in London* (Oct. 2006), 6–10

el-Khazen, Farid, *The Breakdown of the State in Lebanon 1967–1976* (2000)

—— *The Making and Politics of the 1943 National Pact* (Oxford, 1991)

Khoury, Gérard D., *La France et l'Orient arabe: Naissance du Liban moderne* (2009 edn)

—— ed., *Selim Takla 1895–1945: une contribution à l'indépendance du Liban* (Beirut, 2004)

Kiel, Machiel, *Studies on the Ottoman Architecture of the Balkans* (Aldershot, 1990)

Kinglake, A. W., *Eothen* (1919 edn)

Kinross, Lord, *Ataturk: The Rebirth of a Nation* (Nicosia, 1981 edn)

Kitromilides, Paschalis M., ed., *Eleftherios Venizelos: The Trials of Statesmanship* (Edinburgh, 2006)

—— Enlightenment, Nationalism, Orthodoxy: Studies in the Culture and Political Thought of South-Eastern Europe (1994)

Knight, William, Oriental Outlines, or, a Rambler's Recollections of a Tour in Turkey, Greece and Tuscany in 1838 (1839)

Kober, Marc, Entre Nil et sable: écrivains d'Egypte d'expression française (1999)

Koker, Osman, Souvenir of Liberty: Postcards and Medals from the Collection of Orlando Carlo Calumeno (Istanbul, 2008)

—— ed., Bir zamanlar Izmir (2009)

Kolodziejczyk, Dariusz, Ottoman–Polish Diplomatic Relations 15th–18th Century: An Annotated Edition of Ahdnames and Other Documents (Leiden, 2000)

Kontente, Léon, Smyrne et l'Occident, de l'Antiquité au XXIe siècle (Montigny, 2005)

Korais, A., Mémoire sur l'état actuel de la civilisation en Grèce (1803)

Kouyoumdjian, Ohannes Pacha, Le Liban à la veille et au début de la guerre: mémoires d'un gouverneur 1913–1915 (2003)

Kramer, Gudrun, The Jews in Modern Egypt 1914–1952 (1989)

Kupferschmidt, Iri M., 'Who needed department stores in Egypt? From Orosdi Back to Omar effendi', International Journal of Middle East Studies, 43, 2 (Mar. 2007), 175–92

Kurat, Y. T., 'How Turkey drifted into World War I', in Kenneth Bourne and D. C. Watt, eds., Studies in International History (1960)

Kusel Bey, Baron de, An Englishman's Reminiscences of Egypt (1915)

Kutluoglu, Muhammad H., The Egyptian Question (1831–1840) (Istanbul, 1998)

La Motraye, A. de, Voyages du Sr. A. de La Motraye en Europe, Asie et Afrique, 2 vols. (La Haye, 1727)

Lacouture, Jean, and Lacouture, Simone, L'Egypte en mouvement (1957)

Lagnado, Lucette, The Man in the White Sharkskin Suit (New York, 2007)

Lamartine, Alphonse-Marie-Louis de Prat de, Correspondance Générale de 1830 à 1848, 2 vols. (1943)

Lampson, Sir Miles, Politics and Diplomacy in Egypt: The Diaries of Sir Miles Lampson 1935–1937 (Oxford, 1991)

Landes, David S., Bankers and Pashas: International Finance and Economic Imperialism in Egypt (1979 edn)

Larsson, Theo, Seven Passports for Palestine: Sixty Years in the Levant (Pulborough, 1995)

Laurens, Henry, 'La France et le califat', Turcica, 31 (1999)

—— Les Origines intellectuelles de l'expédition d'Egypte. L'Orient islamisant en France (Istanbul, 1987)

Le Bruyn, Corneille, Voyages au Levant, 6 vols. (The Hague, 1732)

Lees, Andrew and Lees, Lynn Hollen, Cities and the Making of Modern Europe 1750–1914 (Leicester, 2007)

Lehmann, Joseph, All Sir Garnett (1964)

Lemos, Andreas G., The Greeks and the Sea (1976)

Leprette, Fernand, Egypte: terre du Nil (1939)

—— La Muraille de silence: Notes d'un Français d'Egypte pendant la guerre (Cairo, 1942)

Leon, Edwin de, Egypt under its Khedives (1882)

Leune, Jean, Une revanche, une étape (1914)

439

Levene, Mark, 'Port Jewry of Salonika between neo-colonialism and the nation state', in David Cesarani, ed., *Port Jews: Jewish Communities in Cosmopolitan Maritime Trading Centres 1550–1950* (2002)

LeVine, Mark, *Overthrowing Geography: Jaffa, Tel Aviv and the Struggle for Palestine* (2005)

Levy, Sam, *Salonique à la fin du XIXe siècle* (Istanbul, 2000)

Liddell, Robert, *Cavafy* (2002 edn)

—— *Unreal City* (1993 edn)

Lincoln, W. Bruce, *Sunlight at Midnight: St Petersburg and the Making of Modern Russia* (2001)

Le Livre d'or du journal La Réforme (Alexandria, 1945)

Llewellyn Smith, Michael, *Athens: A Cultural and Literary History* (2004)

—— *Ionian Vision: Greece in Asia Minor 1919–1922* (2nd edn, 1998)

Long, C. W. R., *British Pro-Consuls in Egypt 1914–1929: The Challenge of Nationalism* (2005)

Loti, Pierre, *Aziyade* (Livre de Poche, 1970)

Loucar, Anouar, *Voyageurs et écrivains français en Egypte* (Cairo, 1956)

Lowry, Heath, 'The Evrenos dynasty of Yenice Vardar', *Journal of Ottoman Studies*, 32 (2008), 1–192

Lushington, Mrs Charles, *Narrative of a Journey from Calcutta to Europe, by Way of Egypt, in the Years 1827 and 1828* (1829)

Lusignan, Livio Missir de, *Vie latine de l'Empire Ottoman* (Istanbul, 2004)

Maasri, Zeina, *Off the Wall: Political Posters of the Lebanese Civil War* (2009)

Mabro, Robert, 'Nostalgic literature on Alexandria', in Jill Edwards, ed., *Historians in Cairo* (Cairo, 2002)

McBride, Barrie St Clair, *Farouk of Egypt* (1967)

McCarthy, Justin, *Death and Exile: The Ethnic Cleansing of Ottoman Muslims 1821–1922* (Princeton, 1995)

MacGill, Thomas, *Travels in Turkey, Italy and Russia*, 2 vols (1808)

Mackridge, Peter, 'The myth of Asia Minor in Greek fiction', in Renée Hirschon, ed., *Crossing the Aegean* (Oxford, 2003)

McLeave, Hugh, *The Last Pharaoh: The Ten Faces of Farouk* (1969)

MacNiven, Ian S., ed., *The Durrell–Miller Letters 1935–1980* (1988)

Madden, R. R., *Travels*, 2 vols. (1827)

Maehler, Herwig, 'The Mouseion and Cultural Identity', in Anthony Hirst and Michael Silk, eds., *Alexandria, Real and Imagined* (Aldershot, 2009)

Mahfouz, Naguib, *Autumn Quail* (1990)

—— *Miramar* (2000 edn)

Makdisi, Jean Said, *Beirut Fragments: A War Memoir* (New York, 1990)

Makdisi, Ussama, *The Culture of Sectarianism: Community, History and Violence in Nineteenth-Century Ottoman Lebanon* (Berkeley, 2000)

Malarkey, James M., 'Notes on the psychology of war in Lebanon', in Halim M. Barakat, ed., *Towards a Viable Lebanon* (1988)

Malet, Sir Edward, *Egypt 1879–1883* (1907)

Malkin, Irad, and Hohlfelder, Robert L., *Mediterranean Cities: Historical Perspectives* (1988)

Mango, Andrew, *Ataturk* (2000)

Manguel, Albert, 'Once again Troy', in Anna Wilson, ed., *Lebanon, Lebanon* (2006)

Manley, Deborah, and Ree, Peta, *Henry Salt: Artist, Traveller, Diplomat, Egyptologist* (2001)

Manning, Olivia, *The Levant Trilogy* (2003 edn)

Mansel, Philip, *Constantinople: City of the World's Desire* (1995)

—— *Dressed to Rule: Royal and Court Costume from Louis XIV to Elizabeth II* (2005)

—— 'The grand tour in the Ottoman Empire', in Paul Starkey and Janet Starkey, eds., *Interpreting the Orient: Travellers in Egypt and the Near East* (Reading, 2001)

—— *Paris between Empires* (2001)

Marr, David, *Patrick White: A Life* (1991)

—— ed., *Patrick White Letters* (1994)

Marsot, Afaf Lutfi al-Sayyid, *Egypt in the Reign of Muhammad Ali* (Cambridge, 1984)

Matar, Nabil, *In the Lands of the Christians: Arab Travel Writing in the Seventeenth Century* (2003)

Maundrell, Henry, *A Journey from Aleppo to Jerusalem at Easter, A.D. 1697* (1810 edn)

Maurice, Colonel J. F., *Military History of the Campaign of 1882 in Egypt* (1887)

Mazower, Mark, *Salonica, City of Ghosts: Christians, Muslims and Jews 1430–1950* (2004)

Menargues, Alain, *Les Secrets de la Guerre du Liban* (2004)

Mengin, M., *Histoire de l'Egypte sous le règne de Mohammed Aly* (1823)

Mengous, Petros, *Narrative of a Greek Soldier* (New York, 1830)

Mermier, Franck, *Le Livre et la ville: Beyrouth et l'édition arabe* (2005)

Miéville, Sir Walter Frederick, KCMG, *Under Queen and Khedive: The Autobiography of an Anglo-Egyptian Official* (1899)

Millard, David, *Journal of Travels in Egypt, Arabia Petraea and the Holy Land during 1841–2* (Rochester, NY, 1843)

Millie, J., *Alexandrie d'Egypte et le Caire* (Milan, 1868)

Milton, Giles, *Paradise Lost: Smyrna 1922* (2008)

Minutoli, Baroness von, *Recollections of Egypt* (1827)

Missouma, Sakina, *Alger à l'époque ottomane* (Aix-en-Provence, 2003)

Molho, Rena, *Salonica and Istanbul: Social, Political and Cultural Aspects of Jewish Life* (Istanbul, 2005)

Mollenhauer, Anne, 'The Central Hall House: regional commonalities and local specificities: a comparison between Beirut and al-Salt', in Jens Hanssen, Thomas Philipp and Stefan Weber, eds., *The Empire in the City: Arab Provincial Capitals in the Late Ottoman Empire* (Beirut, 2002)

Le Mondain égyptien (Cairo, 1939)

Monroe, Elizabeth, *Philby of Arabia* (1973)

Montefiore, Simon Sebag, *Stalin: The Court of the Red Tsar* (2003)

Montgomery, Viscount, *The Memoirs of Field-Marshal the Viscount Montgomery of Alamein, KG* (1958)

Moorehead, Alan, *African Trilogy* (1944)

Morewood, Steven, *The British Defence of Egypt 1935–1940: Conflict and Crisis in the Eastern Mediterranean* (2005)

Morin, Edgar, *Vidal et les siens* (1989)

Morin, Jean, *Souvenirs d'un banquier français* (1983)

Morris, James, *Among the Cities* (1985)

—— *Farewell the Trumpets: An Imperial Retreat* (1998 edn)

—— *The Market of Seleukia* (1957)

Mott-Radclyff, Charles, *Foreign Body in the Eye: A Memoir of the Foreign Service, Old and New* (1975)

Moustaki, Georges, *Les Filles de la mémoire* (1989)

Murphy, Robert, *Diplomat among Warriors* (1964)

Murray, Hon. Sir Charles Augustus, KCB, *A Short Memoir of Mohammed Ali* (1898)

Murray, Eustace, *The Roving Englishman in Turkey: Sketches from Life* (1855)

Murray, John, *Handbook for Travellers in the Ionian Islands, Greece, Turkey, Asia Minor and Constantinople* (1840)

—— *Handbook for Travellers in Turkey in Asia*, 2 vols. (4th rev. edn, 1878)

Naff, Alixa, *Becoming American: The Early Arab Immigrant Experience* (Carbondale, 1985)

Naggar, Jean, *Sipping from the Nile: My Exodus from Egypt* (New York, 2008)

Nahum, Henri, *La Grande Guerre et la guerre greco-turque vues par les instituteurs de l'Alliance Israélite Universelle d'Izmir* (Istanbul, 2003)

—— *Juifs de Smyrne, xixe–xxe siècle* (1997)

Najjar, Alexandre, *The School of War* (2006)

Napier, Commodore Sir Charles, *The War in Syria*, 2 vols. (1842)

Napier, Lt-Col. Edward, *Reminiscences of Syria and Fragments of a Journal and Letters from the Holy Land*, 2 vols. (1843)

Napoléon III et l'Europe (2006)

Navet-Grenillet, Marie-Cécile, *Penelope Delta et Alexandrie: une femme grecque à la confluence des langues et des cultures* (unpublished thesis, Montpellier University, 1998)

Nea Smyrna (map with history) (Athens, 1999)

Neale, F. A., *Eight Years in Syria, Palestine and Asia Minor from 1842 to 1850*, 2 vols. (1851)

Neguib, Mohammed, *Egypt's Destiny* (1955)

Neumann, Christoph K., 'Decision-making without decision-makers: Ottoman foreign policy circa 1780', in Caesar E. Farah, ed., *Decision-Making and Change in the Ottoman Empire* (Kirksville, 1993)

Nicholls, David, *The Lost Prime Minister: A Life of Sir Charles Dilke* (1995)

Nicol, Martha, *Ismeer; or Smyrna and its British Hospital in 1855* (1856)

Nightingale, Florence, *Letters from Egypt* (1998 edn)

Ninet, John, *Lettres d'Egypte 1879–1882*, ed. Anoua Louca (1979)

Nostitz, Pauline, Countess, *Travels of Doctor and Madame Helfer in Syria, Mesopotamia*, 2 vols. (1878)

Nubar Pacha, *Mémoires* (Beirut, 1983)

Oikonomos, Constantino, *Etude sur Smyrne*, tr. and ed. Bonanventure F. Slaars (Smyrna, 1868)

Olin, Stephen, *Greece and the Golden Horn* (New York, 1854)

—— *Travels in Egypt, Arabia Petraea and the Holy Land*, 2 vols. (New York, 1843)

Olnon, M. Merlijn, 'Köprülü imperial policy and the refashioning of Izmir', in Maurits van den Boogert, ed., *Ottoman Izmir* (Istanbul, 2007)

Owen, H. Collinson, *Salonica and After: The Sideshow that Ended the War* (1919)

Owen, Roger, *Lord Cromer* (2002)

Oztuncay, Bahattin, ed., *100th Anniversary of the Restoration of the Constitution* (Istanbul, 2008)

—— *Hatira-i uhuvvet Portre Fotograflarin Cazibesi 1846–1950* (Istanbul, 2005)

Page, Bruce, Leitch, David, and Knightley, Phillip, *Philby: The Spy who Betrayed a Generation* (1968)

Panayotopoulos, A. J., 'Early relations between the Greeks and the Young Turks', *Balkan Studies*, 21 (1980), 87–95

Pannuti, Alessandro, *Les Italiens d'Istanbul au xxe siècle* (Istanbul, 2008)

Panzac, Daniel, *La Caravane maritime – marins européens et marchands ottomans en Méditerranée (1680–1830)* (2004)

—— *Les Corsaires barbaresques* (1999)

Papadopoulos, Stelios A., ed., *The Greek Merchant Marine, 1453–1850* (Athens, 1972)

Parish, Michael Woodebine, *Aegean Adventures 1940–1943* (Lewes, 1993)

Parmaksiz, Pinar M. Yarmakli, 'A Muslim family in infidel Izmir at the turn of the century: the Evliyazades', in Maurits van den Boogert, ed., *Ottoman Izmir* (Istanbul, 2007)

Paton, A. A., *The Modern Syrians* (1844)

Peach, Ceri, Robinson, Vaughan, and Smith, Susan, eds., *Ethnic Segregation in Cities* (1981)

Pentzopoulos, Dimitri, *The Balkan Exchange of Minorities and its Impact on Greece* (2002 edn)

Pernot, Maurice, *Rapport sur un voyage d'étude à Constantinople, en Egypte et en turquie d'Asie (janvier–août 1912)* (1912)

Peters, Rudolph, *Islam and Colonialism: The Doctrine of Jihad in Modern History* (The Hague, 1979)

Petropoulos, Elias, *Old Salonica* (Athens, 1982)

—— *La Présence ottomane à Salonique* (Athens, 1980)

—— and Emery, Ed, *Songs of the Greek Underworld: The Rebetika Tradition* (2000)

Petropoulos, John A., *Forms of Collaboration with the Enemy: Memoirs of Kanellos Delegiannes* (n.d.)

Peyssonnel, Claude Charles de, *Examen du livre intitulé Considérations sur la guerre actuelle des Turcs* (Amsterdam, 1788)

Philip, John, *Reminiscences of Gibraltar, Egypt and the Egyptian War* (Aberdeen, 1893 edn)

Philipp, Thomas, *Acre: The Rise and Fall of a Palestinian City* (2001)

—— *The Syrians in Egypt 1725–1975* (Stuttgart, 1985)

Philou, Christine, 'To be or not to be Roum in the 1820's', paper given at Ecole Française d'Athenes, Feb. 2006

Picard, Elizabeth, 'Les Syriens, l'envers du décor', in Jad Thabet, ed., *Beyrouth: la brûlure des rêves* (2001)

Pieridis, G. Philippou, *Memories and Stories from Egypt* (Nicosia, 1992)

Pillaut, Julien, *Les Consulats du Levant*, 2 vols. (Nancy, 1902)

Pintak, Larry, *Beirut Outtakes* (Lexington, 1988)

Playfair, Lt-Col. R. L., *Handbook to the Mediterranean: Its Cities, Coast and Islands* (1881)

Pococke, Richard, *A Description of the East*, 2 vols (1743)

Poffandi, S. E., *Indicateur égyptien* (Alexandria, 1892)

Poitou, Eugène, *Un hiver en Egypte* (1860)

Politis, Athanase G., ed., *Le Conflit turco-égyptien de 1838–1841 et les dernières années du règne de Mohamed Aly d'après les documents diplomatiques grecs* (Cairo, 1931)

Politis, Kosmas, 'At Hadzifrangos', *The Charioteer*, 11 (1969–70)

Polk, W. R., and Chambers, R., *The Beginnings of Modernization in the Middle East* (Chicago, 1968)

Le Portrait à Alexandrie dans les collections particulières (Alexandria 1955)

Poullet, M., *Nouvelles relations du Levant*, 2 vols. (1667)

Poumarède, Gérard, 'Négocier près la Sublime Porte: jalons pour une nouvelle histoire des capitulations ottomanes', in Lucien Bély, *L'Invention de la diplomatie* (1998)

—— *Pour en finir avec la croisade: Mythes et réalitiés de la lutte contre les Turcs aux XVIe et XVIIe siècles* (2004)

Pratt, Lawrence R., *East of Malta, West of Suez* (1975)

Presland, John, *Deedes Bey* (1941)

Prousis, Theophilus C., *British Consular Reports from the Ottoman Levant in an Age of Upheaval* (Istanbul, 2008)

—— 'Smyrna 1821: a Russian view', *Modern Greek Studies Yearbook*, 7 (1991)

Psomiades, Harry J., *The Eastern Question: The Last Phase* (Thessaloniki, 1968)

Pückler-Muskau, Prince, *Egypt under Mohammed Ali*, 2 vols. (1845)

Puryear, Vernon J., *Napoleon and the Dardanelles* (Berkeley, 1951)

Queiros, Eça de, *Les Anglais en Egypte* (2008)

Raafat, Samir W., *Cairo, the Glory Years: Who Built What, When, Why and for Whom* (Alexandria, 2003)

Rafeq, Abdul-Karim, *The Province of Damascus 1723–1783* (Beirut, 1966)

Raguse, Duc de, *Voyage de M. le Maréchal Duc de Raguse*, 5 vols. (1837)

Randal, Jonathan, *The Tragedy of Lebanon* (1990 edn)

Rawnsley, Andrew, *The Party is Over* (2010)

Rees, Tom, *Merchant Adventurers in the Levant* (Stawell, 2003)

Reimer, Michael J., *Colonial Bridgehead: Government and Society in Alexandria 1807–1882* (Boulder, 1997)

'Relation de l'île de Chio' (1747), in Antoine Galland, *Recueil des rits et ceremonies du pèlerinage de la Mecque* (Amsterdam, 1754)

Richardson, Robert, *Travels Along the Mediterranean and Parts Adjacent, in Company with the Earl of Belmore, during the years 1816–1817–1818*, 2 vols. (1822)

Ridley, Ronald T., *Napoleon's Proconsul in Egypt: The Life and Times of Bernardino Drovetti* (1998)

Riffier, Jean, 'Les Œuvres françaises et l'invention de la Syrie', in Bernard Delpal et al., eds., *France–Levant, de la fin du xviie siècle à la Première Guerre mondiale* (2005)

Risal, P., *La Ville convoitée: Salonique* (1914)

Ristelhuber, René R., *Les Traditions françaises au Liban* (2nd edn, 1925)

Roe, Sir Thomas, *Negotiations of Sir Thomas Roe, in his Embassy to the Ottoman Porte, from the Year 1621 to 1628 Inclusive*, 2 vols. (1740)

Rogers, Michael, 'To and fro: aspects of Mediteranean trade and consumption in the 15th and 16th centuries', in *Villes au Levant: Hommage à André Raymond* (1990), 57–74

Rondeau, Daniel, *Alexandrie* (1997)

Ross, H. R., *Letters from the East* (1902)

Royle, Charles, *The Egyptian Campaigns 1882 to 1885* (rev. edn, 1900)

Rustum, A. J., *The Royal Archives of Egypt and the Disturbances in Palestine, 1834* (Beirut, 1938)

Sabit, Adel M., *A King Betrayed* (1989)

Sabry, M., *L'Empire Egyptien sous Mohammed Ali et la question d'Orient (1811–1849)* (1930)

Sacerdoti, Annie, *The Guide to Jewish Italy* (Venice, 2004)

Sacré, Amédée, and Outrebon, Louis, *L'Egypte et Ismail Pacha* (1865)

el-Sadat, Anwar, *Revolt on the Nile* (1957)

Sadgrove, Philip, *The Egyptian Theatre in the Nineteenth Century 1799–1882* (Reading, 1996)

—— 'Travellers' rendezvous and cultural institutions in Mohammed Ali's Egypt', in Paul Starkey and Janet Starkey, eds., *Interpreting the Orient: Travellers in Egypt and the Near East* (Reading, 2001)

Saghie, Hazim, 'Crossings: Beirut in the eighties', in Malu Halas and Roseanne Saad Khalaf, eds., *Transit Beirut: New Writings and Images* (2004)

Said, Edward, *After the Last Sky: Palestinian Lives* (1986)

—— 'Cairo and Alexandria', in id., *Reflections on Exile* (2001)

St John, Bayle, *Two Years' Residence in a Levatine Family* (1856)

St John, James Augustus, *Egypt and Mohammed Ali; or, Travels in the Valley of the Nile*, 2 vols. (1834)

Salam, Nawaf, and Sassine, Fares, *Lebanon: A Century in Pictures* (Beirut, 2003)

Saliba, Robert, *Beirut 1920–1940: Domestic Architecture between Tradition and Modernity* (Beirut, 1999)

Salibi, Kamal S., 'Beirut under the Young Turks as depicted by the political memoirs of Salim Ali Salam 1868–1938', in Jacques Berque, ed., *Les Arabes par leurs archives* (1976)

—— *A House of Many Mansions: The History of Lebanon Reconsidered* (2009 edn)

—— 'Maronite historians of Lebanon', in P. M. Holt and B. Lewis, eds., *Historians of the Middle East* (1962)

Sammarco, Angelo, *Les Règnes d'Abbas, de Said et d'Ismail* (Rome, 1935)

Sandalci, Mert, *Max Fuchtermann Kartpostallari*, 3 vols. (Istanbul, 2000)

Sandys, George, *Travels: Containing an History of the Original and Present State of the Turkish Empire* . . . (6th edn, 1670)

Sattin, Anthony, *Lifting the Veil: British Society in Egypt 1768–1956* (1988)

Saulcy, Léon Caignart de, *Carnets de voyage* (1955 edn)

Savidis, George, ed., *C. P. Cavafy: Collected Poems* (rev. edn, 1992)

Sayek, Sybil Zandi, 'Fêtes et processions', in Marie-Carmen Smyrnelis, ed., *Smyrne, la ville oubliée?* (2006)

Sayigh, Rosemary, *Too Many Enemies: The Palestinian Experience in Lebanon* (1994)

Scheikevitch, Antoine, *Hellas? . . . Hélas! Souvenirs de Salonique* (1922)

Scherzer, Charles de, *La Province de Smyrne considérée au point de vue géographique, économique et intellectuelle* (Vienne, 1873)

Schilcher, Linda Schatkowski, 'The famine of 1915–1918 in Greater Syria', in John P. Spagnolo, ed., *Problems of the Modern Middle East in Historical Perspective* (Reading, 1992)

Schmidt, Jan, *From Anatolia to Indonesia: Opium Trade and the Dutch Community of Izmir 1820–1940* (Istanbul, 1998)

—— *Through the Legation Window: Four Essays on Dutch, Dutch Indian and Ottoman History* (Istanbul, 1992)

Schmitt, Oliver Jens, *Les Levantins: cadres de vie et identités d'un groupe ethno-confessionel de l'Empire Ottoman au 'long' 19e siècle* (Istanbul, 2007)

Scholch, Alexander, *Egypt for the Egyptians! The Socio-Political Crisis in Egypt 1878–1882* (Oxford, 1981)

Schroeder, Francis, *Shores of the Mediterranean*, 2 vols. (1846)

Schulze, Kirsten E., *The Jews of Lebanon: Between Coexistence and Conflict* (Brighton, 2001)

Sciacky, Leon, *Farewell to Ottoman Salonica* (Istanbul, 2000)

Scott, C. Rochfort, *Rambles in Egypt and Candia*, 2 vols. (1837)

Seale, Patrick, *Assad of Syria* (1988)

—— *The Struggle for Arab Independence: Riad al-Solh and the Makers of the Modern Middle East* (Cambridge, 2010)

—— and McConville, Maureen, *Philby: The Long Road to Moscow* (rev. edn, 1978)

Seferis, George, *A Poet's Journal: Days of 1945–1951* (Cambridge, Mass., 1974)

Sehnaoui, Nada, *L'Occidentalisation de la vie quotidienne à Beyrouth 1860–1914* (Beirut, 2002)

Seikaly, May, *Haifa: The Transformation of an Arab Society 1918–1939* (1998 edn)

Selwyn, Victor, et al., *Return to Oasis: War Poems and Recollections from the Middle East 1940–1946* (1980 edn)

Senior, Nassau William, *A Journal Kept in Turkey and Greece in the Autumn of 1857 and the Beginning of 1858* (1859)

Senoçak, Bulent, *Levant'in yildizi Izmir* (Izmir, 2003)

Shannon, Richard, *Gladstone: Heroic Minister 1865–1898* (2000 edn)

Sharif, Omar, *L'Eternel masculin* (1977)

Shaw, Stanford J., *From Empire to Republic: The Turkish War of National Liberation 1918–1923. A Documentary Study*, 5 vols. (Ankara, 2000)

al-Shaykh, Hanan, *The Story of Zahra* (1993 edn)

Shepherd's Oriental Yearbook for 1860 (Smyrna, 1859)

Simpson, Michael, ed., *The Cunningham Papers*, 2 vols. (Aldershot, 1999–2006)

Şimşir, Bilal N., ed., *British Documents on Ataturk*, 8 vols. (Ankara, 1984–2006)

Sinoué, Gilbert, *Le Colonel et l'enfant roi* (2006)

Skilliter, Susan A., 'An ambassador's tayin: Edward Barton's ration on the Egri campaign 1596', *Turcica*, 25 (1993)

Smyrna before the Catastrophe (Athens, 1992)

Smyrna, Metropolis of the Asia Minor Greeks (Athens, 2001)

Smyrne: Estudiantina nea ionia (compact disc: Athens, 2003)

Smyrnelis, Marie-Carmen, ed., *Smyrne, la ville oubliée?* (2006)

—— *Une ville ottomane plurielle: Smyrne aux xviie et xviiie siècles* (Istanbul, 2006)

Solominidis, Victoria, 'Greece in Asia Minor: the Greek administration of the vilayet of Aydin, 1919–1922', PhD thesis (University of London, 1984)

Sonbol, Mira el-Azhary, ed., *Beyond the Exotic: Women's Histories in Islamic Societies* (Syracuse, NY, 2005)

Sonnini, Charles-Sigisbert, *Voyage en Grèce et en Turquie fait par ordre de Louis XVI* (1997 edn)

Sotiriou, Dido, *Farewell Anatolia* (Athens, 1991)

Soucek, Svat, 'The Strait of Chios and the Kaptanpaşa's navy', in Elizabeth Zachariadou, ed., *The Kapudan Pasha, his Office and his Domain* (Rethymnon, 2002)

el-Sousssi, Shadia, 'Borrowed words from Italian in Alexandrian Arabic', in Bibliotheca Alexandrina, *Alex-Med Newsletter*, 7 (July 2007)

Spagnolo, John P., *France and Ottoman Lebanon 1861–1914* (1977)

—— ed., *Problems of the Modern Middle East in Historical Perspective* (Reading, 1992)

Spears, Sir Edward, *Fulfillment of a Mission: The Spears Mission to Syria and Lebanon, 1941–1944* (1977)

Spencer, Edmund, *Travels in European Turkey*, 2 vols. (1851)

Sperco, Willy, 'Lamartine et son domaine en Asie Mineure', *Revue de France*, 15 Oct. 1938, 1–22

Stadiem, William, *Too Rich* (1992)

Starkey, Paul, and Starkey, Janet, eds., *Interpreting the Orient: Travellers in Egypt and the Near East* (Reading, 2001)

Starr, Deborah, *Remembering Cosmopolitan Egypt: Literature, Culture and Empire* (2009)

Steensgaard, Niels, 'Consuls and nations in the Levant from 1570 to 1650', *Scandinavian Economic History Review*, 15, 1–2 (1967), 13–55

Stewart, Desmond, *Orphan with a Hoop: The Life of Emile Bustani* (1967)

—— *Turmoil in Beirut: A Personal Account* (1958)

Stochove, Fermanel, *Le Voyage d'Italie et du Levant* (Rouen, 1664)

Stone, Christopher, *Popular Culture and Nationalism in Lebanon: Fairuz and the Rahbani Nation* (2008)

Storrs, R., *Orientations* (def. edn, 1943)

Strachan, Michael, *The Life and Adventures of Thomas Coryate* (Oxford, 1962)

Sturdza, Mihail-Dimitri, *Dictionnaire historique et généalogique des grandes familles de Grèce, d'Albanie et de Constantinople* (1983)

Sulzberger, C. L., *A Long Row of Candles: Memoirs and Diaries 1934–1952* (1969)

Sureau, François, *Les Alexandrins* (2003)

Swan, Rev. Charles, *Journal of a Voyage up the Mediterranean; Principally among the Islands of the Archipelago, and in Asia Minor*, 2 vols. (1826)

Sykes, John, *The Levantine* (1952)

Symes, Sir Stewart, *Tour of Duty* (1946)

Tabbara, Lina Mikdadi, *Survival in Beirut: A Diary of Civil War* (1979)

Tancoigne, J. M., *Voyage à Smyrne, dans l'archipel et l'île de Candie en 1811, 1812, 1813 et 1814*, 2 vols. (1817)

Tapp, A. Griffin, *Stories of Salonica and the New Crusade* (1922)

Tauber, Eliezer, *The Emergence of the Arab Movement* (1993)

Tchentsova, Vera, 'Le fonds des documents grecs (F. 52. "Relations de la Russie avec la Grèce") de la collection des archives nationales des actes anciens de la Russie et leur valeur pour l'histoire de l'Empire Ottoman', *Turcica*, 30 (1998), 383–96

Tedder, Marshal of the RAF Lord, *With Prejudice: War Memoirs* (1966)

Tekeli, Ilhan, and Ilkin, Selim, 'The public works program and the development of technology in the Ottoman Empire in the second half of the nineteenth century, *Turcica*, 28 (1996)

Terhune, A. P., *Syria from the Saddle* (1896)

Terrades, Marc, *Le Drame de l'Héllenisme: Ion Dragoumis (1878–1920) et la question nationale en Grèce au début du xxe siècle* (2005)

Terry, Janice J., *The Wafd* (Beirut, 1981)

Testa, Marie de, and Gautier, Antoine, *Drogmans et diplomates européens auprès de la Porte Ottomane* (Istanbul, 2003)

Texier, Charles, *Description de l'Asie mineure faite par ordre du gouvernement français*, 3 vols. (1849)

Thabet, Jad, ed., *Beyrouth: la brûlure des rêves* (2001)

Thackeray, William Makepeace, *Notes of a Journey from Cornhill to Grand Cairo* (2nd edn, 1846)

Thomas, Hugh, *The Suez Affair* (1986 edn)

Thompson, Victoria, *Losing Alexandria* (Sydney, 1998)

Tignor, Robert, *Capitalism and Nationalism at the End of Empire* (Princeton, 1998)

—— *State, Private Enterprise and Economic Change in Egypt 1918–1952* (Princeton, 1984)

Timofeev, Igor, *Kamal Joumblatt et le tragique destin du Liban* (Beirut, 2000)

Toledano, Ehud R., *State and Society in Mid-Nineteenth-Century Egypt* (Cambridge, 2003 edn)

Tomes, Jason, *King Zog: Self-Made Monarch of Albania* (2003)

Totten, Michael J., 'From Baghdad to Beirut', *City Journal*, 10 Jan. 2010 (online)

Tournefort, M. Pitton de, *Relation d'un voyage du Levant, fait par ordre du Roy*, 2 vols. (1717)

Trading in the Levant (Manchester, 1912)

Travelos, John, and Kokkou, Angelike, *Hermoupolis* (Athens, 1984)

Trimi, Katerina, 'La famille Benakis: un paradigme de la bourgeoisie grecque alexandrine', in Meropi Anastassiadou and Bernard Heyberger, eds., *Figures anonymes, figures d'élite: pour une anatomie de l'Homo ottomanicus* (Istanbul, 1999)

Tucker, Judith E., *Women in Nineteenth Century Egypt* (1985)

Tulloch, Major-General Sir Alexander Bruce, *Recollections of Forty Years' Service* (1903)

Turner, Barry, *Suez 1956* (2007 edn)

Turner, William, *Journal of a Tour in the Levant*, 3 vols. (1820)

Turrell, Ray, *Scrap Book 1809–1922* (Englefield Green, 1987)

Tzalas, Harry F., *Farewell to Alexandria* (Cairo, 2003 edn)

al-Udhari, Abdallah, tr. and ed., *Modern Poetry of the Arab World* (1986)

Ugur, Ugur U., 'A reign of terror: CUP rule in Diyarbekir province 1913–1919', MA thesis (University of Amsterdam, 2005)

Upward, Allen, *The East End of Europe* (1908)

Ursu, J., *La Politique orientale de François Ier 1515–1547* (1908)

Uşakligil, Halid Ziya, *Kirk yil. Anilar* (Istanbul, 1987 edn)

Vacalopoulos, Apostolos E., *The Greek Nation 1453–1669* (New Brunswick, 1976)

—— *A History of Thessaloniki* (Thessaloniki, 1972)

Vailland, Roger, *Choses vues en Egypte* (1982 edn)

Valon, Alexis de, *Une année dans le Levant: voyage en Sicile, en Grèce et en Turquie*, 2 vols. (2nd edn, 1850)

van Droffelaar, Johan, '"Flemish Fathers" in the Levant', in Geert Jan Van Gelder and Ed de Moor, eds., *Eastward Bound: Dutch Ventures and Adventures in the Middle East* (Amsterdam, 1994)

Vatikiotis, P. J., *Nasser and his Generation* (1978)

Vaucher, G., *Gamal Abdel Nasser et son équipe*, 2 vols. (1959)

Veinstein, Gilles, 'Ayan de la region d'Izmir et le commerce du Levant', in id., *Etat et société dans l'Empire Ottoman, xviie–xviiie siècles* (Aldershot, 1994)

—— 'Retour sur la question de la tolérance ottomane', in Bartolome Bennassar and Robert Sauzet, eds., *Chrétiens et musulmans à la renaissance* (1998)

—— ed., *Salonique 1850–1918: la ville des juifs et le réveil des Balkans* (1992)

Velde, C. W. M. van de, *Narrative of a Journey through Syria and Palestine in 1851 and 1852*, 2 vols. (1854)

Verdeil, Chantal, 'Les écoles d'Orient: le réseau scolaire congréganiste en Syrie', in Bernard Delpal et al., eds., *France–Levant, de la fin du xviie siècle à la Première Guerre mondiale* (2005)

Viallon, Marie F., *Venise et la porte ottomane 1453–1566* (1995)

Wailly, Henri de, *Syrie 1941: la guerre occultée* (2006)

Walker, Hugh H., *The Anglo-American Guide Book to Alexandria* (Cairo, 1938)

Walker, Mary A., *Through Macedonia to the Albanian Lakes* (1864)

Walsh, Rev. R., *A Residence at Constantinople, during a Period including the Commencement, Progress, and Termination of the Greek and Turkish Revolutions*, 2 vols. (1836)

Wassef, Magda, ed., *Egypte: cent ans de cinéma* (1995)

Waterfield, Gordon, *Egypt* (1967)

Waugh, Alec, *The Mule on the Minaret* (1964)

Waugh, Evelyn, *The Letters of Evelyn Waugh*, ed. Mark Amory (1980)

White, Patrick, *Flaws in the Glass: A Self-Portrait* (1983 edn)

Wiet, Gaston, *Mohammed Ali et les beaux-arts* (Cairo, 1949)

Wilkinson, Sir Gardner, *Handbook for Travellers in Egypt* (1847)

Williams, H. Noel, *The Life and Letters of Admiral Sir Charles Napier KCB* (1917)

Wilson, Sir Charles Rivers, GCMG, CB, *Chapters from My Official Life* (1916)

Wilson, Field Marshal Lord, *Eight Years Overseas* (1948)

Wines, E. C., *Two Years and A Half in the Navy; or, Journal of a Cruise in the Mediterranean and the Levant*, 2 vols. (Philadelphia, 1832)

Winton, John, *Cunningham* (1998)

Wissa, Hanna F., *Assiout: The Saga of an Egyptian Family* (Lewes, 1994)

Woodruff, Samuel, *Journal of a tour to Malta, Greece . . . and Spain in 1828* (Hartford, 1831)

Woodsworth, Nicholas, *The Liquid Continent*, 3 vols. (2008)

Wortabet, Gregory M., *Syria, and the Syrians: or, Turkey in the Dependencies*, 2 vols. (1856)

Wratislaw, A. C., *A Consul in the East* (1924)

Wright, Arnold, *Twentieth Century Impressions of Egypt* (1909)

Wynn, Antony, *Three Camels to Smyrna: The Story of the Oriental Carpet Manufacturers Company* (2008)

Yeğin, Ugur, ed., *Once Upon a Time . . . Izmir from the Collection of Ugur Goktaş* (Izmir, 2009)

Yehya, Lutfi A. W., 'Alexandria reminiscences of an old historian', *Mediterraneans*, 8 (2006), 365–7

Yiannakopoulos, Georgios A., ed., *Refugee Greece: Photographs from the Archive of the Centre for Asia Minor Studies* (Athens, 1992)

Yurdusev, Nuri, ed., *Ottoman Diplomacy: Conventional or Unconventional?* (Basingstoke, 2004)

Zahlan, Rosemay Said 'George Baldwin', in Paul Starkey and Janet Starkey, eds., *Interpreting the Orient: Travellers in Egypt and the Near East* (Reading, 2001)

Zananiri, Gaston, *Entre mer et désert: mémoires* (1996)

Zimmerli Hardman, Esther, *From Camp de César to Cleopatra's Pool* (Alexandria, 2008)

Zisser, Eyal, *Lebanon: The Challenge of Independence* (2000)

Zogheb, Count Patrice de, *Red Cross and Red Crescent: Work in Alexandria under the Patronage of HRH Prince Mohammed Ali* (Alexandria, 1943)

Illustration Acknowledgements

Courtesy of Ahmet Piristina City Archive and Museum Izmir: 3 below, 4 above, 5 above. akg-images: 8 above. AP Photo/Ahmed Azakir/Press Association Images: 16 above. Courtesy of Hala Cochrane: 13 below. Courtesy of Centres d'Études Alexandrines: 9 centre. Corbis: 2 below (Underwood & Underwood/Bettmann), 6 above, 8 below (Bettmann), 10 above (Bettmann), 12 below (Bettmann), 15 above (Patrick Chauvel/ Sygma), 15 below (Maher Attar/Sygma). Mary Evans Picture Library: 5 below (Grenville Collins Postcard Collection). Fratelli Alinari Museum Collections Florence: 7 above (photo Félix Bonfils-Favrod Collection), 9 below (photo U. Dorès). Getty Images: 1 below, 4 below, 7 below (Roger-Viollet), 10 below (Roger-Viollet), 12 above (Frank & Helen Schreider/National Geographic), 16 below (Joseph Barrak/AFP). Magnum Photos/Abbas: 14. Princeton University Library, Rare Books Division, Department of Rare Books and Special Collections: 1 above (detail of an engraving from Jean Du Mont *Voyages de Mr. Du Mont, en France, en Italie, en Allemagne, à Malthe, et en Turquie*, vol 2 La Haye 1699). Private Collections: 6 centre, 6 below, 11 below. Collection Rijksmuseum Amsterdam: 2 above (David George van Lennep family portrait by Antoine de Favray). TopFoto.co.uk: 9 above, 11 above, 13 above. Courtesy of Antony Wynn: 3 above.

Index

Aydin: railway to Smyrna, 161, 184, 192; changes hands in Turkish–Greek conflict, 206

Baabda, Lebanon, 148
Baalbek: prints, 15
Badaro, Clea, 243, 278
Baer, Robert, 342
Baghdad: Arabic origins, 2; ethnic/religious segregation, 9; zoned, 352
Baghdad Pact, 312
Baghdadi, Maroun and Nayla de Freige, 331
Baladi, Naguib, 264
Balfour-Paul, Glen, 316
Balkan war (1912), 186–7
Balladur family, 230
Balladur, Edouard, 230
Baltaliman, Convention of (1838), 82
Baltazzi family, 3, 45, 167–9, 190, 220
Bank of England: founded, 33
Bankes, William, 16
Banque de Salonique, 177
Barakat, Hoda, 341; *The Stones of Laughter*, 355
Barakat, Nicholas and Victoria, 318, 329
Barbir family, 194
Baring, Evelyn *see* Cromer, 1st Earl of
Barker family, 71, 136, 254–5, 258
Barker & Company (of Smyrna), 160, 254, 277, 282
Barker, Lieut.-Colonel (English POW), 203
Barker, Gabriella, 255, 259
Barker, Sir Harry, 254
Barker, Sir Henry, 255, 258
Barker, Henry Alwyn, 255, 281
Barker, Sir Henry Edward, 107
Barker, John, 62, 95, 107
Barker, Michael, 255, 268, 277, 280–2, 285
Barton, Edward, 9
Bashir II Shihab, Emir, 78–9, 85, 92, 96
Baudrot, Auguste, 134
Bauffremont, Admiral Joseph de, 35, 39
Bawli, Osta, 154
Bayar, Celal, 166, 186, 192
Bayhum, Ahmad Muhtar, 194, 296
Bayhum, Omar, 99, 300
Beaton, Cecil, 258
Beauval, M. de (French consul in Alexandria), 102
Beidas, Youssef, 321
Beirut: as key port, 1, 3, 153; cosmopolitanism, 3, 10, 153; languages, 3, 303; French attack (1520), 6; Russians seize (1773–4), 36–7; modernized by Muhammad Ali, 91, 93, 95; strong Christian element, 91, 98; foreign merchants move to, 92; population, 92, 96, 151, 302; merchant dynasties, 93; rivalry with Damascus, 93, 150, 193; beauty of countryside, 94–5; consulates, 94; Greeks in, 94; British–Ottoman–Austrian force attacks (1840), 95–6; development and administration, 96, 98; character and social life, 97–8, 315–16; schools and education, 97,

149–50, 154, 319; sectarian massacres (1860), 98–100, 149, 154; French intervention and withdrawal (1860–1), 100; French dominance in, 148, 156; municipality, 149–50, 352; printing, publishing and newspapers, 149, 320, 330–1; Europeanization, 150, 153; as provincial capital, 150–1; trade, 150, 152–3; Ottoman resurgence in, 151–2; public clock and timekeeping, 151–2; migration through, 152; port facilities rebuilt and developed, 152; railway and transport, 152; communal unrest, 153–5, 312–13; social life, 153; as centre of Arab nationalism, 193, 296; racial and nationalist tensions, 193–5; welcomes Young Turk revolution, 193; shelled by Italians (1912), 194; in First World War, 199–201; famine, 201; post-1918 status and conditions, 296–7; as capital of Lebanon, 299–30, 344; administration and constitution, 300; as modern business city, 301; and political and social change, 301; women, 301, 309, 320, 341, 355; American University, 302; expansion, 302; Muslim riots in favour of Syria (1936), 303; new port and airport opened (1938), 303; Allied forces enter (July 1941), 305; nationalism, 308; French coup (1943), 309; French give up power, 309; and military coup by PPS, 311–12; privately owned guns, 311; US marines in, 312–13; port further developed (1967 and 1975), 313; capitalism and banking, 314, 347; casino, 314–15, 347; cultural life, 315, 319–20; as spy and press centre, 315–16; buildings and architecture, 318–19; new universities, 319; exiles in, 321; multiculturalism and religious variety, 321; and Arab radicalism, 323; civil war in, 324–33, 335–40; Palestinians dominate, 324; division and 'green line', 329; crosses and symbols, 330; National Front, 333; Israeli air raids on, 335; PLO leaves, 335; casualties, 336; Mufti killed, 339; life during civil war, 340–1; homosexuals in, 341–2; and pacification of Lebanon, 344; revival and redevelopment under Hariri, 344–6; night clubs, 346; Hezbollah in, 349–51; choice between segregation and integration, 352–3; Iraqi refugees in, 352; present status, 355–6; *see also* Lebanon
Beirut Apartment (film), 355
Bekfaya, Lebanon, 337
Bell, C. F. Moberly, 126
Belon, Pierre, 12
Ben-Gurion, David, 179, 286, 316
Benaki family, 137–9
Benaki, Alexander, 291, 317
Benaki, Anthony, 140
Benaki, Daphne, 284
Benaki, Emmanuel, 137, 139
Benaki, G. A., 132
Benaroya, E., 227
Benedetti, Comtesse, 74

INDEX

Hochepied family, 230
Hochepied, Clara Catherine de, 29
Hochepied, Daniel Alexander de, 29
Hochepied, Daniel Jean de, 29
Hochepied, Count Edmond de, 197, 230
Hochepied, Elbert de, 29
Hodges, Col. George Lloyd, 84
Holden, David, 287, 294
Holy League, War of the (1683–99), 34
homosexuality: in Levant, 142–3; in Alexandria, 268; in Beirut, 341–2
Hope, Thomas: *Anastasius*, 52
Hopkinson Pasha, Henry 139
Horowitz, Theodore, 282
horses: in Smyrna, 165
Horton, George, 199, 206
Hoss, Selim al-, 339
Hugo, Victor, 50
Hungary, 7
Husrev Pasha, 79–80, 83
Hussein, King of Jordan, 324
Hussein, Sherif of Mecca, 297
Hussein, Taha, 261, 269, 320
Hussein Pasha, dey of Algiers, 68

Ibn Khaldun, 56
Ibn Sina (Avicenna), 28
Ibrahim, Ezzat, 243
Ibrahim Pasha (Muhammad Ali's son): in Alexandria, 61; friendship with John Barker, 62; in war against Greeks, 70, 75–6; successes against Ottomans, 77, 82; governorship in Syria, 78; ambitions, 79, 81; correspondence with father, 79; and father's dynastic ambitions, 83; introduces conscription, 83; retreats from Syria, 86; unpopularity in Beirut, 96
Ibrahim, Sheikh, 64
Ilhami, Emina, 115
Ilhami Pasha, 105
Impartial, L' (Smyrna newspaper), 160, 230–1
India: British dominance in, 89; Mutiny (1857–8), 109
Inönü, Ismet, 220, 223, 225
Internal Macedonian Revolutionary Organization (IMRO), 179–80
Ioannou, Yorgis, 237
Ionia, 211
Ionian University, 213
Iraq: refugees in Beirut, 352
Iron Duke, HMS, 204, 212–13, 217–18
Iskander, Afifa, 315
Iskanderun, 23, 50
Islam: as foundation of Ottoman Empire, 5–6; and jihad, 5–6, 339; marriage laws, 11; forced conversions to Christianity, 13; increase in Alexandria, 294; *see also* Muslims
Islamic Jihad, 339
Ismail Bey, 87
Ismail Pasha, Khedive of Egypt: claims Egypt part of Europe, 3, 114, 128; succeeds Said as

governor of Egypt, 110; and Dervieu, 111, 113; abdicates, 114; and failed Ethiopian war (1875), 115; strengthens Alexandrian defences, 117; in Alexandria, 128; use of French, 146; Sultan Abdulaziz visits, 168; statue, 241, 288
Ismailis: in Lebanon, 92
Israel: in Arab wars, 266, 311, 322; Egyptian Jews migrate to, 270, 278; bombing campaign in Egypt, 278; invades Egypt (1956), 285, 311; peace with Egypt, 295; state created, 322; air raids on Beirut, 335; invades Lebanon (1982), 335, 338; army organizes massacres of Palestinian refugees in Lebanon, 337; attacks Hezbollah in Lebanon (2006), 349–50; withdraws from south Lebanon, 349; *see also* Jews; Palestine
Issigonis family, 221
Issigonis, Alec, 221
Issigonis, Dimo, 162
Issigonis, G., 174
Istanbul *see* Constantinople
Italian language, 145; *see also* lingua franca
Italians: in Alexandria, 107; occupy Tripolitania, 128
Italy: conquers Libya, 194; takes refugees from Smyrna, 220; ambitions in Anatolia, 232; refugees from Fascism, 243; conquests in Africa, 250; Egyptian hostility to, 251; in Second World War, 252–3, 255; 'human torpedoes' attack British fleet in Alexandria, 256
Ivan IV ('the Terrible'), Emperor of Russia, 13
Izak, Algazi ('Bulbul Salomon'), 228
Izmir *see* Smyrna
Izmir, Gulf of, 16

Jabarti, Abdul Rahman al-, 57, 64–5, 80, 89–90, 143
Jacquemart, Henri Alfred, 112
janissaries, 7, 10, 14, 40, 46–7
Jansen, Maison (interior decorators), 248
Jasad (magazine), 355
Jeddah, 109
Jemal Pasha, 199–201, 297, 307
Jennings, Pastor Asa, 219
Jerusalem: segregation, 352
Jewish Agency, 303
Jews: ghettoized, 10; repressed in Spain, 13; in Smyrna, 24–5, 30, 172, 174, 185, 207, 215, 217; restrictions lifted by Mahmud II, 54; Greek hostility to, 116, 139, 172; schools, 163; in Salonica, 177, 179, 202, 237; women, 185; on Greek liberation of Salonica, 188; in First World War, 202; distrust of Greeks, 207–8; leave Smyrna, 227–8; view of Palestine as homeland, 228; deported to Auschwitz, 237; in Alexandria, 242, 263, 285, 295; and Israeli victories in Arab wars, 266; leave Alexandria for Israel, 270, 278; in Beirut, 313; *see also* anti-Semitism
John Chrysostom, St: *On the Priesthood*, 167

461

John Polycarp, St, Bishop of Smyrna, 24
Johnson, Michael, 324, 336
Jolliffe, Thomas, 56
Jongh, family de, 230, 233
Jongh, Fred de, 230
Jour, Le (newspaper), 304
Journal de Salonique, 177
Jouvenel, Henri de, 300
Jumblatt dynasty, 100
Jumblatt, Kemal, 311, 334, 339
Jumblatt, Mai, 315
Jumblatt, Taymur, 352
Jumblatt, Walid, 339

Kabbani, Nizar, 311, 320
Kamel Pasha, Ahmed, 249
Kamil Pasha, 173, 175
Kamil Pasha, Mustafa (founder of Egyptian
    National Party), 142
Karabekir, Kazim, 232
Karaosmanoglu family, 41, 78, 165, 168
Karatheodory, Constantine, 213
Karolidi Effendi, 185
Kassir, Samir, 349
Katipzade family, 162
Kaya, Şukru, 232
Kayem, Henri el-, 261
Kechriotis, Vangelis, 183
Keller Pasha, 131
Kelly, David, 241
Kemal Bey, Yussuf, 221
Kemal, Mustafa (Ataturk), 76, 162; birth and
    background in Salonica, 178; deposes Sultan,
    182; modernization, 189; on Smyrna, 189–90;
    message to army, 196; leads resistance
    movement against Greeks (1919), 206–7,
    209–10; and General Trikoupis, 212; in
    Smyrna, 214–15; and killing of Armenians,
    215; expels Greeks and Armenians from
    Smyrna, 219; uses Hortense Woods's house as
    HQ, 220; blames Greeks and Armenians for
    Smyrna fire, 221–3; claims Turkey at war
    with Britain, 223; no regrets for Smyrna fire,
    224–5; stays in Uşakligil house (Göztepe,
    Smyrna), 224; courtship, marriage to and
    divorce from Latife, 225, 228–9; leaves
    Smyrna for Ankara, 225, 227; land victories,
    226; revisits Smyrna, 228, 232; assassination
    plot against, 232; authoritarianism, 232;
    equestrian statue, 233; treaty of friendship
    with Venizelos, 235; and fate of Smyrna, 267
Kemal, Yahya, 146
Kemal, Prince Youssef, 243
Keun family, 35, 230
Keun, Bernhard, 45
Khalil, Zeena el-: *Beirut I Love You*, 346
Kharratt, Edwar al-, 244
Khashoggi, Adnan, 283
Khayyat, Winnie, 281
Khazan, Farid and Philippe el-, 200
Khazen family, 93–4

Khoury, Bernard, 346
Khoury, Bsharra al-, 151, 304, 307–9
Khoury, Elias, 323
Khoury, Khalil, 318
Killearn, 1st Baron *see* Lampson, Sir Miles
Kinglake, Alexander: *Eothen*, 55
Kitchener, Lieut. H. H. (*later* Field Marshal Earl),
    123, 128, 131, 147
Klat, Jules, 290
Klezl, Franz de, 51
Koenig (French officer in Egypt), 66
Koleilat, Ibrahim, 313, 327
Konya, Battle of (1832), 77
Köprülü, Fazil Ahmed, Grand Vizier, 22, 27
Köprülü, Mehmed, Grand Vizier, 21
Korais, Adamantios, 44–5
Koran, Holy: and printing, 28
Kraemer, Baron de, 40
Kraemer, Herr (Smyrna businessman), 156
Kuchuk Kainardji, Treaty of (1774), 37
Kulthoum, Oum, 268
Kut, Mesopotamia, 204
Kutahya, 77–8

La Fontaine, Sydney, 192
La Forest, Jean de, 7
Lagonikos, Stefanos, 268
Lahoud, Emile, 347–8
Lamartine, Alphonse de, 86, 93, 167
Lamartine, Julia de, 93
Lamb, Sir Harry, 215
Lampson, Sir Miles (*later* 1st Baron Killearn), 251,
    253, 260
Lascaris, 'Despo', 238
Lascaris, Manoly, 257, 268
Lascaris, Theodore, 7
Lasciac, Antonio, 133
Lausanne, Treaty of (1923), 223, 229
Lawrence, T. E., 95
Lebanese Forces, 335
Lebanon: religious composition and sectarianism,
    91–2, 95, 317; French relations with, 92, 148;
    revolt against Muhammad Ali, 95; French
    language in, 145; territorial expansion, 297–9;
    silk industry, 298; established as state, 299; as
    'new Phoenicia', 304; conflict between Vichy
    France and Britain in, 305–6; in Second
    World War, 306–7; National Pact, 307;
    Arabic as official language, 308; constitution,
    308; elections (1943), 308; nationalism,
    308–10; strikes against French, 309–10;
    independence from French, 310; economic
    union with Syria ends (1950), 311; Palestinian
    refugees in, 311, 322–4, 332, 338–9; PPS coup
    (1961), 311–12; Christian domination, 312;
    confessionalism, 317, 327, 351–2; Arafat in,
    322; relations with Israel, 322; radical Arab
    nationalism in, 323; civil war, 324–33, 335–9;
    army inactivity, 326, 328; presidential election
    (1976), 328; women, 331; dynasties, 334, 352;
    Israel invades (1982), 335, 338; massacres and